The "Who Is Johnny Dollar?" Matter

A CHARACTER PROFILE

AND PROGRAM SYNOPSIS

OF "AMERICA'S FABULOUS INSURANCE INVESTIGATOR,

THE MAN WITH THE ACTION PACKED EXPENSE ACCOUNT"

"YOURS TRULY, JOHNNY DOLLAR"

BY JOHN C. ABBOTT

THE "WHO IS JOHNNY DOLLAR?" MATTER

A CHARACTER PROFILE AND PROGRAM SYNOPSIS
OF "AMERICA'S FABULOUS INSURANCE INVESTIGATOR,
THE MAN WITH THE ACTION PACKED EXPENSE ACCOUNT"
"YOURS TRULY, JOHNNY DOLLAR"
VOLUME ONE
© 2010 JOHN C. ABBOTT

Published in the USA by:

BEARMANOR MEDIA
PO BOX 71426
ALBANY, GA 31708
www.BearManorMedia.com

ISBN-10: 1-59393-087-9
ISBN-13: 978-1-59393-087-5

BOOK DESIGN AND LAYOUT BY VALERIE THOMPSON.

Table of Contents

Dedicated to:
All those wonderful actors, actresses, writers, directors, producers, technical staff and sponsors, who made radio a wonderful place for almost 40 years.

Special thanks also go out to J. David Goldin and Bill Brooks, for their support, and encouragement and most of all, for answering my many questions.
Thanks guys.

Support for this project was also provided by:
Jeanette Berard of the Thousand Oaks Library, Anthony L'Abatte at Eastman House, and Janet Lorenz at the National Film Information Service.

The Golden Age of Radio

From the day of its invention in the late 1920's, until the early 1960's, radio was a magical place where Americans went to find news, sports, and entertainment. And find they did. One could find almost any sort of entertainment on the radio. This was the age of quiz shows, talent shows, soap operas, westerns thrillers, detectives dramas, comedy and variety shows, news, gossip and much more. Everyone gathered around the radio during the World Series when Red Barber or Vin Scully or Mel Allen would describe every nuance of what was happening on the field[1]. Radio presented the presidential campaigns. Radio brought America into President Roosevelt's living room for fireside chats. We heard the blitz of London, the capitulation of the Axis and the demise of the Japanese. Lowell Thomas took us to all sorts of exotic places. Radio took us into committee hearings to hear the Red Scare exposed before our ears. Americans took to Radio, and vice versa. Radio was the next big thing in the entertainment. Next to talking films, radio was the entertainment for everyone, until the numbing of our senses by television.

UNLIKE THE VISUAL NATURE OF MOVIES AND TELEVISION, RADIO REQUIRED THREE THINGS TO BE SUCCESSFUL:

1. A WELL WRITTEN AND DESCRIPTIVE SCRIPT
2. ACTORS WHO COULD PRESENT THE MATERIAL
3. THE IMAGINATION OF THE LISTENER.

When a writer sat down to write a story, dialog was not enough—you had to describe almost everything. When the character walked across the room, the sound effects men made him walk, but the writer had to tell them how. Every action had a sound; a gun shot, a door opening, a creaking step on the stairs up to the haunted attic. When a girl walked into a room, you knew what she was wearing via the description of the observer in the story. That requirement did not

---

[1] I remember an interview on Ed Walker's "The Big Broadcast" program on WAMU FM in Washington, where the interviewee noted that you could walk down the block and never miss a play when a ball game was on the radio.

exist for the movies where everything was naked and exposed to the eyes of the viewer.

It was the imagination of the listener that brought many programs to life. When you turned the lights down, and tuned in **Suspense**, or **Inner Sanctum**, it was the mind's eye that provided the illumination of the story. Ask two listeners what Matt Dillon looked like, and you get two distinctly different answers. Ask how big Fibber McGee's closet was and the answer would vary. The listener was totally in control of the visual aspect of a program. If they wanted the Shadow to look a certain way—he did. Did Walter Denton, the student nemesis of Miss Brooks on the comedy **Our Miss Brooks** have a dimple on his chin? If you were a young and impressionable teenager who liked dimples—he did. It was your program to color in as you wished.

It is the many-hued nature of radio characters that brought about the contents of this book. We know what Johnny Dollar did—he solved cased for insurance companies. But what was Johnny Dollar the man like?

Who is Johnny Dollar?

In February of 1949, America was introduced to an investigator named Johnny Dollar[2]. Johnny was not your average run-of-the-mill, hard drinking, hard hitting, one step behind the crook and one step ahead of the local police detective out to track down murderers, gangsters and thugs. Johnny Dollar was different—his beat was free-lance insurance investigations. He was hired and paid by insurance companies to look after their financial interests in various matters.

Over the course of the next 12 years, and 886 broadcasts, Johnny Dollar entertained audiences via the voices of 6 different actors[3]: Charlie Russell (1949–1950), Edmond O'Brien (1950–1952), John Lund (1952–1954), Bob Bailey (1955–1960), Bob Readick (1960–1961) and Mandel Kramer (1961–1962).

Many other sources have detailed the actors and writers and directors and producers who created and presented the series. But what do we really know about the character? What was he like? What were his habits, predilections and preferences? From listening to over 700 different programs covering every available case, the following profile of Johnny Dollar emerges.

[2] His original name was "Lloyd London"—see Terry Salomonson's YTJD Log Book.

[3] Two other actors, Dick Powell and Gerald Mohr auditioned for the program.

BACKGROUND

There is no concise biography of John Dollar, or Johnny Dollar as he preferred to be called. After all, he was a fictitious character. He could be, or would be, what ever the writer chose him to be. With over 30 individual writers or writing partnerships involved in the creation of his adventures, there would be some variability in his past, his likes and dislike and his habits. Only after listening to his adventures the following comes out:

- EARLY PROGRAMS IN THE SERIES TEND TO INDICATE THAT JOHNNY DOLLAR STARTED OUT AS AN EMPLOYEE OF THE LEGENDARY "PINKERTON" DETECTIVE AGENCY.
- IN PART 4 OF THE "THE BENNET MATTER," THE FOLLOWING INFORMATION IS BROUGHT OUT AS JOHNNY TESTIFIES IN COURT THAT AS OF 1956:
  - JOHNNY HAD 10 PLUS YEARS AS A FREELANCE INVESTIGATOR
  - JOHNNY SPENT 4 YEARS IN THE UNITED STATES MARINES
  - JOHNNY WAS A NEW YORK POLICE DEPARTMENT DETECTIVE SERGEANT 2ND GRADE.

Adding these factors together and doing a little math:

STORY YEAR	1956
INVESTIGATOR EXPERIENCE	-10
US MARINES	-4
NYPD DETECTIVE EXPERIENCE	-4
HIGH SCHOOL GRADUATION AGE	-18
YEAR OF BIRTH	1920

- HOWEVER, IN THE "THE MAN WHO WAITS MATTER" AIRED ON 5/22/1960, JOHNNY MENTIONS THAT HE WAS JUST GETTING STARTED 7 YEARS EARLIER IN 1953.

This would make the Bob Bailey era Johnny Dollar in his mid thirties.

In "The Paradise Lost Matter," and in "The Bad One Matter" Johnny Dollar is asked his age, and the answer is a mumbled thirty something. Not too old to be found attractive by younger women, not to old to go off romping through the woods and pretty much old enough to be settled in his ways and experienced enough to get the job done. In the series, Bob Bailey was in his late thirties to early forties, and quite capable of vocally carrying off the part.

Johnny is a very knowledgeable individual, who always seems to have that special bit of knowledge necessary to cinch a case. Some of that knowledge no doubt came from the school of hard knocks. But, in "The Wayward Heiress Matter" Johnny notes that he met Ginnie Van Doren while they were attending college together in the Midwest.

Other than a direct reference to the U.S. Marines in the Bennett Matter, and a reference of having been a soldier in the CBI (China, Burma, India) Theater of World War II in "The Expiring Nickels And The Egyptian Jackpot" story, there is no direct mention about Johnny's specific military experience. However, in three programs, Johnny is at the controls of a small plane with the inference that he might have been an aviator during World War II. In "The Sealegs Matter," Johnny tells his cohort Oscar Patrick Vladimir Poscaro, played by Parley Baer, that he has a Pilots License. In "The Midnight Sun Matter," Johnny handles the controls of a twin-engine cargo plane, and eventually performs a belly landing after the pilot suffers an attack of appendicitis and a failure of the hydraulic system. In "The Wrong Doctor Matter," Johnny flies a small plane across the border in pursuit of a drug smuggler. In several cases, Johnny uses SCUBA (Self Contained Underwater Breathing Apparatus) gear, and even an old-fashioned helmeted deep-sea diving suit, indicating some possible military training as a diver.

Johnny does own a personal automobile—a "jalopy" he calls it, which is used on some trips, usually after he buys a tank of gas, on the expense account of course. However, Johnny is more apt to jump into a cab, onto a plane or a train to add items to the expense account. In "The Star of Capetown Matter," Johnny even rides in a helicopter to get onto an ocean liner while it is en route. The rental of a helicopter also figures into "The Further Buffalo Matter."

In the beginning of the series, Johnny Dollar was only armed with his wits. As the character, and the nature of the plots developed, Johnny was within close proximity of his gun. It was always on a case with him, either packed in his bags or in a holster. While no specific mention is made, the "typical" detective of the era usually carried his gun in a shoulder holster.

On numerous occasions Johnny makes a reference to his "automatic" of unnoted caliber possibly either a .38 Automatic, or a .45 Automatic. Other references are made to his ".38" revolver, probably a Smith & Wesson .38 caliber "Police Special." However, in "The Shy Beneficiary Matter," he notes that he threw his "automatic" to the ground. In "The Carboniferous Dolomite Matter," the Police Inspector inspects his gun and specifically notes that the clip is full, another inference to an Automatic. In "The Deadly Swamp Matter," a reference is made to his "pretty gun" possibly indicating a nickel finish. In "The Can't Be So Matter" the wife of an insurance agent buddy mentions his impressive gun collection, to which her husband is secretly trying to add a single action Army Colt .45 revolver.

In the Bob Bailey and Mandel Kramer programs, Johnny carries a .38 "lemon squeezer." From the 1890's until the 1930's Smith and Wesson manufactured a hammerless .32 and .38 caliber revolver called a "lemon squeezer." This type of revolver was reportedly popular with gamblers and detectives because it could be safely fired from inside a coat pocket.

In the post 9/11 era, it is somewhat incongruous to think that Johnny Dollar could jump on an airplane, armed and ready to go.

Johnny was a licensed investigator. He was more than willing to show his ID to the police, sometimes with less-than favorable results. As the red scare developed, Johnny also picked up a secret clearance from the FBI. In "The Top Secret Matter" Johnny lists several other clearances, including several military organizations. Having such clearances allows Johnny to handle much more than the usual insurance cases. He was able to go where the political action was, and helped out on a number of cases involving the space race.

The Different Investigator

There was more to Johnny Dollar than the theme of the program. Johnny answered to a "higher" power. A Sam Spade or a Richard Diamond was hired, typically by a person, to right some wrong, find a killer or put a crook in jail. All cases were handled with the hope of getting paid. Johnny Dollar however, worked for insurance companies, an industry known for trust and financial propriety.

When Johnny took an assignment, he was not on his own. He was working to protect the interests of the insurance company, and in turn to protect the interests of the policyholder. When a policyholder must be paid, no matter the circumstances, it was Johnny's job to get the facts and make sure the payment was correct. When the circumstances called "foul," Johnny had to look to the interests of the insurance company that was employing him. In several cases, that was a difficult thing to do. In "The South Sea Adventure" Johnny was hired to find a group of missing policyholders in the south pacific. Once into the investigation, Johnny discovers that the very ones he must protect were the one causing the problems. So there was the matter of keeping his client's property alive long enough to turn them in to the police.

Like all detectives, Johnny was often working on investigations where the police were or should have been involved. The "typical" radio detective was usually either one step ahead of the police, or the prime suspect of the police. Johnny Dollar was put in the position of working along with the police. For the most part, this was a professional and mutually rewarding experience, as Johnny was able to provide additional footwork to the police, or in some cases go where the police could not go. In a number of cases, Johnny notes that he is able to "cut a deal" with the suspect for the return of jewels or stolen money, something prohibited to the police. In "The Protection Matter" Johnny goes one step further and gets the necessary information by administering a beating to a former gangster.

The relationship with the police was not always cordial. Because of his ability to offer deals and the need to maintain confidentiality, Johnny frequently withheld information from the police. On occasions that put Johnny on a collision path with the police, who were out to solve the crime. Johnny was threatened with arrest, and was arrested on several occasions. He was ordered off cases and had his license threatened numerous times as a form of unfair leverage.

Personal

As an individual, Johnny Dollar gave no reference to either parents or siblings. In "The Matter of the Medium, Well Done Part 3," he does state that he does not have a brother, even though he had told a medium that he did. But there were no other familial references in the programs available.

Johnny was a confirmed bachelor but really enjoyed the company of an attractive young lady. There were several women who seemed to play an important or recurring part in Johnny's life:

- CAROL DALHART, DAUGHTER OF THE CANTANKEROUS DURANGO LARAMIE DALHART
- BETTY LEWIS, A BUSINESS WOMAN BENT ON TRAPPING JOHNNY INTO MARRIAGE, WHICH HE WOULD HAVE LOVED TO DO, EXCEPT FOR HIS JOB.
- MARY GRACE MARSHALL, A NEW YORK FASHION DESIGNER WHO ONLY APPEARS ONCE, AND IS KILLED AFTER SPENDING A CHUMMY, PLATONIC WEEKEND WITH JOHNNY.

Many other relationships were inferred, and many hearts were broken, but Johnny remained a bachelor right to the end. While all of the Johnny Dollars were comfortable around women, Charles Russell played a particularly womanizing character, which by the end of the Edmond O'Brien run had mellowed quite a bit. Maybe he had just grown up by then.

In "The Henry J. Unger Matter" Johnny gave his address as 390 Pearl Street, an apartment in Hartford, Connecticut, the heart of the American insurance industry. There actually is a Pearl Street in Hartford. Today the 390 Pearl Street address is a parking lot. In "The Calgary Matter" his phone number was given out by the operator as "Stanley 3469." In the Dick Powell audition program, Johnny says that "he lives in Hartford, Connecticut, or at least that is where he pays rent." The apartment is a walk up and is described as being nicely furnished. As it was described in "The Date With Death Matter" the apartment has a den and a small kitchen with a rear entrance out to the fire escape. It seemed to be your typical professional bachelor apartment.

There is generally no indication of his appearance. We can only assume he is around six feet tall, probably of medium build and very attractive to women. (Was there ever a detective who was repulsive in appearance?) In "Milford Brooks III," Johnny says that, in case you want to give a Christmas present, he wears a size 42 suit, 15 1/2 inch shirt with 33 inch sleeve, and a 7 3/8" hat. No doubt these measurements fit Dick Powell to a "T." In "The Man Who Waits Matter," Johnny notes that in order to effect a disguise, he had to use dye to darken his light hair, and peroxide to lighten his normally darkly tanned skin. In "The Wayward Truck Matter," Johnny is told that he fights pretty well for a skinny guy. As with most "men of action" in the 1950's and 60's, Johnny was a cigarette smoker.

Johnny also was one who enjoyed fine dining as many entries in his infamous expense reports were for meals at nice restaurants. At the same time, he was not above grabbing a sandwich on the go or even skipping a meal when the action required otherwise. Johnny was not above finding comfort in a bonded form of nourishment, both in his room at night, or with clients. Both Charles Russell and Edmond O'Brien would, when asked if they were on a case, reply, "Yes, a case of Kentucky bonded." The earlier Johnny Dollars tended to be bourbon and cognac drinkers; Bob Bailey and later Johnny's were scotch drinkers. No fizzy, umbrella-topped drinks for these guys.

Johnny Dollar always seemed to be a snappy dresser. While nothing specific was mentioned, he seemed to fit the business suit and hat standard of the day (see above for a wardrobe description). In "The Smokey Sleeper Matter," Johnny is described as wearing "a blue shirt and a bow tie." In "The Short Term Matter," Johnny mentions a cashmere sports coat. Even when out fishing, there was no mention of what he was wearing, other than fishing clothes.

On his many adventures he was always doing things that could only bring joy to the heart (and pocketbook) of the local haberdasher. Things like jumping into the Everglades or the 20 Mile Swamp to protect himself, climbing down into ravines to find a body or wrecked automobile, or traipsing all over town at night, all while dressed in his business attire. A number of expense accounts included replacement clothes.

Johnny Dollar was a departure from the "hard-core" fast-fisted cynical tough-guy detective. He could be tough. In the "The Clinton Matter—Part 4," Johnny shows his tough side by demanding that the sheriff of a crooked town resign. In several other cases, he is not afraid to order autopsies be performed, issue court orders or convince someone that his face would look much prettier without Johnny's fist in it.

But at the same time, Johnny could show a tender, even compassionate side. He was not afraid to give someone, especially a pretty girl, a shoulder to cry on. Often Johnny would look the other way when what was right went against what justice called for. In a couple of cases, he even donated his expense account to the local charity or even worked gratis if the case was one where taking his expenses was not the correct thing to do.

Johnny was an admirer of the other sex, but remained a confirmed bachelor. The most consistent reason was that it would be unfair to tie someone down to a guy who did not know from day-to-day if he would be home for dinner, or even home. Johnny once told a travel agent that he only bought one-way tickets because sometimes he did not know if he would be coming back. He seemed to have a bit of remorse over his occupation from time to time, but he never strayed from the case or gave up. On at least one occasion, he traveled all over the country to avoid what he thought was going to be a shotgun wedding!

Occupational Hazards

There is another aspect to Johnny Dollar that is somewhat troublesome. In every episode, almost without exception (although there were a few) there were two occurrences that could be relied on:

1. SOME ONE WOULD DIE, AND
2. JOHNNY WOULD BE KNOCKED UNCONSCIOUS BY A HIT ON THE HEAD WITH SOMETHING—USUALLY THE BUTT OF A GUN.

It is the second occurrence which must have made Johnny's head look like a phrenologist's nightmare with it's numerous bumps, gashes, gullies and chasms inflicted by over 12 years worth of abuse. One wonders why Johnny did not stammer and lumber around like a punch-drunk fighter.

Another occupational hazard held by all detectives is the risk of being shot, and working for insurance companies does not spare Johnny from that danger. Over the course of 12 years, Johnny is shot 13 times. The cases involved are:

THE EIGHTY FIVE LITTLE MINKS
THE LLOYD HAMMERLY MATTER
THE BALTIMORE MATTER
THE SAN ANTONIO MATTER
THE MACORMACK MATTER – PART 5
THE TODD MATTER – PART 5
THE MIDAS TOUCH MATTER – PART 5
THE DENVER DISBURSAL MATTER
THE VIRTUOUS MOBSTER MATTER
THE PERILOUS PARLEY MATTER
THE INFORMER MATTER
THE WELL OF TROUBLE MATTER
THE SKIMPY MATTER

For the superstitious, bear in mind that there are a number of missing programs that might adjust the above number.

Recreation and Hobbies

For Johnny Dollar there was only one sport, fishing, either on the job or on vacation. Many of the programs were woven around the "Lake Mojave Resort" in Arizona, or at Earle Poorman's Sarasota, Florida, beach home. Johnny was willing to wet a line where ever opportunity and a body of water presented it self. Fishing locations included the Gulf of Mexico, the Pacific around southern California, Lake Tahoe, the Esophus River in New York State, and Lake Mojave Resort. Most of the dialog was pretty general, but in the "The Blue Rock Matter" the author of the script, Jack Johnstone goes into a nice bit of detail regarding what type of trout flies to use in the early season. I know the details are correct, as I am more than familiar with the joys and frustrations of being humiliated by a wily trout, while standing in freezing water with a fly rod in my hands! Jack Johnstone was also quite a fisherman, and would often go to the real Lake Mojave, and fish with his real friends Ham Pratt and Buster Favor. Jack even patented a fishing hook called the Sure-Strike hook that was mentioned in several programs.

Johnny also liked beach activities, whether swimming or snorkeling, or discussing a case with a lovely young lady poolside. In several cases, Johnny seems to be a boxing fan and occasionally goes to the track. In "The Picture Postcard Matter" Johnny takes to a pair of skis. In "The Short Term Matter" Johnny starts the case by relating the previous weekend's major activity; falling on his back in a chair-lift accident that requires him to wear a steel-ribbed corset, another skiing reference.

Income

The basic premise of the program is the "action packed expense account" created in the process of completing his investigations for his employers. But there is more to be had in examining the details.

The early Johnny Dollars always seemed to be one step ahead of their creditors, although they always seemed to have the cash to jump on an airplane (long before frequent flier miles) or a train (when trains still ran). Johnny even takes a bus on several occasions to get to the scene of the case. Near the end of the Bob Bailey series, Johnny notes the use of his "personal" American Express credit card. There are also several references to grabbing a hand full of "American Express Travelers Checks" on his way to the airport.

The major issue with the expense account, and the underlying theme of the program, tends to be the "padding" of the expenses for any given case. The term "incidentals" shows up regularly, as do the names of top grade hotels. There was no "Motel 6" for Johnny Dollar, unless that was the only place available. In "The Parakoff Policy Matter," Johnny adds $700 to the expense account for a trip to Miami to recover from a cold caught in Ohio. When Dick Powell auditioned for Johnny Dollar, he adds a $318 bracelet for his girlfriend "Butter" to the tab in "Milford Brooks III." In retrospect is it interesting to listen to Johnny wrap up a case, having traveled all over the country, with an expense account of less than $200. In a report at the end of the cases, I have recapped the expenses of each of the actors who played Johnny Dollar, and have adjusted them for inflation to 2006 values. The adjusted figures help to see not only the relative cost of the trips, but give a perspective on price inflation also. Sometimes there was not even an expense account. On several occasions, Johnny even ended up working gratis for a good cause.

But there is more to the picture. A close listening reveals that in addition to expenses, Johnny's pay was tied to the face value of the policy, or the goods stolen. It seems that almost everyone in the world had a huge diamond or emerald necklace in the 1950's, and most of these ended up being stolen. Sometimes, like the Canary Diamonds, they were stolen twice!

It would seem that in cases of fraud or other occurrences that would render a policy null and void, Johnny got a percentage of the face value of the policy. In the case of stolen items, there was a fee based on the insured value of the property recovered. In "The Suntan Oil Matter," Johnny tells Mrs. Galloway that he gets 10-30% of the value of a piece of stolen jewelry when he recovers it. In some cases, when he was really trying to get out of a case or was just irritated at the agent requesting his time, or Johnny was in need of money, there would be a "fee" or "commission" added to make the case worth his time. In several cases, there was a reward for the arrest of a criminal, which went to Johnny.

Other clients bestowed gifts and rewards on Johnny as well. Alvin Peabody Cartwright was one such client; Durango Laramie Dalhart was another. Both lavished relatively large amounts of cash or expensive gifts on Johnny whom they both counted on, for professional services and as a good friend. In "The Merry-Go-Round Matter," Alvin Cartwright gives Johnny a money clip covered with diamonds as a Christmas present.

Another interesting item is the radio broadcasts of his cases. Starting with "The Blooming Blossom Matter," Mr. Blossom notes that he listens to Johnny's radio programs. In "The Winsome Widow Matter," the program actually starts with Johnny telling Pat McCracken that he is in Hollywood to meet with Jack Johnstone about the broadcasting of his cases. Johnny even runs into Jack Johnstone's brother Doug in several stories that take place in Corpus Christi, Texas. In a number of later episodes, Johnny is recognized by his voice (which is his undoing in at least one case), and many clients and contacts make reference to hearing the stories on the radio. In "The Big H. Matter," Johnny is even contacted by an elderly radio fan for help. The unmentioned aspect of the Hollywood angle is that Johnny Dollar would likely have been paid for the stories, providing yet another source of income for Johnny.

During the later Bob Bailey series, and especially at the end of the Mandel Kramer episodes, there are blatant plugs for the CBS affiliate located in the city of the investigation. The Bob Bailey, John Lund and Mandel Kramer characters enlist the aid of the local CBS news departments in their investigations. In "The Missing Missile Matter," "The Wayward Kilocycles Matter" and "The Vociferous Dolphin Matter" Johnny enlists the aide of a CBS sound engineer, Bob McKenny to provide technical assistance.

All things considered, in an era when the average household income was less than $6,000, and a $25,000 policy was big stuff, Johnny Dollar tended to live pretty well, but always seemed to act as if the wolf were at the door. Johnny lived in a walkup apartment, and drove a jalopy, and did mention some investments in the stock market. So one wonders where his money went.

The Final Chapter Matter

After the final episode of Yours Truly Johnny Dollar aired in September 1962, Johnny Dollar disappeared from the airwaves. There was no closure, just the finality of dead air. The abruptness of the end raises an interesting question: what would have happened to Johnny Dollar if Jack Johnstone had been given the opportunity to close out the character gracefully? How would the series have ended, what would have become of the man with the action packed expense account?

What follows below is my attempt to provide an answer to these questions. There are several typical closure mechanisms available. Johnny could just be killed off or disappear on his last case or he could just get tired and retire. There are many options, but the following scenario, in my mind, outlines the final days of Johnny Dollar.

NOTE: THE TEXT BELOW IS WRITTEN WITH BOB BAILEY IN MIND, SO I HAVE TRIED, PROBABLY VERY POORLY, TO WRITE AS IF BOB WERE READING THE TEXT BELOW. ADDITIONALLY, MY MIND'S EAR HEARS WILL WRIGHT AS MR. FARNSWORTH, AND VIRGINIA GREGG AS BETTY.

THE FINAL CHAPTER MATTER

(*Phone rings*)

Johnny (*yawn*) Dollar.

"Mr. Dollar, this is Webster T. Farnsworth and I represent. . ."

"I'm sorry Mr. Farnsworth, but I am not interested in a new case right now. I have been out of town on a case for five weeks and I'm really tired." I mumbled into the phone.

"Mr. Dollar, I am not calling to hire you for your services. I represent Alvin Peabody Cartwright and"

"Oh, no! What has poor old Alvin gotten himself in to this time?"

"Well Mr. Dollar, I do understand you were previously involved in some insurance matters with Mr. Cartwright. But I am calling on an entirely different matter. I regret to inform you, Mr. Dollar, that Mr. Cartwright has died."

"Died? Alvin? How did it happen? Was foul play involved?"

"No, Mr. Dollar. Alvin's passing was quite natural. He had been ill for some weeks and died peacefully in his sleep four days ago. We have been trying to contact you, but the phone was never answered. Now I understand why. Mr. Dollar, can you come to Los Angeles for the funeral? It is quite important that you do so."

"I'll grab the first flight."

(*Theme Music*)

Expense Account submitted by special investigator Johnny Dollar to, well this one is really to me. The following is an accounting of expenditures during my involvement in "The Final Chapter Matter."

"After returning home at 3:00 AM from another tiring and very frustrating case, I found a telegram under my apartment door urging me to call a Mr. Farnsworth, an attorney in California. I was not ready for another case, and it was too late to call, so I made a note to return the call in the morning, or rather much later that day after a well-deserved rest. At 10:45 that morning, I received a call from Mr. Webster T. Farnsworth advising me of the passing, four days ago, of my old friend and client Alvin Peabody Cartwright. Poor old Alvin had been in ill health for weeks, and had died peacefully in his sleep. I immediately advised Mr. Farnsworth that I would catch the first available flight to Los Angeles to attend the services for my dear old friend. Mr. Farnsworth advised me that I should be prepared to attend the reading of the will the day after the funeral. It was just like Alvin to remember his friends with a last thank you."

"I shaved and showered, packed a fresh suitcase and threw my swimming trunks in for good measure. After a long, cold and frustrating five weeks chasing down a gang of insurance scam-artists I needed a rest. So I planned on spending a week in the sun and surf around San Diego after the funeral."

"Expense Account Item one: cab fare, incidentals and plane fare to Los Angeles: $295.45"

"After wiring Mr. Farnsworth of my travel arrangements, I caught an early evening jet flight to Los Angeles, settled back and napped most of the way. I arrived in Los Angeles at 9:15 PM, and was unexpectedly met by one of Mr. Farnsworth's associates, who took my bag and informed me that I would be staying at the Cartwright estate. The drive to Alvin's mansion was pleasant and a familiar one, as I had been to the estate several times on business. I was shown to a suite of rooms and informed that there would be a breakfast buffet on the patio for Mr. Cartwright's friends at 9:00 AM the next morning. I was still tired, so I went to bed and slept through the night, time change and all."

"At 9:00 AM I went downstairs and was met at the bottom of the long winding staircase by George Reed, Alvin's insurance agent and advisor. George was and old friend and we expressed our pleasure to see each other, but lamented the circumstances. On the large balcony outside the dining room our mutual friend Pat McCracken, who had acted as the Universal Adjustment Bureau intermediary on several cases involving Alvin, met us for breakfast."

"On the balcony were about a two dozen others; executives of the various companies Alvin had set up over his long and profitable lifetime, his personal staff and old friends. At 10:30 we were all ushered into the Library for a very sedate and short memorial service. Alvin had never wanted a formal funeral, so we were not surprised that there was no coffin in the room. Mr. Farnsworth orchestrated the service at which there were three speakers: his longtime secretary, his legal advisor Mr. Farnsworth, and his friend George Reed. The whole event was over in barely over thirty minutes."

"After the service, I introduced my self to Mr. Farnsworth."

"I am sorry I had to awaken you the other day, Mr. Dollar, but we had been trying to reach you for four days." Farnsworth told me.

"Unfortunately, I was out on a case. In my business I am rarely home. Did you contact my service?" I asked.

"No, we had your home number in Mr. Cartwright's file and there were very explicit instructions to make sure you were called immediately. You must have been a very good friend of Mr. Cartwright's, Mr. Dollar."

"Alvin, er, I mean Mr. Cartwright and I were associated professionally. I handled some insurance related matters for him, and some personal matters as well. He was quite a character."

"Yes. Knowing Mr. Cartwright as I did, I can only imagine what he had you involved in. The poor man was a bit flighty and addled at times, but he had a business mind that was just as sharp in his final weeks as it was forty years ago."

"Flighty is an understatement. Some of his cases made for the funniest of the all the broadcast programs I worked on for Jack Johnstone over at CBS radio."

"Well, I am not much of a radio or television person Mr. Dollar, so I will have to get my staff to find some of the programs to listen to. While I am talking about my staff, I will send a car for you here tomorrow at 9:00 AM. Mr. Cartwright's Last Will and Testament will be read in my offices at 10:00 AM tomorrow, and your presence is most important."

"I had planned to stay until tomorrow afternoon, and then head for the beach in San Diego for a week of vacation."

"Very good. I will see you tomorrow morning, Mr. Dollar."

"During the service we all had learned that Alvin had wished to be cremated and have his ashes spread at sea. At 1:00 PM I joined a small group of chosen friends who were driven to his yacht 'The Alpecar'. We sailed out to the area beyond the Channel Islands and very somberly spread the ashes of Alvin Cartwright over the waters. It was quite fitting that a Sea Otter came up, looked around, winked and then dived down into the waters during the ceremony."

"The rest of the day was spent with George and Pat talking about old times. We managed to find a good restaurant near by and went out for drinks and dinner. "

"Expense Account Item two: Dinner for three at the "Surfside Restaurant": $57.89. I shocked no one by picking up the check, but Pat wondered aloud how I was going to get Alvin to pay for it."

"At 9:00 AM sharp the next morning there was a car and driver to take me to the offices of Mr. Farnsworth in Beverly Hills. In the wood paneled and somber conference room of Farnsworth's office were gathered a variety of people. Some were quite obviously executives of Alvin's various companies, while others looked like they had worked for, or known Alvin personally over the years."

"Most of the bequests were generous amounts given to Alvin's employees, some old friends and his business associates. But it was the last part of the will that left me speechless. Having no immediate family, Alvin had established a foundation to direct the activities of his far-flung financial interests, and he had named me, Special Investigator Johnny Dollar to be Chairman of the Board of the Alvin Peabody Cartwright Foundation. Needless to say, I was flabbergasted. Being an insightful man, Alvin knew that that I could not maintain my activities as an investigator and direct a foundation that would oversee almost five hundred million dollars. So Alvin left me another most unexpected surprise. Alvin provided a $5,000,000 cash bequest to allow me to lessen my schedule and help me make time for my new responsibilities without making for a financial burden! Like I said, I was flabbergasted!"

"After the meeting adjourned I approached Mr. Farnsworth."

"Mr. Farnsworth, are you really sure about this foundation thing? I am not sure that I am the executive type, or at least the type of high power executive you are looking for. I have spent the past twenty years chasing people, being shot at and the hit on the head. I do not want to appear ungrateful or disrespectful, but I think that you and Alvin have made a mistake here."

"No, Mr. Dollar. I believe it is you who are wrong. Let me explain. For the past year, after Mr. Cartwright suspected that he was ill, we looked for someone who could run the foundation in the manner Mr. Cartwright wanted it run. We interviewed over 200 well-qualified executives, and after each meeting, Mr. Cartwright would say that he wished he could find another Johnny Dollar, a man he could trust implicitly. He wanted a man with four qualities. First the man had to be honest above suspicion. Secondly, the man had to be able to stand toe-to-toe with someone, look him in the eye and tell him 'NO!' Thirdly we wanted a man who could wade through the smoke and fluff of a problem and find the facts and act accordingly. Lastly, we wanted a man who would look out for the interests of the foundation and all associated with it. Mr. Cartwright knew you were the man for the job."

"Well, I am flattered, but still I. . ."

"Mr. Dollar, Johnny. Let me reassure you that you will not flounder alone in this position. You will have the assistance of the finest law firms, accountants and auditors in the country. You will not be alone.

"You may not know this, but Mr. Cartwright followed your cases very closely, to the point of buying a sizeable interest in the Universal Adjustment Bureau. He watched how you dealt both with the small penny-ante policyholders and the industrialists who were out to fleece anyone they could. Mr. Cartwright was positive you were the right man for the job."

"But this is such a change from what I am doing now. I do not even know the others I am supposed to work with, let alone how to evaluate or protect anything. I feel like I have just been launched into space on one of those new guided missiles."

"Johnny, let me tell you a story. I was born on a hardscrabble farm in Alabama. My father never had more than a dollar to his name, but he taught me how to work hard. In high school I had to literally fight my way on to the basketball team so that I could have a pair of shoes that fit. I worked my way through college and law school. When I got to my first real legal job, I did not think I could pour water from a boot and hit the floor with it. But, a mentor at the firm told me something that got me through. The oldest partner of the firm called me into his office on the first day and told me that the only thing separating me from the other attorneys there was experience. He told me I was just as smart as anyone there, I just did not know the ropes. His advice was to learn how to manage the ropes, and everything else would take care of it self. And it has. Johnny, my advice to you is to learn the ropes and you will excel. There is no magic here. This position is no different than working on one of your investigations. In some ways it will be the same job you have been doing very well for many years. The only difference is, you get to approve your own expense accounts."

"Well, Mr. Farnsworth if"

"Please, my friends call me Webb, and you are my friend now Johnny."

Ok, Webb. I guess I need to think like Tarzan and learn the ropes. Thank you very much for your confidence in me. And I promise to take it easy on the expense accounts for once!" Did I say that?

"After completing the necessary paperwork with Mr. Farnsworth, who is now "Webb" and who promised me that I would not be overwhelmed by my new duties, we met with several other members of the foundation, and I was given a very thick binder to read on my vacation."

"Later that day I caught a flight to San Diego for that week at the beach."

"Expense Account Item three, well, with money in my pocket and a new set of responsibilities I think that accounting for my expenses as I have done for so many years is somewhat unnecessary now, as this account is on me."

"I spent a short week at the beach, enjoying the sun, swimming in the pool, snorkeling down near Mexico and doing a little deep-sea fishing. But the binder was always there to lull me to sleep each night. I was tempted to take a quick trip to see my friends Buster and Ham at Lake Mojave Resorts, but I decided to get back to cold, snowy Hartford. After all, I still had not unpacked my bags from my last case."

"Expense Account Item four, well old habits are hard to break."

"I arrived home in Hartford and spent a busy day unpacking, catching up on the mail, paying some bills and making my dry cleaner a happy man with the accumulation of a month's dirty clothes. After a night of strangely fitful sleep, I called my service only to find out that the Universal Adjustment Bureau was looking me."

"I called Pat Fuller at his office and listened to the case, which would have taken me to the jungles of South America once again. I told Pat that, for the first time I would need to think about the case before accepting it."

"I left the offices and walked around snowy Hartford for several hours just thinking. After thinking about the changes in my life over the past week and a long day of contemplation, I went to a public stenographer and had her prepare several letters for the next day."

"On a cold mid February morning, I made a series of early phone calls, sent some wires and visited a number of my most loyal employers in Hartford to give them an unwanted message; Johnny Dollar has retired. I explained why at each of my stops, and after both congratulations and pleas for my services "for just one more big case" the deed was done. Johnny Dollar, the man with the action packed expense account was no longer available."

"After the insurance company meetings, I made my way to the office of my dearest and closest gal-friend, Betty Lewis. I surprised the receptionist Lucy by showing up unexpectedly. Lucy told me that Betty was in a meeting that had already gone an hour over the scheduled time, so I decided to sit and wait. After 45 minutes and four magazines, the conference room emptied and Betty finally burst out of the room talking angrily to a younger man about really botching the presentation to a major client."

"What were you thinking? That presentation was nowhere close to the approach you were told to use! And you event spelled the man's name wrong!" the young man is told. Betty was so involved with sending the man off to his office to start trying to fix the damage that she walked right past me, into her office, slamming the door in the process. I looked at a surprised Lucy who then buzzed Betty to tell her that I was here.

"Johnny? Here?" Betty came rushing out, pleasantly surprised to see me yet apologetic about walking past me.

"That's ok, Betty. I sort of sensed you were busy, " I told her " but I need your help right now on a major case I am working on."

"Johnny, you know I would do just about anything for you, but today, no, this week has just gone down the drain and I need to recover a botched presentation to keep a major client. It really is important. You understand don't you?" she said, looking like she was ready to either pull her hair out or cry or both.

"Sure I understand, but I only need you for an hour, and it has to be today, right now." I told her. "Come on, I'll buy you lunch and you can help me start this project. It will only take a few minutes, and you really could use a break right now. Who knows, you might actually like working on this project."

"Johnny, what is so important that you have to come into my office without an appointment, not that you need one, and take me off on one of your crazy wild-goose-chase insurance investigations? Can't it wait until next week? After all, I have not seen you for, well for months. I really need to salvage this project. I know your job is important to you, but this project is important to me. It is maybe the most important project of my career, and maybe the last one if I cannot salvage it."

"Betty, what I want you to do for me is even more important than your project. It will only take half an hour at most if we skip lunch. Come on, we can start on it now." I told her pulling on her arm.

"Look, Johnny, I can't leave right now. What is so all important that is can't wait for a week?" she told me, starting to get angry.

"Look, all I need you to do is get in a cab with me, run down to City Hall and get a marriage license with me. You will be back in plenty of time to deal with your client. Maybe even with a new perspective on it."

"Johnny, if all you need is someone to sign a paper, I will get Lucy to call our Notary and. . .what did you say!"

"You heard me, Miss Betty Lewis. Johnny Dollar has retired. I have a new job, and I think that it is about time I stopped stringing you along and settled down. Now are you coming with me?"

Lucy and I picked Betty up and put her on the sofa in her office after she fainted. After recovering for a few minutes I told Betty of my new job with the foundation and my plans to retire and move to Florida. I told her I wanted to build a little beach house, maybe somewhere close to my friends Earle and Mike Poorman. Then I would spend my days fishing with Earle, tending to my job at the foundation and most importantly of all, trying to be a good husband to Mrs. Betty Dollar. Suddenly the turmoil of the office was forgotten, and after dictating a series of instructions for Lucy, Betty and I ran off to catch a cab for City Hall.

Over the next month I worked on settling my affairs, collecting my outstanding expense account payments, starting the plans for a move to Florida and attending a few board meetings. Betty was even able to rescue her client, at the cost of a brash young up-and-coming account manager who is now probably working on a loading dock somewhere licking his wounds!

On a bright Saturday in April, Miss Betty Lewis became Mrs. Johnny Dollar before an overflow crowd of family, clients and friends. Pat McCracken was my best man and Betty's college roommate was her maid of honor. My old fishing buddies Buster and Ham from Lake Mojave Resort were there. Randy Singer came up from New York and the boys from Virtue, South Carolina were there. That living-doll Carol Dalhart Johnson came, with a note from her Uncle Durango who was ill, her husband William, and a wink-in-her-eye offer to dump William if I would change my mind about marrying Betty. Insurance agents from all over the country were there, some of who owed their jobs to my work. Even my friend Louis Du Marsac, "les char gris" from Paris, France was there, albeit with a gendarme handcuffed to his left wrist, a sly grin on his face and a solemn promise to keep his right hand in his own pockets.

Jack Johnstone and the actors from my CBS Radio program came. Parley Baer and Howard McNear were up to their usual tricks and even put on a little "roast" during the reception. Jack even arranged for the CBS Television staff in New York to come and film the wedding as a present. Some of the footage even made the national evening news with Walter Cronkite that Sunday.

After almost 20 years of investigations for agents and clients all over the country, the gifts from my associates looked like a catalog from a well-heeled department store. At one point, I think I recognized an antique silver tea set on the gift table that had almost gotten me killed. I shot a quick glance to Pat McCracken only to get a quizzical look as Pat went looking for the punch bowl. All in all a fine day was had by all, even though the party lasted well into the next morning.

The next day Betty and I left for a two-week honeymoon in Bermuda and the

Bahamas, where the hotels mysteriously seemed to lose the bills and champagne appeared mysteriously every night. Well rested and happy, Betty and I returned to Hartford to clean out my apartment at 390 Pearl Street. Even after 20 years of odd hours, strange visitors and more than a few late rent payments, the landlady and my old friends in the building were in tears as they watched the moving van being packed.

Unfortunately another bit of bad news came for us as we were packing up. Carol Dalhart Johnson called to tell me that her uncle, Durango Laramie Dalhart, had died that night. According to his wishes, he was buried quietly with no fanfare on his little farm in Bum Spung, Oklahoma. But there was a letter for me that Durango had written shortly before his death that required my presence.

Betty and I flew to Enid, Oklahoma, and drove to Bum Spung where we met with Carol and William, who is now the attorney for Durango's business interests. We read the letter under a cottonwood tree in the yard of his farm, beside that ramshackle little house he loved so much. In the letter, Durango recalled his life and the adventures he and I had shared together, including the time he chased me across the country as I ran from him, thinking he was after me with a shotgun to make me marry Carol. As a token of thanks for my friendship to both him and to Carol, Durango left me 10,000 shares of Dalhart Industries stock and a position on the board of directors. Once again, my life had taken on a new and unexpected dimension.

So it is no more "Mr. Special Investigator" for Johnny Dollar. No more long flights, long nights and bullets whizzing past my ears. No more spending hours pouring over insurance policies and watching shady characters. My activities have now turned to board meetings and financial dealings.

Betty and I finally were able to get to Sarasota and move into our new house on the beach. Earle and Mike Poorman welcomed us like long-lost children. Our life has settled down to trips for board meetings in Los Angeles and Dallas, regular trips to Lake Mojave Resort, fishing with Earle on the Gulf of Mexico and most of all, enjoying life with a wonderful woman named Betty Dollar. Betty has me eating right, she convinced me to stop smoking and I have almost learned how to beat her at tennis, but I still think she cheats with the scoring.

Expense account total, well there is no amount of money that can pay for the happiness I now have with Betty. I have lost two wonderful friends, but life has dealt me a new hand, which I, or rather we, are still trying to deal with. I still jump each time the phone rings during the night, but now it is Earle wanting to sneak out early to fish for Tarpon or Snook before it gets too hot. So, as I close out this final matter, I can only say,

Yours Very Truly,

Betty and Johnny Dollar.

And this is where the story of Johnny Dollar should have ended. It leaves plenty of opportunity for some enterprising writer to pick up the story and create new life for Johnny Dollar, the man with the action packed life being lived with one hand in Betty's, and a fishing rod in the other.

Program-Related Information

The program stuck to a general premise over the entire run of the series. A client hired Johnny to resolve an insurance matter. Hopefully, Johnny would not spend more than the client was going to save! In the process, a variety of cases, presented by a stellar gathering of voices were presented to the listening audience.

THE CASES:

As an independent investigator, Johnny Dollar was free to pick and choose his assignments. Early on, the option tended to be to accept or be poorer than he was. Later in the series, there was reticence over some types of cases, but others—where there was money to be had—were accepted regardless of the circumstances. Most of his cases were for insurance or related financial companies. However, Johnny did work for individuals, as in the case of "The Case of Bonnie Goodwin" where King Hart, a gangster hires him. Johnny also worked several cases for himself, as in "The Mickey McQueen Matter" where he looks into the death of his old, personal friend police officer Mickey McQueen.

Over the run of the series, Johnny handled almost every type of insurance matter. Cases included:

- TRACKING DOWN MISSING BENEFICIARIES
- EXPOSING FRAUDULENT CLAIMS
- INVESTIGATING APPLICATIONS FOR LARGE POLICY AMOUNTS
- FINDING LOST POLICY HOLDERS
- RECOVERING LOST JEWELS AND OTHER PROPERTY
- ACTING A BODY GUARD TO LOVELY WOMEN—AND A FEW UGLY MEN
- INVESTIGATING MANUFACTURING ACCIDENTS
- ARSON, MAYHEM AND THE OCCASIONAL TALKING DOG OR SINGING MOUSE!

During the mid-late 1950's a number of cases involved espionage by "a certain unfriendly country" (I wonder who that was?). As the space race picked up speed, several cases involved a rocket-fuel or space capsule related theme.

More often than not, murder was involved. Johnny often solved cases that the Police should have. Johnny always seemed to know who to call for information, whether it was to Randy Singer of the NYPD, or some famous scientist or professor who just happened to have a vital piece of information.

ACTORS:

Reviewing the many other excellent publications that review the broadcast history of Johnny Dollar, there are a number of names that reappear, some in recurring roles. Some of the most noted radio, screen and television actors stepped up to a microphone opposite Johnny Dollar.

Among the many stars were Virginia Gregg, Parley Baer, Howard McNear, Vic Perrin, Harry Bartell, John McIntire, Willam Conrad, Hy Averback, Sam Edwards, John Dehner, Will Wright, Lou Krugman, Jack Johnstone, Bill Johnstone, Roy Glenn, Byron Kane, Ed Begley, Jim Nusser, Herb Vigran, and many many, more—too many to mention. Many of these names represent voices familiar to many. Many made the transition to television. Many were motion picture stalwarts. Some played a recurring role, such as Howard McNear as Alvin Peabody Cartwright and Parley Baer as Jake Kessler and Larry Dobkin as Pat McCracken. The interesting thing about radio is that, due to the non-visual presentation, and consummate skill of many of these actors, they could play numerous characters in the same program—each with their own voice and character.

THE WRITERS AND PRODUCERS:

Yours Truly, Johnny Dollar was in a sense brought to life by the writers who penned the stories. The table below lists the writers for the programs that I have detailed in this book. There are others, but I have no information who wrote the numerous missing programs.

STORY TOTALS BY WRITER

WRITER(S)	STORY COUNT
ADRIAN GENDOT	1
ALLEN BOTZER	2
BLAKE EDWARDS	28
BLAKE EDWARDS, DICK QUINE	1
CHARLES B. SMITH	11
CHARLES SMITH	1
DAN SANFORD	1
DAVID CHANDLER	1
DON SANFORD	2
E. JACK NEUMAN	25
E. JACK NEUMAN, GIL DOUD	1
E. JACK NEUMAN, JOHN MICHAEL HAYES	3
GIBSON SCOTT FOX	1
GIL DOUD	79

GIL DOUD, DAVID ELLIS	14
JACK JOHNSTONE	261
JOEL MURCOT	3
JOHN DAWSON	23
KATHLENE HITE	1
LES CRUTCHFIELD	23
MORTON FINE, DAVID FRIEDKIN	2
PAUL DUDLEY, GIL DOUD	36
PAUL FRANKLIN	1
ROBERT BAINTER	1
ROBERT RYF	15
ROBERT STANLEY	4
SAM DAWSON	1
SIDNEY MARSHALL	21
TONY BARRETT	2
UNKNOWN	2

It fell on the producer to coax the characters out of the actors in each program. The table below lists the producers for the programs compiled here:

PRODUCER SHOW TOTALS

PRODUCER	SHOW TOTAL
BRUNO ZIRATO, JR.	64
FRED HENDRICKSON	17
GORDON HUGHES	2
GORDON T. HUGHES	13
JACK JOHNSTONE	259
JAIME DEL VALLE	181
NORMAN MACDONNELL	3
NORMAN MCDONNELL	2
RALPH ROSE	1
RICHARD SANVILLE	7
UNKNOWN	3

Based on the above information, if one were to choose a father figure for Johnny, the honor would fall on Jack Johnstone. It was to Jack, who was already a successful writer and producer, that the task fell to revive Johnny Dollar in 1955. Not only did Jack bring in a different format, but he brought in a stellar cadre of radio actors to bring life to the programs.

Eventually Jack undertook both the writing and directing/producing responsibilities for the program. Under Jack's aegis, the program was able to last until September of 1962, when *Yours Truly Johnny Dollar* and *Suspense* ended their runs as the last dramatic programs on radio. Interestingly, Jack wrote the programs for both final broadcasts.

RECURRING CHARACTERS:

Over the run of the series, there were a number of recurring characters, either as contacting agents, clients, or helpers. Some of the more notable are:

Randy Singer, NYPD 18th Precinct: Randy was an old friend who invariably helped Johnny out with information, and an occasional hand out of a deep situation.

Earle Poorman[4], Sarasota Florida: Earle was a good friend of Johnny, as well as an insurance agent who called him in to resolve difficult cases. . .and to go fishing in the Gulf of Mexico.

Ham Pratt & Buster Favor[5], Lake Mojave Resorts: As the owner and manager of the resort, Ham and Buster were always on hand to provide the necessary local information, and to make sure the boat was ready for fishing after the work was done.

Pat McCracken, Universal Adjustment Bureau: The Universal Adjustment Bureau was a fictitious policy claim-clearinghouse. As the manager, Pat was able to provide Johnny both cases and logistical assistance.

Betty Lewis, favorite girl friend: Betty was a business woman who, while desperately wanting to get Johnny's ankle into a marital bear trap, was smart enough to know that the time was not right. Betty figured in several cases as the "secondary" lead.

Durango Laramie Dalhart, of Bum Spung, Oklahoma: Durango, a retired oil/cattle/real estate millionaire, had the habit of walking around with a small fortune in cash in his pocket—and paying all his bills in cash. On one occasion he even laundered his money—literally!

Alvin Peabody Cartwright, slightly forgetful eccentric millionaire: This role fit Howard McNear to a "T." Poor Alvin was loaded but so addle brained he would forget whom he was calling in the middle of a phone call. While seemingly gullible, he was no man's fool in the final analysis.

George Reed, Floyds of England: As a representative of the fictitious "Floyds of England (read Lloyds of London) who always had a wacky case to be handled whether it was a singing mouse or a talking dog or Durango Dalhart.

---

[4] Based on conversations with my friend Bill Brooks, who was a friend of Jack Johnstone's, Earl and Mike Poorman were real friends of Jacks.

[5] Based on conversations with my friend Bill Brooks, who was a friend of Jack Johnstone's, Ham

Louis Du Marsac, les char gris ("The Grey Cat"): This was a French underground character played with a distinct Peter Lorre accent. While the character knew everything that happened in the underground, he quite often cheated himself out of money while dickering over the amount of money he was trying to extort out of Johnny Dollar.

One notable feature of the broadcast series is that on two different occasions during the Bob Bailey episodes (during "The Open Town Matter" and "The Curse of Kamashek Matter"), the star took a few moments to give heartfelt thanks to all of those who had taken the time to write in. Each used the words "You will never know how much your letters meant to us." The announcement also included a promise to answer every letter.

In "The Look Before The Leap Matter" in 1960 during National Brotherhood Week[6], Bob gives a very heartfelt plea for the principles of the event. Bob also gave messages around the Christmas and Thanksgiving holidays as well.

---

[6] Tom Lehrer fans will no doubt remember his rendition of "National Brotherhood Week" with a somewhat less gentle side.

Case Synopses

I personally have listened to every available episode of "Yours Truly, Johnny Dollar" I am aware of. My personal collection is over 700 programs. Additionally, I spent a busy week in the Thousand Oaks Library reviewing the scripts in the KNX collection, which added over 75 programs to the book. The information below is a synopsis of the story line for every program I have either listened to or reviewed. I have tried to recap the writer, producer, announcers and music providers when available in the broadcast. I have referenced at least two other external sources where cast and crew information is available there.

THE FORMAT OF THE SYNOPSES IS AS FOLLOWS:

SHOW DATE:	DATE ON WHICH THE PROGRAM AIRED.
SHOW TITLE:	THE NAME OF THE PROGRAM. WHERE MY NAME VARIES FROM THE USUAL NAME, IT IS BECAUSE I HAVE EITHER CORRECTED SPELLING OR BASED THE NAME ON THE TITLE PAGE OF THE SCRIPT.
COMPANY:	THIS IS THE COMPANY OR INDIVIDUAL WHO HAS HIRED JOHNNY FOR THE CASE
AGENT:	WHERE AVAILABLE, THE AGENT OF THE COMPANY
EXPENSE TOTAL:	THIS IS THE TOTAL OF EXPENSES FOR EACH CASE.
CAST:	WHERE AVAILABLE, THE CAST OF THE PROGRAMS. DEPARTING FROM THE PRACTICE OF OTHER AUTHORS, I HAVE OPTED TO LIST ACTORS EXACTLY AS THEY WERE CREDITED. THEREFORE, YOU WILL FIND ENTRIES FOR DICK CRENNA AND RICHARD CRENNA, BILL CONRAD AND WILLIAM CONRAD, ETC. I HAVE OPTED TO DO THE CAST CREDITS THIS WAY TO PROVIDE A REFERENCE POINT TO CHANGES IN HOW ACTORS REFER TO THEMSELVES.
SYNOPSIS:	A RUNDOWN OF THE CASE—INCLUDING WHO DONE IT. IF YOU DON'T WANT TO KNOW—DON'T READ IT!
NOTES:	INFORMATION OR FACTS IN THE CASE I FIND INTERESTING, ANY AKA'S FOR THE STORY, THE ANNOUNCERS AND MUSIC PROVIDERS, ETC.

The synopses below are divided into seven sections; one section for each of the primary actors, and one for the several audition programs which are available. In each of these programs I have endeavored to spell the names of the directors, writers and actors as accurately as possible. I have relied on the information available from a review of the scripts, J. David Goldin and Terry Salomonson for most of this information, as well as assorted tools on the Internet, such as the "Internet Movie Database" and the researcher's friend, Google.

In the case of characters in the radio programs, I have tried as much as possible to apply a reasonable transliteration to sounds and have relied on the above resources where possible. "Smith and "Jones" are easy; "Ah Mei" and "Arnesson" are a little harder.

Where geographical locations are noted, I have tried to locate them. Native peoples and regions are located and described to the extent possible.

Section 1:
Charles Russell

Charles Russell was the first regular actor to play the Johnny Dollar character. The role that Russell played was of a sarcastic, irreverent, droll and somewhat lecherous person. Johnny always got the bad guy, but he always seemed to get the girl as well—sometimes to his undoing and always, it seemed "on" the expense account. Each of the Russell cases included an alternative title, sometimes two. An additional feature added after the initial programs was an opening comment about the case. An example is the opening of "The Search For Michelle Marsh": "Sure, they may have plenty of blue blood in Boston, but from what I just saw, they've got plenty of the other kind too."

This Johnny is not so much of a hard-boiled detective. He does his job and yet wonders why. He is not afraid to stick his nose into trouble, but he often wonders why he does it. The first Johnny Dollar has no hesitation to add pleasure and personal items to the expense account, much to the chagrin of his employers.

The following are the cases of the Charles Russell "Johnny Dollar."

SHOW:	THE PARAKOFF POLICY
SHOW DATE:	2/11/1949
COMPANY:	EAST COAST UNDERWRITERS
AGENT:	
EXP. ACCT:	$1,230.20

SYNOPSIS: Johnny is already in his room when he checks into the Valley Hotel in Benton, Ohio. Johnny asks to leave his card and sees the room number the clerk put it in and goes to the room. Johnny knocks and announces himself as a bellboy with a special delivery package from Hartford. Inside the room is Eric Barker, the defense attorney for the policyholder Parakoff. Johnny questions Barker and learns that Parakoff killed Harland Wolf, who was the owner of the insurance policy and his business partner. Barker tells Johnny that Mr. Parakoff was caught running away from town with the murder weapon in his possession. Supposedly Parakoff shot Wolf in self-defense after an argument.

Johnny goes to visit Mrs. Marsha Parakoff and is met at the door by a woman with red hair and green eyes and wearing a negligee. Johnny comments on how well she furnishes the living room where Johnny asks her what she knows and she tells Johnny that the District Attorney had told her to keep quiet. But she willingly tells Johnny all of what is in the newspapers. Her story is that the she is the Vice President of the Highland Coal Company. Johnny makes a comment about his anthracite heart feeling very bituminous, but Marsha does not catch the references to coal. She was alone with Wolf talking about the business when her husband comes home and shoots Wolf with a .38—hence the case. Marsha asks Johnny to throw some more wood on the fire in the fireplace for her. Johnny goes out to get a damp piece of wood—they burn slower.

Some time later Johnny calls for a cab and walks down the snow-covered sidewalk where he is stopped and told to get out of town by two police officers. They have the guilty man and do not want any trouble. The men beat Johnny up but he lifts a wallet from one of them in the confusion. The cabby arrives and takes Johnny to his hotel room where Johnny expenses medicinal supplies—bonded. The next morning Johnny has the contents of the wallet photographed and mails the photos to Hartford. Johnny then meets with the DA, Edwin Byrum. Johnny tells him what happened to his face and Byrum plays ignorant of any involvement by the local police. Johnny is told that the indictment will be handed down tomorrow.

Johnny phones Barker and arranges to borrow photos of the crime scene. The photos arrive and Johnny examines pictures of the crime scene, and it turns out that Wolf and Parakoff were standing face-to-face when Parakoff was shot. Bullet placements in Parakoff's body indicate that a left-handed person shot him. Johnny makes an appointment to see Barker at three and goes to look into the owner of the wallet he got the night before. Johnny goes to the disreputable address of the wallet's owner, Ben Arnold, and finds his wife there with a black eye. In a small room Johnny finds a police coat the "CPD" on the buttons. Johnny goes to see Barker and tells him about the fake police who beat him up while wearing out of town uniforms. Johnny wonders if Marsha set Johnny up.

Johnny figures that if Wolf dies she gets the money from the insurance being the widow of the beneficiary, and she gets the coal company. Barker admits to Johnny that Marsha and Wolf had been having a romance. Johnny figures that Marsha shot her husband and convinces Wolf to take the blame and claim self-defense. Wolf gets a light sentence, or no sentence and then gets the girl. Johnny notes that he photos indicate a left-handed shooter and Barker tells Johnny that Wolf is left-handed, so he decides to go to see Marsha to see if she is left handed.

At the Parakoff house, Johnny builds a fire and asks Marsha to light it, which she does with her right hand. Johnny asks Marsha to call the DA and change her story. Johnny tells her that her husband was killed by a left handed man and that Marsha had killed her husband and phoned Wolf to convince him to take the rap for her. As Marsha cries Johnny tells her that she changed her story after Wolf was arrested and told the DA that Wolf had been after her to leave her husband and threatened to kill him. Marsha begs Johnny to stop and Barker comes in and agrees with her. Barker tells Johnny that he wants the wallet and Johnny tells him of the photos he took, but Barker is not convinced. Johnny tells Barker that he was the one who arranged for the men to beat him up. Johnny notes that Barker is holding the gun in his left hand and accuses him of shooting Parakoff. Marsha tells Barker to shoot Johnny and rushes for the gun. Johnny throws Marsha into Barker and a fight for the gun begins. Johnny manages to shoot the gun into the ceiling and knocks Barker out.

Johnny has lunch with the DA and they agree that the defense was working harder for a conviction that the prosecution and that everyone was guilty: Barker of murder, Marsha of being an accessory before and after the fact, and Wolf for conspiracy to defraud. Johnny notes that he had to take a side trip to Miami Beach to recover from a cold he caught rolling in the snow.

NOTES:

- "THE NEXT HALF HOUR HAS ITS BAGGAGE PACKED TO TAKE A TRIP WITH AMERICA'S FABULOUS FREELANCE INSURANCE INVESTIGATOR. AT INSURANCE INVESTIGATION HE IS AN EXPERT—AT MAKING OUT HIS EXPENSE ACCOUNT HE IS AN ABSOLUTE GENIUS."
- JOHNNY BUYS TWO ONE-WAY TICKETS BECAUSE HE IS NOT ALWAYS SURE HE WILL COME HOME.
- $1 DOLLAR TIPS TO TAXIS AND BELLMAN.
- $7.00 BONDED MEDICAL SUPPLIES AFTER THE BEATING.
- JOHNNY NOTES SOME SKILLS AS A POOLROOM PICKPOCKET.
- IN THE FINAL STRUGGLE, THE .38 MURDER WEAPON FIRES 7 TIMES.
- THE MID-PROGRAM COMMERCIAL IS FOR THE PROGRAM "SING IT AGAIN."
- LIETH STEVENS PROVIDES THE MUSIC FOR THE SERIES.

Producer: Richard Sanville   **Writers:**   Paul Dudley, Gil Doud
Cast: Unknown

SHOW:	THE SLOW BOAT FROM CHINA
SHOW DATE:	2/25/1949
COMPANY:	ORIENTAL WEST CARGO BONDING COMPANY
AGENT:	MR. FUNDY
EXP. ACCT:	$1,407.00

SYNOPSIS: Johnny flies to San Francisco, California in answer to the letter from Oriental Bonding and has lunch on Fisherman's wharf. Johnny cabs to the office of Mr. Fundy, who gives Johnny a ticket to Singapore and tells Johnny that Oriental has insured a cargo of Tin, but the ship has been held up for three weeks. An expediter investigated the delay, and several mechanical failures were reported. Johnny tells Fundy what he needs a good plumber. Johnny is told to look for William Harrison at the Crown Colony Hotel and he will fill in the details. Johnny only has hours to get the boat moving, as more delays will cost them $2500 per day. Johnny looks forward to a night on the town, but is told his plane leaves in two hours.

Johnny reports a loss of $240 teaching a plane passenger how to play poker on the trip. In Singapore Johnny gets a room at the Crown Colony and goes to Harrison's room where the door is open and Johnny finds a calling card from his old friend, trouble. Johnny searches the dresser and the bathroom where the toothbrush is still wet. In the trashcan Johnny finds a swizzle stick with "The Colliard Tea Bar" stamped on it. Johnny goes to the bar, overlooking the harbor. The bartender gives Johnny bourbon and is told that Harrison has been in every night with the chief engineer of the Shanghai Wayfarer, a really nice guy and big tipper. For $20 Johnny gets his name, Frank Moore. Johnny goes to the docks by rickshaw and tips the driver $1. The gangway watch stops Johnny with a large knife and tells Johnny that Moore has been stabbed and is in the morgue and that the police are holding a girl. Johnny visits the British Chief Inspector who has never heard of Harrison. Johnny looks at the body, and Moore had been "sunk with a hole in one." A large stack of crisp $20 bills in the wallet makes Johnny wonders if Moore was taking money to delay the sailing. A picture, signed by Shandra, the girl who had been released by the police reminds Johnny that the man who said, "never the twain shall meet" should have met her. Johnny learns that she works in the Wordlow Bar on Maylay Street. Johnny goes to the bar and asks for Shandra and is told that she is not there tonight. Shandra shows up and asks why Johnny is asking for her and tells Johnny that he either wants secrets or has secrets to sell. Johnny asks if she knows Harrison, but she does not know him and tells Johnny that maybe he was lonely and does not want to be found tonight. She tells Johnny that they should go to her house to have a drink where they do not have to whisper.

At Shandra's house Johnny spots a Louisville Slugger baseball bat on the wall with the words "Remember the US Marines" on it. Johnny and Shandra relax and she wants to know Johnny better, and she does when Johnny stops talking but Johnny wonders how Shandra knew that Harrison was missing tonight. Two men with guns break the door open, and Shandra joins them. One man is a bald fat man with three chins, the other a punk with a sneer and arms too long for him. Johnny is tied to a chair and Shandra tells them that Johnny is looking for Harrison and Moore, which is why she called them. The punk tells Johnny that he using his head better than Harrison did. Johnny is told he can prevent Harrison's death and his if he cooperates. Johnny is offered 750 pounds for the information they want. The man threatens to slit his tongue to make him talk but Johnny and replies "Nuts!" Johnny is beaten and wakes up tied up in the dark where another voice says "hello" and asks Johnny who he is. The other man is Harrison, and Johnny tells him that he is trying to find him. Johnny tells him that the men, Roseline and Corgy have offered him 750 pounds for "it," what ever "it" is. Harrison tells Johnny that "it" is a package that Moore had asked him to drop off with Shandra. She was not there, so he took it to her house where he hid the package in the bottom drawer of a chest. Harrison tells Johnny that Moore had been a good friend, and he wanted to make sure that Shandra got the package rather than those two. Johnny tells him that all three are working together, and Harrison calls himself an idiot. Johnny is sure that Moore was murdered for the package. The door opens and a voice Johnny recognizes enters the room. Johnny recognizes him as the gangway watch at the Shanghai Wayfarer. The man, named Roark, tells Johnny that he wants the package. Johnny tells him he is only interested in getting the ship underway, and Roark tells him that will happen as soon as he gets the package. Johnny convinces Roark to untie them. Johnny hits him and runs from the room. Johnny goes to Shandra's house and breaks in. Johnny tells Shandra he knows where the package is, and she tells Johnny that with the package they can be happy for the rest of their life. Johnny goes to the bedroom and takes the package from the chest and opens it to find a stack of money—$500,000 in fresh, green American twenties. Shandra tells Johnny they are counterfeit, made in China. Moore brought them for Roseline to take to the states, but Roseline was delayed so Moore created the accidents. Moore then decided to keep the money, but Roseline caught up to him and killed him. A car drives up, so Johnny ties up Shandra and locks her in the closet with a mouth full of money as a gag. Johnny takes the baseball bat and waits by the door. Roseline walks in and is decked with the bat, as is Corgy. Johnny takes their guns when Roark comes in telling Johnny that he will take over. He tosses Johnny his wallet, which contains his US Treasury ID. Roark tells Johnny that he was too close to the payoff to tell him who he was. The money has been coming through Singapore for months, and Roseline was the ringleader. Johnny asks Roark, since he is with the Treasury, to help him fill out his income tax. Johnny expenses, among other things, $200 for a new suit and $375 for entertainment while waiting for his plane after the ship sails.

Notes:

- **The case Title is "The investigation of Delayed Cargo aboard the Shanghai Wayfarer."**

- COMMERCIAL BREAK #1 IS FOR THE JACK BENNY PROGRAM ON SUNDAY, WITH CLAUDE RAINES.
- THE NEXT ADVENTURE IS "THE STAR OF HADES DIAMOND."
- THERE IS A PROMO FOR GANGBUSTERS AND PHILLIP MARLOW AT THE END OF THE PROGRAM.
- JOHNNY EXPENSES A SUIT TO REPLACE ONE RUINED IN THE SHANGHAI RIVER BUT HE WAS NEVER THROWN INTO THE RIVER.

Producer: Richard Sanville   Writers: Paul Dudley, Gil Doud
Cast: Unknown

◆   ❖   ◆

SHOW: THE ROBERT PERRY CASE
SHOW DATE: 3/4/1949
COMPANY: AMERICAN CONTINENTAL LIFE INSURANCE
AGENT: MR. GORDON
EXP. ACCT: $1,263.00

SYNOPSIS: Johnny takes a night train to New York and cabs to Mr. Perry's New York City import office at exactly at 9:00 AM. Susan the receptionist buzzes him in and the office explodes. Perry had thought his life was in danger and now he is dead. Johnny gives the receptionist some water to drink as the occupants of the building stream in. Everyone is told to leave and Johnny explains to Susan that someone hooked up a bomb to the buzzer to kill Perry. Mr. Perry left last night and someone must have come in afterwards and rigged the bomb. Susan tells Johnny that his next appointment was to be with his partner Van Brooten, who came from Holland to pick up a check dissolving the partnership. Christine, the wife, was due later to finalize the upcoming divorce. The fire department arrives and Johnny tells them someone will get burned when the cops arrive. The police arrive and conduct an investigation. At eleven Van Brooten comes in to pick up the check. Johnny tells Van Brooten that Perry is dead, but Susan is confused. Susan gives Van Brooten the check and he leaves.

Johnny calls American Continental and tells Mr. Gordon what has happened. Johnny is told to stay on the case, and Mr. Gordon asks if the death could have been suicide. Johnny tells Gordon that trying to prove "suicide" to enable the suicide clause would require a "Santa" clause. Johnny will talk to the wife to see if fraud is involved. Johnny cabs to the apartment of Christine Perry. Christine tells Johnny who he is and why he is there, and Johnny wonders about he motives. She tells Johnny that she knows very little about her husband's friends since she left him. She tells Johnny that she was with a friend, Al Donovan at the Club Caprice. Her husband was there also with Susan. Al Donovan enters the apartment and slugs Johnny after he starts asking questions. Al tells Christine that he was not with her at the club, and that she was supposed to be there with her husband talking about the divorce. Johnny listens from the floor as Christine and Al leave the apartment. This case is becoming interesting.

Johnny follows Al in a cab and after a car ride with Christine, she jumps out and Johnny follows Al to a police precinct. Johnny speaks with the police and they tell Johnny that Al Donovan has made a full confession to bombing the office. Donovan told the police he was in love with Mrs. Perry and planted a bomb in the office. Johnny thinks he is trying to cover up something.

Johnny searches Perry's office and learns that Van Brooten was bald and had been getting toupees from Perry for years. In the files Johnny learns that Al Donovan was Perry's former. Mrs. Perry comes in and finds Johnny in the office. She tells Johnny that she wants to talk to someone and thought Johnny might be there. She tells Johnny that Al's confession is bogus. Johnny tells her that Al was Perry's bodyguard until the day before the blast. Christine tells Johnny that she wants to tell the truth and Johnny tells her to call the police. Christine pulls a gun on Johnny and Johnny pulls the phone from the wall as Christine wishes him success in the investigation. After she leaves Johnny discovers that Susan the receptionist was a former ordnance technician who wired bomb fuses!

Johnny goes to Susan's apartment and meets her when she comes in. Johnny tells her about Al's confession, but Susan thinks he is covering for Christine. Johnny mentions the Club Caprice and Susan tells him that she was there with Perry. Mrs. Perry was there with a man Susan did not know, but Perry did. Susan tells Johnny that she has worked for Perry for four years. The doorbell rings and Susan is shot as she answers the door. Susan is shot once and Johnny can find no one in the hallway. Susan is sure that she will be arrested. She tells Johnny that the man in the office was a phony and she was shot because she was trying to blackmail him. Susan tells Johnny the man's hotel name and faints.

Johnny goes looking for the phony Van Brooten in the Nelson Hotel. Johnny cannot find any Dutch names so he gets the rooms that the maids have not been able to make up and starts looking. Johnny finds pay dirt in room 427. Johnny gets the man out of the room with a phony fire alarm. Johnny gets into the room and beats the name, Van Zandt. Van Zandt tells Johnny that the real Van Brooten is drugged in the next room. Van Zandt had known Van Brooten in Amsterdam and knew about the sale of the company. Van Zandt had drugged Perry's cocoa and set up the bomb in the office. Van Zandt did not know how Susan had known he was a phony. Johnny tells Van Zandt that Perry was sending his partner gray wigs, my red headed friend! Johnny wires the insurance company that they will have to pay Christine, who was only guilty of trying to stay on the right side of a hot tempered boy friend. Christine had lied about the Club Caprice because she had been out with the real Van Brooten who was trying to convince her not to divorce his friend Perry. Johnny expenses a fine of one thousand dollars and no sense for setting off the false alarm.

NOTES:
- SLIGHTLY DIFFERENT OPENING MUSIC FROM PREVIOUS PROGRAM.
- THERE IS ONLY ONE $1 TIP.
- THE MID-PROGRAM COMMERCIAL IS ABOUT THE $60 MILLION THE RED CROSS NEEDS.

- THE ANNOUNCER GIVES A PROMO FOR THE JACK BENNY SHOW WITH RONALD AND BENITA COLEMAN NEXT SUNDAY.

Producer: Richard Sanville   **Writers:** Paul Dudley, Gil Doud
Cast: Unknown

◆ ❖ ◆

SHOW: MURDER IS A MERRY-GO-ROUND
SHOW DATE: 3/11/1949
COMPANY: NUTMEG STATE CASUALTY AND BONDING COMPANY
AGENT:
EXP. ACCT: $692.18

SYNOPSIS: Johnny travels to Talladega, Alabama to investigate a series of accidents at the Funfair and Weatherly Entertainment traveling circus. Johnny cabs to the circus and talks to the employees but none of the employees are willing to talk about the accidents. After being slugged Johnny is awakened by a man who asks him what he is doing there. The man is Shanty Brennan the manger. Over a drink Johnny tells Brennan that the show is reported to be clean, but is plagued by accidents for ten straight nights. The owner, Louisa Pepper comes in and Johnny feels that she is too friendly. Johnny tells her he is with the insurance company and she wants Johnny to find out who is responsible for the accidents as someone is out to get them. And, the cost of extra protection is costing too much. They know their help and trust them. Louisa tells Johnny that a former employee, Carter Lacy, is the only one to have a grudge—but he is in jail for attempted murder—or is he? Johnny agrees to find out if Carter is still in jail. Brennan tells Johnny that Carter was jailed for the attempted murder of Myrtle Pepper, Louisa's niece.

Johnny finds out that Carter has been paroled and has been following the show for two weeks. Johnny calls the hotels in town and finds one with Carter registered there. Johnny cabs to the Sunshine Hotel and arranges to meet Carter in a cafe. Carter tells Johnny that he is going to settle some scores. Carter tells Johnny that two of the three key people will be dead soon, and one of the three will help him. Louisa Pepper, Shanty Brennan and Myrtle Pepper, the snake charmer, are the targets. Cater tells Johnny that he was an innocent bystander and was hurt, just like the people in the accidents. Johnny hires a detective to follow Carter and returns to the circus. Johnny looks for Myrtle and tells her he has a message from Carter Lacey. Myrtle lets Johnny in and he tells her about the threat to two if the people at the circus. Myrtle leaves to tell Shanty and Louisa and Johnny finds black book. Johnny goes to see Louisa and find Myrtle there. Myrtle has told Shanty who was going to feed her snakes. All three go to the snake tent and find Shanty Brennan feeding the snakes—literally.

Johnny takes Myrtle and Louisa to their tent and Johnny tries to figure out who is next. Johnny gets Louisa's gun and puts it on the table between Louisa and Myrtle, in case Carter shows up. Johnny gets the car keys so that the car and trailer cannot be moved. Johnny calls the police and a cab. Johnny cabs to Carter's hotel and finds Carter gone. Johnny picks the lock and finds Myrtle Pepper strangled in Carter Lacy's room. Johnny calls the police and tells them to send in the second team. Johnny finds some old newspaper clippings in the room along with Carter's parole papers. Johnny leaves and finds Carter in the hallway. Johnny tells Carter that Carter was sent up for Grand Larceny not attempted murder like Brannan had told Johnny. Johnny tells him about a bankbook he found where $60,000 had been deposited into a bank the same year Carter was sent up for Grand Larceny. Johnny suspects a double cross as the money went to a bank account for the Peppers and Brennan.

Johnny goes back to the circus and Louisa lets him into the trailer. Johnny tells her that he had talked to Carter and that Myrtle is dead. Johnny hints that Carter never meant to do anything him self, he would just let others fight among themselves. Johnny tells Louisa that Myrtle was strangled by someone with long fingernails, but Carter bites his nails. Louisa pulls the gun on Johnny but Carter shows up with a gun. Johnny tells Carter that the state will take care of Louisa, but Carter wants to hear her squeal. Johnny leaves to find a rope when he hears shooting. Johnny starts the car and takes the trailer onto the highway. Johnny is shot at attracts the police with some reckless driving.

Johnny buys cigars for the local police and pays Carter's hotel bill, as Louisa had shot him.

NOTES:
- A WORD OF ADVICE—GO TO THE HEAD OF A CIRCUS FIRST FOR INFORMATION.
- A SLOW TAXI RIDE GETS A NICKEL TIP.
- MID-WAY HOT DOGS ARE NO THOROUGHBREDS.
- THERE IS A COMMERCIAL ABOUT JOHN LUND IN ESCAPE.
- EXPENSE ACCOUNT TOTAL—ONLY $692.18? "I MUST BE SLIPPING!"
- THE FINAL COMMERCIAL IS ABOUT THE SPIKE JONES SHOW, WHICH HAS MOVED TO SATURDAY.

Producer: Unknown   **Writers:**   **Paul Dudley, Gil Doud**
Cast: Unknown

◆ ❖ ◆

SHOW: **MILFORD BROOKS III MATTER**
SHOW DATE: 3/25/1949
COMPANY: HONESTY LIFE INSURANCE UNDERWRITERS
AGENT: AUSTIN FARNSWORTH
EXP. ACCT: $1,182.23

SYNOPSIS: Johnny cabs to Farnsworth's Hartford, Connecticut office where there is a struggle going on. Johnny slugs the man Farnsworth is fighting with to keep away from the window and closes it. Johnny sits on the man's head to keep him from killing Johnny. Johnny is told that the man is Farnsworth's most important client, and is insured for two million dollars. The man is Milford Brooks, III and the policy is to allow the heirs to pay the inheritance taxes when he dies. But because of his life style, he has no heirs and no money, so he is trying to get money by killing himself. He came in today and changed the beneficiary and demanded $500,000 in cash. Since there was no loan provision in the policy he told Farnsworth to either get the money or pay off on the policy. The new beneficiary is a notorious gambler named Harold Hatcher. Farnsworth wants Johnny to protect Brooks. Johnny tells him that since he will have to work twice as hard to keep somebody from killing Brooks, or having him kill himself, he will have to be paid twice as much. Johnny is told to give Brooks something to live for, an interest in life. Johnny gets an inspiration and pulls out his little black book. Rudi? No, her favorite expression is "Drop dead!" Bernadine? No, she would be the new beneficiary by midnight. Butter! She's the one. Johnny calls Miss Theodora Buts in New York at Hudson 2-4292. Johnny tells Butter he is coming and he asks her to reserve a table for dinner, and that he will be there in a couple hours. Johnny buys a bottle of Brandy to keep Brooks quiet on the drive to New York. As they pass the Yale Bowl, Brooks gives a "Boola, Boola" for dear old Eli. Brooks tells Johnny that he loves someone very much and hates someone very much and passes out again. Johnny muses about the case as he drives the Merit Parkway. He is sure that Brooks owes Hatcher a bundle, so Hatcher must have forced Brooks to make him the new beneficiary. But why the suicide threat, unless he was trying to get away from Hatcher. At Butter's apartment Johnny puts Brooks on the couch where he passes out. Over a root beer Johnny tells Butter all about the case. Johnny sees a big boat and wishes he could sail away with Butter—but she tells him it is the 125th street ferry. Johnny tells Butter that he has a Dad's old-fashioned root beer, and is ready for one on Mom's new-fashioned kisses. Johnny tells Butter that she is what Brooks is supposed to live for, and she slaps him. Johnny talks his way out of the situation and Butter apologizes. The phone rings and the call is for Johnny. Farnsworth asks about Brooks and wants to talk to him. Johnny goes to get him, but Brooks is gone with Butter.

Johnny has lost both Brooks and Butter and so Johnny goes to look for them. Johnny searches the neighborhood and decides to get help from a higher source. Johnny calls Lt. Fisher at Missing Persons. Johnny asks him about Butter and is told to call Dorothy Dix. Johnny asks him about Brooks, and is told they think they know where he is—the Hudson River. His coat was found in the 125th street ferry with a pack of matches with the initials "HH." Johnny goes to the club owned by Hatcher and is met by a blond who asks Johnny who he is looking for. She is Jeanelle, and knows Hatcher. Johnny tells him he wants to see Hatcher about a friend—Brooks. She recognizes that Johnny is not a cop or a society friend of the Brooks. She tells Johnny where Hatcher's office is and that he won't have any trouble, as Hatcher sent her to check him out—and he is all right. Johnny goes to the office and tells Hatcher who he is and why he is there and about Brook's disappearance. Johnny asks where Brooks is and Hatcher tells Johnny he was driving around when Brooks disappeared. He tells Johnny that

Brooks owes him a couple hundred thousand, so he would not bump off his own assets. Hatcher knows nothing about the insurance policy, but Johnny tells him he will get 2 million if Brooks is found dead. Hatcher tells Johnny that he will never be able to prove anything. The intercom buzzes and Hatcher is told the police are there. The police take Hatcher to headquarters and Johnny goes to talk to Jeanelle. Johnny tells her about the conversation and she tells Johnny that she told Hatcher he would get in trouble about the policy. Brooks owes Hatcher money, and there is a note in Hatcher's office that Brooks is supposed to get back when Hatcher is made beneficiary. Johnny is sure that Jeanelle is trying to sell out Hatcher. They go to the office and Johnny searches the closet until he finds the note in the top desk drawer. Johnny also finds something in his closet that could turn into a bond fire. Johnny tells Jeanelle he found what he was looking for and leaves. Johnny gets a cab (dollar tip) and waits until Jeanelle comes out and gets one also. Johnny follows her to 72nd where he stops a block behind her and runs to the building, and old garage. Inside Johnny goes to upstairs ands hears Brooks plotting with Jeanelle. Johnny rushes in and slugs Brooks and Jeanelle tells Johnny that he is hers. Johnny tells them that were silly to plant the matchbook. They should have planted a lighter, as there is one in every suit Hatcher owns and that he never carries matches. Johnny accuses Brooks of insurance fraud and asks where Butter is. Brooks tells Johnny that he had to take her with him when he left, but he put Butter into a cab to the energy hospital. Hatcher comes in and tells Johnny that he has had enough fun. He tells Johnny that the police had counted the turnstiles at each end of the ferry, and they matched. So Brooks was not really missing. He came to the garage because he always knows where Jeanelle goes. Johnny tells Hatcher that they were trying to frame him and that they made a real mistake by trying the fraud. Hatcher is ready to shoot Brooks when Johnny tackles him and knocks him out, but not before Brooks is shot. The police arrive and Johnny goes to see Butter in the hospital. She tells him that they had to cut off some of her hair to put on the bandages. Johnny tells her that Brooks is in the same hospital

NOTES:
- COMMERCIAL BREAK #1 IS FOR THE JACK BENNY PROGRAM.
- IN THE DICK POWELL AUDITION, JOHNNY SPENT $318 ON A BRACELET FOR BUTTER.

Producer: **Richard Sanville**   **Writers:**   **Paul Dudley, Gil Doud**
Cast: **Unknown**

◆   ❖   ◆

SHOW: STOLEN PORTRAIT
SHOW DATE: 4/1/1949
COMPANY: FINE ARTS SECURERS
AGENT: FREDERICK KIMBLE

EXP. ACCT: **$1,563.40**

SYNOPSIS: Johnny flies to London, England to look for a stolen portrait of the Duke of Massen. Johnny loans his coat to a seatmate who is fighting to keep his meal down. The passenger goes to get some water from the stewardess and disappears out the back door of the plane in Johnny's topcoat!

In London, Johnny meets Dexter Morley who appreciates the fine arts but who does not have the money to either buy them or travel to see them. He has set up a program to get the top twelve museums of the world to loan pictures out to him. The Duke's picture was the first one to be shown and was stolen on the first night! Johnny gets the address of the museum and Dexter tells Johnny that he is going to France that day. Johnny buys a paper to read of his adventures on the front pages. Johnny meets Dexter's assistant, Muriel Harding. Johnny tells her about what happened on the plane and she shows Johnny where the paining was stolen, along with the frame. Muriel has gone over the museum with Scotland Yard and is sure that she can save Johnny a lot of trouble. Muriel provides Johnny with a complete list of all the known art thieves in Europe complete with address for the two who are not in prison. Criminology fascinates her.

Johnny cabs to Scotland Yard and meets with Inspector Carrew at Scotland Yard who tells Johnny that no one has filed a claim of loss, and they cannot act until someone does. Johnny asks if Muriel is known by Scotland Yard and shows Carrew the list. On his way to the Mount Royal Hotel, Johnny naps wonders about Muriel and the incident on the plane. At the hotel Johnny is almost run down by a car (worse than the bloody buzz bombs replies the doorman). Johnny is sure he has been set up as a pigeon.

After a nap, and shower, Johnny goes to dinner at Ketners. Johnny goes to the flat of the first thief on his list and lets him self in to find a wood burning stove blazing away, the painting of the Duke on a table, and a dead body with it's head parted down the middle. Johnny searched for a phone and finds a door that spits bullets at him.

Johnny drops to the floor and hers someone leaving through a window. Johnny goes to see Miss Harding and tells her he has called the police and taken the painting to Scotland Yard. Muriel tells Johnny that the thief probably tried to shoot Johnny, but Johnny is not convinced. Johnny tells her he has a yearning, burning deep inside to break some ones neck. Johnny calls New York collect to report in. While Johnny waits Muriel offers Johnny a drink, but Johnny wants to join her on the couch. Muriel tells Johnny about her days in the Royal air force as he kisses her. The phone call comes in and Johnny learns that the frame is also insured for $10,000. Back to work after he calms his nerves with Muriel.

Johnny goes back to the flat of the thief and finds a very curious form of ashes—diamonds! Johnny cabs to Morley's office and finds a cabinet shop in the basement—and a gun in Morley's hand. Johnny is sure that Morley was the one who shot at him earlier that day. Johnny tells Dexter that he is in charge of a smuggling racket, but Morley only wants the diamonds. Johnny tells him that the diamonds are in a cab with a burnt out license light, so only Johnny knows which cab it is. Johnny tells Morley that has each picture is sent to him the frame would be filled with diamond and moved around the world. But a burglar interrupted the plan, so now Johnny will get his. Morley slugs Johnny with his gun. When Muriel tries to get in through a window, Johnny slugs Morley with his gun. Muriel tells Johnny that she was only trying to help and had followed him. Johnny shows her the diamonds that are in his pocket.

Johnny flies home to avoid a wedding and buys Muriel a cookbook to divert her interest on criminology. Any Expense account errors in Johnny's favor were due to confusion over the exchange rates!

NOTES:
- AKA: "WHO OPENED THE SEASON ON CANVAS BACKED DUKES"?
- JOHNNY NOTES HE PADS HIS EXPENSE ACCOUNT TO MAKE A LIVING.
- TIP TO THE CABBY, 2 BOB
- $14 FOR A BOTTLE OF MEDICINAL SCOTCH.
- THERE IS A 5-SCHILLING LIMIT ON DINNER PRICES. JOHNNY'S DINNER IS CHICKEN WITH CREAMED, BOILED, AND ROASTED BRUSSELS SPROUTS!
- JOHNNY STATES THAT "THERE IS A YEARNING, BURNING DEEP INSIDE" TO BREAK SOME ONES NECK—NICE QUOTE OF JEROME KEARNES
- THERE IS A SMALL EXPENSE ITEM FOR BROMO SELTZER TO FIGHT THE BRUSSELS SPROUTS IN GANDER, NEWFOUNDLAND.
- THERE IS A COMMERCIAL FOR OZZIE AND HARRIET.
- THE FINAL COMMERCIAL MENTIONS THE FOLLOWING PROGRAMS: THE FAMILY HOUR OF STARS, OZZIE AND HARRIET, JACK BENNY, HELEN HAYES, EVE ARDEN, AMOS N' ANDY, LUM AND ABNER, SAM SPADE, LIFE WITH LUIGI AND IT PAYS TO BE IGNORANT.
- MUSIC IS BY MARK WARNOW

Producer:	Richard Sanville	Writers:	Paul Dudley, Gil Doud;
Cast:	Unknown		

◆　❖　◆

SHOW:	THE CASE OF THE $100,000 LEGS
SHOW DATE:	4/15/1949
COMPANY:	HIGHWORTHY INSURANCE UNDERWRITERS ASSOCIATION
AGENT:	HARVEY ANTHONY
EXP. ACCT:	$948.76

SYNOPSIS: Johnny is paged at the track and expenses the $60 he lost because of a hasty bet. Harvey tells Johnny to fly to Hollywood, California and act as a bodyguard to Marilyn Majors whose legs are insured for $100,000 for 48 hours as part of a publicity policy. Johnny will be there, if American Airlines co-operates.

Johnny flies to Los Angeles and goes to the penthouse apartment of Marilyn where he finds the door open and the body of Marilyn very dead in a cheesecake position, with a bullet hole where an earring should have been. Johnny calls Anthony to tell him the bad news but it gets worse. Johnny is told that

Highworthy also insures her life with double indemnity for death by violence. While Johnny is on the phone about to call the police when he is told by a young girl (who is wearing a tobacco brown dress so round, so firm, so fully packed) to hang up the phone with a .32 caliber convincer. She tells Johnny that she came there to kill Marilyn but some one beat her to it. The girl takes Johnny to the bedroom and puts him against the wall as she searches for a packet of letters apparently written by her husband who had just committed suicide over them. Johnny gets locked in a closet and uses a nail file and an ink pen to push the carpet down to let air in. Johnny overhears the girl call the police and tell them that the killer is in the closet. Then Johnny hears a man come in, accuse her of blackmailing him and then shoot the girl with 6 shots in the back. He takes the letters and leaves.

Johnny escapes the closet with a hard kick. Johnny looks around the apartment and finds letters from two other men, one named Baron and one named Lawrence, and suspects the "old badger game." The police arrive and naturally blame Johnny for the murders. Johnny shows his ID to the police who call him an insurance dick. Johnny prefers "freelance special insurance investigator—it keeps his rates up. Johnny tells the police what had occurred and why he is there. Johnny's only witness is the dead girl. Johnny tells them about the letters and the man who came in and shot the girl. An officer finds Johnny's nail file, pen and a .32 stuffed in a shoe in the closet. Johnny tries to explain but spends the night in the LA City jail, cell number 36.

Johnny relates how he had envisioned staring at bars on this case, but not jail bars. Police Lt. Roach talks to Johnny and tells him that the evidence points to his innocence. He tells Johnny that the gun in the closet is the one that called Marylyn. Roach tells Johnny that Marylyn had been playing a high stakes Badger game, and that the fire department should be handling the case. Johnny suggests that there is a third set of letters floating around, as the murder grabbed the wrong letters. Johnny wants to clear his name and get his job done so he suggests planting a newspaper article stating that the murderer got the wrong letters and that Johnny has them in his hotel room. Roach agrees to publish he story and Johnny asks for fighter coverage. Johnny gets out and gets a paper with the fake story, his picture and his hotel name in it.

Johnny goes to dinner and returns to his hotel. In his hotel room he finds a woman, Mrs. Alice Lawrence Hill, in a negligee. Her husband is in the lobby and knows Johnny is in the room. She wants the letters. If she doesn't get them, her husband will shoot Johnny for attacking his wife. Johnny is sure that he will get killed when Hill gets there and tries to talk her out of going further. There is a knock at the door and Mr. Baron comes in with a gun and wants the letters. Baron threatens Johnny and he tells both of them that he does not have the letters. When the phone rings Johnny fakes a conversation with the police to an empty line. Johnny recognizes Baron's voice from the closet and figures Lawrence Hill killed Marylyn. Johnny mutters dangerous words into the phone to get Baron close enough to bean him with the phone. Johnny kicks the gun under the bed and Johnny beans Baron with a water jar. Johnny pulls Mrs. Hill from under the bed where she is trying to get Baron's gun. Johnny tells Alice that her husband did not see Johnny come in, because he used the back door. As Johnny gets the gun from under the bed Lawrence Hill comes in. Alice screams at him to shoot, and he shoots Baron. Johnny shoots Hill from under the bed.

After the police finally show up Johnny yells at Roach for not having protection in the hotel. Johnny tells him who the bodies are and how he shot Hill from under the bed. Roach tells Johnny that no one saw him come in. Johnny tells him that he came in the back door.

NOTES:

- AKA: WHO PUT YOUR COMPANY OUT ON A LIMB?
- JOHNNY MENTIONS AMERICAN AIRLINES
- HE IS NOT CARRYING HIS GUN IN THIS CASE
- THE MID-PROGRAM COMMERCIAL IS FOR THE $50,000 JACKPOT ON THE PROGRAM SING IT AGAIN.
- QUOTE FROM IN JAIL—WHO EVER SAID STONE WALL DO NOT A PRISON MAKE HAS A BETTER CHANGE OF GETTING OUT OF BARTLETT'S QUATIONS THAN I HAVE OF GETTING OUT OF JAIL.
- NEWSPAPER COSTS 7 CENTS
- EXPENSE ACCOUNT INCLUDES $167 FOR "ENTERTAINMENT" IN HOLLYWOOD.
- MUSIC IS BY MARK WARNOW
- THIS PROGRAM STARTS WHAT I CALL THE "UM" ENDING, WHERE JOHNNY SIGNS OFF "YOURS TRULY—UM—JOHNNY DOLLAR."

Producer: Richard Sanville   **Writers:** Paul Dudley, Gil Doud
Cast: Bill Conrad, Unknown

◆ ❖ ◆

SHOW: THE CASE OF BARTON DRAKE
SHOW DATE: 4/22/1949
COMPANY: AMERICAN PIONEER LIFE INSURANCE
AGENT: W.K. GREEN
EXP. ACCT: $1,482.63

SYNOPSIS: After a $100 expense item for being awakened at 9:00 AM, Johnny goes to "Old Stonewalls" office for his assignment. Johnny is greeted by Chickie, the receptionist, and tries to wrangle a date. Johnny goes in to see the General, or rather Mr. Green. Green tells Johnny about Barton Drake, who is insured for $30,000 and disappeared almost 7 years ago in 1942. After his car plunged in to a river during an attempt to escape the police, he disappeared. Drake gave his occupation as Hardware Store Manager, but Johnny remembers he was generally acknowledged to be a thief. In one week, Drake will be declared legally dead, and his wife has started proceedings. However, the NYPD Missing Persons Squad saw Barton Drake on the television watching a boxing match!

Johnny drives to Bridgeport to review the files on Drake and then to Drake's home on Long Island, New York where he meets Mrs. Stella Drake—dressed in a negligee and a diamond necklace while eating a genuine English kipper for breakfast at 2:00 PM. Johnny tells her that she has a good change of getting her husband back, but Stella is not too happy to hear that her hubby is not dead but works up some appropriate suffering. Johnny is told to leave so that she can think. On the way out, Johnny cuts the phone lines and watches the house. Johnny follows Stella downtown to a phone booth where (after writing down the number she calls) he listens to her arrange to meet someone at the usual place in twenty minutes. The usual place is the ladies room at Union Station. Mrs. Drake then goes to the Commodore Hotel and gets a room. Johnny gets a room on a different floor and hires the house detective to keep an eye on her. Johnny buys a portable phonograph and a Frank Sinatra record (65¢). He then calls the number, fakes a radio call-up quiz and arranges to deliver a bunch of goodies (see below) to the winner. Johnny plays the Sinatra record "Night and Day," and Mrs. Knott is the winner! When he delivers the prizes he finds an old lady in a wheelchair. While Johnny is grilling Mrs. Knott about her background, Barton's wife comes in, and Mrs. Knott turns into Barton Drake with a set of brass knuckles.

Johnny wakes up to hear Barton Drake yelling at his wife about trying to collect on the policy. Drake ties Johnny to a chair and drives him to the beach. Johnny is tied up and thrown on to a boat and sent to sea. Johnny manages to turn the boat around by using his body as a rudder and ends up on an island. On the island Johnny wakes up to Fred Kindly who wants to be paid for the damage to his dock in Slate Island. Fred tells Johnny that for $500 in canned food he will take Johnny to shore. Johnny agrees and signs the contract for food as "Ali Khan."

Johnny gets back to Drake's apartment and finds an empty apartment. Unfortunately, Drake has split with the baggage Johnny bought him. Stella comes in and she tells Johnny that she does not know anything. Johnny tells her that she is guilty of fraud and she tells Johnny that Drake never left New York, and had been using the disguise for years. Johnny takes Stella's bag and discovers that she is heading south. Stella tells Johnny that Barton is leaving in an hour and a half on the Orange Blossom Special. Johnny tells Stella that the train leaves in 30 minutes.

Johnny makes a quick call to Travelers Aid and tells them to hold his dear old crazy aunt who thinks she is a honey bee, and who is going to throw herself in front of the Orange Blossom Special. Johnny rushes to the station and finds the police and the Travelers Aid folks have Drake surrounded, but they still think that he is just and old lady. Johnny slugs Drake and gets slugged by a policeman.

Johnny goes back to Mr. Green's office and Chickie tells Johnny that the General is so happy that Johnny has saved the company $30,000 that he has taken the morning off to celebrate by playing golf. Chickie agrees to help Johnny complete his expense account so that they can go out for the evening. Johnny tells how, after waking up, that the police discovered that Mrs. Knott was Drake when the police took him to the hospital! Drake and his wife were put in jail, as they are guilty of Insurance fraud. Mr. Kindly gets $500 of canned food. $500 of canned tomatoes with no labels on the can! Yours—um—Truly, Johnny Dollar.

NOTES:
- AKA "HOW I PLAYED DUCKS AND DRAKES WITH A DRAKE WHO DUCKED."
- $1 TIP TO THE CABBY
- JOHNNY DERISIVELY NOTES THAT "OLD STONEWALLS BELT NEVER STOPPED FIGHTING THE BATTLE OF THE BUSINESSMAN'S BULGE" AND "THOSE WHO SERVED CAN BE JUST A S PROUD AS THOSE WHO FOUGHT"
- APPLIANCES JOHNNY BOUGHT WERE A SUNBEAM MIXMASTER FOR $39.50; A HOOVER VACUUM FOR $79.50 AND GLADIATOR SUITCASES FOR $89.50.
- FRANK SINATRA SINGS "NIGHT AND DAY" ONLY LOG ENOUGH TO GIVE THE TITLE OF THE SONG.
- THE MID-PROGRAM COMMERCIAL IS FOR PHILLIP MARLOW (THE CLOAK OF KEMEHAMEHA) AND GANGBUSTERS (THE CALLOUS KILLER).
- THERE IS A PUBLIC SERVICE ANNOUNCEMENT FOR THE AMERICAN CANCER SOCIETY FUND DRIVE.
- MUSIC IS BY LIETH STEVENS

Producer:	**Richard Sanville**	**Writers:**	**Paul Dudley, Gil Doud**
Cast:	**Parley Baer, Unknown**		

SHOW:	HERE COMES THE DEATH OF THE PARTY
SHOW DATE:	7/17/1949
COMPANY:	PREMIER LIFE & CASUALTY COMPANY
AGENT:	
EXP. ACCT:	$1,434.67

SYNOPSIS: Some people feel that for a quick divorce, bullets are much cheaper than Lawyers.

Johnny goes to Reno, Nevada (where the husbands pay off faster than the slot machines) and goes to the Broken Ring Ranch and meets the manager, B. T. Bates, and a young lady named Francine. Johnny is being hired as a "social director" to keep an eye on a guest, Mrs. Nora Craven, who is afraid her husband Arnold wants to kill her. If she dies before the divorce, he gets the $100,000 policy.

While talking to Mr. Bates Johnny hears Nora scream. It seems that a ranch hand, Slim, had given Nora a present, a .38 with a broken barrel and was

Showing Nora how to use it when it went off. Johnny tries to ride a horse, finds a snake in his room and is wounded at a dance in his role a social director.

Johnny decides on a preemptive strike and takes Nora to town to meet her husband, but he is not there. Johnny goes back to the ranch to find Nora's husband in her room. Johnny is knocked out and wakes up to fine Francine in the room—dead. Slim walks in to find Johnny and Francine and tells Johnny that firing the gun for Nora was his idea. Johnny goes to Francine's room to find Nora there. Johnny searches her purse and finds a Photostat of a marriage license proving that Francine has been married to Arnold for two years. Arnold arrives and Johnny tells him about his bigamy and killing Francine, who was going to tell Nora. Arnold fires the gun he had given Nora, but the barrel explodes and Arnold is killed.

NOTES:
- AKA: "THE CASE OF THE POISONOUS GRAPEVINE."
- MUSIC IS BY LIETH STEVENS
- STORY INFORMATION OBTAINED FROM THE KNX COLLECTION IN THE THOUSAND OAKS LIBRARY

Producer:	Norman Macdonnell	Writers	Paul Dudley, Gil Doud
Cast:	Vivi Janis, Jack Kruschen, John Dehner, Anne Morrison, Paul Dubov		

◆　❖　◆

SHOW:	WHO TOOK THE TAXIS
SHOW DATE:	7/24/1949
COMPANY:	NUTMEG STATE LIABILITY UNDERWRITERS
AGENT:	
EXP. ACCT:	$1,100.00

SYNOPSIS: "Everybody knows a taxi driver likes being over tipped, but you can't blame them for not liking being tipped over."

Johnny travels to New York City and the Apex Cab Company. Johnny meets with Gordon McKissick who has just had another cab stolen and is rushing to the site. So far 12 cabs have just vanished on the streets of New York. Johnny tells him that he wants facts, but McKissick tells him it might just be competition.

After a cab ride to 13th & East River, Johnny finds cabby George Brandon beaten. All Brandon can tell Johnny is that a small guy who talks funny was involved and then he dies.

Johnny visits the 11 other victims, Johnny has three clues: 1.) A team of a small man and a huge man with a seersucker suit were involved; 2.) Only the uniform hats were stolen; 3.) McKissick is a former bootlegger, bookmaker and an ex-con.

Back at the cab office, Johnny tells McKissick what he has learned, but McKissick is angry at the idea that he was faking the thefts for the insurance. Johnny orders all the cabs off the street until the case is cleared up, or he will have the insurance cancelled. By 5:00 PM all the cabs are in and by 5:30 the place is deserted except for the night watchman.

Marita Guastilla visits at 6:00 looking for a purse lost in a cab. Johnny takes Marita to a local bar to find out what she is really about. She tells Johnny that she only came from Spain two weeks ago, and took the cab at ten minutes before four. Johnny suggests that they go and look at the cab registers to see which cab she rode in. But Johnny notes that Sherry is more the drink for Spanish ladies, but Marita sure can belt down a martini. Johnny is sure that she is in a hurry to get something out of a cab.

Back at the garage, the gate is open and the night watchman is gone. "Bridewell!" moans Marita. Marita runs away and Johnny goes in to find the guard lying on the floor—and a .38 in his ear held by a huge man with a Sidney Greenstreet type voice. He is Mr. Bridewell, and the guard is ok. His partner Victor comes in and is unable to find something in the cabs. Johnny invites Johnny to go with him to his hotel.

Johnny has made up his mind that there is something hidden in one of the cabs. Johnny goes to Bridewell's hotel where he hears Bridewell's life story, and is told that Marita is notching but a common thief. Victor comes in and is ready to search Johnny for something. Bridewell offer Johnny $7500, but Johnny replies "Nuts!" Bridewell tells Johnny the story of the "Scarlet Madonna": It is an emerald fashioned in 1256 with an image of the Madonna on one side. It is the Scarlet Madonna because everyone who has owned it has died, including a pirate who had it braided into his beard.

Victor slugs Johnny and searches him. Victor finds Johnny's gun and ID and in the ensuing argument over what to do, Johnny slugs Victor and runs down to the street where he runs into Marita.

In a cab Marita tells Johnny that she owns the Scarlet Madonna and was smuggling the stone into the country. Marita realized that she was being followed by Victor and Bridewell, so she left the stone in the seat of one of the cabs and is looking for it now. Johnny takes Marita to a small hotel and checks her in. While Marita is taking a bath, Johnny steals her clothes and leaves.

Back at the garage, Johnny finds the night watchman who tells Johnny he had told Bridewell that McKissick had searched the cabs. Johnny goes to the office and discovers McKissick holding the stone and bartering with Victor, who shoots McKissick. Johnny beats Victor and takes the Madonna from McKissick's hand. Bridewell comes in and asks for the Madonna. Bridewell Johnny gives Johnny his ID and a letter of authorization. Bridewell turns out to be a British Insurance Investigator "with a fantastic and highly successful career." However because he looks and sounds like Sidney Greenstreet, people normally assume he is the villain. Bridewell is authorized to recover the stone for the museum from which Marita and Victor had stolen it. Bridewell gives Johnny the address where he had hidden the cabs.

Johnny buys a dressing gown and gives it to Bridewell to give to Marita before he turns her over to the police. Johnny decides to stay in New York to rest up for a while.

NOTES:
- AKA: WHO TOOK THE TAXIS FOR A RIDE?
- DIFFERENT OPENING THEME MUSIC.
- MUSIC IS BY LIETH STEVENS
- THE ANNOUNCER IS ALLEN BOTZER
- START OF THE OPENING WISE CRACKS.
- WITH THE "SCARLET MADONNA," AT STAKE THIS SOUNDS JUST LIKE THE MALTESE FALCON, WITH A WONDERFUL IMITATION OF A SYDNEY GREENSTREET LIKE CHARACTER NAMED BRIDEWELL
- THE DRINKS WITH MARITA ARE MARTINIS.
- $1.95 FOR AN EVENING GOWN FOR THE NAKED MARITA.
- $6.10 FOR A BOTTLE OF "MOUTHWASH"
- $400 ADVANCE FOR RESTING ON HIS LAURELS—OR POSSIBLY EVEN BRIDEWELL'S LAURELS
- THE MID-PROGRAM COMMERCIAL IS A SPOT FOR THE WORLD'S GREATEST SCIENTIFIC ENTERPRISE—THE ARMED FORCES.

Producer: Norman McDonnell   **Writers:** Paul Dudley, Gil Doud
Cast: Herb Butterfield, Jack Kruschen, Paul Dubov, Lillian Buyeff, Lou Krugman, Junius Matthews, Jan Arvan

SHOW: HOW MUCH BOURBON CAN FLOW UNDER THE BRIDGEWORK
SHOW DATE: 7/31/1949
COMPANY: NATIONAL SURETY & LIFE INSURANCE COMPANY
AGENT:
EXP. ACCT: $2,063.00
SYNOPSIS: "I had to go all the way to Hawaii to be taught that a pineapple is sometimes just another word for a bomb."

Johnny goes to Honolulu, Hawaii to look into the $100,000 policy on Peter Neeley, who has been drinking because of a half-caste girl named Dai Soon. Johnny goes to a bar and the bartender tells Johnny that Peter has been drinking and that his sister has been trying to break of the relationship with Dai. Johnny goes to Peter's apartment and meets Dai. She tells Johnny about the dock strike that is affecting the Pineapple factory. Peter comes in drunk and gets into a fight with Johnny and loses.

Sylvia Neeley arrives with Mr. Fenger, who manages the Neeley factory. Peter gets angry with Sylvia because Peter wants to change the beneficiary of the policy. Sylvia leaves and Johnny takes Peter to a doctor, but is attacked and Peter is kidnapped. Johnny goes back to the apartment to find Dai looking for the insurance policy. Johnny ends up being tied up and given a parting kiss by Dai, who leaves. Later a clerk comes in and unties Johnny and tells Johnny that Dai took a cab. Johnny fins the cab and it takes him to the waterfront where the longshoremen are on strike. Johnny talks his way onto the Island Traveler only to see Dai dive into the water just before the ship explodes "in the biggest explosion since Mona Loa erupted in 1946."

The fire department fights the fire while Johnny feels that Peter was forced to sign the policy because Fenger was losing money at the plant, and that the boat was really shipping munitions rather than fruit. Sylvia and Fenger show up and are anxious about the thought of murder. Johnny gets onto the ship and discovers that the cargo really is fruit. In the process Johnny finds a cat trying to get back into the boat. On a hunch Johnny takes the cat to a local herbalist, Dr. Fu, who confirms Johnny's suspicions about the cat.

Johnny goes to his hotels and is called by Dai, who tells Johnny that she blew up the boat to save Peter, who is ok. Dai tells Johnny that Peter knows that Sylvia and Fenger are smuggling narcotics out in cans of pineapples.

Johnny picks up Peter and they go to Sylvia's and Fenger's apartments, but they are not there. They then go to the plant. Johnny goes in and it shot at by Fenger, who is on top of the pineapple slicer. Johnny works his way up to a control panel, but Fenger has Johnny covered. Johnny throws a pineapple at the control panel, starts the conveyor belt, causing Fenger to be sliced like his pineapples.

NOTES:
- AKA: "BEING THE SABBATH, LETS ALL GO HAVE A PINEAPPLE SUNDAE"
- THE ANNOUNCER IS ALLEN BOTZER
- MUSIC IS BY LIETH STEVENS
- STORY INFORMATION OBTAINED FROM THE KNX COLLECTION IN THE THOUSAND OAKS LIBRARY

Producer: Norman Macdonnell   **Writers**   Paul Dudley, Gil Doud
Cast: Wilms Herbert, Georgia Ellis, Larry Dobkin, Doris Singleton, John Dehner, Don Diamond, Edgar Barrier, Barney Phillips

SHOW: THE CASE OF BONNIE GOODWIN
SHOW DATE: 8/7/1949
COMPANY: KING HART
AGENT:
EXP. ACCT: $0.00
SYNOPSIS: "I hope Saint Peter is listening. This report may one day qualify me for that pass through the pearly gates. The case almost rushed me up there."

Johnny comes home late on Saturday night to find a party going on in his apartment—a party of one, King Hart a noted New York gangster. Hart wants Johnny to find a Bonnie Goodwin so that he can change the beneficiary of his $100,000 insurance policy. According to the policy Bonnie must sign it before the beneficiary can be changed. Johnny wants to turn down the case because he cannot check King's credit, but King has a full wallet. Johnny suggests that King hire Phillip Marlow, Sam Spade or Richard Diamond who would sing him a song. King is allergic to detectives, so he wants Johnny to find the girl. Johnny is told that Bonnie Goodwin is in Chicago and that Hart had run the accounting department at Leavenworth for five years. Johnny wants the assignment in writing and a $3000 advance, which Hart agrees to.

With a $3,000 advance in hand, Johnny heads to Chicago, Illinois (traveling first class per Hart's instructions) to look for Bonnie, first checking into the Ambassador Hotel. The first stop is Bonnie's last boarding house, the Muriel Arms. The switchboard operator tells Johnny that Bonnie was last seen around "Emma's Place," a local bar. Johnny goes to Emma's and the bartender, Joe Emma, tells Johnny to look at the Flagler Apartments. After 18 other stops there is still no sign of Bonnie. (Her heart was no express train because it made a lot of stops") At the last place Johnny is only a couple of hours behind the last move-out.

As Johnny leaves a girl carrying a suitcase stops Johnny on the street. She is Janie and claims to be a friend of Bonnie. Johnny notices a tail and they head to a bar in two different cabs. At the bar, Johnny mentions the insurance, at which the girl asks if Hart is dead. When told he is not, she says that Bonnie will never sign away the only thing she has. When Janie leaves the two goons who followed them enter the bar. Johnny creates a disturbance to stop them and runs out the back door. Janie heads out the back and is killed. The next morning Johnny hears on the hotel room radio that the girl was identified as Bonnie Goodwin, ex-girl-friend of King Hart.

Johnny is upset that he had been looking for Bonnie with Bonnie! King Hart calls Johnny from the airport and tells him that Joe Emma had called him with the news. Johnny tells him to take his case and, well Johnny quits and will report what he knows to the police. Johnny goes to the morgue to find an address in the girl's belongings and learns that her roommate, Janie Page had identified the girl. Johnny goes to see the Janie and finds her packing. Janie tells Johnny that Bonnie knew too much about too many people and was afraid. Janie tells Johnny Hart had wanted to marry Bonnie but she said no. Also, Joe Emma is an enemy of Hart and had slit up with Hart over Bonnie.

Johnny works up a plan to expose the killer by planting a false story in the papers about the misidentification of the body. Johnny takes up residence in Janie's apartment, makes some coffee and sandwiches and waits by the phone. The first person to show up is Hart. Hart comes in while Johnny fakes a phone call to the police. Hart tells Johnny that the body in the morgue was not Bonnie's. When Hart gets too close Johnny slugs him with the phone and hides him in the closet. Johnny is calling the police when Joe Emma and a friend name Angie show up. Joe wants Bonnie, but Johnny tells him she is not there. Joe goes to the closet and Hart jumps from the closet and a fight ensues and Joe and Angie are knocked out. Hart tells Johnny that the body in the morgue is not Bonnie's and wants to know where she is. As the Police show up, Johnny agrees to pass a message to Bonnie for him.

Johnny plays cupid and over dinner tells Bonnie how Hart feels about her. Bonnie tells Johnny to tell Hart that she is going back home. Johnny, in an altruistic move gives Bonnie the $3,000 he had gotten from Hart and tells her to get a long way away. Johnny buys a beer for Hart, who is not happy with the results and tells Johnny to forget about the $163.55 in expenses!

NOTES:
- AKA: "SHE WAS UNDER TWENTY ONE, BUT THAT DIDN'T MEAN SHE WAS INVOLVED WITH NOTHING BUT MINOR VICES," OR "MURDER AIN'T MINOR"
- REFERENCES MADE TO SAM SPADE, PHILLIP MARLOW AND RICHARD DIAMOND (WHO WILL SING A SONG FOR YOU)
- A REFERENCE IS MADE TO BEING TAUGHT BY AN OLD PINKERTON AGENT THAT, "BEING AN INVESTIGATOR IS LIKE BEING A MAIL MAN WITH NO ADDRESS ON THE LETTER."
- EXPENSES INCLUDE $22.50 TO REPLACE A RADIO HE TURNED OFF WITH HIS FIST.
- THE MID-PROGRAM COMMERCIAL IS FOR THE PROGRAM "CALL THE POLICE" AND SAM SPADE.
- ROY ROWAN IS THE ANNOUNCER
- MUSIC IS BY LIETH STEVENS

Producer: Gordon T. Hughes   **Writers:** Paul Dudley, Gil Doud
Cast: Paul Dubov, Martha Wentworth, Lou Krugman, Georgia Ellis, Jeanne Bates, Larry Dobkin

SHOW: DEATH TAKES A WORKING DAY
SHOW DATE: 8/14/1949
COMPANY: GREAT COLUMBIAN LIFE INSURANCE COMPANY
AGENT: HARRY DEL HUBBEL
EXP. ACCT: $823.00

SYNOPSIS: **Take off your lipstick and pucker up sweetheart, here comes the kiss of death.**

Johnny drives to the estate of the deceased at Loyal House.

The housekeeper, Miss Sarah Trammel meets Johnny and tells him that the widow is out shopping. Miss Trammel has worked for the household for 30 years. "Loyal, er, Mr. Martin was an expert on Victorian furniture" Johnny is told. In answer to the unasked question, yes, Miss Trammel was provided for in the estate. Johnny says he is investigating the murder so the murderer is not paid off. "People waste a lot of murders that way" He tells her.

Police Lt. Marquette is in the library in which only two things were out of place—a suit of armor and a case of shiny new hunting rifles. Lt. Marquette tells Johnny that the body of Mr. Martin was found after dinner and had two bullet holes in it. According to Lt. Marquette, there are four suspects; a wife who was too young, the housekeeper who was in love with the deceased, the brother was broke and brooding and the body guard, a detective.

Johnny decides to start with Nick Bulotti, the bodyguard. Johnny meets with him after a horseback ride, and he tells Johnny that he had nothing really to say, but the police told him to stay put.

Marty, the brother was entertaining a bottle of 20-year-old brandy that was much too young for the book he was reading. It seems that the young wife had asked him to come and protect her from her husband. Joy-Anne, the widow comes home and goes swimming in a bikini that would "get her pinched on the Riviera!" Joy-Anne tells Johnny that Marty had introduced her to Loyal. But Loyal gave her everything but love, and when she went looking for it, the housekeeper informed Loyal and he became a madman. The housekeeper was upset with Joy-Anne because she had always assumed that Loyal would marry her. So Joy-Anne is going to enjoy what little free time she has left. Johnny to check up on the housekeeper who Johnny finds in the library wiping off the desk in violation of police orders to keep out. She tells Johnny that she always cleaned at that hour of the day otherwise Loyal would get mad. Lt. Markwood comes in and orders Johnny to take her to her room and then come back. On the way, there are 6 shots fired in the library. Johnny goes back to the library and finds Lt. Marquette dead holding a shotgun and an open window.

While searching the body, Bulotti comes in. The only clue Johnny can find, which Lt. Marquette would have wanted to share was an entry in his new notebook "Check tattooing diameter. Recheck penetration." Johnny asks Bulotti to keep quiet. He also asks the others who have now gathered to go back to their rooms. Outside Johnny looks for clues and finds a .32 revolver in the grass. The gun has 6 empty chambers and lipstick on the grip. Johnny wonders if it could it be a red herring? Sgt. McDougal arrives and Johnny tells him what happened and gives him the gun. The gun is the same caliber which killed Loyal, but why was Lt. Markwood holding an unloaded shotgun when he was shot? Johnny gets more puzzling information from Sgt. McDougal. The autopsy showed two bullet holes, 1 1/2 inches apart, which did not penetrate too deeply. Every thing pointed to the bullets being fired from 300 yards. The witnesses were split on whether 1 or 2 shots were fired on the night of the killing.

Johnny goes to the ballistics lab and discovers that the ballistics people had found powder burns, called tattooing, on the body indicating a close firing of the weapon. Also, the .32 was the weapon that killed both people. A .32 owned and licensed to Joy-Anne Martin, who looked better in a bathing suit than she will in the electric chair.

Johnny goes to see Joy, and gets her out of the shower. When quizzed about a gun owned by her, she says that her gun is in the dresser. When she gets up to get it, the gun is gone. She says it must have been stolen, and there are too many people who would love to frame her. When asked if she remembers any thing else, she says that she remembers hearing shots two days before the killing while she was out horseback riding. They came from a walnut grove. Just as Johnny kisses her, the police he had called showed up, and Joy-Anne is taken into custody after she slaps Johnny.

Next morning Johnny goes looking for the walnut grove and pondering why everyone heard one shot, and there were two bullets in the body. In the hollow trunk of a tree Johnny finds a peck of cotton waste with powder burns in it. Johnny is hit on the head and sees Marty running back to the house. Johnny chases Marty back to the house and hears 6 shots. Johnny finds Bulotti standing over Marty. Bulotti says that Marty had drawn on him, so he shot in self-defense. Johnny suggests Bulotti go to police headquarters and register his story.

Johnny calls Sgt. McDougal and tells him that Marty had just been shot and the killer was on his way to the office. Johnny tells McDougal that Nick and Marty had arranged to fire the .32 into the cotton waste to get the bullets. The bullets were then packed into a shotgun shell and fired at close range by a shotgun. Johnny tells him that he knew that Bulotti was the accomplice because he had said Marty drew on him, but Marty was unarmed.

NOTES:
- AKA: INVESTIGATION OF THE POLICYHOLDER LOYAL B. MARTIN
- AKA "HOW NOT TO TAKE A VACATION IN FAIRFIELD COUNTY."
- THE SCRIPT TITLE PAGE LISTS "DEATH TAKES A WORKING DAY" AS THE SHOW TITLE.
- THE ANNOUNCER IS ROY ROWAN
- MUSIC IS BY LIETH STEVENS
- STORY INFORMATION OBTAINED FROM THE KNX COLLECTION IN THE THOUSAND OAKS LIBRARY

Producer: Gordon Hughes   **Writers**   Paul Dudley, Gil Doud
Cast: Herb Vigran, Larry Dobkin, Jack Edwards Jr, Doris Singleton, Lois Corbett, Bill Bouchey

SHOW: OUT OF THE FIRE INTO THE FRYING PAN
SHOW DATE: 8/21/1949
COMPANY: CORINTHIAN LIABILITY & BONDING COMPANY
AGENT:
EXP. ACCT: $1,463.00
SYNOPSIS: "Mrs. Perkins won the prize, but I got in the biggest pickle at the county fair."

Johnny is Bodyguard to a Grand Blue Ribbon Champion Spotted Portland China Hog, Rosie Baron of Iowa.

Johnny travels to Carver, Iowa and goes to the county fair grounds looking for the 980-pound hog he is assigned to protect. Johnny is told that Rosie Baron is known as Rollo around here. As Johnny approaches the Swine building, loud noises are heard. As Johnny rushes in, a man rushes out. Once inside, Johnny discovers that a brooch has been stolen from Mrs. Hortense Tiller whose husband owns Rollo. Johnny is told that someone stole the brooch while Mrs. Tiller was having her photo taken. The Sheriff Harry Blewit comes in and accuses Johnny of being in cahoots with the man seen running out as Harry saw something passed between them. Johnny tells the sheriff why he is there (as a piggy-sitter) and suggests to the sheriff to get the pictures developed and look for the thief in the pictures. (Say, that gives me a idea!)

Johnny finds Rollo eating yams and meets Alva Anderson, who raised Rollo the pig. The owner, Worthington Tiller shows up and wants Johnny's picture taken with his wife and the pig. Tiller tells Johnny not to worry about the brooch as it is insured. Tiller also notes that he paid $10,000 for the pig, which is insured for $25,000, and does not want anything to happen to Rollo. When Tiller remind Johnny of all the publicity he will get, Johnny just hopes his publicity will not be an obituary that reads "Johnny Dollar no longer am, He gave up his life for a great big ham."

To pass the afternoon guarding Rollo, Johnny talks to Alva and vice versa, but the conversation is all about pigs. When Tiller relieves them, they go to dinner for baked ham, of course. The sheriff finds Johnny and informs him that he had rushed the pictures from the camera to the state capital, and there was a known criminal in it, "Little Rocky" from Arkansas! He has the brooch and is on the loose.

The grand march starts and Johnny goes to watch. As Rollo's truck and trailer pass by, Johnny sees that the driver is Little Rocky from Arkansas. After an unsuccessful attempt to tackle the truck, Little Rocky and Rollo get away.

Johnny is helped up and questions Alva as to where to get rid of a hot pig. Johnny gets the price of pork, and is sure that Little Rocky is not interested in selling Rollo. The sheriff finds Johnny and tells him that he saw Johnny's performance and does not believe Johnny was trying hard enough. Johnny asks the sheriff to loan him a car but there is no way as there is only one county vehicle. On the way to the Ferris wheel to scout out the country (Say, that gives me a idea!) Johnny asks if another pig could smell out the mash in Rollo's feeding trough and lead them to Rollo. It's possible says the sheriff. (Say, that gives me a idea!)

Johnny tricks the sheriff onto the Ferris wheel where Johnny drowns the engine with lemonade and strands Harry at the top. Johnny goes back to the Swine building to talk to Tiller. Johnny tells him that the only one who is in trouble now is the insurance company. Tiller does not like it when Johnny accuses Mrs. tiller of losing the brooch to get the insurance money for it. Tiller tells Johnny that his father had the same thing happen to him. He bought a prize pig at a fancy price and then had it stolen from him. Johnny asks if he should arrest Alva and Tiller tells Johnny that it is up to him. Johnny searched the fair grounds for Alva. As Johnny goes to the swine building Johnny sees Little Rocky with a bag over his shoulder forcing Alva out the back door. Johnny steals the sheriff's car and follows Rocky to a building outside of town where the pig and another man is. As Johnny listens at the window, he learns that the man had hidden the brooch in a yam, and the pig must have eaten it. After going through all the yams, they have not found the brooch. The men argue about killing Rollo and Alva is very upset.

Johnny "has a idea," and throws in a yam as a diversion, Johnny rushes in and slugs the thieves and rescues Alva and Rollo. Rollo is delivered to Tiller and is told that the brooch is inside him. Tiller gets Rollo ready for his next appearance at a slaughterhouse the next day and Alva is upset at losing Rollo. Johnny and an upset Alva go to dinner, a vegetable dinner. Johnny buys Harry a new badge to appease him. Johnny notes that the Sheriff was using a pig to track down Rollo at a distillery on the wrong side of town. Johnny wonders what else you can eat with eggs for breakfast.

Yours—um—Truly, Johnny Dollar.

NOTES:
- AKA: "THE PRIZE HOG BODYGUARD," OR "HOW YOU CAST MY PEARLS OF WISDOM BEFORE SWINE."
- THE MID-PROGRAM COMMERCIAL IS FOR LUX RADIO THEATER, CALL THE POLICE AND SAM SPADE.
- CURRENT PORK PRICES ARE $23.50 PER LB.
- ROY ROWAN IS THE ANNOUNCER.
- MUSIC IS BY LIETH STEVENS

Producer: Norman McDonnell   **Writers:** Paul Dudley, Gil Doud
Cast: Parley Baer, Jack Kruschen, Sammie Hill, John Dehner, Junius Matthews, Anne Morrison, Paul Dubov, Pinto Kolveg (Rollo)

SHOW: HOW I TURNED A LUXURY LINER INTO A BATTLESHIP
SHOW DATE: 8/28/1949
COMPANY: OLD CALEDONIA SECURITY INSURANCE COMPANY
AGENT:
EXP. ACCT: $2,747.27
SYNOPSIS: Well, now I know one quartet that wishes it could sing My Body Lies Under the Ocean

Johnny goes to New York City and buys seasickness pills and passage to Le Havre on the S.S. Atlanta. Onboard Johnny has dinner with Roberta Cobb, the owner of a $75,000 diamond bracelet, which she is wearing. While talking to Roberta, Aunt Cobina comes to the table to tell Roberta that her stateroom has been torn apart. Johnny inspects the cabin and calls Murdock, the ship's detective. Once under way, Roberta starts working on the male passengers while Johnny watches the bracelet. Johnny meets one of the passengers, Duke Cornwall, who Johnny is suspicious of when he heard Duke tell a man named Foley that they will have a profitable voyage. Johnny talks to Murdock who is familiar with Cornwall, and Eddie "The Faker" Foley, both of whom are fast operators. Johnny tells Roberta, but she tells Johnny that he is just jealous. Johnny continues to follow Roberta for two more days.

When the boat arrives in Le Havre, Roberta is not wearing the bracelet. Johnny goes to her room and sees the bracelet. Johnny goes in to get it and is knocked unconscious.

Johnny wakes up to Murdock slapping him. Roberta comes in and learns that the bracelet is gone and is angry, especially since Cornwall dumped her. Johnny watches the customs agents search both Cornwall and Foley, but they find nothing. Johnny joins Roberta, Aunt Cobina, Cornwall and Foley on the train to Paris. In Paris Johnny follows Cornwall and Foley through a number of bars until they meet a contact that hands Cornwall a small package containing the bracelet. Johnny follows Cornwall to the Hotel Ritz and up to the second floor room of Roberta Cobb. Cornwall slaps Roberta and accuses her of passing paste. Johnny tells Roberta that she was flashing the bracelet to set up Cornwall, and that the bracelet was stolen in front of Johnny to collect the insurance. Roberta gives Johnny the fake bracelet. Roberta gets a call from the desk for Johnny. The desk clerk tells Johnny that Aunt Cobina is on her way up. Johnny tells Roberta that "Aunt" Flora Cobina is not her aunt, and that she has a record for selling stolen jewels. Flora comes into the room and Roberta throws a vase at her while Johnny takes the real bracelet from her hair.

NOTES:
- THE ANNOUNCER IS ROY ROWAN
- MUSIC IS BY LIETH STEVENS
- JOHNNY NOTES THAT HE HAS BEEN A DETECTIVE FOR 10 YEARS.
- STORY INFORMATION OBTAINED FROM THE KNX COLLECTION IN THE THOUSAND OAKS LIBRARY

Producer: Norman Macdonnell   **Writers** Paul Dudley, Gil Doud
Cast: Lynn Allen, Lois Corbett, Larry Dobkin, Paul Dubov, John Dehner

SHOW: THE EXPIRING NICKELS AND THE EGYPTIAN JACKPOT
SHOW DATE: 9/4/1949
COMPANY: CONSTANT SUN TRADING COMPANY
AGENT:
EXP. ACCT: $5,350.40
SYNOPSIS: "I always say, if you take a trip halfway around the world you gotta expect you'll get your ticket punched."

Johnny travels to French Indo China and then to Calcutta, India (9 dreary hours at 20,000 feet sucking oxygen) to assist an old Army buddy, Chaplain Joe Blessing who stayed in India to save souls in his recycled Army Quonset hut church. Joe tells Johnny that he wants Johnny to save another man's soul. Here is Calcutta, William Briggs has evidence that will free a man condemned to hang the next day in Cairo, Mr. Lionel Brooke-Nickels, who owns the Constant Sun Trading Company. Brooke-Nickels' cousin is Miles Atkinson, a big wheel in Egyptian government, who wants the business is framing him for a murder Miles committed. Johnny is to take Briggs (who is a leper) and the evidence (a loaded and armed Luger) to Cairo via chartered cargo plane.

On the Horizons Unlimited plane, Joe's assistant Frankie gives Johnny the loaded Luger, which Johnny pockets. Frankie and Johnny compare stories of losing horses during the trip. After a refueling stop in Bombay, they stop in Aden for servicing and pick up a stowaway, Miss Fate Fabian who is quite a dish, as usual. Johnny takes $500 as payment for passage to Cairo and good behavior. Johnny is happy to spend the flight with Fate. An ambulance meets the plane in Cairo, Egypt only it is not an ambulance and both Briggs and Frankie are kidnapped.

After Briggs is taken Johnny attempts to fire at them with the Luger, but Johnny finds that it is missing from his coat. Fate has it in the bathroom, but she does not know how it got there. Johnny takes a wild cab ride into Cairo to find Briggs. Johnny accuses Fate of being involved, but she denies it, even after Johnny tells her all about what is going on. Johnny goes to the police and meets with the Chief Inspector, who is Miles Atkinson! Miles takes the gun from Johnny, and tells Johnny that Frankie has been arrested for killing Briggs. At gunpoint, Miles tells Johnny the entire story of how he killed a man and framed Brooke-Nickels. Fate commends Miles for making a full and voluntary confession and that Miles is going with them. When Miles tries to fire the Luger, but it is empty. In an attempt to escape, Miles kills the lights and runs for the roof turning off the lights as he goes. On the roof, Miles tries to hold Fate and Johnny off with a fire hose. Fate opens the hose valve all the way and whips Miles off of the roof and down onto the gallows in the courtyard.

Johnny thanks Fate who tells Johnny that she had unloaded the gun on the plane. Fate tells Johnny that she is an undercover agent for the Police Inspector General. Johnny and Fate get Brooke-Nickel and Frankie released and Johnny heads back to the airport. Mr. Brooke-Nickel meets with Johnny and agrees to pay all of Johnny's expenses. He also agrees to build a proper Church for Joe Blessing. A Johnny heads back to Calcutta to say goodbye to Joe, and buys a custom blackjack for Fate.

NOTES:

- "YOURS, UMM, TRULY" SIGNOFF
- JOHNNY NOTES HE MET JOE BLESSING WHILE HE WAS A SOLDIER IN THE "CBI THEATER" WHICH WAS THE "CHINA BURMA INDIA" THEATER
- JOHNNY BUYS A BLUE SUEDE BLACKJACK FOR FATE—HOW ROMANTIC!
- THE MID-PROGRAM COMMERCIAL IS FOR HORACE HITE'S YOUTH OPPORTUNITY SHOW
- JOHNNY UN-HOCKS AN OLD "AIR MEDAL" UPON RETURN TO HARTFORD. AFTER ALL THAT FLYING, HE NEEDS ONE

- JOHNNY TAKES A VACATION AND WILL COME BACK ON SATURDAY, OCTOBER 1
- ROY ROWAN IS THE ANNOUNCER
- MUSIC IS BY LIETH STEVENS

Producer: Gordon T. Hughes   **Writers: Paul Dudley, Gil Doud**
Cast: Georgia Ellis, Parley Baer, Paul Dubov, Jack Edwards

◆ ❖ ◆

SHOW: THE SEARCH FOR MICHELLE MARSH
SHOW DATE: 9/25/1949
COMPANY: TRI-STATE LIFE & CASUALTY INSURANCE COMPANY
AGENT:
EXP. ACCT: $786.00
SYNOPSIS: **"Sure, they may have plenty of Blue blood in Boston, but from what I just saw, they've got plenty of the other kind too."**

Johnny goes to Boston, Massachusetts to look for Michelle Marsh who was reported missing by her sister. Michelle is insured for $25,000. Johnny gets to her last know address just in time to see a man gunned down with carbines by two men in a car. Johnny goes to the victim and the dying man's last words were "Michelle Marsh." Johnny makes a quick visit to her apartment and searches it finding only a book of matches for "Boston's Best Bar by Far, Flannery's Bar." Back outside, Johnny meets Lt. Bell and gives him a very detailed breakdown of the killers; after all he is paid to pay attention to details. Johnny learns that the dead man was also a detective with a good business and a bad reputation. Johnny tells Bell about Michelle and why he is looking for her, and what the dead man had told him.

A visit to the apartment manger, Mrs. Macy, uncovers nothing except that Michelle had irregular hours, and was last seen leaving with a suitcase and a man, supposedly her employer. She only got mail from someone in Chicago.

Johnny questions the neighbors and learns nothing more. Johnny goes dinner and then to Flannery's Bar and asks for a double rye. Johnny asks for "Blackie" and gives the bartender a description of Michelle's boy friend. A big guy named Roxy takes Johnny outside and tells him that the description is that of Louie Marine. On the way out of the bar with Roxy, Johnny is met by a hail of carbine fire that is met with submachine gun fire.

Johnny discovers that he had been saved by the police and is probably being used as a pigeon. Johnny goes to his hotel and after reading the afternoon paper Johnny calls Lt. Bell and tears him apart for putting Johnny's name and hotel and why Johnny was in town into the papers. Bell tells Johnny that it must have been a misunderstanding. Lt. Bell tells Johnny that the dead detective was named Bernard Knight and that he was hired by Roxy Morris to find the girl. Johnny is sure that Louie Marine probably killed Knight.

Michelle calls Johnny the next morning. She tells Johnny to stop looking for her. Johnny tells her that she was waiting for Roxy to come from Chicago when Louie showed up. She thinks Johnny is guessing but agrees to meet Johnny at the Gangplank Bar on Chelsea Street near the Navy Yard. Johnny visits a North Boston "Undertaker" and pays for information. Johnny learns that Roxy Morris was suspected of stealing $75,000 in a payroll robbery. Roxy left for Chicago and left the money in Boston.

In the bar Johnny meets Michelle who confirms the story. Michelle adds that Louie Marine had tricked Michelle out of $20,000 by telling her that Roxy had sent him for it. Later Louie told Michelle that he had lied and that he would call the police if she turned him in or told Roxy. Then he made her give him $15,000 more. Now Roxy is back and he wants ALL of the money, which Michelle doesn't have.

Johnny sets up a plan with Michelle and the police: Michelle will arrange to meet Roxy. The undertaker friend will arrange for Louie to meet Roxy. The police will meet all three. The place is the Bunker Hill Monument (Don't fire until you see the red in their eyes) at 3:00 PM.

Johnny walks up to the observation platform early and finds an unconscious Michelle with a suicide note beside her. Johnny hers a shot and starts down the steps where he meets Roxy and baits him to go up by saying Louie Marine is upstairs. Roxy goes upstairs and slugs Johnny. Johnny then meets Louie who escorts Johnny to the observation deck. Johnny reaches the observation deck top see Roxy. Johnny goes up and ends up standing between Louie and Roxy. Suddenly Michelle screams and pulls Johnny's leg out from under him while Roxy and Louie shoot each other.

Johnny carries an unconscious Michelle to the hospital to have the remaining poison pumped from her stomach; apparently she took too little the first time. Then he goes to Lt. Bell to find out why he did not show up until an hour later. The reason: He forgot to set his watch back after the time change!

NOTES:
- AKA: "She Came In Like A Lion, But Went Out On The Lam," or "She Should Have Been Banned In Boston."
- "Yours, umm, Truly" ending
- I hear Michelle MARCH when I listen to this program
- The first car was a tan club coupe with Mass tags 3R165
- The carbines were .30 cal. Army issue
- Johnny shows up on Saturday night next week.
- Music is by Lieth Stevens

Producer: Gordon T. Hughes   Writers: Paul Dudley, Gil Doud
Cast: Bill Bouchey, Charles Seel, Dorothy Lovett, Larry Dobkin, Myra Marsh, Vic Ryan

SHOW:	THE FISHING BOAT AFFAIR
SHOW DATE:	10/1/1949
COMPANY:	INTERCONTINENTAL MARINE INSURANCE COMPANY
AGENT:	
EXP. ACCT:	$1,264.28

SYNOPSIS: "This you can really call a fish story, and I was the live bait!"

Johnny flies to the Pacific Deep-sea Canning Company in San Pedro, California where he meets Mr. Walton who wants his $400,000 for the two fishing boats he lost at sea with no survivors and only two bodies. Walton agrees to assist Johnny then insurance fraud is mentioned. Captain George Carpo, Fleet Captain, meets Johnny but he does not know what happened, but he has never lost a boat in five years. Carpo tells Johnny it will be a miracle if the finds the boats.

Johnny goes to the Coast Guard and meets with Lt. SG Myles Endikett. The Coast Guard report says that the bodies show signs of a violent explosion, and that means scuttling to collect the insurance.

Johnny goes to the Cormorant Bar and finds Carpo talking to a woman and then leaves. Johnny goes in and talks to the girl. Johnny tells her who he is and she tells Johnny she has a tough job. The girl, Anita Vargaves, is willing to talk somewhere else for money, as Carpo lives upstairs. Johnny takes Anita to another bar where Roscoe Walton shows up and is angry because Johnny is with HIS girlfriend. Johnny decides to get lost.

Johnny goes to the local police and asks them to look into dynamite purchases, then goes back to Carpo's place. While walking up the steps he hears 6 shots and runs in to find Carpo shot and barely alive and Johnny notices that he was beaten. A man walks in and accuses Johnny of killing his friend.

Johnny finds himself with a dead man at his feet, and a gun at this head. Johnny explains what has happened, and the man identifies himself as Cricket who was there to talk business with Carpo. Johnny tells him who he is and Cricket tells him that he is in the salvage business. Cricket tells Johnny that Carpo's face met with a "Monkey's Fist." Cricket explains the purpose of the knot, and Johnny asks about a woven ships bumper on the wall. Before the police arrive they leave and go to Cricket's boat, a surplus Navy PT boat where, over some Tchaikovsky and a drink, Cricket agrees to find the sunken boats for salvage rights and a $5,000 fee, returnable if he is unsuccessful. After agreeing, Johnny goes to Carpo's office where he finds a floor safe with a gold ingot in it. Walton and Anita show up with a gun. Johnny accuses Walton of smuggling Mexican gold, but Walton does not know what he is talking, so the struggle and Johnny knocks him out with the ingot.

Johnny gets the $5000, calls the Coast Guard and then heads out to sea with Cricket. After arriving in the San Clemente area, they spend an hour searching for the lost boats. The wrecks are located and a diver goes down and confirms that the boats are there.

Johnny has to go down to make it official, so he dons the old-fashioned diving suit, complete with helmet, lead shoes, rubber hoses and a canvas suit, not very zoot!

While on the bottom, Johnny finds the boats and the gold hidden in the ships bumper. Cricket calls to Johnny over the intercom and tells Johnny he is not going to come up but will suffer an "accident." Johnny tells Cricket that he has found the gold and hidden it, so he has to come up.

Upon arriving at the surface, actually at the end of the hoist, Johnny sees a full-scale battle going on with the Coast Guard. Johnny cuts his suit with a diving knife and it falls on Cricket.

After a cab trip to the police, Cricket tells all: while in Cleveland he had noticed a nationwide series of small gold thefts. He discovered that the gold was being melted into ingots and shipped to the orient. He wanted to intercept the gold and make a tidy profit. It was Carpo who was helping him get the gold and transfer it to the tuna clippers.

Johnny buys chocolates for Anita, who is in jail as an accomplice.

NOTES:
- **AKA:** "The Tuna were running and so was everyone else," or "I caught a fishing boat but you should have seen the one that got away!"
- The commercial is for the Edgar Bergen program, which starts on Sunday
- Cricket is described as a "Thomas Mitchell Type." Mitchell played forgetful Uncle Billy in "It's a Wonderful Life"
- "Yours, umm, Truly" ending
- Wilbur Hatch does the music for this program
- The Red Skelton program starts tomorrow
- Paul Masterson is the announcer

Producer: Gordon T. Hughes   **Writers:** Paul Dudley, Gil Doud
Cast: Willard Waterman, Larry Dobkin, Paul Dubov, Junius Matthews, Edmond MacDonald, Georgia Ellis

◆   ❖   ◆

Show: The Racehorse Piledriver Matter
Show Date: 10/8/1949
Company: Lloyds Underwriters Association
Agent:
Exp. Acct: $1,449.22
Synopsis: "This is a horse on me. But I did find out that in the race for life and death, the police laboratory is where they make the photo finish."

While buying cigarettes (18 cents) Johnny is approached by Nettie Montana, the short Johnny Longden, a former jockey and small guy. Nettie has an offer for Johnny about a horse and $50,000, but he can't talk in public so they go to Johnny's apartment. In Johnny's apartment Nettie tells Johnny about the racehorse Piledriver. The horse made a lot of money for Nettie, but Piledriver hasn't won since Nettie retired after an accident in Central Park. The current owner has him insured for $50,000 and is going to kill him because he can't win and can't go to stud. Nettie is willing to pay Johnny to save Piledriver. After an OK from the insurance company, Johnny and Nettie head for the Hiawatha Racetrack, outside of Chicago, Illinois.

At the track Nettie warns Johnny to look out for Lilah, as she is dangerous to men like Johnny. Johnny meets Lilah Bushnell, the daughter of the owner Col. Faraday Bushnell. Johnny tells Lilah that he is interested in buying Piledriver but Lilah assures Johnny that "daddy would nevah sell Pahledrivah as he is one of the family!" Lilah shows the horse to Johnny he tells her he hopes to make the horse win again. Lilah kisses Johnny just as her boyfriend Leo Corbett shows up and blows up at her. Johnny slugs Leo just as the Colonel shows up Lilah and Leo leave and explains to Johnny that Leo is a fellow horse owner and a very jealous man. Johnny tells the colonel that he is glad that Leo is not James J. Corbett.

Johnny meets Nettie in a bar and learns that Corbett owns fast horses but is suspected of running his horses slow to build up the odds and then cashes in by running them fast. Johnny tells Nettie that he offered the Colonel $60,000 for Piledriver pending approval his private vet from California. Against Johnny's advice, Nettie is going to the stable to personally guard the horse.

Johnny gets a room for $3 and settles in for the night only to be awakened by sirens heading towards the stables. Johnny goes into the barn in the landlady's 1929 Ford and learns that Nettie had gone into the barn. Johnny goes in and finds Piledriver's stall padlocked. Johnny breaks the door and gets the horse out and then finds Nettie in the stall unconscious on the floor. Johnny drags Nettie outside and finds a horseshoe imprint on his very dead head.

Lilah runs up and sees Nettie, and Johnny tells her to get lost. The Colonel runs up and is shocked that Nettie is dead, as he was his best jockey. Johnny accuses the Colonel of trying to kill Pile driver and takes Nettie to the morgue in Chicago.

Later that morning Lilah calls wants to talk to Johnny. Johnny tells her to pick him up so they can drive to the country. Lilah denies all Johnny's accusations that the Colonel is out to kill Piledriver. She tells Johnny that her father owes Leo $50,000 from betting on Piledriver and Leo has told the Colonel to kill the horse and he has agreed, but Lilah knows he will not. Lilah tells Johnny that she kissed him to prove to Leo that he would not get everything he wants. Johnny goes to the Chicago police where Lt. Craig tells Johnny that the autopsy confirmed that Nettie was hit with a new horseshoe, not one on a horse. It also had to have been swung by a person, and not a horse. Johnny calls a meeting at the track offices with the Colonel and Leo. The colonel arrives and is ready to sell Piledriver to Johnny. Leo shows up because Johnny had called him. Johnny tells them that the fire was set and that Nettie's lungs were full of smoke. Johnny wants to test their lungs for residual smoke to see who killed Nettie. The Colonel hesitantly agrees, but Leo bolts out the door. Leo runs out onto the roof (see the notes below) with Johnny in hot pursuit. On the grandstand roof, Leo shoots at Johnny, but he is a lousy shot. Leo fights with Johnny and runs again. Leo tries to escape down the downspout, but it collapses and he is killed.

The final expense item is dinner for two with Lilah, $34.80—only $8 of which was for dinner. The rest was listening to her life story.

NOTES:

- AKA: "HE WOULD HAVE BEEN OFF HIS DEED IF I DIDN'T KNOW MY OATS," OR "IT'S GREAT TO GET A KICK OUT OF LIFE AS LONG AS IT IS NOT A KICK IN THE HEAD."
- JOHNNY BUYS LUCKY STRIKE CIGARETTES (LUCKIES).
- LEO IS COMPARED TO JAMES J. "GENTLEMAN JIM" CORBETT—HEAVY-WEIGHT PRIZEFIGHTER.
- THE COMMERCIAL IS FOR THE SATURDAY PROGRAMS PHILLIP MARLOW, GANGBUSTERS AND ESCAPE. THERE IS A SINGING "CBS" COMMERCIAL AT THE END.
- DURING THE PROVERBIAL CHASE SCENE, THERE ARE TWO RACES GOING ON—THE ONE ON THE TRACK "AND THERE THEY GO!" AND THE ONE ON THE ROOF WITH BOTH COMMENTARIES GOING ON AT THE SAME TIME—VERY FUNNY!
- WILBUR HATCH PROVIDES THE MUSIC FOR THIS PROGRAM
- PAUL MASTERSON IS THE ANNOUNCER

Producer: Gordon P. Hughes   **Writers: Paul Dudley, Gil Doud**
Cast: **Bill Conrad, Doris Singleton, Jerry Hausner, Herb Butterfield, Hal March**

◆   ❖   ◆

SHOW: DR. OTTO SCHMEDLICH
SHOW DATE: 10/15/1949
COMPANY: AMERICAN VOLUNTEER LIABILITY INSURANCE COMPANY
AGENT: HOMER SHALLY
EXP. ACCT: $1,211.69
SYNOPSIS: "What does a doctor do when a doctor needs a doctor?"

Johnny takes a cab to the office of American Volunteer where Homer Shally apologizes for an argument they had about Johnny's $1 tips on his last expense account. The insurance company has issued a malpractice policy to Dr. Otto Schmedlich, in Los Angeles (doesn't anything happen in Hartford?). It covers accidental malpractice, but they want to prove criminal malpractice. The company has paid 2 claims to this quack so far and the local authorities are looking into him, but they cannot find anything.

Johnny flies to Los Angeles, California and, after 11 phone calls, goes to Dr.

Schmedlich's office where he meets nurse Doreen, the receptionist and asks her for a date. Doreen tells Johnny that there is no way she would be caught dead with him. Later that night in a restaurant Johnny tells Doreen he is an "insurance man" and would like to get a list of the doctor's patients, after all a lot of healthy people go to the doctor and worry about their health. Johnny takes Doreen home and tells the cab to wait. $28 later Johnny goes to his hotel.

Next morning Johnny gets to the office early to get the list from Doreen. While eyeing the list, surprise, the doctor is also early. After telling the doctor that Johnny is a patient, the doctor gives Johnny an exam for a back problem. The exam the doctor gives includes a hypo of a liquid lullaby. As Johnny goes out, he sees the doctor going through his jacket for the list and his ID.

When Johnny wakes up, he is in a room with padded walls, a bad taste in his mouth and a ringing in his head. Johnny realizes he is in a mental institution and pounds on the door. His nurse, a man named Forgey tells Johnny that the boss will see him just before supper. The boss is Dr. Doreen Smith. While he waits, Johnny makes a blackjack out of his shoes and a ripped-up bed sheet. At 4, Forgey shows up with Doreen. Johnny slugs Forgey when he comes in and pulls Doreen into the room. Doreen tells Johnny to go back to Hartford. Johnny locks Doreen and Forgey in the cell and takes her keys. Johnny notes that the cell is in an out-of-the-way country house with no other visitors. Johnny borrows Doreen's car and drives to a gas station. At a phone booth Johnny calls the one name he remembers (A. A. Aaron) and fakes a pharmacy survey, and gets the name of Schmedlich's favorite pharmacy. Johnny goes to the pharmacy and while talking to the pharmacy manager Mr. Anjoy, Johnny learns that most of Schmedlich's prescriptions are refillable, dangerous and habit forming. Johnny also memorizes a list of clients from the narcotics book in Anjoy's office.

Johnny finally finds one client at home, Millicent Royal, a blue blood type. She tells Johnny that Dr. Schmedlich is a wonderful doctor. Johnny threatens to tell her father that he thinks she is not being honest and she gets angry. Millicent's estranged husband Bill shows up and Johnny decides to leave.

After a shower, a drink and a thinking session at this hotel room Johnny wonders why he has not called the police. After four drinks Millicent calls and wants to talk. Johnny tells her to tell him what she wants to say over the phone because, usually when he goes to see someone, they wind up dead. Johnny goes back to Millicent's apartment and, yep, she's dead.

A call to the Dr. Schmedlich's phone service tells Johnny that he is going to the office. When Johnny gets there the lights are on and Bill is waiting inside. He tells Johnny that he didn't kill Millicent. He tells Johnny that Dr. Schmedlich had hooked her on narcotics and then blackmailed her to not tell the family. When she called Schmedlich and told him she was going to tell, Schmedlich killed her. Now Bill is going to kill Schmedlich using a hand grenade he had kept from Guadalcanal. When the Doctor comes in, Bill pulls the pin and throws it at Schmedlich. Johnny kicks Bill, and then kicks the grenade out into the hallway. After the explosion, Bill beats Schmedlich while Johnny watches. Johnny stops Bill with a portable typewriter before he kills Schmedlich.

PS, Johnny calls the police.

The final expense items include round trip air fair to Palm Springs and dinner for three—Johnny, Haig and Haig.

Johnny warns Shally that if he reacts to this expense account like he did to the last one, he will need a doctor.

Notes:

- AKA: An Apple A Day Sent The Doctor Away, or It Couldn't Have Happened To A Bigger Worm.
- $1 tip to office.
- Shally tells Johnny, "When I want a laugh, I tune in Jack Benny"
- Dr. Schmedlich office visit was $50.
- Russell stammers three, once on "submitted" and once on "identification," once on "word."
- Champagne is described as "Rich people's 7-Up"
- The commercial is for the Edgar Bergen program.
- Haig and Haig scotch mentioned at the end.
- Cast is from RadioGOLDINdex
- Music direction is by Wilbur Hatch
- The announcer is Paul Masterson

Producer:	Unknown	**Writers:** Unknown
Cast:	Willard Waterman, Betty Lou Gerson, Lawrence Dobkin, Paul Dubov, Georgia Ellis, Edmond MacDonald	

Show:	Witness, Witness, Who's Got The Witness
Show Date:	10/22/1949
Company:	Max Krause Bail Bond and Insurance
Agent:	Max Krause
Exp. Acct:	$500.71

Synopsis: "In this case most of the principles are out on bail. It put me out on a limb."

Max Krause arrives at Johnny's apartment with a bad cigar and a potential loss of $50,000. Max put up bail for two prosecution witnesses against gangster Leo Porcina, and both have disappeared. Max's insurance contacts recommended Johnny, who has a good reputation, except for padding the expense account, but who doesn't do that, right? Johnny gets a $1,000 advance to find Glenn "Nippy" Cochran and Dan Patterson.

Johnny goes to New York City and heads for the apartment of Nippy's sister, who uses the stage-name Mona Doyle. Johnny gets into the building with a delivery boy and goes to Mona's apartment. Johnny tells her why he is there and tells Mona he hires some radio writers to work things out for him. Mona does not know where Nippy is and would not tell Johnny if she did. She tells Johnny that everything she has came from Nippy, including being introduced to Leo Porcina. Johnny and Mona have a couple of drinks and then Leo shows up. He offers Johnny the opportunity to work together to find Nippy and Dan, because their disappearing makes him look bad. But Johnny turns him down.

On the way out, Johnny notices the chauffeur of Leo's limo following him. Johnny takes a cab to Dan Peterson's apartment, but the chauffeur is there when he gets to the apartment. The chauffeur tells Johnny that he is Dan Patterson! Dan suggests they go somewhere to talk and slugs Johnny.

Johnny wakes up with a .45 headache on the floor of the back seat of the limo, with a hose coming in from the exhaust pipe. Johnny is able to plug up the hose with a handkerchief and waits to see what will happen.

Dan stops the limo and takes Johnny out. Johnny slugs him with a rock and takes his gun. When Dan wakes up, he tells Johnny that Leo made him do it, and what Leo says, you do. Johnny gets Dan to tell him that they are in New Jersey. Dan tries to run, and Johnny shoots him and then deposits him with a police doctor.

Johnny goes to New York and calls Mona. She tells Johnny that Nippy has come back and killed Leo. Johnny picks up Mona and goes to Leo's apartment where Johnny finds Leo dead, with a knife wound in his chest. Mona tells Johnny that she was in the back room and heard voices. When she came back in, Nippy was standing over Leo.

They go back to Mona's apartment and, after almost being seduced by her charms, and a "Johnny Walker for Johnny Dollar" Johnny wakes up. Johnny wonders why would someone who had turned state's evidence kill someone the state was going to kill? Then he figures it out. Leo was up on tax charges and Mona was holding some of the money for him. If the police find out, Mona would go to jail, and Nippy provided everything for Mona.

The seduction does not work. "I'm not human, I'm an insurance investigator!" Johnny calls the police and turns Mona in for murder. Johnny plants a phony story in the newspaper outlining how he had used a tape recorder to get the confession. Johnny goes to the hotel, after getting some adhesive tape. In his room, Johnny tapes the phone books to his chest and waits.

Nippy shows up and tells Johnny that Mona's confession is phony. Johnny tells Nippy that a friend killed Leo but that does not fit Nippy. Nippy tries to throw a knife into Johnny's chest, but it bounces off the telephone books. Johnny throws a chair and Nippy and finally knocks him out. Johnny expenses a trip to the doctor to get the adhesive tape removed with alcohol. The expense account also includes $367.25 entertaining Mona for her forgiveness!

Signed: "Yours (clink, clink) ummm Truly, (ahhhhh) Johnny Walker, I mean Dollar!"

NOTES:
- **AKA: HE SAID GIVE ME LIBERTY OR GIVE ME DEATH, AND GOT BOTH, OR "WITNESS, WITNESS, WHO HAS THE WITNESS?"**

- JOHNNY TELLS MONA "I HAVE A COUPLE OF RADIO WRITERS WORK THINGS OUT FOR ME."
- THE COMMERCIAL IS FOR THE PROGRAM "PEOPLE'S PLATFORM."
- SEVERAL REFERENCES TO JOHNNY WALKER SCOTCH—THE BEST IS: "JOHNNY WALKER FOR JOHNNY DOLLAR JOHNNY ON THE SPOT!"
- PAUL MASTERSON IS THE ANNOUNCER
- MUSIC DIRECTION IS BY WILBUR HATCH

Producer: Gordon T. Hughes   **Writers:** Paul Dudley, Gil Doud
Cast: Sidney Miller, James Nusser, Georgia Ellis, Paul Dubov, Ed Max

◆   ❖   ◆

SHOW: THE LITTLE MAN WHO WASN'T THERE
SHOW DATE: 10/29/1949
COMPANY: WEST COAST UNDERWRITERS
AGENT: BRADFORD L. COATES
EXP. ACCT: $942.08
SYNOPSIS: "If you're looking for murder, I know a man who can get it for you wholesale."

Johnny receives a postage due letter assigning him to a case in San Francisco, California. Mr. James Yarbow had a $20,000 policy on his wife, which was cancelled the day before she died due to non-payment of the premium. Yarbow claims to have had a hand in the "accidental" deaths of 12 other West Coast policyholders.

Johnny goes to San Francisco and meets with Mr. Coates. Coates tells Johnny that the 12 deaths in question have totaled $250,000. Mr. Yarbow has had a perfect alibi for each of the 12 deaths. All of the deaths involved an automobile accident, except for one where a pilot died. Johnny asks for a list of policyholders, only to see if it would be easy for Yarbow to get it also. Johnny asks for a $50,000 policy on him self—just in case.

Johnny gets Yarbow's address and the address of the 12 victims, rents a limo with chauffeur and starts interviewing. The "tears were falling like monsoon rains in Burma" at each family, but none of the families knew a man named Yarbow.

Johnny then goes to Yarbow's house and starts watching. When Yarbow leaves his house dressed in a black trench coat and carrying a black satchel, Johnny breaks in through a window and explores the house. Yarbow's house looks like a crime museum, full of guns, books, evidence and Mr. Yarbow!

Yarbow holds Johnny at bay by telling him that the room and the roses in the rug are wired to booby traps. Yarbow tells Johnny that crime is his hobby. He has items from the Black Museum in Scotland and items from all over the country. Yarbow knows who Johnny is and why he is there. Yarbow continues his rant about the unpaid policy on his wife. Yarbow tells Johnny that he gave the money to his wife and she spent it, and he can prove it. When Yarbow lowers his guard to open a drawer, Johnny slugs him while he is standing on a big red rose on the floor. The phone rings and, trying to imitate Yarbow, Johnny answers. On the phone is Martha, calling from the office, who tells Johnny that there has been another accident killing two more policyholders—and Johnny is Yarbow's alibi!

Johnny searches Yarbow for a gun and then looks in the black satchel and finds an old Army tank radio receiver wired to a transmitter in the house, which is what allowed Yarbow to hear Johnny enter the house.

When Yarbow recovers, Johnny tells him that Martha had called, but Yarbow is sure that she told him nothing. Yarbow shows Johnny the insurance policy he was reaching for. Johnny locks Yarbow in the most secure room in the house, the bathroom. Yarbow protests in horror, as he does not want to be locked in the room where his wife died!

Johnny calls the state police and confirms the accident information given him by Martha. Then Johnny calls Coates and arranges to meet him in his office. At the office Johnny and Coates search the personnel files for "Martha" and find three, but only one was in the office that night, Martha Kinsey.

Johnny goes to Martha's apartment and wakes her up and tells her who he is. Martha says nothing other than Yarbow has paid her for information (everyone does it) and Yarbow is smart, he told he so. The only thing Johnny really gets is that Martha is in love with Yarbow. Johnny then visits the doctor who did the autopsy on Yarbow's wife. She died of a cerebral hemorrhage after falling in the shower. On the way back to Yarbow's, Johnny realizes that 1) The alibis are too perfect; 2) Yarbow cared more about the policy money than losing his wife, and 3) Yarbow is crazy and a murderer! Now Johnny has to get the evidence.

At Yarbow's, Johnny searches the house until he finds the evidence he is looking for, while being careful not to step on the roses on the carpet!

Yarbow is taken from the bathroom and Johnny confronts him the fact that he had nothing to do with the accidents. Martha was the once supplying him with the information Yarbow had used to threaten the insurance company with. Johnny shows Yarbow the evidence of his wife's murder, the one piece of evidence he should not have kept; a piece of pipe with a faucet on it. The pipe he used to murder his wife. Martha comes in and they both attack Johnny. Martha throws an urn and misses, but Yarbow chases the urn as it rolls towards a rose on the rug, which explodes on a booby trap killing Yarbow.

Johnny buys Martha a three-month subscription to "Love Life Magazine" to read in jail. Then there is dinner on fisherman's Wharf diving for pearls, Pearl's earring that fell in the barrel of clams from which dinner was being picked.

Yours, ah Truly, Johnny Dollar.

NOTES:
- **AKA: "THE LITTLE MAN WHO WASN'T ALL THERE, OR IN MOST CASES THERE AT ALL," OR "THE UNPAID PREMIUM PAYOFF"**
- **THE BLACK MUSEUM WAS ALSO THE NAME OF A MYSTERY SERIES HOSTED BY ORSON WELLS**

- THE COMMERCIAL OF FOR THE GROUCHO MARX SHOW, BING CROSBY, GEORGE BURNS AND LUM AND ABNER

Producer: Gordon T. Hughes   Writers: Paul Dudley, Gil Doud
Cast: Jay Novello, Martha Wentworth, Paul Dubov, GeGe Pearson,
             Larry Dobkin

◆   ❖   ◆

SHOW: THE SOUTH SEA ADVENTURE
SHOW DATE: 11/5/1949
COMPANY: SEVEN SEAS MARITIME UNDERWRITERS ASSOCIATION
AGENT: ENOS MCCARTLE
EXP. ACCT: $3,286.44

SYNOPSIS: "The only reason I took this case on a savage island off the coast of New Guinea is I'd been having a bout with a bottle of "Old Fairy Godmother" and I was hoping to run into a native who would shrink my head!"

Johnny travels to Port Moresby, Papua, New Guinea, buys some new tropical clothes and goes to the offices of Seven Seas where he meets Mr. Narky. Johnny confirms that a group insurance policy was sold to Grand East Development Corporation, who used it to provide $50,000 polices as an inducement to get divers and executives for the pearling fleet. So far 2 men are dead and 4 are missing. Narky tells Johnny that the police have their own problems, and that the government officials might get to it in three months, so Narky is just waiting for Johnny.

Johnny charters the "Kitty Wake" captained by Steve Granger for the trip to Tun-Yutan. Granger arranges to leave at 5:00, and Johnny is told to bring a .45!

Once at sea, Johnny starts to enjoy being on the boat. Granger meets Johnny on deck and tells Johnny that there is another unnamed passenger going to Tun-Yutan. On the trip the other passenger stays in his cabin claiming seasickness, but the cabin boy says he eats like a horse.

The next evening the boat arrives at Tun-Yutan. The captain starts the engine and works his way through the reef. Just short of the reef the captain orders an about face. There is a pearling lugger on the beach with a native strangled and hanging from the foremast!

Suddenly the other passenger, Matt Keely shows up on deck with a gun in each hand and orders everyone aft. When Granger orders the crew to abandon ship in Kanaka—the local language, Keely kills them and then orders the boat towards shore. Once on shore, Johnny and Granger are taken to a hut surrounded by 12 dead natives apparently killed by the .30 cal. water-cooled machine gun protruding from the window. In the hut they meet Portez. Johnny tells them that he is there to take care of them and they laugh. Keely offers Granger $500 for his boat which is worth $50,000. Some how the offer of $500 or death seems fair. They need the boat to get off the island and will be at sea for a couple months. A very ugly, fat woman, Princess Papalya, comes into the room and is brusquely pushed back into the other room by Portez. Granger slugs Keely, then Johnny lunges out for Portez. Granger is shot and then Keely is hit with a chair swung by the Princess! Then the lights go out.

Johnny dreams of being in a hammock, with a pretty girl and a parrot, and wakes up to the first two! (And he remembers his copy of "Tales of the South Pacific" is 17 days overdue from the library) The lovely girl he is with, Ponta tells Johnny that Papalya slugged Johnny and brought him to her village. **Papalya likes Johnny**, and saved him for herself! Ponta explains that Keely and Portez were pearl divers who went bad and killed the natives and stole all the pearls. The natives had stopped diving, so Keely kidnapped the princess and held her for ransom until they started diving for pearls again. Johnny learns that the dead natives had tried to save the princess and were killed by Portez and that the Princess is now hiding in the mountains. The ugly part is that now Johnny has to protect Keely and Portez as they are insured by Seven Seas for $50,000 each!

The next morning there is more shooting as the natives try to get at Keely and Portez who Johnny must protect. Johnny wonders why Keely and Portez do not leave, so Ponta gives Johnny a black pearl that Papalya had sent for him. Keely and Portez want it also. But Johnny has a plan. Johnny disguises Ponta to look like the Princess and goes to tell Keely and Portez that he will trade the pearls and the Princess if they will leave the next morning.

The next morning Johnny and Ponta leave early to get to the boat but Keely and Portez are there early too. Johnny opts to swim out to the Kitty Wake and waits for daylight. At dawn Keely sees the natives coming out with his binoculars. So that Keely does not spot the fake princess, Johnny creeps up onto the boat and pushes Keely overboard, and then slugs Portez. When Johnny checks on Keely, the Princess Papalya is beating him with a paddle. She had pulled rank on Ponta because, "**She like Johnny!**"

Keely and Portez are turned over to the police and Johnny recommends that their policies cancelled. Johnny buys a tattoo for the Princess Papalya. The last expense item, 48 cents, is for overdue fines at the library. Never did read the book. It would be an utter waste of time for a man who has known Ponta!

NOTES:
- AKA: "SOUTH OF THE EQUATOR THINGS CAN GET HOT IN MORE WAYS THAN ONE!," OR "MOTHER CALL MY DRAFTBOARD; I'M LEAVING THE COUNTRY AGAIN"
- JOHNNY STUTTERS ON THE WORD "SING"
- A PEARLING LUGGER IS A TWO MASTED SHIP WITH A DIAGONAL SPAR TO HOLD THE SAIL.
- "TALES OF THE SOUTH PACIFIC" WAS WRITTEN BY JAMES MICHNER AND A. GROVE DAY.
- KANAK: A NATIVE MELANESIAN INHABITANT OF NEW CALEDONIA.
- THE COMMERCIAL IS FOR THE CBS PROGRAMS SING IT AGAIN, GENE AUTRY, VAUGHN MONROE, GANGBUSTERS, PHILLIP MARLOW, JOHNNY DOLLAR AND DANNY CLOVER—THE CBS SATURDAY NIGHT LINEUP.

- PAUL MASTERSON IS THE ANNOUNCER
- MUSIC DIRECTION IS BY LIETH STEVENS

Producer: Gordon T. Hughes   **Writers:**   Paul Dudley, Gil Doud
Cast: Willard Waterman, Mary Shipp, D. J. Thompson, Tom
             Holland, Clark Gordon, Larry Dobkin

◆   ❖   ◆

SHOW: THE MELANIE CARTER MATTER
SHOW DATE: 11/12/1949
COMPANY: MISS MELANIE CARTER
AGENT:
EXP. ACCT: $0.00
SYNOPSIS: "The most popular sport in Boston's Charles River is rowing in
one-man skulls, or rather it was the most popular sport that is, until they
took to beating on one man's skull—MINE!"

Johnny goes to Boston, Massachusetts and meets Melanie Carter who lives in
a chrome and black wheelchair in a flat right out of the last century. Melanie had
gotten a telegram of his assignment, as she has no telephone. Melanie is taken
aback when Johnny reminds her of an old flame from her youth. She tells Johnny
that she was once happy, but as for today and tomorrow, who knows.

Melanie tells Johnny that many years ago her husband was murdered by his
brother, who then died. She not only got all of the insurance, but she also adopted
the brother's children and raised them. Now they are destroying her mind by
trying to kill her.

Johnny first checks out the financial arrangements for the heirs and they have
a frugal stipend to live on. Johnny then goes to visit the nephew, Chalmers Carter
and is met by the wife, Crystal. Johnny is told that her poor hubby is out on
business—he is always out on business, but will call before he comes home, but
she wants to have fun. Johnny looks like a fun guy in that "nice" suit.

Johnny unfolds a plan: he is a "finder" for a California man who has some oil
property to develop, and Johnny is looking for investors with a lot ($120K) of
money. Would hubby be interested? Boy would he be interested. "He just needs
one big chance!"

Back at his hotel, Johnny finds a note from Chalmers who is at the Bay Shore
Trotters Club, watching the horses work out. Johnny gives him the oil spiel,
including the 27% tax write-off. When Chalmers says he probably can raise the
$120K, "George," a fellow horse watcher reminds Chalmers that he owes George
$500,000!

Johnny goes to the niece Sophia Carter and gives her the spiel. She first must
rely on the advice of her business manager, but decides she can raise the money.

Johnny goes back to Melanie's flat and finds the door open and Miss Carter
standing at the telephone she does not own! She is telling Joe to bring Rocky to
her place as she has a job for them. She wants to get rid of someone. Johnny

watches the flat from across the street. When Joe and Rocky go in, Johnny follows and listens at the keyhole. Johnny hears "Grandma" tell Joe and Rocky that she has had Dollar followed, and Dollar is trying to get the niece and nephew to kill her. Now she wants Dollar out of the way, and she means "out of the way!" Suddenly Joe sees Johnny's shadow under the door. Joe and Rocky grab Johnny and rough him up before taking him out of the apartment.

Johnny is "taken for a ride" in a cab to Joe's hotel room where the boys tell Johnny that they want a piece of the action. They think that Johnny is hustling the heirs with a phony oil stock scam. They figure that since they are getting money from "Grandma," they want some of Johnny's action too so Johnny agrees to cut them in. Incidentally they met Grandma when, while breaking and entering, she nailed them with a musket and then hired them for odd jobs. Johnny suggests they go back and watch to see who kills Grandma, so they can work on getting the insurance money.

They all go back to Melanie's flat to find the police there. By claiming he is a Boston Globe reporter Johnny finds out that a friend of the Commissioner called for help, and by the time the police got there, the dame was dead. By saying he will get his name in the paper, Johnny gets Officer Fred Moser to fake an arrest, which sends Joe and Rocky fleeing. A couple blocks later, Johnny gets a cab to Chalmer's place. He is out on business, but Crystal is alone and wants company! In the middle of an embrace, Chalmers comes in (and he didn't call either!) and threatens to thrash Johnny, so Johnny has to slug him.

Johnny then goes to Sophia's place, breaks in and sees several things; the Charles River he has been crossing all day, an open drawer with the impression of a missing revolver in the dust, and Grandma holding the gun on Johnny. Johnny takes the gun from Grandma after firing 3 shots into the ceiling. In the other hand is a letter she was trying to steal from Sophia's desk. The note is from Melanie's husband to Sophia telling his favorite niece that his wife has finally succeeded in killing him, as she did his brother when he came to his rescue and she ran over him with her carriage. It is not too hard to see that Sophia has been blackmailing Grandma and Sophia was the dead body at the Carter flat, where she had gone to get the $120.000.

Grandma goes to the police on Johnny's arm to give a dignified surrender. Chalmers gets a pipe and slippers to help his home life, Joe and Rocky get a pass on the River Queen sightseeing boat and Officer Moser gets his name published, on a check for $50.

Expense Account total—you won't be able to pay it where you are.

NOTES:
- AKA: WHO'D LIKE TO ROCK THE OLD DOLL TO SLEEP, OR "THE UN-NICE NIECE AND THE CHARMING YOUNG RAT WHO PUT THE FEW IN NEPHEW."
- JOHNNY'S "NICE" SUIT IS NEW YORK CITY- $185 RIGHT OFF THE RACK.

Producer: Gordon T. Hughes   **Writers: Paul Dudley, Gil Doud**
Cast: Larry Dobkin, Unknown

Show:	**The Skull Canyon Mine**
Show Date:	**11/26/1949**
Company:	**Old Caledonia Insurance Company**
Agent:	**Oscar Wheaton**
Exp. Acct:	**$947.99**

Synopsis: "I knew when I went to the desert that anyone who plays around with cactus is liable to get stuck. But I didn't remember another way of saying death is going west."

While working on a case at dinner, Johnny is contacted by Oscar Wheaton. Johnny is told that two years ago Old Caledonia had invested in a working gold mine in Twin Buttes, Arizona. Two months ago profits suddenly dipped by 50%. Johnny is to find out why!

Johnny flies to Twin Buttes and is met by Jackie who drives him in a jeep 23 miles, over no road, to the mine. Johnny's cover is that he is an efficiency expert hired by the company.

At the mine Johnny meets Nugget, the barking dog, and Doyle the manager who gives him the books to review. Doyle knows of no problems at the mine, but things could be better considering they must cart the ore 8 miles by mule train to the smelter. Then Johnny goes to the mine with Doyle.

On the way in on a burro propelled dynamite cart, Johnny hears drilling. Just before a blast goes off Johnny is told to open his mouth and close his eyes by Doyle who then instructs the miners to get the ore loaded. Johnny asks to see the rest of the mine, but Doyle tells his that this is the only face being worked.

After a steak dinner (burro steak maybe?) Doyle goes to the mine and Johnny talks to Jackie. She tells Johnny that she is the secretary and bookkeeper. She came out to the mine to marry the former manager, but he disappeared.

Johnny goes to the bunkhouse and meets a muleskinner named Kangaroo, his roommate. Johnny tells him that he plans to go with him the next morning to deliver the gold ore to the smelter. Johnny is starting to suspect that Doyle is working the mine for himself and keeping the profits.

The next morning on the way to the smelter, while Kangaroo is murdering "Mule Train," the mule wagon is buzzed by an airplane at Halfway Rock and is then surrounded by horsemen. The pilot lands and introduces himself. He is "El Puerco," the pig, because he is as ugly as one. El Puerco wants the gold, not the unrefined ore in the back, but the $30,000 in pure gold under the wagon seat.

The gold is loaded into the plane. Johnny and Kangaroo are tied to a stake and the mules are tied around them. El Puerco tells them that he will then buzz the mules, and they will kick Johnny and Kangaroo to death. Too bad Kangaroo knows how to calm angry mules, except for the one who kicks Johnny as Kangaroo is warning him to "never trust a mule."

Johnny wakes up to Nugget licking his face, and Jackie tending his head. Jackie's clothes are torn. She tells Johnny that she and Doyle were going to run away, but the plans have changed. Jackie tells Johnny that Kangaroo has taken the mules back to the mine. Jackie also tells Johnny that she suspects that Doyle had killed her intended husband Larry, and was milking the mine. She had only acted interested in Doyle to find out more. Now she wants to help Johnny expose Doyle. She knows that there is a refinery in the mine, which is where the pure gold comes from. The charts to the mine are in the safe and she has the combination.

Back at the mine the Saturday night square dance is in progress. Johnny and Jackie go to the office and find the safe open, along with El Puerco's dead mouth. Johnny goes looking for Kangaroo. A miner tells Johnny that Kangaroo was looking for Doyle who was in the mine.

At the mine entrance shots are heard and Jackie thinks it was Kangaroo who was shot. Johnny goes in to investigate and finds Doyle dead. He calls for Kangaroo, but another wounded man answers—it is Larry! Johnny gets to him just as he dies. Johnny discovers that Kangaroo was out feeding his mules and was not in the mine.

Johnny figures out that Larry, Doyle and El Puerco were working together and started double-crossing each other.

Final expenses include a cable to Old Caledonia recommending that Jackie be made mine manager, and 32 ounces of snakebite prevention—in case a snake ever bites him.

Expense Account Total, $947.99. Which is just about as much sense you can make it without making it a dollar.

Yours, (No charge for that double talk) Truly, Johnny Dollar.

NOTES:
- AKA: "MR. BONES, WHO WAS THAT LADY I SEEN YOU WITH LAST NIGHT?" OR "MESSING WITH A MULE TRAIN IS ONE GOOD WAY TO KICK OFF."
- STAMMERS ON "REMEMBER" IN INTRO.
- DINNER ($12.80) WAS LIVER AND DUMPLING SOUP, VEAL PAPRIKASH, CHERRY STRUDEL AND COFFEE. THE CASE WAS AN ECCENTRIC MILLIONAIRESS WHO WANTED TO MARRY JOHNNY FOR HIS MONEY.
- MR. BONES REFERS TO THE OLD BLACKFACE MINSTREL SHOWS
- THE SONG KANGAROO "SINGS" REFERS TO "MULE TRAIN" BY FRANKIE LAINE.
- "MAKING HISTORY AT TANFERAN" WHEN THE HORSEMEN ATTACK REFERS TO THE FORMER TANFERAN RACE TRACK, A JAPANESE ASSEMBLY AREA IN WWII.
- THE SNAKE BITE REMEDY IS AN OLD W. C. FIELDS ROUTINE.
- PAUL MASTERSON IS THE ANNOUNCER
- MUSIC DIRECTION IS BY LIETH STEVENS

Producer: Gordon T. Hughes   **Writers:** Paul Dudley, Gil Doud
Cast: Doris Singleton, Willard Waterman, Don Diamond, John Dehner, Fred Howard

Show:	**Bodyguard To Anne Connelly**
Show Date:	12/3/1949
Company:	**Ambassador Life & Casualty Insurance Company**
Agent:	**Franklin Haley**
Exp. Acct:	$845.30

Synopsis: **"This case looked refreshing at first. It took me to Milwaukee, the brewing capitol of the USA. But it occurred to me later, for a guy who appreciates a good head on a glass of beer, I take lousy care of my own."**

Johnny has just started a library "who done it" mystery book "The Playful Siamese" when Franklin Haley calls. Haley thinks crime fiction is trash. "They'll never get a penny of mine (oh yes I will, mutters Johnny!)." It seems that Miss Anne Connelly fell in with a man named Neal Grafter. On the eve of their wedding, Neal was arrested for grand theft. Neal is being paroled tomorrow. Anne is penniless and has a large policy; therefore Johnny has been assigned to protect her, and leaves on a 6:30 flight to Milwaukee, Wisconsin. Johnny takes the book, with him, but gets little reading time on the flight due to a blown fuse.

He arrives at Anne Connelly's fashionable house and is admitted by the maid Cora. Miss Connelly informs Johnny that Miss Connelly "should be home when the joints close. Want a straight slug or a highball?" Cora it turns out is Miss Connelly's personal maid and a former specialty dancer. When Johnny tells Cora that he thought Connelly was penniless, which is why Johnny was hired, Cora tells Johnny that Anne needs a bodyguard like she needs a foster mother. She has all sorts of boy friends, like Ray Merrick with whom she is out with tonight. Cora also tells Johnny that she has never heard of Grafter. When Johnny compliments Cora on her wardrobe, Cora says that she has free use of Connelly's clothes, except for a few upper pieces that are too small.

Johnny waits on the couch and reads his book until Anne and Merrick, who is a lawyer, come home at 2:30 AM. When challenged about the nice house and the penniless plea, Merrick tells Johnny that they went to the insurance company because they have no idea how long protection would be needed, as there is no telling when Grafter will show up. Ray leaves and tells Johnny to call him if anything comes up.

Everyone goes to bed and Johnny checks the doors, turns out the lights and snuggles up on the couch, like a Fakir, with his book. Later Cora comes out to talk, dressed only in a nightgown. She tells Johnny that Merrick and Connelly were giving him a boatload of untruths. She has personally seen Anne's bankbook, and she can afford J. Edgar Hoover!

While they are talking, a window breaks, there are shots, and Anne screams. While running to her bedroom, Johnny sees an open window and a shadow by the garage. He rushes out to the garage and runs into a huge arm that reaches out and nearly strangles him. It is Neal Grafter.

When Johnny asks Grafter about being in prison, Neal doesn't remember anything about prison. He only remembers a room with bars and screaming people, and doctors. He knows that he didn't kill Anne because she wasn't in her bed. Was she with Johnny! Johnny tries to reason with him, but it only gets his throat grabbed again. Finally Neal leaves and Johnny goes inside.

Back in the house Johnny pulls the shades and confronts Anne with Neal's talk of doctors and bars like in a mental hospital. Since it was Cora's bed that was shot at, Johnny realizes that Anne had set Cora up as a pigeon.

Anne admits that Neal was in a mental hospital and had escaped over a month ago. The police had watched for a while, but gave up when he didn't show. She had no insurance, so Merrick bought some and called the insurance company to get protection.

The next morning Johnny gets a call from the hospital confirming that Neal was a paranoid schizophrenic, is dangerous, and would try again, probably tonight.

Johnny sets up a lie. Johnny tells Anne and Ray to go out as usual, he and Cora will stay. Johnny hides in the yard by the incinerator as it snows waiting for Neal. At 4:00 AM Johnny sees a shadow by the house. After breaking the window glass, shots are fired into Anne's window. Johnny tackles the shadow at the window and nails his target with a furnace poker. The shadow is Ray Merrick!

Back inside Johnny calls an ambulance for Anne. Cora is very distraught primarily because Anne still owes her a week's pay. Anne ends up in the hospital with a 50/50 chance and Ray Merrick is in jail for Insurance Fraud. Ray was going to kill Anne and blame it on Neal, who was caught that morning and returned to the hospital.

NOTES:

- **AKA: "IT MAY HAVE BEEN LOVE AT FIRST SIGHT. BUT THE LAST SIGHT WAS DOWN THE BARREL OF A .45 AUTOMATIC."**
- **JOHNNY IS DRINKING JOHNNY WALKER AND SODA**
- **WHILE ON THE COUCH JOHNNY FEELS LIKE A FAKIR: A MUSLIM OR HINDU RELIGIOUS MENDICANT, ESPECIALLY ONE WHO PERFORMS FEATS OF MAGIC OR ENDURANCE.**
- **BOB STEVENSON IS THE ANNOUNCER**
- **MUSIC DIRECTION IS BY LIETH STEVENS**

Producer: Gordon T. Hughes **Writers:** Paul Dudley, Gil Doud
Cast: Betty Lou Gerson, William Conrad, William Johnstone, Sandra Gould, John Dehner

SHOW: THE CIRCUS ANIMAL SHOW MATTER
SHOW DATE: 12/10/1949
COMPANY: BRITTANIA UNDERWRITERS ASSOCIATION
AGENT:
EXP. ACCT: $152.70

SYNOPSIS: Johnny travels to Brunswick, Georgia to the animal circus of Maxmillian Sandro. Max is working with a singing elephant when Johnny gets there. Sandro tells Johnny that he has just acquired a new black leopard named "Ashanti" which is insured for $20,000. But some one has tried to steal her. Sandro saw the attempt but was not able to trace who did it. Additionally, Tex Randall, who sold Sandro the cat, has upped his price.

When Johnny sees the cat pacing in its cage, "My feet wanted to run but my eyes could not leave the cat." Fortunately there was a gorgeous set of steel bars in the middle.

Tex shows up. He tells Johnny that he had caught the cat in Togo, and was watching it to protect his investment. The price has gone up because the trip was more expensive than first planned. He also had seen the attempted robbery and had received a gaping knife wound for his diligence.

When Tex leaves to go to town, Angela, an "Ava Gardner type woman" shows up. Angela tells Johnny that she is Sandro's daughter, and that she likes cocktails, dining and dancing, which Johnny tells her, is on the agenda for later. Angela leaves to get ready for tonight.

While watching the cat pace, Johnny sees a light it the cat's eyes then a knock on his head that does not put him out. He is grabbed from behind in a double hammerlock and pushed towards the cat's cage. Suddenly, cocktail hour is over and the lights are out.

When Johnny wakes up, the cat is gone, and Tex is dead with claw marks across his head. The police are called and while waiting for the police, Johnny searches Sandro's trailer and finds a "friendship tree" made up of Christmas cards, including one from Angela in San Francisco, regretting that she will not be able to be with him this year!

Angela enters the trailer with a well-armed man she calls Ben, who suggests they retire to his hotel room to discuss the location of the cat, and Johnny agrees. At the hotel room, Johnny makes a big mistake—he calls the man "Ben" and is rebuked. Johnny is told that the man's name is Sir Bennett Montford and only his closest friends may call him by the familiar term "Ben." Montford tells Johnny that he is a big game hunter and is well trained in the proper use of a high-powered rifle. He wants to know where the cat is. He gives Johnny a story that the local people in Togo worship the cat, and are offering $100,000 in gold to get the cat back. Montford's assistant Harold is called to help convince Johnny to talk, but Johnny calls Montford's bluff and walks out. Whew!

Back at the circus, Sandro shows up, and tells Johnny that he has been in hiding. He admits to killing Tex, who was trying to kill Johnny, by pushing Tex into the bars of the cage. Johnny suggests going to the cat to lure Montford there ($100,000 of cheese even makes a mouse look dangerous), but Sandro objects until Johnny threatens him with the police.

Johnny and Sandro drive to the barn where the cat is still pacing in its cage. Montford, Angela and Harold show up armed to the teeth. Montford is now prepared to kill the cat to get at a fortune in diamonds hidden in the cage by Tex Randall. Sandro tries to protect his cat by opening the cage to let it escape. As the cat flies across the room, Montford gets a paw full of claws across the face and is killed. Fearing the cat, Angela and Harold disappear. Johnny gives his story to the police who put out an APB for Angela and Harold, Sandro heads to Okefenokee swamp with a group of men to look for the cat.

Johnny has a word of advice for the insurance company: don't insure the men who are looking for the cat! If you want to throw away your money, throw it at me!

Signed "Yours Truly, Johnny ummm 'Frank Buck' Dollar"

NOTES:
- AKA: "ALL THEY NEEDED WAS A CLOWN UNTIL I SHOWED UP"
- AKA: "I ONCE THOUGHT I WANTED TO RUN AWAY TO THE CIRCUS, THIS ONE I WANT TO RUN AWAY FROM."
- FRANK BUCK WAS A FAMOUS ANIMAL HUNTER AND PROVIDER FOR ZOOS AND CIRCUSES.
- CAST FROM RADIOGOLDINDEX
- MUSIC IS BY LIETH STEVENS
- BOB STEVENSON IS THE ANNOUNCER.

Producer: Unknown   **Writers:** Unknown
Cast: **Lynn Allen, Lawrence Dobkin, William Conrad, Parley Baer**

◆ ❖ ◆

SHOW: HAITI ADVENTURE MATTER
SHOW DATE: 12/17/1949
COMPANY: AMERICAN FEDERATED LIFE INSURANCE COMPANY
AGENT: HARVARD HUNTINGTON
EXP. ACCT: $424.70
SYNOPSIS: "The encyclopedia says that the island of Haiti can be called San Domingo, Santa Domingo, or Hispaniola. Well after my visit there, I could suggest several more things they can call it, but they probably wouldn't get past the censors."

Johnny is called, just as he is about to go to a show, to the office of Mr. Harvard Huntington. Harvey tells Johnny that Ralph Gordon, the black sheep scion of the Hartford Gordons, is insured for $100,000. The beneficiary is either charity or a wife, if he has one. Ralph is on his boat in Haiti and is dying—of a voodoo curse. Ralph's older brother, Thomas who is also in Haiti, reported the information.

Johnny flies to Port au Prince, Haiti, buys some tropical clothes, and goes in search of someone to help find Gordon. In a bar Johnny runs into Cap Regan, American expatriate (courtesy of the Feds), who tells Johnny that Gordon's boat is in the harbor without a crew because they refused to work for a drunken captain. Regan rows Johnny out to Gordon's boat—a filthy yacht—and is met by a woman in a pair of clam diggers and an off shoulder tee shirt. The woman is

Edwina, Ralph's wife. When Johnny explains why he is there and asks to see Ralph, she agrees and takes Johnny below. Johnny only gets as far as the locked cabin door when he is met by abusive shouts and cries for more wine. Edwina explains to Johnny that a woman called Maria LaSalle has put a curse on Ralph after he cursed at her. Edwina gets angry when Johnny suggests she is after the money and the ship's bos'n invites Johnny to leave. Johnny goes to see Thomas Gordon, who agrees that the voodoo curse is trash and requires only a susceptible mind. Thomas tells Johnny that Ralph is only looking for escape through alcohol. "Call on me for anything" and "Let me know what you learn" are the reassuring words of the good doctor as Johnny leaves.

Johnny and Regan go in search of Madam LaSalle and find her hut in a cane field. Madam LaSalle tells Johnny that Gordon will die tonight in the wind and rain, and her magic is the key. When Johnny doubts her magic, she throws something into the fire that causes Johnny to stagger out of the hut gasping for breath and nearly passing out. When he recovers he goes into the hut and finds small pieces of photographic film. So much for magic. (See notes).

Johnny goes back to the boat in a gathering storm. On the boat, Johnny overhears Edwina talking to some one. Johnny then knocks out the bos'n when he comes out on deck. Johnny then accuses Edwina of plotting with Madam LaSalle to kill Ralph, which she denies. She tells Johnny that she is only plotting to divorce Ralph and marry the boson. Johnny and Edwina go back to Madam LaSalle and Johnny confronts her with the film scam. When threatened with the police she admits that a man put her up to the phony curse. She tells Johnny that the man needs the storm so that the portholes on the boat will be closed. Edwina tells Johnny that only the food, which she cooks, and champagne is brought onto the boat. A visit to the local liquor shop confirms that a case of champagne has just been sent to the boat, packed in dry ice. A call to Thomas confirms that dry ice in a closed cabin could asphyxiate a drunken man.

Johnny finds Regan and, for $20, Johnny gets him to row out to the boat in the storm. (It was raining hard enough to require a seeing-eye seal.) When they near the boat, Regan is shot in the leg and Johnny decides to swim for the boat. When Johnny gets to the boat, dear brother Thomas is holding a gun on Johnny! The bos'n pushes Thomas off of the boat, and Johnny breaks down the door to Ralph's cabin and carries him up to fresh air.

Thomas goes to jail (he wanted control of the family fortune, not Ralph's insurance). Ralph and Regan go to the hospital.

NOTES:
- **AKA: THE NIGHTS WERE BLACK, BUT THE MAGIC BLACKER.**
- **THE COMMERCIAL NOTES THAT THE ORANGE BOWL TEAMS (SANTA CLARA AND KENTUCKY) WILL BE HONORED ON THE VAUGHN MONROE PROGRAM TO FOLLOW.**
- **JOHNNY KNEW THAT PHOTOGRAPHIC FILM MADE OF CELLULOSE AND NITRATE GIVES OFF NITRIC OXIDE AND NITROGEN DIOXIDE WHEN BURNED. BOTH ARE WORTHY OF ANY GAS CHAMBER.**

- **MUSIC BY LIETH STEVENS**

Producer:	Ralph Rose	Writers:	Paul Dudley, Gil Doud
Cast:	Betty Lou Gerson, Daws Butler, Sylvia Syms, Ben Wright, Ken Christy, Howard Culver, Tim Graham		

◆　❖　◆

SHOW:	THE DEPARTMENT STORE SWINDLE MATTER
SHOW DATE:	12/24/1949
COMPANY:	INDUSTRIAL INSURERS INCORPORATED
AGENT:	EVAN STEVENS
EXP. ACCT:	$511.50

SYNOPSIS: "It was the week before Christmas and all through the house, a creature was stirring, and boy what a rat!"

A hand written message delivered to Johnny's apartment summons him to the office of penny-pinching Mr. Stevens. Evans tells Johnny that the Association of Department Stores of Greater Manhattan has reported a number of robberies. A man impersonating a sales person will take an order for a large item and then disappear. Evan gives Johnny a check for his "usual retainer."

Johnny heads for New York City on the 7:03 "Bankers Special" train where he watches the bankers practice shaking their heads and whispering "no." At the association offices, Judy Whitehall is assigned to help Johnny. Judy tells Johnny that they have a general description of the man and that all the store detectives and sales staffs are watching for him. Just as Johnny is getting his Letter of Identification, Judy and Johnny learn that another store has been hit. They are told that a man was buying a camera when a little girl took his picture. The man then shot a store detective and grabbed the girl and the camera and ran off. And, the man is still in the store.

Johnny and Judy go to the store and find the manager, Mr. Sandler in the camera department going crazy. He tells Johnny that the girl was found wrapped in a 9 by 12 oriental carpet ($123.50) but without the camera, which probably was not loaded anyway.

Johnny talks to the little girl, Bobbie, and she is no help as she just cries until Johnny gets her with the old "better-be-nice-to-Santa" trick. Johnny then gets news that the store detective is dead. Now it's murder. Johnny goes and tells Santa (5th floor—Dante's Inferno, Jr. Grade) what is going on and then Bobbie and Judy come in. Bobbie tells Santa that all she wants is an air rifle. After telling Santa all about the event, a descriptive drawing of the man is made, including the details of Bobbie's teeth marks in his hand, and it is given to the guards. Johnny has lunch is in the tearoom with Judy. Lunch is the "Shoppers Special."

After lunch Johnny learns that the store Santa has been found tied up in a closet. It seems that the killer was playing Santa and Bobbie told him all! Then Johnny learns that the Santa costume has been found about the same time as a woman was shot in the Junior Lingerie Department. Sandler tells Johnny that she was lost on the stairs looking for the ladies room, and the man shot her and ran down stairs to sporting goods where he got several guns and ammo.

The police arrive, the store is emptied and the police start searching from the roof down. Johnny and Sandler start from the bottom floor. On the first floor Johnny and Sandler are shot at. After getting Sandler to create a diversion, Johnny shoots the display case the man is standing on, but he runs down to the shipping department. Johnny runs after him and, after finding the man and engaging in a fight with a hammer, Johnny nails the man is into a crate and blacks out.

The next morning Johnny wakes up in the hospital with Judy standing beside him. Judy tells Johnny that the man got away, and Johnny gets up and runs to the store. In the shipping department, the manager tells Johnny that the crate Johnny had nailed shut has been shipped out to upstate New York. The funny thing is, the merchandise meant for the box was found on the floor. But the manager tells Johnny that he knows where the box is going. The merchandise was the manager's charitable contribution for the unfortunates who will be spending the holidays away from home. . .at the state prison in Ossining!

Expenses included $12 dinner for Judy, and $10 for medical supplies for the CBS soundmen Bern Shurry and Billy Gould who had to break all the glass during the show.

The expense account may be high, but isn't everyone this time of year?

NOTES:
- AKA: "HOW I PLAYED SANTA CLAUS AND ALMOST GOT LEFT HOLDING THE BAG," OR "GOING FOR A SLEIGH RIDE WITHOUT THE BENEFIT OF SNOW CAN BE TOUGH SLEDDING"
- THIS IS THE FIRST PROGRAM TO MENTION A RETAINER.
- THE SHOPPERS SPECIAL IS CREAM CHEESE, WALNUTS, WATERCRESS AND PINEAPPLE ON WHOLE WHEAT.
- AT THE END, THE ANNOUNCER'S MIKE MUST HAVE BEEN TURNED OFF, AS HE HAS TO START TWICE.
- BOB STEVENSON IS THE ANNOUNCER
- MUSIC BY LIETH STEVENS

Producer: Gordon T. Hughes   **Writers:** Paul Dudley, Gil Doud
Cast: Connie Crowder, Georgia Ellis, Jay Novello, Parley Baer, Marlene Ames, Paul Dubov

SHOW:	THE DIAMOND PROTECTOR MATTER
SHOW DATE:	12/31/1949
COMPANY:	AMERICAN CONTINENTAL INSURANCE COMPANY
AGENT:	ROBERT FERRY
EXP. ACCT:	$1,142.89

SYNOPSIS: This was not only the end of the old year—it was almost the end of mine.

Johnny goes to the office of Robert Ferry who tells Johnny that a rich, old widow has a diamond necklace worth $250,000 that is kept in a bank vault. Robert wants Johnny to take the diamond to her so that she can wear it to a party, after which Johnny will return it to the bank vault. Johnny is not sure until Robert gives him a ticket to Honolulu, Hawaii.

Johnny goes to San Francisco to catch a flight to the islands. Johnny spots a man who looks familiar. The man introduces himself as Wayne Franklin, former thief. Wayne recognized Johnny from a newspaper article that describes how Johnny will be bringing the Star of Hades diamond to Honolulu. Wayne also points out a man who de describes as a detective who is following him. In Honolulu, Hawaii Johnny goes to the Royal Hawaiian Hotel where Mrs. Bettsworth keeps a beach house. At the beach house Johnny meets Thomasina, Mrs. Bettsworth's niece. She tells Johnny that she was the one who put the article in the paper, and hopes that the diamond will be stolen. If is it, she will get a third of the insurance money, which she will use to help others at Warm Springs Georgia, where she had been a patient. Mrs. Bettsworth arrives with here son Nikki, who is in debt and tries to hit Johnny. Mrs. Bettsworth thinks Johnny's name is funny, so he tells her that he paid two radio writers for the name. Johnny gives her the stone. Johnny tells her about Franklin and how the kids want the money. When she gets uppity, Johnny locks her in her room until the party.

Mrs. Bettsworth is let out for the party, at which Johnny spots Franklin in the orchestra. The lights go out, Mrs. Bettsworth screams and the diamond is gone. The police are called and the guests are searched and released when nothing is found. Johnny suggests to Mrs. Bettsworth that she issue a $10,000 reward for the return of the stone. Suddenly there are shots and Johnny runs outside to find that the police have shot Franklin. Franklin tells Johnny that the detective really was his accomplice and dies before telling Johnny where the stone is. Johnny goes in to talk to Mrs. Bettsworth, who tells Johnny that the diamond is the only important thing. Johnny grabs Thomasina, carries her up the stairs and shows her the diamond in a chandelier. Thomasina gets the diamond and Johnny gives it back to Mrs. Bettsworth. Johnny tells her that when the lights went out, he slid down the banister, grabbed the necklace and hid it in the lights. Johnny tells Mrs. Bettsworth he will take the diamond back, and might tell the police if she does not pay Thomasina the reward, which she gets.

NOTES:
- AKA: "YOU LEAD A DIAMOND, MOTHER, AND THE GAME WILL REALLY GET STARTED"
- STORY INFORMATION OBTAINED FROM THE **KNX** COLLECTION IN THE THOUSAND OAKS LIBRARY

Producer: **Writers**
Cast: **Unknown**

SHOW: THE FIREBUG HUNTER MATTER
SHOW DATE: 1/7/1950
COMPANY: EASTERN INSURANCE COMPANY
AGENT: ARNOLD WHELAN
EXP. ACCT: $410.00
SYNOPSIS: I didn't make any New Year's resolutions, but if I had, one of them would have been to take no more arson cases. Ouch! They get hot in more way than one.

Johnny is in Palm Springs trying to recoup from the New Year when he is called to San Diego, California. Johnny meets with Mr. Sheridan who introduces Johnny to a local investigator named Crowley. Johnny is told that George Duke has policies on five buildings, three of which have burned. Crowley has learned that Duke was convicted of arson in 1941 when he burned a garage. Johnny goes to the police who suspect Duke, and a partner named Menkoff of running a car theft ring, and the burned garage was used to pain and renumber the cars. Johnny then goes to the Ohio Hotel and starts following Duke. On the third night Johnny spots a girl and a drunk go into the hotel. Shortly afterward the girl leaves and the hotel catches on fire. Johnny calls the fire department and goes to the hotel where he meets Duke coming out. Johnny confronts Duke who tells Johnny that he was on the fourth floor, and that Johnny can prove nothing.

The fire is out in about forty minutes, and all of the guests but one, Geraldine Marlow, are accounted for. The fire is determined to have started in her room, and a body was found on the stairs. Geraldine arrives and must get into her room to find Carl, who was sick and had passed out. Johnny tells her that Carl started the fire with a cigarette on the bed. The body of Carl is later identified to be a legal Houdini and a gang lord. Crowley calls Johnny and tells him that Carl was poisoned, and Johnny tells him to find out more about Geraldine.

Johnny goes to the hotel and finds Geraldine shot. George Duke is there but claims that someone threw the gun into the room when she was shot. Johnny goes to a local bar to look into Geraldine and Carl. The Bartender tells Johnny that Carl was not with a girl the previous night. Later the body is identified by Carl's fourth wife, Lucille Taylor based on a watch found on the body. Lucille tells Johnny that she last saw Carl at 8:30, and Johnny notes that the fire was at 9:00. Lucille tells Johnny that a girl was to take Carl to meet a man from LA about a payoff, but the man in the room was a stand-in, Jules Menkoff, who handled the car ring.

Johnny calls the editors of the newspapers and entertains them while giving them the story that he is investigating the fire and can prove that Carl is still alive. Johnny waits for Jules to appear, but Carl comes to the room. While he is talking to Johnny there is a knock and Jules is there and wants proof that Carl is alive. Carl tells Johnny that he saw Jules start the fire, and Jules calls him a liar and pulls a gun. Both shoot, but Carl shoots Jules.

Johnny apologizes to George Duke, and Carl is held and released when it is learned that he saved Johnny's life.

Notes:

- **AKA: "Press Out My Asbestos Dinner Jacket, Mother, I'm Going To Smoke"**
- **Music is by Lieth Stevens**
- **The announcer is Bob Stevenson**
- **Story information obtained from the KNX Collection in the Thousand Oaks Library**

Producer: **Gordon T. Hughes**   Writers   **Paul Dudley, Gil Doud**
Cast: **Fay Baker, Rita Lynn, Herb Butterfield, Willard Waterman, Sidney Miller, Paul Dubov, Edmond MacDonald, Larry Dobkin**

Show: **The Missing Chinese Stripper Matter**
Show Date: **1/14/1950**
Company: **Apex & Great Northern Bonding Company**
Agent: **Phineas Perch**
Exp. Acct: **$611.44**

Synopsis: This time I went on a personally conducted tour of San Francisco's Chinatown, and Johnny Dollar got a new slant on life.

Johnny goes to San Francisco, California, and meets with Phineas Perch, who has a broken arm. Johnny is told that Wu Sin was given a six-week work permit and Apex has the bond. But Wu Sin has disappeared. Phineas has some information that Wu Sin had been beaten. A girl had called and told Phineas that Wu Sin had called her boss and told him not to look for her.

Johnny goes to the Almond Pit Bar and meets Eddie Foo. Eddie tells Johnny that he was told to hire the girl and was paid to employ her. She was good for business and he ants her back. Eddie will not tell Johnny who paid him, and is told to come back later. Johnny eats dinner and in his fortune cakes is a message that the man Johnny is looking for is a killer named Lo Hoo Pur. Johnny goes to the police and learns that the police have turned the case over to the Feds. Johnny learns that Pur is suspected of Arson, but it was not proven. Johnny is told to let it be known that he is looking for Pur, and he will find Johnny.

Johnny goes to a number of bars, and Pur finds him. Johnny asks about the girl and Pur takes Johnny to a back room where he is beaten, pushed into a trashcan, and rolled down a hill.

Johnny wakes up in the hospital where police lieutenant Fischer tells Johnny that he is being sued. The trashcan he was in hit a 1949 Caddy, and the owner is suing. Johnny is called by Eddie Foo and told that he is in love with Wu Sin, and that she has some problems with immigration. Eddie tells Johnny that she is hiding in Sausalito. Johnny goes to the address in Sausalito and gets in to talk to Wu Sin. She tells Johnny that she is in trouble, but does not know why. Johnny tells her who he is, and that she is being lied to. Wu Sin tells Johnny that a friend will be back at midnight, and Johnny tells her to keep him there.

Johnny goes back to his hotel and finds Edie Foo in his room, dead. Johnny calls Lt. Fischer and leaves a message for him to come to Harbor House Hotel. The lieutenant arrives and Johnny tells him his story. Johnny and Lt. Fischer drive to Sausalito armed with a riot gun and tear gas. There is a car in the drive and the lights are on. The police surround the house and are shot at. Johnny gets a gun from Lt. Fisher and climbs into an ashcan and rolls into the house. Wu Sin shoots at Johnny but he gets the gun, and finds the body of Lo Hoo Pur. Johnny tells her that she finally will be staying in the country.

Wu Sin was brought into the country to work as an entertainer, but was taken into Mexico for a form of entertainment not related to this report. Wu Sin killed Lo when he threatened to expose her.

NOTES:
- AKA: "THE SEARCH FOR THE MISSING CHINESE STRIPPER WU SIN," OR "SHE DIDN'T HAVE MUCH TO HIDE, SO WHY DID THEY HIDE HER?"
- THIS IS THE LAST CHARLES RUSSELL SHOW
- THE ANNOUNCER STATES: "WE HOPE YOU WILL BE LISTENING AT THIS TIME NEXT WHEN CBS PRESENTS A SPARKLING NEW COMEDY OF COLLEGE LIFE 'YOUNG LOVE.' "
- THE ANNOUNCER IS BOB STEVENSON
- MUSIC IS BY LIETH STEVENS
- STORY INFORMATION OBTAINED FROM THE KNX COLLECTION IN THE THOUSAND OAKS LIBRARY

Producer: Gordon Hughes   **Writers** Paul Dudley, Gil Doud
Cast: David Ellis, Parley Baer, Edmond MacDonald, Vanessa Brown

Section 2: Edmond O'Brien

The Johnny Dollar played by Edmond O'Brien was a much different person. O'Brien tended to be a much more hard-boiled and cynical person. Edmond had a much harder voice with a faint New York accent and a clipped manner of speech. These characteristics portrayed his voice is that of a hard person. This Johnny Dollar was not one to fool around. There were jokes from this Johnny Dollar, but they were much darker than Charles Russell's quips. In "The Yankee Pride Matter" after Carl Bush tells Johnny that the insurance company is on the short end of the deal, Johnny says he know all  about that "I bet on Notre Dame last weekend." There was no nonsense allowed from the aggrieved widow or the philandering playboy.

This Johnny Dollar was all business and would not pull either his verbal or physical punches. Not that he was heartless. In "The Virginia Towne Matter," Johnny totally realized that the girl has been shortchanged and gives her a break in allowing her time to raise the money for the jewelry. At the end of the case, he even donates his expense check to the defense attorney. His cold-blooded nature shows itself in "The Yankee Pride Matter" where Johnny shoots "The Major" to prevent him from leaving the room. In "The Stanley Springs Matter" Johnny shoots Norman Stager to prevent him from walking out on him. Both instances were against unarmed men and premeditated, yet not fatal. Other Johnny Dollars tended to shoot only after being shot at.

The following are the Edmond O'Brien Johnny Dollar cases.

SHOW:	**THE LOYAL B. MARTIN MATTER**
SHOW DATE:	**2/3/1950**
COMPANY:	**GREAT COLUMBIAN LIFE INSURANCE COMPANY**
AGENT:	
EXP. ACCT:	**$823.00**

SYNOPSIS: Johnny drives to the estate of the deceased—a mausoleum like manor—Loyal House.

The housekeeper, Miss Sarah Tompkins meets Johnny and tells him that the widow is out shopping. Miss Tompkins has worked for the household for 30 years. "Loyal, er, Mr. Martin was an expert on Victorian furniture" Johnny is told. In answer to the unasked question, yes, Miss Tompkins was provided for in the estate. Johnny says he is investigating the murder so the murderer is not paid off. "People waste a lot of murders that way." He tells her.

Police Lt. Marquette is in the library in which only two things were out of place—a suit of armor and a case of shiny new hunting rifles. Lt. Marquette tells Johnny that the body of Mr. Martin was found after dinner and had two bullet holes in it. According to Lt. Marquette, there are four suspects; a wife who was too young, the housekeeper who was in love with the deceased, the brother who was broke and brooding and the body guard, a detective.

Johnny decides to start with Nick Balotti, the bodyguard. Johnny meets with him after a horseback ride, and he tells Johnny that he had nothing really to say, but the police told him to stay put.

Marty, the brother was entertaining a bottle of 20-year-old brandy that was much too young for the book he was reading. It seems that the young wife had asked him to come and protect her from her husband. Joy Anne, the widow comes home and goes swimming in a bikini that would "get her pinched on the Riviera!" Joy tells Johnny that Marty had introduced her to Loyal. But Loyal gave her everything but love, and when she went looking for it, the housekeeper informed Loyal and he became a madman. The housekeeper was upset with Joy because she had always assumed that Loyal would marry her. So Joy is going to enjoy what little free time she has left. Johnny goes to check up on the housekeeper who is in the library wiping off the desk in violation of police orders to keep out. She tells Johnny that she always cleaned at that hour of the day otherwise Loyal would get mad. Lt. Marquette comes in and orders Johnny to take her to her room and then come back. On the way, there are 6 shots fired in the library. Johnny goes back to the library and finds Lt. Marquette dead holding a shotgun, and an open window.

While searching the body, Balotti comes in. The only clue Johnny can find, which Lt. Marquette would have wanted to share was an entry in his new notebook "Check tattooing diameter. Recheck penetration." Johnny asks Balotti to keep quiet. He also asks the others who have now gathered to go back to their rooms. Outside Johnny looks for clues and finds a .32 revolver in the grass. The gun has 6 empty chambers and lipstick on the grip. Johnny wonders if it could it be a red herring? Sgt. McDougal arrives and Johnny tells him what happened and gives him the gun. The gun is the same caliber which killed Loyal, but why was Lt. Marquette holding an unloaded shotgun when he was shot? Johnny gets more puzzling information from McDougal. The autopsy showed two bullet holes, 1 1/2 inches apart, which did not penetrate too deeply. Every thing pointed to the bullets being fired from 300 yards. The witnesses were split on whether 1 or 2 shots were fired on the night of the killing.

Johnny goes to the ballistics lab and discovers that the ballistics people had found powder burns, called tattooing, on the body indicating a close firing of the weapon. Also, the .32 was the weapon that killed both people. A .32 owned and licensed to Joy Ann Martin, who looked better in a bathing suit than she will in the electric chair.

Johnny goes to see Joy, and gets her out of the shower. When quizzed about a gun owned by her, she says that her gun is in the dresser. When she gets up to get it, the gun is gone. She says it must have been stolen, and there are too many people who would love to frame her. When asked if she remembers any thing else, she says that she remembers hearing shots two days before the killing while she was out horseback riding. They came from a walnut grove. Just as Johnny kisses her, the police he had called showed up, and Joy is taken into custody after she slaps Johnny.

Next morning Johnny goes looking for the walnut grove and pondering why everyone heard one shot, and there were two bullets in the body. In the hollow trunk of a tree Johnny finds a peck of cotton waste with powder burns in it. Johnny is hit on the head and sees Marty running back to the house. Johnny chases Marty back to the house and hears 6 shots. Johnny finds Balotti standing over Marty. Balotti says that Marty had drawn on him, so he shot in self-defense. Johnny suggests Balotti go to police headquarters and register his story.

Johnny calls Sgt. McDougal and tells him that Marty had just been shot and the killer was on his way to the office. Johnny tells McDougal that Nick and Marty had arranged to fire the .32 into the cotton waste to get the bullets. The bullets were then packed into a shotgun shell and fired at close range by a shotgun. Johnny tells him that he knew that Balotti was the accomplice because he had said Marty drew on him, but Marty was unarmed.

Expense account items 2-9 are $624 in entertainment of Joy Ann.

NOTES:
- AKA: "DEATH TAKES A WORKING DAY," OR "HOW TO TAKE A VACATION IN FAIRFIELD COUNTY"
- O'BRIEN STAMMERS SEVERAL TIMES.

- JOHNNY ANNOUNCES HIMSELF TO JOY AS THE HARTFORD HAWKSHAW—
  A REFERENCE TO A CHARACTER IN THE 1863 TOM TAYLOR PLAY "THE
  TICKET OF LEAVE MAN"
- COTTON WASTE IS THE MATERIALS LEFT OVER FROM THE COTTON GINNING
  PROCESS AND USED AS A RAG OR ABSORBENT.
- EDMOND O'BRIEN CONTINUES THE "UM" ENDING FOR THIS PROGRAM.
- CAST DATA FROM RadioGOLDINdex

Producer: **Writers:**
Cast: Irene Tedrow, Ted de Corsia, John Dehner, Walter Burke,
                  Jeanne Bates, Ed Begley

◆   ❖   ◆

SHOW: THE S.S. MALAY TRADER SHIP
SHOW DATE: 2/10/1950
COMPANY: INTERCONTINENTAL MARINE INSURANCE COMPANY
AGENT:
EXP. ACCT: $0.00

SYNOPSIS: Johnny goes to Savannah, Georgia and signs on to the S. S. Malay
Trader as a seaman. The ship is a rusty old liberty ship in the process of loading
rattan-covered bales.

At the top of the gangplank is an officer cleaning his nails with a knife. He is
chief officer Halstaff who assigns Johnny to the 4-8 watch and to his quarters.

In his quarters, Johnny meets Al Roter, a marine investigator for
Intercontinental. Al has been onboard since the ship left Singapore. Johnny
learns that the company has had some run-ins with customs, and bought a lot of
crude rubber just before the devaluation of the British pound. Half of it burned
with an insurance loss of $100,000. Now the cargo is worth more lost than sold.
Al thinks that the ship is heading for Corpus Christi and then to Mexico.

Halstaff calls Johnny and tells his to sign his papers in the shipping office
where he meets Ah Mei, (yes, ahhhh me!) a half-caste Malay who is the daughter
of the owner. She is also Halstaff's girl friend who wishes she could go with him
to be with her father who is going on the ship. While Johnny is signing his
papers, Ah Mei notices that his hands are so nice, and she has seen all kinds.

Johnny takes up his duties and wonders about the interest Ah Mei has in his
hands; could they be a tip-off? And why would the owner go on the ship—to
smell his rubber burn?

The next day the ship departs and Johnny is sure "the sailors life is not for
me." Later he talks to Al, who feels that something is fishy, but cannot tell what.
They go on deck, and while Johnny distracts the lookout, Al goes into the #2
hold. After 10 minutes, Johnny heads back to his cabin and hears a disturbance
and the sound of running feet. Johnny finds Al Roter dead, with a knife wound
in the back of his neck. Johnny goes to the owner and reports a killing and
demands the Coast Guard be called. While arguing with the owner, Johnny hears

a "Man over Board" call. The owner, to find out what is going on, calls Halstaff who tells him that he saw a seasick man leaning over the rail and fall over when the ship pitched. He is circling the ship now.

Johnny is on his way to radio the Coast Guard when the boilers start exploding. The crew panics, and in the confusion Johnny gets to inspect the #2 hold area where he finds blood on the cover and a pocketknife, the one Halstaff was using. When he opens the hold he sees the real reason for the explosions, burning cargo!

At dawn the ship finally sinks and there is no evidence of her presence except the loose hatch covers. Johnny makes his way back to the Malay Traders office in Savannah and sees Ah Mei, who is surprised to see him, as Johnny had been reported missing. Johnny tells her he is missing because he did not report himself in the confusion. Johnny shows her his ID, and accuses her of complicity in the destruction of the cargo. She claims total ignorance of a plot. A daughter does not question her father. She cries and Johnny is convinced she is innocent.

Johnny calls a chemist, and asks a question about the specific gravity of crude rubber. The chemist says it should float, but Johnny notes that it didn't. Johnny asks Ah Mei about movements from the warehouses, and then tells Ah Mei to tell her father he is in the warehouses and to meet him there.

Johnny goes to the warehouse and finally finds what he is looking for, crates of crude rubber which should have been off the ship, but which will now be sold for a profit after an insurance payoff. Halstaff comes into the warehouse with a gun. Johnny tells him that he has the knife Halstaff used to kill Roter. But Halstaff says that even if he confessed there is no body. "Who says that there is no body?" asks Johnny. When Halstaff tries to search Johnny, a fight ensues and Halstaff ends up in police custody. Johnny had bluffed about the body, but Halstaff sang to the police and the ship owner was innocent of the murder but guilty of insurance fraud.

Expense Account total: because of Al Roter, his friend's death and the ugly taste it left, "this one is one me"

NOTES:
- AKA: THE SHIP WITH NO PORT OF CALL.
- LIBERTY SHIP: THE LIBERTY SHIP WAS USED BY THE US IN WWII TO TRANSPORT GOODS TO THE FRONT.
- RATTAN: A CLIMBING PALM USED ESPECIALLY FOR WALKING STICKS AND WICKERWORK
- THERE ARE A NUMBER OF SHIP RELATED TERMS USED IN THIS PROGRAM: TOPPING-LIFT, A LARGE AND STRONG TACKLE, EMPLOYED TO SUSPEND OR TOP THE OUTER END OF A GAFF, OR OF THE BOOM OF A MAIN-SAIL AND FORE-SAIL; SUCH AS ARE USED IN BRIGS, SLOOPS, OR SCHOONERS. A PREVENTER: AN ADDITIONAL ROPE, EMPLOYED AT TIMES TO SUPPORT ANY OTHER, WHEN THE LATTER SUFFERS AN UNUSUAL STRAIN, PARTICULARLY IN A STRONG GALE OF WIND. DEFINITIONS FROM WILLIAM FALCONER'S DICTIONARY OF THE MARINE—THE SOUTH SEAS PROJECT

- SPECIFIC GRAVITY: THE RATIO OF THE DENSITY OF A SUBSTANCE TO THE DENSITY OF SOME SUBSTANCE (AS PURE WATER) TAKEN AS A STANDARD WHEN BOTH DENSITIES ARE OBTAINED BY WEIGHING IN AIR.
- CAST INFORMATION FROM RadioGOLDINdex
- ROY ROWAN IS THE ANNOUNCER
- MUSIC IS BY LIETH STEVENS

Producer: **Writers:**
Cast: Barton Yarborough, Elliott Reid, Lillian Buyeff, William Conrad, Robert Griffin

◆ ❖ ◆

SHOW: MR. & MRS. ARBUTHNEL TRUMP
SHOW DATE: 2/17/1950
COMPANY: NATIONAL FIDELITY LIFE INSURANCE COMPANY
AGENT:
EXP. ACCT: $763.90

SYNOPSIS: Johnny is asked to go to North Dakota and notes that he is sent to North Dakota in the winter and Miami in the winter. Johnny is asked to look into two old duffers who are insured for $80,000. They are threatening to kill them selves.

Johnny travels to Highbridge, North Dakota to look into Mr. and Mrs. Trump. They are insured for $80,000 and are going to kill themselves. At the train station, Johnny gets a ride on the local pung to the Trump home but the driver will only take Johnny to the gate. He is scared and wishes those folks were dead. He has been receiving packages from Africa and India labeled "Dangerous—Do Not Open—DEADLY." He tells Johnny that whatever was in those packages was alive. Johnny says he will call when he is ready to leave, but is told there is no phone there.

At the Trump place, Johnny walks up the snow-covered driveway in a fresh set of automobile tracks. A young man greets Johnny and tells him to come in. Johnny is told not to take off his coat he won't be staying long. The house is hot, humid and filled with orchids. Johnny is told to join the Trumps for coffee. At the dinner table Johnny explains that he has the papers to change the beneficiaries, but asks isn't killing your selves rather drastic?

Mrs. Trump explains that noted alienists have found them sound of mind. They have had a happy life and owe the world something. With all the threats of A-bombs and H-bombs and UFOs, which are the prelude to destruction—after all Mr. Trump knows these things—He READS! They want to leave the world the beginnings of a new humanity. The current beneficiary, their niece Hope is wasteful. The new beneficiary Erwin Harper will use the money to continue their plan. And their plan?

Johnny is taken to the basement to see a maze of lead and concrete bunkers lined with cages of snakes! Johnny is told that when life on earth is erased, the snakes will be released to recreate humanity, just as Masterson said in 1903. Machines will feed the snakes for 100 years if necessary, and Erwin will continue their work with the insurance money. Johnny says that they are entitled to their opinions, but they are still wrong. He will let them sleep on it and let them sign the papers in the morning.

Johnny wants to borrow a car, but is told that there is no car here. They have been barred from the property for years, including tonight!

Johnny is shown to his room and spends the night thinking about the situation. Just as he is about to drop off, he hears what he fears. Hisssss. Hisssss. Johnny grabs a shoe and turns on the light, ready to kill the hissing non-venomous radiator. Then Johnny hears a woman scream in the hallway. Johnny slips on his shoes and opens the door to see a girl lying on the floor. He bends over to look, and is knocked unconscious. When Johnny wakes up, the girl is gone and Mr. and Mrs. Trump are telling him he must be careful when he walks in his sleep. They tell Johnny that they saw no woman when they got to Johnny. When Johnny tells them about the tire tracks, they look out the window and see nothing. Johnny tells them that the drifting snow took care of the tire tracks and his footprints, so he must not be there either! The Trumps say it must have been a nightmare. Johnny takes them to his room to sign the papers immediately, but the papers are gone.

The Trumps go back to bed, and Johnny goes to Erwin's room. He tells Johnny that he knows nothing of a girl, and heard no scream. Now, Johnny is starting to get mad.

Johnny searches the house looking for Hope. Back in his room, he hears a car trying to start. Johnny jumps from his window into the snow and goes to the car where Hope is trying to get away and they go back inside. Hope is a very attractive girl with an ugly gun she pulls from a shoulder holster. She tells Johnny that she has every right to the money and will do everything to thwart their plans, as the Trumps are fools. She tells Johnny that that Erwin will take the money and run, as he already has a ticket to South America. She had gone to him and confronted him with the facts and it was he who slugged her outside of Johnny's room. She tells Johnny that she has thrown the switch to release the snakes, and they are outside freezing right now. Erwin comes into the room with a gun, and is ready to kill both of them. Johnny tells Erwin not to move, as a snake has found it's way into the house and is coiled up behind him. Erwin accuses him of faking and moves toward Johnny. The snake (yes there was a snake) strikes Erwin. Erwin recognizes it as a bushmaster, the most deadly of their snakes. He manages to shoot the snake, and then kills Hope and dies.

With no snakes and no beneficiaries, the Trumps are left with no purpose. Johnny suggests that Mr. Trump research a machine to fight the UFOs. He calls it the "Flying Cup." Yours uh Truly? Johnny Dollar

NOTES:

- **AKA: "HOW THE GRAVEDIGGER'S SPADES CAME NEAR TO BEING TRUMPS."**

- A pung is a low box-like sleigh drawn by a single horse.
- An alienist is the old term for psychiatrists.
- Johnny wants some Old Harper referring to Old Harper bourbon
- The bushmaster is a deadly South American viper.
- There is a plug for O'Brien's newest movie, DOA.
- This is the first program using the "phone call" opening.
- Roy Rowan is the announcer
- Music is by Lieth Stevens

Producer: Jaime del Valle   **Writers:**   Paul Dudley, Gil Doud
Cast: Peggy Weber, Parley Baer, Hugh Thomas, Dick Ryan,
Jess Kirkpatrick, Mary Shipp.

Show: The Disappearance of Bruce Lambert
Show Date: 2/24/1950
Company: Great Corinthian Life Insurance Company
Agent:
Exp. Acct: $456.90

Synopsis: Johnny is called and asked why he is not down here, as his train leaves in 45 minutes. Johnny tells the caller he is taking a quick course in ancient history. He wants to be able to speak his language in case he finds him alive.

Johnny travels to the Brighton Arms Hotel in New York City to meet with Marcia Lambert, sister of the missing archeologist Bruce Lambert, who has disappeared after his return from Egypt. Marcia had called the insurance company because she does not want any publicity or police involvement.

Marcia tells Johnny that her brother had been working on a remote dig in Egypt. She had stayed in the village. After telling her that he does not trust her and threatening to walk out, Marcia tells Johnny that they had smuggled some artifacts into the country. The artifacts were an obsidian statue and a scarab; both were possibly very valuable. Her brother is not a strong man as he had been involved in an accident in Egypt and his arm and shoulder are in a cast. She gives Johnny a picture of Bruce for ID purposes.

Johnny goes to check with the crew of their boat, but it had sailed. Johnny checks with Customs. They have a record of Lambert coming in with one suitcase and one piece of statuary, no duty paid. Johnny then starts checking with the cabbies and notices a small well dressed man watching him from behind a newspaper. Cabby #782 remembers seeing the Lambert, but he paid him more to keep quiet than Johnny is paying for him to talk. After a $20 bribe, the cabby takes Johnny to a dingy hotel. A bribe to the room clerk gets Johnny a passkey to Lambert's room where he finds the obsidian statue. Johnny wonders why, if this thing is so valuable, does he not care for it better? His thoughts are interrupted by a small man with a small "lady's gun" who wants to know where

Lambert is. The man tells Johnny that Mr. Drummond will pay Johnny $2000 to find Lambert. The man waves the gun in Johnny's face, and Johnny takes it from him and slugs him for good measure. In the man's jacket Johnny finds an Egyptian passport in the name of Ammon Hixis. Johnny leaves Hixis in the room and leaves a note with the desk clerk telling Lambert not to go into the room, but to call Johnny.

Johnny goes back to Marcia and confronts her with Ammon Hixis' visit. He bawls her out for withholding information and tells her "he just stopped doing things her way." If anyone calls, he will be in his room. In his room, Johnny gets a call from Lambert. Johnny explains who he is and what his sister has told him. Lambert tells Johnny that Marcia is his fiancée, not his sister. Johnny tells him to meet him at Marcia's room. Johnny gets there first and goes in. Johnny meets Lambert in the corridor to tell him that Marcia is in the bathroom, dead. Johnny takes Lambert up to his room to get his story and to prepare an alibi for the police. Lambert tells Johnny that he had met Marcia in the hospital after his accident, and that she knew about the artifacts. Lambert gives Johnny the scarab to hold onto. He tells Johnny that he does not know Hixis or Drummond. Also, Lambert tells Johnny that his life had been threatened twice on the voyage over.

Johnny and Lambert go back to Marcia's room to meet with the police. In the room the police find a prescription bottle with the name of Dr. Ammon Hixis. Johnny suggests that Lambert be taken to police headquarters. Johnny also suggests that the police doctors x-ray the casts.

After dinner, Johnny goes to this room and finds Hixis and Drummond there. They weave a tail about the value of the scarab and how it will open up vast new oil fields if they can get it from Lambert. When Johnny says that he has it, the story changes. They tell Johnny that they had lied about the geegaw; they want Lambert. The phone rings and Johnny answers it. The police are calling to tell Johnny that they have x-rayed the cast and found over $300,000 in narcotics in it. They are on their way over. When Johnny tells Drummond that the call was from the police, Drummond tells Johnny how he and Hixis had used Lambert to carry theirs drugs for them. Marcia was involved also but stupidly fell in love. They decide to wait for Lambert to show. Hixis goes into the bathroom with the gun, and Drummond sits on the bed. There is a knock on the door, and Johnny tells Lambert to come on in, thus tipping the police. The police bust in and Hixis shoots Drummond when he is shot.

Drummond will live, and Lambert is placed in a private hospital until he recovers. Johnny sells Lambert a policy on the artifacts.

NOTES:
- **AKA: "THE ARCHEOLOGIST WHO NEVER SHOULD HAVE LEFT HIS TOMB."**
- **EDMOND O'BRIEN DROPS THE "YOURS, UH TRULY" ENDING**
- **ROY ROWAN IS THE ANNOUNCER**
- **MUSIC IS BY LIETH STEVENS**

Producer: Jaime del Valle   **Writers:** Paul Dudley, Gil Doud

Cast: Virginia Gregg, Jay Novello, Ed Begley, John Dehner, Pat McGeehan

◆   ❖   ◆

SHOW: ALEC JEFFERSON, THE YOUTHFUL MILLIONAIRE
SHOW DATE: 3/7/1950
COMPANY: GREAT CORINTHIAN LIFE INSURANCE COMPANY
AGENT: BOB DOUGLAS
EXP. ACCT: $711.00

SYNOPSIS: Bob calls Johnny and asks how quickly Johnny can leave for California. Johnny tells him right away, as his big toe needs defrosting. Bob tells Johnny that Alec Jefferson has disappeared, and it might be murder.

Johnny travels to Los Angeles, California to look for a missing millionaire, Alec Jefferson. Johnny goes to Rebel Wildcatters, Inc. and meets Mars Flaherty, Jefferson's partner. Mars has been looking for Alec but he has turned up nothing. Mars tells Johnny that he is wasting his time and money. Mars tells Johnny that Great Corinthian was the executor of Jefferson's trust, and had financed the venture. It was Jefferson's money and Mars' brains. Johnny is told that Jefferson had irritated many on the site with too much money and too many of other men's women. He was last seen one week ago.

Johnny tries to talk to the oilfield workers, but they tell him nothing. Johnny goes to Jefferson's apartment on Sunset Strip. Inside, the color scheme is "hangover green." There are loosely strewn women's clothes lying around and a loosely strewn woman in the bedroom who Johnny discovers is Jefferson's wife Ada. Johnny makes coffee and they talk. She tells Johnny that she needs money and has been waiting for a week. She knows Flaherty, as she was his girl friend. She had reported Alec missing and has no idea why he has gone.

Johnny leaves and notices someone watching him from across the street. Johnny uses the old "slow walk-away, quick turn" routine to get close to the car. Johnny tells the driver that he looks like an old friend. Johnny slugs the driver and takes him to an empty house in the suburbs to search his wallet. The man is Phil Wilkins, a private detective. When Phil wakes up, he tells Johnny that he was watching the girl, and he knows who Johnny is. Phil tells Johnny that Flaherty had him beaten up when he had tried to sell Flaherty some information on Alec. Phil tells Johnny that Flaherty and Jefferson have some sort of queer deal. The papers are in the safe and he has the combination.

Johnny goes to the office with Wilkins. They get into the office; get the agreement from the safe and leave. In the car they find Flaherty in the back seat with a gun. Flaherty tells Phil to drive to his house as Jefferson is there, quite dead!

On the way, Flaherty tells Johnny that he was out all day, but has no witnesses. He is sure that someone has planted the body there to frame him. At Flaherty's house, Johnny looks at the body, and finds an earring beside it. Flaherty recognizes it as one he had bought for Ada. Flaherty tells Johnny that he had married Ada in Mexico in '45. She had taken Alec to Mexico and married him without divorcing Flaherty.

Flaherty, Phil and Johnny go to Ada's apartment and confront her. She says she never got any earrings from Flaherty and they are not going to pin anything on her. Johnny accuses her of marrying both men so that she could collect in case one died. Ada struggles with Johnny and he calls the police. After reporting to the police that he has a murderer, Johnny slugs Flaherty. He tells everyone that Flaherty is the murderer. In the struggle with Ada, Johnny had noticed that she did not have pierced ears. The earrings that Flaherty said he bought were for pierced ears.

The police investigation finds no fingerprints on the firewood used to kill Alec, but they do find splinters under Flaherty's fingernails.

NOTES:
- **AKA: "HOW I GOT A WILDCAT OIL OPERATION BY THE TAIL," OR "THE YOUTHFUL MILLIONAIRE"**
- **AKA: "HOW THEY WERE DRILLING FOR OIL, BUT WHAT THEY STRUCK WAS ME."**
- **THERE IS A PLUG FOR O'BRIEN'S NEW MOVIE, DOA**
- **ROY ROWAN IS THE ANNOUNCER**
- **MUSIC IS BY LIETH STEVENS**

Producer: Jaime del Valle   Writers: Paul Dudley, Gill Doud
Cast: Michael Ann Barrett, Ed Max, Tony Barrett

◆   ❖   ◆

SHOW: THE EIGHTY-FIVE LITTLE MINKS
SHOW DATE: 3/14/1950
COMPANY: MUTUAL LIABILITY
AGENT: ED BONNER
EXP. ACCT: $384.16

SYNOPSIS: Ed calls Johnny very early in the morning and tells him to get up and get his gumshoes on. Ed has $300,000 coverage on Elwood Faver's fur department. Now he does not have a fur department, as 85 mink coats have been stolen.

While in Boston, Massachusetts, Johnny is assigned to the theft of 85 mink coats from the Elwood Faver Department Store. Johnny arrives at the store by cab just in time to see the night watchman, Kronen, loaded into an ambulance. Inside the store, Johnny meets Lt. Delaney and reviews the case. Johnny is told that someone broke into the store, opened the safe with the combination, removed the furs and shot the night watchman. Dmitri Stroganoff, head of the fur department, and a very agitated man, reported the theft. Stroganoff just knew something would happen that day, and it did. When Stroganoff meets Johnny his spirits lighten. Johnny has his $300,000, yes? Johnny tells him that he is only an investigator. Stroganoff tells Johnny that the "Insurance company always says two words, PAY PREMUIM. Now I have two words, PAY STROGANOFF!" Stroganoff then gives 23 pages of statement to the police: at 8:45 Stroganoff discovered the theft, called Mr. Favor and then the police. Stroganoff tells them that no one had the combination except himself.

While Johnny and Lt. Delaney are talking over lunch (ham sandwiches and a beer) a call comes in that the night watchman has died without saying anything. Johnny then finds out that there was another watchman in the store, Al Reedy. Johnny goes to talk to Reedy. He tells Johnny that he had been on duty all night. He sat in his office and was listening to the radio all-night and heard nothing and knows nothing. Now leave him alone.

Johnny checks Reedy's personnel records and finds nothing. Then on a hunch, Johnny goes to the Middleton Safe Company to talk to the owner about the safe. Johnny finds the owner, Mr. Middleton, standing in a new safe that will be shipped to South America the next day. Johnny is told that no one could open the safe without the combination. Based on the serial number of the safe, D4536, only Middleton, Mr. Danner the chief engineer and Stroganoff knew the combination. Johnny asks to talk to Danner, but he cannot, as Danner is dead.

Back at his hotel, Lt. Delaney meets Johnny. He tells Johnny that the police have found a body in the Charles River that had been shot with the same .32 used to kill the night watchman. After a fruitless night at police headquarters, Johnny gets three hours sleep before Ed Bonner calls. Johnny tells him he is working hard on the case but Bonner is adamant about getting the case settled and Johnny sounds rattled. Johnny gets ready to leave and is met at the door by Stroganoff, who tells Johnny that one of the mink coats has been mailed to the store in a dirty cardboard box! At the store Johnny searches the coat and finds a ticket stub for the "Country Club Dance." A call to the country club uncovers a familiar name on the list of attendees, Patricia Reedy. Johnny goes to see her, and Johnny tells her that he had seen her at the dance and how nice she looked in the mink coat. Her father interrupts and takes Johnny outside to talk. Reedy reiterates to Johnny that he did not help with the robbery and that he has a record. He tells Johnny that after serving time, he got married and had a daughter. His wife died and he is trying to help his daughter to have a nice life. He had borrowed the mink coat for the dance and had returned it. He tells Johnny that he had borrowed other things, and told Patricia that the company let him borrow things. Johnny shocks him by telling him that he believes him, and will forget the incident for the time being. Reedy is really shocked. On the way out, Reedy tells Johnny that the man the police found in the river was Ted Grey. Johnny goes to the store and checks the personnel records. Johnny discovers that Grey had worked for the store two weeks earlier, and was fired for insubordination. Johnny goes to Grey's apartment and finds nothing except 14 phone numbers written on the wall next to the phone. Johnny calls each one of the numbers and call number 8 hits the jackpot. Johnny calls Delaney and tells him where he is going. Johnny then goes to the Middleton Safe Company as he had recognized the voice of Mr. Middleton on call #8. Inside the plant, Middleton shoots at Johnny.

Middleton offers Johnny $100,000 to not turn him in, but Johnny declines the offer. Johnny asks if Middleton is using the same .32 he used to kill Grey and Middleton tells Johnny "No, I have a Luger this time. A Luger with a special sight!" He tells Johnny that he had shot Grey because Grey had reported that there were 85 minks in the vault, but only took out 84, so he was cheating Middleton. Middleton fires again, but the special sight is of no use. Johnny is shot in the shoulder and Middleton is mortally wounded. Before he dies, Middleton tells Johnny that the furs are in the vault heading for South America.

At dinner the next night with Patricia Reedy, Johnny gets a frantic call from Ed Bonner. One of the minks has been stolen! Johnny reassures Ed that it will show up, and then tells Patricia "You look lovely in mink." Johnny stays in Boston a few more days, sight seeing, until Patricia's eyes start saying marriage!

NOTES:
- JOHNNY IS SHOT FOR THE FIRST TIME.
- THE ANNOUNCER URGES THE AUDIENCE TO COMPLETE THEIR INCOME TAX FORMS.
- MUSIC IS BY LIETH STEVENS

Producer:	Jaime del Valle	Writers:	E. Jack Newman, John Michael Hayes
Cast:	Harry Bartell, Joseph Kearns, Hans Conried, Bill Johnstone, Howard McNear, Gloria Blondell		

◆ ❖ ◆

SHOW:	STUART PALMER, WRITER
SHOW DATE:	3/21/1950
COMPANY:	BRITANNIA CASUALTY AND LIFE
AGENT:	
EXP. ACCT:	$635.24

SYNOPSIS: Miss Ramey calls Johnny from Britannia's legal department. Johnny asks if a murderer is executed, does the policy pay off? She has never seen that happen, but Johnny tells her to put on your make up. It is likely to happen any minute.

Johnny goes to Chicago, Illinois to look into the arrest of Stuart Palmer, who is insured for $100,000. The beneficiary is Neal Beasley.

Johnny goes to see Stuart in Jail. Stuart tells Johnny that he does not want his help and that no one recognizes his greatness. Lt. Carrigan tells Johnny that Stuart was present when a wino was killed and was holding a cue like the one used to kill the man. Palmer tells Johnny that he hangs out in the west-end area to get background for his material—he writes crime stuff.

Johnny goes to see Stuart's wife, Marion. Her response is "why go after him. He is not guilty of anything bad." When Johnny tells her that Stuart has been arrested for murder, she says his lawyer Mr. Martin will spring him. Johnny is told that Stuart used to write for the radio, but he quit to write a play about crime. Now he lives with his subjects. She is sure that Stuart is going to get his play produced. With no money coming in, Johnny wonders how Stuart can afford so much insurance with no money.

Johnny goes to see George Michealkoff, Stuart's former agent. He tells Johnny that Palmer is crazy, too artsy. And his play? It is probably sitting in the bottom of Halstein's desk. Want to read a copy? He tells Johnny that so far Palmer has been bailed out twice and is washed up. The problems all started with Neal Beasley, who Johnny has heard of.

Based on a tip from a wino named Roscoe, Johnny goes to the west-end to look for Beasley and finds him in the Atomic Tavern. Johnny finds Beasley and tells him why he is there. According to Beasley, Palmer is a good man, but fate gets everyone. Johnny sees Palmer enter and then leave when Palmer spots Johnny. Johnny chases Palmer and as he turns a corner, Palmer turns and shoots, killing a newsboy.

Johnny chases Palmer, but loses him after a block. Johnny is looking for a phone when Lt. Carrigan shows up, Johnny tells him the whole story. But why Palmer would shoot at Johnny is the $100,000 question. A general alert is issued for Palmer.

Johnny calls the local agent for Britannia and tells him to cancel Palmer's policy as quickly as possible, but it will be tomorrow until the agent can do anything. The agent will call Hartford tonight and see what he can do. Johnny then goes to see Mrs. Palmer to tell her the news, but she will not believe him. Johnny is sure that he wants the police to kill him so that she can get the insurance. The phone rings and it is Stuart, who hangs up. Then the police show up.

Johnny tells Lt. Carrigan what he knows and Carrigan is sure that they will have to stop Palmer with a gun. Johnny then goes back to see Beasley who knows where Palmer is but won't tell. Beasley also tells Johnny that Palmer had offered him $10,000 to help him, but he does not want the money. Beasley reluctantly agrees to take Johnny to Palmer. When they get to the room where Palmer is, Palmer tells Beasley "Good work. Bring him in quickly." What kind of plot is this Johnny wonders? Inside Palmer tells Johnny that Beasley helped him plan the whole thing, but Johnny won't be around to tell any body. When Johnny tells him that his policy has been cancelled, Palmer still plans to go on.

The police show up, and have Palmer's wife with them. She comes in and begs Palmer to give up and that she is not interested in the money. Palmer rejects her plea, goes out shooting and is killed by the police.

The policy is not cancelled in time, but Johnny is sure that the lawyers will find a way out. Beasley is in jail for sixty days for attempted Insurance Fraud. Johnny almost forgets to mention that Mrs. Palmer notified him that Stuart's play will be produced on Broadway.

NOTES:
- **AKA: "THE MAN WHO WROTE HIMSELF TO DEATH"**
- **THE PROGRAM I HAVE IS A REHEARSAL PROGRAM.**

- THE MID-PROGRAM COMMERCIAL IS FOR THE BING CROSBY PROGRAM ON WEDNESDAY WITH MILDRED BAILEY AND CLIFTON WEBB,
- ROY ROWAN IS THE ANNOUNCER.
- MUSIC IS BY LIETH STEVENS
- THERE IS A PLUG FOR DOA

Producer: Jaime del Valle;   **Writers:**   Gil Doud, David Ellis
Cast: Lurene Tuttle, Larry Dobkin, Bill Bouchey, Bill Grey, Jack Kruschen, Herb Butterfield

◆　❖　◆

SHOW: THE MISSING MASTERPIECE
SHOW DATE: 3/28/1950
COMPANY: BAY STATE BONDING AND LIABILITY
AGENT: DOUG STRAND
EXP. ACCT: $68.30

SYNOPSIS: Doug Strand calls and has a big bonding case for Johnny in Boston. Johnny tells Doug that he is already working on a case in Hartford, also bonded. Doug tells Johnny that a picture insured for $250,000 has just been stolen.

This case took place in Boston, Massachusetts, but turned out to be no tea party.

Johnny travels by car to Boston, to look into the theft of "The Village Scene" painted by Peiter Breugel. The painting was stolen from the Maudan Gallery, and is insured for $250,000. At the gallery, Johnny meets with Teresa Maudan, the owner's daughter. Teresa tells Johnny that Caesar Ritto, a local art appreciator, owns the painting. She is upset because she had urged Ritto to show the picture.

Mr. Maudan comes in and tells Johnny that he is discouraged because the police do not know anything about art. If the picture is not found, he will be forced to close the gallery and move to start again. The gallery is his life and he had brought most of the work from Salzburg after the Anschluss. He also shows Johnny window the thief had come in through.

Mr. Maudan has offered a $5,000 reward, but Mr. Ritto does not seem to care. He has also tried to protect his daughter from Ritto.

Johnny goes to talk to Sgt. Himes of the police. Sgt. Himes is glad to have Johnny on the case and is glad for Johnny's help. This case seems to be different and the police are looking for the frame too.

Johnny is told that Ritto is supposedly a liquor distributor who made his money in the black-market during the war. Ritto was also up before the Senate for buying contracts. Johnny mentions that fraud charges against Ritto might be easier to prove than finding the picture. Johnny goes to Ritto's house on Beacon Hill where the butler admits him. Johnny meets Lily Swanson, the girlfriend of Ritto who wonders if Johnny is the friend Ritto has been sitting up with. She warns Johnny about Teresa (she is poison) and is tired of Ritto. He wants refinement now, when he used to be interested in burlesque houses and going out to visit sick friends at night. Ritto comes in, there are words between them and Lilly slaps him and leaves.

Johnny talks to Ritto who seems to have an answer for everything. When Johnny tells him that there is a clause that requires prior notice before moving the picture, Ritto say he will find another clause that will nullify that one.

Johnny leaves and watches Ritto's house. A "long cold time later" Johnny sees Ritto leave, and then Lily goes out and Johnny follows her. It is obvious that she is going to the gallery, so Johnny tries to beat her there. Johnny gets to the back window just in time to hear a woman scream and 3 shots. Johnny goes in to find Ritto alone with two bullet holes in him.

Johnny calls an ambulance and the police and asks Ritto what happened, but Ritto says nothing other than the gallery is where he meets Teresa. After talking to the police and saying nothing incriminating, Johnny goes to see Lily, who only asks if Ritto is dead. Johnny tells Lily that he knows she went to the gallery, but Lily said she was going to see what Ritto and Teresa were up to, but she changed her mind. Johnny continues to question her while he searches the house for the painting, but finds nothing. Johnny goes to the Maudan residence where he talks to Teresa, while her father is in his studio. Teresa Tells Johnny that Ritto is her fiancé. She was there when Ritto was shot, but Ritto had told her to leave. She is marrying Ritto because she is tired of being the daughter of a poor man. Ritto is going to be rich and she wants to be a rich man's wife. Teresa's father comes in and is very distraught over what he heard.

The next morning Sgt. Hines calls to say that the paining had been returned for the reward. On the way to the gallery, Johnny ponders A.) Why was the painting stolen in the frame, B.) Why did Maudan not mention that he was an artist, C.) Ritto knew nothing about art but was not upset, D.) Maudan offered a reward, but he was a poor man. Was it a diversion because he knew he did not have to pay the reward?

At the gallery, Johnny finds Maudan and two pictures, the original and a copy. Maudan tells Johnny that he faked the theft as an act of love for his daughter. He hoped he could hold on to Teresa with the money, but he fears it is too late. Ritto comes in and sees the duplicate and gets angry. Maudan accuses him of bringing shame to his daughter and the family, and then he shoots Ritto. Teresa comes in from the car and cries. She tells Johnny that Ritto knew the copy was being made. He knew her father was going to give the copy to Ritto and sell the original, but he did not care. Maudan is turned over to the police.

"The next time anyone assigns me to find a masterpiece, my expense account will be a masterpiece of overstatement!"

NOTES:
- **AKA: "THE VILLAGE SCENE MATTER"**
- **THE ANSCHLUSS WAS THE ANNEXATION OF WESTERN AUSTRIA BY HITLER.**
- **JOHNNY MENTIONS HAVING TICKETS FOR SOUTH PACIFIC.**
- **THERE IS NEW MUSIC AT THE CLOSE OF THE PROGRAM.**
- **THERE IS A PLUG FOR DOA**

- ROY ROWAN IS THE ANNOUNCER
- MUSIC IS BY LIETH STEVENS

Producer: Jaime del Valle   Writers: Paul Dudley, Gil Doud,
Cast: Tyler McVey, Charles McGraw, Walter Burke, Lillian Buyeff,
             Robert Griffin, James Nusser, Joan Banks

◆ ❖ ◆

SHOW: THE STORY OF THE BIG RED SCHOOLHOUSE
SHOW DATE: 4/4/1950
COMPANY: GREAT CHESAPEAKE FIDELITY INSURANCE COMPANY
AGENT: PAUL MCGRAW
EXP. ACCT: $3,227.00

SYNOPSIS: A man calls Johnny and tells him he has $500 for him. Johnny guesses that the mystery voice is Julius Caesar, but it is Western Union assigning Johnny to go to Manhattan, Nebraska and get a room in the Cheyenne Hotel. The Western Union man tells Johnny that he was stationed in Manhattan during the war. It makes an army camp look like the Promised Land.

[skip]

Johnny is talking to the architect Bill Garrett. Garrett tells Johnny that he had designed the school. The city agreed to build it and Garrett has sent to study at the Sorbonne in Paris. When he returned, the building exterior was his, but the interior was made up as they went along.

Johnny goes to see the builder, Big Jim Madden. Johnny finds an angry crowd is at his home. Johnny uses his ID to get past the guards and into the house. Johnny meets Madden who tells him that the city construction committee saw no reason for the boiler explosion. Madden tells Johnny that the janitor was drunk and did not watch the boilers. Johnny is told that the city will rebuild the school from the Insurance money. Madden gives Johnny 50 pages of building specifications for him to review.

Johnny goes to see Mike Degerra, the building inspector. Vivian Degerra is there dressed in a negligee and nursing a drink, but there is no sign of Mike. After Johnny notes signs of his absence, Vivian admits that Mike had left three months earlier.

Johnny then calls the insurance company's head office and reports that everything about the case is rotten. McGraw tells Johnny that he is sending eight additional agents to help Johnny.

Back in his hotel room, a man walks into the room and collapses with three bullet holes in him. Johnny searches the body and discovers that it is Mike Degerra. Johnny takes the body to the morgue. The police hold Johnny overnight until the hotel staff finally concurs that Degerra came into the wounded.

Back in the hotel, Johnny meets with the nine agents who have arrived. Johnny briefs them on the case, and tells them to not push anyone around, but not to be pushed around. Carl and Chip are to go after Degerra's background and finances, etc. Rob and Tip are to find out about Madden. Paddy and Ralph are to look into the janitor Stankovitch. Rocky and Jerry look into everything else.

Later that morning the Mayor comes in and talks to Johnny about the deplorable situation. He tells Johnny that the city will give its complete cooperation. The Mayor outlines the history of the school project, but nothing new is learned. Johnny asks the mayor about the purchase orders for the school. The mayor does not know where they are, but he will look for them. He also tells Johnny that the city will file a claim for the insurance.

Johnny receives a call from Carl who has learned that Degerra had made four $1,000 deposits, but his salary is only $7,000. Johnny goes to see Mrs. Degerra who is now wearing a slinky black mourning dress and a poor mourning act. She tells Johnny that she did not know where the money came from, but it went for other women. Now with out a husband and no insurance, she needs help. Johnny agrees to get her a $2,000 policy for the right information. She tells Johnny that the money came from Universal Rock Company, which is owned by Madden's brother. Mike had come back to ask Madden for more money and had gotten shot for his efforts.

On the way back to the Hotel Johnny ruins into Bill Garrett. He tells Johnny about a law he believes exists that says that a citizen may commit a crime to prevent a bigger crime. Bill tells Johnny that he had gotten his former secretary to steal a file from the mayor's office. The file was a folder containing the purchase orders for the school. Johnny mails the file to the insurance company for protection. Johnny goes to see the mayor and calls him a liar because he had the purchase orders. The mayor tells Johnny that he was going to go after Madden but did not know how. Johnny tells him that the insurance will never be paid and that the mayor should give himself up to the police.

Back at the hotel, Johnny gets more information from two witnesses. Later, three tough guys walk into his room and suggest that he go with them. Johnny is escorted from the hotel, but is met outside by his investigators who take care of the tough guys. After being slapped around, they tell Johnny that Madden had ordered them to take Johnny to the rock company. Johnny and the boys go to Universal Rock and surround the main building and Johnny goes in with K. G. As they go in, there are shots and Jim Madden falls down the stairs dead. Johnny and K. G. go in to see Mrs. Degerra shoot the mayor. Johnny disarms her, and calls an ambulance. As the mayor dies, he tells Johnny that the whole plot was his idea. He and Madden had made over $100,000 on the deal. Degerra had wanted more money to keep quiet so the mayor had him killed. As the mayor dies, he asks, "Why is there always a falling out among thieves?"

NOTES:

- THERE IS A PLUG FOR **DOA**.
- IN THE PROGRAM, PAUL MCGRAW TELLS JOHNNY THAT HE IS SENDING EIGHT AGENTS TO ASSIST JOHNNY. WHEN THE MEN ARRIVE, JOHNNY LISTS NINE MEN: RALPH HAYCRAFT, CARL ROYAL, CHIP HANIGAN, PADDY PHILLIPS, ROCKY ANDROSANO, JERRY KATAY, TIP MILLER, ROB CORNIEL

AND **K. G. PETERSON. WHEN ASSIGNMENTS ARE GIVEN, K. G. PETERSON IS NOT LISTED.**

- **THE ANNOUNCER, ROY ROWAN, ERRS ON WATERMAN'S NAME, CALLING HIM "WILLER"**
- **MUSIC IS BY LIETH STEVENS**
- **THIS PROGRAM WAS ALSO DONE AS "THE CLINTON MATTER" WITH BOB BAILEY**

Producer:	Jaime del Valle	Writers:	E. Jack Newman, John Micheal Hayes
Cast:	Victor Perrin, Elliott Reid, Hy Averback, Clayton Post, Bill Conrad, Virginia Gregg, Willard Waterman		

◆ ❖ ◆

SHOW:	THE DEAD FIRST-HELPERS
SHOW DATE:	4/11/1950
COMPANY:	GRAND INDUSTRIAL INSURERS
AGENT:	BILL HUDSON
EXP. ACCT:	$520.25

SYNOPSIS: Bill Hudson calls and tells Johnny that there have been a lot of deaths at the Cornell Steel plant in Pittsburgh, and it looks like murder to him.

Johnny travels to Pittsburgh, Pennsylvania to look into a series of five murders at the Cornell Steel Company. At Cornell, Johnny meets Joel Barrett, the manager. Johnny learns that all of the dead men were First Helpers. Barnett explains that each Melter Foreman is responsible for several furnaces and has a First Helper on each furnace. The first helper has a second helper and they have Cinder Snaps. There was no common denominator in the accidents, except that each of the men was a senior worker who knew and followed the rules.

Johnny hires on as a cinder snap and goes to work, and boy does he work! Johnny gets to know Andre, who enjoys showing him the ropes. "Remember the rules and you will be OK" Johnny is told. Andre tells Johnny that the men who were killed were careless.

Johnny meets Joe Poland, who is a gruff man. To Joe, Johnny looks like an office type. When Johnny mentions Kirk Brody, the last man killed, Joe tells him that Kirk was his friend. Johnny meets Fred, who is another first helper, but he worries about his family and wonders when he will get his blue slip or have an accident. Fred knows that the other men were killed.

Johnny goes to Brody's cold-water flat to see his widow. She tells Johnny that she knew something was going to happen and warned her husband to be careful. She knows her husband was murdered, as all the men are worried about their jobs. She tells Johnny that he should go talk to Barrett.

At the office, Johnny tells Barrett of the rising tensions and the men's fright. Barrett tells Johnny that all the killed men were alone when they were killed.

Johnny looks at the employment records. Johnny tells Barrett that he had discovered that each of the men was alone when killed, that they were killed by seniority, that Barrett had posted a memo saying there would be layoffs by seniority but that Barrett knew the company was not laying men off. Barrett says that his job is to boost productivity.

Johnny goes to Mike and tells him he is with the insurance company and warns him that, as the senior man he is next. Later that evening, Mike is cleaning his furnace when a huge man dressed in an asbestos suit attacks him and throws him off of the furnace killing him.

Johnny chases the killer but only gets a fall and a safety lecture from the plant manager. Johnny gets the key to the locker room from the main office and searches the lockers. In Mike's locker Johnny only finds a wallet and a picture. In Andre's locker Johnny finds the asbestos suit, complete with a tear in the arm. Joe Poland comes in sick and tells Johnny that Andre is on furnace #10. Joe tells Johnny that he saw Andre wearing the suit, and that he does not like Andre. Johnny puts the suit in the office and goes to find Andre. Johnny finds Andre who invites Johnny home for some good French food. Johnny goes with Andre and meets his wife. Andre throws Johnny out when Johnny tells him that he found the suit in his locker.

Johnny goes to the office and takes the seniority list and goes to get some sleep. Johnny goes to his room and before going to sleep Johnny notices that Andre's name is next, so Johnny goes to see him. When he gets there, Andre is dead and Andre's wife tells Johnny that a big man had killed him and that the suit was a plant. Johnny takes a cab back to Barrett's office. Johnny blames himself to Andre's death and gets Joe Poland's address, as he is next on the list. Johnny and Barrett go to Joe's flat, but his wife says that Joe is not home. Johnny searches the flat but finds nothing. The wife says that Barrett is to blame for everything and spits on him.

On the way out Barrett expounds his management theory on Johnny: Men work better under pressure. If Johnny worked as a supervisor in a steel plant for 10 days, he would know that. Johnny calls the police and goes to find Joe in the plant. Johnny finds Joe on furnace #12 cleaning the furnace. Joe knows that he is on the top of the seniority list now, and no one is going to take that from him. Joe tells Johnny that he will get a raise now. No one can take his job from him. As Joe moves to grab Johnny he shoots Joe four times. Finally Joe grabs Johnny's throat and Johnny fires one last time into the heart and Joe falls into the molten steel and disappears.

At the funeral they bury a block of steel and Joe's wife calls Barrett a murderer. Johnny's last action is to have Barrett removed as supervisor.

NOTES:
- THERE IS A LOT OF SLANG USED IN THE STEEL INDUSTRY HERE.
- THE MID-PROGRAM COMMERCIAL IS FOR THE BURNS AND ALLEN SHOW
- ROY ROWAN IS THE ANNOUNCER, WHO PLUGS DOA
- MUSIC IS BY LIETH STEVENS

Producer: Jaime del Valle   **Writers:** Gil Doud, David Ellis
Cast: Joe Forte, Junius Matthews, Jack Petruzzi, Raymond Burr, Jack Kruschen, Kay Stewart, Peggy Webber

◆ ❖ ◆

SHOW: THE STORY OF THE 10:08
SHOW DATE: 4/18/1950
COMPANY: SHIPPER'S INDEMNITY
AGENT: HARRY POULDEN
EXP. ACCT: $312.00

SYNOPSIS: Harry calls and tells Johnny to take a plane to Buffalo. They have a blanket policy on the Atlantic Central Railroad, and a train car has been robbed. Get up there—and watch your expense account!

Johnny goes to Buffalo, New York to look into a boxcar robbery on the Atlantic Central Railroad. Harry warns Johnny to watch his expense account!

In Buffalo, Johnny meets Eath Grimms, a "cinder bull" for the railroad. Eath tells Johnny "the rail road runs six gully jumpers to Rochester each day. Five hours after leaving she jerks up at Batavia so the clowns can water her down. That's when the donigan noticed a brownie is open and half the gig is gone. He wangdoodles a copperbuster up the line." Johnny seems to understand that the brakeman found the boxcar open and called ahead to the telegraph operator.

The boxcar in question had a mixed cargo and the bookkeepers are trying to determine what was in it. The train only stopped for the water, and for a passenger train to pass it. The yard workers had seen a blonde woman hanging around asking questions claiming she was a reporter, but Eath had checked and none of the papers had a reporter named Ruth Smith.

Johnny guesses that the crooks followed the train in a truck and picked up merchandise thrown from the train along the road. Grimms is impressed that Johnny pretty much has it figured out. Now, to find the merchandise.

Johnny and Grimms go out looking for evidence in Grimm's army surplus jeep. Along a road beside the right of way, they find a number of tire tracks indicating someone was going towards the tracks. At a shanty they find a man named Bogardus who had seen a yellow truck with no writing on it, which had headed back to Buffalo.

Johnny and Grimms go back to town and start looking for the truck. Johnny is called by Eath, who tells Johnny that the police have found the truck wrecked in a ravine. The driver, Rick Blakey, lives long enough to tell Johnny to look for Jake. Jake had slugged him and run him into the gully. As the cargo is loaded, Johnny finds a card for a bar with a message, "Jake 8:00 Tuesday. Her is always there." Johnny goes to the Horseshoe Bar and Grill, and after bribing the bartender with a five spot, who recognizes Johnny as a cop, to signal if Jake comes in, Johnny waits. Later the bartender leaves and Johnny follows to find him hanging up the phone. He tells Johnny that Jake had just called looking for his glasses. He tells Johnny that Jake will be in his room, #210 at the Embassy

Hotel. Johnny goes to the hotel but there is no room 210. On the way out Johnny is "escorted" to an alley where Johnny meets a tall well-dressed man, Jake. Jake asks Johnny why he is looking for him. The accomplice named Trench slugs Johnny and frisks him.

When Johnny wakes up, he goes and finds the bartender and slaps him around for setting Johnny up. Johnny finds out that Jake is Jake Samuels and that he has a partner named Trench, but he does not know where Jake lives.

Tired and groggy, Johnny gets a room in the Imperial Hotel. As soon as he checks in, Grimms comes to his room. The cargo has been checked and the only thing missing is a barrel of jeweler's rouge worth $247 being shipped to Boston by Ralph Morton, who runs a jewelry shop. It was being sent to Michael Agelson in Boston. Next morning Johnny rents a car and drives to the Morton's store. On the way in, Johnny notices a man watching from across the street. In the shop Johnny finds Morton and a snappy blond woman. When Johnny mentions that the rouge was stolen, Morton drops the item he is working on. Morton tells Johnny that he did ship the rouge. The woman drops something when Johnny says that the thieves are guilty of murder. Morton tells Johnny that his rouge is a special formula liked by a man in Boston who designs jewelry.

Johnny leaves and approaches the man across the street who then leaves. Johnny follows him to a drug store where the man is eating a butterscotch sundae. Johnny learns that the man is Ben Sanchez, a private detective. Ben thinks that Morton is a fence for jewels stolen from the Arcadia Company, where $250,000 in jewels was stolen. Ben tells Johnny that Morton has a record but he can't prove he is guilty of fencing anything even though he lives in an $85,000 house.

The blonde leaves and Johnny follows her to a nondescript house. As he is standing in front of the house, the same man from the night before puts a gun in his back, takes Johnny's gun and tells him to go in. Inside the house Johnny hears a woman and a man who are arguing over money. Then an angry Jake comes in with the girl from the store. Johnny tells Jake what he is working on, and about the girl he saw in Morton's shop. The girl is angry because Jake owes her $45,000 for the $300,000 in jewelry. Jake tells her to leave and Trench insults her. She opens the door, turns and shoots Trench twice with an automatic. She tells Jake she wants the money now, but he tells Andrea that he does not have it. Johnny convinces the girl that if she gives him her gun, he will try to square it with the police. The alternative is the gun or a murder rap. She gives in and gives Johnny her gun. The police are called and they take over. Jake had hired Andrea to get information about Morton for $50,000, which she never got. Morton was shipping the Arcadia jewels to Boston in the barrel of rouge, which the police recovered. Expenses include a new foam rubber seat for Eath's jeep.

NOTES:
- MY PROGRAM IS A REHEARSAL PROGRAM.
- JOHNNY IS CHARGED 50¢ FOR A DRINK.
- THERE IS A LOTS OF RAILROAD SLANG SOME, OF WHICH I CANNOT VERIFY

- THE COMMERCIAL IS FOR THE BING CROSBY PROGRAM ON WEDNESDAY
- IN THE PROGRAM, GRIMMS SPELLS OUT AGELSON'S NAME, WHICH IS THEN PRONOUNCED ADELSON
- ROY ROWAN IS THE ANNOUNCER, WHO PLUGS DOA.
- MUSIC IS BY LIETH STEVENS

Producer: Jaime del Valle   Writers: E. Jack Newman, John Michael Hayes

Cast: Ted de Corsia, Pat McGeehan, John Dehner, Harold Dryanforth, Bill Bouchey, Jeanne Bates, Clayton Post

◆   ❖   ◆

SHOW: THE PEARL CARRASA MATTER
SHOW DATE: 4/25/1950
COMPANY: PIEDMONT MUTUAL LIFE INSURANCE COMPANY
AGENT: BOB CASE
EXP. ACCT: $712.55

SYNOPSIS: Bob Case calls Johnny to tell him that a girl pulled from the East River was a policyholder. Johnny tells Bob to go to the police to find their killer. Bob tells Johnny that they know who killed her, and he is being executed right after midnight. Bob wants to know about the victim.

Johnny drives to Sing Sing Prison and talks to Marty Pruit in his cell on death row where Marty is playing solitaire. Marty is Pearl's murderer. He tells Johnny that he was paid $5,000 to kill Pearl, but he refuses to tell Johnny anything about who hired him. Marty tells Johnny to leave this case alone as it is an ungodly mess.

Johnny goes to the New York City police and speaks with Lt. Goldberg about the case. The only thing he can add is Pearl's last address on the Eastside. Johnny goes to the boarding house and talks to the manager who tells Johnny that Pearl had no visitors, and received no mail. She only went out twice a day for about an hour. Johnny spends the rest of the day looking for a possible post office box within half an hour of the boarding house. The next day Johnny finds a grocery store with a mail drop, and a letter for Pearl Carrasa forwarded from the Rambeau Club in Las Vegas. Johnny calls Bob Case and gets authorization to travel to Las Vegas.

Johnny flies to Las Vegas, Nevada and in the Club Rambeau Johnny strikes up a conversation with a girl at the bar. When Johnny mentions Pearl's name, she suddenly has to get back to work. Johnny asks the bartender about Pearl and is escorted back to the office of Peter Barren, who sports a red scar across his face.

When Johnny mentions that he is looking for Mrs. Carrasa, Barren gets really aggravated. After a few minutes of verbal sparring, Barren tells "Mike" to take Johnny to see Mrs. Carrasa. On the way out the door, four other men join Johnny and Mike and beat Johnny. When Johnny wakes up, Barren wants to know how Johnny knows Pearl. Johnny tells Barren about the policy and goes unconscious.

After a visit to a doctor and two days rest, the girl Johnny met in the bar visits Johnny in his room. She tells Johnny that she is scared to death, but does tell Johnny to tell Pearl never to come back. When Johnny tells her that Pearl is dead, she tells Johnny that the casino is really a front for drugs brought up from Mexico. She leaves Johnny to catch a bus out of town. As Johnny looks out the window, the girl is shot in the doorway of the bus.

Johnny gets to the girl's body just ahead of a deputy sheriff and tells him what happened. Johnny gives Johnny his ID and tells him about the case. The deputy tells Johnny that he knows that Pearl had gotten involved with Pete Barren and left town. Johnny is told that the police have been watching Barren, and that the Carrasa family is one of the finest names in town. They have been suspected of involvement in drugs but they have no evidence.

Johnny takes a cab to the Carrasa estate and is escorted to the library by the butler. In the library, Johnny tells Mr. Carrasa about Pearl, who is saddened to hear of Pearl's death. Mrs. Carrasa rushes in worrying about whether the palms have been watered for the music club meeting tonight. When Johnny tells Mrs. Carrasa of Pearl's death, she is not sorry. She had brought shame on the family by bringing her "friends" to the house. Why, she actually wanted to marry one of them! Johnny can take the check back, as she does not want it. Johnny leaves the insurance papers and leaves.

On the way out of the house, Johnny sees Barren drive in. Johnny goes to the sheriff and tells what he saw. They both go back out to the estate. The butler is arrested at the front door to keep him quiet. As they enter the library, Barren is telling Mr. and Mrs. Carrasa about the murder of Pearl, who knew too much and was going to tell. Barren tells Mr. Carrasa "things like this happen." He retorts, "things like THIS happen," pulls a gun and shoots Barren. When the police take the gun from him, Mr. Carrasa tells them that everything was his wife's fault. He had a tile business after the war, but she wanted more. Nice clothes, nice houses and nice friends and sophistication! When Pearl brought a nice boy in, she humiliated the boy and then told Pearl to get out of the house. Mrs. Carrasa had gotten involved with Barren to get money and that lead to involvement with drugs. She had involved herself with the very people she wanted to avoid. Johnny takes the check and leaves. Johnny thinks the check should be used to clean up the respectable slums, but that is not his decision.

NOTES:
- THERE IS A LOT OF INTERESTING BACKGROUND CHATTER IN THE CASINO WHEN JOHNNY COMES IN AND ON THE WAY TO PETER'S OFFICE.
- THE MID-PROGRAM COMMERCIAL IS FOR THE BURNS AND ALLEN PROGRAM ON WEDNESDAY
- ROY ROWAN IS THE ANNOUNCER
- MUSIC IS BY LIETH STEVENS
- THE ANNOUNCER GIVES A PLUG FOR DOA.

Producer: Jaime del Valle   **Writers:** Gil Doud, Davis Ellis
Cast: Hy Averback, Joseph Kearns, Bill Johnstone, Bill Conrad, Martha Wentworth, Sarah Selby, Virginia Gregg, Howard McNear

◆ ❖ ◆

SHOW: THE ABEL TACKETT MATTER
SHOW DATE: 5/2/1950
COMPANY: CORINTHIAN LIFE INSURANCE COMPANY
AGENT: MR. HOUSE
EXP. ACCT: $4,075.80

SYNOPSIS: Johnny is called by Mrs. Tackett, and she agrees to see Johnny that afternoon.

Johnny goes to the New York City apartment of Mrs. Tackett where he is welcomed to the sounds of recorded tribal drum music. Johnny tells Mrs. Tackett that he is going to British North Borneo to look for her husband, who has not written for 5 years. Mrs. Tackett tells Johnny that her husband had last written that he was lost and was trying to find his purpose in life. Johnny tells her that he is probably looking for a dead man, but she insists that Abel is alive; maybe he has just stopped writing. Johnny reminds her that if Abel is dead, she gets $750,000 in insurance. But at 24, she wants for believe that he is still alive.

Johnny travels to the Philippines and gets on a cargo ship as "super cargo." At dinner, the captain asks why Johnny is going to Borneo. Johnny tells him that he is looking for a man no one has probably heard of, Abel Tackett. "TACKETT!" screams the captain. The captain tells Johnny that everyone in South Asia knows the name of Tackett. He lifts his shirt to show Johnny a scar across his chest, inflicted by Abel Tackett. "Something happens to men out here," the captain tells Johnny. Bursts of temper usually follow the mention of Tackett's name.

In Sandakan, Borneo Johnny looks up the secretary to the Assistant District Manager who describes Tackett as a fabulous fellow, a man of mystery who is looking for something but who is probably dead. He can arrange for Johnny to go inland the next day on a supply lorry.

Johnny meets a woman named Inez who knows Tackett. Her husband is dying of fever, but she knows Tackett is alive and can get Johnny to him. The woman's husband dies, and she visits Johnny in his hotel room. She tells Johnny that she knows who sent supplies to Tackett just a month ago. Johnny reluctantly accepts her offer.

At a trading post, Johnny meets a man named George Brown, who has been trading there for 10 years. For $500 he can take Johnny to Tackett, but he will kill Tackett when he finds him. Brown had a good and peaceful trading relationship with the Dayak headhunters, but Tackett had gone in and upset the peace.

Johnny discovers that in the jungle, conversation is a waste of breath. On the first night, Johnny tells Brown that he did not want to take Inez along, but she insisted. Brown tells Johnny that Tackett is a troublemaker and is always stirring up the natives. Inez tells Johnny that Tackett had never talked to her about his wife, and that the trouble Tackett had in Manila was because the locals thought he was afraid of them. On the 3rd day, they find the body of a native who had been killed by headhunters and left on the trail as a warning. On the whole trip, Inez, Brown and Johnny are all at odds over what they will do to Tackett. Inez loves him, Brown wants to kill him and Johnny wants prove he is alive so that he can go home to his wife.

Finally on the 6th day, in a driving rain, they arrive at the small village of Longwye in Dutch Borneo. There is no sign of life in the village. As they make their way to the shack of Abel Tackett, the drums of the Dayak Mamapalu, or "return from hunting" ceremony start. At the shack, Johnny and Brown both enter to find Abel Tackett dead. Tackett had been killed by the headhunters. There is no positive ID, but the body is presumed to be Tackett.

Back in New York Johnny confronts Mrs. Tackett with the news of her husbands death, "He died from fever." Johnny tells her. Johnny tells her to go to the probate court and have him declared dead based, on the evidence he has. She declines insisting that Abel is alive somewhere, and could have changed his identity. Johnny leaves a "young woman slowly dying."

On this trip, Johnny relates that "I became an expert on pure unadulterated frustration!"

NOTES:
- MY PROGRAM IS A REHEARSAL COPY
- THE MID-PROGRAM COMMERCIAL IS FOR "YOU BET YOUR LIFE," WITH GROUCHO MARX
- BRITISH NORTH BORNEO IS NOW MALAYA.
- DUTCH BORNEO BECAME PART OF INDONESIA.
- THE DAYAK ARE THE INDIGENOUS PEOPLES OF THE AREA AND WERE HEADHUNTERS.
- ROY ROWAN IS THE ANNOUNCER, WHO PLUGS DOA.
- MUSIC IS BY LIETH STEVENS

Producer: Jaime del Valle   Writers: Gil Doud, David Ellis
Cast: Ben Wright, Maria Palmer, Tudor Owen, Raul Chavez, Chris
             Kraft, Dan O'Herlihy

◆   ❖   ◆

SHOW: THE HAROLD TRANDEM MATTER
SHOW DATE: 5/9/1950
COMPANY: CLAYSON MUTUAL ASSURANCE CO
AGENT: JACK BARTON
EXP. ACCT: $706.82

SYNOPSIS: Jack Barton calls and gives Johnny the policy number 245-7809. Los Angeles, amount $1,115,000, beneficiary Mabel Trandem, insured is Harold

Trandem. There is no official problem, but the company is unhappy to hear that here has been an attempt on Mr. Trandem's life. He is insured for $1,150,000 and his wife Mabel is the beneficiary. Johnny is to go out unofficially to make sure that Trandem is ok.

Johnny travels to the Bel Aire, California mansion of Trandem and is escorted to the terrace. A scowling Mr. Trandem tells Johnny that he has taken precautions and does not need Johnny's help. While Trandem is talking to Johnny, he is shot and killed. The staff and bodyguard come in and everyone accuses Johnny. The bodyguard tells Johnny that he will get fired for letting Trandem get shot, so why don't they exchange information. Johnny relates that the only thing he saw was a puff of blue smoke from the bushes. The police are called and they only find some bent twigs and nothing else.

After the police leave, Johnny talks to Mabel, the wife. He tells her that the last word Trandem had said was "Lilah" and Johnny wants to know who was she. Mabel tells Johnny that Lilah Whinnig was all Trandem ever talked about. When Johnny reassures her that the killing will not prevent her from collecting on the policy, Mabel is glad, as the money is the only thing he left her and the Jessie Fredrica Mission. She tells Johnny that she had been a waitress until Trandem met her. She had plenty of everything, but she still hated him. The closer you came to him, the more you hated him Johnny is told. Mabel said she was going to get a small apartment and a couple of Siamese cats, as she has always wanted a cat.

Johnny goes to Lilah's apartment but no one answers. Johnny looks through the window and sees Lilah on the floor with a .38 caliber hole in her temple. The police are called and spend their time going over Trandem's love letters to Lilah. The phone rings and the police answer. It is from the Jessie Fredrica Mission— the boys miss Lilah. Will she be coming down soon? Not likely is the answer.

Johnny goes to the rescue mission and talks to Miss Fredrica, who mistakes Johnny for a client, even though he is pretty clean. Johnny tells her of the two murders and arranges to hang around and talk to the boys. Johnny spends his afternoon talking with a lot of confused old men. Johnny strikes up a conversation with "Little Ben" who knew Trandem. Ben knew Trandem, and he had given Ben tips in the market, but he had lost it all. But Trandem had worked his way back up from the bottom. Ben points to one man at the mission who hated Trandem and Lilah more than everyone else, Bill Sanderson. Trandem and Sanderson were partners, but Trandem had cheated him out of his brokerage business and sent Sanderson to skid row.

Johnny goes to get some dinner and finds Little Ben dead upon his return. Sanderson then approaches Johnny and takes him from the mission at knifepoint. In an old storefront, Sanderson tries to work Johnny over but Johnny eventually gets the upper hand. When Johnny confronts Sanderson with the killings of Trandem and Lilah, he manages to escape. Johnny calls the police and then goes back to talk to Mabel.

Max the bodyguard meets Johnny and tells Johnny that he has been fired. Max spins a wild story to Johnny, who is skeptical. Johnny agrees to let him tag along "on the swindle sheet." Johnny finds Mabel with a new cat and she tells Johnny that she does not know Sanderson. When Johnny sees a letter from Sanderson and plane tickets for 6:00, she pulls a gun and tells Johnny that Sanderson had killed Trandem for her. She tells Johnny that she should have married him first. Mabel does not believe Johnny when he tells her that Sanderson has killed Lilah and Ben. She locks Johnny in the library and leaves. Johnny calls Max, who was taking a nap and fires him! Johnny runs out in time to see Mabel driving away. Johnny calls the police and advises them of what is happening. Johnny notes that there are too many cab rides on his expense report and asks they can send a car for him and take him to the airport. Lt. Vincelli and Johnny wait at the gate but they do not show up. Johnny notes he felt "like Drew Pearson when his predictions come true." Johnny and Vincelli then go to a roadblock south of Capistrano and wait. After dark, a car breaks through the roadblock and Johnny and Vincelli give chase. Johnny manages to shoot out a tire with a rifle and the car crashes killing both Sanderson and Mabel.

After a week, Johnny gets ready to leave. He visits Miss Fredrica at the mission and gives her a gift in the form of a check for $1,150,000. The mission had been the second beneficiary of the policy.

NOTES:
- CAST INFORMATION FROM RadioGOLDINdex
- ROY ROWAN IS THE ANNOUNCER
- THE MID-PROGRAM COMMERCIAL IS FOR "DOCTOR CHRISTIAN," A PROGRAM WRITTEN BY THE AUDIENCE
- THE INSURANCE POLICY WOULD BE WORTH OVER **$9,600,000** IN 2006 DOLLARS
- DREW PEARSON WAS A POLITICAL MUCKRAKER DURING THE 1940's AND 50's
- JOHNNY MAKES A REFERENCE THAT THERE ARE TOO MANY CAB RIDES ON HIS EXPENSE ACCOUNT

Producer: Unknown   **Writers:** Unknown
Cast: Eda Reiss Merin, Edwin Max, Gloria Blondell, James Eagles, Junius Matthews, Raymond Burr, Ted Osborne

SHOW: THE SIDNEY RYKOFF MATTER
SHOW DATE: 5/16/1950
COMPANY: EAST COAST UNDERWRITERS
AGENT: EDWARD HOLLY
EXP. ACCT: $982.28

SYNOPSIS: Edward Holly calls Johnny. Johnny is told that East Coast has a policy on Sidney Rykoff who is a pugilist and who has been kidnapped.

Johnny goes to see Mr. Holly who tells Johnny that Rykoff will die in seven hours at midnight if the $25,000 in ransom is not paid. This is a delicate matter and the police have not been called. Rykoff also has a policy for $100,000, so the payoff is an easy decision for the company. Johnny gets the money, a list of serial numbers and charters a plane to Kansas City, Kansas. Over Ohio the plane runs into a storm, and the pilot wants to land. Johnny tells him there will be a dead man in the morning if he does not get to Kansas City.

Johnny arrives in Kansas City at 11:40 and goes to the designated place in a local cemetery and is met by a man. Johnny gives the money to the man and is told he will be told where Rykoff is.

The next morning Johnny goes to the Southern Athletic club, Rykoff's "headquarters" and talks to Madill, his manager who says that Rykoff is probably out drunk somewhere. Johnny is told that Rykoff likes to drink bourbon and milk when he is in training. Rykoff has a good right cross but has not been doing too good lately. His wife is a nice person but can be a demon. She bosses Rykoff around. If Rykoff loses, he sleeps in the hall.

On the way out, Al Basumian approaches Johnny. Al tells Johnny that it is not time for Rykoff's binge. Rykoff's next binge is not due until September. Al tells Johnny that he handles bets for the fighters.

Johnny goes to see the wife and tells her that her husband has been kidnapped. She tells Johnny that Rykoff comes in when ever he feels like it. Johnny asks who knew of the $100,000 policy, and only his manager Madill and her knew about it. She tells Johnny that she does not hang around with losers and did not arrange to kidnap Sidney. A man named Mickey Snell comes in and Mrs. Rykoff yells at him for losing a fight. She backs him out of the apartment and reaches for a wrought iron candlestick on the mantle but Mickey runs. Johnny leaves and follows Mickey to a bar. Mickey tells Johnny that he knows Rykoff and had been beaten by him a couple of times. Mickey tells Johnny that Rykoff was winning now. Johnny arranges to meet Mickey at his hotel later. Johnny goes outside and waits to follow Mickey. Mickey comes out and at a street corner a car runs Mickey down. Johnny tells the police what he saw and the story about Rykoff. The police search Mickey's pockets and find only his ID and a lot of cash. Johnny looks at one of the bills, and it is a fifty from the ransom money.

Johnny reviews the evidence and considers that Mickey died either because of Al Basumian's gambling ventures, the insurance held by Madill, or the old "kidnap yourself and collect the ransom" racket, the latter being the most probable. The next morning Johnny walks to Rykoff's apartment and confronts the wife with the kidnapping plan. She tells Johnny that she is tired of hearing about Rykoff. Rykoff had a lousy contract with Madill, so there was no way to win much. Johnny tells her that she is in debt and needs money so maybe she faked the kidnapping, wrote the ransom note and would collect twice. The police show up and tell her that Rykoff's body has been found on the highway. There is little reaction in her face as she gets the news. She tells Johnny that she feels like she did when she got paroled for burglary and "a couple of other things." She did not know if Rykoff loved her or hated her but he fought when she taunted him.

Johnny goes to the morgue and looks at the body and learns that the cause of death was a heavy instrument to his head.

The next morning, Johnny gets an early call from Al Basumian asking him to come over immediately. Johnny goes to Al's place, where Johnny is taken to the basement and shown a gold trophy with caked blood on it, hidden in a box of ashes. Al tells Johnny that he was cleaning the furnace when he found it. Johnny asks Al if he made up the plan for a cover and tells him to call the police. Al pulls a gun instead. On the way up the steps Johnny elbows the light switch and ducks as Al shoots at him. Johnny over powers Al and leaves him out cold on the floor. Johnny picks up the trophy and heads to Rykoff's apartment. Johnny should have called the police and left town, but he had to resolve the insurance and the ransom money. The door is open when he gets there and the wife is talking to some one with a familiar voice. Johnny goes down the street and calls the police and tells them to give him five minutes. Johnny sneaks in the apartment, places the trophy in a clean spot on the mantle and lights a cigarette. The wife comes in and Johnny suggests that there is something different in the room and points to the mantle. She sees the trophy and tells Johnny that no one is going to stop them. Mrs. Rykoff tries to hit Johnny, but he overpowers her. The man comes back and so do the police.

The wife confesses that she had killed Rykoff in an argument and had Larry hide the body. They sent in the ransom note and Larry collected the ransom. Larry also put the trophy in Basumian's basement.

The police also raid Basumian and shut down his gambling operation.

NOTES:
- MY PROGRAM IS A REHEARSAL
- THE MID-PROGRAM COMMERCIAL IS FOR BURNS AND ALLEN
- ROY ROWAN IS THE ANNOUNCER
- MUSIC IS BY LIETH STEVENS
- EDMUND O'BRIEN'S UPCOMING NEW MOVIE THE "LOS ANGLES STORY"

Producer:	Jaime del Valle	**Writers:**	Gil Doud, David Ellis
Cast:	Howard McNear, Howard Culver, Walter Burke, John McIntire, Bill Grey, Jeanette Nolan		

SHOW:	THE EARL CHADWICK MATTER
SHOW DATE:	5/23/1950
COMPANY:	TRI-STATE LIFE INSURANCE COMPANY
AGENT:	LELAND SCARF
EXP. ACCT:	$1,575.30

SYNOPSIS: The Ambassador Travel Agency calls and confirms Johnny's travel arrangements to travel to Bermuda on Pan American flight 134 from LaGuardia. The agent asks Johnny if he is going on vacation and Johnny tells her he is going there to look up a dead man.

Johnny goes to the Tri-State office to hear the story of a woman who has seen Earl Chadwick. Earl had embezzled $30,000 and disappeared in 1945. His wrecked boat was found and he was presumed drowned. Earl was declared dead in 1947. Johnny meets Mrs. Marshall, who had just been to Hamilton, Bermuda Mrs. Marshall knew Earl and saw him in a bar in Hamilton (they were slumming). She talked to him but he denied being Earl. Mrs. Marshall found out that Earl was using the name of George Brewster. Johnny is told that the wife, Grace, had remarried to a business associate of Chadwick.

Johnny goes to Bermuda and checks in with the local police. Johnny learns from the chief inspector that the Brewster character is clean. Johnny goes to his hotel and memorizes the picture of Chadwick. That night Johnny goes to the bar where Chadwick was last seen. After several hours, the man comes in. Johnny takes him to his table and explains why he is there. Brewster tells Johnny about meeting some old fat dame who thought she knew him, and agrees to meet Johnny at noon the next day at his house.

Johnny goes to the address and a woman answers the door. She lets him in, and Johnny looks over the papers left there. Brewster comes back and Earl now agrees to go back to Johnny's hotel, where he outlines the whole story. He had embezzled $10,000 and given the money to his wife, who was supposed to meet him in Mexico City after the insurance policy had been paid. But, she never showed up. Chadwick is now ready to go back to the states.

Johnny and Earl fly to New York and go to the home of his former wife Grace, and her husband Harold Anderson. Grace and Harold deny that the man with Johnny is Earl. Johnny leaves and asks about proof of his identity, but Earl has destroyed a lot of his records. Johnny tells Earl to go to his former dentist and get a full set of x-rays. Earl tells Johnny that he can be trusted but, just to be sure, Johnny hires a detective, Landreau, to follow Earl. Later Johnny goes to see the dentist, Dr. Homer Fields who gets Earl's old x-rays and compares them to the ones just taken and there is no match. Johnny questions the dentist about possible robberies of the records or mis-filings to no avail. Johnny asks where someone would go to get a set of x-rays. Dr. Fields tells Johnny that a dentist would only give x-rays to someone if they were their own. Johnny thanks him and leaves.

Johnny then goes in search of a paper trail for Earl at the hall of records and the police and finds nothing. Johnny checks with Landreau who reports that Earl had gotten wise to him. He followed Chadwick and saw him purchase a gun at a pawnshop. Johnny goes to the Anderson's hoping Earl is not there. The Anderson's are sure that someone has discovered the details of the case and is impersonating Earl. The man knows too much, Johnny says, to be an impostor. Johnny tells them that Earl has only made one mistake. Earl admits to taking $10,000 but $30,000 was taken.

Johnny goes back to the hotel and finds Earl there with the gun. He tells Johnny that he was scared, and being Brewster was getting dull. Johnny takes the gun away from him. Johnny tells Earl that the x-rays did not match and is sure that Anderson had switched them. Landreau calls and Johnny arranges for him to get a fake driver's license for $500. Johnny has Landreau call Anderson and tell him he has proof that Earl is alive and the proof is for sale. Anderson arranges to come to the office. Anderson arrives at 11:30 as Johnny and Earl watch from the back room. Anderson agrees to pay Landreau $15,000 for the license. Anderson has $1,500 with him and reaches for the money only to pull a gun. Johnny rushes out and Anderson kills Earl. The police are called and the Armstrongs give their statement confessing their crime. The wife had convinced Earl to steal the $10,000 and Harold had taken an additional $20,000. Johnny is not proud if his part, but he was paid to find a dead man.

NOTES:
- CAST INFORMATION FROM RadioGOLDINdex
- ROY ROWAN IS THE ANNOUNCER

Producer: **Writers:**
Cast: **Lillian Buyeff, Tudor Owen, Virginia Gregg, Walter Burke, John Dehner, Ben Wright, Ted Osborne**

◆   ❖   ◆

SHOW:	THE PORT AU PRINCE MATTER
SHOW DATE:	5/30/1950
COMPANY:	AMERICAN FEDERATED LIFE INSURANCE COMPANY
AGENT:	HARVARD HUNTINGTON
EXP. ACCT:	$424.70

SYNOPSIS: Dr. Colby calls and tells Johnny that he is behind on his shots and needs booster for diphtheria, small pox, typhoid, cholera and tetanus, if he can find room. Johnny asks where he is going to get the shots, as it is a long flight to Haiti, and the plane seats are uncomfortable, at best.

Johnny is called, just as he is about to go to a show to see Detective Story, to the home of Mr. Harvard Huntington. Harvey tells Johnny that Ralph Gordon, the black sheep scion of the wealthy Hartford Gordon's, is insured for $150,000. Ralph is on his boat in Haiti and is dying of, and this is pure nonsense, of a voodoo curse. Harvey got his information from Ralph's older brother Thomas, who is a doctor and also in Haiti, reported the information.

Johnny flies to Port au Prince, Haiti, buys some tropical clothes, and goes in search of someone to help find Gordon's boat. In a bar Johnny runs into Cap Regan, who tells Johnny that he has been there since before repeal, courtesy of a couple of prohibition agents. Cap tells Johnny that he can pay Cap to row Johnny out to Gordon's boat. Johnny tells Cap that he is with an insurance company. Cap tells Johnny that Gordon has been here for two months, and everyone on the crew has left. Gordon was always drunk and the crew refused to sail with him. Johnny is shown the boat and Cap tells him it is as filthy as a scow. At the boat, Johnny is met by a woman in a pair of clam diggers and an off-shoulder tee shirt. The woman tells Johnny that she is Edwina, Ralph's wife. When Johnny explains why he is there and asks to see Ralph, she agrees and takes Johnny below. Johnny only gets as far as the cabin door where he is met by abusive shouts and cries for more wine. Johnny mentions the curse and Edwina tells Johnny that a man called Papa Luar has put a curse on Ralph after he cursed at him. Edwina knows Thomas and they hate each other. Edwina gets angry when Johnny suggests she is after the money and the ship's bos'n invites Johnny to leave. Johnny goes to see Thomas Gordon at the Hotel Francois, who agrees that the voodoo curse is trash and requires only a susceptible mind. Thomas tells Johnny that Ralph is only looking for escape through alcohol. "Let me know what you learn" are the reassuring words of the good doctor as Johnny leaves.

Johnny and Cap Regan go in search of Papa Luar in a gathering storm and find him in a hut in a cane field. Johnny goes down a path to Papa Luar. Inside the hut Papa Luar tells Johnny that Gordon will die tonight in the wind and rain, and his magic is the key. When Johnny doubts him magic, he throws something into the fire that causes Johnny to stagger out of the hut gasping for breath and nearly passing out. When Johnny recovers he goes into the hut and finds small pieces of photographic film. Johnny notes that film made of cellulose and nitrates puts out nitric oxide and nitrogen dioxide when burned. A combination that would meet the demands of any gas chamber.

Johnny and Cap goes back to the yacht in a gathering storm. On the boat, Johnny overhears Edwina talking to the bos'n. When he comes on deck Johnny knocks him out. Johnny then accuses Edwina of plotting with Papa Luar and the bos'n to kill Ralph, which she denies. Edwina tells Johnny that she is tired of her husband drinking himself to death and is only plotting to divorce Ralph and marry the bos'n. Johnny and Edwina lock up the bos'n go back to Papa Luar who does not know who Edwina is. Johnny confronts him with the film scam. When threatened with the police he admits that a man put him up to the phony curse. Papa tells Johnny that the man needs the storm so that the portholes on the boat will be closed. The man had also given Papa the film to use on Johnny. Edwina tells Johnny that only the food, which she cooks, and champagne is brought onto the boat. Johnny goes to the local liquor shop learns that a case of champagne has just been sent to the boat, packed in dry ice. A call to Thomas confirms that dry ice in a closed cabin could asphyxiate a drunken man. Johnny tells him to send for a pullmotor. If it is too late, maybe he can use it

Johnny finds Regan and Johnny gets him to row out to the boat in the storm. When they near the boat, Regan is shot in the leg and Johnny decides to swim for the boat. When Johnny gets to the boat, dear brother Thomas is holding a rifle on Johnny! The bos'n pushes Thomas off of the boat, and Johnny breaks down the door to Ralph's cabin and carries him up to fresh air. Johnny gives Ralph artificial respiration to save a policyholder.

Thomas goes to jail (he wanted control of the family fortune, not Ralph's insurance). Ralph and Regan go to the hospital. Johnny buys a bottle of voodoo perfume for Edwina. Hopefully she will use it on her husband.

NOTES:
- THIS PROGRAM IS ESSENTIALLY THE SAME SCRIPT AS THE CHARLES RUSSELL VERSION OF 12/17/1949, WITHOUT HIS WISE CRACKS.
- THE CAP REGAN CHARACTER SPEAKS WITH A BRITISH ACCENT.
- THE VOODOO SHAMAN IS CALLED PAPA LUAR.
- A PULLMOTOR IS AN AMBULANCE WITH A SPECIAL RESPIRATION UNIT ON IT
- THE MID-PROGRAM COMMERCIAL IS FOR THE GROUCHO MARX PROGRAM ON WEDNESDAY
- ROY ROWAN IS THE ANNOUNCER AND PLUGS O'BRIEN'S UPCOMING MOVIE "711 OCEAN DRIVE"
- MUSIC IS BY LIETH STEVENS

Producer: Jaime del Valle   **Writers:**   Gil Doud, David Ellis
Cast: Willard Waterman, Earl Lee, Ted de Corsia, Charlotte Lawrence, Lou Krugman, Byron Kane, Dick Ryan, Clayton Post

SHOW: THE CALIGIO DIAMOND MATTER
SHOW DATE: 6/8/1950
COMPANY: INTERCOMMERCIAL INSURANCE COMPANY OF AMERICA
AGENT: HENRY GLACEN
EXP. ACCT: $65.34

SYNOPSIS: Henry Glacen calls to ask Johnny if he has heard of the Caligio Diamond. Henry tells Johnny that the $200,000 Caligio diamond is missing. The owner, Mr. Benson was found murdered the previous evening.

Johnny goes to the Benson residence in Hartford, Connecticut and meets with the daughter, Betty. She tells Johnny that her father had purchased the diamond in Italy three years earlier in Italy for $200,000. Johnny is told that the stone has a strange history as all of its owners have died violently. She tells Johnny that she was out with her fiancé until 3:00 AM and found her father in the library when she came home. Her father kept the stone in his safe. Only her father, her mother and the family attorney, Mr. Corrigan, who has free access to the house, knew the combination.

Johnny goes to meet with Mr. Corrigan. During a brief discussion interrupted by phone calls, Johnny learns that Benson and Corrigan had been schoolmates and Corrigan had last seen Benson two weeks earlier. Mrs. Benson arrives and Johnny is escorted out the back office door, but he stays to listen. "Darling, you look lovely in black," he tells Mrs. Benson as he kisses her and Johnny listens. Johnny hears that Corrigan is divorcing his wife and they will go to Bermuda when they get married. Johnny tries to leave but trips on the carpet and is caught by Corrigan and Mrs. Benson. After some "small talk" about ethics, Johnny agrees to keep the meeting from the police, for the time being.

On the street Johnny is stopped by a man, who offers him information. The man pulls a gun and tells Johnny to get into a car and then slugs him. Johnny wakes up in his torn up apartment with both his head and the phone ringing. Henry Glacen wants an update, but all he gets is a request for a doctor from Johnny who passes out. Henry comes over and tells Johnny that he does not want the police called. Johnny feels that the man who slugged him is looking for something.

Betty calls to say that the police have found the gun that killed her father, in her purse!

Johnny gets to police headquarters and meets with Lt. Parnell, an old buddy, who is on the case. Johnny is told that Corrigan is on the way, and that Betty's prints are all over the gun, but she knows nothing about it. She tells Johnny that she has not used that purse for a long time. Corrigan and Bob Gorman, the fiancé, show up and everyone starts questioning everyone else's motives. When asked if Corrigan had visited with Mrs. Benson, he claims the Fifth Amendment.

Johnny leaves and goes to Corrigan's apartment and finds an IOU from Benson for $2,000. He goes to Bob Gorman's apartment and finds a bill from a detective agency. Johnny then goes to police headquarters and finds a picture of a tall, thin man with a well-trimmed moustache.

Back at his apartment, Johnny finds a tall, thin man with a well-trimmed moustache drinking his bourbon ("This is lousy bourbon!"). The man wants the diamond and starts to leave. After the man tries to shoot Johnny, he slaps him around to find out what his angle is, but his story changes several times. Originally he worked for Corrigan, and then Mrs. Benson and finally he tells Johnny that he works for the Gorman Detective Agency. Johnny tells him that his name is Vic, and that Gorman had hired him to get the stone, but when he got there it was gone and Benson was dead. Vic had slugged Johnny because he thought that Johnny had the diamond. Johnny calls Bob Gorman and asks him to come over. When Bob gets there Johnny tells him that he had just talked to his employee Vic Hastings. Bob denies hiring Bob, but admits that he hired Hastings to find the stone, because he wanted it. He had crashed a party to case the house, but ended up falling for Betty. Gorman pulls a gun and excuses himself. Johnny calls Lt. Parnell and asks him to arrest Bob Gorman. Johnny goes back to the Benson house and confronts Mrs. Benson. She tells Johnny that she knows who has the diamond. She tells Johnny that Gorman had a violent temper. Johnny accuses her of framing Berry with the gun when Corrigan shows up. Johnny overpowers Corrigan takes him to the police.

Johnny states that this case hinged on a big guess that paid off. Mrs. Benson and Corrigan confess to the robbery. The police get Gorman and Hastings. Betty will probably be looking for a new boyfriend.

As for the expense account, "that's pretty cheap."

NOTES:
- THE TITLE OF THIS PROGRAM IS CHANGED, BASED ON THE SCRIPT TITLE PAGE.

- AT THE END THERE IS A STATEMENT THAT "I TOLD THEM MY GUESS AND WITH THE AUTHORITY OF AN ILLINOIS JUDGE THEY SWALLOWED IT." THIS IS EITHER AN OBSCURE AXIOM OR A SCRIPTING ERROR AS THE CASE TAKES PLACE IN HARTFORD.
- ROY ROWAN IS THE ANNOUNCER
- MUSIC IS BY LIETH STEVENS

Producer: Jaime del Valle   **Writers:**   Gil Doud, David Ellis
Cast: Wally Maher, Jane Webb, Bill Johnstone, Virginia Gregg, Stacy Harris, Bill Bouchey, Harry Bartell

◆　❖　◆

SHOW: THE ARROWCRAFT MATTER
SHOW DATE: 6/15/1950
COMPANY: GRAND EAST LIFE AND LIABILITY INSURANCE COMPANY
AGENT: MILLARD SNELL
EXP. ACCT: $940.20

SYNOPSIS: Mr. Snell's secretary calls Johnny about the policies on the three missing Arrowcraft cruisers. In the past two weeks three have sunk with no survivors. The next of kin are each suing for a million dollars.

Johnny flies to Los Angeles, California, rents a car and drives to Newport Beach where Mr. Snell has chartered a boat. They are going out to find the latest boat to be hit. Snell tells Johnny that another boat has been lost. So far that is four boats that have been lost with eleven fatalities with only seven bodies recovered.

At dawn they find the boat awash in the ocean swells. Johnny goes aboard and finds the body of a young girl floating face down in the cabin. Johnny examines the boat and the body, which has a strange bruise behind the ear. The body is taken to the charter boat and they head back. Snell is upset at finding the girl. Johnny tells Snell that he boat was registered to Chester McNeal. After talking to the police, Johnny goes to talk to Dr. Saine at the morgue. Johnny is told that the girl was Antonia Caruso, who was identified by her mother. Johnny mentions the bruise and the doctor agrees that a gun might have caused the bruise, and the hair braids might have softened the blow. Johnny wonders if she might have been thrown overboard and been alive and climbed back into the boat and died. Without the permission of the family there would be no autopsy.

Johnny goes to see the girl's mother, who is deeply upset. The daughter was going to marry Chester McNeal, whose father owned the boat. Chester loved her and she had worked hard to make sure that Antonia had what her parents didn't.

Back at the hotel, Mr. Snell is white-faced. Johnny learns that Fred Crocker, the local Arrowcraft agent has been killed in a hit-and-run accident. The papers relate that the Arrowcraft office had been ransacked earlier that day.

Johnny goes to the Arrowcraft office and looks through the papers for a list of customers, which is missing. Johnny is sure that someone is looking for something and killing people in the process. Johnny thinks that Crocker was in the office when it was searched and killed later.

Johnny throws a little party for members of the local press, and gets them to print a story based on what he thinks is happening. The next day the story runs, along with one about a night watchman who is in the hospital after catching a prowler on an Arrowcraft boat. At the jail Johnny questions the prowler, Jerry La Barber, but he is a hard character and says nothing to Johnny, besides his lawyer is on the way. Johnny is sure that La Barber is hiding something.

Johnny is able to contact 2 Arrowcraft owners and searches their boats and finds nothing. Johnny and Snell head back to the hotel with a bottle of Cognac to mourn the death of the night watchman.

Later, a woman calls Johnny from a phone booth and wants Johnny to meet her at a bar in Long Beach. She has something to say. Johnny carefully goes to the bar, and is met by a man with a gun who escorts him outside to a car where the girl, Gwen, is driving. They drive to a secluded area where Gwen tells her story. Johnny is told that a man named George Masterson runs a chain of furniture stores, which is a front for the Mafia. She has written down everything she knows and told Masterson that the letter was hidden on an Arrowcraft boat. She feels that all the deaths are her fault because she just picked the Arrowcraft name out of the air. She did not go the police because she has a record.

Gwen gives the letter to Johnny and drives away. Johnny gets a hotel room, and reads the letter, the hottest document in California! The next morning Johnny mails the letter to the FBI. Johnny then goes to Masterson's office and beats him for the death of the boating victims, and then calls the police.

The FBI puts Gwen in protective custody. The crime ring is broken, and so far the DA has 75 counts against Masterson.

NOTES:
- THIS IS THE FIRST PROGRAM FOR THE WRIGLEY GUM MANUFACTURERS, WHO SPONSORS THE PROGRAM FOR SEVERAL YEARS.
- ALL COMMERCIALS FOR THE WRIGLEY PROGRAMS ARE FOR WRIGLEY GUM.
- EDMOND O'BRIEN CAN SOON BE SEEN IN "711 OCEAN DRIVE."
- BOB STEVENSON IS THE ANNOUNCER
- MUSIC IS BY LIETH STEVENS

Producer: Jaime del Valle   **Writers:** Gil Doud, David Ellis
Cast: Howard McNear, Jeanne Bates, Clayton Post, Harry Bartell, Hy Averback, John McIntire, Jeanette Nolan

◆ ❖ ◆

SHOW: THE LONDON MATTER
SHOW DATE: 6/22/1950
COMPANY: U.S. TREASURY DEPARTMENT
AGENT: MARK NELSON

EXP. ACCT: **$1,580.20**

SYNOPSIS: Mark Nelson calls to ask Johnny to assist the Treasury Department with a smuggling ring. Johnny goes to the Commonwealth Hotel and gets the details from Mark. The Feds have allowed a shipment of drugs from India to enter the country via Seattle, and then on to Beverly Hills to the home of the actress Dorothy Rivers and her director husband Broderick Green. Now, they are going to London, England to make a picture and their trunks are the only things that have left the house. Only one person, Lorraine Miller the confidential secretary, is going with the trunks, the other servants having been discharged.

Johnny goes on board the boat, and gets final instructions from Mark. Johnny is told that Inspector Finch of Scotland Yard will meet him in England. The ship's detective Clarence Doud has been told Johnny would contact him. Also, Lorraine Miller's brother is on the boat traveling under the name Miles Fanning.

Johnny meets the hazel eyed, auburn haired Lorraine and explains why he is there. When she tells Johnny how exciting his job must be, he tells her "I once got to baby sit a pig named Rollo who had swallowed a brooch."* They arrange to have drinks and dinner in her suite that night. After dinner they are talking in Johnny's stateroom when a porthole suddenly opens and Johnny sees a man's face. Johnny is told that the man he saw was her ex-husband and he will have to leave and not see her any more on the boat.

Johnny goes to see the ship's detective and asks him to keep an eye on Fanning. Johnny will check back with him every night. For five nights Johnny has to deal with watching the passengers.

On the night before docking, Lorraine comes to see Johnny and apologies for her behavior. The phone rings and Johnny disguises a call from Doud, (who reports to Johnny that Lorraine and Fanning had met after dinner) as a request for a fourth at bridge. Lorraine leaves and Johnny pours himself a long drink. As soon as he tastes the drink Johnny knows he has been drugged.

Johnny wakes up to the voices of a doctor and another man who turns out to be Inspector Finch. Johnny tells them that Lorraine probably drugged the whiskey while he was on the phone. Finch tells Johnny that everyone is off the boat. The trunks were taken to their destination, and will be unpacked by Scotland Yard agents. Also, Fanning is being followed.

Finch takes Johnny to his flat to recover. That afternoon a call comes in and the police report to Finch that the trunks are empty of drugs. Johnny and Finch go to the Yard to get the names of possible purchasers for the drugs. Mark Nelson calls and Johnny updates him on the lack of drugs in the trucks. Mark will call the states to double check that the drugs actually left.

A call comes in with the news that the man following Fanning has been shot. Finch issues Johnny a gun to replace his, which he left on the boat, and they head to the flat to Fanning's flat to find Doud dead. The police officer tells Johnny and Finch that Fanning was carrying a portmanteau when he left. Johnny surmised that Doud had carried the drugs off the ship, taken them to Fanning and argued over the split and Fanning shot him.

Johnny and Finch go to Lorraine's flat but she is not there. They wait for a while and she shows up. Johnny confronts her that he knows who Fanning is. She breaks down and tells Johnny that her brother came back a different man after the war, and was always in trouble. She tells Johnny that Fanning is on his way to Tangiers. Johnny and Finch get the name of the ship and head there. After ensuring that the crew is off the boat, the police go on, and in the usual hail of bullets Fanning is killed and the drugs recovered.

Johnny arranges that Fanning's is the only name that will hit the papers.

NOTES:
- DETECTIVE DOUD IS WEARING "CONGRESS GAITERS"—ELASTIC-SIDED LOW BOOTS
- ROLLO THE PIG WAS IN THE CHARLES RUSSELL PROGRAM OF 8/21/49
- RadioGOLDINdex NOTES THAT TUDOR OWEN AND BEN WRIGHT PLAY DOUBLE PARTS IN THIS SHOW
- BOB STEVENSON IS THE ANNOUNCER
- MUSIC IS BY LIETH STEVENS

Producer: Jaime del Valle   Writers: Gil Doud, David Ellis
Cast: Wally Maher, Virginia Gregg, Herb Butterfield, Dan
            O'Herlihy, Tudor Owen, Ben Wright, Alec Harper

◆   ❖   ◆

SHOW: THE BARBARA JAMES MATTER
SHOW DATE: 6/29/1950
COMPANY: MONARCH LIFE INSURANCE COMPANY
AGENT: FRANK GABER
EXP. ACCT: $344.59
SYNOPSIS: Frank calls and asks if Johnny is free for a week. Mrs. Martin James has disappeared in Denver. Her husband is a wealthy contractor and she is insured for $200,000. Johnny hopes she is not dead, but Frank tells him the police say there is little possibility of anything else.

Johnny flies to Denver, Colorado to look into the disappearance of Mrs. Barbara James. Johnny meets with Detective Lt. Harrison and gets the details of the case. Mr. James is 50 and had married Barbara, who is 28, three years ago in Reno. Mrs. James first husband was under contract to a movie studio. Mr. James had given her everything she wanted to keep her happy. She was reported missing 6 weeks ago and there has been no trace of her since.

Johnny goes to James' mansion and meets a very old looking Martin James. James tells Johnny that he does not know why she ran off. She married him for money and he married her for her youth. James tells Johnny that he had come home one night and quarreled with her. She left and has not been seen since. James does not know any of her friends, but maybe Johnny should talk to Bennett at the Yellow Bird Café and Nightclub. James always felt that Bennett was the first one on her list. James tells Johnny "if you find her, tell her she need not come back."

Johnny goes to see Bennett at the Yellow Bird café, a blue-lighted nightspot. Bennett tells Johnny that he does not know where she is. Bennett tells Johnny that he had been seeing her at one time, but she gave him the brush. "I hope you find her dead." Johnny talks to a girl at the dice tables. She confirms that Barbara had given Bennett the brush. She also tells Johnny that Bennett started his place with money he borrowed from Barbara. Johnny also tells Johnny that Barbara's first husband, Fred Vogel, is in town. Bennett stops Johnny and asks him what the girl told him. Johnny mentions the husband and tells Bennett not to fire the girl.

Johnny goes to Vogel's hotel and follows him into his room at 3 AM. Vogel tells Johnny that he has not seen Barbara for over three years. Vogel tells Johnny that he had gone to New York to make money and she was gone when he came home. Vogel has been in town for two months. Vogel tells Johnny that came to town to see Barbara but he was afraid to see her, now he can't leave until she is found.

Next morning Lt. Harrison calls to report that Dorothy Weller, a dice girl from the Yellow Bird, was found on the highway shot four times. Johnny and Harrison go to the apartment of the girl. In the girl's closet Johnny and Harrison find a lot of expensive clothes. A call to the store where they were sold, Martin Rifling, tells Harrison that Dorothy had made over $3,000 in purchases and paid the bill herself.

Johnny goes to see Bennett again and accuses him of killing Dorothy because she was blackmailing him over Barbara James. Bennett tells Johnny that he and Barbara were going to run off and Dorothy was sent to tell Barbara where to meet him. Johnny accuses Bennett of paying money to Dorothy to keep quiet about him and Barbara and suspects that some one was paying Dorothy to keep quiet about what happened at the James house.

Johnny goes back to the James place and demands the truth. By the swimming pool, Johnny tells James that he came home to find Barbara packing to leave with Bennett, and Dorothy was with her. When Johnny tells James that Dorothy is dead, he admits that he came home to find Barbara packing. There was a big fight, and he was paying Dorothy to keep quiet about the quarrel. Johnny and the police now focus on murder and search the estate several times over the next three weeks, with James following along and smiling.

Johnny is looking on the patio one day when Mr. Dolf comes up and asks to clean the pool. Dolf tells Johnny that he had designed and built the pool. It is made of steel and gunnite. A real quality job. He had started on May 23 and sprayed the gunnite on May 26. Mr. James wanted the pool filled in 10 days, but Dolf told him that gunnite needed 28 days to cure. So on the 25th, when Barbara disappeared, the pool was just a hole in the ground! Johnny shocks Dolf by telling him to dig up the pool! James laughs at Johnny and his police order and tells Johnny that he will have his job. When the bottom of the pool is dug up, Dolf finds a loose area underneath. Johnny and Lt. Harrison dig in the loose soil and find a grave. James tries to run away and holds Johnny at bay with a gun.

Johnny takes the gun away from him and tells Harrison that James will not need a new swimming pool.

Martin James had buried by Barbara James under the pool. It was a good tomb. Made to last a lifetime, but it was not deep enough.

NOTES:

- GUNNITE IS A FINE CEMENT WHICH IS APPLIED UNDER PRESSURE FROM A SPRAY GUN.
- BOB STEVENSON IS THE ANNOUNCER, AND PLUGS "711 OCEAN DRIVE."
- MUSIC IS BY LIETH STEVENS

Producer: Jaime del Valle   Writers: Gil Doud, David Ellis
Cast: Howard McNear, Parley Baer, Jack Moyles, Jean Spaulding, Jay Novello, Stacy Harris

◆ ❖ ◆

SHOW: THE BELLO-HORIZONTE RAILROAD
SHOW DATE: 7/6/1950
COMPANY: SWANSON INDUSTRIAL INSURANCE CORPORATION
AGENT: GEORGE DONNELLY
EXP. ACCT: $1,492.54

SYNOPSIS: George Donnelly calls and tells Johnny that they are having engine trouble. Swanson has a substantial policy on the Bello-Horizonte Railroad, but losses have been extensive. They have conflicting reports and it is either insurance fraud or murder. Johnny tells him that either his luck, it is probably both.

Johnny travels to Rio de Janeiro, Brazil, Brazil to look into a series of accidents on the Bello-Horizonte Railroad. In Rio, Johnny meets with Benjamin Hulley, president of the railroad, who is in the hospital. Hulley tells Johnny that there have been four accidents killing 20 people. One set of reports says they were accidents; one says sabotage. Johnny is told that the railroad hauls manganese, and Peter Yaradan is the main competition. Yaradan has offered to buy Hulley out, and has spread rumors, but Hulley tells Johnny that he will never sell. Johnny arranges to investigate, and Hulley arranges for a car and driver.

Johnny is assigned a driver named Sica, who tells Johnny who he is and why he is there—but he will not find anything. Sica tells Johnny that he is not really a driver; he is a poet. Sica takes Johnny to meet with Henry Meyers, who had filed the accident reports. His wife tells Johnny that Henry knew nothing about the busted pins. Henry comes in and tells Johnny that he knew the pins were sawed but let the locomotives go out anyway. He was scared and reported the wreck as an accident. Another man saw them too and let the train out, but Johnny will have to find out who that man was. Johnny goes back to the hotel and waits, while playing Monopoly with Sica. Henry Meyers calls and tells Johnny to come back as he is ready to talk. Johnny goes back to find Meyers shot. Before he dies, he tells Johnny "Go to Vervita." Johnny tells Mrs. Meyers that

Henry is dead and she rushes in screaming that she knew they would get him. While Johnny is talking to Meyer's wife about who Vervita is, a man with a gun comes to take them all to Mr. Yaradan. Yaradan holds a gun on Johnny and suggests that he should take a rest to help his investigation. Yaradan tells Johnny that all the stories Hulley tells about him are false. Yaradan suggests that Johnny should work for Yaradan, as the wages would be better while he was still alive. Johnny pulls a lamp over on Yaradan, jumps from a window and runs to the hotel. Johnny writes up an account of what he knows so far and leaves it with the notary in the San Carlos Hotel and sends a series of telegrams. Johnny then goes back to Yaradan and demands the release of Mrs. Meyers and his driver. Johnny tells Yaradan that he will have a report sent to the police if he is not back at the hotel in two hours with the others. He also wants an apology and information: who is Vervita? Yaradan tells Johnny that the railroad has been on the verge of bankruptcy for two years and has offered to buy Hulley out. Yaradan could use the railroad to consolidate his hold on the manganese fields and be a rich man. Yaradan tells Johnny that Hulley is sabotaging his own railroad. Yaradan offers $10,000 for Johnny not to file the report, but Johnny declines and they all leave.

Johnny learns from Mrs. Meyers that there was one survivor of the crashes, a man named Vervita. He is living in the mountains and only she knows where he is. Vervita was a fireman and saw someone pull a hand switch that put two locomotives on the same track. Johnny and Sica take a locomotive to the area and then walk to the cabin of Vervita. Mr. Vervita tells Johnny that Meyers was the one who pulled the wheel pins. Vervita is throwing Johnny out when he is shot. Johnny runs after the shooter, but he gets to the locomotive, overpowers the engineer and leaves. The locomotive is moving too fast and derails on a curve and crashes down an embankment. Johnny and Sica go over the wreckage and find a wallet. Inside is a card for the "Railway Engineers of South America," issued to Benjamin J. Hulley.

Johnny finds the car Hulley had driven to the cabin. Hulley is suspected to have hired Meyer's killer. The railroad is in receivership, and Yaradan was forced out of the country by public resentment at Johnny's report. Johnny notes that this case had him stumped right up to train time.

NOTES:
- BOB STEVENSON IS THE ANNOUNCER, AND PLUGS "711 OCEAN DRIVE."
- MUSIC IS BY LIETH STEVENS

Producer: Jaime del Valle   **Writers:** Gil Doud, David Ellis
Cast: Bob Griffin, Francis X. Bushman, Anthony Barrett, Martha Wentworth, Joe Du Val, Jack Kruschen, Ted de Corsia

SHOW: THE CALGARY MATTER
SHOW DATE: 7/13/1950

COMPANY:	**ALLIANCE BONDING COMPANY**
AGENT:	**MR. MATTHEWS**
EXP. ACCT:	**$1,180.00**

SYNOPSIS: Johnny gets a mysterious call from "Johnny Doe" about a robbery at Calgary Products in Camden. If he is interested, check the Alliance office and be home at 10:00 the next night.

Johnny goes to the Manhattan offices of Alliance Bonding to speak with Mr. Matthews who admits that there had been a robbery at Calgary, which had been kept quite due to similarities with another unsolved crime, the Brink robbery. Johnny gets the details on the robbery and Matthews gives Johnny clearance to work on the case.

That night Johnny gets a call from Philadelphia at 10:05 (the operator puts the call through). A girl tells Johnny not to call the police. She tells Johnny that a friend of the man who called Johnny wants to surrender to the New Jersey DA. If you are interested, go the Branford Hotel in Bridgeport, Connecticut and check in as Charles Randall from Boston, you will be contacted.

Johnny goes to the hotel, located on the waterfront, and checks in. Johnny is met by a man who tells him to leave only his car keys in the room and to come with him. The man tells Johnny that he is only helping someone out. They crisscross the area to make sure that Johnny has not been followed, and head towards Long Island. They drive down a dirt road and arrive at a cabin where a young girl meets Johnny. She tells Johnny that the man had decided to leave, as it was not best to meet yet. Johnny complains about a plot out of "dime detective," but the girl gives him a case containing money from the robbery. She tells Johnny that the man wants to turn state's evidence and that he wants immunity and protection. Johnny says it will take two days to see what he can arrange, but immunity is never offered. They will call Johnny daily at 10:00PM.

Johnny goes to Trenton and talks to the District Attorney. Johnny is told that immunity is out of the question, but protection can be arranged. Johnny drives home and waits. On the second day he gets a call from Boston instructing him to meet in a rural area north of Boston. Johnny is told that he is being followed but can lose them. Johnny is given instructions and drives to the area. Later that night a man who introduces himself as Gannett meets him. Gannett is not armed agrees to the terms offered by the DA, and they drive to Trenton watching for tails, but that is not the problem. When Johnny and Gannett get out of the car, Gannett yells "Al! No! Al Don't!" and is shot six times from the crowd. Later the police identify Gannett as Professor Arnold Gannett, LLD, Professor of Law at Russell University in New Haven!

Johnny now knows that the police have been looking in the wrong place! Johnny goes to the cabin on Long Island Sound and meets the man from the hotel. Johnny tells him that Gannett is dead, and Johnny is told that the girl is Gannett's wife. Johnny wakes the girl and tells her of Arnold's death. She cries and tells Johnny that she does not know who killed him. Johnny learns that the other man is Earl Becker, a gardener at the University who knew Gannett and fished with him. Gannett told him that he was involved in the robbery, and that

Gannett asked him to help him surrender. Mrs. Gannett tells Johnny that Gannett taught criminal psychology. His class had been discussing the Brink robbery and Gannett had a theory that it had been done by non-criminals. The theory grew into an obsession with him. He pulled the Calgary job to prove his theory. His students number in the 100's, but there is a list at his home.

Johnny, Earl, and the girl drive to the Gannett home in New Haven, Connecticut, while trying to beat the police. Johnny searches the files and finds a list or 100 names from the 1949-50 class, but there is one name that Johnny wants. Johnny slips out when the police arrive and goes to visit a particular name.

Johnny meets with Mr. Matthews of Alliance Bonding. His son Albert is packing for a canoe trip to Vermont. Johnny confronts Albert with the facts and he confesses to being involved, along with two other law students. Albert had used information from his father's insurance files to get the details.

Johnny wonders how many other crimes are committed by respectable people the police will not suspect.

NOTES:
- JOHNNY'S PHONE NUMBER IS "STanley 3469"
- JOHNNY'S CAR IS A GREEN COUPE.
- BOB STEVENSON IS THE ANNOUNCER, AND PLUGS "711 OCEAN DRIVE."
- MUSIC IS BY LIETH STEVENS

Producer: Jaime del Valle   Writers: Gil Doud, David Ellis
Cast: Ted Osborne, Florence Lake, Bill Bouchey, Virginia Gregg, John Dehner, Terry Kilburn

SHOW: THE HENRY J. UNGER MATTER
SHOW DATE: 7/20/1950
COMPANY: ASSOCIATED INSURANCE COMPANIES OF NEW ENGLAND
AGENT: CAL PORTER
EXP. ACCT: $50.39

SYNOPSIS: Cal Porter calls to warn Johnny that Henry J. Unger is out of prison and looking for Johnny there in Hartford, Connecticut. Cal wants Johnny on the payroll to look into Unger for them.

Johnny sends a night letter to the prison asking for details. The doorbell rings and Johnny finds Eileen Kennedy there. She comes in and Johnny makes her a drink. Eileen is a former girl friend and their conversation is polite but tense. She asks why Johnny sent her a telegram asking her to come here at 7:30? Johnny tells her that he did not send her a telegram. The doorbell rings and Johnny opens the door to find Henry J. Unger and another man, Ferdie, who invite them selves in. Eileen tries to leave, but is prevented from doing so by Unger. Ferdie ties Johnny to a chair, his sleeve is pulled up, and Ferdie sticks a needle into a "nice big blue bulgy vein" on his right arm and Johnny goes out.

When Johnny wakes up, he has a terrible hangover, his gun is in his hand and a dead Eileen is on the carpet. Johnny checks his gun, which has been fired twice, and his watch, which says 10:20PM—three hours since Unger had come. Johnny hears the maid yelling that he had killed her and calling for the police. Johnny staggers out of the apartment and makes his way to the home office of a friend, Dr. Norwich. The doctor takes a blood sample, a gastric analysis and suggests that Johnny had been injected with alcohol. Dr. Norwich tells Johnny that the injection could have been self-inflicted, and a good attorney could prove that. Johnny gets a "Swiss bath" of ice-cold water, some vitamins and coffee to sober up.

Johnny goes to the "Last Chance Café" to talk to an informant who tells Johnny, for twenty-five dollars, that Unger comes there daily. Unger walks in and Johnny confronts him. Johnny asks him if it was revenge. Unger says that Johnny will never be able to find any proof, as it was a perfect crime. Johnny pulls his gun to force a written confession but police Lt. Sawyer puts him under arrest for the murder of Eileen Kennedy.

At the jail a lawyer is called for Johnny, who recounts what happens to Sawyer, but cannot prove anything. Sawyer tells Johnny that Eileen was shot twice, and that gastric analysis showed she had alcohol in her system. The bullets match the gun Sawyer took from him, a .38 automatic. Johnny's lawyer, Joseph P. Harris talks to Johnny and they discuss the case. Johnny is unable to provide anything that will prove he is innocent. Johnny is told that it will be a tough one.

At the trial, "The State of Connecticut vs. John Dollar," Dr. Norwich testifies about the levels of alcohol in Johnny's blood and stomach. Rochelle Haberstan, Eileen's roommate, confirms that Eileen and Johnny were friends two years ago, and were going to get married. She testifies that Eileen had gotten a telegram, and hoped that Johnny would not ask her to marry him. Lt. Harvey Sawyer testifies that a search of the apartment found four empty liquor bottles each with a few drops left in them. Johnny is curious, as he only saw three bottles! Against his attorney's wishes Johnny asks to be put on the stand.

Johnny says that he can prove he is innocent. After recounting the testimony about the bottles, Johnny points out that a man who empties 3.5 quarts of liquor in less than 3 hours would not be able to put a hypo in he right arm with his left hand. Johnny relates that only Unger had a motive to cause him harm. Johnny tells the jury that the next witness, the elevator operator will testify that Unger and Ferdie came to his apartment. At hearing this, Unger panics and bolts, but is caught by the police. Ferdie confesses and Unger is booked. Too bad there is no elevator in his building!

Notes:
- Eileen notes Johnny has gotten rid of a Rodin statue—probably "The Thinker"
- Eileen and Johnny were almost married.
- Johnny's gun is a .38 automatic, but he opens the breech and

SEES IT HAS BEEN FIRED TWICE. I CHECKED WITH THE LOCAL POLICE WHO
CONFIRM THAT YOU MUST EITHER CHECK THE CLIP FOR MISSING ROUNDS,
OR COUNT SHELL CASINGS. YOU CANNOT TELL JUST BY LOOKING AT THE
BREECH.

- JOHNNY LIVES AT 390 PEARL STREET IN HARTFORD.
- BOB STEVENSON IS THE ANNOUNCER, AND PLUGS "711 OCEAN DRIVE."
- MUSIC IS BY LIETH STEVENS

Producer: Jaime del Valle   Writers: Gil Doud, David Ellis;
Cast: Raymond Burr, Bill Conrad, Lou Krugman, Jeanne Bates,
           Sidney Miller, Mary Shipp, Parley Baer, Herb Butterfield

◆ ❖ ◆

SHOW: THE BLOOD RIVER MATTER
SHOW DATE: 8/3/1950
COMPANY: TRISTATE LIFE & CASUALTY COMPANY
AGENT:
EXP. ACCT: $740.00

SYNOPSIS: Johnny gets a call from Blood River. Deputy Tom Grey tells Johnny
that there is no transportation from Divide, so he will pick Johnny up. Colburn
has not recovered, and may not live until tomorrow.

Johnny travels to Blood River, via Parkinson and Divide to investigate the
shooting of a policyholder, Max Colburn. There is a $50,000 policy to be split
between the son Frank and the daughter Mary. When Johnny arrives in
Parkinson, he is called to the local hospital where Mr. Colburn has been moved.
The deputy sheriff, Tom Grey, tells Johnny that Colburn had been shot four
times with a .45. Johnny learns that the hired woman Millie had found him. She
said a man had come to the door and asked for a meal. Mr. Colburn had sent the
man away, but the man had shot him. He was moved to the hospital to get
better treatment. Johnny and Tom go into the room with the children to wait.
Max is described as a huge man, who was a legend in the area. His son Frank is
a big man also. At 6:15 that evening, Max finally dies. The doctor tells Tom that
being shot at point-blank range, he really did not have a chance. Max was a fine
man, and the doctor hopes they find the killer. Frank yells at Tom for bringing Max to the hospital and spending too much time with Mary.

Johnny goes to Blood River, a small town deep in a valley between two tall
mountains. The next morning Johnny and Tom go to the Colburn ranch to
interview the hired woman Millie. Duke the barking dog meets them and then
Millie lets them in. Millie recounts to Johnny how a man had come to the door
after dinner and asked for food. She had gone to the sitting room to tell Mr.
Colburn, who went to the kitchen, yelled at the man who then shot Mr.
Colburn. Millie would be able to recognize the man, who had a coat with a
newspaper in the pocket. Johnny is told that Randy, the other hired man had
come from the bunkhouse, but he saw nothing. "Franky, I mean Mr. Colburn"

was out working and got back later. Tom tells Johnny that Millie never quite grew up inside. Tom tells Johnny that they had found the gun, wrapped in a newspaper. Johnny and Tom start to leave when a man, George Baxter, rides up. Baxter tells Johnny that the posse has found Elmer Brice and they are taking him to the jail. Tom tells Johnny that Brice was a hired man who Max Colburn had fired after he killed a colt.

When Johnny and Tom get back to the jail, a mob is starting to form. Millie comes in and identifies Brice as the killer. Brice is brought in and proclaims his innocence. He admits going to the ranch but only to get a meal. After all Colburn owed him that after ruining his reputation over the accidental death of the colt. Besides, he never owned a gun. Baxter comes back and the mob is angry. There are shots, and Tom and Johnny try to move Brice to a more secure location, but the crowd overpowers them. Later Tom and Johnny find Brice's body hanging from a bridge outside of town. Tom tells Johnny that Max was special, as he was going to divide up his land and sell it at reasonable prices to his neighbors. Johnny hands Tom a receipt for Brice's belongings signed by George Baxter. Tom tells Johnny that Brice could not read. Johnny wonders why he was carrying a newspaper if he could not read it. Or did he learn to read, and not to write"? Tom goes to Parkinson to report to the authorities and Johnny goes back to the Colburn ranch. On the way Johnny is stopped by a group of men who tell Johnny that Brice must have hung himself. Johnny confronts them with Brice's innocence.

At the ranch Johnny talks to Frank, who tells Johnny that everyone should have a trial, referencing Brice's lynching. Mary screams that Frank had killed his father and runs out crying to go to the sheriff. Frank explains that he had angrily told his father to kill himself or he would. The argument was over the father's plan to divide up the ranch and sell it to his neighbors. Besides, he was out riding fences when the shooting happened. Frank tells Johnny that he is going to lay low for a while and Johnny tries to stop him. Millie comes in with a gun and tells Frank that he has to kill Johnny. She tells Frank that she lied and that she had killed his father for him. She had killed Max after Brice had left. She did it all for Frank. When Frank tells Millie they are finished, she shoots him twice, and Johnny takes the gun.

Frank will survive, Millie is in jail, and there was no fraud, so the policy will be paid.

NOTES:
- THE ANNOUNCER PLUGS EDMOND O'BRIEN'S MOVIE, "711 OCEAN DRIVE"
- BOB STEVENSON IS THE ANNOUNCER, AND PLUGS "711 OCEAN DRIVE."
- MUSIC IS BY LIETH STEVENS

Producer: Jaime del Valle   **Writers:** Gil Doud
Cast: Bill Conrad, Virginia Gregg, Junius Matthews, Sammie Hill, Clayton Post, Tyler McVey, Dave Light, Howard Culver

SHOW:	**THE HARTFORD ALLIANCE MATTER**
SHOW DATE:	**8/10/1950**
COMPANY:	**COSMOPOLITAN ALL RISK INSURANCE COMPANY**
AGENT:	**BARTON KEEFE**
EXP. ACCT:	**$180.00**

SYNOPSIS: Johnny is called by Barton Keefe about a building fire there in Hartford, Connecticut. The man who set the fire has been caught, and Barton wants Johnny to talk to him.

Johnny takes a cab to the Hartford Alliance building where he meets Barton. Clarence Pickett, who has an office on the third floor, owns the building. A police officer had caught a boy running from the building.

Johnny goes to Police headquarters and meets Sgt. Broderick who tells Johnny that the boy they are holding will say nothing. The boy admits to Johnny that he set the fire and wants what is coming to him. He wants no trial, and tells the police just put him away. He is a clean-cut boy with clean hands and fingernails, not a troublemaker type. When the police take a snapshot, the boy goes ballistic and is put in his cell.

Johnny goes to the city offices and looks into Pickett's finances, which are not good. Pickett has been losing money in the stock market. Johnny finds Pickett at the fire scene and he tells Johnny that his office is right over where the fire started. Johnny tells Pickett what he has learned and Pickett gets angry. Pickett does not want to go to the police and identify the boy, but relents when Johnny threatens to get a court order.

At the jail, the boy tells Johnny and Broderick that Pickett paid him $50 to start the fire and owes him another $50. Pickett gets mad and walks out saying he never paid anyone to do anything. The police psychiatrist thinks that maybe the boy saw Pickett's picture in the paper. He is well bred and educated, but something is eating at him. Johnny wonders if the boy had a loan that he could not pay back.

Johnny goes to the ruins and talks to a workman who is trying to get a safe out of the Loan Company office on the first floor, but there is another one just like it that fell from the employment office on the second floor. As they are working to remove the safe, someone pushes debris down on them from one of the upper floors, injuring the workman.

Johnny talks to Barton and tells him of the accident and Barton tells Johnny that the workman is unconscious in the hospital. Johnny goes back to the jail and talks to the boy and tells him that he lied about Pickett and that there s something in the building he wants, but the boy will say nothing. Johnny then gets a lead on the boy's identity from Pine Orchard. Johnny goes to the resort town of Pine Orchard and talks to Mrs. Landry, who recognized the boy as Billy Brandon. The family is from Chicago but has an estate in Pine Orchard. The father is in Florida fishing right now. Johnny is told that Mr. Meaks the gardener told Mrs. Landry that the maid had just gone and left the house open. She thinks that the maid had come from the Hartford Alliance Employment Agency that is located in the building that burned.

Back in Hartford, Johnny checks the files for the maid, Belle Muir, but finds nothing. A check is made on Benjamin Price who owns the employment agency and they find a lot! Johnny learns that Price has a record for fraud.

Johnny learns that the workman has died, so now it is arson and murder. Johnny goes to see Belle Muir who tells Johnny that she had worked for the agency for about a year. She left the Brandon estate because no one was there. She is surprised about Billy, as he was such a nice boy. She is surprised that Price has a record. On the way out, Johnny pauses at the door and hears Belle make a call. "He was here" started the conversation. Johnny goes to see Price who tells Johnny that Bell is going to marry him and that she has nothing to say. Johnny says he saw Price in the building, and he will get him for murder but Price denies being there.

Billy's father, a big defense attorney in Chicago, shows up at the jail and after beating around the bush and a claim of blackmail by Johnny, Mr. Brandon comes out with the truth. Mr. Brandon tells Johnny that Billy had been involved in a traffic accident in Chicago that killed a woman. Mr. Brandon admits that he had bought off the only witness and Billy was acquitted. The maid had over heard a conversation with the witness and told someone. The father had made a payment to a man, and he can recognize him. They all go to Price's apartment with a warrant and the father fingers him as the man he paid the money to. The police arrest Price after a brief struggle. The policy will be paid. The son is charged with Arson and the father is put out of business. Price and Bell are charged with Fraud and murder.

NOTES:
- BOB STEVENSON IS THE ANNOUNCER, AND PLUGS "711 OCEAN DRIVE."
- MUSIC IS BY LIETH STEVENS

Producer: Jaime del Valle   Writers: Gil Doud
Cast: Hy Averback, Ken Christy, Raymond Burr, Gil Stratton Jr,
             Howard McNear, Ted Osborne, Peggy Webber

◆　❖　◆

SHOW: THE MICKEY McQUEEN MATTER
SHOW DATE: 8/17/1950
COMPANY: HARTFORD POLICE DEPARTMENT
AGENT:
EXP. ACCT: $0.00
SYNOPSIS: Johnny's old friend Mickey McQueen, an old style Irish cop in Hartford, Connecticut calls him and wants to talk.

Mickey come to Johnny's apartment at 2:00 in the morning, but just can't say what he wants to. Mickey tells Johnny that he is being moved to a desk job, but there is "murder being planned and being done" but no one can stop it. Mickey leaves and the next day Johnny goes to Mickey's apartment. Johnny is met by a distraught woman who points Johnny to a small door, a closet containing Mickey's uniforms and a dead Mickey McQueen, hanging from the clothes pole with his belt. The woman is Mickey's wife Thelma. She is young and attractive, with natural platinum blonde hair. She tells Johnny that she was leaving Mickey and had come back to get her clothes. He was a kind and wonderful person, with not an enemy in the world. She tells Johnny that she had met Mickey after his wife had died. Johnny tells her that he thinks Mickey was murdered. A search of the apartment finds nothing, so Johnny calls the police and leaves.

That afternoon Johnny follows Mickey's beat and talks to his friends. At the Cedrick Hotel, Johnny talks to the house detective, Ned Martin. Johnny tells him about Mickey's visit and Ned tells Johnny that he had talked to Mickey last night and he seemed down about his new desk job. Ned tells Johnny that Mickey's wife, Thelma Weaver, and had done time in Joliet. Ned tells Johnny to drop the case, but Johnny wants to know more. If you want to find out more, see Fred Ku at the Calcutta Club, but don't tell him I sent you, adds Ned.

Johnny goes to see Fred Ku, who is half oriental. Johnny feels he could retire from 10% of the bail posted by the customers in the bar. Fred takes Johnny to the office and tells Johnny that Mickey was a nice guy and that he did not take payoffs and but he left Fred alone. Fred tells Johnny that he did not know Mickey's wife. Fred is called out of the office and Johnny looks around for another exit. The door opens and Thelma comes in, and points a Colt .25 automatic at Johnny when he mentions Thelma Weaver.

Johnny throws ink on Thelma and is able to get the gun away from Thelma and tells her he knows of her past. She tells Johnny she had met Mickey after his first wife had died. She tells Johnny that she got out of prison and gave her friends in Chicago the slip. Mickey had arrested her for vagrancy and came back the next day to bail her out. She had used Mickey's soft side to get information for her friends from Chicago, who are outside in the bar. Mickey was being transferred to the Police Armory, and the boys wanted the keys. They wanted explosives for a jewel robbery at the Marquat Building. Roy Weaver, her husband had threatened to tell Mickey she was a bigamist unless Mickey helped him. She tells Johnny that Roy had taken the keys from Mickey and then Roy killed Mickey. Johnny tries to leave, but Roy comes in and objects. Roy thanks Thelma for warning him. Johnny is taken to an old wine cellar and slugged.

When Johnny wakes up he discovers he is in an old wine cellar filled with burglary tools. Johnny figures out the situation and tries to find a way out. When the door opens, he fakes being unconscious and hears the men take out the tools to the cars where Fred has the explosives from the Armory. After the men leave with Thelma, Johnny tries to force his way out. Johnny hears the door open and Ned Martin is there. He tells Johnny that a woman had called to say Johnny was locked in the bar and something was going to happen. Johnny tells Ned what is planned and Ned takes Johnny to the area of the Marquat Building, where

Johnny sees the cars being unloaded. Johnny sees Thelma walking towards him. Roy calls to her and she turns and fires into the first car, igniting the cordite powder, which explodes. Thelma is shot but she turns on the ground and hits the second car, which explodes.

Johnny gets to her in time for her to say that Mickey would be proud of her. She tells Johnny that they cannot send her back to Juliet, and then she dies. Ray Weaver lives long enough to sign a confession that he killed Mickey McQueen.

NOTES:
* BOB STEVENSON IS THE ANNOUNCER, AND PLUGS "711 OCEAN DRIVE."
* MUSIC IS BY LIETH STEVENS

Producer: Jaime del Valle   **Writers:** Gil Doud
Cast: Bill Conrad, Virginia Gregg, Ben Wright, Jim Nusser, Dan O'Herlihy

◆ ❖ ◆

SHOW: THE TRANS-PACIFIC EXPORT MATTER
SHOW DATE: 8/23/1950
COMPANY: CORINTHIAN LIABILITY & RISK
AGENT: AL HARPER
EXP. ACCT: $3,544.00

SYNOPSIS: Al Harper at Corinthian has a job for Johnny, but he won't like it. However the commission will be big. The policy is for $200,000 and Johnny will have to travel to Hong Kong. Johnny is not scared yet. The policyholders are people they have had trouble with before. "Remember the Trans Pacific Import Export outfit?" "Yeah, I sent flowers to the widow." Johnny tells Al. Johnny is scared, but he will take a crack at it.

Johnny flies to Hong Kong, which is in turmoil. At the American Consul, Johnny meets Miss Verdas, secretary to the Consul, Mr. Grover. Johnny meets with Grover and after some small talk over the turmoil of war and a review of the case, Grover agrees to help Johnny with letters of introduction and phone calls. Johnny tells him that the previous case was settled because the investigator was killed.

Johnny arranges to get a room at a hotel owned by Miss Verdas' Portuguese father. The room is stark, but Miss Verdas comes to visit. Johnny offers her a cigarette or scotch, and she informs Johnny that he is being followed. Johnny is told where to look, and spots the man outside. She stays only a few minutes, but long enough to tell Johnny about a love song being sung out side and that she is looking for an American to take her out of China. She hates it here and is very impatient. She has no Portuguese relatives to help her.

The next day Johnny goes to see William Meadow, owner of Trans-Pacific. Mr. Meadow is clearly aggravated at the insurance company and is on the defensive, which infers guilt to Johnny. After Johnny is thrown out, he spends the rest of the day looking for former employees to get their stories. After an interview with the accountant, Franklin Abbott and two others, the case is starting to form. When Johnny gets back to his hotel, Miss Verdas is waiting for him again in his room. She stays and they talk.

The next day Johnny speaks with a Fire Brigade supervisor, who tells Johnny that the fire was definitely set, and that timing devices were used. He gives Johnny pictures and statements that he has photocopied and sent to Hartford. On the way back to the hotel, his tail is missing, but Johnny finds him in his room with a police badge and Miss Verdas dead on the floor.

Johnny tells the constable that she had gotten to the room before Johnny and someone thought her shadow on the blinds was his. The constable tells Johnny that he had been following him at the orders of Mr. Grover at the Consul.

A confused and distraught Johnny is driven to the police Superintendent Clyde's office to give his statement. He tells Clyde that he is convinced that Will Meadows had the girl killed and wants him arrested. Johnny goes to see Mr. Grover about his escort, and Grover knows about Verdas. Johnny tells Grover that Verdas is dead because of him, and that this case has been bad on his nerves. Johnny is sure that that Verdas was killed because the killers thought she was Johnny. After leaving by the back door to lose his tail, Johnny walks back to the hotel, puts his automatic in his pocket and goes to Will Meadow's home. The houseboy tells Johnny that Meadow is not home. Johnny convinces him to tell Johnny where Meadow is. Johnny gets the location, a cottage on Repulse Bay. Johnny calls the police to and tells them to meet him at the cottage. At the cottage the police arrive just as Johnny calls Meadow, who is surprised to see him. Johnny wants him to go back to town and they exchange shots and Meadows is killed. The police say that by shooting first, Meadows admitted guilt and allowed Johnny to defend himself. Nothing good came out of this assignment except saving your company some money it didn't know it had."

NOTES:
- THIS PROGRAM WAS USED AS THE AUDITION FOR GERALD MOHR AND JOHN LUND.
- ANOTHER REFERENCE TO AN AUTOMATIC HANDGUN.
- DURING THE EARLY 1950S THERE WAS A GREAT DEAL OF ANGST OVER POSSIBLE WAR WITH IN CHINA BETWEEN THE RED ARMY AND THE NATIONALISTS.
- THERE IS A COMMERCIAL FOR PHILLIP MARLOW AND SONGS FOR SALE IN THE MIDDLE OF THE PROGRAM.
- BOB STEVENSON IS THE ANNOUNCER, AND PLUGS "711 OCEAN DRIVE."
- MUSIC IS BY LIETH STEVENS
- THE HOLLYWOOD THEATER FOLLOWS THIS PROGRAM
- THERE IS AN ANNOUNCEMENT FOR THE NEED FOR BLOOD DONATIONS FOR THE RED CROSS

Producer: Jaime del Valle   **Writers: Gil Doud, David Ellis**

Cast: Tudor Owen, Lillian Buyeff, Hy Averback, Robert Griffin, Hal March, Dan O'Herlihy

SHOW:	THE VIRGINIA BEACH MATTER
SHOW DATE:	8/31/1950
COMPANY:	EAST COAST UNDERWRITERS
AGENT:	CARL BREWSTER
EXP. ACCT:	$855.75

SYNOPSIS: Carl Brewster calls Johnny about a bodyguard case. Miss Janice Browning, who is living in Virginia Beach, Virginia, was engaged to Mark Robeson. Robeson was arrested for robbery and will be released from the state prison in Richmond tomorrow. He has promised to kill her.

Johnny cabs to Carl's office and learns about the case. Johnny reviews what he knows, and tells Carl that Janice probably deserves what she gets. Johnny is told that the husband was sent up for robbery. Janice is penniless but has a policy therefore Johnny has been assigned to watch her. Carl has met Janice, and it will not be an unpleasant assignment.

Johnny travels to Virginia Beach and arrives at Janice's beach cottage house where Johnny is met by the maid Betty, a honey blonde in shorts and a halter-top. Betty was not told about any investigator coming, but lets him in. When Johnny tells Betty that he thought Janice was penniless, which is why Johnny was hired, Betty knows nothing of her finances. She has done ok, though. She is out right now with George Masters.

At 5:00PM Janice and George come home. Janice sends Betty to the beach and talks to Johnny. She tells Johnny that she really did not know what else to do. She last saw her fiancé six months ago and told him she was finished with him. Robeson told her that he would kill her when he got out. Johnny tells her to cancel their evening plans, and they all settle down for a long night.

Around 11:00 Betty comes out of her bedroom and talks to Johnny. She tells Johnny that she had not gone to the beach, but had searched Janice's room. She found a wedding picture dated 1947. Shots ring out and Janice screams. Johnny runs outside and finds Mark Robeson standing by the window firing an empty .38 Police Special. Mark tells Johnny that he will not go back to the hospital as Johnny looks like a doctor. He is not going back. Mark tries to strangle Johnny but stops and disappears into the night.

Johnny goes in and confronts Janice with the things Mark had said. Johnny asks why she had set Betty up as a patsy. Janice tells Johnny that using Betty was George's idea, as was telling the story about Mark getting out of jail. She had tried to get detectives and the police to handle the case, but not one wanted to touch it. Going to the insurance company, she tells Johnny, was George's idea. She also tells Johnny that Mark was her husband and has been in a mental hospital in Pennsylvania but had escaped.

After talking to Janice, Johnny decides to not drop the case. Johnny calls

Dr. Becker, who had treated Mark. He agrees to come over and calms Janice, and talks to Johnny about Robeson's condition. Johnny is told that Mark is insanely jealous and will probably come back.

Janice calls George, but he does not answer the phone. Johnny borrows the doctor's car and they drive to George's house where there is a light on, but no one answers the door. Johnny and Janice go in and find George strangled in his study, with a .38 lying on the desk, the same gun Mark had used earlier. The police are called and Johnny takes Janice back to the cottage and Dr. Becker sedates her.

The next morning, Janice tells Johnny that she was in love with George, and that Mark knew George. She had borrowed from the insurance policy to pay for Mark's hospital bills. Betty screams and tells Johnny that Mark is back, but there is no trace of him outside. That afternoon Betty is put on a bus for New York. Johnny goes to George's house and a deputy lets him look though the papers in the desk. In a ledger, Johnny finds an entry for a $20,000 loan to Janice. Johnny also notes a $5,000 loan against the policy in April. Johnny leaves and makes a call to the insurance company and they tell Johnny that the policy is for $50,000 and George is the sole beneficiary.

Johnny meets with the doctor and they develop a plan to deal with Mark. That afternoon Johnny parades Janice around in her bathing suit to lure Mark. Later she sits in front of a window. After that, Johnny waits outside. Finally at 10:30 Mark shows up. Johnny stops him and tells Mark, "I am George Masters," but Mark tells Johnny that it was his fault that she was not in the room. Johnny walks into the light and Mark recognizes him as a doctor. Mark tells Johnny that Masters is dead and he will not go back to the hospital. He grabs for Johnny but this time Johnny is able to slug him. Johnny had figured out that Masters had given Mark the gun and told him to shoot Janice, but he had made a mistake and fired into the wrong room. When Mark came back he killed George because he had made him make a mistake.

NOTES:
- THIS IS A VARIATION ON "THE ANNE CONNELLY MATTER" OF 12/3/49. THE NAMES AND LOCATION ARE CHANGED AND THERE ARE MINOR CHANGES IN THE PLOT.
- THE EXPENSE REPORT INCLUDES $500 AS PAYMENT FOR DECEIT.
- BOB STEVENSON IS THE ANNOUNCER
- MUSIC IS BY LIETH STEVENS

Producer: Jaime del Valle   **Writers:**   Gil Doud
Cast: Howard McNear, Bob Sweeney, Virginia Gregg, Jeanne Bates, Hy Averback

◆　❖　◆

SHOW: THE HOWARD CALDWELL MATTER
SHOW DATE: 9/30/1950

COMPANY: BRITANNIA LIFE INSURANCE COMPANY
AGENT: MR. NATHAN
EXP. ACCT: $1,050.00

SYNOPSIS: Mrs. Caldwell calls to tell Johnny that her son is dead; she feels it as only a mother could.

Johnny goes to the Caldwell country estate. Johnny relates that Mrs. Caldwell was the answer to the question of why boys left home. She tells Johnny that she made Howard share everything. At age 23 he left for San Francisco and was studying to be an artist. He had met some people and enrolled in a school, the Orlando School of Art. Johnny is told that Howard wrote to say that it was better he not come home, and he will never see his mother again. He wrote that he is not mentally equipped for life.

Johnny calls Mr. Nathan of the insurance company. Mrs. Caldwell's lawyer told her to call. Johnny is told that there is a $200,000 policy on Howard. Johnny goes to San Francisco, California and goes to last known address where the manager opens the apartment. Johnny finds Howard's clothes are still there. The manager tells Johnny that he knows none of Howard's friends. Johnny searches the apartment and only finds mail from his mother, and a collection of match folders with dates. Johnny also finds a folder of sketches of a beautiful woman.

Johnny goes to the Art school where Mrs. Orlando tells Johnny that Howard had stopped coming to class. Johnny shows her the sketches, and she confirms that they are Howard's work, but she does not know the model.

Johnny visits the bars on a list he made from the matchbook covers, most not worth remembering. At "The Stop Sign" Johnny asks for Howard. The bartender does not know Howard, or the girl in the picture. However, a man in the bar knows Howard Caldwell. Johnny goes outside with him and gets into a car and meets another man, and they drive off. They tell Johnny that they have been waiting for someone to show up. They tell Johnny to drop the matter, as it is for the best. Then they take Johnny to his hotel.

Early the next morning, a phone call tells Johnny to buy an Examiner and look at the headlines. Johnny gets a paper, and finds the headline: "Syndicate head found slain in auto trunk—Benjamin Miller western gang chief found dead." Johnny reads the article and learns that Miller was found in an abandoned car. On page four Johnny sees a picture of Nora Rush in Los Angeles, the girl Howard had drawn. Johnny catches a United Airlines flight to Los Angeles and goes to Nora's Ardmore address. When he gets there Nora is still in her robe. She tells Johnny that she knows why he is there. She tells Johnny that she does not know where Howard is and cries. Johnny searches the house and finds a picture of Howard. Johnny tells Nora that he saw the sketches, and that a few other people have seen them. "How could he have been so stupid?" she tells Johnny. There had been nothing to link them together. She tells Johnny that Howard had killed Miller with her gun. Nora explains that she was going with Miller after she came from Chicago. She met Howard at a party and there was just something about him. They would meet in bars and then go to her place where he sketched her. Ben Miller saw him meet her and Ben hit her. Howard got angry and killed him and Howard had help moving and hiding Miller's body. Everything was ok until Johnny came. Johnny asks Nora why two friends would help? She tells Johnny that no one wanted Howard to take a wrap for killing Miller. She does not know where Howard is, and her bothers are flying in and will be there by noon.

After noon, Nora's brother Al arrives. Johnny tells Al that he will not call the police until they talk. Al tells Johnny that Nora fell for Howard. Ben stirred up mud about her past and Howard killed him. Johnny thinks it makes more sense if they were protecting their sister. Al agrees to take Johnny to Howard. They drive to an apartment and Johnny knocks on door. Johnny opens the door to find an empty apartment. Johnny slugs Al and goes back to Nora's house.

Howard is there in bedroom, lying on the bed crying. Howard is glad that Johnny came. He tells Johnny that Nora didn't want me, just my name and money. Howard admits he killed Miller. He tells Johnny that he has lived with low class people and started to think like them. This was the first thing he has done by himself. Howard tells Johnny that Nora says he is a snob. Johnny turns Howard in for murder and the others as accessories.

NOTES:
- JOHNNY TAKES UNITED AIRLINES.
- THERE IS A PLUG FOR O'BRIEN'S NEW MOVIE "WAR PATH"
- ROY ROWAN IS THE ANNOUNCER
- MUSIC IS BY WILBUR HATCH

Producer: Jaime del Valle   **Writers:** Gill Doud
Cast: Lurene Tuttle, John McIntire, Bob Sweeney, Hy Averback,
             John Dehner, Jeanne Bates, Jeanette Nolan

◆ ❖ ◆

SHOW: THE RICHARD SPLAIN MATTER
SHOW DATE: 10/7/1950
COMPANY: CORINTHIAN LIFE AND LIABILITY INSURANCE COMPANY
AGENT: BRUCE HARVARD
EXP. ACCT: $375.00
SYNOPSIS: Bruce Hardwick calls and has a case or Johnny. A policy was found at the scene of a murder without a body. Bruce wants Johnny to investigate.

Johnny travels to New York City and is met by homicide Sgt. Burns at the apartment of Richard Splain. Johnny looks through the apartment and Sgt Burns tells Johnny that Richard Splain rents it. There are signs of a violent struggle, but no one heard anything. Johnny finds part of ship model and tells Sgt. Burns that he will talk to Splain's wife and beneficiary.

Johnny goes to the apartment of Splain's wife Clara, a dumpy blonde. She tells Johnny that they had split up. A man named Mark Barnes opens the door and is protective of Clara. Johnny explains she is the beneficiary of $35,000 policy. She tells Johnny that Splain was either in port or at sea, as he was a ship's carpenter. Mark tells Johnny that Splain would not call his wife when he came home. They want a divorce, but lawyers cost money. Clara tells Johnny that maybe Splain is not dead but someone else was killed.

Johnny goes to back Splain's flat. Sgt. Burns is gone so Johnny tells the guard that he is working with Burns to get in. Inside Johnny finds Splain's ships papers, and his last ship was the Tangier. Johnny also finds a small address book. Johnny copies names until there is a knock on the door and a man enters. The man tells Johnny that he thought Splain was in. The man acts panicky but does not know where Splain his. He tells Johnny that he liked to talk about foreign places with Splain. Johnny pays him $10 for talking. Johnny then tails the man to his apartment where the name on the door is Paul Krell. Johnny calls Sgt. Burns and updates him. Burns tells Johnny that he has gone to Splain's ship but did not get anything. Sgt. Burns will call Johnny if anything turns up.

Next morning the phone rings. It is Clara Splain, and she must see Johnny immediately. She tells Johnny that the police have arrested Mark, and Splain's body has been found. She tells Johnny that Mark told the police nothing, but Mark could not prove where he was. She tells Johnny that she left Dick because he smuggled dope in model ships, and it is important to tell Johnny now.

Johnny ponders the ship models, Krell as a possible user, and the address book. Back at the apartment the police are there along with the body of Paul Krell who has been beaten. Johnny chides Burns for not calling and a nasty Burns threatens to arrest Johnny for meddling by sneaking in to the apartment earlier. Johnny tells him that he only came for the name of the ship. Burns tells Johnny that the only change to the apartment was an open drawer with a torn envelope in it. Johnny leaves before he locks horns with Burns, as the address book is gone. Johnny keeps quiet about the book and meeting Krell.

Johnny goes to Mrs. Splain and asks if she knows Krell, and she does not. Johnny asks Clara where Mark was last night and she tells Johnny that Mark was with her. She asks Johnny why would she tell him about the narcotics if the story were not true. Clara shows Johnny a model and opens a hidden compartment. She tells Johnny that she does not know who Splain's customers were.

Johnny goes to Krell's apartment and learns Krell was just a friend. Johnny goes to the next name on the list, Mr. Kentner. He does not know Splain but gives himself away when Johnny tells him Splain is dead. "That's bad," replies Kentner. He admits to Johnny that he bought ships models. He last saw Splain a week ago and had met him through a friend.

The next two stops uncovered nothing. Johnny goes to see Francine Wells and her father opens door as Francine was expecting Fred. Johnny tells him that it is important to talk to her and he lets Johnny in. Francine tells Johnny that he must have come to the wrong place, as she has never heard of Splain. When told Splain sold narcotics, she is shocked. Johnny tells her he is trying to find out who killed Splain and she admits she saw Splain last week. She was introduced to him by a friend and bought narcotics from him. Johnny shows her the list but she does not know anyone in it. Johnny gives her a business card and leaves.

Other visits give similar results; the people bought drugs from Splain. Johnny visits J. L. Tucker who knew Splain's wife and tells Johnny that she was shilling for Splain. Johnny calls Clara and she tells Johnny that Tucker had called and was looking for someone, so she told him about Dick. She was stiff and did not know what she was doing.

After dinner and drinks Johnny meets Francine Wells on his hotel floor. She tells Johnny that she was no angel. After a party in Pennsylvania, someone got drugs, and that was the start. Now it has ended. She killed Splain. She tells Johnny that she went to Splain without money and he laughed, so she beat him. She cannot go on as she killed Krell also. Haven't I done enough?

Johnny calls on Mr. Wells. Johnny is looking for evidence, an address book. Mr. Wells admits that Francine confessed to cover him. He saw her and learned the truth and he killed Splain to protect her.

NOTES:
- THERE IS A PLUG FOR O'BRIEN'S NEW MOVIE "WAR PATH"
- BOB STEVENSON IS THE ANNOUNCER
- MUSIC IS BY WILBUR HATCH

Producer: Jaime del Valle   **Writers:** Gil Doud
Cast: Herb Butterfield, Raymond Burr, Howard McNear, Joe Gilbert, Bill Bouchey, Barry Kroger, Mary Lansing

◆   ❖   ◆

SHOW: THE YANKEE PRIDE MATTER
SHOW DATE: 10/14/1950
COMPANY: TRI-STATE INSURANCE COMPANY
AGENT: CARL BUSH
EXP. ACCT: $2,686.00

SYNOPSIS: Carl Bush calls and offers Johnny a fat commission in Singapore. Mechanical breakdowns are holding up a cargo ship.

Johnny goes to the office and talks to Carl. Johnny is told that Maritime Insurance is a risky business. Johnny knows about bad bets—he bet on Notre Dame last Saturday. Johnny is told that the Yankee Pride has a cargo of tin bound for a West Coast defense plant. There is a time clause on deliveries, and Tri-State loses 2% per day on $300,000. Johnny is told that Vincent Ells is the local agent. Carl tells Johnny that he will send bouquet of bourbon to plane.

Johnny flies to Singapore and goes to Tri-State office and talks to Ells, who tells Johnny that the unexpected is commonplace in Asia. Johnny is told that this could be a dangerous mission, as another adjuster has been killed. The agent was Chinese so the police aren't too concerned. He had gone to the Yankee Pride and never arrived. Death is not rare in here in Singapore. Johnny is told the investigator has a brother and Johnny gets the address. Ells warns Johnny to proceed with caution.

Johnny goes to the ship and meets with the Chief who has malaria. Johnny tells him why he is there. The chief tells Johnny that a bearing is being flown in from Hong Kong. Sabotage is not likely as bearings go and generators fail all the time. The chief tells Johnny that he will talk to the captain, so come back tomorrow.

Johnny goes to see the brother of the dead agent. The rickshaw driver waits and Johnny goes to the door. The man will not talk about his brother but lets Johnny in after Johnny tells him why he is there. Johnny is told that his brother was killed for his job or some other reason. He does not want to die and knows nothing. A man came here before police did and warned him not to talk to police. He was an Englishman who works for someone else. His brother's last words were about a woman. There was always a new woman. She is Malayan and he did not mention her to the stranger. Johnny is told that the girl, RanDee works in a bar and there is where his brother met her. "Leave and do not come back" Johnny is told. On the way out shots ring out and the brother is shot, but Johnny does not go back. Johnny goes to the bar on Malabar Street after being unable to find a phone to report the shooting. The bar is crowded and Johnny orders a Scotch and asks for the girl. The bartender tells him to sit at a table and the girl comes to serve him. Johnny tells her that a friend told him about her. She tells Johnny that she learned English from a missionary school. She tells Johnny that the agent, Koo Fu Soon was no friend. She did not want to meet him again, as he made fool of himself, as he was lonely. Are you lonely? Come to my house after work. Johnny goes to her house and she does not lie about not knowing that Koo Fu Soon is dead. She tells Johnny that he is in trouble. As she mixes a drink, a man breaks in and tells Johnny that he is going for a ride. Johnny tries to fight and is knocked unconscious. When Johnny wakes, up he is in a mansion where he is introduced to the "Major." Johnny is told "You will accomplish nothing until I allow you to." Johnny is told that the chief engineer will move ship on his order, and that the ship is going to Mexico. The Major tells Johnny that "One can buy anything, including petty official signatures, as Major has power." He will let Johnny go on with his work, as Johnny is a petty pipsqueak. Johnny is told to tell the insurance company that the Major will cover their losses. Two men, named Earl and Roy, take Johnny to his hotel. Johnny had seen the man's name, "Major Ralph Dixon" on an envelope, and he is a power mad man.

Next day Johnny calls Ells and asks, "Who is Dixon?" as he claims to be behind the problems with ship. Johnny tells Ells to look into the ship's papers and Dixon's visa and to check customs. Johnny will start at the other end, as he knows his way around the bottom.

Johnny goes back to RanDee and tells her there is going to be trouble. He will turn her in and no one will believe her. She tells of people who are afraid of an invasion and are sending their gold out of the area. The Major is in charge of shipping the gold out on ships. There is an estimated $100 million in gold being shipped. She tells Johnny that Mr. Ells is as greedy as everyone else, and he has been bought. If Johnny is wise, he will get out. Johnny goes to Ells' home where there is no answer at the door. In a window Johnny sees Ells, dead with pistol in his hand. Johnny goes to the hotel and gets his automatic and heads to the Major's place. Johnny forces his way in and tells the Major that Ells is dead. The Major tells Johnny that "He was weak and did not appreciate the Major's strength." Johnny tells him that there is only one way to stop the Major, to kill him; as he is a man of influence only in his own mind. Johnny is going to take him to the police as he knows about the gold and will stop the scheme. The Major only replies that he is late for a meeting at the club and starts to leave. As he walks out of the room laughing Johnny shoots the Major. The police arrive and arrest the Major. The gold is seized when it arrives. The Yankee Pride will sail only two days late.

NOTES:
- ANOTHER REFERENCE TO AN AUTOMATIC HANDGUN.
- FIRST TIME JOHNNY ACTS PREEMPTIVELY.
- MUSIC BY ALEXANDER COURAGE.
- THERE IS A PLUG FOR O'BRIEN'S NEW MOVIE "WAR PATH"
- BOB STEVENSON IS THE ANNOUNCER

Producer: Jaime del Valle   **Writers:**   Gil Doud
Cast: Virginia Gregg, Bob Sweeney, Tutor Owen, Bill Johnstone, Wally Maher, Jack Kruschen, Ben Wright

◆   ❖   ◆

SHOW: THE JACK MADIGAN MATTER
SHOW DATE: 10/21/1950
COMPANY: STROOL BAIL BOND
AGENT: MANNY STROOL
EXP. ACCT: $2,720.00
SYNOPSIS: Manny Strool calls Johnny. He needs Johnny to save him $50,000. He provided bail for two witnesses who then disappeared, and Manny wants to talk to Johnny.

Johnny phones New York to check on Manny Strool's reputation, which is good enough for the courts. Manny tells Johnny that Jack Madigan forced him to put up the bond. Madigan wanted the men out on bond and now they have disappeared. Manny came to Johnny because the police don't care and detectives can be bought. Manny was referred to Johnny by his insurance contacts. Manny has learned that Johnny is honest, but tends to pad the expense account, but who doesn't. Manny gives Johnny the details on Nippy Bruno and Max Kraus. Johnny wants a $2,500 retainer before starting.

The check comes the next day, so Johnny goes to New York City. Johnny entertains a reporter friend and asks about Madigan. Johnny learns that much has been written about Madigan, and people have disappeared before.

Johnny takes a cab to the house of Nippy Bruno's sister, Vivian Brown an actress. A man answers door and announces Johnny. Vivian tells Johnny that he must have come to the wrong place, as she has not seen Nippy in years. The man, who is called "Red," pulls a gun and Johnny is searched. Vivian and Johnny sit and wait until Jack Madigan arrives. Johnny tells Madigan that he did not expect to find Madigan and the sister of a witness together. Madigan apologizes for the gun and tells Johnny that his reputation is ill deserved. He wants the men to testify. He has decided to tell all, he is tired and going straight. Johnny declines an offer of money from Madigan to stop snooping.

Johnny leaves, gets a cab, and sees Red watching him from a window. After making sure the cab is not being followed, Johnny goes to Max Kraus' apartment, only to find that Red is there. He tells Johnny that he is Max Kraus. He tells Johnny that he has to do something with Johnny, so he takes him outside and heads for a car but is gunned down in the alley. Johnny leaves the scene because the dead man is not Max Krauss. Johnny goes to Manny Strool who tells Johnny that the phony description of Kraus was a mistake.

Johnny calls Vivian, who tells Johnny that Jack had left after he got a phone call. She wants Johnny to come up. Johnny takes a chance and walks to the apartment where she answers the door and lets him in. Johnny searches the apartment and finds no one there. Vivian tells Johnny that she wanted to tell Johnny where Nippy is, and that she is involved too. Jack knew things would happen and he told Vivian that he will have government eating out of his hand. She is ratting on Madigan because he cared only for himself. He is the one that wanted Max Kraus killed. Vivian had called Nippy at his hotel earlier but now there is no answer. Vivian tells Johnny that Nippy is in a hotel on Lexington Avenue. Johnny takes Vivian to his hotel room for safety and then goes to Madigan's address and sees police in front of the building and a body in the sidewalk, Jack Madigan's body.

Johnny goes back to his hotel room and tells Vivian that Jack is dead. Johnny wants Vivian to go to the police, as she needs protection, but she won't go, as they would love to blame her. "It is easier to be rotten," she tells Johnny. Vivian then tells Johnny that she will give him Nippy. They go back to her apartment, and Nippy is there. Johnny tries to talk Nippy into giving up, but Nippy tries to kill Vivian and Johnny slugs him. Johnny calls the police and Vivian is held as an accessory.

Johnny talks to Strool and tells him not to make bail for her. Johnny tells Manny that he will never work for him again, and wait till you see my expense account! The expenses include an item for $2,500 in miscellaneous expenses, and Johnny is holding the retaining fee until this matter is settled

NOTES:
- THIS IS AN ADAPTATION OF "WITNESS, WITNESS, WHO HAS THE WITNESS" BROADCAST ON 10/22/1949 WITH CHARLES RUSSELL. THE NAMES ARE DIFFERENT. FOR INSTANCE IN THIS CASE, ONE OF THE WITNESSES, MAX KRAUS, IS THE NAME OF THE BAIL-BONDSMAN WHO HIRES JOHNNY.

- THERE IS A PLUG FOR O'BRIEN'S NEW MOVIE "WAR PATH"
- DAN CUBBERLY IS THE ANNOUNCER
- MUSIC IS BY WILBUR HATCH
- "SING IT AGAIN" IS NEXT, AND THE PRIZE IS **$5,000**

Producer: Jaime del Valle   **Writers:** Gil Doud
Cast: Sidney Miller, John Dehner, Clayton Post, Jeanette Nolan, John McIntire

◆　❖　◆

SHOW: THE JOAN SEBASTIAN MATTER
SHOW DATE: 10/28/1950
COMPANY: CORINTHIAN LIFE INSURANCE COMPANY
AGENT: MR. SEMPLIN
EXP. ACCT: $356.75

SYNOPSIS: Johnny calls Boston and gets the name of the police contact for the Joan Sebastian case from Mr. Semplin and it told to see Lt. DeRosa. Johnny asks if the police have a theory yet, and is told they do not. So it is either murder or suicide.

Johnny rents a car and drives to the Boston, Massachusetts police headquarters. Johnny meets Lt. DeRosa and tells him that the insurance company is nervous about a possible suicide case. Johnny tells DeRosa that the girl's mother is the beneficiary and an invalid. Johnny leans that the mother has taken up with an old boy friend. DeRosa tells Johnny that the girl was found in shallow water near a bridge and did not look like a typical suicide. The bridge was too low, and a suicide never does it without taking off their coat and shoes, and her purse is missing. She was 21 yrs old and pretty. Johnny is told that the inquest will be in two days. Johnny tells DeRosa that he wants to dig up his own background information.

Johnny goes to the site where the body was found. Johnny notes that the placement of body indicates she was going towards Boston, not away from town. Johnny goes to Joan's apartment and talks to Mary O'Neal, Joan's roommate. Joan tells Johnny that Joan's death is a great shock. She never thought she would do anything like this. She tells Johnny that she expected some trouble, as Joan lived too fast after her mother went into the hospital. There were just too many men. One boyfriend is Harold Correy, who is a truck driver for North American Van Lines. Mary tells Johnny that Joan saw other men when he was gone. Johnny asks to look at Joan's things and Mary takes him to Joan's room. Johnny goes through a locked dresser with nothing but clothes, expensive perfume and jewelry, and a key with a heart shaped head. Johnny keeps the key, as he wants to find out who made it.

Johnny calls North American Van Lines and is told that Correy is out of town and is due back at 3AM. Johnny calls Joan's employer and goes to see Mr. Hollis at his home, where Johnny meets Mrs. Hollis. Mr. Hollis knew nothing of Joan's private life, as he had no right to know, but he did know of Joan's invalid mother. Johnny tells Hollis that he thinks there was only one man, not many. Johnny asks for the names of Joan's coworkers and Hollis tells Johnny he will get the names of the co-workers if Johnny will call in the morning.

Johnny goes to see Correy at 10:30. Johnny tells Correy that the case looks like murder. Correy tells Johnny that Joan would never kill herself. Correy tells Johnny that he left Wednesday morning on a run, and Johnny suggests that he could have killed Joan before he left. Correy gets angry and tells Johnny that he wanted to marry Joan and throws him out.

Johnny calls DeRosa and learns that the cause of death has been ruled suicide, as the autopsy says Joan died of carbon monoxide poisoning. Lt. DeRosa thinks that someone probably moved her body to avoid embarrassment. Johnny goes to see Lt. DeRosa to see the autopsy report, which points to car exhaust but also shows a severe concussion. Johnny shows DeRosa the key and asks if he can find out where it was made.

Johnny goes to see Paul Anderson, the boyfriend of mother. Paul tells Johnny that the mother was 17 when Joan was born. He met Joan first, and realized she was an opportunist. He did what he could for the mother, and did not send her to a home to get her out of the way. Paul does not know anything about a gold key, but tells Johnny that Joan was heading for a bad end with no one to blame but her self.

Johnny goes to see Correy and talks to him in a near by café. Correy tells Johnny that he is going out again, as he cannot take the pressure any more. Johnny talks to six of Joan's co-workers and finds nothing. Johnny goes to Lt. DeRosa and learns that the police have found the goldsmith who made key. Johnny goes to talk to him, and he is positive, as it has his mark on it, "CF" for Cedrick Frost. Frost does not know for whom he made it, for but searches his records and finds a gold key made in March for J. E. Carter. The gold key was made from a key to a cottage and was a surprise for his wife. Johnny tells Lt. DeRosa about the cottage, but DeRosa cannot assign men to search cabins in the area, as it is a county responsibility. Johnny searches real estate companies in the area and on the 3rd day hits pay dirt. Johnny finds an agent who remembers renting a cottage to J. E. Carter in March. Johnny and the agent go to cottage, where Johnny sees tire tracks in a lean-to garage, and a stained rug, among other things inside. On the way out, Johnny locks the cottage door with the gold key.

Johnny goes to Mr. Hollis and tells him that he thought he would get away with it. He had rented the cottage and bought Joan the key. Hollis admits that he was infatuated with Joan and wanted to break it off. Joan left the cottage and committed suicide in car. Johnny tells him of the bloodstains and Hollis agrees to go to the police. When Hollis asks Johnny what had convinced him Johnny tell Hollis that he had found a Wall Street Journal addressed to Hollis in the cottage. Mrs. Hollis comes in and tells Johnny that she killed Joan. She had gone to the cottage and waited inside killed the girl and carried her to the car.

Remarks: "I don't know what sticklers the Massachusetts courts of law are, but Joan Sebastian was not killed by the wronged wife. She was unconscious but alive when Hollis put her into the car trunk. She died there by carbon monoxide."

NOTES:
- THERE IS A PLUG FOR O'BRIEN'S NEW MOVIE "WAR PATH"
- DAN CUBBERLY IS THE ANNOUNCER
- MUSIC IS BY WILBUR HATCH

Producer: Jaime del Valle   **Writers:**   Gil Doud
Cast: Virginia Gregg, Howard McNear, Virginia Eiler, Wally Maher, John Stevenson, Bill Johnstone, Raymond Burr

◆   ❖   ◆

SHOW: THE QUEEN ANNE PISTOLS MATTER
SHOW DATE: 11/4/1950
COMPANY: TRI-STATE INSURANCE COMPANY
AGENT: WILLIAM CARTER
EXP. ACCT: $365.35

SYNOPSIS: William Carter calls Johnny and tells him that the idiot cousin of a company vice president has sold a $15,000 policy on a pair of antique pistols. Carter wants Johnny to see that the pistols are delivered, as someone has tried to steal them twice.

Johnny goes to the Tri-State office and meets Leonard Bonny, who has been injured. Bonny tells Johnny that he was attacked in Liverpool before boarding a ship, and in New York. On neither time did he have the pistols with him. Johnny sees the pistols in a leather box; two graceful flintlocks with a faint name etched on them. The pistols are going to Arthur Worthing of 272 Medford Street in Boston. Johnny is to deliver them, and Bonny will wait in Hartford.

Johnny takes a plane to Boston, Massachusetts and goes to the office of Arthur Worthing, who is happy to see the package. Worthing tells Johnny that James Freeman Norwhich made the pistols in 1705. They were fashioned during Queen Anne's rule, and have had a colorful history. These guns have caused many murders, and many murdered for them. The insurance policy is in force until Johnny delivers them to purchaser who is Mr. or Mrs. Jack Rawlins Bride. Johnny is to deliver the pistols to them and tell them that Bonny or Worthing will contact them.

Johnny goes to the Bride address and gives the package to Mrs. Bride who screams when she sees it. Mr. Bride comes in and tells her that he will take care of the matter. Johnny is told that he will not get a signature from him. Bride asks if Bonny is here in America, and who Worthing is. Bride tells Johnny to get out with his fake form and pistols. "Your bluff won't work," he tells Johnny. Johnny goes back to Worthing, but the shop empty and for rent.

Johnny sends a telegram to Tri-State and goes back to his apartment where the phone is ringing. Johnny tells Mr. Carter that Bride had called the pistols blackmail. Carter tells Johnny that he cannot find Bonny. Johnny tells Carter that he wants no part of this matter. Later Johnny looks over the pistols and decides that they are nothing worth $20,000. The engraved name on the pistols was "Bride" and the date is 1704. What was it all about?

Next morning Johnny gives the pistols to Tri-State and starts on another case. That night the Bride's butler meets Johnny at his apartment. He wants the pistols and does not like the story that they are in the Tri-State vault. As Johnny is told "Please get them in the morning," he is hit with a needle and collapses.

Johnny wakes up to the voice of Bonny. It is after 9:00 PM and Johnny sees that his apartment is torn up and Bonny's arm is no longer in a sling but filled with a Webley automatic. Bonny mumbles about the problem being Worthing's fault. Johnny and Bonny go to see Worthing in a shabby hotel in Boston. "We are in a mess as pistols are locked up" Bonny tells Worthing. Worthing tells Bonny that the pistols are not important now. They have served their purpose. Now the plan is blackmail the Brides to keep secret a two-year-old murder.

Bonny calls the Brides and leaves. The Brides arrive an hour later and meet with Worthing. Worthing tells them that the pistols are locked up, and cannot be delivered. Worthing tells the group that the Brides had their uncle, the Duke of Pembroke murdered. The estate went to the Brides and the other relatives just nibbled at the edges. Worthing and Bonny will keep quiet about a murder in October 8,1948 when a killer hired by the Brides killed the Duke. The theft of the pistols was the motive. Bonny is where proof of guilt lies and he might need more money some day. Mr. Bride will pay $5,000 to Bonny at their house, the rest later. Mrs. Bride is hysterical and wants to go to the police, as too many people know what happened. After the Brides leave, Worthing has his own plans for Johnny, who jumps him and overpowers him. Worthing is searched; his wallet has no ID. In the lining of his coat is a card: "Arthur P. Worthing, CID, Scotland Yard."

Worthing wakes up and tells Johnny that he was posing as blackmailer. The scheme is intricate but he obtained the Bride's confession with Johnny as a witness. The trial in England got no information, so Worthing had to turn criminal. Johnny is told that Bonny was hired to kill the Duke. If they kill Bonny, they will confess to the other murder. Worthing tells Johnny that the Duke was Worthing's friend. Worthing calls the police and Johnny goes to the Brides home with Worthing. Johnny hears angry voices in the library as the police take their positions. Inside Bonny is shot and the police rush in. The Inspector got what he wanted: Bonny is killed and the Brides arrested. Expense account item #6 is $150 for miscellaneous items. You have to admit I deserve something for what I went through!

NOTES:
- WEBLEY PISTOLS WERE MANUFACTURED IN GREAT BRITAIN.
- THERE IS A FREEDOM OF WORSHIP COMMERCIAL TO SUPPORT YOUR CHURCH.
- EDMOND O'BRIEN'S LATEST FILM IS WAR PATH

- BOB LEMOND IS THE ANNOUNCER
- MUSIC IS BY WILBUR HATCH

Producer: Jaime del Valle   **Writers:** Gil Doud
Cast: Ben Wright, Bill Conrad, Dick Ryan, Jeanette Nolan, Dan O'Herlihy, Tyler McVey

◆   ❖   ◆

SHOW: THE ADAM KEGG MATTER
SHOW DATE: 11/11/1950
COMPANY: GRAND EAST ALL RISK INSURANCE COMPANY
AGENT: AL BEGNEY
EXP. ACCT: $230.40

SYNOPSIS: Al Begney calls and Johnny asks him what he insured that he should not have, or are you inviting me to dinner? Johnny tells him that he gets three types of phone calls: social, business and people who want money, creditors or other wise. All tells Johnny that the jewels from the Kegg burglary are insured for $120,000. Is Johnny free? Unemployed yes; but not free.

Johnny travels to New York City to see Begney. They go together to see Mr. Kegg, who is a Broadway angel and an unlikable person. Mrs. Kegg answers the door and shows Johnny a newspaper that was left at the door with a note "see page 3 col 2." Johnny sees an antihistamine ad that has been changed to read: "Histime stops at sign on your cold cash insist at histime." The price has been changed to $98,000. There are instructions to go to a phone booth in Montclair at Maple & 7th, 10:30 tomorrow. Begney tells Johnny to pursue the ransom offer, but Kegg wants noting to do with it. Johnny is told that the Keggs were out for the evening and the jewels were in a locked box in a locked drawer. Johnny talks to Danny, the bellboy operator. Danny tells Johnny that he has been in the apartment, and put out the paper every morning but today. Danny tells Johnny that he lives in Queens, and that the maid lives in Montclair, but has just resigned.

Johnny talks to the police who have found only some smudged fingerprints, and they are canvassing the known fences.

Johnny rents car and goes to Montclair. At a phone booth near a bowling alley a car double-parks and Johnny is told to get into the car and not to cause trouble. Johnny tells the man that the ransom money is to be paid by the Insurance Company. Johnny tells the man he is staying at the Hotel Langley and walks back to his car.

Johnny visits Millicent Weaver the maid. She tells Johnny that she told the police she quit for personal reasons. She has a personal code of ethics. She also knew the location of Jewels.

Back at the hotel there is a message for Johnny to meet a girl in booth #1 in the bar. Johnny goes to the bar and meets Mrs. Kegg, who is scared. She tells Johnny that Danny the bellboy has been killed, and she has to talk. She cries and tells Johnny her story. She is not feeling sorry for herself, but is afraid of what her husband will make of it. She tells Johnny that Danny was killed by a hit and run driver. She relates that she only had the privilege of wearing the jewels until Kegg divorces her, which is in the works. She admits that Adam will rant and rave over this and goes home.

The police did not print Danny's death in the paper. Johnny gets a phone from Hartford. Al Begney tells Johnny that Kegg wants to drop the whole matter. Johnny tells Al he can't do it as it will look like they pulled off rather than uncover a murder.

Johnny goes to see Kegg and asks why he wants the investigation dropped. Are you afraid of what will come to the surface, that you might have faked the robbery? That Danny knew the setup and you killed him? Johnny tells Kegg that the investigation can't be dropped and Kegg tells him to go ahead if he insists.

Johnny goes to the police and tells them of the meeting in Montclair. Johnny also learns that Danny's death was an accident, and that the driver, a Miss Linquist from Florida, has given herself up. Johnny calls Tri-State to give up the case. There is a knock and Mrs. Kegg is at his door. She tells Johnny that knows man in Montclair. His name is Stanley Griffin, and she used to date him. He is a musician and lives in the village. Johnny goes to visit Stanley who tells Johnny that the stuff is in his apartment, and that he will make a statement in front of Kegg. Stanley opens a suitcase and gets the jewels. At the Kegg apartment, Stanley gives the jewels to Mr. Kegg. He tells him that Mrs. Kegg was going to share profits, and will now share the blame. Griffin leaves to give a statement to the police. He tells them that he did it to get her away from Kegg, but she threw him out so he made it look like she helped him. He was drunk and crazy and wanted to see her in prison with him.

This whole matter is a cloud of smoke. The death was inconvenient; and it was a rare type of burglary, done for revenge by jilted man.

NOTES:
- EDMOND O'BRIEN'S LATEST FILM IS WAR PATH
- DAN CUBBERLY IS THE ANNOUNCER
- MUSIC IS BY WILBUR HATCH

Producer: Jaime del Valle   **Writers:** Gil Doud
Cast: Stacy Harris, Lamont Johnson, Jeanette Nolan, Jack Moyles, Hy Averback, Paula Victor, Raymond Burr

◆ ❖ ◆

SHOW:	THE NORA FAULKNER MATTER
SHOW DATE:	11/18/1950
COMPANY:	GREAT EASTERN LIFE INSURANCE COMPANY
AGENT:	JIM MORRIS
EXP. ACCT:	$1,120.40

SYNOPSIS: Jim Morris calls and asks, "Are you working on a case?" "Bonded Kentucky yes, but not insurance" answers Johnny. Jim tells Johnny that a woman in California wants to buy a $200,00 insurance policy, but the agent thinks she is holding back. Jim has decided to investigate.

Johnny travels to the Los Angeles, California office of Great East to see Mr. Snyder, who gives Johnny the Faulkner folder. The husband is the beneficiary and Mrs. Faulkner would pay 6 months of premiums in advance, but she wanted to know when policy is in effect.

Johnny goes to the house and talks to the neighbors who give varying accounts of Faulkner, who lives with her husband and mother-in-law. At the Faulkner house, Johnny meets the mother in-law who has iron gray hair and is losing the battle to stay young. "Who is she seeing in Los Vegas?" Johnny is asked. "You're not the detective? You're not from the agency?" She tries to cover by telling Johnny that it is just a little game she plays. She tells Johnny that she knows nothing of a policy, but Nora does not tell her everything, and she is clever. Nora is always maneuvering to get her husband's affections. Johnny is told that Nora rushed Anthony into marriage in 1942, and while he was in army she partied. Andrew comes in and tells Johnny that he does not know of an insurance policy. Nora has not said anything to him, but he never knew what Nora is thinking. She relies on a psychic, Madam Starr.

Johnny goes to visit the psychic. Johnny asks her why Nora is so anxious to buy insurance. "Who are you?" she asks Johnny. "You mean you don't know?" chuckles Johnny. She tells Johnny that she only offers Nora advice and that she is not a psychic. Nora has been coming for advice and she tries to help. Nora has been under severe mental strain the last few years. She wanted more tangible protection for her life. Everyone has reasons for protection. Johnny is told that Nora is in the Flamingo Hotel in Las Vegas.

Johnny flies to Las Vegas, Nevada on a Western Airlines excursion coach. Johnny goes to the Flamingo Hotel and checks in. When he mentions Mrs. Faulkner to the clerk, the sheriff is called. Johnny is told that she has been poisoned and is in the hospital. Johnny shows his ID and deputy sheriff Wood tells Johnny of the poisoning. Johnny is told that she is too ill to talk and is with her personal doctor. The sheriff has talked to mother, and she fainted. Johnny goes to the hospital room, and Dr. Brooks tells Johnny that Nora is resting, but Nora tells Johnny that she could not stand it any longer and took some poison and destroyed the remains. Johnny thinks the story sounds phony. Johnny tells Nora that her life is very unhappy and that she is lying to protect someone. Dr. Brook tells Johnny that a bottle of the vitamin tonic Hadicol is Nora's hotel room, and it might be the source of the poison. They go to the room and Dr. Brooks accidentally drops the bottle in the sink. The sheriff scoops up some and puts it in a container. In the lobby Johnny meets the managers of the hotel, Max Lewis and Nev Gilbert. The sheriff tells Johnny that the boys will take care of him. Johnny goes to the bar with Max who tells Johnny that he knows nothing of Nora. Max talks to Joe Rosenberg, the credit manger, who tells Johnny that he had signed for a $500 check, which limits the amount of checks cashed.

Andrew and his mother show up after midnight and are told Nora will recover, and the mother is so relieved.

Later that night Johnny is reading in bed when the phone rings. The sheriff tells Johnny that he is back at the hospital, and Nora has been shot. Johnny goes to hospital and learns that Nora is dead, but had named her husband before she died. Johnny is told that Dr. Brook was out for coffee when Nora's husband came in. The doctor tells Johnny that Andrew had threatened to kill her said no one would suspect him because he loved her. Nora wanted a motive, so she bought the insurance. Dr. Brook did not know everything until that night. She told him that Andrew's mother had driven her to it and that she wanted to give him another chance. Anthony had come in briefly the day before and flew back. He arranged the poison when she would not go back with him. Andrew was a deranged war casualty and Nora was terrified of him yet defended him. The sheriff has a search underway and will call out some more men.

Johnny and the sheriff wait, as Los Vegas only has one road and in the desert, the roads end somewhere so they wait for a radio report. The desert is a tough place and the sheriff gives some local color. A railroad section house calls with a sighting. When Johnny and the deputy get there, Anthony is hiding in a culvert. Both ends are covered and Johnny calls into the culvert. Anthony shoots once, then five more shots. The sheriff fires 11 times and then there is no answer. The sheriff asks who carried his life insurance.

The son was guilty in fact. Now the mother must start life alone knowing the guilt was hers.

NOTES:

- JOHNNY DRINKS RYE AND SODA
- JOHNNY NOTES TO HIS SEATMATE ON THE PLANE TO LAS VEGAS THAT HE USED TO LIKE TO FISH BUT THERE IS NOT MUCH TIME FOR IT NOW. HE IS ALWAYS GOING TO START.
- THERE IS A PLUG FOR WESTERN AIRLINES.
- THE SHERIFF TELLS JOHNNY THAT AN OLD PROSPECTOR WAS HIT IN THE FACE WITH A DROP OF WATER AND IT TOOK A BUCKET OF SAND TO WAKE HIM UP, AND THE OLD STORY ABOUT IT BEING SO HOT A STARVING COYOTE WAS CHASING A RABBIT AND THEY WERE BOTH WALKING. LATER IT WILL BE SO HOT THAT ANDREW WILL CRAWL ONTO THE ELECTRIC CHAIR TO COOL OFF.
- DAN CUBBERLY IS THE ANNOUNCER
- MUSIC IS BY WILBUR HATCH

Producer: Jaime del Valle   **Writers:** Gil Doud
Cast: Parley Baer, Jeanette Nolan, Herb Butterfield, Lee Patrick, John Dehner, Tim Graham, Virginia Gregg, Wilms Herbert, Victor Perrin, Clayton Post

SHOW: **THE WOODWARD MANILA MATTER**
SHOW DATE: **11/25/1950**
COMPANY: **COLUMBIA ALL RISK INSURANCE COMPANY**
AGENT: **RALPH WEADEN**
EXP. ACCT: **$3,940.00**

SYNOPSIS: Ralph Weadon calls to tell Johnny that the take from the burglary is $75,000 and that an American clerk has disappeared.

Johnny goes to Manila, Philippines to investigate a burglary and is met by Floyd McDonald and Irving Morgan of the Woodward Hardware Company who take him directly to the office. Johnny is told that the safe was found open on Monday morning with $75,000 missing. The U. S. headquarters required them to keep the money on hand for monthly shipments home. Then Floyd and Irving disagree over Dan Blake the clerk. Floyd trusts him and Irving feels he is guilty. He has been missing four days, but it is easy to drop out of site in the area.

Johnny goes to his hotel and orders Gimlets while he waits for his luggage. Later Johnny goes to the police and talks to Sgt. Malvar who is not looking for Dan Blake. He has captured the thief; a local man named Miguel who cannot tell where he was that night, and was robbing another store last night. Johnny talks to Miguel and he tells Johnny that he does not have the money. If he had money, then why would he steal 5 pesos? Johnny thinks it is easier for Malvar to grill Miguel than look for the real person.

Johnny goes to the Woodward office and meets Charlotte Page, the niece of owner. She shows Johnny the office layout, and Johnny tells her that it looks bad for Dan. She tells Johnny that she saw him occasionally and knows of no problems. Johnny is shown the office safe, which is under the rug in the office. Everyone trusted Dan, but he did not know the combination. Johnny gets Dan's address from payroll records and goes to Dan's room. Form the contents of the room, Johnny learns that Dan was a student of the Philippines and traveled widely there.

Johnny goes to the police and tells Malvar of Dan's travels in the islands. Malvar tells Johnny that Dan has been found and taken aboard a ship. He was shot many times and is dead. The ship captain knows it is Dan because the man had mentioned his name before he died. Johnny calls Floyd but he is out so Johnny tells Charlotte to tell Floyd to come and look at the body. Charlotte is saddened to hear Dan is dead. Later, Floyd and Johnny go to look at the body and Floyd confirms that it is Dan. They are told that Dan was found in a dugout in Tayabas Bay. Captain Covar, the captain of an inter-island schooner found him. He was alive for a while but the money was not found on him. Floyd and Johnny rent a boat to find Capt Covar, and find his boat, the "Sea Nymph" to be a wreck. They go onto the boat and talk to Captain Covar who tells them that Malvar thinks that Covar has the money and that he better give it to him. Covar tells Johnny that he found the man in a dug-out Morro craft. He lived 15-20 minutes and said little. Covar gets angry, as the police are getting papers to search his boat. Covar tells Johnny that plenty could have happened on the way to Tayabas Bay, as the Huks would do anything for money. Johnny and Floyd leave the boat, and Johnny is not sure of Covar as he may be lying. Later, Johnny sees in Malvar's report that the crew says that Dan said nothing as the Huks had killed him. Johnny learns from Malvar that McDonald is deep in debt, so maybe he used Dan as a patsy, as there is no reason for Dan to have done it. Malvar tells Johnny that it is not wise to question McDonald, as he is a man of honor.

Johnny goes to see Irving Morgan, who tells Johnny that he has heard that the money is gone, as Floyd had said so. Irving also tells Johnny that the Huks can be handy to have around. "How much do you know of McDonald's personal life?" asks Johnny, "Does he owe you money?" Irving tells Johnny that Floyd is not the kind of man to do such a thing. Floyd has dinner at the Merchants Club every day, so question him at home, as Irving wants to stay away from this thing.

Johnny goes to see Floyd at his home, and a man comes out of the front door, Capt. Covar. "Forget you saw me," he tells Johnny as he runs away. Johnny goes to the house and meets Charlotte, who tells Johnny that Covar had come to see her, and hit her because he wanted the money. She tells Johnny that she had the money and was holding it for Dan. They wanted to get away to have a life of their own.

Johnny calls Malvar and meets him at the harbor police, and they go out after Covar. Malvar tells Johnny the police Doctor says Dan was choked to death. They find Covar 30 minutes after leaving. The police open up with a machine gun, and Covar fires back, hitting a searchlight. Covar's crew turns on him and he shoots them. The police machine gun cuts Covar down, and Johnny goes aboard to find the money.

Charlotte was arrested but the money did not add up to the amount claimed.

NOTES:
- THE HUKS, OR HUKBALAHAPS WERE NATIVE PEOPLE WHO REBELLED AGAINST THE GOVERNMENT AFTER WWII.
- THE MORO WERE A GROUP OF MALAY MUSLIMS STILL ACTIVE TODAY.
- DAN CUBBERLY IS THE ANNOUNCER
- MUSIC IS BY WILBUR HATCH
- EDMOND O'BRIEN'S NEW MOVIE IS "WAR PATH"

Producer: Jaime del Valle   **Writers:** Gil Doud
Cast: Bill Conrad, Lillian Buyeff, Robert Griffin, Bill Johnstone, Hy Averback, Jack Kruschen

◆ ❖ ◆

SHOW: THE JACKIE CLEAVER MATTER
SHOW DATE: 12/09/1950
COMPANY: SIERRA ALL RISK
AGENT: CARL MASON
EXP. ACCT: $280.00

SYNOPSIS: Carl Mason from Sierra All-Risk calls Johnny and asks him to assist in looking for a policy beneficiary who has disappeared. Carl got a letter from the client last week and does not understand why she has disappeared so quickly.

Johnny meets Carl Mason, who tells Johnny about the death of Howard Shumaker who had left a $40,000 policy to Jackie Cleaver, his ex-wife. Mason's last letters from Jackie came from Manchester, New Hampshire. Now she has disappeared.

Johnny rents a car and drives to the address in Manchester, which is a convalescent home. The manager, Mr. Foresland, tells Johnny that Jackie has moved out, and that she probably is in Middleton. She had no visitors and got checks from California twice a month. Johnny gets an address from the local post office and drives to Middleton where she has moved out of the ratty hotel she was staying in. The manager thinks she went to New Haven and mentions also getting alimony checks from California. On the way out, a little man tells Johnny that he can help Johnny find Jackie, as she is a friend and maybe she does not want to be found. He will call Johnny the next day.

Johnny calls Mason from his apartment to tell about the man he met, and that he thinks Jackie is in the run. As soon as Johnny hangs up, there is a knock on the door. At the door is the man with a friend named Bert who invite them selves in and ask Johnny about Mason. The small man, who is named Happy, finds Mason's card, and as Johnny tries to get it back he is slugged. Johnny is told to stop looking for Jackie, as there is going to be trouble. Bert leaves to go to the hotel to see Mason while Happy waits, and then leaves after 25 minutes. Johnny goes to the hotel and finds a dead man in the bathroom — Bert! The police are called and Lt. Schiller gets Johnny's story and "encourages" Johnny to continue with his investigation.

Johnny wires a detective agency in California for information on Mason and Jackie, and then goes back to the hotel in Middleton to find more about Happy. The desk clerk tells Johnny that his name is Snell Chapman, and that he has a girlfriend there in the hotel. Johnny is told that Snell hangs out at a couple bars in the area. Johnny tells the manager to have Happy call if she sees him, and starts visiting the bars. At the first one, Johnny orders a dark rum and gets no information from the bar tender. On the way out, Happy meets Johnny in the parking lot. He knows that Bert is dead, but he can get Johnny in touch with Jackie. Johnny tells him that the police want to talk to Jackie too. Happy will call Johnny the next morning.

In the morning Johnny gets a reply from the agency in California. Mason is a disbarred lawyer who worked for a syndicate on the West Coast; and Jackie was the star witness who helped break up the syndicate. Mason calls Johnny and wants to give up. He tells Johnny that he killed Bert in self-defense and needs Johnny's testimony. Johnny agrees to meet him after noon. Happy calls and agrees to meet Johnny at Lt. Schiller's office at 11:30. Johnny meets Happy and Jackie at Lt. Schiller's office. She is surprised that they know what they do, as her testimony was supposed to have been kept quiet. She also tells them that her lawyer in Los Angeles sends the money as part of her testimony agreement.

Later, Johnny goes to meet Mason at a drug store. Mason tells Johnny that Jackie talked because she was a plant from the rival syndicate who moved in after the first one was broken up. They leave for the police and Happy meets them on the street and kills Mason. Happy is arrested and the police are looking for Jackie.

Johnny hardly expects Sierra to pay his expenses, but hopes they will learn what goes on behind their back.

NOTES:
- EDMOND O'BRIEN'S NEW MOVIE IS "WAR PATH"
- DAN CUBBERLY IS THE ANNOUNCER
- MUSIC IS BY WILBUR HATCH

Producer: Jaime del Valle   **Writers:**   Gil Doud
Cast: Ed Begley, Dick Ryan, Mary Lansing, Sidney Miller, Tim Graham, Virginia Gregg, Hy Averback, Jim Nusser

SHOW: THE LELAND BLACKBURN MATTER
SHOW DATE: 12/16/1950
COMPANY: PLYMOUTH INSURANCE COMPANY
AGENT: BOB HALL
EXP. ACCT: $345.75

SYNOPSIS: Bob Hall calls to tell Johnny that Gene Rymer, another investigator, and a friend of Johnny's has been killed in Charleston, South Carolina, and that his wife was with him. Johnny accepts the case, noting "You cannot hunt for trouble without finding some." Johnny is told that Gene Rymer was looking into the death of Leland Blackburn who was bludgeoned to death in his study.

In Charleston Johnny goes to see Gene's wife Barbara, who was an old flame of Johnny's before she married Gene. She tells Johnny that Gene had made her come; that he beat her; and that he had found out about a man she was seeing. She said she would like to have killed Gene for the things he had done.

Johnny goes to police and meets Lt. Simms, who tells Johnny that Blackburn was killed in his home; that he was a stockbroker; that his wallet was empty, and that the family has refused an autopsy. Johnny is told that Gene was found in alley near Magazine Street; shot three times with a .32, but Blackburn would have never set foot in that part of town.

Johnny goes to the Blackburn home and meets with Mrs. Blackburn, and the son Roland. Johnny is told that the Blackburns are a fine old southern family whose name must not be dragged into murder. Roland suspects a plot and wants his father's killers punished. Mrs. Blackburn tells Johnny that she was in bed at the other end of the house. Roland had gone to the kitchen and found Leland, who was a charitable, honest and pious man. She tells Johnny that she hopes to join him soon. Johnny calls Lt. Simms to pass on the statement of Roland and his suspicion that he knows more. Lt. Simms tells Johnny that he had checked their finances and they were fine.

Back at his hotel Johnny is met by the house detective, Hal Brands. He tells Johnny that he had been paid by Gene to watch his wife, and that she had a visitor named George Richards just before Gene was shot. Richards has gone back to New York. Johnny goes to Barbara and tells her he is angry that she lied. She tells Johnny that she did not know George was coming. She told him to leave, and that no one would find out. She tells Johnny that neither she nor George killed Gene. Right now, Johnny tells her, you need witnesses or the police will arrest you. Johnny searches for alibis for George but gets nowhere.

Johnny goes to see Lt. Simms and is told that he is in real trouble for not telling them about Gene's troubles with his wife. Johnny tells Lt. Simms that Gene had a mean streak, and that she was a friend. Also, all the evidence is circumstantial. Johnny wonders if Richards had set up a phony meeting to kill George? Barbara is brought in for questioning. The autopsy report comes in and discloses that Blackburn was a narcotics user.

Johnny goes to see Mrs. Blackburn and tells her of the required autopsy and the results. She tells Johnny that they thought they were doing the right thing, but Gene had found out. Blackburn had been buying from two men named Miller and Stone, who were blackmailing him. They had come to force him to buy more drugs, and then they killed him. Johnny is told that Gene had gone to meet the men and was killed.

Johnny gets the address and decides to go there alone. Johnny forces his way into the apartment and ends up shooting Miller as he runs out. Miller talks to the police and Stone is caught.

Back in Hartford, Barbara calls, but Johnny says he is on another case and has to earn a living. Goodbye.

Personal note: Cops should never marry. They are away from home too much and leave too many widows.

NOTES:
- JOHNNY SAYS HE LEARNED THE BUSINESS AS A PINKERTON AGENT.
- JOHNNY REFERENCES CARRYING AN AUTOMATIC.
- DAN CUBBERLY IS THE ANNOUNCER
- MUSIC IS BY WILBUR HATCH
- EDMOND O'BRIEN'S NEW MOVIE IS "WAR PATH"

Producer: Jaime del Valle   **Writers:** Gil Doud
Cast: John Dehner, Jim Nusser, Jeanette Nolan, Georgia Ellis, John McIntire, Larry Dobkin

◆ ❖ ◆

SHOW: THE MONTEVIDEO MATTER
SHOW DATE: 12/23/1950

COMPANY: **WASHINGTONIAN INSURANCE COMPANY**
AGENT: **BILL BRANDON**
EXP. ACCT: **$1,650.00**

SYNOPSIS: Bill Brandon calls Johnny and tells him that an English woman has been found dead in South America. The London Investment Group wants Johnny to investigate the death.

Johnny flies to Montevideo, Uruguay and gets a room at the Hotel Madrid. Johnny then meets with Inspector Alcira and learns that Mrs. Madeline Furness has been killed. Her husband Roger owns a meatpacking plant, and their son Keith lives with them. The killing was four days ago, and the gardener Raymon del Gado found the body. Mrs. Furness was killed with a blast from a shotgun.

Johnny goes to the Furness home where Ramon is working. He tells Johnny that "she was a bad woman and he was a bad man." Johnny meets Keith, who is a stepson. He tells Johnny that his father did not kill her for the £5,000 insurance, and that Madeline was a schemer. Johnny is shown a picture of Madeline, who is a much younger woman. Keith tells Johnny that he goes to school in England, and that the body was found between their home and the house of Jack Strong, their neighbor.

Johnny meets with Mrs. Strong, who is in a wheelchair. She tells Johnny that there was a division between Madeline and her stepson. Johnny notes that Roger Furness must have found out about his wife's escapades with Mr. Strong. Everyone heard the gunshot, and money probably was the motive.

Johnny meets Mr. Furness, and he tells Johnny that he needs the money from the insurance. He admits that he knew about his wife and Strong. Keith comes in and tells Johnny that he killed his stepmother. Keith is arrested and jailed, but under questioning he is unsure of the facts.

Johnny goes to the Strong residence and sees Mrs. Strong walking inside the house. Once inside she is in the wheelchair again. She tells Johnny that she hurt her back in a hunting accident, and is not supposed to walk. She admits to Johnny that she knew about her husband and Madeline. Mr. Strong comes in and attacks Johnny, who slugs him. Johnny goes to see Mr. Furness and accuses him of hiding behind his son's confession. On the way out, Furness is shot at the front door. Inspector Alcira later tells Johnny that del Gado is a common name, but they are looking for Ramon. Later he is arrested and admits to the killings. He tells the police that they killed his grandson with their automobile after his daughter had died.

NOTES:
- THIS PROGRAM IS REPEATED ON **9-3-52**
- THE ANNOUNCER IS DAN CUBBERLY
- MUSIC IS BY WILBUR HATCH
- EDMOND O'BRIEN'S NEXT FILM IS "WAR PATH"
- STORY INFORMATION OBTAINED FROM THE KNX COLLECTION IN THE THOUSAND OAKS LIBRARY

Producer: Jaime del Valle   **Writers**   Gil Doud
Cast: Ben Wright, Terry Kilburn, Lillian Buyeff, Jay Novello, Lou Krugman, Tudor Owen

◆   ❖   ◆

SHOW: THE RUDY VALENTINE MATTER
SHOW DATE: 12/30/1950
COMPANY: COUNTY COURT, KINGS COUNTY
AGENT:
EXP. ACCT: $10.85

SYNOPSIS: Rudy calls Johnny from Leavenworth prison and reminds Johnny that in 1940 he sent Rudy to prison, along with his wife and lawyer. Rudy is ready to settle up now.

Johnny goes to New York City and is almost hit by a car. A witness tells Johnny that the streets are not safe with all the drunk drivers. Johnny goes to the police and talks to Sgt. Foss who searches the records. Johnny learns that Rudy was convicted of robbing a delicatessen, and was identified by the owner. Later the gun and money were found in his room. Rudy had been arrested for Auto theft in 1939, and assault in 1940. He was 17 at the time. Johnny gets the address and goes to read the trial transcript. Johnny learns that the attorney was William P. Capper, who is now a successful lawyer. Johnny goes to see Capper and talks to him. Johnny is told that Rudy has also contacted Capper, but he calls it just talk.

Johnny goes to his hotel and wires the prison. The prison officials tell Johnny that Rudy got mail from Sybil Miller on 16th Street. Johnny goes to see Sybil and asks for Rudy, but she tells Johnny that he is not there. Johnny tells her of the threats and she tells Johnny that Rudy had promised to forget about the past. Sybil tells Johnny that Rudy has gone to Buffalo. Johnny goes to see Rudy's brother Anthony at a newspaper-cigar stand he runs. Johnny meets Rudy's wife Pat, and Anthony tells Johnny that Rudy has not contacted them, but he will send Rudy's wife out of town for protection. Johnny gets a telegram from the prison that tells him that Rudy had spent time in the mental ward and attempted suicide, but is all right now. Johnny is then called by Rudy's wife, who tells him that Tony has been killed by Rudy.

Johnny goes to the apartment and meets Lt. Maxwell who tells Johnny that they have picked up Rudy's wife Pat. Johnny tells him that he has no description for Rudy.

Sybil comes to Johnny's hotel and tells Johnny about Tony. She argues with Johnny and accused him of planting the gun. She tells Johnny that only a framed man would kill his brother, and gives Johnny a description of Rudy. Johnny calls Capper and learns that he is on his way to Florida. Johnny goes to his hotel and meets Rudy at his door. Rudy tells Johnny that he has talked to Sybil, and that Rudy did not kill Tony. Rudy tells Johnny that he went to Buffalo to look for a job, and was driving a blue 1939 Plymouth coupe (Not the car that almost ran Johnny down). Rudy tells Johnny that his lawyer was responsible for putting the money in his room. Johnny convinces Rudy to give him self up to the police.

Johnny goes to see Pat and discovers that she is dead. Johnny goes to Capper's apartment and tells him that he was paid to throw the case, and calls him an ambulance chaser. Capper tries to bribe Johnny, and then pulls a gun.

Remarks: As I said at the outset, I do not expect the County Court, Part One to honor this statement. It would be fair and equitable to work out payment for a witness. It looks like I made that position again at Capper's forthcoming murder trial, and for me it'll be a waste of time. I know he is guilty."

NOTES:

- THE ANNOUNCER IS CHARLIE LYON
- MUSIC IS BY EDDIE DUNSTEDTER
- STORY INFORMATION OBTAINED FROM THE KNX COLLECTION IN THE THOUSAND OAKS LIBRARY

Producer:	Jaime del Valle	Writers	Gil Doud
Cast:	Sidney Miller, Bill Johnstone, Jack Moyles, Jeanette Nolan, Joseph Kearns, Clayton Post, Tom Hanley, Bill James		

◆ ❖ ◆

SHOW:	THE ADOLPH SCHOMAN MATTER
SHOW DATE:	1/6/1951
COMPANY:	CORINTHIAN ALL-RISK INSURANCE COMPANY
AGENT:	HAROLD WARNER
EXP. ACCT:	$150.80

SYNOPSIS: The secretary for Harold Warner calls. Harold wants to meet Johnny for lunch to talk about a policyholder in Allentown, Pennsylvania who was poisoned.

Johnny meets with Harold and is told that Adolph Schoman was in the steel and concrete business in Pennsylvania. Schoman held $150,000 in personal insurance and $200,000 with the company as beneficiary. The family also includes his wife Amelia, and children Eric, Max and Gertrude. Schoman was 80 and known to run the house like a factory. He died last night.

Johnny goes to Allentown and meets with Mrs. Schoman who tells Johnny that her husband was an invalid and had cancer, which had been kept form the public. Johnny is told that he did not kill himself; that would be a sign of defeat. The children have no ambition and just hang around for the money, and the local doctor, Dr. Buchholtz has an office in town.

Johnny goes to see Dr. Buchholtz and is told that Adolph was a fool. Gertrude is an old maid, Max is an alcoholic and Eric is in an unsuccessful marriage with Betty Elliot, a model or working girl, which is below the family standards. Johnny goes to see Betty, but she does not want to talk other than to tell Johnny that she does not live with Eric because he is a slave to the family. Betty thinks that the mother killed Adolph. At the inquest it is determined that someone administered an alkaloid poison, and that there was an abrasion on his hand.

Johnny meets with the children and none of them remembers hearing anything. While they are talking Amelia screams and Johnny rushes upstairs to find poison in a glass of water. Amelia is ok, but Johnny calls the doctor. When Dr. Buchholtz arrives Johnny gives him the glass, which he says contains belladrine. Amelia tells Johnny that she does not want the police called. When Johnny insists, he is told to leave, and take the glass with him. On the way out Max tells Johnny that Betty is pregnant. Johnny goes to talk to Betty, who tells him that Eric is to be disinherited. Johnny goes back to Amelia and tells her that Erick is to be charged by the police. Johnny tells her that she killed her husband because he wanted to disinherit Eric because of Betty and the child.

NOTES:
- THE ANNOUNCER IS DICK CUTTING
- MUSIC IS BY WILBUR HATCH
- THIS STORY WAS DONE BY BOB BAILEY AS THE AMELIA HARWELL MATTER, WITH A REVERSAL OF VICTIMS
- STORY INFORMATION OBTAINED FROM THE KNX COLLECTION IN THE THOUSAND OAKS LIBRARY

Producer: Jaime del Valle   **Writers** Gil Doud
Cast: Virginia Gregg, Joe Du Val, Jeanette Nolan, Dick Ryan, Francis X. Bushman, Stacy Harris, Edgar Barrier

SHOW: THE PORT-O-CALL MATTER
SHOW DATE: 1/13/1951
COMPANY: GREAT EASTERN INSURANCE COMPANY
AGENT: BOB REDDEN
EXP. ACCT: $450.60

SYNOPSIS: Bob Redeen calls and Johnny is told to drop his current assignment. There has been a series of robberies in San Francisco. Bob wants Johnny to get right on it.

Johnny goes to San Francisco, California and meets Lt. Clark who tells Johnny about the four robberies at the Port O'call Savings and Loan. The first was at 9:15, the last at 10:55. The same group of 8-10, men who appeared to wear makeup, did all of the jobs; and only one person talked and used a falsetto voice. So far the take is $47,000. Johnny is told that the police are searching the usual places, so Johnny and Lt. Clark can only wait.

At 5:00 PM a call comes from missing persons that a Mrs. Gier has reported her husband missing. Johnny and Clark talk to Mrs. Gier, who tells them that her husband drives a cab and has not had an accident, and that she has three kids and a roomer. Johnny tells her of the robberies and is told that her husband would never get involved in a robbery. She leaves and the police put a tail on her. Johnny wonders if the robbers could have used a cab.

Johnny talks to the cab company drivers and discovers that a driver, Mike Landini missing. Johnny goes to see Lanini's apartment manager and looks through the apartment, but learns nothing.

The next day a body is found. Mrs. Gier is called in and is very upset, but it is not her husband. Johnny follows her to her home and asks why she is so upset. She tells Johnny that she had never seen a body before. Back at police headquarters, Mr. Prince from the bank tells Johnny and Lt. Clark that he remembers seeing a man with a manicure and a ring. Johnny remembers that the body had a manicure and a missing ring. The police report in that no one has seen Mrs. Gier, but they have not seen the roomer either, and Johnny wonders where he is. The police get two neighbors to identify the body as Mrs. Gier's roomer. Johnny goes to the Gier home with Lt. Clark. They search the room and hit pay dirt — drawings of the bank branches and a list of names. Mrs. Gier tells Johnny that the roomer is named Ted Grace, was a salesman; got no mail, but had phone calls from the same man, and hung out at the Furlong Bar.

Johnny goes to the bar, orders a Rye and Soda, and asks the bartender for Ted, or Tony. The bartender tells Johnny that he knows no one by those names. On the way out, an old man calls the bartender "Tony." Johnny doubles back and watches Tony make a phone call. Johnny calls Lt. Clark and they confront Tony. Under pressure he admits to participating in the robberies, and tells them that the organizers were 3 ex-cons from the east. Tony knew there would be trouble when the killing started. Tony gives Lt. Clark the name of the motor court where the three men are.

Lt. Clark and Johnny join other officers at the motor court in a rainstorm. Lt. Clark is shot going up to the door and two of the robbers die in a hail of bullets. Lt. Clark dies on the way to the hospital.

It is probably not important but the gunfight showed up on page two of the papers, the storm got page one.

NOTES:
- JOHNNY IS DRINKING RYE AND SODA
- EDMOND O'BRIEN'S NEW MOVIE IS "WAR PATH"
- DICK CUTTING IS THE ANNOUNCER
- MUSIC DIRECTION IS BY WILBUR HATCH

Producer: Jaime del Valle   **Writers:** Gil Doud
Cast: Howard McNear, Ed Begley, Hy Averback, Jim Nusser, Virginia Gregg, Janet Scott

SHOW: THE DAVID ROCKY MATTER
SHOW DATE: 1/20/1951
COMPANY: BRITANNIA LIFE INSURANCE COMPANY
AGENT:

EXP. ACCT: **$840.75**

SYNOPSIS: Miss Beale, the travel agent calls Johnny with his travel arrangements: National Airlines to New Orleans then Pan American to Managua, Nicaragua and a train to San Juan del Sur, Nicaragua. Why not make round trip reservations she asks; I'm not always sure I will come home from these trips Johnny replies.

Johnny goes to New York, and gets information on David Rocky from the Maritime Union Hiring Hall. Johnny tells them that David had missed his ship and was unaccounted for. When asked why Johnny is going to all this trouble, Johnny tells them that David just became a millionaire. Johnny flies to San Juan del Sur and meets with Mr. Wahl of the shipping line. Wahl tells Johnny to go back to Hartford as Rocky is in jail for murder for knifing a man in a drunken brawl. When asked why the shipping company had not reported it, Wahl says one must be careful not to annoy the Guardia. Johnny discovers the Guardia were formed by the US Army, and are a force to be dealt with carefully.

Johnny goes to see Rocky in the jail where Sergeant Ortega says that Rocky cannot be seen. Why? Because I say he is guilty, now leave! Johnny threatens to go to the American Counsel and is allowed ten minutes. The cell has no lights so Johnny uses a match for light while David holds his ID. Johnny tells David that his adoptive father, Titus Morgan has died and left him $1.5 Million and $50,000 in insurance. David tells Johnny that he does not remember what happened that night. He was drinking with friends, and remembers nothing. He tells Johnny that he liked Emiliano Sagasa and had no reason to kill him. He was with Emiliano, his wife Misha, a girl named Alicia and his coworkers Dave Light and Chris Binstead. David tells Johnny that he wishes he had stayed home with his adoptive family. Johnny thinks David is innocent, as there is no motive and the knife has not been found. Johnny sends a wire to Hartford and requests that a lawyer be sent to represent David.

Johnny meets with Misha Sagassa, who is an attractive girl who likes Americans because they always bring her presents, and that made her husband angry. She did not see the killing, as she was outside with Alicia. She tells Johnny that she heard talking and then Chris came out and said, "Dave killed Emiliano." Johnny wonders if he could have meant Dave Light? Johnny tells Misha of David's inheritance and how he must learn the truth.

Johnny goes to see Chris Binstead. He tells Johnny that he saw Misha wake David up, some words were said and David killed Emiliano with a knife. Johnny goes back to the hotel and there is a message from Wahl telling him that Misha has been looking for Johnny and wants to see him immediately. Johnny goes to Misha and she tells Johnny that she has found the knife, which the Guardia had not even looked for. She tells Johnny that she just was thinking about it and looked behind a chest and there it was. Johnny takes the knife and tells Misha not to tell anyone anything about this. Johnny charters a plane and takes the knife and his wallet to be processed for fingerprints. Later Johnny goes to see David Rocky, who tells of his being adopted and how he just did not fit into the high-society life of this adoptive father, so he just left. Later, Johnny learns that a lawyer is on the way and that the report on the prints is back, so he goes to the only place he can go. Johnny goes to see David and tells him that the prints on the knife were his; he had murdered Emiliano Sagasa.

The lawyer thinks there is a good change at a second-degree murder plea. But $1.5 million is worth waiting for.

NOTES:

- THE INSURANCE AND ESTATE ARE WORTH OVER $12,000,000 IN 2006 DOLLARS—DEFINITELY WORTH WAITING FOR.
- EDMOND O'BRIEN'S NEW MOVIE IS "THE REDHEAD AND THE COWBOY"
- DICK CUTTING IS THE ANNOUNCER
- MUSIC IS BY WILBUR HATCH

Producer: Jaime del Valle   **Writers:** Gil Doud
Cast: Lillian Buyeff, Bill Conrad, Jack Moyles, Tyler McVey, Edgar Barrier, Jay Novello

◆ ❖ ◆

SHOW: THE WELDON BRAGG MATTER
SHOW DATE: 1/27/1951
COMPANY: FINANCIAL SURETY
AGENT: JIM WALDO
EXP. ACCT: $65.80

SYNOPSIS: Jim Waldo calls Johnny and tells him that it still looks bad, and Dr. Bragg is still unconscious and the hospital is only admitting the police.

Johnny goes to the Redlands Hospital in Hartford, Connecticut, but the guard will not let Johnny in, and will only tell him that Dr. Bragg has been shot.

Johnny goes to Dr. Bragg's house and meets Lt. Gregory who tells Johnny that Dr. Bragg was in the study and was shot twice, and the gun was not an automatic. Mrs. Bragg was upstairs and heard the shots. The next day Johnny goes to the hospital with Lt. Gregory and they are told that Dr. Bragg is dying. They go into the room to get a deathbed statement, and Dr. Bragg asks if Ethel is there. They leave and Johnny tells Lt. Gregory that Mrs. Bragg is named Gwen, and Ethel Johnson is the nurse.

Johnny goes to see Mrs. Bragg, and she asks Johnny if her husband asked for "her," and admits that she has lost her husband a long time. Johnny goes to see Nurse Ethel Johnson who tells Johnny that she loved the doctor, but his wife refused to give him a divorce. Ethel shows Johnny a letter from a psychiatric patient whose wife died in an operation, and accuses Dr. Bragg of killing her. Johnny visits Lt. Gregory, and tells him about the letter. Lt. Gregory tells Johnny that his younger brother Floyd is the man who wrote the letter. Lt. Gregory tells Johnny that he tries to be a good cop, and will arrest his brother if necessary. The ballistics report comes in and Dr. Bragg was shot three times by a .32 revolver from a distance of seven feet.

Johnny goes to see Mrs. Bragg and she denies what Johnny tells her about the divorce. Johnny searches the study and finds the accounts are in arrears, another patient had died in an operation, and the doctor had been sued but won the case. Johnny goes to see Floyd at his job, but he is not there. Later that night Johnny finds Floyd at home and tells him about the letter. Floyd wants to confess to keep his brother out of trouble. Johnny tells Lt. Gregory about the conversation the next day. Johnny goes to the doctor's office the next day with Sgt. Bell and finds a box with .32 caliber shells inside of it. Johnny calls Lt. Gregory and arranges to meet him at his office. Johnny and Lt. Gregory go to see Ethel to confront her about the ammunition and Mrs. Bragg's denial of a divorce request. Ethel gets the gun and tries to shoot her self and fires once after Johnny grabs the gun. She admits that she had gone to see Dr. Bragg and had argued with him. She followed him, and shot him in his study.

NOTES:
- THE ANNOUNCER IS DICK CUTTING
- MUSIC IS BY LUD GLUSKIN
- EDMOND O'BRIEN'S NEXT MOVIE IS THE RED HEAD AND THE COWBOY
- STORY INFORMATION OBTAINED FROM THE KNX COLLECTION IN THE THOUSAND OAKS LIBRARY

Producer: Jaime del Valle   **Writers**   Gil Doud
Cast: Howard McNear, Bill Bouchey, Bill Conrad, Lee Patrick, Stanley Farrer, Virginia Gregg, Clayton Post, Wilms Herbert, Jim Nusser

◆   ❖   ◆

SHOW: THE MONOPOLY MATTER
SHOW DATE: 2/3/1951
COMPANY: CORINTHIAN ALL-RISK INSURANCE COMPANY
AGENT: MR. BRANDT
EXP. ACCT: $63.80

SYNOPSIS: Mr. Brandt calls about a fire but there are no details. It is the Monopoly Club in Waterbury.

Johnny rents a car and drives to Waterbury, Connecticut. The fire department is still on the site as Johnny arrives. Later the fire is under control and Johnny talks to the fire inspector, Captain McReedy. The fire started inside; the building is less than five years old and is licensed for public use. The alarm came in at 11:00 AM. The owner has gone home. The firemen find proof of arson—a Molotov cocktail.

Johnny goes to see the owner, Gerald Hobson. He was at the site but his nerves got the best of him, so he went home. Thank goodness for the insurance. The business specializes in the game Monopoly, harmless entertainment for the factory workers. Johnny asks about gambling, but Hobson denies anything.

Johnny tells him that gambling debts could cause someone to burn the building. Hobson tells Johnny that a man had come by last week and made him pay for protection—he paid $100 and told the police who found nothing.

Johnny goes to see McReedy about the possibility of extortion. Sgt Winnick from the police arrives and they talk about Hobson. The police had gone to see Hobson, but no one else had reported anything. They thought a transient had taken Hobson.

Johnny goes back to Hobson to tell him that he is under suspicion for setting the fire. His story of the protection racket did not hold up. Johnny is not as cautious as the police. Johnny tells Hobson he has looked into his finances and Hobson gets angry. He is in need of $18,000 and the insurance would help. Johnny goes back to Hartford and gets a call from Winnick the next morning. Winnick tells Johnny that Hobson's story is on the level—there was another protection racket try this morning and a shooting at a bowling alley.

Johnny drives back to Waterbury and meets Winnick at the bowling alley. The dead man was a bystander. The owner, Mr. Roblinski is upset. He shot the man when they told him he was a foreigner and had to pay to work in the city. Carl came in and one of the men shot Carl. Roblinski shot the other man and the shooter got away. The wounded man is Paul Loaner from Chicago. The police are searching for the other man.

Johnny and Winnick go to the hospital to talk to Loaner, who has little to say. Johnny tells him that he talked while he was unconscious but he does not believe them and is not going to talk. They found a gun but Loaner says it is not his. Winnick says Roblinski told them Loaner was alone, to get information. He had a partner but does not know his name. To trick Loaner, Winnick blurts out Bert Lucas' name and Loaner is tricked into admitting Bert was his partner. Mr. Hobson comes in and Johnny apologizes for suspecting him. Hobson does not recognize Loaner. Loaner says both of them torched the Monopoly club because Hobson went to the police. They should have taken $500. On the way out, a nurse has a call from Loaner's wife. Johnny tells her that Paul is all right. She is just down the street. She will meet him downstairs so she will not have to talk to anyone. She knew something bad would happen. The wife tells Johnny that Bert Lucas was with Paul. She knows where Bert is. He is at the place they burned down, and he knows he killed the man at the bowling alley.

Johnny gets Winnick and they go to the Monopoly Club. The police go in with their Thompsons and look for Bert. They call for Lucas and are shot at, wounding an officer in the stomach. Lights are brought into the building and Lucas tries to run, but is cut down.

NOTES:
- THE ANNOUNCER IS DICK CUTTING
- MUSIC IS BY WILBUR HATCH
- THIS IS THE SAME STORY BROADCAST WITH JOHN LUND, BUT WITH A DIFFERENT CAST

- **STORY INFORMATION OBTAINED FROM THE KNX COLLECTION IN THE THOUSAND OAKS LIBRARY**

Producer: Jaime del Valle   **Writers**   **Gil Doud**
Cast: Sammie Hill, Joe Du Val, Tony Barrett, Parley Baer, Herb Butterfield, Ted Osborne, Howard Culver, Kay Stewart

◆   ❖   ◆

SHOW: THE LLOYD HAMMERLY MATTER
SHOW DATE: 2/10/1951
COMPANY: GREAT EASTERN INSURANCE COMPANY
AGENT:
EXP. ACCT: $2,350.00

SYNOPSIS: Johnny calls Frank to cancel dinner and tells him that he is going to Port Moresby, New Guinea. A man killed in 1942 has been seen alive.

Johnny flies to San Francisco and goes to the S.S. Hanford Star to talk to the first officer, Mr. Carlson. Johnny tells Carlson that he heard about him writing to the Hammerly family about Lloyd. Carlson tells Johnny that he had trained with Lloyd, and had gone to the South Pacific with him in 1942, and Hammerly was his navigator. Carlson was sick one day, and did not fly a mission to Gona where the plane was shot down and Lloyd was killed. Carlson tells Johnny that he saw Lloyd at the Canberra bar in Port Moresby. He recognized the slouch of his shoulders and called his name. The man turned and looked and walked away. Carlson asked the bartender, who was named Felix, who the man was, and he was given the name Bill Meadows.

Johnny flies to Port Moresby, gets a room in a Chinese hotel, and goes to the Canberra Bar. The bartender tells Johnny that Felix is dead, and that Bill Meadow owns a flying company, Papua Lines. Johnny goes to the office and learns that Bill is on a flight to Wau, and will be back the next day. Johnny goes to the local police and talks to Constable Staire, who does not know Meadow, and tells Johnny that men's pasts do not matter there.

Johnny goes to see Mrs. Meadow and tells her why he is there. She tells Johnny that she does not know anyone named Hammerly, and that the story scares her. She tells Johnny that she met Bill four years ago, and they have a son he insisted on naming Lloyd. The next day Johnny meets Bill Meadow, and half of his face is scarred from burns. Bill tells Johnny "so it happened," referring to being recognized. Bill tells Johnny that he has been a coward for not going home. He asks Johnny about his family, and Johnny tells him that his father died 2 years ago. Bill asks Johnny to meet him later at his home. Johnny wires the insurance company about the meeting and about Felix being dead. Johnny goes to meet with Bill and his wife and Bill tells Johnny that he flew on A-20's during the war, and on his last flight the plane was shot down near a group of whites trying to escape the Japanese. They helped nurse Lloyd back to health and after the war he picked a new name and bought new identity papers. Bill asks what will happen, and Johnny tells him that the insurance company will probably ask for their money back from the family. Johnny is not sure what the Army will want to do, and that he will not take Bill back with him. Bill tells Johnny that he will not go back. Johnny tells him about Felix the bartender being killed and leaves.

Johnny goes to his hotel and is attacked and shot three times. Johnny wakes up in the hospital to the voice of Constable Staire. Johnny is told that he was shot at and hit with one bullet. Some natives have been arrested, and one had Felix's watch. The next morning Johnny and Constable Staire go to see Meadow, but he is not home, and has gone on a flight in monsoon weather. They rush to the airfield and the radioman is in contact with the plane, which is coming back from Wewak. Johnny and Constable Staire watch as the plane fails to clear a hill and crashes attempting to land, killing Bill and his wife.

NOTES:
- THE ANNOUNCER IS DICK CUTTING
- MUSIC IS BY WILBUR HATCH
- JOHNNY IS SHOT FOR THE 2ND TIME
- EDMOND O'BRIEN'S NEXT MOVIE IS THE RED HEAD AND THE COWBOY
- STORY INFORMATION OBTAINED FROM THE KNX COLLECTION IN THE THOUSAND OAKS LIBRARY

Producer:	Jaime del Valle Writers Gil Doud
Cast:	Jack Kruschen, Dave Young, Dan O'Herlihy, Francis X. Bushman, Virginia Gregg, Barton Yarborough

◆　❖　◆

SHOW:	THE VIVIAN FAIR MATTER
SHOW DATE:	2/17/1951
COMPANY:	PLYMOUTH INSURANCE COMPANY
AGENT:	
EXP. ACCT:	$150.00

SYNOPSIS: Johnny is called by a man with a tip for the police. He tells Johnny that an insurance company stands to lose $12,000 on a fur coat. Check with Carl Schmidt the jeweler and Oscar Minch the dressmaker in the Bronx. Johnny is also told to check with Homicide and ask about Van Courtland Park.

Johnny calls homicide and is told to come immediately. Johnny goes to New York City and meets with Lt. Maguire and tells him about the call. Johnny is shown the file on a body that was found by a truck driver. There were no labels in the clothes and the shoes and purse were missing. Johnny calls the insurance company and gets a list of 14 names. Johnny goes to see both Schmidt and Minch, and neither of them knows anything. Johnny goes back to the police and learns that the body has been identified by Mrs. Kaley as her sister, Vivian Fair.

She tells Johnny that her sister always had men troubles and did not know right from wrong. Johnny calls the insurance company and learns that a policy had been issued in 1949 for a fur coat and two bracelets. Johnny goes to the apartment of Vivian and finds it a mess. Johnny finds a pair of shoes by the sofa, and there is a bloodstain on the heel. Johnny also finds a book that outlines her social life and blackmail. Johnny also finds a ledger book for a loan to her brother-in-law Vincent Kaley.

Johnny goes to see Mrs. Kaley. While he is there Lt. Maguire breaks in to search to search the apartment and asks Johnny about Vincent. Johnny is told that Vincent killed Vivian because she laughed at him, and that Vivian did not want him around because he was a cheap moocher. Johnny goes to see Mr. Schmidt again, and after searching his records finds a sale for a sapphire pendant, which Johnny forwards to Lt. Maguire. Johnny goes to his hotel and gets a message from the anonymous caller, who has seen the papers. He tells Johnny that Vincent did not kill Vivian. Johnny is told to meet the caller at a fruit stand on 59th street. Johnny goes and buys a paper and sees a story about a wife killing her husband. Johnny meets with Vincent Kaley, and he knows who killed Vivian. Vincent tells Johnny that he had lost his job as a machinist and had borrowed money from Vivian, who loved to laugh at people who had to borrow money. She told Vincent to go away and bragged to him about her insurance. He had told some men named Lester and Jerry about the insurance and gave them a key to the apartment. Lester and Jerry waited for Vivian in her apartment, and she hit Lester during the robbery. Vincent was supposed to get part of the money, and gives Johnny their address. Johnny takes Vincent to the police, and they go to the address for the men. The police find Lester in the apartment, and he blames Jerry for killing Vivian.

NOTES:
- THE ANNOUNCER IS DICK CUTTING
- MUSIC IS BY WILBUR HATCH
- STORY INFORMATION OBTAINED FROM THE KNX COLLECTION IN THE THOUSAND OAKS LIBRARY

Producer: Jaime del Valle   Writers   Gil Doud
Cast: Stacy Harris, Wally Maher, Sidney Miller, Jeanne Bates

SHOW: THE JARVIS WILDER MATTER
SHOW DATE: 2/24/1951
COMPANY: BRITANNIA LIFE INSURANCE COMPANY
AGENT:
EXP. ACCT: $540.00
SYNOPSIS: Johnny calls Mr. Mitchell Kendall, the defense attorney for Alma Wilder, to tell him that he is coming to look into the murder but the insurance

is not a factor.

Johnny goes to Farmington, New Mexico where the newspaper is reporting that the grand jury is ready to indict Alma for murdering her husband. Mr. Kendall tells Johnny that Alma has confessed, and that he was hoping for a self-defense and temporary insanity plea. Johnny tells Kendall that Alma gets no insurance. Kendall tells Johnny to be careful if he goes to the ranch, as the Wilders are hated people. Russell, the twin of Jarvis, has all of Jarvis' bad qualities.

Johnny goes to the Wilder ranch and talks to an old ranch hand. After gaining his confidence, the hand tells Johnny that Alma didn't shoot anyone. He had heard Jarvis yelling. When he came out of his cabin, he saw Alma lying on the ground on her belly with the gun beside Jarvis. Johnny goes to see the police for details of the shooting. Johnny then visits Alma, who is 24. She tells Johnny that Jarvis was a cruel man. She is happy in jail, the happiest she has been in three years. She wants to forget her past life. Johnny asks if someone killed Jarvis for her, but she tells Johnny that she has no friends, and was not allowed out of the house. "Now leave me alone" she tells Johnny.

Johnny goes to see Kendall and asks why a woman would stay with a man she hated. Kendall tells Johnny that she had left once before, and Jarvis had beaten her. Johnny tells Kendall of his theory and Kendall is interested. Johnny goes to the police and they are interested. They agree to perform a paraffin test and to do tests on the rifle. Johnny goes to see Russell Wilder, who tells Johnny to get out. Johnny tells Russell that he came to investigate the insurance claim and was told there were no problems. Russell gets belligerent when Johnny tells Russell that he killed Jarvis. Why were you out at 11 PM? What did you have to gain? Russell tells Johnny that he saw her kill Jarvis, and that he does pretty much what he thinks ought to be done.

Johnny goes to see Alma again and asks her about the night of the killing. She tells Johnny that she was trying to leave and had taken a rifle with her. Jarvis caught her and she shot him. Johnny is suspicious, as Johnny asks her about the rifle, and she does not even know how to cock the rifle. Johnny is then summoned to see the chief deputy. He tells Johnny that in looking at the murder weapon, they have found dirt in the butt plate. He also tells Johnny that the coroner's report also showed teeth marks on Jarvis' arm. They tested a similar rifle and got dirt into its butt plate. Johnny confronts Alma with a story that she was trying to leave and Jarvis tried to stop her. She bit him, and the rifle dropped to the ground and went off. She finally admits to Johnny that his theory is what really happened. She wants to stay in jail, as Russell said that if the police did not convict her, he would kill her, and Russell always does what he says he will do.

Alma is losing her freedom but spending it in a hospital where she is expected to recover.

NOTES:

- EDMOND O'BRIEN'S NEW MOVIE IS "THE REDHEAD AND THE COWBOY"
- DICK CUTTING IS THE ANNOUNCER

- MUSIC IS BY WILBUR HATCH

Producer: Jaime del Valle   **Writers: Gil Doud**
Cast: Parley Baer, Tim Graham, Bill Conrad, Herb Butterfield,
          Mary Lansing

◆   ❖   ◆

SHOW: THE CELIA WOODSTOCK MATTER
SHOW DATE: 3/3/1951
COMPANY: WASHINGTONIAN LIFE INSURANCE COMPANY
AGENT: SAM MILLER
EXP. ACCT: $73.60

SYNOPSIS: Captain Lyle Woodstock returns Johnny's call. Woodstock tells Johnny that there is no trouble with his wife's disappearance. At least not yet. Johnny rents a car and drives to Bridgeport, Connecticut to meet with Captain Lyle Woodstock—captain only because he owns a 64-foot schooner. Lyle says that he has discharged the servants and had lied to Mr. Miller about fearing for his wife's life. He had wasted money on a detective, David Slater, to follow his wife and asked the insurance company for help. Woodstock gives Johnny a folder about his wife, who is 27. He met her in Mexico and married her. They both like adventure. Woodstock is suspicious as Celia has been seeing too much of Dr. Masterson in town. She sees him three times a week but she seems very healthy. Now she had disappeared. Johnny goes to see Slater, who tells Johnny of the doctor visits and of losing her on a train to New York City after taking $2000 from the bank. Slater had overheard a phone conversation with a man named Sprague. Johnny decides to tell Woodstock he is dropping the case as he gave up chasing wives a long time ago. At the Woodstock house, a nervous man with a gun meets Johnny at the door. Johnny is locked in a closet and the man leaves. Johnny breaks out of the closet and finds Celia Woodstock on the floor shot. Johnny tries to call the police but the phone is dead, so he calls the police from a neighbor's phone. The police arrive and take Celia to the hospital. Johnny tells his story to Lt. Al Jester. Johnny remembers the man carrying a cheap nickel-plated .32. The police find another body upstairs and Johnny goes up with Lt. Jester.

In a bedroom they find Capt. Woodstock with a .38 beside him. He has been shot in the back. Johnny gets a room and the next day he talks to Dr. Masterson's former nurse, Janet Squire. Janet tells Johnny that she did not know of any romantic involvement between Dr. Masterson and Celia Woodstock, nor does she know a man named Sprague. Johnny checks in with Jester and learns nothing. Johnny goes to see Dr. Masterson who wants his name kept out of the papers. He tells Johnny that that Celia came to him for a sinus condition. She seemed satisfied with her husband and looked forward to a trip to South America. He tells Johnny that during one visit Mrs. Woodstock became hysterical when the receptionist mentioned a call for "Mrs. Emile Sprague." Johnny reports in to Lt. Jester and learns that Celia was shot with a .38, Lyle by a .32; and there is no sign of Sprague. Around midnight Celia recovers consciousness and at 3 AM talks to Johnny and Jester. She tells them that she was in the house when Emile killed Woodstock and that she is really Mrs. Sprague. She married Lyle in Mexico and Emile found out and wanted money. She met him in New York and gave him the $2000. Then he followed her to Bridgeport and forced her to take him to see Lyle. Lyle shot her and Sprague shot Lyle. Emile has an apartment on Commerce Street.

Johnny and Jester go to the apartment around 3:30 AM and surround it. Johnny sees Sprague watching them from the window as they go in. Johnny calls on a pay phone and urges Sprague to surrender. He tells Johnny that he shot Woodstock because he though Celia was dead. Sprague runs from the apartment shooting and is killed.

I understand that the lawyers are now working to kick the bigamist wife out of the estate.

NOTES:
- EDMOND O'BRIEN'S NEW MOVIE IS "THE REDHEAD AND THE COWBOY"
- DICK CUTTING IS THE ANNOUNCER
- MUSIC IS BY WILBUR HATCH
- MY FAVORITE HUSBAND IS PREVIEWED
- VAUGHN MONROE IS ON NEXT

Producer: Jaime del Valle   **Writers:** Gil Doud
Cast: Francis X. Bushman, Jim Nusser, Ted Osborne, Lurene Tuttle, Bill Johnstone, Tudor Owen, Ray Hartman

◆   ❖   ◆

SHOW: THE STANLEY SPRINGS MATTER
SHOW DATE: 3/10/1951
COMPANY: FINANCIAL SURETY
AGENT: ED BEST
EXP. ACCT: $0.00

SYNOPSIS: Ed Best from Financial Surety calls about a problem with a cotton plant they own in the southwest. Someone says that illegal activities are being carried on.

Johnny cabs to "Insurance Row" and meets Mr. Best. Financial Surety has received an anonymous letter about illegal shipments. While it may be a crank, they do not want to go to the Feds without evidence.

Johnny travels by plane, train and bus to get to Stanley Springs, a dusty depression in the desert. Johnny checks into the only hotel and is immediately approached by a girl named Ann. She lives in the hotel and wants to talk. Johnny thinks her curiosity might be a good way to check out strangers. Johnny tells her that he is in town researching a magazine article.

Johnny goes to the Stanley Springs office and meets Norman Stager the manager. Stager tells Johnny that they are a small outfit, just like others, and that there is a lot of work to do this week, so Johnny will have to talk to people after hours. Stager introduces Mr. Phillips, the chief clerk, and Mr. Childs, the shipping clerk. Phillips is surprised when he meets Johnny and Stager sees it. Childs takes Johnny to the loading dock to watch bales being loaded. When Johnny returns Phillips is gone, and he is told that he went home sick. "Maybe he worries too much. You might want to go see him, he might be sicker than you think" Stager tells Johnny. Johnny goes to Phillips' house but no one answers. Johnny enters and sees a picture of Ann on the coffee table. That night, Johnny goes to hear Ann entertain and asks about Phillips. She tells Johnny to go away and she will see him at 4:00AM when she gets off. Later she comes to Johnny's room and asks Johnny who he really is. When Johnny asks if she were expecting someone from the east, she tells Johnny that Phillips had smuggled a letter out of town. She tells Johnny that Stager is smuggling narcotics, that Phillips found out and Stager would not let him leave town. She knows about it, and she cannot leave town either. Johnny tells her that he will call the Feds, but Ann tells him that there is only one phone in town, and it is in Stager's office. Johnny goes out and is met by Childs and another man. Childs tells Johnny that he saw Phillips came home last night around 9:00. Johnny goes to Phillips' home and finds him there with a .38 in his hand and a hole in his temple and another faint clue. The deputy sheriff is called and the body is taken out and the room examined. Johnny goes to see Ann and tells her of Phillips death. He tells Ann to stay in his room and let no one in. Johnny walks towards the bus depot followed by two men who are ready to keep him off a bus.

After breakfast, Johnny goes to the office and tells Stager that Phillips was not a suicide. Johnny tells him that he had smelled chloroform. Johnny tells Stager that they both know that Phillips was chloroformed and that someone put the gun in his hand and helped him pull the trigger. Stager is told that he has been sitting on a good thing for a long time, and the town is a front for his operation, but he cannot control Johnny. Stager tells Johnny to keep his empty accusations to himself. When Johnny tries to use the phone he is beaten and told it is for employees only. Johnny goes to the hotel room and Ann fixes his wounds. When asked why she is so calm, she tells Johnny that she has been afraid of many other things. She leaves and Johnny never sees her again.

Johnny goes to the office with his automatic. Childs is there and Johnny threatens to kill him of he does not tell him where Ann is. Childs says he does not know, so Johnny asks for Stager. Johnny threatens again to kill him and Childs takes Johnny to Stager in one of the warehouses. Stager tells Johnny he is in trouble for beating Childs. He does not know where Ann is and is tired of Johnny's nonsense and walks off. Johnny shoots Stager and wounds him to stop him from leaving. Johnny asks Childs to take him to the sheriff, as he wants to be arrested.

Johnny gets a lawyer, Ann is found alive and the Feds come to investigate. His expense account is not complete, as he is mailing it from jail.

NOTES:
- THE PROGRAM ANNOUNCES SPECIAL GUEST "YOURS TRULY, OLGA SAN JUAN" WHO WAS A RADIO AND MOVIE STAR OF THE 40'S AND 50'S WHERE SHE WAS TYPICALLY CAST AS A GORGEOUS LATINA SPITFIRE. SHE WAS ALSO MARRIED TO EDMOND O'BRIEN AT THE TIME
- EDMOND O'BRIEN'S NEW MOVIE IS "THE REDHEAD AND THE COWBOY"
- DICK CUTTING IS THE ANNOUNCER
- MUSIC IS BY WILBUR HATCH

Producer: Jaime del Valle   **Writers:** Gil Doud
Cast: Ray Hartman, Bill Conrad, Herb Butterfield, Olga San Juan

◆ ❖ ◆

SHOW: THE EMIL LOVETT MATTER
SHOW DATE: 3/17/1951
COMPANY: COLUMBIA ALL-RISK
AGENT:
EXP. ACCT: $93.45

SYNOPSIS: Johnny is called by Sgt. Wybeck, who tells Johnny that the widow is still too sick to see. The girl is with her mother, a great motive for suicide.

Johnny goes to New York City and meets the mother-in-law of Emit Lovett, Mrs. Mueler, who is with Sgt. Wybeck. Johnny learns that Emit has a criminal record. She tells Sgt. Wybeck that Emil was a fence and shows Johnny and Sgt. Wybeck where Emil was shot three times in the back while in his pajamas. The police find $500 in the bedroom, and a bolt of cloth. They wonder how Emil got that much money working in a poultry store for $35 a week.

Johnny goes to see Mrs. Mueler, who tells Johnny that she is ashamed of Emil. He was a thief and she did not talk to him. Johnny meets a "chunky brunette" wearing a negligee and mules who is Emil's wife Lila. Mrs. Mueler leaves, and Lila tells Johnny that she did not know her husband too well. He had brought the cloth to make curtains from, and always seems to have money. She tells Johnny that she was told to go for a walk just before Emil was killed, and a neighbor told her of the killing.

The police report showed that no one heard the shots that night. The parole board knew that Emil had met Rose Delancey, and her boyfriend Frank is brought in. He tells the police that he knew Emil, but denies killing him, even though he was seeing Rose. The police identify the bolt of cloth as coming from a robbery, which confirms that Emil was a fence.

Johnny goes to see Rose and she tells Johnny that she has known Emil for six years, and denies going with Frank. Johnny rushes to Lila's apartment where he meets Sgt. Wybeck, who tells him that two hoodlums broke in and one was shot and has been taken to the hospital. Lila is questioned, but does not know the men, who wanted to know who killed Emil. Her mother-in-law was shopping at the time. The police decide to take Lila in. Johnny goes to the jail to talk to

Joseph Maschiano in his cell. Joe has a record, and tells Johnny that he did not kill Emil, and tells Johnny to see his lawyer Charles Hagan.

Johnny goes to see Hagan, who accuses the police of going by the regulations to solve the murder. He tells Johnny that Joe and his associate were doing their own investigation, and that if Emil were a fence, his customers would not kill him. Johnny calls Sgt. Wybeck and he tells Johnny that there have been a number of robberies on the eastside, but there has been little progress, and a good fence is the reason. Johnny goes back to see Joe, and he tells Johnny that Emil was an important man, and the boys miss him. Johnny visits Lila in jail, and Mrs. Mueler yells at her. Johnny tells Lila that she killed Emil, and she admits that she shot him with his own gun. She shot him because she just got sick of him.

NOTES:
- THE ANNOUNCER IS DICK CUTTING
- MUSIC IS BY WILBUR HATCH
- STORY INFORMATION OBTAINED FROM THE KNX COLLECTION IN THE THOUSAND OAKS LIBRARY

Producer:	**Jaime del Valle**	**Writers**	**Gil Doud**
Cast:	**Bill Conrad, Jeanette Nolan, Mary Lansing, Herb Butterfield, Jack Moyles**		

◆   ❖   ◆

SHOW:	**THE BYRON HAYES MATTER**
SHOW DATE:	**3/24/1951**
COMPANY:	**CORINTHIAN ALL RISK INSURANCE COMPANY**
AGENT:	
EXP. ACCT:	**$180.80**

SYNOPSIS: Johnny gets a call from a man who has information about the Byron Hayes killing. The caller is Roy Corona, the chief suspect and he wants to talk. A friend will tell Johnny where he is to be picked up.

Johnny goes to New York City to work on the Byron Hayes murder, but there is little information to go on. Johnny gets a call from Roy Corona who wants to talk. Roy tells Johnny where he is to be picked up, and Johnny goes out to wait. A car picks up Johnny and he is taken to meet Roy. Roy tells Johnny that he is the natural suspect because his girl friend was seeing Byron when he got out of prison. He has witnesses, but they are all ex-cons too, and the police would not believe him. Roy tells Johnny that he was waiting outside her apartment and overheard Byron telling Rita that he could no longer pay her, and that he was not going to see her anymore. Roy is sure that she was blackmailing him. He left the apartment and she shot him. Johnny agrees not to tell the police yet.

Johnny goes to see Rita Cobb, who tells Johnny that she only knew Byron casually. He was just an acquaintance. Johnny goes to see Mrs. Hayes, who is adamant that her husband was much too upright and respectable to have been seeing her, and was not paying her. Rita was lying. Johnny goes to Rita and asks why she is withholding information. She says she only met Hayes once or twice. Johnny asks her about Arnold Smith and Earl French, who were her "friends" also. Johnny asks if she was blackmailing them too. She tells Johnny that she was afraid to tell about the others. Johnny leaves and calls Rita from the corner and, as suspected, her phone is busy as she is warning someone.

Later Johnny gets a call from Earl Fisher in his hotel room. Earl wants to talk to Johnny confidentially. He tells Johnny that Rita had threatened him, and he must look after his reputation. Johnny leaves to meet Earl at a bar and is shot at as he exits the hotel. A police patrolman takes Johnny's statement and Lt. Middleton arrives. Johnny tells him of the lead from Rita and tells Middleton that he must keep his source confidential. Johnny has no proof that Fisher tried to shoot him, so Middleton goes to arrest Rita. Johnny calls the bar but the bartender does not know an Earl Fisher. Johnny goes to the Hayes residence and gets tough with Mrs. Hayes. She seems to be worried more with her reputation than her dead husband. Johnny suggests that maybe she shot him. Mrs. Hayes finally admits to knowing about Rita and the blackmail. She tells Johnny that she thinks the death is her fault, as she was over righteous and forced Byron to go to Rita. She tells Johnny that a man had come to her and told her about Rita and she confronted Bryon with the information. She gives Johnny a perfect description of Roy Corona!

Johnny tells Lt. Middleton of the conversation and they question Rita. She calls the money she got "loans." Byron had come by for a visit and after he left she heard shots. She came out and found him in the hallway. Johnny tells her that they have proof of blackmail and are going to charge her with murder. Later Johnny gets a call from Roy and he admits that he killed Hayes and wants to give up. Come and get me before I change my mind. Johnny calls Lt. Middleton and they go to the location where Roy is. There is an exchange of gunfire, but Roy is not killed. Roy tells Johnny that he started the whole thing when he got out of prison and found out Rita was seeing other men. He wanted to frame her but Johnny tells Roy that Rita has confessed and the murder weapon was found in her apartment.

Johnny reports that Earl Fisher was brought in for questioning and released; but Johnny saw his wife, and Mr. Fisher is a condemned man.

NOTES:
- EDMOND O'BRIEN'S NEW MOVIE IS "THE REDHEAD AND THE COWBOY"
- THERE IS A MID-PROGRAM COMMERCIAL FOR GANGBUSTERS
- DICK CUTTING IS THE ANNOUNCER
- MUSIC IS BY WILBUR HATCH

Producer: Jaime del Valle   **Writers:** Gil Doud
Cast: Jim Nusser, Lee Patrick, Jeanne Bates, Ed Begley, Jack Moyles

SHOW:	THE EDWARD FRENCH MATTER
SHOW DATE:	4/7/1951
COMPANY:	TRI-STATE INSURANCE GROUP
AGENT:	
EXP. ACCT:	$2739.50

SYNOPSIS: Mrs. French calls and Johnny advises her that the insurance company has authorized him to look for her son Edward French in the Malay States.

Johnny travels to Chicago to speak with Mrs. French. Johnny learns that Edward had left the states to manage a tea plantation with his English wife. The tea was sold to the Jewel Tea Company. On a trip to Singapore, Edward had disappeared. Johnny is looking into the matter for Tri-State.

Johnny travels for a week to get to the Singapore tea merchant Mr. Neeps who tells Johnny that French had been there and had left after one day. Johnny is told not to worry, as French is impulsive and does things people tell him not to.

Johnny takes an armored train to Raub, Malaysia and is met by an armored jeep for the trip to the police. Johnny learns that Constable Whitlow, who had filed the report, has been killed in an attack by the bandits. Constable Downes advises Johnny that the bandits have just attacked the neighboring plantation owned by Mr. Stuart. Downes thinks that kidnapping may be the cause of French's disappearance, as the vehicle is missing and the body had not been found, and that is most unusual. Johnny takes the armored police jeep to the French plantation and notes the well-armed enclosure. Johnny meets Mrs. French. As she is explaining that Edward had driven to Singapore, gunfire erupts. Keith Stuart arrives, fleeting glances are exchanged with Mrs. French, and a warning is given for an impending attack that night. Johnny is told to spend the night. Unable to sleep, Johnny goes to the veranda and overhears Keith and Mrs. French talking and there is no doubt they are involved in a plot concerning Edward. The attack comes and Johnny is given a Thompson sub-machine gun and joins in fighting off the 100 insurgents.

Johnny goes to Constable Downes and asks him to call a meeting of all the plantation owners so that he can talk to Mrs. Stuart alone. The meeting is called and Johnny goes to speak with Mrs. Stuart, who is a frail fever-wracked woman who knows of her husband's affair with Mrs. French. She tells Johnny that any future plans Keith might have will concern her, unless he kills her first, and sometimes she wishes he would. She does tell Johnny that her husband was gone for some time a month ago, when Edward disappeared.

Johnny goes to the French plantation and is met by Keith, who knows he has been to see his wife, but warns Johnny that she makes up things in her fevers. Johnny tells him of overhearing the conversation on the veranda. Mrs. French comes in and denies Keith's involvement and says the natives killed her husband. Johnny tells them that the police are searching for alibis and Keith admits he had met French on the road and shot him. Johnny takes his gun and they go back to the Stuart plantation and are met by a man—Edward French! French tells Johnny and Keith that he had stayed alive after Keith had shot him. Now Keith will die, and he shoots Keith 6 times.

French had made his way to a local hospital where he had recovered anonymously. Now he is being held for murder.

NOTES:
- EDMOND O'BRIEN'S NEW MOVIE IS "THE REDHEAD AND THE COWBOY"
- DAN CUBBERLY IS THE ANNOUNCER
- MUSIC IS BY WILBUR HATCH

Producer: Jaime del Valle   Writers: Gil Doud
Cast: Jeanette Nolan, John McIntire, Tudor Owen, Maria Palmer,
                 Dan O'Herlihy

◆   ❖   ◆

SHOW: THE MICKEY MCQUEEN MATTER
SHOW DATE: 4/14/1951
COMPANY: HARTFORD POLICE DEPARTMENT
AGENT:
EXP. ACCT: $0.00
SYNOPSIS: Johnny's old friend Mickey McQueen, an old style Irish cop in Hartford, Connecticut calls him and wants to talk.

Mickey come to Johnny's apartment at 2:00 in the morning, but just can't say what he wants to. Mickey tells Johnny that he is being moved to a desk job, but there is "murder being planned and being done" but no one can stop it. Mickey leaves and the next day Johnny goes to Mickey's apartment. Johnny is met by a distraught woman who points Johnny to a small door, a closet containing Mickey's uniforms and a dead Mickey McQueen, hanging from the clothes pole with his belt. The woman is Mickey's wife Thelma. She is young and attractive, with natural platinum blonde hair. She tells Johnny that she was leaving Mickey and had come back to get her clothes. He was a kind and wonderful person, with not an enemy in the world. She tells Johnny that she had met Mickey after his wife had died. Johnny tells her that he thinks Mickey was murdered. A search of the apartment finds nothing, so Johnny calls the police and leaves.

That afternoon Johnny follows Mickey's beat and talks to his friends. At the Cedrick Hotel, Johnny talks to the house detective, Ned Martin. Johnny tells him about Mickey's visit and Ned tells Johnny that he had talked to Mickey last night and he seemed down about his new desk job. Ned tells Johnny that Mickey's wife, Thelma Weaver, and had done time in Joliet. Ned tells Johnny to drop the case, but Johnny wants to know more. If you want to find out more, see Fred Ku at the Calcutta Club, but don't tell him I sent you, adds Ned.

Johnny goes to see Fred Ku, who is half oriental. Johnny feels he could retire from 10% of the bail posted by the customers in the bar. Fred takes Johnny to the office and tells Johnny that Mickey was a nice guy and that he did not take payoffs and but he left Fred alone. Fred tells Johnny that he did not know Mickey's wife. Fred is called out of the office and Johnny looks around for another exit. The door opens and Thelma comes in, and points a Colt .25 automatic at Johnny when he mentions Thelma Weaver.

Johnny throws ink on Thelma and is able to get the gun away from Thelma and tells her he knows of her past. She tells Johnny she had met Mickey after his first wife had died. She tells Johnny that she got out of prison and gave her friends in Chicago the slip. Mickey had arrested her for vagrancy and came back the next day to bail her out. She had used Mickey's soft side to get information for her friends from Chicago, who are outside in the bar. Mickey was being transferred to the Police Armory, and the boys wanted the keys. They wanted explosives for a jewel robbery at the Marquat Building. Roy Weaver, her husband had threatened to tell Mickey she was a bigamist unless Mickey helped him. She tells Johnny that Roy had taken the keys from Mickey and then Roy killed Mickey. Johnny tries to leave, but Roy comes in and objects. Roy thanks Thelma for warning him. Johnny is taken to an old wine cellar and slugged.

When Johnny wakes up he discovers he is in an old wine cellar filled with burglary tools. Johnny figures out the situation and tries to find a way out. When the door opens, he fakes being unconscious and hears the men take out the tools to the cars where Fred has the explosives from the Armory. After the men leave with Thelma, Johnny tries to force his way out. Johnny hears the door open and Ned Martin is there. He tells Johnny that a woman had called to say Johnny was locked in the bar and something was going to happen. Johnny tells Ned what is planned and Ned takes Johnny to the area of the Marquat Building, where Johnny sees the cars being unloaded. Johnny sees Thelma walking towards him. Roy calls to her and she turns and fires into the first car, igniting the cordite powder, which explodes. Thelma is shot but she turns on the ground and hits the second car, which explodes.

Johnny gets to her in time for her to say that Mickey would be proud of her. She tells Johnny that they cannot send her back to Juliet, and then she dies. Ray Weaver lives long enough to sign a confession that he killed Mickey McQueen.

NOTES:
- THIS IS A REPEAT OF THE 8-17-50 PROGRAM. THE PROGRAM IS ESSENTIALLY THE SAME SCRIPT WITH MINOR CHANGES IN THE SMALL TALK AND DESCRIPTIVE LANGUAGE. THE BACKGROUND MUSIC IN THE BAR IS DIFFERENT. SOME CAST MEMBERS ARE DIFFERENT.
- EDMOND O'BRIEN'S NEW MOVIE IS "THE REDHEAD AND THE COWBOY"
- DICK CUTTING IS THE ANNOUNCER
- MUSIC IS BY WILBUR HATCH

Producer: Jaime del Valle   Writers: Gil Doud
Cast: Bill Conrad, Martha Wentworth, Herb Butterfield, Jack
           Moyles, Ray Hartman

SHOW: THE WILLARD SOUTH MATTER
SHOW DATE: 4/21/1951
COMPANY: GREAT EASTERN INSURANCE COMPANY
AGENT:
EXP. ACCT: $373.00

SYNOPSIS: Lou Creager calls Johnny and tells him that the boat belonging to Willard South has been found. It was empty and there were signs of trouble. Lou will meet Johnny at the police dock.

Johnny goes to Charlotte Amalie, Virgin Islands to investigate the disappearance of Willard and Georgina South. Johnny meets with Lou Creager who tells Johnny that he boat was found with no one on board. Johnny meets Officer Shoi who is investigating the case and he shows Johnny a bullet in the woodwork and bloodstains on the deck indicating that maybe someone pushed them overboard. Johnny is told that a lot of people disliked Mr. South, especially men whose wives were involved with Willard. Shoi shows Johnny a cut rope used to trail a dinghy, and Lou confirms that South always trailed a small skiff behind the boat.

Johnny goes to see Willard South's foster-mother but meets his brother Paul, who lives in Florida. The brother tells Johnny that he had been out searching as well. Johnny mentions Willard's bad reputation and is told that he had a lot of enemies. Johnny is told that the trip was a special occasion so that Georgina could talk to Willard. Mrs. South arrives and tells Johnny that she has come to expect bad things from Willard. She is sorry for Georgina because she let her marry Willard, who is a beast.

Johnny meets Celeste Roberston who was seen with Willard recently. She tells Johnny that she is on the island getting a divorce. She admits that she has spent some time with him over the past several weeks, but had nothing to do with any murder or anything else.

After the Coast Guard planes and boats come back from searching for the small skiff, a radio report is received that Georgina South has been found alive. Johnny and Shoi go to meet the boat that found Georgina. Captain Bracken tells Shoi and Johnny that he found the skiff with her in it, and that she is going directly to Doctor Garr. Bracken tells them that she had seen her husband shot and thrown overboard.

The next day, Johnny and Officer Shoi go to see Georgina South. She is able to recount how she and Willard had left for Calibra and were stopped by a boat claiming that they had run out of gas. A man from the boat came on board and shot Willard. The other man robbed her, and threw Willard overboard. Georgina was set adrift in the skiff. The doctor tells Johnny that Georgina is in good shape because she had shelter and water in the skiff. Officer Shoi agrees to wire the prisons in Puerto Rico to check for escapees who might have killed Willard. Johnny goes to the waterfront to look at the boats again and is stopped by Captain Bracken and Johnny tells him about the possibility of escaped prisoners doing the job. Bracken tells Johnny that it would be fitting if convicts had killed Willard. Johnny examines both boats and finds nothing.

After gets a reply to Shoi's wire, Johnny decides to use the lack of clues as a weapon. Johnny goes to see Lou Creager and asks why he was so quick to help, and Lou tells him that the thought that Johnny needed help and offered it. Johnny tells Lou that he had showed him a cut line on the boat, but the line on the skiff was not cut. Why? You were able to find her when the Coast Guard could not because you knew where she was. Johnny tells him that a doctor will be there to prove that Georgina did not spend three days adrift. Creager gets angry and Bracken has to break up the fight. Johnny goes to see Georgina at home. Mrs. South tries to protect her but Johnny accuses her of knowing the truth like everyone else does. Johnny tells her that she should have know she could not have gotten away with it, as there were too many mistakes made. Mrs. South tells Johnny that both of her sons were adopted but Willard was a beast, the worst of heredity and environment. She tells Johnny that she is the murderer, and she had to kill Willard before he destroyed everyone! Johnny thinks the confession is a fake, but it turns out to be true. There was a lot of conspiracy involved, and the trial will be very interesting.

NOTES:
- THE CLOSING CREDITS ON THIS BROADCAST GIVE THE ACTORS AND THEIR ROLES: IRENE HUBBARD IS EVANGELA, JAN MINER IS GEORGINA, GILBERT MACK IS LOU, FRAN LAFFERTY IS CELESTE, ED LATIMER IS SAM, MAURICE TARPLIN IS SHOI, BERNARD LINDROW IS THE DOCTOR
- THE ACTORS ON THIS SHOW ARE DIFFERENT THAN THE USUAL POOL OF ACTORS.
- THE MID-PROGRAM COMMERCIAL IS FOR "SING IT AGAIN"
- THERE IS A PUBLIC SERVICE ANNOUNCEMENT ABOUT THE DANGERS OF FOREST FIRES.
- EDMOND O'BRIEN'S NEW MOVIE IS "THE REDHEAD AND THE COWBOY"
- OLEN TICE IS THE ANNOUNCER
- MUSIC IS BY WILBUR HATCH

Producer: Jaime del Valle   **Writers:** Gil Doud
Cast: Irene Hubbard, Jan Miner, Gilbert Mack, Fran Lafferty, Ed Latimer, Maurice Tarplin, Bernard Lindrow

◆ ❖ ◆

SHOW: THE MONTH-END RAID MATTER
SHOW DATE: 4/28/1951
COMPANY: COLUMBIA ALL RISK INSURANCE COMPANY
AGENT:
EXP. ACCT: $396.50
SYNOPSIS: Lt. Arnesson calls and tells Johnny that he can come down to the

hospital whenever Johnny is ready. The driver is not going to live, and the loss is almost $250,000, and very little of the cash was marked.

Johnny goes to Kansas City, Missouri to investigate the $250,000 robbery of an armored car used by the Andover Department Stores. Johnny learns that the receipts from a three-day sale were being picked up when the armored car was robbed. One guard is killed and the driver, Carl Biller, is wounded and expected to die. Johnny meets Lt. Arnesson in the hospital and he tells Johnny that the wounded men were shot in cold blood, which means they might have known their killers. Two cars were used in the robbery to box in the truck in a loading zone. The robbery division has heard rumors of a gang forming in town. While talking to Lt. Arnesson, Johnny learns that the driver has died.

Johnny talks to Mrs. Biller in the hospital. She tells Johnny that she knew something would happen, what with all that money. Johnny notes that the robbers had shot the guards in cold blood, so maybe they did it to silence men who knew them. She knows of no reason why Carl would have been involved in a robbery. Johnny tells Lt. Arnesson about the interview, and he decides to send two officers to watch her.

The next day, Johnny and Lt. Arnesson meet with Emile "The Count" Ordall, an informant. Emile tells Lt. Arnesson has heard about a gang moving in from Chicago, but knows nothing about the Andover job. Emile knows only about men named Pinky, Ross, Shorty and "The Mick." Emile does not want to tell more, as he might get shot too. Lt. Arnesson is sure the money is in town and sends a wire to Chicago asking for information.

After leaning more about the case, Johnny goes to see Mrs. Biller again, and asks her about Betty Claire and why her husband was seeing the wife of a known criminal who just got out of prison. She tells Johnny that she was going to tell the police about her. She had written to the bonding company warning them. She tells Johnny that her husband had seen Betty after her husband had been paroled. She tells Johnny that Carl did not come home the night before the robbery and had come home only to change clothes. Mrs. Biller hopes Betty gets hurt like she has been hurt.

Johnny and Lt. Arnesson go to the apartment of Betty Claire. There is no answer at the door so they unlock the door and find Betty, choked to death in the kitchen.

There are signs of a struggle and a newspaper in the apartment indicates that Betty had died after Carl Biller. Later that day, the police find a body in a garage in the East Bottom area. The body has a receipt for a package, which is claimed by the police, and contains $15,000. Johnny, Emile and Lt. Arnesson go to the morgue and Emile recognizes the body as Earl Norworth, a known criminal in Kansas City. Lt. Arnesson tells Emile that he might have been bought, and gives Emile until 10:30 to find out what he can from the streets.

The police sweep the city and the jails fill. A known associate of Arnold Claire is brought in and he tells Johnny and Lt. Arnesson that Claire is trying to go straight, and is looking for a job and was not involved. The man tells them that he was with Claire and Betty until 2AM before the robbery and that Biller was not there, which is different from what Mrs. Biller had said he was. A delivery boy can verify that there were only three people there. The man does not know about Betty being killed and tells Lt. Arnesson that Claire is staying in a shack by the river. As they get ready to leave, Lt. Arnesson is told that Emile has been killed. Lt. Arnesson is going to miss him, as he was a good honest stoolie.

A check of the delivery boy confirms that only three people were in the apartment that night. Lt. Arnesson, Stone and Johnny go to the shack to pick up Claire. Claire is taken without a fight and blames Stone for ratting on him and Stone tells Claire that she has gotten him involved in a murder. Claire admits that he had been trying to go straight, but he had killed his wife. He had killed her because she was involved in the robbery. Mrs. Biller had called him the night her husband died, and told him that Betty had planned the job so that he would be blamed and go back to prison. So he went to see her and killed her. Claire knows one man who was in the robbery, and names him to the police. That man leads to another and that one to another until the gang from Chicago is located in a house. Johnny learns that one of the men from Chicago, Ross Degnen, killed the guard only because he was high on narcotics. The police surround the house as the men try to escape in a car. There is a shootout and the gang members are killed, and all but $2,000 of the money is recovered.

Remarks: Johnny talked to Mrs. Biller and learned that she had talked to Arnold Claire and told him that Betty had set up the robbery, and she got her revenge for murder. The company owes Mrs. Biller a debt of gratitude.

NOTES:
- THE MID-PROGRAM COMMERCIAL IS FOR "SING IT AGAIN"
- EDMOND O'BRIEN'S NEW MOVIE IS "THE REDHEAD AND THE COWBOY"
- DICK CUTTING IS THE ANNOUNCER
- MUSIC IS BY WILBUR HATCH
- THERE IS A PUBLIC SERVICE ANNOUNCEMENT ABOUT THE DANGERS OF HOUSE FIRES

Producer: Jaime del Valle   Writers: Gil Doud
Cast: Herb Butterfield, Joe Du Val, Virginia Gregg, Sidney Miller, Peter Leeds, Edgar Barrier

◆   ❖   ◆

SHOW: THE VIRGINIA TOWNE MATTER
SHOW DATE: 5/5/1951
COMPANY: PLYMOUTH INSURANCE COMPANY
AGENT:
EXP. ACCT: $0.00
SYNOPSIS: Roy Underwood calls and tells Johnny to come over and he will tell where the stolen jewels are and who stole them.

Johnny goes to New York City, gets a room at the Hotel Bentley, and meets with Roy Underwood in the midst of a party where Johnny is interrupted by a particularly drunken girl. Johnny gives Underwood a list of the stolen jewels and is told that the description of the jewels is correct. Underwood tells Johnny that Virginia Towne stole them. She was at a party in the apartment and he saw her leave with them. He did not call police so he could allow her to think twice. The jewels were in a dresser drawer. She put them on, he told her to take them off and she refused. Johnny gets the address for Francis Adams, a friend of Virginia's. Johnny goes to the apartment of Francis and meets Virginia at the door. She tells Johnny that the jewels were not stolen, as he gave the jewelry to her. Johnny tells her that without proof of ownership, the jewels belong to the insurer, who is Roy Underhill. She must give them back or Underhill will go to police. She tells Johnny that she cannot give them all back as she has sold a bracelet at a low price to get money to live and needs $1500 to cover the price. She tells Johnny that she had told Underwood she didn't want to see him any more and he laughed at her. Phil Kelly, a friend of Virginia's comes in and his hands clench as he hears the story. He tells Johnny that Underwood had put Virginia in shows using his advantage. He had enjoyed her until he tired of her. Phil then tells Johnny that he stole the jewels to cover for her. Johnny does not want to see her arrested, so he tells Virginia that he will stall Underwood for two days. That is the best he can do and will check back tomorrow. The next day Johnny checks in, and Phil is out raising money. On the third day, Virginia tells Johnny that the bracelet has been cut up, so they cannot get it back. She tells Johnny, "The next time you see me you won't be my friend, just another man with evidence," and wants to go out for a drink. Next day Johnny goes to see Underwood, with the jewels. The missing piece is listed for $2400, and Underwood signs the claim form. "I cannot afford to be taken advantage of every young thing that happens along" he tells Johnny.

Johnny gives his report to the police and goes to his hotel to pack. Lt. Brinker comes to his room and tells Johnny that the jewels are missing again, and that Underwood has been shot to death in his apartment.

Johnny is told that Alice Breen, the drunken woman at the first party, had heard screaming and entered the apartment and found Underwood dead. She is being held as a material witness. Johnny goes over his story to police and wonders if Virginia Towne could have re-stolen the jewels. Lt. Brinker tells Johnny that Underwood was ruthless in getting rid of women. The police allow Johnny to work alone in getting the facts from Virginia, even though the police know that Johnny had found Virginia before his report said he did. Johnny goes to the apartment and both Virginia and Francis are gone. Johnny finds Phil, and he has not heard of the killing and does not know whereabouts of Francis or Virginia. He tells Johnny that maybe she is looking for Johnny.

Phil takes Johnny to Virginia, in a room near the waterfront. Johnny tells Virginia that Phil brought him and tells her that Underwood is dead. She tells Johnny that she is hiding because she did not want to be arrested. She came here to hide from Underwood. "You have lied to me, and I believed them because I wanted to" Johnny tells her. Johnny tells Virginia that the police learned that

Underwood bought all of the pieces at an auction last year. Johnny tells her that the jeweler says he told you he was going to cut up the bracelet. "I gave you three days, and now I am in trouble. I must clear myself with the police by taking you in." Johnny takes Virginia to the police in Phil's cab.

Lt. Brinker questions Virginia for two hours and then releases Breen. When Johnny leaves he sees Phil outside the police station. Johnny asks him to take him to his hotel, and Phil tells him that he knows she did not do it, as she told him with her eyes. Phil tells Johnny that he killed Underwood. He knew the family and she is a good girl. Johnny tells Phil that he police have the jewels, as Virginia had told them where she took them after she killed him.

Johnny directs the insurance company to send the expense check to Charles Hagen, attorney for the defense.

NOTES:
- THE MID-PROGRAM COMMERCIAL IS FOR "SING IT AGAIN"
- THERE IS A TRAILER AT THE END TALKING ABOUT THE THREATS OF COMMUNISM AND THE NEED TO BUY DEFENSE BONDS.
- EDMOND O'BRIEN'S NEW MOVIE IS "THE REDHEAD AND THE COWBOY"
- DAN CUBBERLY IS THE ANNOUNCER
- MUSIC IS BY WILBUR HATCH

Producer: Jaime del Valle   **Writers:**   Gil Doud
Cast: Ramsey Hill, Jean Wood, Virginia Gregg, Jack Moyles, Ed Begley

◆   ❖   ◆

SHOW: THE MARIE MEADOWS MATTER
SHOW DATE: 5/12/1951
COMPANY: WASHINGTONIAN INSURANCE COMPANY
AGENT: BILL BRANDON
EXP. ACCT: $110.40

SYNOPSIS: Bill calls Johnny about a double murder in Boston, a girl and her mother. Bill heard about it on the radio, and there is a $50,000 policy that is a week old.

Johnny drives to Boston, Massachusetts and goes to the scene of the murder. The police and the bodies are still there. Johnny meets Sgt. Foley who tells him that the girl was stabbed twice, and her mother was strangled. The other daughter, Celia, found the bodies, and is the second beneficiary on the policy. Johnny goes to talk to Celia, who is 24, and meets her husband Peter. Peter tells Johnny that Marie liked to hurt people. Irwin Dodge, who works for the phone company, is one of those. Johnny calls a number of other men, and finds out that Marie had been involved with Peter also. Johnny calls Sgt. Foley and learns that the mother was a sculptress, and that Marie was a model. Johnny goes to see Irwin Dodge, and he tells Johnny that her mother was always pushing her, and that her father had been thrown out of the house because he was not good enough for them. Irwin tells Johnny that the father works in a leather shop. Also, Peter married Celia to be near Marie.

Johnny goes to Marie's apartment and the doors are locked. A neighbor tells Johnny that Marie came in around 1:30 that morning. Johnny goes to see the father, Chester Meadows, and learns nothing. Johnny goes to see Sgt. Foley and learns that Marie had been married to Mark Feedler for three days, and that Mark has skipped town.

The next day Feedler is captured by the police. He tells them that he loves his wife, and had dinner with her that night. They had kept the marriage a secret from Marie's mother. He had been out of town looking at a cabin. Mark is released, and Johnny thinks that the mother killed Marie when she found out she had married. The autopsy report gives a sharp triangular weapon as the cause of death. Johnny goes to the leather shop, and then to a hotel looking for Mr. Meadows. Johnny finds him, but he does not want to talk. Johnny calls the police and he is taken to a hospital to sober up. Johnny goes to see Celia who tells Johnny that her father could not have killed Marie or her mother, and that she and Peter had been at home with friends.

Johnny goes to the apartment with Sgt. Foley and tells him that the case rests on who could get into the locked apartment. Johnny spots a tree outside, and remembers that Dodge works for the phone company. Johnny goes to see Dodge and tells him about cleat marks on the tree outside the apartment. He throws his linesman cleats at Johnny and tries to run, but Johnny stops him and he confesses to killing Marie and her mother.

NOTES:
- THE ANNOUNCER IS DAN CUBBERLY
- MUSIC IS BY WILBUR HATCH
- STORY INFORMATION OBTAINED FROM THE KNX COLLECTION IN THE THOUSAND OAKS LIBRARY

Producer:	Jaime del Valle	Writers	Gil Doud
Cast:	Pat McGeehan, Ted Osborne, Robert North, Jeanne Bates, Herb Butterfield, Bill Johnstone		

◆ ❖ ◆

SHOW:	THE JANE DOE MATTER
SHOW DATE:	5/19/1951
COMPANY:	NEW YORK POLICE DEPARTMENT
AGENT:	
EXP. ACCT:	$0.00

SYNOPSIS: Lt. William Sexton of the New York police calls Johnny. He wants Johnny to come down and identify a "Jane Doe" who was found in Central Park with Johnny's name and phone number in her pocket.

Johnny goes to New York City, and goes to the morgue, but cannot identify the body. Over lunch Johnny thinks that he might know the girl, but cannot remember from where. Johnny meets with Lt. Sexton who tells Johnny that the body was found at 8:30 in Central Park by a delivery truck. She had been killed by a blunt instrument and thrown from a car. Johnny sees the note and recognizes his handwriting. Johnny goes home and searches his files, and finds eight cases that might be relevant. Johnny starts calling the names for the cases, and the fifth name was Sybil Miller. Johnny calls the apartment but is told that Sybil is married and has moved to Kansas or Nebraska. Johnny asks if she was a friend of Rudy Valentine. The manager remembers that a girl visited there two weeks ago and Mr. Koesler talked to her.

Johnny goes back to New York and talks to Mr. Koesler. He remembers seeing the girl, but does not know her name. He does remember that she wore a waitress' uniform with "IB" on it. Johnny starts a search of restaurants and goes to Inez's Basement Bar and Grill where he talks to Munsey and Burke who are hesitant to talk until Johnny mentions murder; then they tell Johnny that "they did it." Johnny is attacked and knocked out. Johnny wakes up in Central Park and goes to his hotel where he gets fixed up and then goes to see Lt. Sexton and tells him about the bar. Johnny is told that an apartment manager has identified the girl as Margaret Nelson. The manager told the police that he girl was not working, and came from the Middle West. Johnny and Lt. Sexton go to see the manager, Mr. Brimley, and he tells them that the girl came to town recently. Johnny and Lt. Sexton go to the bar and see Burke who tells them that they have not had a waitress for three months, and her name was Mary Keats. Johnny asks him who they" were and he admits that Mary was selling drugs for Munsey and sold up to $15,000 a night. She left and the buyer, who is named Noland, killed her. Burke tells Johnny that Brimley also bought drugs from her also. Munsey comes in, see the police and runs away and is shot three times.

NOTES:
- THE ANNOUNCER IS DICK CUTTING
- MUSIC IS BY WILBUR HATCH
- STORY INFORMATION OBTAINED FROM THE **KNX** COLLECTION IN THE THOUSAND OAKS LIBRARY

Producer: Jaime del Valle   **Writers**   **Gil Doud**
Cast: **Raymond Burr, Virginia Gregg, Howard McNear, Peter Leeds, Tudor Owen, Jim Nusser**

SHOW: THE LILLIS BOND MATTER
SHOW DATE: 5/26/1951
COMPANY: GREAT NORTHERN BONDING & SURETY
AGENT:

EXP. ACCT: **$308.90**

SYNOPSIS: Pat Shade, a private detective working for the bank, calls Johnny. He tells Johnny that he knows Lillis, and he is a nice kid. Pat wants to know if Johnny wants to get together and compare notes. Johnny has no notes, but he will be glad to pick Pat's brain.

Johnny goes to Chicago, Illinois to look into the disappearance of a bank messenger and $80,000. Johnny meets Pat Shade, a detective who works for the bank. Pat knew Henry Lillis and thought he was a bright kid. He had a good reputation because he was bonded. His father had died some years ago and Henry has worked to help support his mother. Johnny goes to see Mrs. Lillis, who is an attractive woman of forty. She tells Johnny that she knows the police suspect her son, but she is sure that Henry did not do it. She relates that she has not tried to meddle in her son's life and let Henry work out his own life. She knew of Henry's friends except for Raymond Lockhart, who works at a gas station. Johnny goes to talk to Ray. Ray tells Johnny that knew Henry and that Henry had a temper at times. Ray tells Johnny that Henry had a girl friend that had a car and that she was a "used dish." She had a strange name, but Ray cannot remember it, but her father worked at the bank. "Was the last name Shade?" asks Johnny. Yeah, that's it. Lillian Shade was her name.

Johnny meets with Pat Shade again. Johnny tells Pat that he has not told the police about Lillian yet. Pat tells Johnny that his daughter is away visiting with friends somewhere. Pat tells Johnny that she was no good, just like her mother and had started running around at thirteen. Pat tells Johnny that he did not know that she was seeing Henry. Pat thanks Johnny and tells him he will tell Sgt. Dyer immediately.

Next morning Sgt. Dyer calls Johnny to tell him that Henry Lillis has turned himself in. Sgt. Dyer tells Johnny that Henry told them that he had had a fight with an accomplice named Saunders, had hitchhiked into town to surrender and is in the hospital. Johnny and Sgt. Dyer go to see Henry in the hospital. Henry tells Johnny that he had pulled the robbery with Lillian Shade and gone to a house in Lake Bluffs with Lillian. He tells Johnny that her father had warned him about her once, but he ignored him. He relates that he had met Lillian were in the same boat, as they both wanted the things they did not have. She told Henry that she would not marry him unless he was rich. She also told Henry that she had blackmailed some man to get the money for the car. She was always talking about the money Henry carried, so she waited for four days until Henry had a big delivery and then disappeared to the house in Lake Bluff. Later a man named Red Sanders, or maybe it was Saunders, showed up and Lillian told Henry that she was just using him, and told Henry to leave. Henry had a fight with the man and left without any of the money. He had to hitchhike into town, but only a minister would pick him up because of his torn clothes. The police issue and APB for the man and Lillian Shade. Johnny and Sgt. Dyer go to the house in Lake Bluffs and find a car parked to the side of the house. Johnny and Sgt. Dyer go in and find evidence of a fight and Lillian Shade in the kitchen, dead. The lab boys are called and Johnny goes to see Pat Shade to follow an idea. Pat tells Johnny that after he talked to Johnny, he got drunk in the hotel bar. He went home and does not remember anything. When Johnny tells Pat about where he went and that Lillian is dead, Pat is afraid Johnny is trying to accuse him of doing it. Pat tells Johnny that he was so drunk that if he did kill Lillian, he would not remember it.

Johnny goes to see Sgt. Dyer and reads the lab report. There is only one place to go. In the hospital, Johnny confronts Henry with the lack of car prints from Red Sanders car. There was only one set of car tracks, Lillian's. After being confronted with the facts, Henry admits that she had become scared and wanted to take the money back. He lost his temper and killed her because he thought she was faking, but she wasn't. In his next statement, Henry tells the police where he buried the money, so the company will not lose. But that is more than you can say for the two parents involved, either the deserving or the undeserving.

NOTES:
- THIS PROGRAM IS FROM A REHEARSAL DISK. IN THE OPENING, EDMOND O'BRIEN TELLS PAT SHADE THAT HE WILL "PICK UP YOUR BRAIN" AND THE WHOLE CAST ROARS IN LAUGHTER.
- JOHNNY MENTIONS THAT HE HAS AN EXTRA BOTTLE OF WHISKEY IN HIS BAG.
- EDMOND O'BRIEN'S NEW MOVIE IS "WAR PATH"
- BOB LEMOND IS THE ANNOUNCER
- MUSIC IS BY WILBUR HATCH

Producer: Jaime del Valle   **Writers:** Gil Doud
Cast: Herb Butterfield, Jeanette Nolan, Tony Barrett, Tim Graham, Gil Stratton Jr.

◆ ❖ ◆

SHOW: THE SODERBURY, MAINE MATTER
SHOW DATE: 6/2/1951
COMPANY: BRITANNIA LIFE INSURANCE COMPANY
AGENT:
EXP. ACCT: $84.90
SYNOPSIS: Edward Whiteman calls Johnny to assist in the investigation of Mr. Soderbury's murder. Johnny wants to talk with Ed as he was riding with Mr. Soderbury when he was killed. Ed tells Johnny that he has just left constable Remmin, and he has found the place from which the shots were fired. Ed arranges to meet Johnny in front of his hotel.

Johnny goes to Soderbury, Maine, a small New England village, to investigate the murder of the town's leading citizen, George Soderbury. Ed Whiteman tells Johnny that there was a celebration in town to mark the reopening of a World War II factory. Whiteman tells Johnny the factory was originally built to handle government contracts during World War II, and that the town's people are against the influx of outsiders and their ways. Fathers do not have their sons to work the farms and daughters marry outsiders. During the parade Mr. Soderbury was shot. The deputy sheriff Fred Remmin has found the place where the shots came from, the roof of a store that has stairs in the back. In the parade Mr. Soderbury was in the first car with the windows opened. Fred Remmin comes from the roof and tells Johnny that there are a lot of excellent marksmen in the town. The prime suspect is Ben Sutherland who lost his oldest son in an accident at the plant and has another son who will be sixteen soon.

Johnny learns that he Soderbury family has controlled the town for three generations, but is not well liked. The sole survivor of the family is George's younger sister Bert. Johnny and Remmin go to see Ben Sutherland, who is not home. His wife tells Johnny and Fred that he left last night and that she will not tell them where he is as she is keeping a trust. Remmin is sure that Ben has left and not gone through town, so he knows where he went. Remmin calls the county authorities and arranges for the body to be picked up for the autopsy.

Johnny goes to see Beth Soderbury that evening and meets Lawrence Taft there. Lawrence leaves and Beth tells Johnny that she was educated in England and does not feel like part of the town. George, her brother, was not famous for making friends, but he knew what he was doing was forcing change on the townspeople. Johnny asks about Ben Sutherland, and she knows that Ben is angry. As they are talking Beth's dog "The General Scott" starts barking and shots ring out. Johnny goes to investigate and finds that The General has been wounded and that the whole village has turned out. Johnny calls Remmin and search of the area turns up nothing so Johnny goes to his hotel. On the way Remmin tells Johnny that Ed Whiteman came when the factory opened and that Taft was an orphan who was raised by George Soderbury. He was a smart man who worked in the factory, but was not happy. He was thick with Beth and would kill himself before he would harm George. Whiteman was an outsider brought in to work in the factory.

Next day the county picks up the body and the State Police bring in Ben Southerland. Ben tells Johnny and Fred that he heard of George's death when the police stopped him. Ben tells Johnny and Fred that he had taken his son to work on a farm away from the factory. He then went out to get drunk for the first time in twenty years and had a fight with some men in Brighton.

All but forty of the town's people have been checked by Fred and Johnny when the county reports that George had been shot with a 250/3000 caliber rifle. Four people are identified who own that type of rifle, including Ben Sutherland. The rifles are tested, and the results show that the murder weapon was not among them.

Johnny requests that Remmin to hold a meeting with Ed Whiteman, Lawrence Taft and Beth Soderbury on some pretense while Johnny looks for something. Johnny takes less than an hour to find some torn clothes and another rifle in a closet and goes to the killer. Johnny meets with Beth and tells her that Lawrence is the killer. Beth calls Lawrence and Johnny tells him he has found the torn clothes and the gun. Johnny tells Lawrence that he was outside listening when the dog barked and he shot it. Johnny tells Lawrence that he was an important man the last time the factory opened, but he has been left out this time. Lawrence admits that he had tried to kill Ed Whiteman for Beth. He was ashamed that Ed Whiteman had been brought in and that people were laughing at him. He had tried to shoot Ed, but missed and killed George—his dearest friend to whom he owes everything.

Johnny relates that Beth was right when she told Johnny that anyone with generations of background in an insular village like that takes a chance when he comes out, to say nothing of a half-generation Hartfordian when he goes in.

NOTES:
- THIS PROGRAM IS A REHEARSAL
- EDMOND O'BRIEN'S NEW MOVIE IS "WAR PATH"
- BOB LEMOND IS THE ANNOUNCER
- MUSIC IS BY WILBUR HATCH

Producer:	Jaime del Valle	Writers:	Gil Doud
Cast:	Robert North, Howard McNear, Virginia Gregg, Larry Thor, Sammie Hill, Herb Butterfield, David Light		

SHOW:	THE GEORGE FARMER MATTER
SHOW DATE:	6/9/1951
COMPANY:	GREAT EASTERN LIFE INSURANCE COMPANY
AGENT:	MR. MITCHELL
EXP. ACCT:	$33.65

SYNOPSIS: Mr. Mitchell calls Johnny at 5:30 AM and tells Johnny to be in the New York office when it opens. George Farmer has died and the wife has put in for a $100,000 double indemnity claim.

Johnny drives to New York City and meets with the Great Eastern manager who tells Johnny that Mr. Mitchell must have been sure that Johnny would take the case. Johnny tells him that Mr. Mitchell is familiar with Johnny's bank account. Johnny is told that George Farmer was on vacation at the Sportsman's Retreat when he was burned to death in a fire. His wife has filed a claim for $100,000. Dr. William Evans, an insurance doctor calls with important news, so Johnny rushes to his office. Outside the Equitable Building, Johnny meets Dr. Evans who is on the sidewalk where he had jumped from his office. Johnny is taken to see Lt. Briggs when he tells the officers on the street the name of the body. I just guessed, Johnny tells Lt. Briggs. Lt. Briggs tells Johnny that nobody saw Evans being pushed. Johnny goes to see Mrs. Farmer. She tells Johnny that she has already talked to the insurance investigator and that she does not know a Dr. Evans or who sold the policy to her husband. Johnny leaves and finds who sold the policy. Johnny then takes the subway to the home of Martin Ames where his wife is crying. She tells Johnny that her husband has just been in an automobile accident and is in the hospital. Johnny rushes to the hospital with Mrs. Ames and meets Lt. Briggs there. While Mrs. Ames waits for the doctor to come, Lt. Briggs tells Johnny that Ames was involved in a hit-and-run accident and is dead. Lt. Briggs tells Johnny that before he died, Ames told the police that a car had run him off the road.

Johnny and Lt. Briggs go to Mrs. Farmer again and ask her why two men who knew her husband were dead? She tells them that she did not know either of the men. When asked why did she not go to the Catskills this year with her husband, she tells them that she had gone there for fifteen years and was tired of it. She tells Johnny that her husband had smoked in bed occasionally, but she had already told the investigator that and Johnny should talk to her attorney. She tells Johnny that she in entitled to the money. Johnny leaves and suggests to Lt. Briggs that they drive up to the Sportsman's Lodge to find out how Mrs. Farmer knew that an investigator has been up there already.

Johnny and Briggs drive to the Sportsman's Retreat and speak with the foreman, a man named Pop Sloan. Pop offers breakfast and tells them that the same people stay there every year. Mr. Phillips owns the resort, and will be there that afternoon. Lt. Briggs remarks to Johnny about how beautiful it is there and Johnny reminds him that "his soul is showing." Pop tells Johnny that everyone is out fishing and that Mr. Farmer usually brought his wife with him. If she had come this year, she might have saved him. Everyone had hiked up to Willow Peak when the fire broke out, but Farmer did not go as he had trouble with his legs. Doc Combs has looked at the body, and is out fishing now. Later that morning Mr. Phillips the owner arrives from the city. Phillips tells Johnny that he was on his way to the lodge when the fire broke out. He knew Farmer, who was a quiet man. He had started a small fire two years ago, but his wife had saved him. Farmer usually stayed for his whole vacation and was very stingy. Dr. Combs comes in and tells Johnny that he knew Farmer and had identified the body by finding the broken wrist. "What broken wrist?" Johnny asks. George Farmer had broken his right wrist just a week before he came up to the lodge. Johnny has Briggs call the precinct to find out when and where the wrist was treated. Johnny thinks he can prove that Farmer was murdered. The police call back and Johnny learns that Farmer broke his wrist on the 26th, and that it was treated at the Olive Hospital. Johnny is told that Farmer got to the lodge on the fourth and died on the eleventh. However the policy went into effect on the 22nd, and the first claim was for the death, not the broken wrist. Johnny and Briggs go back to talk to Mrs. Farmer.

Johnny and Lt. Briggs confront Mrs. Farmer with what they know. She tells Johnny that her husband did not have a broken wrist when he bought the policy, and broke the wrist later. She tells Johnny that she had come to the insurance doctor with her husband and Johnny reminds her that she did not know Dr. Evans. Lt. Briggs tells her the signature on the policy does not match the one on his driver's license. Mrs. Farmer screams at Johnny to leave as he tells her how she sent someone else in to take the physical and forged her husband's name, so who helped you? Mr. Phillips comes in with his gun and removes all doubt about who helped her. There is a gunfight, and Phillips is killed. Mrs. Farmer tells Johnny that she and Phillips had fallen in love but he had planned the whole thing. Phillips had gone to Dr. Evans for the physical and Ames had sold him the policy and he killed them both. Mrs. Farmer will probably get the second degree for complicity, and the insurance company can cancel the policy.

NOTES:
- DICK CUTTING IS THE ANNOUNCER
- MUSIC IS BY WILBUR HATCH
- EDMOND O'BRIEN'S NEW MOVIE IS "WAR PATH"
- STARTING TOMORROW, GUY LOMBARDO IS REPLACING JACK BENNY FOR THE SUMMER, AND MARIO LANZA IS REPLACING EDGAR BERGEN AND CHARLIE MCCARTHY

Producer:	Jaime del Valle	**Writers:**	Blake Edwards
Cast:	Hy Averback, John McIntire, Herb Butterfield, Harry Lang, Jeanette Nolan, Virginia Gregg		

◆ ❖ ◆

SHOW:	THE ARTHUR BOLDRICK MATTER
SHOW DATE:	6/16/1951
COMPANY:	CORINTHIAN ALL RISK INSURANCE COMPANY
AGENT:	
EXP. ACCT:	$77.30

SYNOPSIS: Dr. Carr calls Johnny and advises him that Arthur Boldrick is lucky to be alive. Johnny can see Boldrick later that evening. Sgt. Wright hopes that Boldrick will talk to Johnny, as he is not the police.

Johnny goes to the Emergency Hospital in Hartford, Connecticut to talk to Arthur Boldrick who tells Johnny he was shot by a man in the alley behind his garage and cannot remember what he looked like. Arthur thinks that the man was after his car keys, and when Arthur pushed him the man panicked and shot him. Arthur cannot give a good description of the man and asks Johnny if his wife can come to see him, as he sure wants to see his wife.

Johnny goes to the police and gives his report about a man in blue work clothes or overalls with a small caliber gun to Sgt. Wright. Johnny goes to see Mrs. Velma Boldrick who lives in an area called "an older part of town" rather than a slum. Velma Boldrick shows Johnny where the shooting took place and tells Johnny that she heard shouting and ran outside but saw no one. Johnny is sure that the neighbors should have seen something at that time of the evening. A neighbor, Will Wheeler, comes over and chides Johnny for bothering Velma. Will tells Johnny what he knows and relates to Johnny that theirs is a rotten neighborhood with rotten people. Johnny mentions that the wounds are aggravating an injury to a lung obtained in the war. Johnny goes to see Sgt. Wright and meets Mrs. Cole who tells them that she was working in her garden and saw a tan or brown car driving up the alley at the time of the shooting. She though the car was backfiring, but learned later it was gunfire. Sgt. Wright tells Johnny that so far nothing fits; almost everyone saw nothing and one person sees a car.

Johnny goes to see Arthur with Sgt Wright and accuses Arthur of protecting someone. They tell Arthur of the conflicting evidence and Arthur finally admits to them that he was seeing his ex-wife without telling anyone. He was hurting her husband, his wife and the neighbors. Arthur has a relapse and is near death. Johnny and Sgt. Wright go to see Anna, the ex-wife, and Thomas Hood her husband. Sgt. Wright tells her that Arthur told them that her husband had shot him. Johnny is told that Thomas is out of town on business and left at four. Since Boldrick was shot at five thirty he had left in plenty of time to shoot Arthur. Johnny is also told that Thomas has a tan sedan. Anna begs Johnny not to tell her husband about them, as he does not know anything. Anna will not tell Johnny where Thomas is, as she does not want him to find out about them. Johnny and Sgt. Wright go back at the hospital and learn that Arthur had given a deathbed statement naming Thomas as the shooter. Johnny goes back to see Velma to tell her of the statement, and Will the neighbor is there. Will is told about the statement, and is surprised that Thomas Hood would kill Arthur. Will does not know if Velma knows about the first wife.

Back at police headquarters, a Mr. Mandel comes in to say that he might have been the car in the alley. He was delivering a repaired radio in the area and drove down the alley on the way home. He did not hear any shots as the alley is bumpy, and his car has a lot of loose bolts and is very noisy. Johnny and Sgt. Wright go to see Velma after reviewing the facts. She tells Johnny that she knows Arthur has died and only knew about the affair when Will had told her that day. After a few well-placed accusations by Johnny, Velma breaks down and admits she shot Arthur. He was going to see Anna and had told Velma where he was going. She tells Johnny that Will had lied and admits that she went out side and shot him.

Johnny thinks that Velma will get a "widows special" for second-degree murder and will be out in two years. So the insurance company will have that long to figure out how to cancel the policy.

NOTES:
- EDMOND O'BRIEN'S NEW MOVIE IS "WAR PATH"
- JOHNNY DOLLAR IS MOVING TO WEDNESDAY NEXT WEEK AT 9:00
- THE NEXT CASE IS ANNOUNCED AS THE "THE MALCOM WISH MATTER"
- DICK CUTTING IS THE ANNOUNCER
- MUSIC IS BY WILBUR HATCH

Producer: Jaime del Valle   Writers: Gil Doud
Cast: Edgar Barrier, Parley Baer, Jeanette Nolan, John McIntire,
             Wally Maher, Virginia Gregg, Jeanne Bates, Harry Lang

SHOW: THE MALCOLM WISH, MD MATTER
SHOW DATE: 6/20/1951
COMPANY: WASHINGTONIAN LIFE INSURANCE COMPANY
AGENT:
EXP. ACCT: $577.40

SYNOPSIS: Mrs. Wish calls to ask about her husband's disappearance. She is quite frightened, and Johnny sets up an appointment to see her.

Johnny goes to San Francisco, California and calls on Mrs. Wish. Cecil, the daughter of Dr. Wish, meets Johnny at the door. She tells Johnny that she has something to talk with him about, but has to meet Johnny somewhere. They agree to meet at the Hotel Cleveland coffee shop at noon. In the morning room Mrs. Wish tells Johnny that her husband had received an emergency call at 9:00 P.M. and rushed out without telling her where he was going, and that he would be back in an hour. She has called Dr. Huber, Malcom's business partner for a list of his patients. Johnny takes a cable car to meet with Dr. Huber who has noticed a change in Doctor Wish over the past several months. Johnny is told that Dr. Wish is fifty-two and seems tired and not satisfied with life. Dr. Huber says it may be amnesia but probably not. Dr. Huber will provide Johnny the list of Dr. Wish's patients in the afternoon.

Johnny goes to his hotel to meet with Cecil, but she had left a message saying that she could not make it and Johnny could call her after two. When Johnny leaves the hotel, he notices a blonde man tailing him. Johnny goes to meet Lt. Hughes and the man follows. Lt. Hughes has no information for Johnny and can only wait. Lt. Hughes knows nothing of the man tailing Johnny and suggests that Johnny leave him on the hook. Johnny takes a roundabout trip to Dr. Huber's office and the man is still with him. Johnny goes back to his hotel and calls Cecil. She apologizes for not meeting Johnny and agrees to meet Johnny in his room at 8:30 that night. Johnny tells her he will call the police if she does not show. Johnny spends the rest of the afternoon visiting the doctor's patients to lead the tail away from the hotel.

That evening Johnny returns to his hotel to find Lt. Hughes at his door, and no Cecil. Lt. Hughes tells Johnny that the hat and shoes of Dr. Wish had been found with a suicide note on the Golden Gate Bridge.

Johnny leaves to go to the Wish residence and notes that the tail is gone. Johnny and Lt. Hughes confront Mrs. Wish with the news. She tells Johnny that they had been a happy couple, and maybe she had been blind. Johnny talks to Cecil about what she knows. She tells Johnny that her father has reached that "dangerous age" and had been seeing another woman named Ann Movius. Cecil has talked to her anonymously and she seemed to be a nice person. Cecil knows nothing about the man who was following Johnny. Cecil gives Johnny the address for Ann Movius and Johnny and Hughes go there and find no one there. Inside they a suit coat with dried blood and a label from Carson City, Nevada.

In the bedroom they find surgical dressings soaked with blood, a sales slip for a coat and shirt and a Nevada newspaper. The headlines covered a trio who had robbed a bookie and one of whom was shot. Johnny talks to the neighbors and the manager, none of who knew Ann or had seen an injured man.

Johnny goes back to see Lt. Hughes and learns that the man tailing Johnny was named Ned Ring, a criminal from Carson City. The Nevada police have a record for Alan Movius. An alert is sent out and Ned is captured at the airport. At police headquarters Ned is questioned. Johnny tells him that he had followed Johnny all day, but Ned denies it. After Ned is told what Johnny and Lt. Hughes know, Ned realizes his cohorts have abandoned him. He tells Johnny that Alan Movius is the one who was shot. They had shot the bookie and fled to San Francisco where one of the men, Alan Movius, had a sister who knew a doctor. They tricked the doctor to come over and were holding him. Johnny gets a description of the others when a call comes in from Petaluma. A pharmacist there was suspicious of a prescription he had been given for sedatives. A Dr. Wish had written the prescription. Johnny and Lt. Hughes drive to Petaluma and locate the criminals at a motel. When they knock on the door, Dr. Wish answers, and tells them that the others are in the bedroom dead. He tells Johnny that he had poisoned them with the prescription he had obtained for Alan Movius. Dr. Wish then collapses from the same drug and is rushed to a hospital and is saved. Not only is Dr. Wish a three-time murderer, but it is premeditated as well.

NOTES:
- MUSIC IS NOW PROVIDED BY EDDIE DUNSTEDTER AT THE ORGAN
- THE MID-PROGRAM PROGRAM IS FOR GEORGE RAFT AS ROCKY JORDAN
- SOME CATALOGS LIST THIS PROGRAM AS THE MALCOM WISH, MARYLAND MATTER, BUT THE MD IS CORRECTLY REFERENCED AS MEDICAL DOCTOR
- EDMOND O'BRIEN'S NEW MOVIE IS "WAR PATH"
- DAN CUBBERLY IS THE ANNOUNCER

Producer: Jaime del Valle   **Writers:** Gil Doud
Cast: Jeanette Nolan, Virginia Gregg, Ray Hartman, Bill Bouchey, Tony Barrett, Lou Krugman

SHOW: THE HATCHET HOUSE THEFT MATTER
SHOW DATE: 6/27/1951
COMPANY: FINANCIAL SURETY COMPANY
AGENT:
EXP. ACCT: $1,182.75
SYNOPSIS: Inspector Sayler from Scotland Yard calls Johnny to advise him that Inspector Findley is ill and that he has taken over the Scott jewel case. Sayler asks

if Johnny has been brought in because the Yard's reputation has fallen since the Stone of Scorne was stolen. Perhaps he and Johnny will have better luck.

Johnny goes to London, England and meets with Inspector Sayler who tells Johnny that Inspector Finch was very complementary about his work. Johnny is told that Mrs. Scott was staying at a house in Surrey and had a number of jewels stolen during a party. Johnny tells Saylor that Mrs. King has been known to be selling her jewels lately at below market prices. Johnny learns that Mrs. King has been seen with a man named Norman King. The loss of these jewels is around $100,000.

Johnny is driven to Hatchet House in Surrey see Mrs. Scott, but is told that she is out. Garrett the butler tells Johnny that he has worked there for a long time and only "genuine" people were at the party. The maid, Millie Hackey comes in and tells Johnny that the jewels were not the only scandal there, as Mrs. Scott has talked derisively of her former husband and that Mr. King is a slimy leech. She is only a working girl who knows right from wrong, and will be getting married soon, maybe next month. While Johnny is waiting in the library, Mrs. Scott calls the butler and says she will be in London at the Claridge Hotel for the night, so Johnny returns to Scotland Yard and updates Sayler. Sayler recounts Inspector Finch's report that they should look into collusion between King and Millie, and Johnny calls New York to check on Norman King. Johnny goes to see Mrs. Scott at her hotel. She tells Johnny that she suspects one of the servants, as things got pretty confused after 11:00PM. Johnny tells Mrs. Scott that Norman Kings has a record for forgery and stealing from rich old women and that he has disappeared. Mrs. Scott tells Johnny that she and King are the same types of people. They know what they want and they want money.

Later that night Sayler calls to report that one of the jewels was found at a murder site in Lime House. Johnny and Sayler drive to the scene where the body of George Kinsey is in a grubby room in a grubby part of town. He had been beaten and was found by a bootblack who owed him money. A brooch found in the room is identified as one of Mrs. Scott's. A woman named Gloria Stokes comes into the room and tells them that she had come in to see Kinsley and is taken in for questioning. Johnny learns that Gloria is married to Leonard Stokes, and has not seen him in three days and went to see Leonard to see if he knew where her husband was. She knew Kinsey was no good and that her husband spent too much time with him. When told of the robbery, she tells them her husband was not involved as he doesn't have the brains.

Johnny goes to Hatchet House to meet Mrs. Scott, who apologizes for letting Johnny see a part of her last night that she does not like. She tells Johnny that Norman is on a boat to New York. He left because he thought his record would come out, so he left before he was asked to leave. Johnny shows her a picture of Kinsey and Stokes, and she recognizes neither. Mrs. Scott tells Johnny that he doesn't like her, but Johnny tells Mrs. Scott "your physical part does not match up with a mental apparatus that deserves it" and she slaps him. The servants are shown the pictures and Garrett thinks he might have seen one of the men. Sayler questions the people in the village and finds a few who recognize Kinsey.

Back in London, Sayler gets a report that Leonard Stokes is on a train. Johnny and Sayler board the train and locate Stokes. Stokes admits that he did not kill George. He tells Johnny that George had picked him up and taken him to Seven Oaks and he waited outside Hatchet House while Kinsey went in to see a friend, a gardener. Kinsey came back and showed him the jewels on the way back to London. Kinsey had only taken one of them to give to someone. Later a police report shows that lip rouge was found on Kinsey's body, so Johnny and Sayler go to see Millie. Millie admits that she left the door open for Kinsey. He had promised to marry her and when she went to see him in London, he had told her to get lost so she killed him. He had called her a "stupid country girl," so she killed him.

The jewels are recovered, Millie arrested and Mrs. Scott departs for the Isle of Capri.

NOTES:

- THE STONE OF SCORNE, OR THE CORONATION STONE WAS HOUSED IN WESTMINSTER ABBEY AND STOLEN BY SCOTTISH NATIONALISTS IN 1950.
- THE MID-PROGRAM COMMERCIAL IS FOR SUSPENSE, WHICH WILL AIR THE PROGRAM "THE SECRET OF DR. WALTER'S PRIVATE LIFE"
- EDMOND O'BRIEN'S NEW MOVIE IS "WAR PATH"
- DAN CUBBERLY IS THE ANNOUNCER
- MUSIC IS BY EDDIE DUNSTEDTER

Producer: Jaime del Valle   **Writers:** Gil Doud
Cast: John McIntire, Ben Wright, Tudor Owen, Jeanette Nolan, Virginia Gregg

◆   ❖   ◆

SHOW: THE ALONZO CHAPMAN MATTER
SHOW DATE: 7/4/1951
COMPANY: TRI-STATE INSURANCE GROUP
AGENT:
EXP. ACCT: $672.08

SYNOPSIS: Lt. Schock calls Johnny to ask who Johnny is, and what his involvement is with the Alonzo Chapman killing. Johnny tells him he is working on the case for the insurance company. Johnny tells Schock that he heard about the case last night and got there that morning.

Johnny goes to Los Angeles, California and meets with Lt. Shock and is updated on the case. Johnny is told that Chapman had met a girl in a bar. They had stayed for a while and then left and were walking down the alley to her car when he was shot but not robbed. The girl, Norma Sales, had told the police that she had met Chapman that night.

Johnny goes to see Norma with Lt. Shock. Norma tells Johnny that she vaguely remembers last night. She relates how she had met Chapman in the bar, and they were just talking. He asked her to go to dinner with him, so they left and walked down the alley, as her car was closer that way. Norma tells Johnny that she has no boyfriend who would have been jealous. They were just walking down the alley and a man jumped from behind a trash box and shot him. Norman is not sure she would recognize the shooter.

Lt. Shock writes the Cleveland police for more information on Chapman. Johnny talks to the bartender in the bar. He remembers Chapman letting the girl have his chair at the bar, as it was crowded at that hour. They moved to a booth after a while and then left. Johnny goes back to see Lt. Shock who tells Johnny that Mrs. Chapman is in town and might have a motive. Johnny goes to see Norma's roommate and confirms that she has no boyfriend.

Johnny goes to see Mrs. Chapman who tells Johnny that she is not fond of her husband. He was attractive to women and knew it. She knew that something like this would happen, and now it has. Johnny goes to back see Lt. Shock and tells him of the conversation. Lt. Shock tells Johnny that he has learned that Mrs. Chapman was seeing a man named Nicholson who has left Cleveland and has not been seen since. Johnny and Lt. Shock go to see Mrs. Chapman and confront her with the information on Nicholson. She admits to seeing him, and tells Johnny that they had a lot in common. She last saw him on Wednesday of last week. Johnny asks if he could have killed her husband, but she denies that she had told Nicholson where her husband was when he called her on Friday. She does admit that she and Nicholson had fought over her not pushing her husband for a divorce and gives the Lt. Shock a picture of Nicholson.

Johnny takes the picture to the bartender and a bargirl, neither of which recognize Nicholson. Johnny takes the picture to Norma, and she thinks maybe it might be the shooter, but she is not sure. Later that day, Nicholson is no longer a suspect. The Ohio police have found his body in his car. He had been drunk and had a fatal accident.

Johnny finds a vital clue in the newspaper. Max Gerber, a local mobster had been staying at the same hotel as Chapman and was shot the previous night. Johnny goes to the morgue to see Gerber, and then visits Norma. He confronts Norma with the facts that she had left work sick the afternoon of the shooting and that she had never been to that bar before. Johnny asks Norma if she was paid to meet Chapman. Johnny shows Norma pictures of Alonzo Chapman and Max Gerber. She tells Johnny that she thinks that they are pictures of the same man. She then panics and admits that some men had said that they wanted her to distract Gerber as he owned them some money. She was hired because she was young and blonde. They only wanted money from him.

The second murder was a gangland murder; the first murder was an accident because the mobsters had pointed out the wrong man.

Notes:
- Edmond O'Brien's new movie is "War Path"
- Johnny Dollar moves to 9:30 next Wednesday
- Dick Cutting is the announcer
- Music is by Eddie Dunstedter

Producer: Jaime del Valle   **Writers:** Gil Doud
Cast: John McIntire, Hy Averback, Harry Lang, Jeanette Nolan,
               Virginia Gregg

◆   ❖   ◆

SHOW: THE FAIRWAY MATTER
SHOW DATE: 7/11/1951
COMPANY: COLUMBIA ALL RISK INSURANCE COMPANY
AGENT: SAM HARRIS
EXP. ACCT: $0.00

SYNOPSIS: Sam Harris calls to alert Johnny of a Fairway Airlines plane crash in Hartford, Connecticut. Sam is sure that a bomb caused the accident, and thirteen people were killed. The company wants to place responsibility and do what ever it can. Contact the airline representative Mr. Reed.

Johnny goes to the scene of the crash. The plane had been airborne less than a minute when it exploded and destroyed two houses on the ground killing at least 6 people. Johnny meets a hysterical Carl Reed of the airline who is talking to an equally hysterical Mrs. Goodhugh about a daughter she fears was on the plane. The daughter was on the plane, but she has not been told yet. Carl tells Johnny that the explosion was in the tail of the plane; that the CAB is on the way; and that the State Police are in charge of the investigation.

Johnny goes to find Captain Jim Lenhart of the State Police in the hangar where the bodies are being collected. They wonder if the crash was murder with a motive, suicide, or just a maniac.

The next day Johnny learns that nitroglycerine was the explosive. A tip to the police brings in Wilbur Wheeler, a maintenance worker for the airlines for questioning. Wilber is very nervous and asks what the police have on him. He admits that he had been in love with Shirley Goodhugh, a stewardess, and had fought with a copilot when Wilbur learned that Shirley was going to marry him instead. Wilbur had threatened the copilot and his plane, and knew that made him a suspect. He had heard of the crash on the radio and came back to work to help out. After questioning he is released and a police tail is placed on him.

Johnny relates that on the list of dead passengers, one man named Rupert Stone could not be located because of bogus information. Johnny and Capt. Lenhart go to visit a Mrs. Graham who is distraught over the loss of her husband. She tells Johnny and Capt. Lenhart that her husband had gone to Boston to visit his brother's grave, as he was a religious man. On the way out Jim calls this case a rotten mess and admits that he could not ask Mrs. Graham if her husband's cancer could have caused him to commit suicide. They leave to go have a drink, but are interrupted with the news that the explosive was found to have been in a first aid box in the rear of the airplane.

Wilber Wheeler is brought in for more questioning. After a very nervous interview Wilber tells Capt. Lenhart that he has worked for the airlines for a year and a half, yet does not know about the first aid kit carried on by Miss Goodhugh. Wilbur denied knowing anything about the nitroglycerine. Wilbur is held for a lie detector test and an interview with the police psychologist. Johnny and Jim search Wilbur's room and find no radio, which Wilbur said he had listened to, and no newspapers are found.

On the next day the lie detector test proves negative and the psychologist says that Wilbur has a severe guilt complex. Carl Reed calls to report that another stewardess named Alice Turner is missing and a search of her apartment uncovered her shot dead. Johnny and Capt. Lenhart go to the apartment and Carl tells them that she was originally scheduled to fly on the plane that crashed but had switched at the last minute with Shirley Goodhugh. Johnny is told that the stewardesses often switched flights among themselves. It seems now that the case against Wilbur is not very sound. Johnny and Capt. Lenhart go to visit Mrs. Goodhugh and learn nothing new other than Shirley was called shortly before the flight and that one of the girls was sick. They are told that there were six girls in Hartford who swapped flights if one was sick. Johnny and Capt. Lenhart talk to the other girls and learn nothing.

On the way home a man named Moran meets Johnny in the hallway of his apartment and he wants to talk. Moran tells Johnny that he knew Alice and that he was to blame for the accident. Moran tells Johnny that a man named Arthur Church was using Alice as a courier for drugs, which were carried in the first aid kit. She wanted out and Moran was hiding her. Alice had arranged a meeting with the Feds and Church had found out and killed her. Moran warned her to stay hidden and she had gotten Shirley to take her flight. Moran also tells Johnny that Church had hidden the explosives on the plane in Alice's kit, which was kept at the airport and picked up by Shirley.

Johnny and the Capt. Lenhart go to Church's apartment with Moran. Moran goes in and calls for Church, but he opens fire and kills Moran, and Capt. Lenhart kills Church.

The expense account total is $25.95, but the total is hardly important compared with the losses of others so, just forget it.

NOTES:
- THIS PROGRAM IS REPEATED BY JOHN LUND ON 1/5/1954
- THE CAB, OR CIVIL AERONAUTICS BOARD, WAS THE FORERUNNER OF THE FAA.
- "THE FRONT PAGE" COMEDY IS ON THE BROADWAY PLAYHOUSE TOMORROW NIGHT
- THERE IS A PUBLIC SERVICE ANNOUNCEMENT FOR DEFENSE BONDS AT THE END OF THE PROGRAM.
- EDMOND O'BRIEN'S NEW MOVIE IS "WAR PATH"
- DAN CUBBERLY IS THE ANNOUNCER
- MUSIC IS BY EDDIE DUNSTEDTER

Producer: Jaime del Valle   **Writers: Gil Doud**

Cast: Peter Leeds, Ray Hartman, Martha Wentworth, Bill Bouchey, Vic Perrin, Virginia Gregg

SHOW: THE NEAL BREER MATTER
SHOW DATE: 7/18/1951
COMPANY: GREAT EASTERN INSURANCE COMPANY
AGENT:
EXP. ACCT: $556.70

SYNOPSIS: Dr. Hamill, the local coroner calls Johnny, and Johnny wants to talk to him. Dr. Hamill is convinced that the death was from natural causes. Johnny tells him he has a letter that raised doubts.

Johnny flies to a city not to be disclosed by the insurance company. Johnny goes to visit Dr. Henry Richards, the man who wrote the letter about Neal Breer. Johnny is told that Breer, who was 26, was a part owner of a service station with Westley Birtcher. Neal started having convulsions and supposedly died of a heart attack. Dr. Richards confirms that Neal had a heart condition, but bismine could also have caused the symptoms. Dr. Richards has reviewed the records, and Johnny tells him he will order an autopsy. Johnny goes to see the coroner about the autopsy and is told that he relies on the opinions of the doctors, and that Johnny will have to go to the family for permission to do an exhumation and autopsy.

Johnny develops the background of Neal Breer, and is told to leave the case alone. Johnny goes to the widow, who is shocked at the suggestion of an autopsy. Johnny goes to see Neal's father, and he will not order the autopsy. Johnny goes to his hotel and has had a number of calls from a hysterical man. Johnny asks Hazel, the operator, to listen in if the man calls again. Later, the man who identifies himself as Alan, calls Johnny and tells him to stop the investigation and leave town. Johnny is causing trouble and will be hurt if he continues. Johnny goes to see Hamill who tells Johnny that a toxicologist is on the way, and that the body will be ready. After the tests, the cause of death is found to be bismine. Johnny calls Dr. Richards, and he is happy about the results. He tells Johnny that he does not know where to get bismine. Johnny goes to see Neal's father who tells Johnny that he was not happy when his son eloped with that girl. The business partner had told him that Neal was down in the mouth lately. Johnny goes to see Wesley Bircher who tells Johnny that Neal had seemed to lose interest in things. Everyone was surprised at the marriage because the wife was so strong willed. She threw herself at Neal after her boyfriend went away to medical school. The old boy friend was the son of Dr. Richards. Johnny gets the details of the day, and then goes to see Mrs. Breer. She denies murdering Neal and tells Johnny that she did not love him. Johnny tells her that Alan had called to warn him, and she tells Johnny that she had wanted a divorce and Neal refused. It was then that Alan decided to poison him.

NOTES:

- THE ANNOUNCER IS BOB STEVENSON
- MUSIC IS BY EDDIE DUNSTEDTER
- STORY INFORMATION OBTAINED FROM THE KNX COLLECTION IN THE THOUSAND OAKS LIBRARY

Producer: Jaime del Valle **Writers** **Gil Doud**
Cast: Ralph Moody, Edgar Barrier, Joe Du Val, Jeanne Bates, Mary Shipp, Tony Barrett, Peter Leeds

◆ ❖ ◆

SHOW: THE BLIND ITEM MATTER
SHOW DATE: 7/25/1951
COMPANY:
AGENT:
EXP. ACCT: $1,074.00

SYNOPSIS: [The first half of this program is missing, but it takes place in Santa Barbara, California.] Johnny tells Madelon that her husband hired the detective. She tells Johnny that she loved Keith and did not kill her husband, and does not own a gun. Johnny is told that her husband knew about Keith, but would not give her her freedom. The police arrive and Johnny goes back to his hotel. On the way Johnny spots a cab with a blonde in it. Johnny follows her into the bar and is paged by Ed Belasco who tells Johnny that Keith has been arrested. Ed arranges to meet Johnny at the Harbor Pier.

Johnny goes to the pier where Belasco tells Johnny he can name the killer for $2,000, saving the insurance company $100,000. Johnny agrees to pay $1,000, and just as Belasco tells Johnny that the killer is John Foresyth, Mrs. Ridgeley's first husband, he is shot. Johnny takes his .38 and sees a man by a building. Johnny shoots and the man starts running.

Johnny goes to see Madelon and spots blood on the floor. She tells Johnny that the houseboy cut his finger. Johnny tells her about Belasco and the private detective. She tells Johnny that her husband lives in Santa Barbara, but she has not seen him in fifteen years. As they are talking Forrest Graham comes in bleeding and tells Johnny that he had changed his name when he moved. Graham tells Johnny that he planted the blind item to make Ridgeley jealous and hired Belasco. Madelon hooked up with the piano player and he was sent to the cabin to ask for her freedom. Graham tells Johnny that he killed Ridgeley and collapses.

Remarks: Graham was John Foresyth all right, and he's lying in the morgue beside Belasco. Between them I don't think they'll be able to think of six pallbearers. Keith Tucker was released and Mrs. Ridgeley is being arraigned and will probably get her share for complicity. If you feel charitable some Christmas, just think of how much money I saved you. . ."

NOTES:
- INCOMPLETE SCRIPT
- MUSIC IS BY EDDIE DUNSTEDTER
- EDMUND O'BRIEN'S NEXT FILM IS "WAR PATH"
- STORY INFORMATION OBTAINED FROM THE KNX COLLECTION IN THE THOUSAND OAKS LIBRARY

Producer: Jaime del Valle   Writers   Blake Edwards,
                                                    Dick Quine
Cast: Hy Averback, Jack Moyles, Jack Kruschen, Virginia Gregg, Ted Osborne

◆ ❖ ◆

SHOW: THE HORACE LOCKHART MATTER
SHOW DATE: 8/1/1951
COMPANY: WASHINGTONIAN LIFE INSURANCE COMPANY
AGENT:
EXP. ACCT: $583.85

SYNOPSIS: Bruce Ewell, the attorney for the Lockhart estate calls Johnny. He wants to arrange a meeting to discuss how to solve a $200,000 question. Mr. Ewell still does not know who died first.

Johnny travels from Santa Barbara to Los Angeles, California to work on a new case. The Lockharts had been killed early Monday morning in an auto accident on the Pacific Coast Highway. The police had received a call about the accident from an all-night garage. Mr. Ewell needs Johnny to find the girl who reported the accident to the operator of the garage, as $200,000 rests on who died first, the husband or the wife. Johnny and Bruce agree to place information ads in the paper to ask the girl to contact them.

Johnny rents a car and drives to the garage. The owner, Mr. Gallagher, tells Johnny that a girl rushed in, woke him up, and told him there was an accident and then disappeared. Gallagher cannot remember exactly what she said even when Johnny tells him why it is so important. Johnny explains that the Lockharts were co-beneficiaries of the life insurance policy, and each had left a different second beneficiary. So who was alive last would matter to the two beneficiaries. Gallagher remembers that the girl had blue eyes, wore very heavy makeup, maybe stage makeup, had a headscarf, bare legs and high heels and had headed back towards Los Angeles. Johnny drives to the scene of the accident and finds a sheer drop-off to the beach. Johnny drives to the Sheriff's office, and a look at the photos tells him that the driver must have fallen asleep.

Johnny goes to the Lockhart mansion to meet the two beneficiaries, who have never met. Michael Adams, 27, of Seattle is the son of Mrs. Lockhart and is not used to being around money. Gail, 23, was the daughter of Mr. Lockhart and totally upset by Michael's insensitivity. Michael tells Johnny that he knows that he is an outsider, but $200,000! Wow!

Mr. Ewell and Johnny agree to post a $1,000 reward for information leading to the girl. After seven days an apartment manager calls Mr. Ewell with information and Johnny goes to see her. She tells Johnny that one of her tenants, Susan Lee, had moved out Monday, with a month's rent paid. She was a "specialty dancer" and had told the manager that she would come for her mail. Johnny looks through the mail and finds a bill from a photographer. A visit to the shop yields a picture of the girl, Susan Lee.

Mr. Ewell is convinced by Johnny to leave the ads running for a while. Johnny drives to the Santa Monica club where Susan worked. The manager, Mr. Cobley, tells Johnny that Susan has just dropped out of sight. He had read about the accident but cannot understand why she was headed towards Los Angeles, as she got off her last show at 12:45 AM and the accident was at 2:00 AM. Cobley tells Johnny that a girl named Lameen Dunn had picked up Susan's last paycheck. Johnny gets the address and goes to see Lameen. She tells Johnny that Susan has made her promise not to talk, but something happened that night, and it was probably over the man that she married. Lameen tells Johnny that Susan had married a man named Philip Roberts in Mexico. He traveled a lot and she would meet him in a cabin several times a week. Susan came there that morning and told Lameen that she had to get out of town. Lameen tells Johnny that Susan also used to get flowers from a "masher" in San Diego and never read the cards. Lameen tells Johnny that she had brought the flowers home on Sunday and read the card, which said, "As usual if you ever need me." Johnny gets the card with the florist's name and goes to San Diego and gets an address from the florist. Johnny visits the address and finds a hysterical Susan. She tells Johnny that she has read about the reward in the papers and cries about not killing him; that she was going to meet him but another car was there. She heard a woman's voice say that he was his wife and call him Carl and then there were shots. But she left and did not kill him. You are trying to trick me. I do not care what she says.

Johnny takes Susan to the police who go to the cabin and find a man and a woman shot to death. The man was a bigamist and his wife had found out and killed him and her self. Susan had seen the accident and tried to help but there was nothing to do. Johnny goes to see the beneficiaries and Mr. Ewell tells them that Susan had testified that Mrs. Lockhart was still alive when Susan saw her. Michael is ecstatic. $200,000 for being born to the right mother!

Johnny remarks that in his opinion the money went to the wrong person.

NOTES:
- COMMERCIALS ARE BACK TO WRIGLEY SPEARMINT GUM
- EDMOND O'BRIEN'S NEW MOVIE IS "WAR PATH"
- BOB STEVENSON IS THE ANNOUNCER
- MUSIC IS BY EDDIE DUNSTEDTER

Producer: Jaime del Valle   **Writers:** Gill Doud
Cast: Howard McNear, Hy Averback, Barbara Whiting, David Young, Virginia Gregg, Eddie Marr, Mary Jane Croft

SHOW:	THE MORGAN FRY MATTER
SHOW DATE:	8/8/1951
COMPANY:	BRITTANIA LIFE INSURANCE COMPANY
AGENT:	
EXP. ACCT:	$136.65

SYNOPSIS: Lt. Barbe calls Johnny and tells her that Mrs. Fry was sent home after she identified the body. Come on down and get the details.

Johnny goes to Boston, Massachusetts where he learns that the body of Morgan Fry has been found in the Harbor after being there two days. The only clues were special shoes that were traced to a chiropodist. Mrs. Fry thought her husband was on Wall Street. Robbery is ruled out as the body was shot too many times. The policy is for $125,000, split between the wife ($50,000) and the company ($75,000). Johnny goes to see Mrs. Fry, who tells Johnny that she last saw her husband three days ago, and that he would often go away for several days. On the way out the maid, Millie tells Johnny that when Mrs. Fry went to Detroit recently, Mr. Fry had a woman in the house. Johnny goes to talk to Joseph Miller, the partner of Fry. He tells Johnny that he thought Fry was going to take the 5:40 train to New York, and that another woman was impossible. He does remember the secretary telling him that a woman had called for Fry.

Johnny calls Barbe and is told that he has learned nothing. Lt. Barbe receives a call and learns that Mrs. Fry has swallowed some pills, and the maid had called the police. Johnny goes to the Fry home and talks to Millie who tells Johnny that Mrs. Fry came into the kitchen and said "what have I done?" Johnny goes to the hospital and Mrs. Fry tells him that she found out about the "other" woman and felt cheated. The woman had called and told her about the affair. She said that Morgan had told her to tell her if anything happened to him because he had been making illegal investments.

Johnny and Lt. Barbe go to see Miller, who is ready to talk. Miller tells them that he and his family have been threatened also. Miller tells them that they had invested some money in an organization that was building a racetrack in Nevada. The next investment was to buy some gambling equipment. The man they dealt with was Ernest Nebbie. Fry was killed when he discovered that the money was really used to buy narcotics. A man named Phillip Dean had called after the killing, and Miller gives them the address. Johnny and Lt. Barbe go to see Dean, who denies killing Fry, but is ready to go to the police. Dean goes into his room to get his things and tries to run away but is shot outside by the police. Dean is saved in the hospital, and the woman was never found.

NOTES:
- THE ANNOUNCER IS BOB STEVENSON
- MUSIC IS BY EDDIE DUNSTEDTER

- **STORY INFORMATION OBTAINED FROM THE KNX COLLECTION IN THE THOUSAND OAKS LIBRARY**

Producer: Jaime del Valle   **Writers**   Gil Doud
Cast: Bill Conrad, Edith Tackna, Virginia Gregg, Ted Osborne, Larry Thor

◆   ❖   ◆

SHOW: THE LUCKY COSTA MATTER
SHOW DATE: 8/15/1951
COMPANY: NYPD Homicide
AGENT:
EXP. ACCT: $0.00

SYNOPSIS: Louise Costa calls Johnny and tells him that something is wrong. Lucky is working on a case, and she has not heard from him for over a week. Can I talk to you?

Johnny details the case of Frank "Lucky" Costa. Johnny meets with Louise, who is hesitant to talk. She tells Johnny that Lucky has changed; something a wife can see; and that the change has been going on for a month. She thinks Lucky is involved with another woman as he has made her think that he was hiding something. Supposedly Lucky is in San Francisco working on a divorce case. Louise asks Johnny to look into the matter for her.

Johnny goes to see Frank's brother Joe in Hartford, Connecticut. Joe tells Johnny that he had talked to Lucky for the last time a month ago. Joe asks Johnny if Lucky ever told him about his first wife or his prison time. Joe tells Johnny that Lucky spent over a year in prison for grand theft over the first wife, some 12 years ago. Johnny is told that the first wife, Hazel Mackie, had called Lucky about a month ago. He was going to see her, so Joe called it quits as a brother. Joe tells Johnny that Hazel is in New York.

Johnny goes to New York City to see Hazel, and she tells Johnny that she does not know where Lucky is now, but he is working on a case for her. She tells Johnny that she needed a bodyguard and called Lucky. She tells Johnny that she had changed her mind about an old boyfriend and needed a bodyguard as the man, George Meyers, had told her he would get her. So Lucky is looking for George for her. Johnny is told that when this is over, Lucky can go back to his wife.

Johnny does not tell Lucky's wife for two days. On third day, George Meyers is found shot dead, shot by an "unknown assailant." Johnny calls Joe and visits him at lunch to tell him of the case. Joe is told that Lucky was supposed to guard Hazel from Meyers, but now it comes out that $200,000 is still unfound from the robbery twelve years earlier, and Johnny thinks that maybe Hazel knows where it is. Johnny tells Joe that he must go to police with the news to stay clean with the police. After all, Louise started it, he tells Joe, who walks off angry. "What a sour racket" Johnny mutters to himself.

Johnny goes back to New York and goes to see Hazel. She tells Johnny that Lucky is gone, and that he had killed George Meyers. She tells Johnny that George had followed her to Lucky's hotel. George was waiting in the lobby and pulled gun on them when they left and Lucky shot him. Johnny tells her that his theory is that Lucky agreed to kill Meyers for a share of the $200,000 and asks Hazel where the gun is. "Did you hire a detective as a ploy to kill George and hide behind his license?" Johnny asks Hazel, but she tells Johnny that she knows nothing about the money. Johnny tells Hazel that he will call the police as they can hold her as a material witness.

The police are called, and Lt. Carl Bilder takes Hazel in, and the apartment is searched. Johnny finds a check stub that shows that Lucky had been paid for one weeks work. The phone rings, and it is Lucky. He asks Johnny what he is doing there, and where is Hazel? Johnny asks Lucky to come in and talk, but he does not want to meet anywhere and hangs up. Lt. Bilder tells Johnny that the exits to New York are covered. Lucky's clothes are still in the hotel, so there is no idea what Lucky will do.

Johnny goes to police headquarters where Hazel keeps to her story, a well-rehearsed statement that he police cannot prove otherwise.

Three days later Joe calls Johnny from Hartford and wants to talk. Johnny goes to see Joe who invites him in. He tells Johnny that he is no better than a rat now. Lucky had called him and needs money. Joe told Lucky to call back tonight after 7:00 and Johnny will talk to him.

The call comes in and Johnny agrees to meet Lucky at 10:00 the next night. When Johnny meets Lucky, he tells Johnny that he needs money. Lucky tells Johnny that Hazel double-crossed him, and used Johnny set up the double-cross. She had only told Lucky about Johnny being there after he had killed Meyers. He tells Johnny that he knew how she was. Now he is lost, with no options and there is no way out now. Johnny starts to leave and Lucky pulls a gun. Johnny tells Lucky to use it. Johnny walks out and Lucky does not shoot. The police go in and Lucky is killed in a gunfight. Johnny records that his confession is useless, and that the police cannot charge Hazel, but you should bring her in and grill her until she talks.

NOTES:
- JOHNNY NOTES THAT 5 YEARS AGO HE AND LUCKY WORKED FOR A BIG DETECTIVE AGENCY
- EDMOND O'BRIEN'S NEW MOVIE IS "WAR PATH"
- BOB STEVENSON IS THE ANNOUNCER
- EDDIE DUNSTEDTER

Producer: Jaime del Valle   Writers: Gil Doud
Cast: Virginia Gregg, Gloria Blondell, Hy Averback, Peter Leeds
             Sidney Miller

SHOW: THE CUMBERLAND THEFT MATTER
SHOW DATE: 8/22/1951
COMPANY: CORINTHIAN ALL-RISK INSURANCE COMPANY
AGENT:
EXP. ACCT: $834.75

SYNOPSIS: Deputy sheriff Dunlap call Johnny to tell him that the inventory of the Cumberland Theft amounts to $85,000. Johnny is also told that the Cumberland's maid will be coming back late from Los Angeles.

Johnny travels to San Clemente, California, and gets a room at the hotel. Johnny then goes to the bus station with Deputy Dunlap to meet the maid. Johnny is told that thefts are rare in the area, and that the Cumberland's moved from Cincinnati when he retired. Mrs. Cumberland had inherited the jewels from her mother. Johnny meets Mabel Winder when the bus arrives and they go to the Cumberland home where Mabel is told of the robbery. Mabel tells Johnny that noting unusual happened the night before. The only people who came to the house the next day were the mailman and James Dawes from the Abbott Dairy, but he never came into the house. Mabel denies stealing the jewels, and tells Johnny that she went to Los Angeles to visit a friend and missed the regular bus because there were too many people. Johnny learns that the jewels were in a metal box, and Mrs. Cumberland had not worn them for a long time.

Johnny goes to the local docks to meet Mr. Cumberland, who is just returning from a fishing trip with three albacore tuna. Mr. Cumberland is not upset about the loss and assures Johnny that Mabel could not have taken them. Johnny calls the bus company and learns that the busses were not crowed, like Mabel had said. Johnny goes to see Mabel with Deputy Dunlap, and she denies everything. Johnny even tells her about a son born during World War I that she gave away. Mabel finally admits taking the jewels and hiding them because her son needed money.

Johnny goes to Los Angeles and learns that Mabel's son, Randolph Ord, was born in Duluth in 1914 and was known by the police. Johnny meets Sgt. Maine who tells him that Ord is wanted for murder, and was last seen in Omaha where he committed an armed robbery. Johnny talks to Mabel in the jail, and she tells Johnny about her son and how his grandparents had told him about her. He had written to her, and she had stolen for him and was proud of it.

Ord's accomplice, Jack Wilson, is arrested and is questioned by Sgt. Maine. He admits to being in the bus station to find a locker. He got the key from Ord, whose mother had mailed it to him. Wilson tells Johnny that Ord is in Glendale. Johnny goes to the address, but Ord is gone. Johnny goes to the bus station and spots Ord. Johnny chases him and Ord is shot twice.

NOTES:
- **THE ANNOUNCER IS DAN CUBBERLY**

- Music is by Eddie Dunstedter
- Story information obtained from the KNX Collection in the Thousand Oaks Library

Producer: Jaime del Valle   **Writers**   Gil Doud
Cast: Parley Baer, Virginia Gregg, Howard McNear, John Stephenson, Larry Thor

◆   ❖   ◆

Show: The Leland Case Matter
Show Date: 8/29/1951
Company: Tri-State Insurance Group
Agent:
Exp. Acct: $496.13

Synopsis: Mrs. Case calls Johnny about the disappearance of her husband. Johnny tells her that he is with the insurance company and Johnny wants to talk to her.

Johnny goes to New York City to meet Mrs. Case and stops at the police Missing Persons office and meets with Sgt. Dilko. Johnny tells Sgt. Dilko that the previous Mrs. Case had reportedly tried to kill Mr. Case but nothing was proved. Johnny is told that the current Mrs. Case reported him missing. He is age 47 and owns statewide chain of grocery stores, Case Inc. Nothing is missing from the apartment or from his bachelor apartment at the office. Sgt Dilko relates a lot of missing person cases with the world conditions. Johnny is told that the current wife is much younger than Mr. Case, and is very attractive.

Johnny goes to see Mrs. Case, and she is afraid of the reasons why her husband would have disappeared. She tells Johnny that she reported him missing on impulse and hates the all stories in the papers. She tells Johnny that they have a normal marriage. She had called her lawyer, Paul Frater, and he told her not to worry. She tells Johnny that she did not know any of her husband's business associates. She thinks they are holding back information and is angry and confused and does not know what to do. She accuses Johnny of thinking that she married Leland for his money, but she didn't.

Johnny goes to see Paul Frater. "Now add an insurance company to the suspicious grasping wife" Johnny is told. Johnny is told that it would be best if everyone left him alone. Mr. Case needed a rest and is probably in the country. Frater tells Johnny that he would not tell Johnny if he knew where Mr. Case was. Frater tells Johnny that he will talk to the wife when she gives her the divorce papers. She may have been happy, but Leland was not. There have always been scheming women, and Mrs. Case is a cheap upstate beauty contest type with only a high-school education. Is there no way to stop this idiocy? Johnny talks to Leland's other friends and retraced his last steps to no avail.

Two days later Mrs. Case calls Johnny and she must see him as soon as possible. She tells Johnny that a man has called and demanded money. She is told that

Leland is ok but they must have $10,000. She has until noon tomorrow to get the money. A man will call her to tell where to deliver the money. Johnny convinces Mrs. Case to work with the police to get to the men who have her husband. The next day Johnny alerts Sgt. Dilko while Mrs. Case gets the money. At 11:30 the phone rings. Johnny listens on the phone as the man agrees to the $8,600 that Mrs. Case has been able to get. Mrs. Case is told to take the money in a newspaper to a bus stop, and that a man will meet her at 11:50. They leave for the drop spot. Mrs. Case goes to the bus stop and a man asks her for her paper. Johnny grabs for the man and slugs him.

Sgt Dilko has the man, Eugene Lamson, and is checking out his address. Johnny questions Lamson and he does not know anything about Case. He tells Johnny and Dilko that he was just trying to get money from the wife. He had seen the article in the paper and tailed her, and there is nothing more. Lamson is told the FBI is on the way over, and Johnny starts to feel that Case is dead. The police go to Lamson's address and find an empty apartment.

On the next day, Johnny gets a call from Sgt. Dilko who tells him about a call he had received from a hospital in White Plains. They have a man who meets Case's description. Johnny and Sgt. Dilko drive to the hospital and meet the patient who calls himself by the name "White." Johnny brings a picture that positively identifies the man as Leland Case, but the man does not know who he is. White recognizes the pictures as being of him. White tells Johnny that he only remembers getting off a train in White Plains and being attacked by men on the railroad tracks who took everything he has. Johnny tells White of his background and White remembers nothing. White goes back to New York with Johnny and Sgt. Dilko and meets Frater and Mrs. Case. There is no show of recognition by White of anyone there. Also, White knows nothing of running a large business. Johnny and Sgt. Dilko leave White with his wife and Frater and White tells Johnny that he thinks he will be ok. On the way out, Johnny thinks he saw a wink from White, but then again the light was not too good.

NOTES:

- THIS IS A REHEARSAL RECORDING WITH NO MUSIC.
- THE CAST CREDITS ARE NOT GIVEN, BUT HOWARD MCNEAR AND PARLEY BAER ARE CLEARLY RECOGNIZABLE.
- DAN CUBBERLY IS THE ANNOUNCER

Producer:	Jaime del Valle	**Writers:**	Gil Doud
Cast:	Howard McNear, Parley Baer, Virginia Gregg, Larry Thor, John Stephenson		

SHOW:	THE RUM BARREL MATTER
SHOW DATE:	9/12/1951
COMPANY:	PLYMOUTH LIFE INSURANCE COMPANY

Agent:

Exp. Acct: $43.55

Synopsis: Johnny calls Detective Walter Kirk to report a shooting. Johnny is told that it was part of a liquor store robbery and the owner was killed.

Johnny meets with Hartford, Connecticut Det. Kirk and tells about the cab ride and seeing a man shot. Kirk tells Johnny that the owner said the men were carrying water pistols, and that $300 was taken, but $500 was left in the cash drawer. Johnny goes to talk to Mr. Mueler, a quiet man who tells Johnny that a real gun was held on him. He let the man out, and then shot him at the door, but he was not the one with the money. Johnny gets a description of the others and learns that the victim had a tattoo on his left arm. Later Johnny gets a photo of the tattoo and starts looking for the artist. Johnny goes to Bridgeport and talks to the owners of the tattoo parlors there and finds nothing. Johnny then goes to Providence where a man recognizes the technique as that of Ron Curci in Boston. Johnny drives to Boston and meets with Curci who remembers giving the tattoo to a man with two brothers who all got the same one. Johnny calls Det. Kirk who is not in. Johnny learns that he is investigating another shooting at the Rum Barrel Liquor store. Johnny goes to the store and learns that Mr. Mueler was shot, and that the shooter emptied the gun into him. Mr. Landry, the partner of Mueler arrives and Johnny asks him why Mueler shot the robber. He tells Johnny that Mueler wanted someone to try because he did not like being pushed around.

Johnny and Det. Kirk go to see Mrs. Kline, who was a witness to the shooting. She tells Johnny that Mueler had laughed about the killing. A man came in and called Mueler by name made him sit in the floor and shot him. The next day Det. Kirk is called by Thomas Magill, who knows the killer. Johnny and Det. Kirk go to see Magill, who admits to shooting Mueler. He tells Johnny that he and his brothers robbed the store to get money to send to their sister, who is in a hospital on Colorado. They came in with water pistols and Mueler said he was covered by insurance and begged them to take the money. When they were leaving he shot their brother David on the way out.

Johnny thinks that the confession was false, but he does verify that the sister is in the hospital.

Notes:
- The announcer is Dan Cubberly
- Music is by Eddie Dunstedter
- Story information obtained from the KNX Collection in the Thousand Oaks Library

Producer: Jaime del Valle   Writers   Gil Doud
Cast: Bill Conrad, Ted de Corsia, Edgar Barrier, Herb Butterfield,
                Virginia Gregg, Hy Averback

SHOW:	**THE CUBAN JEWEL MATTER**
SHOW DATE:	**9/19/1951**
COMPANY:	**INTERCONTINENTAL INDEMNITY & BONDING COMPANY**
AGENT:	**ROGER STERN**
EXP. ACCT:	**$708.83**

SYNOPSIS: Roger Stern calls Johnny about a job. "Bring a suitcase with summer clothes, you are going to Cuba."

Johnny goes to New York to meet with Stern. Johnny is told that Mrs. Lenore Carter had $800,000 in jewels stolen three months ago and now the insurance company must pay off. William Carnes, who was in on the robbery knows where the jewels are. The police in Havana are holding him for extradition on federal charges. Johnny is told that the insurance company wants to know where the jewels are before Carnes is put away. Johnny is to find out where the jewels are before Carnes is extradited. Also, there is a bonus if you succeed.

Johnny travels to Havana, Cuba and goes to the jail to meet with Carnes. Johnny poses as a reporter to get into the jail and question Carnes about the jewels. While Johnny is in the cell with Carnes, a man comes in with the police chief held at knifepoint and kills the guard, opens the cell and Carnes leaves. "A friend sent me," the man tells Carnes. The man with the knife apparently knows who Johnny is and tells him to leave too. Johnny follows Carnes to a dark cantina and asks the barkeeper where Carnes is. The bartender does not like Johnny, so Johnny pulls his gun and suddenly the bartender remembers that Carnes went to see Maria. Johnny goes upstairs to Maria's room, and Johnny describes her as a good reason to uphold the good neighbor policy anywhere. Maria tells Johnny that she does not know where Carnes went and tells Johnny to leave. Johnny offers her a $300 bonus for information, and she gives Johnny an address to go to. Johnny has to check to see if his hair is on fire as he leaves. Johnny goes to #3 Avenida Porfidio, breaks down the door as quietly as possible and finds Carnes diving for a dresser drawer. Johnny points his .38 at Carnes and asks him where the jewels are. Carnes offers to make a deal, but Johnny only wants the jewels, so Carnes tells Johnny they are in a bedpost. The man with the knife comes in and thanks Carnes for telling him where the jewels are, and takes the jewels and Johnny's gun. The man tells Carnes that a friend told him to let Carnes out but he decided to take the jewels. The man leaves and Carnes hits Johnny with a metal bedpost.

When Johnny wakes up, it is night, and all seems lost. He goes to his hotel and calls Mr. Stern to update him. Johnny tells Stern that he wants the name of the person who gave the tip to Stern, but he cannot divulge that information. As Johnny is talking the police show up with Sgt. Evans of the NYPD who wants to know who let Carnes out. Sgt. Evans wants the story, so Johnny tells him why he is there, except for Maria and the jewels. Sgt. Evans tells Johnny that he will call New York and Johnny is told to stay put. After talking to Sgt. Evans, Johnny goes to see Maria. She is singing and points to her room with her eyes. Johnny goes up to her room, and Maria comes up and makes herself comfortable. After some small talk she tells Johnny that Carnes came there three months ago, and he was "the best one around" and always seemed to have money. She tells Johnny that she was the only one Carnes spent time with. Johnny describes the man with the knife, but she does not remember seeing the man. As they are talking there is a knock at the door and Sgt. Evans comes in and he wants to talk to Johnny. On the way outside Sgt. Evans tells Johnny that Intercontinental did not hire Johnny, and that Stern is out of town. Sgt. Evans wants to arrest Johnny, but Johnny spots Carnes by the door. They follow Carnes and Evans is shot. Johnny follows Carnes and Johnny wounds him. Carnes finally runs out of ammunition as Johnny gets to him. Carnes tells Johnny that his fellow thief in the Carter job got him out, Roger Stern. Carnes dies and Johnny goes after Stern. Johnny calls the airport for arriving flights from New York, and one is due in an hour. Johnny goes to the airport and waits for Stern's flight in a cab. Sterns catches a cab and is followed by Johnny to a building. Johnny breaks in and hears the man with the knife trying to convince Stern that he does not have the jewels. Roger Stern gives the man the old "count to ten before he shoots him" routine and at ten the man tells Roger that the jewels are in his hat. Johnny interrupts the argument and the man throws a knife and kills Stern. Johnny shoots the man and the Jewels are found in a leather bag his hat. The final story is that Stern needed money and had given Carnes the combination to the safe but Carnes cheated Stern. Roger found him in Havana and hired Johnny. Johnny has saved intercontinental $800,000 and Roger Stern was an employee of the company when he hired Johnny, so please pay the bonus promised by Stern. If it takes longer than two weeks, send it to the Cantina del Gallo where Johnny is going for vacation.

NOTES:
- JOHNNY IS CARRYING A .38 REVOLVER.
- TOMORROW NIGHT IS "THE FBI IN PEACE AND WAR"
- EDMOND O'BRIEN'S NEW MOVIE IS "WAR PATH"
- DAN CUBBERLY IS THE ANNOUNCER
- MUSIC IS BY EDDIE DUNSTEDTER

Producer: Jaime del Valle   Writers: Blake Edwards
Cast: Ted Osborne, Jack Kruschen, Barney Phillips, Nestor Paiva, Lillian Buyeff, Stacy Harris

SHOW: THE PROTECTION MATTER
SHOW DATE: 9/26/1951
COMPANY: COLUMBIA ALL RISK INSURANCE COMPANY
AGENT: PHILLIP MARTIN
EXP. ACCT: $101.92

SYNOPSIS: A call comes in from Phillip Martin about Mr. Bennie Waxman who owns a deli that burned last night. It happened last night and it was arson. Come on down.

Johnny goes to New York City and Mr. Waxman's apartment. The police are there and Waxman tells Lt. Parkinson that he did not commit arson. Lt. Parkinson tells Johnny that an incendiary device was used. Johnny tells Lt. Parkinson that the Insurance was for $20,000, and Lt. Parkinson tells Waxman that he will not get the money. Lt. Parkinson tells Johnny that they are sure he is guilty and are pressing him hard as a man died in the fire. Waxman tells Johnny that Waxman makes a good living but only has $600 in the bank. Waxman tells Johnny that he gave $5,000 to his daughter who they cannot find. Waxman tells Johnny and Lt. Parkinson that she is on a vacation and that he does not want the insurance money. Lt. Parkinson leaves and Johnny talks to Waxman. He tells Johnny that cannot prove he is innocent. Johnny asks him what he is afraid of, and Waxman claims he is only nervous. Johnny tells Waxman that the $5,000 excuse is pretty weak. Johnny leaves and thinks about the case. Johnny is sure that Waxman is scared, but of what?

Johnny goes to the 15th precinct, and Lt. Parkinson is in his office. Over a cup of coffee they discuss the case. Lt. Parkinson admits that Waxman did not start the fire and that he is riding him to get information on a well-controlled protection racket. Lt. Parkinson tells Johnny that he is scaring Waxman to try and get information from his friends. Lt. Parkinson thinks that maybe the daughter was kidnapped; but Waxman has been beaten up and is not the type to pay protection. Why would he burn the store if he paid the $5,000 to the racket? As they are talking Lt. Parkinson gets a phone call from Angelino Giuseppi, who wants to talk.

Johnny and Lt. Parkinson go the deli and talk to Angie. Angie tells them that he has evidence that Waxman did not burn the store. "Them guys who collect the money each week did it." he tells Lt. Parkinson. Angie freezes up and Johnny spots two men crossing the street. The men come in and tell Angie that they want the envelope. Lt. Parkinson recognizes one of the men named "Red" and is shot. Johnny shoots the men and Lt. Parkinson tells Johnny that the man with the red hair was named Dillon, and worked for Dutch Fischer and then dies.

When the police arrive, Johnny explains what had happened to officer Brenners, who offers Angie protection. Brenners tells Johnny that the other owners are threatened. Angie tells Johnny that the men have his daughter but Angie wants no more trouble, as he must think of the others. Angie relents and tells Johnny and Brenners that the men took Waxman's daughter because he would not pay. Angie is told that the store was a lesson to the others after Waxman paid the $5,000 to get his daughter back. Angie tells Johnny that she is supposed to be freed tonight.

Johnny looks at mug shots and gets Dillon's record, and he is a bad boy. From the records Johnny learns that Dutch Fischer is still in prison. The FBI calls and they identify the other man as Lou Fleischman, who went up on a robbery charge with Dillon. Brenners checks the files and finds that a fourth man, George

Biulotti is related to the other three. Biulotti's record is pulled and Brenners recognizes him as George Bivens, a reputable nightclub owner who is clean. Johnny goes to see Bivens at the Yellow Parrot, and slugs Ziggy to get into Bivens' office. Johnny tells Bivens that Dillon and Fleischman and Lt. Parkinson are dead. Johnny tells him about the jobs Bivens had worked with them. As Bivens tries to throw Johnny out a fight ensues and Johnny beats Bivens until he gets the information he wants. Johnny calls the police to pick up Bivens three minutes later. Johnny then goes to a warehouse to meet Brenners. They enter through a window and find an office where two men are holding the girl. Brenners creates a diversion to get the men out of the office and there is a gunfight that kills the two men. Johnny and Brenners free the girl and she is taken to her father. The storeowners are planning a block party.

Make sure the next simple insurance fire is simple. I don't mind helping people out, but I'm too old and too under paid to go back to being a boy scout.

NOTES:
- A NEW TIME IS ANNOUNCED FOR NEXT WEEK SATURDAY, OCTOBER 6.
- THERE IS A PUBLIC SERVICE ANNOUNCEMENT TO SUPPORT THE CRUSADE FOR FREEDOM
- THE VIRGIL AKINS—FREDDIE DAWSON FIGHT FOLLOWS THE PROGRAM.
- DAN CUBBERLY IS THE ANNOUNCER
- MUSIC IS BY EDDIE DUNSTEDTER
- EDMOND O'BRIEN'S NEW MOVIE IS "WAR PATH"

Producer: Jaime del Valle   **Writers:**   **Blake Edwards**
Cast: **Joel Samuels, Bill Conrad, Sidney Miller, Jay Novello, Ray Hartman**

◆   ❖   ◆

SHOW: THE DOUGLAS TAYLOR MATTER
SHOW DATE: 10/6/1951
COMPANY: GREAT EASTERN INSURANCE COMPANY
AGENT: MR. NIBLEY
EXP. ACCT: $181.20

SYNOPSIS: Lt. Reese from homicide calls Johnny and asks if he hired a detective named Douglas Taylor? He was found dead this morning. Come down and answer a few questions.

Johnny goes to the Hartford, Connecticut police headquarters and meets with Lt. Reese. They tell Johnny that they do not know where or when Taylor was killed, as his body was dumped down by the freight yards. His wife told the police that he was working for Johnny. Johnny tells Lt. Reese that he cannot answer questions about the case because it will jeopardize a case worth $500,000, but Lt. Reese wants all the information. Johnny tells him that two men are suspected of insurance fraud and Taylor was tailing one of them. Johnny tells Lt. Reese that he knew Doug for about two years and knew of no troubles with his wife. Lt. Reese tells Johnny that the money is enough to hold Johnny on, but he is told to leave and Johnny knows that he is being followed. Johnny calls Mr. Nibley at the Insurance Company and is told to drop the arson case he is working on. Johnny tells Nibley that Taylor's wife probably knows nothing about the case, but Johnny will check with her.

Johnny goes to see Mrs. Taylor and he tells her that Doug was not killed because of the case he was working for Johnny. She tells Johnny that Doug was a police officer for 12 years, and she has been waiting for this day for 19 years. She is glad Johnny came by. She tells Johnny that Doug never talked about cases or any trouble. Johnny asks about another woman and she tells him that she suspected Doug but never found out anything. She tells Johnny that Henry Farner, his ex-partner, is a hotel detective at the Hotel Milard. As they are talking Lt. Reese arrives and jumps all over Johnny for rehearsing a story with Mrs. Taylor. Lt. Reese tells Johnny that Doug's office has been torn apart by someone looking for something. Lt. Reese tells Johnny to get the case cleared up, or he will put him out of business.

Johnny goes to see Henry Farner, who saw Doug last week. He seemed fed up over something, and had said that there was going to be a change, without his wife who Farner describes as a jealous creep. He has no idea what the change was going to be. Farmer tells Johnny that she could be capable of killing Doug, as she was strange.

Johnny goes back to the Taylor home and sees the lights go on. Johnny knocks at the door and a man with a gun opens the door. The man tells Johnny that he had hit Mrs. Taylor in the bedroom, and tells Johnny that Doug was too filthy to stay alive and too dirty rotten to live. He leaves and shoots as Johnny tries to follow. Johnny holds back and realizes that he was young and out of his head with fear. The plain-clothes man was nowhere to be found and Doug's killer disappears into the night.

Mrs. Taylor was ok but hysterical, and the police are called. She tells Johnny that the man was going to kill her, and that Doug had ruined two lives so he killed him. She tells Johnny that she has never seen the man before. Johnny is sure the man is the same one that broke into Doug's office. When Lt. Reese arrives, Johnny tells him that he had not tried to lose the tail, and asked what had happened. Johnny gives Lt. Reese a description of the boy, including the Smith and Wesson .38 with a black rubber grip and a class ring on his hand. Lt. Reese accuses Johnny of firing the shots, but Johnny tells him he is not carrying his gun. Lt. Reese accuses Johnny of hiding the gun, but Johnny tells him he is being an ass, and to stop riding his badge so that they can work together on the case. Johnny tells him that it is obvious that Doug had something on the stranger. Lt. Reese tells Johnny that they had gone through the house and office and had found nothing.

The next day Johnny sees his name in the papers as an investigator whose involvement is not clear. That night the boy comes to Johnny's apartment. He tells Johnny that Doug had brought Johnny in for protection. He had told Doug that he could not pay anymore and that he wants the file Doug has on him. Johnny tells the boy he believes him and tries to reason with him. The boy says that Johnny had come to Doug's apartment and that his name was in the paper, so he must have the file. The boy starts to leave and the door buzzes, but it is just a delivery boy. Johnny tries to get him to give himself to the police, but the boy is really nervous and will not give up, as he would rather die instead. He has to protect the family. The boy tells Johnny that his father had hired Doug to investigate the boy two years ago, and Doug had been blackmailing the family ever since. Johnny leaves the apartment with the boy and the police stop him on the street. Shots are fired and the boy is cut down with a submachine gun.

The father, Judge Pardette and the family was hit by scandal, which is what the boy was trying to stop.

NOTES:

- THE MID-PROGRAM COMMERCIAL IS FOR OUR MISS BROOKS AND THE EDGAR BERGEN SHOW, WHICH RETURN TOMORROW NIGHT
- THERE IS A PUBLIC SERVICE ANNOUNCEMENT FOR CARE AND FOOD GIVEN TO THE FAMILIES OF YUGOSLAVIA.
- THIS PROGRAM WAS MODIFIED AND DONE AS THE SINGAPORE ARSON MATTER WITH JOHN LUND
- EDMOND O'BRIEN'S NEXT MOVIE IS SILVER CITY
- DICK CUTTING IS THE ANNOUNCER
- MUSIC IS BY WILBUR HATCH

Producer: Jaime del Valle   **Writers:**   Gil Doud
Cast: Ray Hartman, Joseph Kearns, Edgar Barrier, Jeanette Nolan, Hy Averback

◆   ❖   ◆

SHOW: THE MILLARD WARD MATTER
SHOW DATE: 10/13/1951
COMPANY: PLYMOUTH LIFE INSURANCE COMPANY
AGENT: WILLARD DUNHILL
EXP. ACCT: $419.95

SYNOPSIS: Willard Dunhill calls from Plymouth Life Insurance Company and has an assignment for Johnny. A policyholder named Millard Ward was killed on a ship and there is a possibility of fraud. The ship is due in New Orleans tomorrow, and Willard wants Johnny to look into the case.

Johnny goes to New Orleans, Louisiana and meets the "Death Ship." Johnny goes on board with Lt. Tracy and meets the chief mate, Mr. Edward Donovan. Johnny is told that Louis Ratnick is in the brig and the knife is in the body. Johnny is told that Ratnick would say nothing. Donovan tells Johnny that Ward and Ratnick were working together and Ward's body was found in the forepeak. Johnny looks at the murder site and is told that the knife was kept in the forepeak for opening paint cans. Donovan tells Johnny and Lt. Tracy that there had been bad blood between Ward and Ratnick. Johnny meets with Ratnick and he denies killing Ward or having anything to do with Ward's wife. He tells Johnny that he hardly knew Ward's wife and had met her once when he was sick and missed a trip. Ratnick tells Johnny that Ward was alive when he left the locker.

Lt. Tracy questions Ratnick and gets the same story. Johnny and Tracy talk to the crew, who tells them that Ward and Ratnick hated each other. Johnny and Lt. Tracy talk to Ward's wife, who tells them that Ratnick did not kill Ward, and that there was nothing going on between her and Ratnick. She tells them that she does not have too many friends and that she hates New Orleans and is sick and tired of Ward and did not leave him, as he would not last too much longer. As they leave, Mrs. Ward is told to come to the inquest the next day. Johnny then visits the two bars Ratnick hung out in and several people remember seeing Ratnick with Mrs. Ward, and one person tells Johnny he saw them leave separately, but never together.

At the coroner's inquiry, Herbert Massey tells the court that Ward and Ratnick were working together, and that he had found the body. Massey had gone to the forepeak to get Ward and found him with a knife in him and no pulse. The autopsy is read and said that the death might have been a suicide. Johnny goes to see Ratnick and he tells Johnny that he killed Ward in self-defense. Ratnick tells Johnny that Ward had always given him hard assignments and was riding him so he killed him. Ratnick tells Johnny that Ward was trying to hit him with a paint can, so he killed in self-defense. Johnny suggests that Ratnick work on his story and hire a new lawyer.

Johnny and Tracey go to the ship and talk to Massey. They tell Massey that they need more evidence, so they go over what happened. Massey tells them that he noticed nothing out of the usual in the forepeak and that there was no can of paint rolling around. Also, there were no signs of a struggle in the forepeak. Massey tells them that maybe everyone assumes Ratnick was the killer because of the bad blood. Johnny asks Massey who did kill him, and after talking over all aspects of the case, Massey thinks they are trying to blame him.

Johnny and Lt. Tracy go back to headquarters and Massey is investigated, but there is nothing on Massey, nothing on anyone. Johnny goes to see Ratnick and applies some pressure by accusing him of lying. Lt. Tracy tells Ratnick that the self-defense plea was the best thing that his lawyer could come up with. They make him think that Ward's wife that told them something about using him to kill Ward. Ratnick admits that Mrs. Ward was the one who begged him to kill Ward so they could leave New Orleans and live elsewhere. He was alone with Ward and had to do something, so he stabbed him.

There are no remarks as it was a clear case of insurance fraud.

NOTES:
- THE FOREPEAK IS THAT PART OF A SHIP FORMED BY THE ANGLE OF THE BOW.
- THE VAUGHN MONROE SHOW RETURNS TONIGHT

- DAN CUBBERLY IS THE ANNOUNCER
- MUSIC IS BY WILBUR HATCH
- EDMOND O'BRIEN'S NEXT MOVIE IS SILVER CITY.

Producer:	Jaime del Valle	**Writers:**	Gil Doud
Cast:	Sidney Miller, Barton Yarborough, Bill Conrad, Hy Averback, Jeanne Bates		

◆ ❖ ◆

SHOW:	THE JANET ABBE MATTER
SHOW DATE:	10/20/1951
COMPANY:	COLUMBIA ALL-RISK
AGENT:	BOB RUDD
EXP. ACCT:	$2,796.00

SYNOPSIS: Bob Rudd from Columbia All-Risk calls Johnny and asks him to go to Malaysia and offers Johnny a bonus on this case. Johnny is told that an American woman and her daughter were killed there. The woman was the wife of an American planter. Her father got a letter hinting that the truth had been hidden.

Johnny goes to see Bob, who has a letter from Mrs. Abbe's father. He has information from the British authorities that the cause of death was from rebel gunfire. There is a $100,000 policy involved with the daughter as the beneficiary, and the husband as the second beneficiary. Johnny meets with Mr. Stevenson, Mrs. Abbe's father, who has the letter from the authorities in the area.

Johnny flies to Singapore and then on to Penang, Malaysia where he shows Constable Lamb the letter. Johnny is told that the plantations are under attack in that area, and that Mrs. Abbe was killed during an attack. The next day Johnny takes a train to meet Constable Rutherford who is not convinced that the husband killed his wife and daughter. Johnny is shown the official reports, written by the planters, of the attack by the Liberation Army. Johnny compares the handwriting of all the planters to the letter and does not find a match. Johnny goes to the plantation and is attacked on the way, but Johnny is sure that the attack was set up to scare him away. A rescue party arrives and Johnny meets two of the local planter, Gerrish and Strerley.

Johnny arranges to go to the Abbe plantation with Gerrish, and Johnny tells him that he knows that he did not get all of the records, and that one was missing. Gerrish is most uncooperative and will not tell Johnny who the missing planter is. Johnny ends up slugging Gerrish and is taken back to Constable Rutherford, but he is out with the troops who have gone to the Abbe plantation. Gerrish drives Johnny to the Abbe plantation, where Abbe is a drunken wreck. Johnny gets into the compound and talks to Abbe, who admits killing his wife and daughter. Abbe tells Johnny that the rebels had taken Sterley's wife, and she was found later. All of the other planters took an oath to kill their wives rather than let them be taken by the rebels. He tells Johnny that the rebels were inside the house, which was on fire. He shot his wife and daughter but did not have to, because a rescue party arrived. The rebel attack starts, and Johnny notes that murder was committed, but without criminal intent. Johnny did not report that Abbe was found dead after the rebel attack.

NOTES:
- THE ANNOUNCER IS DICK CUTTING
- MUSIC IS BY WILBUR HATCH
- STORY INFORMATION OBTAINED FROM THE KNX COLLECTION IN THE THOUSAND OAKS LIBRARY

Producer:	Jaime del Valle	Writers	Gil Doud
Cast:	Jack Kruschen, Barney Phillips, Lillian Buyeff, Nestor Paiva, Ted Osborne, Stacy Harris, Dan Cubberly		

◆   ❖   ◆

SHOW:	THE TOLHURST THEFT MATTER
SHOW DATE:	10/27/1951
COMPANY:	TRI-STATE INSURANCE GROUP
AGENT:	JIM MADISON
EXP. ACCT:	$77.60

SYNOPSIS: Jim Madison at Tri-State calls Johnny about the Tolhurst fur theft. Johnny is told that a woman has called Jim about the case, but does not want the police called. She wants a call back by three o'clock. Jim wants Johnny to talk to the woman and is willing to work without the police, and will cut corners if Johnny will.

Johnny relates the origins of the Tolhurst theft, which occurred when three men entered a fur store at gunpoint and took $50,000 in cash. The police followed the getaway cars, and a gunfight ensued, but the men escaped. Johnny goes to the Tri-State office to take the anonymous phone call. Johnny talks to the woman, and he tells her that the money is more important than having someone arrested and is willing to work without the police. The caller knows where one of the men is hiding. The man is at the Standing Hotel in Boston using the name Taft, and he is desperate. Johnny drives to Boston, Massachusetts and follows the man named Taft into his room where the man pulls a gun. Johnny shows Taft his identification but Taft tells Johnny that Allen Less hired Johnny to find him. Johnny explains that he only wants the money and will help him to get a break. Johnny tries to convince him to tell what he knows, but to no avail. Johnny tells the man that he has been double-crossed and Taft slugs Johnny and locks him in the closet.

When Johnny wakes up, he searches the room, which is empty, and calls Tri-State and reports the events. Johnny tells Jim Madison that he wants to look into the money angle at the fur store, as there was too much money on hand. Johnny goes to see Mr. Tolhurst the next morning and asks about the money. Tolhurst tells Johnny that most fur purchases are made in cash to make beautiful women more beautiful. And, there are many, many more rich men than there are beautiful wives, as opposed to women, that is. So, if wifey does not get the coat, she does not want to find a check paying for one, or the fur would fly literally. Tolhurst tells Johnny that if the name of one of the purchasers were to become known it could endanger national security and be talked about on the floor of the Senate. Johnny is told that he has no record to indicate who bought the coats, even though it might endanger the insurance claim. Johnny goes to his apartment and the girl from the previous day is calling and she is hurt. Johnny goes to her address and the girl tells Johnny that they beat her because they think she has the money, but she does not have it. They want to know where Fred Surell (Taft) is. The girl tells Johnny that Fred has the money. He is at an auto court on the way to Boston, the Oak Springs Motel. She tells Johnny that her name is Virginia Colley and she knows nothing of the robbery. Fred had left his car there and had told her after the robbery that there was big trouble. Johnny tells her he will have to call the police to stay out of trouble.

Johnny calls the police and tells his story, but is still in trouble. Johnny drives to the motel and meets Lt. Crockett. Inside the cottage there are two bodies but Surell is not one of them. He updates Crockett about the anonymous call and they go back to headquarters to talk. Johnny gives him all he knows, but Lt. Crockett wants Johnny to drop the case and to go home and brush up on police work! Risking his license, Johnny visits the Colley apartment and gets an address for Surell in Princeton, so Johnny goes there. At the address, the landlord tells Johnny that Surell is out of town. Johnny asks to get in to the apartment to leave a note, and the landlord tells Johnny that he can talk to Surell's roommate, a man named Hacker who is there. Johnny talks to Hacker who had heard from Surell a couple days ago because he needed money. Johnny tells Hacker about the robbery, and Hacker knows Al Hudson and Les Vernick, two of Surell's friends. Hacker confirms that Surell had written to him using the name Taft. Johnny is told that Surell's mother has a farm nearby in Tarrington. Johnny searches the room and then goes to the mother's farm after stopping by his apartment to pick up a pocket gun.

At the farm Johnny talks to the hired hand. He knows about the robbery and has sent Mrs. Surell to town to keep the news from her. Johnny is told that Surell will not come here, and that Mrs. Surell is blind and nearly deaf. The hand tells Johnny that Surell has not been back in three years, and that the neighbors had told him to leave, as he is bad. His mother thinks that Fred is in Australia in the hardware business and no one will tell her otherwise.

Back in Hartford the newspapers have the story and there are questions in Johnny's mind. The motel was close to where the car was abandoned so Johnny goes to the site and finds the car. Johnny calls Crockett and asks for assistance. Crockett will see what he can do, and Johnny waits for someone to come back to the car. At sunset, Surell comes back and Johnny tells him that he cannot get away. Surell tells Johnny that the money is buried there and Surell offers him a share. As Surell searches hysterically for the money, Johnny slugs him and takes his gun.

The police finally find the money so the company is not out. Johnny and Lt. Crockett get together, so Johnny is not out, and the girl was nothing. Surell lost his mind over money, and Tolhurst did not lose the universal customer, the wealthy American husband.

Notes:
- Virginia Colley lived at **5860** Stoddard Street, Apt 12. There is a 5860 Stoddard Avenue today in Hartford.
- There is a public service announcement to buy Defense Bonds
- Dan Cubberly is the announcer
- Music is by Wilbur Hatch
- Edmond O'Brien's next movie is Silver City.

Producer: Jaime del Valle   **Writers:** Gil Doud
Cast: Parley Baer, Virginia Gregg, Stacy Harris, Bob Sweeney, Herb Butterfield, Clayton Post, Howard McNear

◆   ❖   ◆

Show: The Hannibal Murphy Matter
Show Date: 11/3/1951
Company: Plymouth Insurance Company
Agent:
Exp. Acct: $734.40

Synopsis: Inspector Treyburt returns Johnny's call about the accidental death of Hannibal Murphy. Johnny is told that Mr. Murphy's death was not accidental. There was a bullet hole in his head.

Johnny goes to Kingston, Jamaica and meets Inspector Treyburt. Johnny is told that Murphy has a wife, a brother and a stepdaughter staying at his cottage, and that the brother and stepdaughter had been visiting him here. Based on the bullet wound, Treyburt has ruled out suicide. Johnny and inspector Treyburt go to see the Murphys, who are described as a family spoiled by money and who could be hated by a lot of people. Johnny is shown the scene of the murder, which is a rocky beach below a cliff where a local boy found the body while fishing. Inspector Treyburt tells Johnny that there are no signs of a struggle and it is confusing as to how the murder happened. Johnny goes to the Murphy cottage where Johnny is met by Felice, the daughter of Mrs. Murphy. Felice tells Johnny that the death was not an accident. Johnny tells her that there will be all sorts of questions, but she is not worried even though she hated him, as he was rotten. Mrs. Murphy comes in and slaps Felice, who has been a "difficult child" and sends her to her room. Johnny is told that the brother, Paul, is out making arrangements. Mrs. Murphy tells Johnny that she knows of no one who would want to kill her husband, and that they do not go out much. She tells Johnny that Hannibal said he was just going to take a walk, as he was not sleepy. Mrs. Murphy tells Johnny that Felice is not guilty, but that she is a poor unbalanced girl full of warped hatreds and misunderstandings and that Felice will say things about Hannibal and me. Johnny leaves and finds Felice outside on the bridal path. She tells Johnny that she is mixed up and thinks that Hannibal is stealing her mother from her. She tells Johnny that she is glad Hannibal is dead. Johnny tells her that he understands the problems of being a stepchild these days, as it is more commonplace.

Johnny tells Inspector Treyburt about the conversations, and he calls Paul Murphy into his office to talk to him that afternoon. Paul tells them that he had gone to bed and Hannibal went for a walk. Hannibal had said nothing about meeting anyone. Inspector Treyburt notes that a .25 cal. pistol was used at close range, so someone was with him or followed him, and robbery is not a motive. Paul has no additional information to give. A few minutes later Paul phones the inspector and asks for an ambulance; as Felice has cut her wrists in a suicide attempt.

Johnny goes to the Murphy residence and speaks with Dr. Gurley who tells Johnny that Felice needs a good psychiatrist. Johnny speaks with Felice who tells Johnny that her mother and Paul killed Hannibal. Felice tells Johnny that last summer her mother had tired of Hannibal and had wanted a divorce. Felice tells Johnny and the Inspector that her parents had argued and Paul and Hannibal left. Later she heard a shot at 11:15. She tells them that Paul came back a few minutes later. She tells Johnny and the Inspector that she has always hated her mother and wants to be taken away from here, as she is afraid. The inspector arranges for Felice to be taken to a police hospital where she repeats her statement. Inspector Treyburt receives from a sporting goods storeowner, Mr. Inness, who tells him that a man tried to sell him a .25 cal. Webley pistol. Inness describes the man, who is English. Inspector Treyburt goes to arrest Paul and Mrs. Murphy who deny the story told by Felice. Mrs. Murphy tells Inspector Treyburt that Felice had lied and that she thinks that Felice killed Hannibal.

Mrs. Murphy and Paul are taken in, although Treyburt tells Johnny that he has no alternative. Johnny goes to the hospital where Felice tells Johnny that she is alone now. She insists to Johnny that she told the truth. Johnny recounts her story detail by detail, but she sticks to it. Johnny prepares to leave, but Treyburt calls and reports that the gun from the store is the murder weapon, and it has been traced to a local criminal, Roy Church. Johnny talks to Church who tells Johnny that Paul was going to pay him 500 pounds to kill Hannibal but welshed on the deal after being paid 100 pounds. He needed money, which is why he sold the pistol. He was supposed to have taken the wallet but Hannibal fell over the cliff. So, Felice really did not see anything. Johnny invites the Inspector to come up and work a simple Hartford murder sometime, as it would do him good.

NOTES:
- LATER THIS EVENING GANGBUSTER TRACKS THE PERFECT CRIME.
- DAN CUBBERLY IS THE ANNOUNCER
- MUSIC IS BY WILBUR HATCH
- EDMOND O'BRIEN'S NEXT MOVIE IS SILVER CITY.

Producer: Jaime del Valle   **Writers:** Gil Doud
Cast: Eric Snowden, Virginia Gregg, Jeanette Nolan, Ben Wright,
Charles Davis, Dan O'Herlihy

SHOW: THE BIRDY BASKERVILLE MATTER
SHOW DATE: 11/10/1951
COMPANY: COLUMBIA ALL RISK INSURANCE COMPANY
AGENT: PHILLIP MARTIN
EXP. ACCT: $137.27

SYNOPSIS: Phillip Martin calls and has a job for Johnny. Carl Baskerville wants to change his beneficiary, as his brother is trying to kill him. Phil wants Johnny to be a bodyguard, and the policy is for half a million. Phil has looked at the records and Carl had sent his brother to prison.

Johnny goes to the Long Island, New York mansion of Carl Baskerville where Collins, Mr. Baskerville's personal secretary, meets Johnny at the door. Collins is 6' 9," and is described by Johnny as "the tallest man I have ever seen." Johnny is taken to see Mr. Baskerville, who is in the garden feeding the birds, and he encourages Johnny to join him (here birdie, birdie!). Mr. Baskerville outlines to Johnny how he has retired after working his entire life to be successful. He tells Johnny that his brother William had been caught stealing $100,000 from the company and Mr. Baskerville was forced to prosecute him. William was to inherit Mr. Baskerville's entire estate, but now he must change the beneficiary as William has sent a letter threatening to kill him. Johnny is told that, after William has a chance to calm down, Mr. Baskerville will put him back in the will. Johnny is also told William had a girl friend, Virginia Carter, who lives in Greenwich Village.

Johnny walks out to get a cab and hears shots. Johnny runs back to the garden and Mr. Baskerville is dead, with a bullet in his heart. Collins comes running out and tells Johnny that he had seen William with a gun. Johnny goes into the house to call the police. While talking to Lt. Brenners, Johnny realizes he has made a fatal mistake. He goes out to the body and discovers the letter is gone.

Johnny goes to Greenwich Village to visit Virginia Carter. At the door Johnny gets the quickest scalding in history as Johnny is met by a lovely woman wearing "something thin enough to make a silkworm hang himself." Johnny is invited in and sits in a very dark living room and has a very hot conversation with Miss Carter. She tells Johnny that she knew William, and that he had shown her a good time. All of her men show her a good time. Johnny spends several hours with her trying to look at her photo album of her men. Finally she shows Johnny a picture of William and tells Johnny that he used to play the saxophone. Johnny leaves and is almost rundown by a car.

At the Musician's Union, Johnny learns William has renewed his card, and is having his mail sent to a swing joint on 52nd street. Johnny cabs to the club and a piano player tells Johnny that William was there but just got up and left around

4:30. For a $5 bribe, Johnny gets William's address. Johnny goes to the address and gets no answer at the door. Johnny is curious enough about noises inside the apartment to open the door to find William swinging from a noose. Johnny is suspicious when he puts the chair under William's feet and they do not touch. He is dangling above the chair. The phone rings and Johnny answers it to hear Virginia's voice. Johnny hangs up and goes back to visit her. Virginia lets Johnny in and makes a mistake by greeting Johnny by name. "Who told you my name?" he asks. After telling her what Johnny suspects, Virginia admits that she had been seeing Collins. She tells Johnny that William and Collins had stolen the money, but only William got caught. Collins had faked the letter to Mr. Baskerville to frame William. As they are talking shots ring out and Virginia is killed. Johnny fires 6 times at Collins and hits him. Before he dies, Collins tells Johnny that he had used Johnny as a witness to frame William, whom he had killed to avoid splitting the money. He had called Virginia and told her to tell Johnny everything so that he could find William and arrange the suicide. Before he dies, Collins says it should be raining, as it is too nice of a night to die.

At the end, Johnny notes that murder isn't so bad. A ride in any New York cab makes a killing look like a Sunday school taffy pull.

NOTES:
- EDMOND O'BRIEN ASKS LISTENER TO DONATE BLOOD FOR THE KOREAN WAR CAMPAIGN.
- DAN CUBBERLY IS THE ANNOUNCER
- MUSIC IS BY WILBUR HATCH
- EDMOND O'BRIEN'S NEXT MOVIE IS SILVER CITY.
- A PROGRAM OF THE SAME TITLE IS BROADCAST ON 3/10/1953.

Producer: Jaime del Valle   **Writers:** Blake Edwards
Cast: Stacy Harris, Bill Bouchey, Howard McNear, Sidney Miller, Virginia Gregg

◆ ❖ ◆

SHOW: THE MERRILL KENT MATTER
SHOW DATE: 11/17/1951
COMPANY: WASHINGTONIAN LIFE INSURANCE COMPANY
AGENT: MR. LAVERY
EXP. ACCT: $378.40

SYNOPSIS: Mr. Lavery calls and asks if Johnny is ready for an assignment. Johnny is to go to a small town near Gallop to look into the death of Merrill Kent. Kent was thought to have died from an accident, but the police have information that leads them to think it was murder. Johnny is told he will have to arrange for an autopsy when he gets there, as Lavery wants to know if Kent was murdered or not.

Johnny travels to Fort Scott, New Mexico where Johnny meets deputy York, the local police department. York tells Johnny that he received a phone call that could not be traced. The caller disguised her voice and told York that Kent had been murdered. Johnny is told that Kent was killed when his horse fell and then dragged him back to his home. York calls the death bad luck. Johnny gets the name of the local physician Doctor Snyder and is not sure that York is happy about him being there.

Johnny visits Dr. Snyder and is met by his nurse, Mrs. Snyder. Johnny meets Dr. Snyder and tells him about the phone call, and Dr. Snyder calls it preposterous. Johnny tells him that he must ask questions and Dr. Snyder tells Johnny that he had been called to the ranch and Kent was dead when he got there. The body was on the ground, and Johnny asks if he could prove that Kent had been in the saddle. Dr. Snyder did not examine the boot or the ankle, as the body was covered with a blanket. Dr. Snyder tells Johnny that Kent had died from multiple fractures to the skull caused by an accident. Johnny tells him that he will order an autopsy, and that a sister from Seattle is on her way in case they need her authority. On the way out Johnny hears a woman crying hysterically inside. Johnny goes back to York's office and learns that Kent was often away on business, and Mrs. Kent did not go with him. York tells Johnny that the people in town are his friends, and he does not want anyone to turn out to be a killer, especially Maxine Kent, who is loved by everyone in the area.

Johnny goes to the Kent ranch and Mrs. Kent, a beautiful woman in her mid twenties, meets Johnny at the driveway. She knows who Johnny is, as her brother had called her. She asks Johnny how she can order an autopsy so soon, and Johnny tells her all she has to do is to sign a paper. She tells Johnny she wants to do what is right.

Johnny goes back to York's office, and is told to go to Dr. Snyder's office and see York there. Mrs. Snyder has killed herself and left a letter claiming she was the caller. Johnny meets York who tells Johnny that Snyder had found his wife and that the letter claims that the call was based on false suspicions about Dr. Snyder and Mrs. Kent. Johnny reads the note, which outlines the suspicions that turned out to be baseless. Having no happiness in her future, it ended with her begging for her husband's forgiveness. Johnny talks to Dr. Snyder who tells Johnny that he is in love with Maxine Kent, but could not divorce his wife unless he were prepared to leave town, which he cannot do. He had broken off the affair and lied to his wife about it. When Merrill was killed, it fueled the doubts held by this wife and drove her crazy. Johnny asks why he said, "killed," and Snyder tells Johnny that his motives are public now, and being wrong does not help. Dr. Snyder tells Johnny that he was in his office when Kent was killed, and his wife had gone out to shop. Johnny tells him that the widow is authorizing the autopsy, and Snyder has nothing else to say. The deputies arrive and Snyder is put in jail. After answering their questions, Johnny goes to the Kent ranch and meets Maxine's brother who tells Johnny that she has gone to Santa Fe. Johnny asks when she left and he tells Johnny that it was before Mrs. Snyder killed her self. Johnny tells him he should get his signals straight as Johnny was talking to her then. Johnny is told that Maxine flew apart when she heard about Mrs. Kent and ran off to Santa Fe. Johnny is told that Maxine had nothing to do with Merrill's death as he was there when the horse dragged him in and he took the foot out of the stirrup. Johnny learns that Dr. Snyder had not been to the ranch for several weeks, after Maxine made him stop. The last time was two weeks ago. He tells Johnny that he was the only one who knew where Merrill was going. Johnny tells him he will have Maxine picked up by the police, and the brother asks him to wait until morning. The next day Mrs. Kent returns and signs the autopsy forms. The body is exhumed and the coroner's report is "death by misadventure at the hands of person or persons unknown." Dr. Snyder and his wife's body are taken to the county seat and Johnny goes over all the evidence with York. Johnny then goes back to the Kent ranch and asks Maxine why she ran out and is told that she just lost her head. Johnny tells her that the death was ruled accidental. Johnny and the deputy had gone out to the area where Merrill had gone and found a rifle he had fired, and where the horse had fallen and dragged him back. Maxine is happy that it is all over, that they believe her now.

Remarks: I'm sorry about the happy ending and the fact that everybody told the truth and that nobody was a criminal, and that the insurance claim is a good as New Mexico gold.

NOTES:
- COMMERCIAL BREAK #1 IS FOR THE GANGBUSTERS PROGRAM, "THE TALKATIVE BOY."
- MUSIC IS BY WILBUR HATCH.
- EDMOND O'BRIEN WILL SOON BE SEEN IN THE PARAMOUNT PRODUCTION "SILVER CITY."
- THE ANNOUNCER IS DICK CUTTING
- EDMOND O'BRIEN TALKS ABOUT THE DUTY OF ALL CITIZENS TO PROVIDE BLOOD FOR THE SOLDIERS INVOLVED IN THE KORAN WAR.
- THE SCRIPT FOR THIS PROGRAM IN THE KNX COLLECTION AT THE THOUSAND OAKS LIBRARY LISTS RAYMOND BURR IN THE CAST, BUT THE ANNOUNCER LISTS RAY HARTMAN.

Producer: Jaime del Valle   **Writers:** Gil Doud
Cast: Ray Hartman, Joseph Kearns, Jeanette Nolan, Edgar Barrier, Virginia Gregg, Hy Averback

SHOW: THE YOUNGSTOWN CREDIT GROUP MATTER
SHOW DATE: 12/8/1951
COMPANY: COLUMBIA ALL RISK INSURANCE COMPANY
AGENT:
EXP. ACCT: $195.20
SYNOPSIS: Sgt. Biggan calls for Chief Allen to update Johnny on the robbery.

Johnny is told that one victim has died and another one can be questioned shortly. Johnny tells Sgt. Biggan that the take on the robbery is up to $48,000. Johnny is told that he can come over for the questioning.

Johnny goes to Youngstown, Ohio to work on a payroll robbery. Johnny is told by Sgt. Biggan that the Youngstown Credit Group is a Savings and Loan set up to provide a check cashing service to plants in the Youngstown area. One of the trips was interrupted by a robbery. Both drivers of the car were thrown from it, and one has died.

Johnny and Chief Edward J. Allen, who had forced the Purple Gang out of Youngstown, go to the hospital to question Charley Watson. Johnny asks Chief Allen why he is involved personally, and the Chief tells Johnny "he has not gotten used to not being a sergeant." Charley tells Johnny that a car had been following them; and it had forced them off the road. Their car, a blue 1948 Plymouth, was taken and they were thrown from it while the car was in motion. Johnny is told that a number of people were familiar with the routine, and Charley gives a list of twelve names that the police check out.

Johnny goes to visit the widow of George Enfield, the man who died. She tells Johnny that she knows nothing and is worried about what to tell the kids and how to pay the bills. She did not know any of George's friends, and only knew that he went bowling a lot at the Highpoint Lanes.

Johnny is worried that the group will break up and the money will disappear. Later that night a tip comes in to the police. A farmer had seen a suspicious car, so Johnny and Chief Allen go to visit the man. He tells them that he saw a blue car pull into a nearby dirt road where it was met by another car. Four men got out and drove back towards town. Johnny goes to the dirt road and finds the car, and a stain is found on the floor. The car is driven to police headquarters where the stain is confirmed to be blood.

The next day, the autopsy on George Enfield shows that he had been beaten, raising the suspicion that knew who killed him. Johnny and Chief Allen revisit Charley Watson, who can add only that he was begging for his life, yet George had said nothing. Johnny goes back to see Mrs. Enfield, who shows Johnny a railroad ticket to California. She tells Johnny that she knew something was wrong, as George had been out late every night for the past two weeks. She tells Johnny that she had called the bowling alley, but George had not been there for three days. She also remembers George talking to a man named Carl at the bowling alley. She wonders why her husband would buy a ticket to California unless he was going to run away.

Johnny calls the police and a known criminal, Carl Huffman, is brought in. The chief reminds Carl that he has had problems with the law before, and tells him to cooperate. Johnny tells Carl that he has been seen with George Enfield, and asks if he was planning the robbery. During the questioning, Johnny tells him there is a witness to the car exchange. When Johnny tells Carl that his prints are on a piece of pipe found on the highway, Carl slips up and admits he was in on the robbery. Carl tells the chief that Bill Loyeck and Verne Clark were also involved, but it was Enfield's idea. Carl also implicates the Thayer brothers, who are back in town. Johnny is told that the Thayers were involved and are the ones who did the killing, as they did not like Enfield. They are back now, and are staying at their former hangout, the Tuxedo Club. The police send men to watch the Tuxedo Club, and plans are made to pick up the Thayers at dusk. On the way Johnny is told all about the Thayers. Loyeck and Clark are picked up and they corroborate Carl's story. The police surround the club and the Thayer brothers try to escape, but are forced back. The police, Chief Allen and Johnny go to get them at 4:30, and the Thayers are killed in a hail of submachine gun fire.

The money was recovered for the most part, and the insurance company got the services of Chief Edward J. Allen.

NOTES:

- FROM THE CONGRESSIONAL RECORD OF 10/25/90: EDWARD JOSEPH ALLEN WAS BORN NOVEMBER 13, 1907, IN ERIE, PA. HE GREW UP IN THAT SOUTHWESTERN PENNSYLVANIA CITY AND, ON MAY 26, 1937, HE MARRIED HIS HOMETOWN SWEETHEART, DOROTHY MAE DAVENPORT. THEY WERE BLESSED WITH TWO CHILDREN AND SIX GRANDCHILDREN. ED BEGAN HIS CAREER AS A PATROLMAN IN ERIE AND LATER WORKED WITH THE FBI DURING WORLD WAR II TO ASSIST FEDERAL AGENTS ON INVESTIGATIONS CONCERNING SABOTAGE, ESPIONAGE, AND SUBVERSION. AFTER THE WAR, HE ATTENDED THE FBI NATIONAL ACADEMY AND IN 1948 BECAME POLICE CHIEF OF YOUNGSTOWN, OH. IN YOUNGSTOWN, EDDIE TEAMED WITH A REFORM-MINDED MAYOR TO DRIVE THE MAFIA INFLUENCE FROM THAT CITY. HIS EFFORTS WON HIM NATIONAL RECOGNITION AND YOUNGSTOWN THE `ALL-AMERICAN CITY' AWARD IN 1950. LATER, IN 1963, HE PUBLISHED A BOOK, "THE MERCHANTS OF MENACE," WHICH ANALYZED MAFIA ACTIVITY IN THE UNITED STATES.
- IT IS TOO BAD THAT REP. DORNAN OF CALIFORNIA, WHO ENTERED THE ABOVE, DID NOT KNOW HIS GEOGRAPHY, AS ERIE IS IN NORTHWESTERN PENNSYLVANIA.
- THE PURPLE GANG WAS A REAL ORGANIZATION OPERATED OUT OF DETROIT
- EDMOND O'BRIEN CAN BE SEEN IN THE PARAMOUNT PRODUCTION "SILVER CITY"
- DICK CUTTING IS THE ANNOUNCER
- MUSIC IS BY WILBUR HATCH.
- THERE IS A PUBLIC SERVICE ANNOUNCEMENT TO GIVE BLOOD TO ASSIST IN THE KOREAN WAR

Producer: Jaime del Valle   Writers: Gil Doud
Cast: Ed Begley, Bill Johnstone, Parley Baer, Virginia Gregg, Tim Graham, Stacy Harris

SHOW:	THE PAUL BARBERIS MATTER
SHOW DATE:	12/15/1951
COMPANY:	BRITANNIA INSURANCE COMPANY
AGENT:	AD MEYERS
EXP. ACCT:	$160.30

SYNOPSIS: Ad Meyers calls Johnny about the newspaper story on the disappearance of Paul Barberis, under somewhat mysterious circumstances. Johnny is told to go the country place in Tylerville, which is where the maid called the police.

Johnny drives to Tylerville, Connecticut, and meets Capt. Slack who tells Johnny that the house was all torn up, but there was no body, the car was gone and there were signs of a beating. Mrs. Barberis is coming up from New York later that day. Johnny is told that Paul Barberis was about 40, a successful criminal lawyer in Waterbury who is divorced and remarried. The wife called the house two days earlier and nothing seemed amiss. Paul Barberis also had come to the cabin unexpectedly. When the wife arrives, Capt. Slack tells her that someone was killed in the cabin, and that she is not to touch anything.

Johnny talks to the maid, who thinks that Mr. Barberis is dead. Johnny goes to Waterbury and talks to Andrew Proust, the partner of Barberis. Proust has no reason to think that Paul had killed anyone.

Johnny goes back to Tylerville and learns that two blankets are missing from the house, and that Barberis' car was the only one to have been there. Capt. Slack gets a call from a man in New Haven who might know something. Johnny goes to meet Mr. Taggert, who tells him that Phillip Ryan runs a service station in the area, and that his wife was killed and Barberis got the killer, Hibson, off. Taggert is sure that Ryan is the one who killed Barberis.

Johnny and Capt. Slack go to see Ryan, who is expecting the police and leaves with them. Ryan is questioned and his confession seems sound. He tells Johnny that he was lured to the house and beat Barberis because he was out of his mind. Later the empty car belonging to Barberis is found in a quarry. The quarry is searched and Johnny goes back to Tylerville. Johnny talks to Ryan's father who tells Johnny that Phillip was a good boy who got upset after the trial. Johnny and Capt. Slack return to the quarry, which is being pumped out. The maid comes there and tells Johnny that she heard Mrs. Barberis call for Phillip. Johnny and Capt. Slack go back to talk to Ryan and go over his story. He tells them that he met Paul Barberis inside the house. He had a key and was supposed to meet Mrs. Barberis there. Johnny talks to Mrs. Barberis and tells her about Ryan's confession. She tells Johnny that she met Ryan at the trial and realized that her husband had no heart. She kept seeing Phillip and was supposed to be there but the husband found out. Phillips was supposed to leave if she did not arrive, and he didn't.

NOTES:
- THE ANNOUNCER IS DAN CUBBERLY

- MUSIC IS BY WILBUR HATCH
- STORY INFORMATION OBTAINED FROM THE KNX COLLECTION IN THE THOUSAND OAKS LIBRARY

Producer: Jaime del Valle   Writers   Gil Doud
Cast: Howard McNear, Raymond Burr, Jeanne Bates, Jeanette
               Nolan, Herb Butterfield, Peter Leeds

◆   ❖   ◆

SHOW: THE MAYNARD COLLINS MATTER
SHOW DATE: 12/22/1951
COMPANY: ATHENA LIFE & CASUALTY COMPANY
AGENT: ED GRIMM
EXP. ACCT: $310.00

SYNOPSIS: Johnny is called by Ed Grimm, who tells Johnny that Maynard Collins was found dead in Colorado Springs, but they think he was dead before the accident. The beneficiary is Delia Collins.

Johnny flies to Colorado Springs, Colorado and meets with Lt. Anders. Johnny is told that the Collins car went off the side of Canyon Road about 10:00 PM, but Collins had been dead for about 2 hours, and had a severe blow to his head. His wife was at the theater in Pueblo at the time. Johnny and Lt. Anders drive to Manitou Springs and talk to the neighbor, Mr. Pinkert who tells him that he heard the crash. Johnny and Lt. Anders go to talk to Mrs. Collins and meet Ralph Turner, her nephew, and Ralph's mother Ada. Their story is that after dinner they went to a movie and Ralph drove them and then went bowling. Maynard did not go because he was supposed to play cards with Mr. Pinkert, but that was called off at the last minute. Johnny is told that Ralph and Maynard are very close, and that the car was left at the house. Johnny verifies that Ralph was at a bowling alley from 7:15 to 10:15. Johnny talks to Mr. Pinkert, who tells them that he was home alone, and that he liked Maynard, but that Maynard and Delia always argued about money. Johnny goes to police headquarters where Clint Bingham comes in and tells them that Maynard had called him around 7:30 about a flat tire. Clint went out and fixed it around 8:00. There was no one home, so he just fixed the flat and left. He tells Johnny that he heard a noise in the brush that sounded like someone running towards the Pinkert house. Lt. Anders tells Clint that Maynard was killed in the brush. A call comes in and Mr. Pinkert has been hit by a car and is in the hospital.

Johnny and Lt. Anders go to talk to Pinkert who tells them that he knew that Clint was at the house and thought he was running away, but he did not see him. Pinkert suggests that Johnny talk to Delia. Johnny goes to see Delia and tells her about the talk of a fight. She tells Johnny that Maynard was paying for Ralph's college bills, but he found out that Ralph was not really trying and would not pay anymore. Supposedly the Dean has not told Ralph yet. Johnny goes to the hospital and learns that the murder weapon was a tire iron. Johnny is called by

Dean Michener. He tells Johnny that Ralph did know that his uncle was removing him from the school because his secretary had told Ralph. Johnny tells Lt. Anders and goes to the bowling alley and talks to the pin girl who tells Johnny that she left the alley at 10:00. However the alley was closed between 7:45 and 8:15 because that is her dinner break. Johnny goes to the jail and Ralph admits knowing about the school. Ralph is told that his prints are on the tire iron and he confesses to walking to the house. He heard a car coming and left and then came back. He knew about Maynard and other women and Maynard was bothering his mother, so he had to kill him.

NOTES:
- THE ANNOUNCER IS DAN CUBBERLY AND DICK CUTTING
- MUSIC IS BY WILBUR HATCH
- STORY INFORMATION OBTAINED FROM THE KNX COLLECTION IN THE THOUSAND OAKS LIBRARY

Producer: Jaime del Valle   **Writers**   Kathlene Hite
Cast: Ed Begley, Gil Stratton Jr, Jeanette Nolan, Virginia Gregg, Howard McNear, Hy Averback

◆ ❖ ◆

SHOW: THE ALMA SCOTT MATTER
SHOW DATE: 12/29/1951
COMPANY: COLUMBIA ALL RISK INSURANCE COMPANY
AGENT:
EXP. ACCT: $0.00

SYNOPSIS: Alan Swain calls Johnny and wants to talk about the Alma Scott murder. He says he did not kill her and wants to talk. Johnny tells Alan he will meet him alone to talk.

Johnny goes to San Francisco, California to investigate the murder of Alma Scott. The police are looking for Alan Swain, who witnesses reported seeing leaving the apartment after the shots were fired. Johnny looks for Alan Swain for two days before Swain contacts Johnny. Johnny waits in front of a photography shop until a woman contacts Johnny, and takes him in a cab to a café near the beach. The woman walks Johnny to the beach where he meets Alan Swain. Alan tells Johnny that he knows he is doing everything wrong and should have gone to the police, but he cannot prove he did not kill Alma. Alan tells Johnny that he and Alma were going to fly to Mexico to be married and then live in Los Angeles. Alan tells Johnny that the reservations are under the name A. J. Hall on CalMexico Airlines. He had used false named because Alma said that there might be people who would be looking for them. Alan tells Johnny that Alma had called him to say that certain people did not want her to leave and that she had changed her mind about going to Mexico and hung up. Alan tells Johnny that he went to the apartment, heard shouting and a gunshot and then ran out. Alan tells Johnny that he has no idea who was in the apartment.

Alan leaves and the woman, who is Alan's sister Helen, takes Johnny to the café and they order drinks. Johnny asks Helen if the killer could have been a woman, as Alma had left a policy to a half sister that cannot be found. Helen tells Johnny that Alma was a bad woman who was using Alan for something and that Alan had no business being mixed up with her. Helen tells Johnny that Alma had previously had been seeing a man named Walter Helms. Helen admits that she had tipped Helms to the marriage plans, but her plans to get Alan away from Alma are not working out. She leaves and Johnny goes to his hotel.

The next day Johnny visits the Scott apartment and talks to the witnesses. After interviewing all of them, their story of seeing only Swain in the hallway is full of holes, as no one was looking for another possible person in the hallway. Johnny goes back to his hotel Johnny and is met by Walter Helms. Walter tells Johnny that he was a friend of Alma's, and wants to get the killer. Walter reassures Johnny that the newspapers have told Johnny the wrong side of him, and that he is really sure that Swain is the killer. Walter tells Johnny that he had found out about Alma leaving with Alan, and had paid her $15,000 to stay. But the check he gave her seems to be missing. Walter tells Johnny that he had given Alma a .32 caliber pistol registered to Walter that seems to be missing. Walter tells Johnny that he wants to "hire" Johnny, but Johnny says that it would be unethical to work for a suspect. Finally Helms tells Johnny that he is going to offer a $20,000 reward for information.

The reward hits the newspapers and Alan calls Johnny about the reward scheme. Johnny tells him to give himself up, as the witnesses are not sure now of what they saw, but Alan is hesitant and must talk to Helen. Lt. Halloran of the police calls to tell Johnny that he has a confession from Helen. Johnny goes to meet Lt. Halloran and tells him that he had met Alan and Helen, but did not have enough to call the police. Lt. Halloran tells Johnny that the comment he had made to Helen about a woman killer had made her think Johnny had something on her, so she turned herself in. Johnny talks to Helen in jail and she tells Johnny that she never thought she would do it, and says she worked for 10 years in burlesque to support Alan. She tells Johnny that she killed Alma when she heard that she and Alan were going to Mexico. Helen had a .32 and shot Alma, waited until everyone left and went out the back door.

Lt. Halloran comes to the cell to tell Johnny that there has been a shooting at Walter Helm's home. Johnny goes there with Lt. Halloran and they find both Helms and Alan Swain shot. Alan tells Johnny that Helms took Alma away from him. Johnny talks to Helms who admits that he heard the shots while standing at the door and admits that he killed her. Alma was going to leave and he could not buy her back.

NOTES:

- JOHNNY DRINKS RYE AND SODA.
- CAST INFORMATION FROM THE **KNX** COLLECTION AT THE THOUSAND OAKS LIBRARY.

- THE MID-PROGRAM COMMERCIAL IS FOR THE EDGAR BERGEN SHOW TOMORROW NIGHT
- JOHN LUND ALSO DID THIS PROGRAM ON **6/16/1953** AS "THE EMIL CARTER MATTER." THE CHARACTERS ARE REVERSED AND THE PLOT SLIGHTLY DIFFERENT.
- THE ENDING OF THIS PROGRAM WAS OBTAINED FROM THE SCRIPT AT THE THOUSAND OAKS LIBRARY.
- DAN CUBBERLY AND DICK CUTTING THE ANNOUNCERS

Producer: Jaime del Valle   **Writers:** Gil Doud
Cast: Jack Moyles, Virginia Gregg, Jeanette Nolan, Herb Butterfield, Hy Averback, Harry Lang

◆ ❖ ◆

SHOW: THE GLEN ENGLISH MATTER
SHOW DATE: 1/5/1952
COMPANY: HARTFORD POLICE
AGENT:
EXP. ACCT: $0.00

SYNOPSIS: This is a personal case based on Johnny's involvement with Glen English. Johnny has known Glen since 1947, and his wife even longer. Glen had studied under the GI Bill and opened a law office in Hartford, Connecticut in 1949. Johnny had occasionally used Glen for legal services and Glen had used Johnny. Glen had called Johnny at 10:30 one night and had asked Johnny to photostat a statement, and told Johnny that he might stop by later, or he will see him in the morning. Johnny read of Glen's death in paper the next morning. Johnny goes to see Glen's widow, Donna. Johnny looks through Glen's papers and finds nothing. Donna tells Johnny that Glen had called her from his office to say that he would be home late, so she went to a movie. She is sad that she will never see him again and wonders what will she do? Donna tells Johnny that she is going to stay with Glen's mother for a while.

Johnny goes to the office and talks to Glen's secretary. She tells Johnny that she had left at 5:00, and that Glen was working late for a new client. Johnny tells her that he will take care of her salary through the next month and looks through the office and finds nothing. Johnny goes to see Lt. Dolger at police headquarters. Lt. Dolger tells Johnny that there is not enough evidence to launch a murder investigation. Johnny tells Lt. Dolger about the evidence Glen had mentioned, and Johnny thinks that Glen was killed on the way over to see him. Johnny tells Lt. Dolger that there is no reason for Glen to be at the intersection where he was killed, except that he was on his way to see Johnny. Johnny gets the reports and the autopsy report details that that there were multiple fractures and internal injuries. Glen's personal effects tell nothing, only a supposition that he was killed. Johnny goes to see Dr. Ramsey about the autopsy. Dr. Ramsey tells Johnny that a car stuck Glen, and the internal injuries indicate that the car was driven fast.

Johnny looks at photos of the accident scene and finds nothing. Johnny turns down a case and goes to look at the accident scene to see if there is anything there. Johnny goes back to see Donna who is ok now, and staying with Glen's mother. Johnny tells her about the new client and she tells Johnny that Glen had been working late for the past two weeks. She tells Johnny that she remembers that their last conversation was a one-sided one and that she had lost her temper. Johnny gets the key to her apartment and searches it. While Johnny is there, the phone rings and Johnny answers. The caller is a man who is calling to talk to Donna. The man wants to tell her that it her husband was murdered, on account of what he told Glen. Johnny is told to go see Warren Kelly. Johnny agrees to pursue the case and the man, whose name is Bruno, agrees to meet Johnny at Caruso's Cafe.

Johnny goes to the café and buys a drink (bourbon and soda, $.60). The bartender directs Johnny to a rear upstairs storeroom where Johnny meets Bruno Vick who apologizes to Johnny for getting Glen killed. Bruno tells Johnny that Glen was going to meet with a notary when three men killed him. Bruno tells Johnny that Warren Kelly is a syndicate boss who is using a contracting company for a front. Kelly killed Ed Waters, who was standing in his way. Bruno tells Johnny that he had helped bury the body, and that Kelly is searching for Bruno all over the country. Bruno tells Johnny that he had told Kelly that he was finished running, and he had gone to talk to Glenn for advice instead of the District Attorney. Bruno takes Johnny to the window and shows Johnny the men who are watching him, Nat Reiner and Alex Shaw, so he cannot go to the police. Johnny goes to call the police so Bruno can give up, but Lt. Dolger is not in. As Johnny is on the phone, Bruno sneaks by him and goes outside. Bruno confronts Nat and Alex and there is gunfire. Bruno is killed and Reiner is wounded. Lt. Dolger shows up and Johnny tells him what happened, that Bruno came out knowing he was going to die. The police find a letter for the District Attorney in Reiner's pocket. The letter tells the details of the Waters killing and Glen's death. Reiner is taken to the hospital and after a back operation Johnny talks to Reiner and tells him that he had talked under the anesthetic and told the police everything. Johnny tells him that he knows where Kelly is and where Waters is buried, and convinces Reiner to tell him about the accident. Reiner tells Johnny that they had followed Glen and Shaw had beaten him and faked the hit-and-run accident after they took the letter.

Lt. Dolger and Johnny go to Alex Shaw's apartment, located in a "sore spot of a building." Johnny and Lt. Dolger break in the door and see Shaw running across the roof. The police open up and Shaw is killed in a hail of submachine gun fire.

If Johnny had been a better friend, he would have walked halfway to meet Glen.

NOTES:

- **THE MID-PROGRAM COMMERCIAL FOR THE NEW PROGRAM, "THE PEOPLE ACT"**

- EDMOND O'BRIEN CAN BE SEEN IN THE PARAMOUNT PRODUCTION "SILVER CITY"
- DAN CUBBERLY AND DICK CUTTING ARE THE ANNOUNCERS
- MUSIC IS BY WILBUR HATCH

Producer: Jaime del Valle   **Writers:**   Gil Doud
Cast: Jeanette Nolan, Jim Nusser, Jeanne Bates, Wally Maher, Jay Novello, Edgar Barrier, Bill Conrad

◆ ❖ ◆

SHOW: THE BAXTER MATTER
SHOW DATE: 1/12/1952
COMPANY: GREAT EASTERN LIFE INSURANCE COMPANY
AGENT: LUTHER BISHOP
EXP. ACCT: $324.10

SYNOPSIS: Luther Bishop calls Johnny and tells him that William Baxter has been killed. Baxter was thrown from this horse in McAlester, Oklahoma where he and his brothers are ranchers. Clay Baxter is in New York, and he does not think that it was an accident. Johnny is to go to the Sheridan Hotel to talk to Clay.

Johnny goes to New York and meets Clay at the Sheridan Hotel. Clay tells Johnny that his brother was not killed in an accident because he was too good of a horseman, and knew how to fall. Bill's wife will inherit the ranch, which is worth between 8-10 million. Johnny and Clay go for drinks and then leave for Oklahoma City and then on to McAlester, Oklahoma. In McAlester Johnny meets Sheriff Billings who tells Johnny that Bill's horse had limped back to the ranch after the accident, and that Luke and Jake Tolliver, who are miners, found the body. Johnny is told that Bill and Clay did not get along, and that Clay bought his ranch after Bill got married. Johnny takes a shower and finds the sheriff feeding his catfish in the swimming pool. Johnny and Sheriff Billings go to the Baxter ranch and Johnny meets Wilma Baxter. Wilma invites Johnny to dinner, but Clay tells her that Johnny is with him. Wilma tells Johnny that she was in town all day on the day of the accident. Johnny takes an agonizing horseback ride to the location of the accident. Johnny is shown the rock that Baxter's head hit and asks if an impression was taken, which it was not. The Sheriff digs up the rock and Johnny goes back to the ranch and meets Frank Kerry, the ranch foremen. Johnny is shown the horse Baxter rode, and notices a swollen hip that looks like it is infected.

Johnny goes back to town and meets with the coroner and gives him the rock. The rock is compared to the wound and it does not match, so Johnny wants an autopsy performed. Johnny and Clay ride out to the Tolliver silver mine and are shot at as they approach. They yell back and forth at each other and Johnny finally gets to go up to the mine alone. The Tolliver brothers confirm that they found the body, and that Baxter was dead when they found him. They tell Johnny that they have saved their money and want to buy some insurance. Johnny manages to leave a half-hour later. Clay lifts Johnny onto his horse and is then shot. Clay's horse runs off, and Johnny is forced to follow him until the horse stops, and Johnny falls off his horse. Clay is taken to the doctor and was only grazed; but Johnny is very sore. Johnny learns that William Baxter did not die from the fracture, but from a long thin instrument that went under his eye and into his brain. Someone then jabbed the horse to make it look like an accident. Johnny goes to the Baxter ranch with a pair of surgical probes he borrowed from the doctor. Johnny goes into the stable and finds what he is looking for. Wilma finds Johnny in the stable and he tells her that William was killed by a woman's murder weapon, a hatpin. Johnny tells Wilma that the Tollivers saw the murder.

Johnny goes back to the Tolliver's mine and tells them about Wilma. Johnny remembers a case in New York where a woman hit a man and then stabbed him with a hatpin. Johnny remembers that a woman planned it, a man did it and they both disappeared. Johnny sets up a trap in the mine with a set of dummies sitting at a table. Later Frank comes in and shoots at the dummies, and the Tollivers get the drop on Frank. Johnny ends up in a fight with Frank, who finally tells Johnny that Wilma had promised him a share of the ranch. Kelly is turned in to the sheriff, and admits that Wilma is wanted in New York.

NOTES:

- THE ANNOUNCER IS DAN CUBBERLY AND DICK CUTTING
- MUSIC IS BY WILBUR HATCH
- STORY INFORMATION OBTAINED FROM THE KNX COLLECTION IN THE THOUSAND OAKS LIBRARY

Producer:	Jaime del Valle **Writers** **Blake Edwards**
Cast:	Howard McNear, Jim Backus, Herb Butterfield, Virginia Gregg, Bob Sweeney, Sidney Miller, Lou Krugman, Dave Light

◆ ❖ ◆

SHOW:	THE AMELIA HARWELL MATTER
SHOW DATE:	7/2/1952
COMPANY:	CORINTHIAN ALL RISK INSURANCE COMPANY
AGENT:	GEORGE PARKER
EXP. ACCT:	$122.35

SYNOPSIS: George Parker calls Johnny looking for an investigator. Mrs. Thomas Harwell has been poisoned on Cape Cod.

Johnny goes to Parker's office and learns that the Harwells are textile heirs, and Mrs. Harwell heads the business. So far there are no details on the poison. Johnny is told that Mrs. Harwell was a domineering person who had $350,000 in total coverage. Johnny rents a car and drives to Cape Cod, Massachusetts. The mansion is described as massive. Johnny talks with Thomas Harwell, the widower, and he tells Johnny that he is used to blunt talk. Johnny is told that Mrs. Harwell was an invalid and had little time left. She despised weakness and never told Thomas if she was in pain. Thomas tells Johnny that he does not approve of the children, as they are a rich woman's children and he was not allowed to father them. Johnny is told that the servants are above suspicion. They are common people and therefore good. Thomas tells Johnny that Dr. Steven is the family physician.

Johnny visits Dr. Stevens who wishes him success. He tells Johnny that Amelia had cancer and could have had an operation, but she would take advice from no one. Now, Thomas is passing from slavery to freedom. Dr. Stevens describes the daughter Maxine as a bitter old maid at 33; the son Dexter is 32 and an alcoholic who has just entered into an unsuccessful marriage. Johnny is told that Amelia could only have lived 2-3 months at most, and that a mercy killing is a possibility. Johnny is told that the poison is unknown and that an inquest will be held this afternoon. Johnny is told that Dexter is married to Gretchen Nielsen, a photographer with a small business there in town, and that she is below their standards.

Johnny visits Gretchen that evening and introduces himself, and she talks to Johnny reluctantly. She tells Johnny that she heard from the butler about the death. She is not living with Dexter, she tells Johnny, because she was thought of as a fortune hunter, and Dexter is a slave to the family. She thought their relationship would drag Dexter from the family, but he was tied to mother's money. Gretchen tells Johnny that Dexter would never kill his mother and that she thinks Thomas did it. Mrs. Harwell was in pain and frightened. Thomas knew it and wanted to help. Also, Gretchen tells Johnny that Mrs. Harwell had made a lot of mistakes.

Johnny calls Dr. Stevens and learns the cause of death was a non-alkaloid poison, one unusual for suicide.

Johnny goes to the Harwell residence and asks to see the children. Johnny meets with them and tells them that the poison used was not a pleasant one. Dexter is talking to Johnny when Thomas cries out in pain. Johnny rushes upstairs to find Thomas barely conscious as he points to a glass of poisoned water. There is no reaction from the children and Dr. Stevens is called. After a short time Thomas is all right as he only took a sip of the water. He wonders who would do this, as he is not ready to follow Amelia. Johnny takes the glass out of the room as Dr. Stevens arrives. The glass has a lot of poison and Dr. Stevens thinks that it is probably canadine. Thomas tells Dr. Stevens that it is unnecessary to report this to police. Johnny notices that there are marks on Thomas' throat, like he was strangled. Johnny tells Thomas, who is feeling better, that he must report this to the police. Thomas asks Johnny, for the sake of the family, why must he report this to the police, as the results were harmless. Thomas tells Johnny that the servants will be fired in the morning. Johnny is adamant about reporting the incident and is told to leave when Johnny says he is calling in the police.

On the way out the children are in the library. Johnny asks why Thomas does he not want to report this, and Dexter points a finger at Maxine, about his marriage, and a baby on the way. Maxine says Dexter stayed because mother would disinherit him. Johnny leaves to give the glass to the police.

Johnny visits Gretchen and tells her of the second poisoning. Johnny hints about the baby and about being disinherited. Gretchen tells Johnny that Thomas was trying to help them, and not even Dexter had suspected. Thomas probably approved of the marriage and Thomas kept the marriage from Amelia, who found out and then died.

Johnny calls Dr. Stevens and then goes to the Harwell estate. He tells Thomas that he can spare Dexter from a murder charge. Johnny speaks to Thomas alone and tells him that police are ready to charge Dexter, but you killed your wife. You gave her the water and she tried to scratch you when you tried to keep her quiet. Thomas admits doing it. He tells Johnny that he has made many mistakes and wants to help the grandchild. He hoped Amelia would approve but she asked for a lawyer, so he killed her.

NOTES:
- COMMERCIALS ARE THE WRIGLEY'S SPEARMINT GUM
- MUSIC IS PROVIDED BY EDDIE DUNSTEDTER ON THE ORGAN.
- EDMOND O'BRIEN'S NEWEST MOVIE IS "THE TURNING POINT"
- THIS IS THE LAST OF THE AVAILABLE EDMOND O'BRIEN SERIES

Producer: Jaime del Valle **Writers:** Gil Doud
Cast: Victor Perrin, John McIntire, Herb Butterfield, Jeanette Nolan, Virginia Gregg, Peter Leeds

◆　❖　◆

SHOW: THE HENRY PAGE MATTER
SHOW DATE: 7/16/1952
COMPANY: HARTFORD POLICE BUNKO SQUAD
AGENT:
EXP. ACCT: $53.00

SYNOPSIS: Hank Page from Page's Printing calls Johnny. He has something that he wants Johnny to look at.

Johnny relates that he had used Hank to print his stationary. Johnny goes to the bar in Hartford, Connecticut where they had arranged to meet and sees Hank run down by a car. Johnny rushes to the body, and Hank gives Johnny a silver cigarette case and tells him to hide it. Hank mentions something about the inside and his wife and then dies. Johnny gives his statement to the police and then goes to the morgue. The police call the death natural causes, which Johnny questions, but will have to wait for the autopsy. Johnny goes to see Mrs. Page and gives her the personal effects. She knew that Hank was going to meet with Johnny, and also tells Johnny that Hank had a heart condition. Johnny asks about the black eye Hank had, and she tells Johnny that Hank had fainted and fallen at home.

Johnny goes to a café and looks at the case, which contains foreign cigarettes and a 100 Florin note. Johnny goes to the office of Van Pelt and Meisner, Commercial Agents, and asks about the currency. Mr. Van Pelt tells Johnny that the cigarettes are his favorites: "Schiesswassers," and that the currency is worth $53.00. Johnny exchanges the note and Van Pelt offers Johnny $500 for the case. When Johnny refuses to sell it, Van Pelt gets angry and tells Johnny to leave, calling him a grave robber.

Johnny goes to eat and as a car approaches, and Johnny is shot at. Johnny wakes up to find a bruise on his chest where the cigarette case had stopped the bullet. Johnny calls the police and is told that the plates on the car belong to Van Pelt. Johnny goes to Van Pelt's apartment and finds Mrs. Page there. She tells Johnny that Van Pelt had called her and, and that she knows nothing about the case. After waiting for an hour, Johnny searches the apartment and finds Van Pelt in the bedroom dead. Mrs. Page tells Johnny that she knew all of her husband's friends, but not much about his partner. She did know that Hank had met Soules in reform school, where they learned the printing business. Johnny searches her purse and then calls the police and leaves her locked in the bedroom.

Johnny goes to Page's print shop where a man tells Johnny that Soules is not there. Johnny asks to come in and the man gets angry. Johnny finally gets in and fights with the man, who is knocked out, along with his accomplice. Johnny finds the press, which is being used to print 100 Florin notes. Johnny grabs the case and some notes and goes to see Soules who tells Johnny that he was worried about the books because Hank had fired the printers two weeks earlier. Johnny accuses Soules of working for Van Pelt, and Soules pulls a gun on Johnny. Johnny gets the gun and Soules admits everything and is taken to the police.

NOTES:
- THE ANNOUNCER IS CHARLIE LYON
- MUSIC IS BY EDDIE DUNSTEDTER
- STORY INFORMATION OBTAINED FROM THE KNX COLLECTION IN THE THOUSAND OAKS LIBRARY

Producer: **Jaime del Valle**   **Writers**   **Gil Doud**
Cast: **Hy Averback, Howard McNear, Harry Lang, Virginia Gregg, Edgar Barrier, Jim Nusser**

◆   ❖   ◆

SHOW: **THE NEW BEDFORD MORGUE MATTER**
SHOW DATE: **7/30/1952**
COMPANY: **CITY OF NEW BEDFORD POLICE DEPARTMENT**
AGENT:
EXP. ACCT: **$213.30**
SYNOPSIS: Johnny is called by the New Bedford police. They have an unidentified body in the morgue. The police found Johnny's business card in her pocket.

Johnny goes to New Bedford, Massachusetts and meets Sgt. Quill who tells Johnny that the girl was a suicide. Her shoes are missing, and she only had a cheap religious medal. Johnny searches for religious supply houses and finds one that sold the particular medal. Johnny is told that it was sold ten years ago to a confirmation class at St. Dismas. Johnny goes to St. Dismas and meets with Father Ames who gives Johnny a list of the 10 girls from the 1946 class.

Johnny goes to see a Mrs. Starza, who tells Johnny that her daughter Julia is gone, but the missing girl is not her daughter and tells him to leave. Johnny is suspicious and leaves but sneaks back in and hears Mrs. Starza being consoled by a man she calls Carl. He tells her that he will take care of Julia by taking her to Chicago. Mrs. Starza wants to see Julia, but is shot by some one. Johnny searches the house and finds a union card and a photo on a dresser. A friend of Julia's comes to the house and tells Johnny that Julia worked at the Apex Fish Company. She started cleaning fish and moved up fast and became the secretary to Carl Hall. Tonia tells Johnny that Julia had some sort of problem, so she had given Julia Johnny's business card that she found in a bathroom at the train station one day. Tonia tells Johnny that Julia's boyfriend is Joe Gorelli.

Johnny goes to see Joe on his boat "The Julia." Joe tells Johnny that Carl Hall made his money as a rumrunner, and then bought some fishing boats. Johnny goes to see Carl Hall who admits that he knew Julia, and hated Joe. Carl tells Johnny that he had given Julia a fur coat for finding a smuggler on one of the boats. Johnny mentions the body in the morgue and Carl telling her mother that Julia would be taken to Chicago, and Carl laughs at Johnny. Johnny slugs Carl and then Joe comes in and kills Carl. Joe tells Johnny that he had killed Julia because he thought he was losing her to Carl.

NOTES:
- THE ANNOUNCER IS CHARLIE LYON
- MUSIC IS BY EDDIE DUNSTEDTER
- EDMOND O'BRIEN'S NEXT FILM IS "THIS IS DYNAMITE"
- STORY INFORMATION OBTAINED FROM THE KNX COLLECTION IN THE THOUSAND OAKS LIBRARY

Producer: Jaime del Valle   Writers   Gil Doud
Cast: Jack Moyles, John McIntire, Francis X. Bushman, Jeanette Nolan, Bob Sweeney

SHOW: THE SIDNEY MANN MATTER
SHOW DATE: 8/6/1952
COMPANY:
AGENT:
EXP. ACCT: $188.00
SYNOPSIS: This is the same story as "The Adam Kegg Matter," with minor

changes to the details and the names. The case takes place in New York City

NOTES:
- THE ANNOUNCER IS CHARLIE LYON
- MUSIC IS BY EDDIE DUNSTEDTER
- STORY INFORMATION OBTAINED FROM THE KNX COLLECTION IN THE THOUSAND OAKS LIBRARY

Producer: Jaime del Valle   **Writers** Gil Doud
Cast: Bill Johnstone, Virginia Gregg, Hans Conried, Eddie Firestone, Elliott Reed, Jeanette Nolan

◆   ❖   ◆

SHOW: THE TOM HICKMAN MATTER
SHOW DATE: 8/13/1952
COMPANY: MAURIE STRAND BAIL BOND
AGENT: MAURIE STRAND
EXP. ACCT: $2,204.06
SYNOPSIS: This is the same story as "Witness, Witness, Who's Got The Witness" and "The Jack Madigan Matter" with minor changes to the names.
     The case takes place in New York City

NOTES:
- THE ANNOUNCER IS CHARLIE LYON
- MUSIC IS BY EDDIE DUNSTEDTER
- STORY INFORMATION OBTAINED FROM THE KNX COLLECTION IN THE THOUSAND OAKS LIBRARY

Producer: Jaime del Valle   **Writers** Gil Doud
Cast: Sidney Miller, Tony Barrett, Raymond Burr, Gloria Blondell, John McIntire

◆   ❖   ◆

SHOW: THE EDITH MAXWELL MATTER
SHOW DATE: 8/20/1952
COMPANY: DR. LUDWIG GOYA
AGENT:
EXP. ACCT: $0.00
SYNOPSIS: Johnny is called by Miss Crane from Dr. Goya's office in Hartford, Connecticut. The doctor needs a detective and asked her to call Johnny.
     Johnny goes to meet Dr. Goya, who is a psychiatrist, and who was a suspect in the Denov murder case. Dr. Goya tells Johnny that her physician had referred Mrs. Maxwell to him. She has told Dr. Goya that she saw a person in the street,

her daughter-in-law, who was accused of killing her son, Carter Maxwell. Mrs. Maxwell arrives and tells Johnny that he resembles the boyfriend of her daughter-in-law, who was jilted by the man. She tells Johnny about a dream she had about the murder weapon and Johnny is to protect her from Edith Maxwell. Johnny is to go to her apartment on the pretext of having her sign some papers.

Johnny goes to the newspapers to review the case and learns that Carter Maxwell was the heir to a large fortune, and was found stabbed. His wife was accused, but Mrs. Maxwell refused to testify to the grand jury. Johnny goes to visit Edith Maxwell, who tells Johnny about being seen on the street, and about the breakdown of Mrs. Maxwell. Edith tells Johnny how much he resembles her boyfriend and they have 2 black velvet cocktails while they talk. Johnny takes Edith to dinner and then to a ball game.

The next day Johnny learns that Mrs. Maxwell is in a nursing home, and takes another case in Boston. When Johnny comes back he goes to see Edith with flowers. Edith reads Johnny a confession to the killing. Johnny goes to see Dr. Goya and quits the case. While they are talking there are screams and Mrs. Maxwell comes in with a .32 and accuses Dr. Goya of sending her to an insane asylum. She tells Johnny that she has shot Edith. Johnny rushes to Edith's apartment where he finds her shot. Edith tells Johnny that she had to save Mrs. Maxwell and get rid of the knife. Johnny reads the confession, which relates that Edith had found the body of her husband and was found holding the knife, but could not remember anything else. Johnny goes to Dr. Goya with the confession and wants him to analyze it, but he tells Johnny that Mrs. Maxwell is in a home. Johnny goes to the hospital to take Edith home, and stays with her while she recovers. Johnny and Edith have an argument and Johnny leaves. Johnny then reads in the papers that Carter Maxwell had committed suicide and that Edith had been trying to protect Mrs. Maxwell from the truth. Johnny arranges to meet Edith in a bar.

NOTES:
- THE ANNOUNCER IS CHARLIE LYON
- MUSIC IS BY EDDIE DUNSTEDTER
- STORY INFORMATION OBTAINED FROM THE **KNX** COLLECTION IN THE THOUSAND OAKS LIBRARY

Producer: Jaime del Valle   **Writers**   Gil Doud
Cast: Virginia Gregg, Joseph Kearns, Lee Patrick

SHOW:	THE YANKEE PRIDE MATTER
SHOW DATE:	8/27/1952
COMPANY:	TRI-STATE INSURANCE COMPANY
AGENT:	CARL BUSH
EXP. ACCT:	$2,686.00

SYNOPSIS: This is a repeat of the previous program on 10/14/1950.

NOTES:

- THE ANNOUNCER IS DAN CUBBERLY
- MUSIC IS BY EDDIE DUNSTEDTER
- **THE LINE-UP** IS ANNOUNCED FOR NEXT WEEK AT THIS TIME.
- STORY INFORMATION OBTAINED FROM THE **KNX** COLLECTION IN THE THOUSAND OAKS LIBRARY

Producer: Jaime del Valle **Writers:** Gil Doud
Cast: Bill Johnstone, Eric Snowden, Jack Kruschen, Ben Wright, Virginia Gregg

◆　❖　◆

SHOW:	THE MONTEVIDEO MATTER
SHOW DATE:	9/3/1952
COMPANY:	WASHINGTONIAN INSURANCE COMPANY
AGENT:	BILL BRANDON
EXP. ACCT:	$1,650.00

SYNOPSIS: Bill Brandon calls Johnny and tells him that an English woman has been found dead in South America. The London Investment Group wants Johnny to investigate the death.

Johnny flies to Montevideo, Uruguay and gets a room at the Hotel Madrid. Johnny then meets with Inspector Alcira and learns that Mrs. Madeline Furness has been killed. Her husband Roger owns a meatpacking plant, and their son Keith lives with them. The killing was four days ago, and the gardener Raymon del Gado found the body. Mrs. Furness was killed with a blast from a shotgun.

Johnny goes to the Furness home where Ramon is working. He tells Johnny that "she was a bad woman and he was a bad man." Johnny meets Keith, who is a stepson. He tells Johnny that his father did not kill her for the £5,000 insurance, and that Madeline was a schemer. Johnny is shown a picture of Madeline, who is a much younger woman. Keith tells Johnny that he goes to school in England, and that the body was found between their home and the house of Jack Strong, their neighbor.

Johnny meets with Mrs. Strong, who is in a wheelchair. She tells Johnny that there was a division between Madeline and her stepson. Johnny notes that Roger Furness must have found out about his wife's escapades with Mr. Strong. Everyone heard the gunshot, and money probably was the motive.

Johnny meets Mr. Furness, and he tells Johnny that he needs the money from the insurance. He admits that he knew about his wife and Strong. Keith comes in and tells Johnny that he killed his stepmother. Keith is arrested and jailed, but under questioning he is unsure of the facts.

Johnny goes to the Strong residence and sees Mrs. Strong walking inside the house. Once inside she is in the wheelchair again. She tells Johnny that she hurt her back in a hunting accident, and is not supposed to walk. She admits to

Johnny that she knew about her husband and Madeline. Mr. Strong comes in and attacks Johnny, who slugs him. Johnny goes to see Mr. Furness and accuses him of hiding behind his son's confession. On the way out, Furness is shot at the front door. Inspector Alcira later tells Johnny that del Gado is a common name, but they are looking for Ramon. Later he is arrested and admits to the killings. He tells the police that they killed his grandson with their automobile after his daughter had died.

NOTES:
- THIS IS A REPEAT OF THE PREVIOUS PROGRAM ON 7-23-52
- THE ANNOUNCER IS DAN CUBBERLY
- MUSIC IS BY EDDIE DUNSTEDTER
- STORY INFORMATION OBTAINED FROM THE KNX COLLECTION IN THE THOUSAND OAKS LIBRARY

Producer: Jaime del Valle   Writers: Gil Doud
Cast: Bob Griffin, Jay Novello, Hy Averback, Jeanette Nolan, John McIntire, Bill Johnstone

Section 3: John Lund

John Lund was the third Johnny Dollar. The initial episodes present Johnny Dollar as a bland, calm and boring person. Part of the problem with this Johnny Dollar, is not the acting ability of John Lund, but the softness of his voice.

John Lund was a successful radio and motion picture actor, with at least 28 movies to his credit. John was able to convey the character, but his voice was too soft, especially after listening to Edmond O'Brien.

The following are the Johnny Dollar programs performed by John Lund.

SHOW:	**THE SINGAPORE ARSON MATTER**
SHOW DATE:	**11/28/1952**
COMPANY:	**GREAT EAST INSURANCE COMPANY**
AGENT:	
EXP. ACCT:	**$2,112.10**

SYNOPSIS: Inspector Brand calls Johnny to advise him that George Douglas is dead.

Johnny travels to Singapore and hires George Douglas to help investigate a case of Arson at a rubber firm, and George has been killed. Johnny meets with Insp. Barnes who tells Johnny that George's body was found on the docks, but he was killed elsewhere, and his wife identified the body. Johnny cannot tell Insp. Barnes about the case, and leaves with the feeling that he is being followed. Johnny calls on Mr. Sawyer the local agent, updates him and tells him that the case is on hold. Johnny visits the widow who tells Johnny that she has been waiting for someone to kill George, and that there was no "other" woman. She tells Johnny to talk to a good friend of George's, Henry Veller, who is the detective at the Hotel Raffles. Insp. Barnes arrives and accuses Johnny of conspiring with the widow. Johnny leaves and goes to see Veller, who is described as a sleazy detective. Veller tells Johnny that he met George in the war and that George had mentioned that there would be a change in his life soon. Veller also describes George's wife as the jealous type.

Johnny goes to see Mrs. Douglas and a man meets Johnny at the door. The man pulls Johnny in at gunpoint and tells Johnny that he hit Mrs. Douglas because she is too filthy to live. The man leaves and Johnny finds Mrs. Douglas in the bedroom. She tells Johnny that the man had said he killed George, and was looking for something. Johnny calls Insp. Barnes and when he arrives, Johnny gives him a description of the man, including the Webley automatic he carried. Insp. Barnes tells Johnny that he had searched George's office and had not found anything.

Johnny goes to his hotel room and the man is there, and he turns out to be a young man and tells Johnny that he wants his file. Johnny tells him that he only hired George, but the boy tells Johnny that George had been blackmailing him for two years, and that his father had hired George. Johnny suggests that Veller may have the file, and the boy hits Johnny and leaves. Johnny calls Insp. Barnes and they go to the Hotel Raffles, but Veller has resigned and is leaving on a ship that night, and the boy had gone to find him. Johnny and the inspector go the Eastern Traveler and arrest Veller. Veller tells Johnny that George had given him an envelope to hold about Max Childress. Insp. Barnes is surprised because Mr. Childress is a very important man in the Customs Bureau. Johnny and Veller leave the ship to try and lure Max. Max stops Johnny and Veller and wants the envelope. Inspector Barnes calls for him to surrender and Max is shot.

NOTES:
- THE ANNOUNCER IS DAN CUBBERLY
- MUSIC IS BY EDDIE DUNSTEDTER
- THIS STORY WAS DONE EARLIER AS "THE DOUGLAS TAYLOR MATTER." THE INTRODUCTION SEEMS TO BE THE CASE MENTIONED IN THE TRANS-PACIFIC AUDITION PROGRAMS
- STORY INFORMATION OBTAINED FROM THE KNX COLLECTION IN THE THOUSAND OAKS LIBRARY

Producer: Jaime del Valle   Writers   Gil Doud

Cast: John McIntire, Eric Snowden, Jeanette Nolan, Jay Novello,
             James McCallion

◆   ❖   ◆

SHOW: THE JAMES CLAYTON MATTER
SHOW DATE: 12/5/1952
COMPANY: NEW YORK MUTUAL
AGENT: CHET GRAHAM
EXP. ACCT: $56.35

SYNOPSIS: Chet Graham, of New York Mutual calls. Chet has to go to California
for a week. Can you watch the office for me for a couple days? Chet will even
give Johnny his tickets to "Wish You Were Here" and his girlfriend. Chet will call
Johnny from California.

This account tells what is not in the papers. Johnny goes to Chet's New York
office and is visited by Miss Jane Stebbins, who is Dr. Clayton's nurse. Dr.
Clayton would like to talk to you in his office, as he is very busy Johnny is told.
Johnny is told that the Doctor is acting strangely and has cancelled all outside
calls. She cries and they go to the office of Dr. Clayton who meets Johnny with
a .32 Iver Johnson pistol. Jane goes to lunch and Dr. Clayton explains to Johnny
that his life has been threatened and that he cannot even load the gun. Dr.
Clayton can't go to the police, as it is a delicate matter. Dr. Clayton tells Johnny
that a patient, Florence Harmon, is suffering from a marriage to her erratic
husband Benjamin and Dr. Clayton had advised her to divorce him. Dr. Clayton
had talked to Mr. Harmon about the health of his wife, but he attacked him and
threatened his life. Dr. Clayton tells Johnny that if he talks to him, Mr. Harmon
might listen. Johnny tells Dr. Clayton to call the police and Dr. Clayton asks
Johnny to do it for Mrs. Harmon.

Johnny goes to see the Harmons and Benjamin opens the door with a gun.
Harmon slugs Johnny and leaves. Mrs. Harmon explains to Johnny about her
husband. She tells Johnny that he attacked her doctor and is mad and liable to do
anything. Johnny goes back to Dr. Clayton's office and Sgt. Tom Bassman is there.
Dr. Clayton and Nurse Stebbins are not there, and Johnny explains the situation.
Nurse Stebbins returns and finds a note from Dr. Clayton saying that he is on
an emergency call, but she does not recognize the address, which is in the
warehouse district. Johnny and Sgt. Bassman go to the address and find the
Clayton's car. A search of the area finds Dr. Clayton's body. The police question the
neighbors, and two people in the area heard the shots. Mr. Harmon had been seen
near a bar in the area and is suspected of luring the Dr. and killing him.

Later that night, Johnny bribes the night watchman to get into Dr. Clayton's
office. Johnny is told that the police had been there earlier and had found Dr.
Clayton's emergency kit. Johnny searches the files, and the patients went from
"Abbott to Zybowski." In the files Johnny learns that Mrs. Harmon was never a
patient, but Mr. Harmon was. Johnny goes to see Nurse Stebbins at her small
apartment and she is upset about the doctor. She tells Johnny that she had

worked for Dr. Clayton five years. "Who was he going to marry?" Johnny asks, "Because the honeymoon has already been planned." Johnny tells her that the doctor had made reservations on the Ile de France for April. She tells Johnny that she does not know anything about them. She tells Johnny that Mrs. Harmon was Dr. Clayton's friend; and they had met when Mr. Harmon was a patient who came in several times and then stopped but Dr. Clayton had been seeing Mrs. Harmon all this time. She tells Johnny that the police had told her about Mr. Harmon's threats. Johnny tells Nurse Stebbins that the wrong man was killed. Johnny goes back to see Mrs. Harmon and Johnny accuses her of using him as a witness for Dr. Clayton in killing her husband. She screams at Johnny that her husband did kill the doctor and throws him out.

Johnny calls Sgt. Bassman from his hotel and explains what he has learned. While Johnny is on the phone, Benjamin Harmon comes into his room with a gun and tells him to hang up. He tells Johnny that he had followed Johnny from his house and wants to know where his law office is. He tells Johnny that Dr. Clayton had called him and told him that a lawyer named Dollar was working on a divorce case for him. He tells Johnny that he did not kill Dr. Clayton. Harmon gets mad and goes for Johnny but Johnny overpowers him and discovers that the gun has not been fired. Harmon tells Johnny that he did not see Clayton and that he was out getting mad and drinking down by the docks. He had called Clayton from a bar and told him where to meet him, but Clayton never showed so he left and heard on the radio that he was wanted. He tells Johnny that Florence had others friends and it would have been too much for him to let her go. He tells Johnny that he is not well and only has a year to live. "They could have waited," he cries to Johnny. Johnny gives him a sleeping pill and confirms what Harmon told him. Johnny goes to Nurse Stebbin's apartment. She tells Johnny that she fell in love with the doctor and knew he was lying and that he was a manipulative man. She tells Johnny that she had followed the doctor and pleaded with him. There was a struggle and the gun went off. Johnny tells her she can prove self-defense, but she tells Johnny that she cannot get off, as she killed Mrs. Harmon an hour ago.

Johnny tells Chet that he did not see his girl, and did not see the musical; he just sat there for three days. Do not call me for a long, long time, if you call at all.

NOTES:

- CHET TELLS JOHNNY HE CAN USE TICKETS TO "WISH YOU WERE HERE" WHICH OPENED JUNE 25, 1952 AT THE IMPERIAL THEATRE (NEW YORK) AND RAN FOR 598 PERFORMANCES.
- MUSIC IS BY EDDIE DUNSTEDTER
- DAN CUBBERLY IS THE ANNOUNCER
- JOHN LUND'S CURRENT MOVIE IS "JUST ACROSS THE STREET."
- THE ILE DE FRANCE WAS A LUXURY OCEAN LINER—SOON TO BE REPLACED WITH TRANSATLANTIC JET TRAVEL. THE FRENCH LINER WAS KNOWN FOR LUXURY FIRST-CLASS SERVICE.

- THIS PROGRAM WAS ALSO DONE BY BOB BAILEY AS "THE SHEPHERD MATTER."

Producer:	Jaime del Valle	Writers:	E. Jack Neuman
Cast:	Virginia Gregg, Victor Perrin, Joseph Kearns, John McIntire, Jeanette Nolan		

◆ ❖ ◆

SHOW: THE ELLIOTT CHAMPION MATTER
SHOW DATE: 12/12/1952
COMPANY: GREAT EASTERN FIRE & CASUALTY
AGENT: DON VICKERS
EXP. ACCT: $516.54

SYNOPSIS: Don Vickers calls and asks Johnny to go to California with him. An office building has burned up and it looks like arson.

Johnny goes to New York to meet Don Vickers and they fly to Los Angeles, California. Don fills Johnny in on Elliott Champion, who is a self-made man who is very aggressive. Johnny is told that Ives has called and told Don that the building was burned, and that Champion is in financial trouble. Johnny is being brought in for protection, along with Vickers and Ives, against Champion who has never been beaten. In Los Angeles, Johnny and Don check into the Statler. The next morning they check in with Norman Ives who tells them that a man was seen loitering in the area of the building, and the description matches Elliott Champion. A newsboy told Norman that he saw a man go behind the building just before the fire started. Johnny is told that the fire was an amateur job and that the setter is not a firebug either. Someone moved five gallons of gasoline into the building that night. Johnny is told that Champion has not been told of these events. Johnny, Don and Norman go over the ruins that day and look at suspects that night.

The next morning Johnny goes to Champion's office where he meets Mildred Champion, who was beautiful but poorly dressed. Johnny asks to see Mr. Champion who yells at Mildred on the intercom. Mildred tells Johnny that he is nice today as Johnny goes in to see Mr. Champion, who knows why Johnny is there. Johnny tells him the fire was arson and Champion tells Johnny that Joseph Harrison is out of prison and that he had sworn he would get Champion for sending him to jail for five years for theft. Champion is certain that Harrison did it. Champion tells Johnny that he saw the story in the papers and that the claim will be paid after the facts are in. Johnny leaves and reviews the trial to substantiate the story. The witnesses identify Harrison and an APB is issued.

Johnny goes to see Mr. Engle, who was Harrison's attorney. Johnny tells Engle that he wants to find Harrison, who has been identified as the man who set the fire. Engle tells Johnny that Harrison was a nice kid but everything was against him. Champion could have let him off, but he poured it on. Johnny tells him that is looks like Harrison is trying to get even with Champion. Engle has not heard from Harrison, so Johnny leaves. Later that afternoon two more witnesses identify Harrison as the man. At 5:00 Mildred calls Johnny and tells him that she knows where Joe is and to meet her at her house in an hour. At 5:30 Champion's lawyer calls and tells Johnny that they will sue if the insurance company does not pay immediately. At 5:38 Norman Ives calls to say that Champion was shot ten minutes ago and is dead.

Johnny goes to the house and sees Champion, shot in the head with a .38, and the police are looking for Harrison. Vickers and Ives arrive and show Johnny proof that Mildred Champion had married Harrison a month before the trial. Now Mildred has disappeared. Johnny had a definite opinion of Mildred but it was wrong. Johnny goes to see Engle again and tells him of Champion's death. Engle tells Johnny that he knew that Mildred was married to Harrison. Johnny tells Engle that Champion was not too good at paying his taxes, but Engle can only tell Johnny that a wife cannot testify against her husband, but everyone else testified against Harrison. Engle feels that Champion was framing Harrison with embezzlement to cover the tax problems. Joe was a nice boy and Engle hopes no one ever finds him. But later that day Joe is found in the county hospital, in the morgue. Harrison had contracted tuberculosis in San Quentin and died of it in the hospital.

Don Vickers calls Johnny and tells him that a man had sold gasoline to a girl who looked like Mildred Champion. Johnny goes to Engle and tells him about Joe. Johnny asks Engle. "Did you help Champion frame Joe"; and Engle tells Johnny that he did not. There is knock at the door and it is Mildred. Johnny tells Engle to hide and shots are fired through the door. Johnny chases after her and shoots her in her car. Johnny gets to the car and she tells Johnny that she wanted to kill Engle, who had helped her uncle. She tells Johnny that she had talked to Joe in prison and thought that Engle had helped to frame him. She had waited five years, only to have Joe die. She tells Johnny that she is not pretty and that no one looked twice at her, but Joe cared and she is dead inside.

Johnny expenses $85.00 that he pampered himself with to help forget Mildred talking about her lover.

NOTES:

- MUSIC BY EDDIE DUNSTEDTER.
- DAN CUBBERLY IS THE ANNOUNCER
- THERE IS A PUBLIC SERVICE ANNOUNCEMENT ABOUT TRAVELERS AID AT THE END OF THE PROGRAM.
- THIS PROGRAM WAS ALSO DONE BY BOB BAILEY AS "THE BENNET MATTER"

Producer: Jaime del Valle   Writers: E. Jack Neuman
Cast: Eddie Marr, Joe Du Val, Joyce McCluskey, Francis X. Bushman, Herb Butterfield

SHOW: THE NEW CAMBRIDGE MATTER
SHOW DATE: 12/19/1952
COMPANY: NEW ENGLAND MUTUAL TRUST & CASUALTY
AGENT: DAVE TAYLOR
EXP. ACCT: $125.00
SYNOPSIS: This is the same story as The Plantagent Matter, and takes place in New Cambridge, Massachusetts. The names change but the plot is the same.

NOTES:
- THE ANNOUNCER IS DAN CUBBERLY
- MUSIC IS BY EDDIE DUNSTEDTER
- THIS IS THE FIRST INSTANCE WHERE A FUTURE JOHNNY DOLLAR PLAYS A ROLE WITH THE CURRENT JOHNNY DOLLAR
- STORY INFORMATION OBTAINED FROM THE KNX COLLECTION IN THE THOUSAND OAKS LIBRARY

Producer: Jaime del Valle   **Writers**   E. Jack Neuman
Cast: Edgar Barrier, Joyce Manners, Robert Bailey, Bill Bouchey, Jeanne Bates

SHOW: THE WALTER PATTERSON MATTER
SHOW DATE: 12/26/1952
COMPANY: DELAWARE MUTUAL LIFE INSURANCE COMPANY
AGENT: MR. ELGIN
EXP. ACCT: $610.13
SYNOPSIS: Mr. Elgin calls and asks Johnny to look into a claim. The case involves Mr. Patterson, who died in 1947, but a friend says he is still alive.

Johnny goes to Wilmington, Delaware and the office of Mr. Elgin. Johnny is told that many people see someone who is dead, but they turn out to be mis-identifications. Two weeks ago, Mrs. Virginia Collier stopped in Tucson and saw Walter Patterson in a Hotel bar and spoke to him. He told Mrs. Collier that his name was Yoler and that he was born in Tucson. Mr. Elgin has contacted the Tucson police who have reported that Yoler had not bought property there until 1947. Mrs. Collier remembered Patterson's limp and Yoler has one too. Patterson went to Amherst but Yoler said he went to Notre Dame, but that did not check out. Johnny gets copies of the paperwork on the policies. Johnny is told that that Patterson was killed in a rented plane in April of 1947 and that his body was never found. Patterson was declared dead and the claim check was issued then. Gloria Ann Patterson is the beneficiary. Mr. Brennan, the family lawyer, got copies of fingerprints and personal papers. Johnny is told that Mrs. Patterson put the money in the bank, and does not know about the sighting.

Johnny spends the day getting more information at the airport and Lt. James Creightson of the Coast Guard, who had conducted the search. Johnny learns that an unreported rescue is possible, but not likely. Johnny goes to Tucson, Arizona sure that he will only find a lot of desert sunshine. Johnny gets a motel room and looks up Sgt. Tyler at the police department. Johnny fills Sgt. Tyler in as to why he is there. Johnny is told that no one knew Yoler until five years ago and that Yoler does not work, but always has money. Johnny is told that Will Yoler does not seem to be hiding from anyone. Johnny visits Yoler and tells him that he is running down the Collier conversation, but Yoler does not remember it. Johnny shows Yoler a picture of Patterson, and he admits that there is some resemblance. Yoler tells Johnny that he was not in the Army and he said that he did not go to Notre Dame and that he told the woman anything to get rid of her. Yoler tells Johnny that he went to Tulane and starts getting nervous. He tells Johnny that he has lived in several cities and was married once in 1944, but Johnny notes that he seemed uncomfortable. Yoler offers to get a birth certificate and other papers for Johnny that afternoon. Johnny asks for a set of fingerprints to prove Yoler is not Walter Patterson and he agrees to give Johnny the prints.

The fingerprints do not match those given to Johnny, so Johnny makes reservations to return home. Yoler calls Johnny and wants to talk and Johnny arranges to meet him at the Arizona Inn. Yoler does not show so Johnny cabs to the house. The front door is open and Johnny calls the police. Johnny tells Sgt. Tyler that Yoler is dead, and that he had been beaten.

The police come and examine the house, which showed signs of a violent struggle. Sgt. Tyler asks Johnny to stick around so that Johnny can help him find a killer, as someone heard or saw something. Three witnesses are found, and one, Mrs. Lucas, tells Johnny that she took a walk that evening and went past Yoler's house and saw him talking to a man who was larger than Yoler with a tweed topcoat, his hat in his hand and red hair. He was there also when she came back. An APB is issued and the cabs companies checked. One cab recorded a man who came in on a plane from the east and used the name Roger Bales. Johnny calls Mr. Elgin and reports in and as he is talking Sgt. Tyler comes in with a wire. Johnny tells him that the war department has come back with a set of fingerprints that match. Mr. Elgin wants to call Brennan, who had supplied the prints, but Johnny tells him not to call Brennan, as he will handle it.

Johnny returns to Wilmington and goes to see Brennan and is met by Mrs. Patterson who tells Johnny that Mr. Brennan is sick. Mrs. Patterson goes upstairs to get Brennan and then starts to leave. When Johnny explains to Brennan why he is there, Brennan tells her to stay. Brennan tells Johnny and Gloria that he had gone to see Walter and had been in a fight with him. Brennan tells Johnny that he will tell this once, and the story will be different in court. Brennan tells them that Walt did not die in the crash but was picked up by a fishing boat and taken to Charleston, South Carolina. Walt had called and had the idea to disappear. Walt hated Gloria, and wanted a divorce. Walt had told Brennan that he could have Gloria for a price: $25,000 a year, which Brennan could afford. Walt just wanted to be away from everything. Johnny tells Gloria that Walt is dead now, really dead. Brennan tells Gloria that he had fought with Walt and killed him. Brennan claims that Walt was going to tell the truth and claim amnesia. It took Gloria five years to decide to marry Brennan and one lousy afternoon for Walter to come back.

It will be up to the courts to prove if Brennan killed Walter Patterson. Johnny is sure Mrs. Patterson is innocent.

NOTES:
- THE MID-PROGRAM COMMERCIAL IS FOR THE PROGRAM "THEATER OF TODAY" ON SATURDAY AFTERNOONS
- MUSIC BY EDDIE DUNSTEDTER
- DAN CUBBERLY IS THE ANNOUNCER
- THIS PROGRAM WAS DONE BY BOB BAILEY AS "THE CHESAPEAKE FRAUD MATTER"
- CAST INFORMATION IS FROM THE KNX SCRIPT COLLECTION AT THE THOUSAND OAKS LIBRARY.

Producer: Jaime del Valle   Writers: E. Jack Neuman
Cast: Fred MacKaye, Herb Butterfield, Stacy Harris, Virginia Gregg, Jeanette Nolan, John McIntire

◆ ❖ ◆

SHOW: THE BALTIMORE MATTER
SHOW DATE: 1/2/1953
COMPANY: ALL STATES INSURANCE COMPANY
AGENT: DON FREED
EXP. ACCT: $294.60
SYNOPSIS: Orin Vance calls and reminds Johnny that he had sent Orin to Ossining seven years ago for the Zeeman Case. Orin wants to do Johnny a favor, and maybe they can work out something. Orin asks Johnny to help him and make some honest money.

A call to Sing Sing Prison tells Johnny that Orin has been released as a model prisoner. Orin arrives at Johnny's apartment, and Orin asks not to be treated like a con. He tells Johnny that his wife would not let him in the house and told him to get a job or she'll divorce him, so he needs a stake to start a business. Orin asks if Johnny remembers the Towner Loan case in Baltimore, the million-dollar theft that was never solved. Orin can help Johnny solve it for half the reward. Orin tells Johnny that he knows two of the six men who did it and gives Johnny one of the stolen bills. Johnny calls Don Freed, who verifies the serial number. Johnny explains the circumstances, learns that there is a $10,000 reward and gets approval from Don to work on the case. Orin tells Johnny that he got the bill from Leonard Torpe in New York. Orin had met Torpe in New York yesterday and Torpe had showed him a stack of money he could not spend. Orin notes that

Torpe was pretty drunk at the time. Orin had looked up the robbery and Torpe fits the description of one of the men. The other man is Harold King who lives in Reno. Orin leaves and will call Johnny in two days.

Johnny follows Orin to the main business section where he buys a ticket to New York. Johnny calls Pete Florian, a detective friend, and asks him to tag along to make sure no one tries to kill Vance. Johnny takes a plane to New York and meets police Lt. Randall. Johnny asks Lt. Randall for a search warrant of Torpe's apartment. Johnny looks at the mug shots that show Torpe has a long record, and Lt. Randall wires Reno to ask them to hold on to Harold King. Johnny and Lt. Randall go to the apartment but they learn that Torpe had moved out the previous morning.

Johnny goes to his hotel and gets a call from Pete who tells Johnny that Vance is in a place at 680 155th street. Johnny cabs to meet Pete and learns that Vance has had visitors, and one of them is Torpe. Johnny and Pete go into the building and knock on the door. Johnny asks for Orrin Vance and Torpe opens the door and tells Johnny that there is no Vance there. Johnny forces the door open and shots are fired and Johnny hears the voice of a man dying.

Johnny is shot twice and is operated on at the police emergency hospital for two .38 gunshot wounds, one in the neck and one in the shoulder. Lt. Randall visits at the hospital two days later and tells Johnny that Pete was killed. Johnny explains how he had hired Pete and about Vance being the tipster. Lt. Randall tells Johnny that Pete had been shot four times but killed Torpe; Vance is in the hospital and the other man got away. Johnny tells Lt. Randall that he was trying to push into the room and everything got fuzzy. Johnny is told that the other man had stolen a car that was found with no prints. Later Vance is able to speak and tells Johnny that the other man was Harold King who wanted to know what Vance had done with the $10 Torpe gave him. Vance tells Johnny that he has reward money coming, so he is not going to die. Two days later Johnny goes to his hotel by ambulance and gets a phone call from a woman who asks if he is interested in finding Harold King. The caller is Melva King. She tells Johnny to meet her at Schraft's Restaurant on 42nd and Broadway, and that she will know Johnny by his pictures in the newspapers.

Johnny goes to the restaurant and meets Melva. She asks about the reward for the Baltimore job and is told she will only get half is she turns in Harry. She tells Johnny that Harry was in on the robbery but she was not involved. She wants a letter from the Insurance Company promising legal assistance if she gets in trouble. She tells Johnny that Harry has $45,000 that he cannot spend as all they got out of the robbery was marked bills. Johnny tells her he will call the insurance company and she agrees to call him in an hour.

Melva leaves and gets into a cab. Johnny follows and Lt. Randall picks him up and they follow her. Lt. Randall surmises that she is offering Harold to Johnny for the reward. Lt. Randall tells Johnny that he had a man following Johnny and that Melva King was from a rich family in Minnesota and got disinherited. Johnny and Lt. Randall follow the cab to a train station in Bucks County and

Melva makes a call but not to Johnny. Lt. Randall thinks that she is working both sides to see who will pay the most. Lt. Randall shows Johnny her file that has 16 arrests. A green caddy pulls up and Melva talks to the men for a while. Lt. Randall orders a pickup and they follow Melva to a motor court. Melva comes out of the room with Harold King, who is wounded. Harold threatens to kill everyone and Johnny and Lt. Randall try to reason with him. Harold tells them that she had been bargaining with both sides while he was unconscious. Harry shoots Melva and Lt. Randall shoots Harold.

Remarks: The men Melva had contacted were part of the six robbers and were arrested and told all. Johnny thinks that Vance deserves half of the reward. He thinks Pete Florian's widow deserves the other half.

NOTES:
- THE MID-PROGRAM COMMERCIAL IS FOR US DEFENSE BONDS AND THE PAYROLL SAVINGS PLAN
- JOHNNY IS SHOT FOR THE 3RD TIME
- DAN CUBBERLY IS THE ANNOUNCER
- MUSIC IS BY EDDIE DUNSTEDTER
- CAST INFORMATION IS FROM RADIOGOLDINDEX

Producer: Jaime del Valle   Writers: E. Jack Neuman
Cast: Tony Barrett, Joseph Du Val, Clayton Post, John McIntire,
             Jeanette Nolan

◆ ❖ ◆

SHOW: THE THELMA IBSEN MATTER
SHOW DATE: 1/9/1953
COMPANY: EASTERN LIFE & TRUST COMPANY
AGENT: MILTON DEFRANCO
EXP. ACCT: $84.15

SYNOPSIS: Milton DeFranco calls about a policy with a beneficiary they can't find. She is missing.

Johnny goes to Milton's office by bus. Milton tells Johnny that the deceased was John Linden who sold newspapers in front of the Metropolitan building. He had purchased two policies in 1940, and the beneficiary is Thelma Ibsen, who was 10 at the time. He bought them because he wanted to do something nice for a little girl. Johnny is told that Thelma Ibsen must be 23-24 now, and that Linden only saw her that one day. Johnny goes to her local address at 113 Brainbridge in Hartford, Connecticut, but she had moved and had lived with an aunt after her parents died in an auto accident. Johnny visits a former work site and learns that Thelma just left one day and never came back. Johnny is told that maybe she went to New York and that Thelma was nice but she had plans of her own. She only talked of meeting someone nice and getting married. Johnny visits the apartment hotel where Thelma had lived, and she had checked out in

December of 1950. Johnny finds a picture in her high school yearbook and a driver's license went into Johnny's file. Two days later, the coworkers are re-questioned and one remembers Floyd Turnbull in New York. Johnny travels to New York City and searches the phone books for Floyd Turnbull. The right one was #5 on the list. He tells Johnny that he had met Thelma in an office and that she had come to New York with him to be married. On December 24, 1950 she walked out of his car at a gas station, and he has heard nothing since. Floyd tells Johnny that Thelma was kind, sweet and gentle and that he had only known her for three weeks. Floyd thinks Thelma was frightened of life and that he offered her the happiness she longed for but she was immature. Floyd tells Johnny that he has not tried to find her. She walked away from the car of her own free will with $2,300 taken from his wallet. "She had to steal it like a common thief" Floyd tells Johnny. Johnny leaves and notes that Floyd was the second elderly man in her life.

Johnny rents a car and checks out Floyd's story. At the gas station Earl Camden remembers Thelma leaving the car and the man waiting for her. Johnny talks to Floyd's sister Edna, who also corroborates the story and tells Johnny that Thelma had left all her clothes there. In New York, the police have a record of her being arrested for disturbing the peace, so Johnny goes there and learns that Thelma had moved. The landlady was talkative and told Johnny that Thelma always had parties and had men visiting her. Johnny goes back to City Hall and looks up the arrest record, and gets the names of the others Thelma was arrested with. Johnny talks to a man named Unger, who gives Johnny an address, so Johnny goes to there. The manager of the building rings her room but no one answers, but he knows she is in. Johnny goes to the apartment in the 15th floor and the door is open. Johnny enters and finds Thelma standing on the window ledge, ready to jump.

Johnny goes in and Thelma tells Johnny that she is going to jump but asks Johnny how he knows her name. Johnny tells her that he knows her, but Thelma does not believe him. Johnny tells her of the picture in the school annual. The manager comes to the apartment and is shocked, so Johnny whispers for him to call the police. She knows that police will try to stop her but they won't, she will jump anyway. She sees a crowd and knows they want her to jump because no one wants to help her. Johnny mentions that Floyd cared for her, but she tells Johnny that she is no good to anyone. She tells Johnny to tell Floyd that she meant to send the money back. Footsteps are heard in the hallway and Thelma shouts hysterically to close the door. She tells Johnny that for the first time she knows exactly what to do and how to do it and that she should have died with her parents. Johnny tells her about the man who bought the policies and how he cared for her. She remembers him and talking about growing up, and that he had told her that she would be a lovely woman. Johnny tells her that he left her $1,000 and shows her the papers. Thelma starts to cry about the "poor old man."

Johnny expenses $3.50 for martinis. This was Johnny's first and hopefully last experience with an intended suicide, but the doctors say she will recover in time.

NOTES:

- THIS PROGRAM WAS ALSO DONE BY BOB BAILEY AS "THE BRODERICK MATTER"
- THE ANNOUNCER IS DAN CUBBERLY
- MUSIC IS BY EDDIE DUNSTEDTER
- JOHN LUND'S CURRENT MOVIE IS "JUST ACROSS THE STREET"

Producer: Jaime del Valle   Writers: E. Jack Neuman
Cast: Tom Tully, Jeanette Nolan, John McIntire, Joe Kearns,
           Virginia Gregg

◆   ❖   ◆

SHOW: THE STARLET MATTER
SHOW DATE: 1/16/1953
COMPANY: TWIN STATE INSURANCE COMPANY
AGENT: KEN RALSTON
EXP. ACCT: $366.05

SYNOPSIS: Ken Ralston calls Johnny from Kansas City, Missouri. Johnny is told that Phil Gardner is an agent in Hollywood who needs help. Gardner is "up to here" in starlets and one of his starlets is insured for $50,000 but her life has been threatened. Johnny asks about the commission, and is told it is fat. Johnny loves Hollywood.

Johnny goes to Hollywood, California out of LaGuardia on flight 601. At the Sunset Ruxton Hotel Johnny flirts with an old friend, Judy the telephone operator. Johnny goes to see Phil Gardner and is directed to the Chez Scotty restaurant across the street. Phil shows Johnny a picture of Toby Drake who Phil says will be a star. Phil tells Johnny that someone wants to murder Toby, and Phil does not want that kind of publicity. A phone is brought to the table and Phil learns that Toby is dead. Phil tells Johnny that her boyfriend called so he would be the first to know. Toby drives Johnny in his jaguar, with the top down, to Toby's apartment. On the couch is her body with a silk stocking around her neck and Det. Cosca, who asks Johnny and Phil about how they found out. Phil recounts the story to Det. Cosca and Phil tells Johnny to find out who did it. "Well, well a little bulge there," says Cosca as he notices Johnny's gun. In the bedroom is the boyfriend Roy Fulton, crying about Toby. Johnny talks to Roy and he tells Johnny that he had come to pick up Toby for a date, found the body and called the agent and the police. Roy tells Johnny that she should have been more careful as she was too beautiful.

Johnny goes to his hotel and Judy tells Johnny that he has a message: "First Toby, then Stella Martin, you can't stop it Dollar." Judy tells Johnny that a man had called, left the message and hung up. Johnny calls Phil, but there is no answer so Judy tells Johnny to call Hollywood Casting. Johnny goes there and gets an address for Stella Martin in Westchester. Johnny goes to Stella's address and a man opens the door. Johnny forces his way in and the man slugs Johnny and knocks him out. Johnny wakes up to find Stella in the bathroom with a silk negligee and a black silk stocking around her neck.

Johnny recognizes Stella from a few B grade movies. Det. Cosca knocks on the door and Johnny tells him what happened. Det. Cosca tells Johnny the police got a phone call about the girl. Johnny tells Det. Cosca about the message and the man, who was about seven feet tall. Det. Cosca finds a note in Stella's hand: "There will be another one tomorrow Dollar." Det. Cosca gets angry with Johnny and throws him out of the house.

The next day Phil calls Johnny and he is accusative of Johnny's lack of protection so Johnny roughs him up a little to get information from Phil about a possible cover-up. Phil tells Johnny that Stella was just a pickup from a Dorcas' drive-in restaurant three months ago. Johnny goes to the drive-in and talks to the manager Mel Dorcas. Johnny talks to Mel who remembers Toby and Stella. When Johnny mentions there might be a third murder, Mel mentions Peggy Brian who was a close friend of theirs, and came to work with them in Toby's car. Mel gives Johnny the address in North Hollywood.

Johnny visits Peggy, who comes to the door hysterical and tells Johnny to go away. She wants to kill Johnny before he can kill her. Johnny takes her gun away and calms her down and tells her that he is there to help. She tells Johnny about a woman who was killed in an auto accident. Toby, Stella and Peggy had been on a trip to Oregon three years ago, and had an accident in which a woman hit them and died. The police said it was not their fault and let them go. Johnny decides to take Peggy out shopping and to Ocean Park to take her mind off of the matter. Johnny calls the Hotel, Roy Fulton and Phil Gardner to let them know of his plans. Johnny takes Peggy shopping and buys her a new dress. Then they go to the amusement park where Peggy figures out what Johnny is doing. In the Fun House, Peggy is having a good time until she sees a tall man. Johnny sends Peggy into a spinning barrel and the man attacks Johnny. Johnny drags him out and he tells Johnny he followed him to be able to get at the killer. The man tells Johnny that Stella was dead when he got there. Peggy screams and there is a man in the mirror. It is Roy Fulton with a gun. Roy shoots at them and Johnny hits him. Roy walks towards Johnny and then collapses. Roy tells Johnny that they killed his wife and then dies.

Johnny tells Ken Ralston to pay Phil Gardner face value of the policy. At least he kept one of the three girls alive, which is luckier than you usually get in Hollywood.

NOTES:
- DAN CUBBERLY IS THE ANNOUNCER
- MUSIC IS BY EDDIE DUNSTEDTER
- JOHN LUND'S CURRENT MOVIE IS "JUST ACROSS THE STREET"
- ACCORDING TO THE SCRIPT, THE WRITERS FOR THIS EPISODE ARE FARGO EPSTEIN AND DAPHNE FENSTER

Producer: Jaime del Valle **Writers:** Morton Fine, David Friedkin

Cast: **Raymond Burr, Dick Ryan, John McIntire, Sidney Miller, Victor Perrin, Virginia Gregg, Jeanette Nolan**

◆   ❖   ◆

SHOW: THE MARIGOLD MATTER
SHOW DATE: 1/23/1953
COMPANY: MARIGOLD POLICE DEPARTMENT
AGENT: WALT YOUNGER
EXP. ACCT: $4.00

SYNOPSIS: Johnny receives a call from Lt. Walt Younger of the Marigold police. Walt tells Johnny that Joe Hickey was killed last night. Can you come up?

Johnny takes a bus to Marigold, Connecticut and meets Walt and Sgt. Cherry. Walt tells Johnny that Joe was found murdered. Johnny tells Walt that Joe did some work for him in Hartford years ago. Walt gives Johnny a letter addressed to him that was found on Joe's body. Johnny reads the letter, which refers to some strange things happening. Johnny tells Walt that he has not heard from Joe for two years. Walt offers to let Johnny get involved to assist them. Johnny and Walt go to the site of the murder where the car was found by the side of the road, with no footprints in the snow. Walt tells Johnny that there was no sign of robbery so maybe it was revenge for a loan or something. Walt tells Johnny that Joe was shot at close range, so he must have trusted who ever did it. Johnny is told that Joes' wife was the last person to see him.

Johnny visits Joe's wife Pat, who thanks Johnny for coming. She tells Johnny that they were having problems and that she was thinking about divorce. She tells Johnny that she was home alone at the time of the shooting and that she did not do it.

Johnny goes to Joe's office and talks to Vivian Asher, who worked for Joe. She tells Johnny that he would find Joe's enemies and that she liked Joe, but there was no romance. She tells Johnny that she did not kill him, and has witnesses. She agrees to go through the files to look for possible enemies. Later Johnny gets the list, which has thirty-five names and addresses. Walt and Johnny interview the people on the list, and they all seemed to hate Joe for pressing them for loan payments, but not enough to kill him. At the Shamrock Bar and Grill, Johnny meets Jim Teal who knew Joe and calls him a bum. He tells Johnny that Joe was a lousy shark who tried to get money from him for a loan Jim paid off months ago. He tells Johnny that Joe came back later to say it was a mistake, but loan companies don't make mistakes. Johnny wonders about the bookkeeping error.

Johnny visits Vivian who tells him that Teal was not on the list, as the list was not complete. Vivian tells Johnny that she had made a mistake and told Joe about it. Johnny asks to see the files, but Vivian tells Johnny to get a search warrant to see the files.

Johnny goes to see Walt about the warrant, but Walt is out. Johnny asks Sgt. Cherry to get him a search warrant but he tells Johnny that it will take a day or so. Johnny also gives Sgt. Cherry an ashtray with fingerprints that he wants checked, as Johnny thinks she might have a background. Walt comes in and they go back to the murder site as Walt thinks someone made a mistake, as the body fell in the wrong place. As they look at the site, five shots ring out and Johnny and Walt drop to the snow. Johnny senses that they have already talked to the killer of Joe Hickey.

The shots came from the road and Johnny hears a car drive away and notices that Walt has been shot twice. Johnny uses his tie to stop the flow of blood in Walt's leg. "At least Exhibit "A" is in his leg" Walt tells Johnny. Johnny takes Walt to the hospital in Hartford and then drives to Joe's office. In Vivian's desk Johnny finds the reason for her not wanting him to look around. Johnny visits Vivian and tells her that he is doing things his way. Johnny shows her $8,000 in delinquent loans recommended by her. She tells Johnny that she got scared and hid them. She tells Johnny that Joe had let her write loans and she made some mistakes. Johnny leaves and watches outside as she makes a phone call. Johnny watches the house for a while, but nothing happens.

The next day, Johnny interviews some of the names on the list of bad loans, and they all have receipts for the payments. At the police office, Sgt Cherry has a report on Vivian from Kansas City. It outlines six arrests and a conviction for both car theft and shoplifting, and she is still wanted in Denver for grand larceny. Sgt. Cherry tells Johnny that she is well liked in town but Johnny mentions the bad loans and the payments she pocketed. Sgt. Cherry thinks that she must have shot Joe when he found out. Johnny and Sgt. Cherry go to arrest Vivian. Sgt. Cherry tells Johnny that he will take no chances as they knock on the door. Vivian opens the door and screams "Cherry" as Sgt. Cherry tries to shoot her. Johnny slugs Cherry and Vivian tells Johnny that Cherry was a policeman in Denver and was blackmailing her to keep from being sent back. She tells Johnny that Cherry had shot Joe when he found out. Vivian tells Johnny that she only wanted to live there and be left alone as Johnny takes her to the police.

Cherry had been a policeman in Denver but was discharged for "conduct unbecoming an officer." The bullets came from his service revolver. Cherry was booked for murder with Vivian as an accomplice.

NOTES:

- THERE IS A **CBS** COMMERCIAL AT THE END FOR **GANGBUSTERS** AND A **CBS** SPOT WHICH SAYS: "AMERICA NOW LISTENS TO **105** MILLION RADIO SETS AND LISTENS MOST TO THE **CBS** RADIO NETWORK"
- DAN CUBBERLY IS THE ANNOUNCER
- MUSIC IS BY EDDIE DUNSTEDTER
- JOHN LUND'S CURRENT MOVIE IS "JUST ACROSS THE STREET"

Producer: Jaime del Valle   **Writers:**   E. Jack Neuman
Cast: Parley Baer, Howard Culver, Vivi Janis, Virginia Gregg, James Nusser

◆ ❖ ◆

SHOW:	**THE KAY BELLAMY MATTER**
SHOW DATE:	**1/30/1953**
COMPANY:	**HEMISPHERIC INSURANCE COMPANY**
AGENT:	**BERT WELCH**
EXP. ACCT:	**$135.40**

SYNOPSIS: Bert Welch calls about going to Broadway to see Lou Waltham. Lou has an insurance application for Kay Bellamy for a two million-dollar policy, but the application does not check out.

Johnny goes to New York City and then to Lou Waltham's soundproof office. Lou tells Johnny that Kay Bellamy is a valuable hunk of talent and that she needs coverage. Johnny tells Lou that he needs more information for the application, so Lou tells Johnny that Kay was a stripper two years ago and now she is making $2,000 a week on radio, but she will not let her picture be taken, not even for movies. Lou tells Johnny that Kay disappears between radio programs and works in burlesque as "Dawn Laviya." Maybe you can talk to her. She is in Boston now.

Johnny flies to Boston, Massachusetts and finds her theater. Johnny goes backstage and sees Dawn dancing with the chorus. Dawn walks backstage and Johnny calls her Kay Bellamy. She tells Johnny that that is not her name. She walks away and a man named Crowel tells Johnny to leave. Crowel knows who Johnny is and why he is there and tells Johnny to tell Lou that Dawn does not need insurance. Crowel promises a personal hunting license from the boss if Johnny comes back. Johnny now realizes that Kay is taking orders from someone.

At a nearby café Johnny sits next to Laureen, a dancer. She tells Johnny that Lutzy Lazario, the dance manager is always giving her a hard time. Just as she starts to tell Johnny about Kay's boyfriend, her ride comes and she leaves. Johnny goes to sit with Lutzy and a dancer named Valerie and tells them that he is scouting for Lou Waltham for dancers for a Broadway play. Suddenly they are interested. Valerie tells Johnny that Dawn can get a lot of money just by marrying her boyfriend, Martin Bayard Cullen III, who is big money. Johnny recognizes the name as connections with a capitol "C." Johnny gets a hotel room and that night he watches the Dawn Laviya show as she takes off all the law would allow. At noon Johnny is awakened by a knock at his door. It is Kay Bellamy. She tells Johnny that she started out in Burlesque and likes it. She tells Johnny that Lou cannot insure her unless she wants him to. As they are talking, the phone rings and Burt Welch tells Johnny that Lou is dead. He has been shot to death.

Johnny returns to New York and goes to Lou's office where Charlie Dyer and the police lab boys are at work. Johnny asks Charlie to let him look through a file drawer for the file on Kay Bellamy. Charlie opens the drawer and Johnny looks at her file and her contract was a dilly, as it allows nothing that would allow people to see her face. The photo file shows her always wearing a hat or veil. Johnny finds one picture that was taken in Mexico, and on her hand was a wedding ring. Back to Boston!

Johnny meets Valerie on the plane and she tells Johnny that she came to meet with Lou Waltham but did not see him. She knows nothing about the murder and won't tell Johnny which plane she took this morning to come to New York. Johnny goes to see Martin Cullen and asks him about Dawn. Johnny tells him that she is involved in a murder and he tells Johnny that Kay has been working him for favor. Martin admits to Johnny that her uncle, Fred, is in the penitentiary and she wanted him to be moved east for the family. Johnny tells Martin that her real name is Kay Bellamy and that Fred is probably her husband. Johnny tells martin that Fred Bellamy was involved in a robbery where a woman drove the getaway car. Martin tells Johnny that she does not like public places and that he must have been taken in. When Martin tells Johnny that Fred is on a train coming east, Johnny tells him to call Washington, as he thinks someone will try to spring Fred. Lou must have found out the same things, muses Johnny. On the way out, Crowel meets Johnny who is ushered into a car and is told to drive. Johnny tells Crowel that he guesses the rest of the gang is going to meet Fred. Johnny drives really fast and tries to run into a truck but Crowel panics and jumps out of the car right into the truck. Johnny drives back to Kay's theater and asks her if she is tired of running. She tells Johnny that she knows Fred is not going to be snatched as Martin had called her. She tells Johnny that she is glad it is over. She tells Johnny that Fred had her watched to keep her in line. Johnny is going to call the police but she tells Johnny that she has already called them. Johnny goes to see Lutzy and asks for Valerie. He tells Johnny that Valerie is in with the manager, Mr. Crowel. Johnny surprises Valerie and he tells her that she has lost a boyfriend. Johnny tells her that she and Crowel had trailed Johnny to New York and had killed Waltham. She tells Johnny that she only went with Crowel, and had heard them arguing and then heard a shot in the office. Johnny accuses her of lying, as the office is sound proof. Valerie pulls a gun and Johnny takes it from her and calls the police.

Lou was never insured and the Kay Bellamy policy was never issued. They do not need to worry about the "missed appearances" clause of her current contract, as she will be missing them for about ten years. The only loss is Johnny's expense account. Johnny notes that he did not expense the pas to the Burlesque Review provided by Lou Waltham, nor the transportation back from Mr. Cullens' as that was provided by Mr. Crowel.

NOTES:
- THE ANNOUNCER IS DAN CUBBERLY
- MUSIC IS BY EDDIE DUNSTEDTER
- JOHN LUND'S CURRENT MOVIE IS "JUST ACROSS THE STREET"

Producer: Jaime del Valle   **Writers:** Joel Murcot
Cast: Raymond Burr, Gloria Blondell, Sandra Gould, Benny Rubin, Jay Novello, Jeanne Bates, Hy Averback

SHOW:	**THE CHICAGO FRAUD MATTER**
SHOW DATE:	**2/6/1953**
COMPANY:	**COLUMBIA ACCIDENT & LIFE INSURANCE COMPANY**
AGENT:	**NILES HARTLEY**
EXP. ACCT:	**$219.77**

SYNOPSIS: Niles Hartley calls Johnny about a broker who wrote a $50,000 policy on Mr. Lane. Mr. Lane has died; he starved to death. Get on an airplane.

Johnny flies to Chicago, Illinois and checks in with Niles, who tells Johnny that a letter has been sent to the Insurance Commission advising them that payment is going to be held up. The sister of Mr. Lane, Lydia Staley has also called about payment on the policy. Niles tells Johnny that she has some trust funds for income, but is upset. Johnny is told that Lane died on the street and was going to be buried by the city until he was identified. A routine post-mortem had been done, and when Niles had checked out the body, it has all sorts of physical problems. Johnny wonders how Lane could have passed the insurance physical done by Dr. Unger. Johnny goes to see Dr. Unger and tells him that he wants information on Christopher Lane. Johnny examines the files and asks Dr. Unger if he signed the letter and if the notes in the file are his. Johnny tells Dr. Unger that he had pronounced Lane physically sound, but he died two days ago. Dr. Unger tells Johnny that if Lane had no heart problem he could have developed one. Johnny tells Unger that Lane died of malnutrition, and Unger cannot explain it, nor can he explain the old heart lesions. Johnny looks at the file copies and asks Dr. Unger to go to the morgue. Dr Unger and Johnny go to the morgue but Dr. Unger does not recognize Lane. Johnny has all of Dr. Unger's employees do the same, and no one recognizes Lane.

Johnny talks to the employees in Lane's apartment, and the elevator operator recognizes the body. She tells Johnny that she had seen him stoned a hundred times and that he was crazy. She tells Johnny that Lane got up at 10:00 AM and went out to get groceries and booze. The janitor, the maid, the doorman and the main desk clerk confirm that Lane had at least 18 months of heavy drinking. Johnny goes to see the sister Lydia, who is foul-tempered and wants to be paid. Johnny tells her that the investigation is for her benefit as well. She tells Johnny that she had not seen Chris for a year and was on good terms with Chris. She tells Johnny that she is widowed and has no children. Her attorney's has told her to sue immediately. Johnny tells her to tell her lawyers that by dying on a public street, the insurance company has learned that he could not have passed the exam. Johnny tells her that Christopher did not take the exam. They are going to find out what happened, but based on the facts, so sue us.

Johnny arranges for Lydia to be watched and goes to visit Mr. Rutherford, the agent who wrote the policy. Rutherford is surprised to hear from Johnny, who confirms that he has checked on Rutherford's 17-year record. Rutherford tells Johnny that he had been looking for a home in Willmette and Lane was the agent. Lane was in the real estate business and had a comfortable income from a trust and did not really work too hard. Lane had bought the policy from Rutherford some time later. Rutherford tells Johnny that Lane was just a client who looked fine. Rutherford tells Johnny that he knows Dr. Unger slightly and had used him professionally. Johnny tells Rutherford that Lane died from malnutrition due to alcoholism. Johnny calls Niles and learns that Lydia is fighting back and that the body has been cremated. Johnny tells Rutherford that he is in trouble, as he would have to have known about the drinking problem if he really had known Lane, and that he is the logical party for collusion. Rutherford slugs Johnny and runs out. Johnny calls Niles and then heads for Lydia's.

Johnny heads for Lydia's place and tells her about Rutherford. Johnny tells her that Rutherford had realized he has just ruined his whole life, but she tells Johnny that she does not know anyone by that name. Johnny questions her about the physical and she is adamant that her brother took the physical.

Niles has a warrant issued for Rutherford, and two days later Rutherford is still missing. Rutherford finally calls Johnny who tells Rutherford that only Johnny and Niles know about the case. Johnny tells Rutherford that if he makes a statement Johnny might be able to get him off. Johnny arranges to meet Rutherford in 15 minutes. Johnny meets Rutherford and Rutherford is pale and shaken. Johnny buys coffee and donuts and Rutherford tells Johnny that he met Lydia Staley right after his wife had died. He was interested in her and asked her to marry him, but she just laughed at him; he was not exciting to her. She told Rutherford that she wanted money and needed $50,000 in cash. Lydia told him about her brother, so Rutherford paid a man to take the physical. Rutherford wanted to cancel the policy, but she was holding the fraud over his head. Johnny tells him to make a statement and the charges will be dropped. Rutherford makes the statement and Johnny arranges for the chares to be dropped and Rutherford leaves town. Before Johnny leaves town he goes to Lydia's apartment to have a release signed. At the door Johnny hears shots and breaks in the door to find Lydia shot. Johnny puts her on the couch and follows a trail of blood to the fire escape. Johnny follows Rutherford to the roof as he fires several times. Johnny gets to the roof and shoots. Johnny runs up and Rutherford tells him that Lydia had laughed at him and that she was planning to run away with some one else and told him that she had just used him. Rutherford and Lydia both died of their wounds.

Notes:
- This program was done by Bob Bailey as "The Lansing Fraud Matter"
- Dan Cubberly is the announcer
- Music is by Eddie Dunstedter

Producer: Jaime del Valle   Writers: E. Jack Neuman
Cast: Jack Moyles, Edgar Barrier, Peggy Webber, Mary Lansing, John McIntire

SHOW:	**THE LANCER JEWELRY MATTER**
SHOW DATE:	**2/13/1953**
COMPANY:	**ALLIED ADJUSTMENT BUREAU**
AGENT:	**PAT CORBETT**
EXP. ACCT:	**$70.25**

SYNOPSIS: Johnny is called by Pat Corbet who tells him that the Lancer jewelry store in Trenton has been robbed, and that Cummings Casualty wants a full report.

Johnny goes to Trenton, New Jersey, gets a hotel room and goes to see Sgt. Ralls who tells Johnny that the robbery occurred at 10:30 Saturday. A man and woman were looking at wedding rings and robbed the store. They took everything, which included $1500 in jewels and a bank deposit for $830. The girl was about 21, and the man was older, about 35. There have been several other robberies in Jersey City, Buffalo and New York with similar modus operandi. A girl matching the description has been picked up and the police are holding her. Johnny goes to the bank and examines the records for the jewelry company and suspects fraud because the bank deposit was too large. Johnny goes to Mr. Lancer and wants an inventory done. He admits that the girl did the robbery, but the cash was only $265.

Johnny reports the information to the insurance company and gets a call about another similar robbery. Johnny goes to the jail and talks to the suspect, Lena Roberts. He tells her that she has been identified in two robberies and offers to help her for information. She tells Johnny that the man was Paul Handley, alias Edward Chamberlain. She tells Johnny that she met Paul at a correctional farm four months ago and describes the robberies to Johnny and tells him that Paul was going to go to South America. She tells Johnny that they have a stolen 1949 Mercury convertible. Johnny learns that Paul has a record for robbery and contributing to the delinquency of minors.

Johnny goes to a woman who he believes is Paul's mother, but she tells Johnny nothing, and he decides to stake out the apartment. Johnny watches the apartment from a bar across the street and sees a former accomplice named Thelma Warton. Johnny talks to her and she has not seen Paul for several days. Johnny calls the insurance company and is told to come home. Johnny goes to the airport and there are shots out front and Johnny spots Handley and follows him into the airport. Handley is confronted and shot and the jewels are found in a bag.

NOTES:
- THE ANNOUNCER IS DAN CUBBERLY
- MUSIC IS BY EDDIE DUNSTEDTER
- STORY INFORMATION OBTAINED FROM THE **KNX** COLLECTION IN THE THOUSAND OAKS LIBRARY

Producer: Jaime del Valle   Writers   E. Jack Neuman
Cast: Clayton Post, Bob Bailey, Jim Nusser, Parley Baer, Virginia
           Gregg, Martha Wentworth

SHOW:	THE LATOURETTE MATTER
SHOW DATE:	2/20/1953
COMPANY:	NATIONAL UNDERWRITERS
AGENT:	
EXP. ACCT:	$219.50

SYNOPSIS: Lt. Dan Mapes calls and Johnny tells him that he is investigating for the Insurance Company. "Enjoy the weather," he tells Johnny, "you won't enjoy the case."

Johnny flies to Denver, Colorado. He had been there in 1947, but Denver had changed. Johnny rents an Avis car and goes to the Cosmopolitan Hotel. At 9:00 Johnny calls Bessie Thompson in the hotel and she tells Johnny to be careful, as everyone involved with this case has seems to die. Johnny buys breakfast (on him) and talks to Bessie. She tells Johnny that she has buried her husband here and will go home. She is 32 and attractive; and maybe someone, well you know. She tells Johnny that the coroner said that Tommy was drunk and walked out on the highway. She asks Johnny if Tommy drank a lot, and Johnny tells her that he never saw him do anything, and that he loved her. Bessie tells Johnny that he had called and said that he was coming home, but he was killed. She knows Tommy was murdered; it was not a hit-and-run. She is sure that he had found something on Latourette. Johnny tells her that he is there to wrap up the details, and Bessie tells Johnny that Tommy's last report is missing. She is sure that he had something and was killed. Bessie tells Johnny that Tommy is in Crown Hill Cemetery, and Johnny tells her that he will send flowers.

Johnny meets Lt. Mapes and reads the police report. Johnny learns that the fire was reported at 2 AM and Mrs. Latourette's body was found in the ashes. The arson men reported that a cigarette had started the fire. Johnny also learns that Tommy had not been in the tavern where he was hit. Johnny asks why was he on Golden Road then? So far there is nothing to tie his death to Latourette. But Latourette will collect $80,000 in property insurance and $17,000 in life insurance to be collected. Lt. Mapes tells Johnny that Latourette was bowling when it happened; had a good home life and is ok financially. The police want whoever ran Tommy down.

Johnny reads all the reports, which outline a story of tragedy, violence and death. That evening Johnny goes to see Mr. Latourette and sees a man through the window that does not move. Johnny knocks and a boy talks to Johnny through the door and tells him that Mr. Latourette is out until tomorrow. Johnny asks to leave some papers, and the boy tells him to leave the papers under the door. Johnny is sure the voice was strained. Johnny opens the door and the boy has a shotgun and Johnny finds Latourette dead and the boy is almost crying as

Johnny talks to him. Johnny tells the boy who he is, and the boy is unsure of that to do as his gun has more work to do. The boy tells Johnny "he killed a man and a woman. He killed Thompson; he ran over him because Thompson found out about his ladylove and Latourette burned his mother in a fire so they could be together. He'll see that they get together real soon!" The man is his father.

Bruce Latourette was young and scared. Bruce tells Johnny to turn around but Johnny won't. Bruce tells Johnny that his father had his mother killed and that the police do not know about Evelyn, but he is going to kill her. Bruce runs out and into his car and drives away. Johnny calls the police and gives them the license plate number for the car to the Police. Lt. Mapes arrives and tells Johnny that Bruce has not been picked up yet. "And who is Evelyn" he asks. Lt. Mapes and Johnny talk to the neighbors and learn nothing.

At 10:15 a girl comes in to see Lt. Mapes. Dorothy Kelly tells Lt. Mapes and Johnny that she has information about Bruce, and that she heard about it on the radio. She tells them that they go to school together, and Bruce has been talking about his mother and has been depressed. Bruce had told Dorothy "they killed her." She also tells them that Bruce's had said that his father had been seeing a woman named Evelyn for a long time and that Evelyn had set fire to the store and killed his mother. Bruce had told all of this to a man named Thompson, and he was killed too. But Bruce did not tell her who Evelyn was, only that she is a skiing instructor somewhere and that Bruce had met her once.

Later a store manager identifies Evelyn Waters as a ski instructor. Lt. Mapes and Johnny go to visit her and she tells them that she does not know Frank Latourette, even after Johnny tells her Frank is dead. "Are you talking to everyone named Evelyn," she asks. Johnny and Lt. Mapes leave but are suspicious and watch the house. Johnny would like to sleep but there are too many things to think about, as this case stinks! Suddenly they see Bruce's car and walk towards it. They call out to Bruce and he shoots at them. Bruce tells them to stay out of the way, as he is going to kill her. He calls to Evelyn and tells her she killed his mother. Lt. Mapes tells Bruce to put the gun down. Bruce shoots and the police open fire and Bruce is hit.

Evelyn is charged with murder and arson. Bruce dies three hours later. Evelyn gives a confession to the fire and tells the police that it was her idea. She had a key and went into the store, saw Mrs. Latourette sleeping and set a trashcan on fire. She tells them that Frank had never talked about a divorce and that the boy had told Thompson about them. Thompson followed them to the tavern and she was driving her car and ran him down. Frank did not have the nerve to do it. He had money but no nerve.

NOTES:
- AVIS RENTAL CAR. $12.50, ABOUT $87 IN 2004 DOLLARS
- CAST FROM RADIOGOLDINDEX.
- DAN CUBBERLY IS THE ANNOUNCER
- MUSIC IS BY EDDIE DUNSTEDTER

- THERE IS A CROWN HILL CEMETERY IN JEFFERSON COUNTY, NEAR DENVER

Producer: Jaime del Valle   Writers: E. Jack Neuman
Cast: Eddie Firestone, John McIntire, Jeanette Nolan, Virginia Gregg, Sammie Hill

◆ ❖ ◆

SHOW: THE UNDERWOOD MATTER
SHOW DATE: 2/27/1953
COMPANY: ALLIED ADJUSTMENT BUREAU
AGENT: RED EAGAN
EXP. ACCT: $491.50

SYNOPSIS: Red Eagan calls and tells Johnny that Mary just had twins. Come on down to my office for two cigars, and bring a suitcase. Red tells Johnny that he has a dead client named Underwood in Rexford, Wyoming. They do not know if it was murder, suicide or an accident. It looks like all three.

Red explains they are in the same old spot, not being a friend for looking into the claim. The widow was called and hung up on Red. Underwood fell from the 4th floor of a hotel, and the policy is $25,000 double indemnity. Underwood also was a major stockholder of the local newspaper. Red tells Johnny to go to the inquest and make sure things are handled right.

Johnny travels by plane, train and bus to Rexford and attends the inquest. The widow, Alice, testifies that she last saw her husband at the hotel that day, and only stayed a few minutes. They called her at 3:00 and told her of the accident. She had gone to talk with him about their divorce. He was in good health and had been drinking lightly. Johnny notes that the widow was 30, with New York clothes, Tiffany rings, and Paris perfume and there was no emotion in her voice. The verdict was death by a fall.

Johnny wires the news to Red and goes to see Sgt. Hannon for the death certificate and the coroner's report. Sgt. Hannon tells Johnny that the insurance company is stuck for $50,000. Johnny is told that Mrs. Underwood was raised here and went to school in the east. Mr. Underwood was rich and was old enough to be her father and he had raised her since she was 14. Sgt. Hannon tells Johnny that she was going to get a lot of alimony, so there was no reason to kill him. Also, Ray was not the suicide type.

Johnny sends a report to Hartford and then gets a phone call from Red, who tells Johnny that the agent in Cheyenne had told him that Underwood wanted to change the beneficiary. But on the morning he died, Underwood changed his mind. Johnny goes to see Mrs. Underwood and asks her about the beneficiary change. Johnny is told that Mr. Underwood had moved out of the house a month ago and that they had had a bitter argument. It was a ridiculous thing and his impulse was to cancel the insurance policy. She tells Johnny that they did not get along, but they made up the day he died. She thinks that the fall was probably due to the argument. Johnny tells her that it seems hard to believe, based on past experience. She tells Johnny that she has told him the truth.

Johnny re-interviews the people in the hotel and then goes to see Sgt. Hannon. Johnny tells him that he has learned that there was no liquor in the room, and that the hotel staff told him that Ray left a call for 11:30 and then called the insurance agent. There was no liquor in the room, but Mrs. Underwood had testified that he had been drinking. Maybe she made it up. Where did he get the drink, if he had one?

Johnny is sure that there is a problem now. Johnny calls Red Eagan and explains that he should cancel the claim and let her sue. Johnny tells Red that she was ready for everyone but you, so she did not know how to handle him when he called. Red is unsure about holding up the claim. Johnny bases his reasoning on instinct, statistics and experience. A young woman and an old rich husband make for trouble. Now she has everything. Johnny wants to file charges for suspected murder. Johnny reminds Red that Underwood did not have a drink, so someone helped her by pushing him out the window.

Johnny meets with Sgt. Hannon and he tells Johnny that Mrs. Underwood is now unsure of the drink, and that the police will start looking for evidence. Johnny goes back to the ranch where a servant tells Johnny that Mrs. Underwood would frequently take trips out of town. He tells Johnny that she would take a small suitcase and the Cadillac, which would come back covered with mud and ice. Mr. Underwood complained about the trips and told her that she should not visit that man. The servant has known Mrs. Underwood for 13 years and had seen her grow up. He was sort of surprised when they married. She was a friend before they married and later they did not seem to be friends. The servant tells Johnny that he will probably be fired for talking like that, but the house is not the same anymore.

A complaint against Mrs. Underwood is issued but not served because the names of three men were uncovered. Only one of the men, a man named Tyler, was nearby, on a ranch 80 miles away. Johnny and Sgt. Hannon go to see him. Tyler tells Johnny and Sgt. Hannon that the Underwoods were both his friends and that he was not seeing Mrs. Underwood on the sly. He tells them that he was in Rexford in December for some shopping. Sgt. Hannon wants to talk to the hired hands and Tyler asks if any action has been taken yet. When told a complaint is ready to be issued, Tyler tells them that Alice's father was a drunk and that Underwood did everything for her, as she needed love. Tyler tells them that he had been seeing her. Tyler tells them that his people would lie for him, but he cannot let her be arrested for something he did. Tyler tells them that he killed Ray Underwood. Tyler had gone to see him and had gone in the back entrance. Ray had called Tyler the night before and was sore. Tyler went to talk but Ray would not let him. Ray swung at him and Tyler pushed him away and he went out the window. That's all.

NOTES:
- **THIS PROGRAM WAS DONE BY BOB BAILEY AS "THE HENDERSON MATTER"**

- RED'S CIGARS COST $3.69 A BOX, SO JOHNNY TELLS RED TO BUY HIM A DRINK INSTEAD.
- THE MID-PROGRAM COMMERCIAL IS FOR "CITY HOSPITAL" ON CBS ON SATURDAY AFTERNOONS
- DAN CUBBERLY IS THE ANNOUNCER
- MUSIC BY EDDIE DUNSTEDTER
- CAST INFORMATION IS FROM RadioGOLDINdex

Producer: Jaime del Valle   Writers: E. Jack Neuman
Cast: Ted Bliss, Jeanette Nolan, Joseph Du Val, John McIntire, Dick Ryan

◆   ❖   ◆

SHOW: THE JEANNE MAXWELL MATTER
SHOW DATE: 3/6/1953
COMPANY: CORINTHIAN LIFE INSURANCE COMPANY
AGENT: MR. SEMPLIN
EXP. ACCT: $266.85

SYNOPSIS: Johnny calls Mr. Semplin in Boston and gets the name of the police contact for the Jeanne Maxwell case. Johnny asks Semplin if the case is murder or suicide?

Johnny rents a car and drives to the Boston, Massachusetts police headquarters. Johnny tells Lt. DeRosa that the insurance company is nervous about a possible suicide case. The girl's mother is the beneficiary and is an invalid. Lt. DeRosa tells Johnny that the mother has taken up with old boy friend. Lt. DeRosa tells Johnny that the girl was found in shallow water near a bridge and that it did not look like suicide. The bridge was too low, and a suicide never does it without taking off their coat and shoes, and her purse was missing. She was 21 years old and very pretty. The Inquest will be in two days. Johnny tells Lt. DeRosa that he wants to dig up his own background information.

Johnny goes to the site where the body was found and placement of body indicates that she was going towards Boston, not away. Johnny goes to Jeanne's apartment and talks to Mary O'Neal, Jeanne's roommate. Mary tells Johnny that it is a great shock to her, and that she never thought Jeanne would do this. She expected trouble as Joan lived too fast after her mother went into the hospital. There were just too many men. One is Harold Correy, who is a truck driver for Seaboard Trucking Company. Mary tells Johnny that Jeanne saw other men when he was gone. Johnny wants to look at her things, and he goes through a locked dresser that contains nothing but clothes, perfume and jewelry, and a gold house key with a heart shaped head. Johnny keeps the key, as he wants to find out who made it.

Johnny calls Seaboard Trucking Company and is told that Correy is out of town and due back at 3 AM. Johnny calls Jeanne's employer and goes to see Mr. Hollis at home, where Johnny also meets Mrs. Hollis. Johnny tells Mr. and Mrs.

Hollis that he suspects murder, as Jeanne did not do any of the things suicides typically do. Mr. Hollis tells Johnny that he knew nothing of Jeanne's private life, as he had no right to know, but he did know of the invalid mother. Johnny thinks there was only one man with enough money to buy her expensive things. Johnny asks about co-workers and Mr. Hollis will get them for Johnny if he will call in the morning.

Johnny goes to see Correy at 10:30 the next morning. Johnny tells Correy that it looks like murder. Correy tells Johnny that she would never kill herself. Correy tells Johnny that he last saw her on Tuesday and left Wednesday morning on a run and Johnny mentions that he could have done it before he left. Correy says he wanted to marry Jeanne and throws Johnny out.

Johnny calls Lt. DeRosa who tells Johnny that the cause of death is suicide as the autopsy says she died of carbon monoxide poisoning. She killed her self and someone probably moved body to avoid embarrassment.

Johnny goes to see Lt. DeRosa and reads the autopsy report, which points to car exhaust but also shows a severe concussion. Johnny is convinced that Jeanne was killed. Johnny shows Lt. DeRosa the key and asks if he can find where it was made. Lt. DeRosa tells Johnny he will do what he can.

Johnny goes to see Paul Anderson, the boy friend of the mother. Paul tells Johnny that the mother was 17 when Jeanne was born. He met Jeanne first and realized she was a cheap opportunist. He did what he could for the mother and did not send her to a home to get her out of the way. Paul does not know anything about a gold the key and says that he knew very little about Jeanne.

Johnny goes to Mary's apartment and she cannot remember anything additional. She tells Johnny that Jeanne had never mentioned Paul Anderson to her, and that she never knew how Jeanne was able to put her mother in a nursing home. Johnny goes to the Seaboard office and follows Correy to a restaurant. He tells Johnny that he is going out again, as he cannot take any more. Johnny talks to six of Jeanne's co-workers and finds nothing. The police find the goldsmith who made key and Johnny talks to him. The jeweler remembers that councilman's wife had come in the same day. The gold key was made for a J. E. Carter. It was made for a cottage on the bay. Johnny tells Lt. DeRosa about the cottage but Lt. DeRosa cannot assign men to search cabins in the area, as it is county responsibility. Johnny searches real estate offices and on the 3rd day hits pay dirt. An agent rented a cottage to J. E. Carter and the rent was paid by cashier's check since May. They go to cottage where Johnny looks through the cottage and locks it with the gold key.

Johnny goes to Mr. Hollis and tells him "you thought you would get away with it." Johnny tells him that he had rented cottage and bought the key. Hollis admitted he was infatuated with Jeanne and wanted to break it off. Jeanne left and committed suicide in the car. Johnny tells Hollis it was not suicide and Hollis agrees to go to the police. Mrs. Hollis comes in and tells Johnny that she had found out about them. She went out and waited and caught them and killed the girl and carried her to the car. "What have I done," moans Mr. Hollis.

NOTES:
- EDMOND O'BRIEN DID THIS PROGRAM AS "THE JOAN SEBASTIAN MATTER"
- NORTH AMERICAN VAN LINES BECOME SEABOARD TRUCKING COMPANY.
- THE CONVERSATION WITH THE JEWELER IS OMITTED AND REPLACED WITH A DISCUSSION WITH THE REALTOR.
- THE EXPENSES ARE LESS $266.85 VERSUS $356.75.
- THE VITAL CLUE, A WALL STREET JOURNAL WITH MR. HOLLIS' NAME IS NOT MENTIONED IN THIS VERSION.
- DAN CUBBERLY IS THE ANNOUNCER
- MUSIC BY EDDIE DUNSTEDTER

Producer:	Jaime del Valle	Writers:	Gil Doud
Cast:	Jeanette Nolan, Howard McNear, Barney Phillips, Ted de Corsia, Virginia Gregg, John McIntire, Dick Ryan		

◆ ❖ ◆

SHOW:	THE BIRDY BASKERVILLE MATTER
SHOW DATE:	3/10/1953
COMPANY:	AGENT:
EXP. ACCT:	$137.27

SYNOPSIS: This is the same at the 11/10/1951 program, except for cast changes. The story takes place on Long Island, New York.

NOTES:
- THE ANNOUNCER IS CHARLES LYON
- MUSIC IS BY EDDIE DUNSTEDTER
- STORY INFORMATION OBTAINED FROM THE KNX COLLECTION IN THE THOUSAND OAKS LIBRARY

Producer:	Jaime del Valle	Writers	Blake Edwards
Cast:	Stacy Harris, John McIntire, Howard McNear, Sidney Miller, Jeanette Nolan		

◆ ❖ ◆

SHOW:	THE KING'S NECKLACE MATTER
SHOW DATE:	3/17/1953
COMPANY:	EASTERN INDEMNITY & INSURANCE COMPANY
AGENT:	MARTY FENTON
EXP. ACCT:	$348.60

SYNOPSIS: Marty Fenton calls Johnny with poetry: "A king there was with his premium paid even as you and I. But he sold his soul for a pot of gold, for rubies and diamonds precious and old, even as you and I." Marty needs help and will meet Johnny at the airport in Miami. There is a king and $250,000 in stones involved.

Johnny goes to Miami, Florida and meets Marty Fenton who briefs him on the case. Johnny is told that King Rawlings is a retired businessman who has a policy on a necklace and someone has attempted to steal the necklace from his safe. The policy renewal is coming up and Rawlings is in financial trouble. Johnny is to go to Los Banos Island the personal island of Rawlings, complete with a collection of, uh people.

Johnny takes a charter plane to the island and is met on the beach by a girl, Nita Valdez. She tells Johnny that she heard him land, and that she has been busy sunbathing. "You have come to see the king about the attempted theft?" she asks and tells Johnny that everyone on the island is a suspect. She tells Johnny not to be concerned about the necklace, because if it is stolen, King will know who did it. Nita tells Johnny that everyone stays for the same reason, money; but she will explain later as Johnny will understand when he meets King. She tells Johnny that she sunbathes there everyday at the same time.

Johnny describes the King residence as a Moorish castle. Once inside, Timothy Harley, King's personal secretary escorts Johnny to the study. "You are here about the necklace? Did Miss Valdez say anything?" Johnny is asked. King Rawlings comes in and Johnny tells him he is there because he is an investigator. Rawlings shows Johnny a substantial safe with scratches on the door. Rawlings tells Johnny that he suspects either Harley or Nita Valdez as they love money and hate him. The safe is opened and Johnny looks at the necklace and tells Rawlings that it is paste, fake jewels. Rawlings has no explanation as the necklace was appraised when the policy was written and no one has the combination to the safe. "I am insured. You have to prove fraud." Rawlings sneers at Johnny.

Johnny calls Marty and updates him, and then Johnny goes outside to find Nita on the veranda, wearing a clinging, silk gown. Johnny wonders if she looks better in the dress or the sun suit? Johnny tells Nita that Rawlings has confirmed that she hates him, and Nita tells Johnny that King acquires people, uses them, and casts them off. But it is easier to stay. She tells Johnny that she is not surprised the necklace is gone, and that he took it. Tim Harley calls to Johnny and asks him if it is true that the necklace is gone. Tim tells Johnny "I wonder if that could account for it. Mr. Rawlings is on the second floor landing. I think he is dead."

Johnny goes to the second floor where Rawlings is "stone cold dead."

Three hours later Marty arrives with Capt. Fuentes of the Havana police. Capt. Fuentes tells everyone that they cannot leave, as murder might be more important than robbery. Johnny tells Capt. Fuentes of the afternoon's activity and Marty is concerned about the jewelry. Capt. Fuentes has Rawling's body flown to Havana and then questions everyone, learning nothing. Johnny goes to Harley's room to talk, and he tells Johnny that Rawlings has a will, in the safe. Johnny asks about a copy of the will, and is told that Señor Chavez might have one in Havana. Johnny spots his half-filled suitcase and asks him why he is leaving. Harley tells Johnny that his employment is terminated and why should Fuentes object. Johnny spots a package in the suitcase and opens it to find money, in crisp $100 bills. Harley tells Johnny that he saved it while working for Rawlings.

Later that night Johnny is smoking a cigarette on the veranda when shots ring out. Johnny fires back into the jungle and waits for Capt. Fuentes. Fifteen minutes later, Capt. Fuentes finds empty shell casings, and discovers that Harley is gone. At the boathouse, Capt. Fuentes discovers that there is a speedboat missing.

Johnny and Marty go to Havana, to meet with Sr. Chavez about the will. Johnny wants to know if Nita or Timothy were named as heirs and is told that the will only named charities and public organizations. Sr. Chavez also tells Johnny that the rumors of financial ruin are false. On the way to the police, Chavez stops Johnny in the hallway with a phone call. Capt. Fuentes tells Johnny that Rawlings had died of natural causes and that Harley has been found dead with the combination to the safe was in his pocket.

Johnny flies back to Miami with Marty. Johnny tells Marty that he is sure the necklace will show up, because it is in your briefcase. Johnny tells Marty that he had figured it all the time, and that all the loopholes had closed, and there was no other reason. Johnny reminds Marty that Rawlings had told Johnny that Marty had made the safe and supervised it's installation, and that the copy of the necklace was too good. Johnny tells Marty that he had given Harley the combination and he made the switch. That is what the money was for, a payoff. Marty tells Johnny that he should have shot him on the veranda, but he tells Johnny that he never could out shoot Johnny.

With all deference to his chosen profession, sometimes this is a lousy business.

Notes:
- In Spanish, "Los Banos" is "the bathroom"
- Commercials are for Wrigley's Spearmint Gum
- Music by Milton Charles
- Charles Lyon is the announcer

Producer:	Jaime del Valle	**Writers:**	Sidney Marshall
Cast:	Jack Moyles, Lillian Buyeff, Tom Tully, Howard McNear, Nestor Paiva, Don Diamond		

◆ ❖ ◆

Show:	The Syndicate Matter
Show Date:	3/24/1953
Company:	Employee Cooperative Group Insurance Company
Agent:	Wilbur Runion
Exp. Acct:	$236.04

Synopsis: Wilbur Runion calls Johnny and apologizes for missing Johnny at the airport. He tells Johnny that he hopes the head office is not mad at him for sending for Johnny. Johnny tells him that four murders put a different light on things.

Johnny goes to Dallas, Texas and contacts Mr. Runion, who tells Johnny that there is little more to know. There have been four murders at the new oil fields, and the men all had been beaten to death, maybe by the same person. Johnny is told that the wife always benefited as the company paid the premiums for the workers. Mrs. Gonzales is due in to pick up the check. She was unaware of the insurance and is due to have a baby soon. Johnny also learns that all of the workers had been new to the fields. Mrs. Gonzales arrives and tells Johnny that her husband did not have a lot of money and worked hard, even when he was injured. There was some accident at the well and he had marks all over him. Runion tells Johnny that another woman had mentioned the same thing. Johnny goes to get a job at the oil field, as there are four openings.

Johnny goes to Tupella, Texas and gets a job at the oil field and immediately meets Bull Farrell, the straw boss. Johnny tells Bull that he has not worked for a long time. Bull tells Johnny that if he needs money, to let him know. Johnny notes that Bull was friendly, too friendly. Johnny goes to the payroll office and asks for an advance on his job, and the clerk tells him to see Bull Farrell. On the way out Bull is waiting for Johnny and directs him to Frankie Robeling, who helps guys along, with a little interest. See him in room 12 at the Tupella Hotel tonight.

Johnny goes to the hotel, and Frankie is waiting for him. Frankie gives Johnny $20 and tells him that he expects $30 back on Friday. Johnny takes the money and asks about a loan form. Don't worry, Frankie tells Johnny, he will remember. On payday, Johnny gets his $32 pay envelope and Bull reminds him that Frankie will want to see him. That night Johnny goes to the hotel where over fifty men are paying money to Frankie. Johnny asks Frankie for more time, and Frankie gives Johnny until next payday, when Johnny will owe $40. Don't be a tough guy Johnny is told, or you might soften up by next payday.

Johnny goes to the bars and tries to talk to the other men. Willie Prescott sits down and wants to talk. Willie tells Johnny that Robeling and Farrell were talking, and it you do not pay up, you will be roughed up. He tells Johnny that a couple of guys have died here, and that most of the guys have families and can't make ends meet. On the walk to the rooming house a girl stops Johnny and asks for help with a butane tank. Several hours later Johnny wakes up after a beating and goes to his rooming house where he passes out again. Bull Farrell visits Johnny the next morning and tells him he should not have gotten drunk. Johnny accuses Farrell of having him beaten, but Farrell denies it and tells Johnny that Prescott is in the hospital. Also, Frankie likes Johnny so Johnny will be back at work.

Johnny sees a doctor and then goes to see the sheriff and explains the situation. Johnny asks him to suppose that you got Robeling trying to beat someone. He expects Johnny to pay next Thursday, and I'll be the pigeon. You arrest them and they will talk. On payday, Johnny goes to Robeling's room to tell him he cannot pay. He will pay the $20 next week but Frankie makes the $20 a gift. While Johnny walks to his room, Bull drives up in a car and he wants to take Johnny to a party. The boys in the car get out and start to beat Johnny until the sheriff shows up. The sheriff tells Johnny that he has put the men who owe Robeling money in protective custody and they have talked. Bull Farrell and the men who tried to beat Johnny are arrested, but do not talk. Outside the jail, Robeling is nervous because he does not know what is going on. Johnny suggests that the sheriff have a guard tell Robeling that Farrell is going to be worked over tonight. Your deputy will be there and they can fake a beating behind the window shades. Then you will fake a confession. What Robeling thinks is going on is what is important. Farrell is brought in and signs a denial paper. Outside Robeling thinks that Farrell has signed a statement and bolts, and the sheriff goes after him. Robeling is arrested in his hotel room, and the syndicate is broken.

Johnny does not include his incidentals and miscellaneous as his oil well earnings covered them, proving that he lives within his means.

NOTES:
- CHARLES LYON IS THE ANNOUNCER
- MUSIC IS BY EDDIE DUNSTEDTER

Producer: Jaime del Valle   Writers: Joel Murcot
Cast: Joseph Kearns, Lillian Buyeff, John McIntire, Stacy Harris,
                  Tom Tully, Virginia Gregg, Parley Baer, Hy Averback

◆   ❖   ◆

SHOW: THE LESTER JAMES MATTER
SHOW DATE: 3/31/1953
COMPANY: CONTINENTAL ADJUSTMENT BUREAU
AGENT: ED TALBOT
EXP. ACCT: $151.22

SYNOPSIS: Ed Talbot calls Johnny and asks him to come on down and work on a case for Corinthian Liability. They have a policy covering the Wallace Cotton Company. There is a $4,185 shortage in the books, and they know who did it; a bookkeeper named Lester James. Your job is to figure out what he did with the money.

Johnny goes to New York City, checks in at the New Westin and then goes to the 17th precinct jail where Sgt. Mangone lets Johnny into meet Lester James, who does not want to be talked to. He tells Johnny that he knows what will happen in court. Johnny tells him that he wants to know what Lester did with the money; and that recovery of the money will affect what happens in court. James has never been in trouble before but just will not tell Johnny what he did with the money.

Johnny describes James as young, dark and tall, not the kind of man Johnny expected to meet. Johnny goes to James' apartment and speaks with the manager, Mrs. Anastasia Denovitch. She tells Johnny that James has no friends and that he never causes trouble. James has no girl friend, and has lived there 5-6 years. Johnny looks through the apartment, a grimy threadbare efficiency apartment. Johnny talks to the local merchants who remember James as a nice person who never had any money.

Johnny goes back to see Sgt. Mangone after the hearing, at which nothing was said. Johnny is told that James has posted his own bail and will leave that evening. After James is released, Johnny follows him to the Empress Theater, and then to his apartment. Johnny knocks on the door, but James does not answer. Johnny breaks down the door and takes James out of the gas-filled apartment. An ambulance is called and James is taken to the hospital. After dinner Johnny goes back to the Empress Theater and talks to the doorman. After Johnny gives him a description of James, the doorman tells Johnny that he comes there to see Margie Cook, who sings here. She is gone for the evening but the doorman calls Margie for Johnny, to see if she will talk to him.

Johnny goes to see Margie Cook and explains why he is there. She tells Johnny that she knows the name, and Johnny asks why James has been seeing her. She tells Johnny that she saw him once. He has given her a number of gifts, some expensive and he also has sent orchids to her every night for about three months. She relates to Johnny that she had gotten a card from him, then the gifts started coming. She saw him once but did not go out with him, as he was different, and had no poise or sophistication. Johnny tells her that James had stolen the money to buy the gifts for her, but he was just a name to her. Johnny tells her that she was something more to him.

Johnny tracks down the gifts and their value totaling $2,780. Johnny tracks down reservations at expensive restaurants where the meal was never eaten that total $835. The florist bills totaled $680. The total was $4,295.

Johnny visits James at the hospital and tells him what he has learned. James is angry that Margie knows what he did. Johnny still has $410 to track down and shows James a list of what he has found. James tells Johnny that he saw her at the office where she was modeling some clothes and he thought money would attract her to him. Johnny suggests that he should have just called her and asked her to have a beer with him; it might have worked.

Margie Cook calls and Johnny tells her that James will probably go to prison, as most of the gifts are non-redeemable. After all the gifts were returned, Lester still owes $2,500. Margie offers to pay the difference for him, as he was the first man who was willing to go out on a limb for her.

James comes to trial, and thanks to Margie, he might get a suspended sentence.

NOTES:
- THIS PROGRAM WAS DONE BY BOB BAILEY AS "THE FORBES MATTER"
- THERE SEEMS TO BE AN ACCOUNTING ERROR HERE. THE LOSS WAS REPORTED AS $4,185, AND JOHNNY IS ABLE TO ACCOUNT FOR $4,295—$110 MORE THAN WAS STOLEN
- CAST CREDITS FROM TERRY SALOMONSON
- MUSIC BY MILTON CHARLES
- CHARLES LYON IS THE ANNOUNCER

Producer: Jaime del Valle   **Writers:** E. Jack Neuman

Cast: **Peter Leeds, Bill Conrad, Bill Johnstone, Virginia Gregg, Clayton Post, Howard McNear**

◆   ❖   ◆

SHOW: THE ENOCH ARDEN MATTER
SHOW DATE: 4/7/1953
COMPANY: HEMISPHERIC LIFE INSURANCE COMPANY
AGENT: HENRY GRANT
EXP. ACCT: $1,879.80

SYNOPSIS: Henry Grant calls and tells Johnny to look at page one in the paper. Johnny is on page four and his second donut, but turns back to see the picture of Mrs. Frank Loring and the Enoch Arden divorce decree for the husband who has been missing for seven years and is legally dead. Henry tells Johnny that Frank Loring was insured for $250,000, and now they have to pay off. Henry tells Johnny that he got a phone call from a nurse in Boston who Saw Frank recently.

Johnny goes to Henry's office and goes over the details of the case. Miss. Ruth Beloine arrives, and she tells Johnny that she worked for a doctor in New York ten years ago, and now works in Boston. She thinks she saw Frank Loring in Boston two weeks ago at the clinic, where he wanted to be vaccinated and gave his name as Michael Walsh. He was going abroad, so she gave him the shots. When she saw the article in the paper his name came to her, as ten years ago Frank had been a patient. Johnny is told that Loring was a character actor who was good at accents and appearances. Henry tells Johnny that a man named Walsh sailed to Chile yesterday on the SS Castile.

Johnny goes to see Mrs. Loring, and a party is in full swing. Freddie tells Johnny that Mrs. Loring is happy as she is getting $250,000 because her husband is dead, and that she is going to Chile. Johnny finds Marsha Loring in the kitchen and tells her that they a common friend: Michael Walsh from Boston. Marsha drops a knife and yells at Johnny to get out. Freddie tries to interfere and Johnny is slugged with a bottle and wakes up in the basement. Johnny has breakfast, wires Henry to hold up payment of the claim pending his investigation and then flies to Colon, Panama Canal Zone.

The SS Castile is in port, and Johnny goes on board to Walsh's cabin, but a steward tells Johnny that Walsh has left the ship after he had gotten a wire last night. Johnny realizes that Walsh is not going to be easy to find.

On the street, a man with a gun stops Johnny and tells him "Jose wants a gift." Johnny offers Jose his watch and slugs Jose as he takes it off. Johnny then asks Jose how he could get out of Panama without notice if the police were after him. Jose tells Johnny that in Porto Bayo there is a bar called "The Geisha Girl" run by Mr. Kamamoto who is very good at making people disappear.

Johnny takes a taxi to Porto Bayo and finds the Geisha Girl Café. Inside, a man with a cockney accent talks to Johnny and asks if Johnny is in trouble. He tells Johnny that Kamamoto is in the storeroom. Johnny goes to the dark storeroom, where a voice speaks and someone knocks Johnny out. Johnny comes to in a room with two men and Mr. Kamamoto, who tells Johnny that he had the exact amount of money in his wallet to pay for passage, over a thousand dollars. They are on a boat, the Okira Matsu, and will sail shortly for South America. Johnny is told that he will be untied when they reach their destination, and that he is hot cargo and that they want to be able to get rid of the hot cargo if stopped by the police.

Johnny is sure that Kamamoto knows he is, as his ID was in his wallet. Jose comes into the cabin where Johnny is tied up, and tells Johnny that they do not want him to finish the trip, and that there are three other passengers on board. Johnny asks Jose to untie him and give him a gun. Jose unties Johnny and he goes out to the main cabin to find the Lorings and Freddie. Johnny tells Frank Loring that he will not get the money, as Freddie will do anything Marsha wants him to do. Freddie loves Marsha and she will probably have him kill you. Marsha tells Johnny that she had been using Freddie, and that he is an idiot. Kamamoto comes in and has Johnny's gun. Johnny tries to bargain with Kamamoto. Loring is paying Kamamoto $5,000 and Johnny lies to Kamamoto by telling him that the policy is for $250,000. Loring tells Kamamoto that the policy is only $25,000 and Johnny suggests bidding to see who will pay Kamamoto the most. Frank and Kamamoto suddenly fire at the same time and Kamamoto is killed. Frank then kills Marsha and Freddie. Jose is in the doorway with Kamamoto's gun and tells Frank that he will kill him. Franks gives Johnny his gun and tells Johnny that he is hit, and that the whole idea was hers. He had hid out like a dog, and she had come to Boston to see him occasionally at first then rarely. Johnny Tells Frank that Marsha never was the lonely type.

NOTES:
- MILTON CHARLES PROVIDED THE MUSIC ON THIS EPISODE.
- CHARLES LYON IS THE ANNOUNCER
- THE TITLE OF THIS STORY COMES FROM WHAT SOME STATES CALL ENOCH ARDEN LAWS WHICH ALLOW A MAN OR WOMAN TO GET A DIVORCE AFTER SPOUSE HAS BEEN GONE FOR A SPECIFIC PERIOD, TYPICALLY 7 YEARS. THESE LAWS WERE PROBABLY BASED ON THE CHARACTER ENOCH ARDEN, IN A POEM BY TENNYSON.

Producer:	Jaime del Valle	**Writers:**	Joel Murcot
Cast:	Stacy Harris, Mary Jane Croft, Howard McNear, John McIntire, Elliott Reid, Sidney Miller, Jeanette Nolan		

◆　❖　◆

SHOW:	THE MADISON MATTER
SHOW DATE:	4/14/1953
COMPANY:	INTERNATIONAL INSURANCE CORPORATION

AGENT: PAUL DUPREE
EXP. ACCT: $525.39

SYNOPSIS: Paul Dupree calls Johnny and asks him to come to his office to meet a girl. She is very pretty and very interesting, and has just told Paul the most interesting story he has ever heard. She just told Paul that she is dead. Johnny tells Paul he better come over.

Johnny goes to the International building to see Paul Dupree where Johnny meets Mrs. Walker who tells Johnny that she is legally dead, and that her husband Dr. Frank Madison has collected on her $10,000 policy. Her real name is Thelma Madison. Dr. Madison lives in Los Angeles and filed a death claim in 1951, and a Dr. Reed signed the Death Certificate. Thelma tells Johnny that a Wanda Thompson had come into the office and was ill. She was taken in and had heart failure in the examination room. In her pocket Frank found an address in Jersey City and called, but the mother had just died. And they were told that Wanda was the only family. She tells Johnny that Frank said that they were in luck and he used her body to be Thelma. Dr. Reed was used to sign the death certificate because he had never met Thelma. Also, she tells Johnny that Frank needed money. Thelma went to New York and Frank was supposed to meet her there. Frank wrote for a while, and stopped and never came. Johnny asks Thelma if she can she prove who she is, but she tells Johnny that she has never been finger printed. Johnny gets list of friends in Los Angeles, and Thelma tells Johnny that she works as a lab assistant in New York. She never got any of the money and is willing to sign a statement even though she can be held criminally liable for fraud. A statement is prepared and signed by Thelma.

Johnny goes to New York City and visits Thelma's apartment. The manager tells Johnny that she is a good tenant. Johnny looks around and finds nothing. Johnny goes to visit Mr. Platt at her office, and her work story checks. Johnny calls Hartford to tell Paul that her story checks out. Paul tells Johnny that the coroner in New Jersey confirms that Mabel Thompson died there, and that Wanda the daughter was not found.

Johnny goes to Los Angeles, California and gets a room at the Statler. Johnny gets a package of pictures and prints for Thelma Walker, rents a car and starts looking.

Johnny visits a Mrs. Quincy who is shown picture and she knows her as Thelma Madison who died a year ago. She was Dr. Madison's receptionist. She tells Johnny that there was no funeral as the body was cremated.

Johnny goes to the police, who have a missing-persons report on Wanda Thompson that was filed by Anthony Rexford. Johnny goes to visit Rexford and he tells Johnny that he knew Wanda and had filed the missing-persons report. He tells Johnny that he had met her in a restaurant and they went to a movie. Then she just disappeared. He last saw her on June 5th, his birthday. He tells Johnny that Wanda did not drink; she just disappeared. Johnny is told that Wanda had come here for her health, as she had a heart problem, but nothing serious. Her doctor was Dr. Madison. Johnny checks with the phone company, but they find no record of a call to Jersey City by Dr. Madison.

Johnny goes to see Dr. Madison and asks him about Wanda Thompson. He tells Johnny that there is nothing in his files, but Johnny tells him that she supposedly came to see him several times. He tells Johnny that is wife was the receptionist but she was not too efficient, and that she is dead. Johnny tells Dr. Madison why he is there, and that he had talked to Thelma Madison about how Wanda had died there and they had collected the insurance. Johnny shows him the picture but he tells Johnny nothing, then he tells Johnny that he has never seen her. Johnny tells Dr. Madison that he has the whole story, but Frank has nothing to say.

Johnny prefers charges and Frank is arrested but he will not talk to anyone about the charges. A wire is sent to Paul Dupree to bring Thelma to Los Angeles, and she arrives the next day. Johnny asks Thelma about her statement about Wanda coming in and dying of a heart condition, and that she had never seen Wanda before. Johnny tells her that the call to New Jersey was never placed. Johnny tells Thelma that Wanda was a patient, and that most of things in her statement are true, some do not make sense, that the case is too good to be real. Johnny tells Thelma that she had planned a premeditated murder, didn't you? Thelma admits that Frank knew about Wanda's condition, and that she had come in to help her sleep, so he took her to the examining room and then claimed that she had died of a heart attack, but she saw a hypodermic on the stand and had given her something. He had it all planned. He called Dr. Reed and told him it was Thelma. She had overheard it and left that night. She is glad it is all over now.

NOTES:
- CHARLES LYON IS THE ANNOUNCER
- MUSIC BY EDDIE DUNSTEDTER
- THIS STORY WAS DONE BY BOB BAILEY AS "THE MCCLAIN MATTER"

Producer: Jaime del Valle   Writers: E. Jack Neuman
Cast: Joseph Kearns, Lillian Buyeff, Parley Baer, Virginia Gregg,
            Tom Tully, John McIntire

◆   ❖   ◆

SHOW: THE DAMERON MATTER
SHOW DATE: 4/21/1953
COMPANY: FEDERAL UNDERWRITERS INC.
AGENT:
EXP. ACCT: $551.10
SYNOPSIS: Lt. Joe Benson returns Johnny's call and Johnny tells him that he is working on the $65,000 National Savings and Loan holdup. Johnny is told that the night watchman has just died. Better come on down.

Johnny goes to San Francisco, California 10 hours after news of the holdup hit Hartford, and Lt. Benson tells Johnny that Bernie Manners, who was one of the four who pulled the job, has just been picked up. Johnny is told that Manners is a two-time loser with 25 arrests, but he only had $2.40 on him. Johnny is taken to see Bernie, but he tells Johnny that he knows nothing, and was in his room sleeping. Bernie tells Johnny and Lt. Benson that he had been driving a truck but was fired. After several hours of questioning Bernie still has nothing to say. Lt. Benson tells Bernie that he has a statement from the watchman that says Bernie was one of the men. Bernie still has nothing to say for several more hours. The phone rings and Lt. Benson is told that the crime lab has found $20,000 in Bernie's car. Bernie finally tells the police that Eddie Page and Jack Ivers and a man named "Chick" are the others who were involved, and that Chick had planned the whole thing. Bernie does not know where they are now. Bernie just drove his car and dropped them at the Fairmont. Bernie tells them that Chick shot the guard for no reason; he just shot him in the back. Bernie gives the police a description and a check of the files uncovers 23 likely suspects.

The next day Johnny learns that the bullets that killed the watchman were from a .45 Colt automatic revolver. Johnny also learns that Ivers was recently released from San Quentin for auto theft, but he had not been seen at his rooming house for two days. Page is two-time loser for armed robbery and is wanted in Denver. He has a sister in Eureka, and the police are talking to her. Johnny talks to the bank auditors and learns that the total is $68,000. Johnny speaks to Hartford and they agree to suspend the insurance claim pending recovery of the money. Johnny calls Lt. Benson, and he has a lead on Page. Johnny cabs to an address on Claire Street where Page's sister had been writing to him. They enter the building and Lt. Benson poses as a deliveryman and Page is confronted. Page shoots but no one is hit and Page is arrested.

Back at headquarters Johnny is told that Page has said nothing, but the police found $15,000 in Page's apartment. Page tells the police nothing about Chick or anyone else. Johnny and Lt. Benson eat and then return to questioning Page. At 10:00 PM a drug store operator calls with a tip. Johnny and Lt. Benson go to the store and talk to Mr. Smith, who has read about the robbery and has found a bill wrapper on the floor. Johnny is told that a man dropped it about twenty minutes ago. Johnny is told that the man bought three bottles of scotch and other things and paid with a fifty and then Smith saw him go across the street to the Alden Hotel. Smith sees the man leaving the hotel and Lt. Benson recognizes him as Jack Ivers. Johnny calls to Ivers and he runs down the alley. Ivers shoots at Johnny and runs down the alley and jumps a fence and goes into an apartment house. Johnny calls to him and there is an exchange of gunfire and Ivers is killed.

Ivers is searched and $12,000 is found in a money belt. Johnny and Lt. Benson go to the hotel and learn that there is a second man in Iver's room, and he is still there. Lt. Benson knocks and then pushes the door open. A man is there "as drunk as you can get."

The man was Chester "Chick" Dameron of Toledo, Ohio who had a 17-year criminal record. 99.39% of the money was recovered. Pretty good for Federal Underwriters.

NOTES:

- THIS IS TOTALLY IRRELEVANT TO THE BOOK, BUT MY FIRST JOB OUT OF THE MILITARY WAS WITH THE NATIONAL SAVINGS AND TRUST COMPANY IN WASHINGTON, DC. I WAS TAKEN BACK IN TIME THE FIRST TIME I HEARD THIS EPISODE AND THE NAME OF THE S&L.
- CHARLES LYON IS THE ANNOUNCER
- MUSIC BY EDDIE DUNSTEDTER
- CAST CREDITS FROM TERRY SALOMONSON

Producer: Jaime del Valle   Writers: E. Jack Neuman
Cast: Bill Johnstone, Clayton Post, Bill Conrad, Peter Leeds,
               Howard McNear

◆   ❖   ◆

SHOW: THE SAN ANTONIO MATTER
SHOW DATE: 4/28/1953
COMPANY: GREAT EASTERN FIDELITY & LIFE INSURANCE COMPANY
AGENT: ED QUIGLEY
EXP. ACCT: $573.49

SYNOPSIS: Ed Quigley calls Johnny and asks "Are you free?" Johnny tells him "If you mean am I available, yes." Ed asks Johnny if he remembers Mark San Antonio the bootlegger? Someone shot him and there is a trust set up for his daughter. The company wants a full report.

Johnny flies to St Petersburg, Florida and rainy weather. Johnny gets a room at the St. Petersburg Hotel and contacts Lt. Benjamin and tells him of the need for a full report. Johnny is told that Mark San Antonio has a big place outside of town, was quiet and stayed out of trouble. San Antonio had called that morning to report two prowlers and a prowl car sent out, but the two men had disappeared. The police investigated and found nothing. The cook had made breakfast for him and found him dead, shot twice from a Luger. The cook just worked there during the day. Johnny is told that Mark just spent his days painting pictures, pretty good ones too. He also listened to music, heavy stuff. Lt. Benjamin thinks San Antonio must have stepped on toes running booze in New York but seemed to have gentled up. Johnny is told that San Antonio paid cash for his house and got a bank statement from New York every month. The lab is still working on the evidence. Johnny is told that San Antonio's daughter and the cook are at the house. The daughter, Edith Randall, had been living with an aunt and did not know Mark was her father until the insurance company told her. Johnny has dinner and talks to Ed about the trust fund.

Johnny cabs to the San Antonio house and meets Mrs. Olson the cook who tells Johnny that she does not want to talk, as it has been a hard day. She also tells Johnny that Miss Randall is upset and cannot talk. Edith comes in and she wants to talk to Johnny. Johnny describes Edith as tall and dark-eyed with a happy mouth. She tells Johnny that she wants to find out more about Mr. San

Antonio. Johnny tells Edith about her father and she learns that she is the daughter of a racketeer. She is 26 and just before she was born her father was on trial for tax evasion. He had set up a trust that reverts to her. It amounts to $50,000. She offers Johnny a drink and they talk about Mark and his activities. She tells Johnny that she was reared far from the San Antonio name. She does not know how long she will be there, or why she came. She has not seen her father yet, but she has seen his life style. She feels much better about him and wants to know why and who killed Mark. Johnny leaves with a warm feeling.

The next morning Johnny talks to Mrs. Olson the cook and learns nothing new. Johnny talks with Lt. Benjamin and there are other developments. Johnny is told that Mark's old partner Jimmy Palalicci was shot in Newark with a Luger, the same gun that shot San Antonio. So now the case now widens as information is gathered on Mark and Jimmy. A day later Johnny goes to see Edith. She tells Johnny that someone has been after her, a reporter who wants a story and that even Hollywood has called and she is frightened. Edith and Johnny walk out of the house and shots ring out. Johnny pulls his gun and there is no one there. Edith cries out and dies in his arms.

Johnny stumbles down to the road and sees a car leaving. Johnny shoots 7 times and the car crashes. Johnny runs to the car where one man gets out and the other man is dead. Mrs. Olson runs up and is told to call the police. The man tells Johnny that he is Giuseppi Ricco, and that the other man was his brother Giovanni. The man wants to die rather than talk to Johnny. Johnny puts his gun to Giuseppi's temple and almost uses his last bullet to shoot Giuseppi but Johnny faints from a shoulder wound.

Lt. Benjamin is there when Johnny wakes up in the hospital. Johnny tells him what happened and learns the Ricco's gun is the same one that killed San Antonio. Johnny is told that the Ricco's are from New York and the police are looking for information. They flew in to town just to get San Antonio and his daughter. Then Johnny learns that Giuseppi Ricco had died. At police headquarters, Johnny learns the Ricco boys were naturalized citizens but their father is missing. He was due to be naturalized soon and the immigration people are looking for him. That night Lt. Benjamin calls and tells Johnny that Pietro Ricco has come in to claim the bodies. Johnny goes to talk to him, and the old man knows that Johnny killed his sons but he will not talk. Johnny learns that Mark San Antonio's will discloses that Mark San Antonio's wife's name was Ricco. Johnny goes to the old man and tells him that his daughter had a daughter. The man tells Johnny that they all had to die, as they were all bad. Pietro tells Johnny that Mark had taken his daughter from Italy and that that Palalicci helped him. Since that time, he has lived only to destroy them all. The daughter had to die as good does not come from a bad man. It was a vendetta.

Pietro Ricco was turned over to the immigration officials.

NOTES:
- JOHNNY IS SHOT FOR THE 4TH TIME.
- THIS PROGRAM WAS DONE BY BOB BAILEY AS "THE VALENTINE MATTER"

- **DAN CUBBERLY IS THE ANNOUNCER ON THE REHEARSAL PROGRAM, AND CHARLES LYON IS ON THE REGULAR BROADCAST PROGRAM**
- **MUSIC BY EDDIE DUNSTEDTER**

Producer: Jaime del Valle   **Writers:**   E. Jack Neuman
Cast: John McIntire, Joseph Kearns, Jeanette Nolan, Virginia Gregg, Jay Novello

◆   ❖   ◆

SHOW: THE BLACKMAIL MATTER
SHOW DATE: 5/5/1953
COMPANY: NATIONAL ALL RISK INSURANCE COMPANY
AGENT: PHILLIP SHORE
EXP. ACCT: $22.68

SYNOPSIS: Philip Shore calls Johnny and tells him that Dale Martin is insured with National, and that a man was killed in his Gym this morning. The police are there right now so you better get over there. Johnny agrees to go, but tells Phil that he does not take off his shirt.

Johnny takes a cab to the gym at 1084 6th Avenue in Hartford, Connecticut. A nervous Dale Martin is there and a police officer tells Johnny that the coroner is due soon. Johnny gets a review of the events, and Dale tells Johnny that Mr. Royal was found in the locker room, and his neck looked broken. There were three assistants and three customers in the gym at the time. Johnny is taken to the rubdown room to look at the body and it is not a very pretty sight. Lt. Nathan, an old friend, arrives with the coroner and everyone in the gym was kept busy. Johnny tells Lt. Nathan that maybe someone was rubbing his neck and got carried away. The police question the men in the gym and there are three prosperous clients, three assistants and six denials. Johnny learns that Bernie Carroll was working with Royal. He tells Johnny that he had sent Royal to the showers and started to work on another customer. Martin tells Johnny that he was just checking on supplies in the locker room. Jack Olsen tells Johnny that he went back to the locker room several times for coffee, and chalk for his hands, as he is new there. Johnny Morgan tells Johnny that he had been past the locker room too. Everyone goes to the police precinct to sign statements and they are released. Johnny goes home with Dale Martin, who offers Johnny some carrot juice. Dale tells Johnny that Royal had been coming there for over a year and that he had a lot of money. Johnny gets a phone call from Lt. Nathan and learns that Royal had a record for blackmail and a safe deposit box key in his suit. Martin gives Johnny the address for Royal and Johnny meets Lt. Nathan there and they search the apartment. Johnny finds an appointment book that has Barbara Carroll's name in it several times. Johnny goes to see Barbara Carroll, who lives with her brother Bernie and Jack Olsen. She tells Johnny that she had been out with Royal several times but he had mentioned nothing. Johnny notices a picture on the piano, and Barbara tells Johnny that it is Jack's father. Bernie asked Jack to move in with them as he was living in a horrible place.

Outside the temperature is 90 and the case is going nowhere. Johnny tells Lt. Nathan that the man in the picture looks familiar, so Johnny goes to the newspaper morgue to look at pictures.

At the newspaper office Johnny gets what he wants. Back at police headquarters, Lt. Nathan tells Johnny that he has the contents of the safety deposit box, and that Royal was blackmailing a number of people. Lt. Nathan has evidence and a list of names. Johnny tells Lt. Nathan that the picture of Jacks father was of a prominent banker named William Barrett, who had jumped from a building. Barrett's name is in the list, so Royal had been blackmailing him. Johnny and Lt. Nathan go to get Jack Olsen. At the Carroll apartment Johnny and Lt. Nathan see Olsen getting into a cab, so they follow it across town to Long Island where the cab drives up to a Sanitarium. They follow Jack inside and talk to the manager. "Which one of you is the patient?" she asks. Dr. Fetter comes out and they explain to him why they are there and he asks, "Which one of you is the patient?" Lt. Nathan is told that Jack is seeing his mother, and her illness is related to her husband's suicide. The shock had driven her to a breakdown. Lt. Nathan drives back to see Dale Martin and Johnny arranges for a visit the next day and asks him to make sure that Jack works on Johnny.

After a vigorous workout, Johnny gets a rub down from Jack Olsen and talks to him. Johnny mentions the picture and asks Jack about his mother, and he tells Johnny that she is dead. Johnny tells Jack that Royal was a blackmailer and tells Jack that his theory that someone in the gym hated him and killed him because he was blackmailing someone else. As jack is massaging Johnny's neck, Johnny asks Jack to suppose that the killer found Royal alone and killed him because he was blackmailing someone close to the killer who could not take it and committed suicide. Johnny suggests to him that he was blackmailing Jack's father and he could not take it and killed him self because he could not pay anymore. Jack finally tells Johnny that he killed Royal. He finishes the massage and goes to the police. Lt. Nathan arrests Jack Olsen and gets a complete statement. Johnny has a drink with Dale Martin but can only see Jack Barrett. Johnny goes to his office and has a fifth of very dry gin that Dale helps him finish. Johnny finally takes a very long drive in the country by himself.

NOTES:
- CHARLES LYON IS THE ANNOUNCER
- MUSIC IS BY MILTON CHARLES
- IN THIS STORY, JOHNNY MENTIONS GOING TO HIS OFFICE RATHER THAN HIS APARTMENT.

Producer: Jaime del Valle   **Writers:** Blake Edwards
Cast: Edgar Barrier, Hy Averback, Hal March, Tony Barrett, Virginia Gregg

SHOW:	THE ROCHESTER THEFT MATTER
SHOW DATE:	5/12/1953
COMPANY:	ALLIED ADJUSTMENT BUREAU
AGENT:	
EXP. ACCT:	$155.42

SYNOPSIS: Johnny receives a collect call from Sgt. Papish, who works in the robbery detail, and he has instructions to call. They have found a mink coat that was stolen six months ago in the Jacoby case in Rochester. Johnny is told that the girl is in the hospital with two bullet holes in her.

Johnny goes to New York City and goes to the New Westin and then to the police where he meets Sgt. Papish. Johnny tells Sgt. Papish that it has been six months since the Rochester theft. Johnny is told that the coat is in the crime lab, and that the girl has no prints on file. Sgt. Papish tells Johnny that the police received a complaint at three this morning and the girl was found in the doorway shot twice. A lady across the street told the police that she saw a car drive up and drop the girl off, but it could be any man in any car. The coat was the only clue, although she was wearing a ring that is unrelated. Johnny tells Sgt. Papish that the claim has been paid off. The phone rings and Sgt. Papish is told that the girl is Eileen Madden.

Sgt. Papish and Johnny go to the address, which is a nice apartment in a nice area. Johnny meets Sgt. Walters of the crime lab, and he tells Johnny that he has not found anything. Johnny and Sgt. Papish meet Mrs. Stromberg from across the hall and she tells them that she met Eileen five months ago, and that her family lives in California. Eileen has several boyfriends, and one of the friends, Bill, has a car like the one seen the night before; he drives a black Cadillac. Bill is described as big and in his mid thirties. Mrs. Stromberg tells Johnny that Bill would give Eileen gifts from time-to-time. Johnny and Sgt. Papish go to the hospital and the doctor gives them two minutes with her. In the room Eileen mumbles "Bill" and tells them that Bill shot her and then she dies at 3:35 PM.

Johnny goes back to the apartment where the police find letters from her father, and a picture signed "Love Bill" in a closet. The police lab reports that Eileen was shot with a Colt .45 automatic, model 1911. Mrs. Stromberg returns and identifies the picture as the Bill who drives the Cadillac. Sgt. Papish gets a call and learns that Eileen had been married in 1951 to Bill Powers, and is divorced. Johnny and Sgt. Papish go to visit Bill Powers and they tell him of Eileen's death. He is stunned and tells them that he saw her just last week. Sgt. Papish tells Bill that she was wearing a stolen mink coat. Sgt. Papish tells Johnny that he noticed the black 1951 Cadillac convertible in the driveway, but he is not the same Bill in the picture. They all go to the morgue to identify the body. Bill tells Johnny that their marriage failed for all the stupid reasons. Johnny wants to prove that she did not steal the coat, and Bill tells Johnny that he knows about Bill Chambers. Sgt. Papish shows Bill the picture and he tells Sgt. Papish that it is Bill Chambers, but he does not know where Chambers lives or works. Bill tells Sgt. Papish that Chambers wanted to marry her but she did not want to. Bill tells them that he had bought a Cadillac because Chambers had one.

The police search their files and there are 24 William Chambers there and none were identified as Bill. The pawnshop detail turns up three more articles from the Jacoby robbery, and the description of the man matches Chambers. The Cadillac is found in a used car lot that morning. Johnny talks to the manager who tells him that the man was nervous and wanted a quick sale. The car provides prints for a William Carlson, who has several aliases and 14 arrests with two convictions for car theft. As the search area widens more stolen property appears in pawnshops. Johnny and Sgt. Papish go to the address provided in the last sale and find a William Courtney there. He is frisked and admits being Carlson and tells Sgt. Papish that he let them find him. He tells them that he did not mean to kill Eileen, and that he will not talk downtown. He tells Sgt. Papish that he has been doing ok with house robberies, and that he met Eileen and they went out several times. He met her the other night, gave her the coat and asked her to marry him. She did not want the coat and said she was going to marry her ex-husband. Then he got mad and shot her. He got tired of running and started unloading the goods. Courtney collapses and tells them that he took some poison when they knocked on the door. Sgt. Papish gives Courtney an antidote that saves his life.

The remaining Jacoby property and other items were found in the apartment and were impounded.

NOTES:
- THIS PROGRAM WAS DONE BY BOB BAILEY AS "THE TODD MATTER"
- THIS IS AN AFRS PROGRAM
- EDDIE DUNSTEDTER PROVIDES THE MUSIC

Producer: Jaime del Valle   **Writers:** E. Jack Neuman
Cast: Bill Johnstone, James Nusser, Virginia Gregg, John McIntire, Jeanette Nolan, Vic Perrin

◆   ❖   ◆

SHOW: THE EMILY BRADDOCK MATTER
SHOW DATE: 5/19/1953
COMPANY: BALTIMORE LIABILITY & TRUST
AGENT: FRANK PRESTON
EXP. ACCT: $738.32

SYNOPSIS: Johnny is called by Frank Preston and told that there is a bad check artist on the loose on the West Coast. So far she has taken $4,500.

Johnny flies to Santa Barbara, California and meets Sgt. Lopez, and then goes to the hotel where the latest check was cashed. Mr. Sheridan tells Johnny that he woman came into the hotel, asked for him by name and acted as if she knew him. She told him that she had just been divorced and ran up a bill for $813. Johnny goes to see Sgt. Lopez and then calls Frank, who tells him that the woman has just struck in Malibu. Johnny goes to the sheriff's office in Malibu and meets Sgt. Pell, who tells Johnny that a local man had just driven her to town. Johnny goes to talk to Mr. Garland who tells Johnny that the woman was recovering from the loss of a child, and he had driven her to the Beverly Glen Hotel, and then to a bar in town.

Johnny drives into Los Angels and goes to the bar, but the bartender has not seen any woman meeting the description. Johnny goes to the hotel and the luggage has not been claimed yet. The next day the police have identified the woman as Emily Braddock, who has a sister in Los Angeles. Johnny goes to see the sister, who is crippled. She is bitter that Emily has not cared for her, but hopes that Johnny never finds her.

Johnny gets a photo of Emily and takes it to Garland who tells Johnny that the photo is of Emily, and that she is in a small hotel in Santa Monica under the name Evelyn Brady. Johnny goes to the dingy hotel and finds Emily and arrests her.

NOTES:
- THE ANNOUNCER IS CHARLES LYON
- MUSIC IS BY MILTON CHARLES
- THIS STORY WAS MERGED WITH THE "THE THELMA IBSEN MATTER" AND BECAME "THE BRODERICK MATTER," PERFORMED BY BOB BAILEY.
- STORY INFORMATION OBTAINED FROM THE KNX COLLECTION IN THE THOUSAND OAKS LIBRARY

Producer: Jaime del Valle   **Writers**   E. Jack Neuman
Cast: James McCallion, John McIntire, Bill Conrad, Stacy Harris, Jeanette Nolan, Joan Banks

SHOW: THE BRISBANE FRAUD MATTER
SHOW DATE: 5/26/1953
COMPANY: COSMOPOLITAN BONDING & INSURANCE CORPORATION
AGENT:
EXP. ACCT: $286.20
SYNOPSIS: Charlie Pantella calls from missing persons and asks if Johnny called about Mr. Brisbane. Johnny tells him he is an investigator for the bonding company and heard about the disappearance from an insurance broker who was one of Brisbane's clients. They have no leads, and Sgt. Pantella invites Johnny to go with him to talk to Mrs. Brisbane.

Johnny flies to Detroit, Michigan, and uses an attorney to issue a writ to impound the records of Brisbane's business, but the police get to them first. Sgt.

Pantella tells Johnny that he has not gotten a lot of information, and that the DA's office is working on the books. Johnny and Sgt. Pantella go to talk to Mrs. Brisbane and she tells them that she last saw her husband two days earlier at breakfast. Sgt. Pantella tells her that he had not gone to his office and she tells him that Mr. Brisbane likes to take the bus to work. Johnny asks about enemies, but she tells Johnny that she knows of no one, and that he never discussed business at home as that was a rule. They have been married for almost 18 years, and she can think of no reason for him to run out. She tells Johnny that she had been out for dinner two days in a row and assumed that her husband was asleep in his room. On Thursday she called the office and learned he had not been there for two days and called the police. The maid told her that she had not made the bed for two days. She also tells Johnny that Mr. Brisbane would often not go to the office, and would stay at home reading and writing in his study. Mrs. Brisbane does not know if anything is missing from her husband's bedroom, but the servants would know. She tells Johnny that he would have a cocktail, but was not a drunk, and that Dr. L. D. Wainer is the family doctor. Johnny questions the servants and learns that Brisbane was a man of careful and precise habits. The study and bedroom are inspected, and it seems Brisbane took only the clothes on his back. Johnny interviews the office staff, but nothing is learned. The District Attorney reports that the business is healthy, and Dr. Wainer reports that Brisbane was in excellent health, for a man in his condition and circumstance. Johnny is told that Brisbane knew how to relax, and had tried his hand at writing occasionally. Brisbane had had a complete physical recently and was in excellent physical and mental health, and no one had noticed any signs of amnesia. Dr. Wainer tells Johnny that he had met Brisbane socially and that Hugh Brisbane had quite a head on his shoulders. Dr. Wainer relates that Brisbane had the ability to quote the classics, and remembers him quoting a Greek, Callicles. He was so impressed he looked up the quotation, and shows it to Johnny. The quote: "But if there were a man that had sufficient force, he would shake off and break through and escape from all this. He would trample underfoot all our formulas and spells and charms, and all our laws that are against nature. The slave would rise in rebellion and be lord over us and the light of natural justice would shine forth." This was quoted to Dr. Wainer on Monday, the day before Brisbane disappeared.

Brisbane's disappearance was complete and final until the District Attorney's men find that $5000 was taken from the savings account. Johnny and Sgt. Pantella visit the bank and talk to the teller, Mr. Cook, who shows them the withdrawal and recognizes Brisbane's picture. Cook tells them that Brisbane had taken out large amounts of money before, and that he took this money in large bills and put the money is a small bag. Cook tells Johnny that Brisbane was in no hurry when he left, like he had no place to go. Johnny verifies that Brisbane had not left with the bag, and all the transportation exits are watched. Sgt. Pantella gets a call from a bar, and the bartender tells him that Brisbane had been there Tuesday night. Johnny and Sgt. Pantella go to talk to the bartender and he recognizes a picture of Brisbane and tells Johnny and Sgt. Pantella that Brisbane stayed in the bar until 2 AM. He was on the phone long distance and Brisbane had asked for $20 in quarters. Johnny contacts the phone company, and a search of their records indicates a call was made to Kenneth Temple in San Francisco. Johnny tries to reach Temple, but is not able to get him on the phone. Johnny vaguely recognizes the name, but cannot place it. Johnny and Sgt. Pantella to go to the Brisbane home and ask Mrs. Brisbane if she knows the name Temple, but she does not know anyone by that name. She tells Johnny that she had been to San Francisco along with her husband two years ago. Sgt. Pantella gets a call from Mr. Temple, who tells him that Hugh Brisbane is there. Hugh talks to his wife and then to Sgt. Pantella. Mrs. Brisbane tells Johnny that Hugh had told her that he was leaving her and everyone else. He was going to take a long sea trip with Temple and would not be back for a year, if he ever came back. He wrote it all in a letter that she should get today. She tells Johnny that she cannot understand why he would want to leave, and that he should have talked to her about it. Johnny tells her that maybe he did, but his doctor was the only one he met who ever listened to him.

"It was true. Hugh Brisbane had just walked out one day and had no intention of coming back for a long, long time. And as far as the police were concerned, there was no way to stop him. As far as we are concerned, we will have to sit on that $25,000 bond and hope that he'll come back to Detroit some day when he gets what ever it is out of his system. There is nothing we can do either."

NOTES:
- COMMERCIAL BREAK #1 IS AN AFRS STORY ABOUT JAMMING OF RADIO SIGNALS.
- THIS STORY WAS DONE BY BOB BAILEY AS THE FIVE PART STORY "THE CALLICLES MATTER"
- QUOTED FROM "GORGIAS" BY PLATO, CIRCA 380 BCE.
- CHARLES LYONS IS THE ANNOUNCER
- MUSIC BY EDDIE DUNSTEDTER

Producer:	Jaime del Valle	Writers:	E. Jack Neuman
Cast:	Jay Novello, Jeanette Nolan, John McIntire, Joe Kearns, Virginia Gregg		

◆ ❖ ◆

SHOW:	THE COSTAIN MATTER
SHOW DATE:	6/2/1953
COMPANY:	FEDERAL INSURANCE & CLAIMS ADJUSTERS
AGENT:	
EXP. ACCT:	$227.50

SYNOPSIS: Introduction missing.

Johnny goes to Toledo, Ohio to investigate 37 stolen merchandise claims, likely a shoplifting ring. Johnny meets with Lt. Sturges and tells him that he is investigating for the insurance companies. Johnny is told that the Maumee Dress Shop reported a coat and dress missing, and then three days later the M'Ladies Shoppe reported a theft. Then more came in, and the last one was just two days ago. The merchandise is usually expensive and always women's clothes in size 10, and none of the articles have been sold. Johnny goes to see Sgt. Grace Beidler, a policewoman who tells Johnny that this thief has good and exclusive taste. Grace thinks that, based on the color of the clothes, the woman recipient has green eyes and short red hair. The choice of clothes colors and cosmetics lead them to the conclusion that the thief's eyes are green, and that the hats are designed for a woman with short hair. Johnny asks Grace "what if someone is doing it for a woman?" Johnny is told that it is impossible to watch all the stores, so they are checking all of the beauty salons for well-dressed redheads. Johnny spends a day and a half studying the reports and agrees with Sgt. Beidler.

Lt. Sturges calls Johnny about a lead and they meet at Cole's Apparel. A clerk there tells Johnny and Lt. Sturges that she saw a woman wearing a green suede coat that had been stolen a month ago. She saw the woman at the cafeteria across the street and is sure the coat is the one. The woman she saw had dark hair and wore glasses. She got suspicious and left in a cab. At the cab company Johnny and Lt. Sturges check the cab records and get an address for the fare. They go to the apartment building and the manager recognizes the coat as belonging to Miss Lillian Jones, who just moved in two days ago. They go upstairs and Lt. Sturges knocks, and the woman answers the door and they go in. The woman denies stealing the coat and tells Johnny that she had her lunch in her apartment. She also denies even having a green suede coat. Lt. Sturges takes her downtown where he discovers that she has a record, one arrest for grand theft a year ago but no conviction. The clerk and cabby identify Miss Jones and the Lt. Sturges searches the apartment. Lillian will not talk and wants to call a lawyer. Later the police return with the coat they found in a hamper. It was positively identified as the stolen coat.

Lillian finally admits to stealing the coat from the Costain home while she was working there as a domestic. Johnny and Lt. Sturges meet with Mr. Costain at his home and tell him about Lillian Jones and the coat. Mr. Costain knows nothing of the coat. He tells Johnny that he had let Miss Jones go, as she did not work out. Johnny is told that Mrs. Costain died last February. Mr. Costain agrees to come in the next day to identify the coat. On the way out, Johnny mentions a photograph of a woman with red hair and green eyes. A check of the neighborhood reveals that the Costains had been there less than a year, and had lived in Detroit before that. Johnny learns that Mrs. Costain had died of a heart condition.

At police headquarters, Costain calls and changes his story and wants to see Johnny and Lt. Sturges. Johnny and Lt. Sturges return to the house where Mr. Costain tells them that he has had a problem with servants and had filed an insurance claim for the coat, which Mrs. Costain had bought before she died. Johnny notes that the coat was stolen after Mrs. Costain died. Mr. Costain tells him that his wife is not dead, and that she will come back and he will have all these beautiful things for her. He tells Johnny that when she went away, he would go out and walk through the stores and would steal the things she liked. He had denied her the thinks she loves, so now he has made it up to her by stealing the things she liked. He tells Johnny that everything is in her bedroom.

NOTES:
- CAST INFORMATION FROM TERRY SALOMONSON.
- CHARLES LYONS IS THE ANNOUNCER
- MUSIC BY MILTON CHARLES

Producer: Jaime del Valle   Writers: E. Jack Neuman
Cast: Hal March, Hy Averback, Edgar Barrier, Virginia Gregg,
             Mary Lansing, Peggy Webber

◆   ❖   ◆

SHOW: THE OKLAHOMA RED MATTER
SHOW DATE: 6/9/1953
COMPANY: UNIVERSAL ADJUSTERS
AGENT: FRANK AHERN
EXP. ACCT: $286.45

SYNOPSIS: Frank Ahern at Universal Adjusters calls and wants Johnny to go to Kentucky to look at a horse that Mr. Calgor has insured for $65,000. The horse was injured and was destroyed.

Johnny goes to Lexington, Kentucky and gets a room at the Southern Hotel. Johnny then goes to the Calgor business office where he learns that Mr. Monroe is no longer at the company and the he will have to see Mr. Calgor. Johnny calls the farm and is told that Mr. Calgor is out. Johnny goes to see Dr. Pierce, the veterinarian. Dr. Pierce tells Johnny the horse was injured by a piece of equipment and injured his leg, and Calgor had the horse destroyed and cremated on the premises. Johnny is told that there are no x-rays and that Dr. Pierce had advised Calgor to have the animal destroyed. Dr. Pierce tells Johnny that Calgor took his word, and asks why he won't. Johnny mails the medical report to a veterinarian in Cleveland and drives to the Calgor farm. Lucy Calgor meets Johnny at the door and is sad about the horse. She tells Johnny that the horse was not injured. Mr. Calgor comes in and slaps Lucy. He tells Johnny that Lucy gets hysterical whenever he shoots a horse. Calgor thinks Johnny is going behind his back by going to Dr. Pierce. Johnny tells him that the claim will not be paid until he finishes his report. Calgor tells Johnny that he fired Monroe for filing the claim so soon. Johnny tells Calgor that he went to Dr. Pierce because that was the logical place to start. Calgor tells Johnny that he is not afraid of Johnny or the insurance company, but Johnny tells him that so far the information is not in Calgor's favor. Calgor tells Johnny that the horse was scared by a mouse, reared back into the machinery and was injured. The trainer, Jim Knight has been fired, and that no one else was there. Calgor tells Johnny that accidents happen and that he gets rid of the animals as soon as possible. Calgor calls Abbott the butler and tells him to throw Johnny out.

Johnny talks to the horse handlers and gets Jim Knight's address in Baltimore. Johnny meets Lucy near the stables and she is more reluctant to talk. She tells Johnny that Red was the best horse they have had in several years.

Johnny checks on Calgor's finances and wires Hartford and Jim Knight in Baltimore. Later, Johnny gets a call from Mrs. Knight who tells Johnny that her son is at the Calgor Farm. Johnny tells her that he left the farm and she tells Johnny that he has not come home. That is not like Jimmy, maybe there is something wrong. Now Johnny is suspicious.

After returning to the farm, Abbott shows Johnny the room where Knight stayed, and tells him that no one saw Jim leave. Abbott tells Johnny that Lucy had driven him around, so maybe she knows where he is. Johnny talks with Lucy again and she tells Johnny that she had been arguing with father for weeks and had used Johnny to get back at him. Lucy tells Johnny that she had been seeing Jim Knight and that her father did not like it. She tells Johnny that she had been looking for an excuse and thinks that maybe her father is mad. She tells Johnny that she does not know where Jim is. Lucy tells Johnny that the Calgors have always been angry people but that her father has not been himself lately. She tells Johnny that he once bought a new car and wrecked it when there was a small problem. She is in love with Jim Knight, and always has been.

Back at the farm Johnny talks with the hands. Later Frank Ahern calls to say that Calgor's finances are good, and that Calgor has not threatened to sue, so maybe he does not have a just claim. Johnny visits Dr. Pierce again and tells him the claim is being denied. Johnny has checked Dr. Pierce out and does not believe his story. Johnny tells Dr. Pierce that Calgor will have to sue and produce Jim Knight, and that means that Dr. Pierce will be required to testify. Dr. Pierce tells Johnny that he has been Calgor's friend for 18 years and that Calgor asked him to lie for him. He tells Johnny that Red was dead when he got there, and that Red was not the horse they thought he was and Calgor just shot him and Knight saw it. Dr. Pierce thinks Calgor is losing his mind.

Johnny drives back to the farm and Abbott opens the door and tells Johnny that this is not a good time to be there. Lucy tells Johnny that father is not in a good mood and that she has been crying because she cannot please him. Calgor walks in and yells at Johnny to take his hands off Lucy or he will kill him too, and then he hits Lucy with his cane and walks out. Johnny calls the sheriff and goes to the stables. Calgor tells Johnny to go away, and warns him that he has a shotgun. Johnny tells Calgor that Dr. Pierce has talked to him. Calgor tells Johnny that he will shoot the whole bunch and shoots at Johnny. Johnny fires back and hits Calgor. As he dies, Calgor tells Johnny that he shot Knight and his body is under the floor of the stable. Calgor asks Johnny "I'm not crazy, am I?" and dies.

NOTES:
- **THIS WAS DONE BY BOB BAILEY AS "THE DUKE RED MATTER"**

- Charles Lyons is the announcer
- Music by Milton Charles
- Cast information from Terry Salomonson.

Producer: Jaime del Valle   Writers: E. Jack Neuman
Cast: Gene Howell, Dave Young, John McIntire, Peter Leeds, Parley
             Baer, Roy Glenn, Jeanette Nolan

◆   ❖   ◆

SHOW: THE EMIL CARTER MATTER
SHOW DATE: 6/16/1953
COMPANY: COLUMBIA ALL RISK INSURANCE COMPANY
AGENT:
EXP. ACCT: $572.00

SYNOPSIS: A woman calls and asks Johnny about the Emil Carter killing. She is Janice Lake and she wants to talk.

Johnny goes to Los Angeles, California where the police are searching for Janice Lake, who had been seen running from Emil's door after shots were fired. Johnny is looking for Emil's brother Frank, the beneficiary. Johnny cabs to the harbor in San Pedro and waits to be met in front of a sporting goods shop. A man asks Johnny for a match and takes Johnny to the girl in a cab. On the way, the man is quiet and bored. Near the beach, the man takes Johnny to Janice who is waiting in a car. Johnny tells Janice that he knows Janice is a former dancer who got involved with Emil. Johnny tells her that she is doing all the wrong things typical of a scared killer. She tells Johnny that she was in the hallway and heard the shots and then ran. She wants to tell Johnny about her side of the story. Janice tells Johnny that she and Emil were going to leave town and live in South America. They had reservations in a different name, as there were friends who would not want him to leave. That night he called and told Janice that he had changed his mind about marrying her. She went to the apartment and heard voices inside, and then shots and she ran. Johnny tells Janice that he will not tell the police, as they will not believe him.

The man and Johnny walk to a café and the man, who Johnny guesses is Janice's brother Frank, asks Johnny why a man would have killed Carter. Johnny tells him that the insurance company wanted that question answered, and about the insurance policy on his brother. Frank tells Johnny that Emil Carter was married to a common law wife and was paying her $1500 a month to keep the secret. Frank had tipped the wife that Emil was leaving for Mexico, and that Janice did not know about the wife. He tells Johnny that he did not think that Janice would go rushing up to the apartment. Johnny learns that the other woman's name is Hazel Carter. Johnny goes to his hotel after deciding that what he learned was too weak to give to the police.

The next day Johnny talks to the residents of the apartment building and learns about the greatest hindrance to investigation, the average eyewitness.

Mr. Samuel Nelson is a composite of the tenants. He tells Johnny that he came out and saw Mrs. Roberts in the hallway. He looked to the rear and saw Mrs. Robinson and heard someone running towards the front. Mrs. Roberts said nothing, but Johnny tells him that she said she did. Now everyone is confused about what they saw and no one can swear to having seen Janice being in the hallway. Johnny mentions a second woman, but Mr. Nelson is confused about what he saw.

Johnny talks to Lt. Scott at homicide, and he is not sure of Johnny's evidence. Johnny tells Lt. Scott that he is not sure that Janice is innocent, and is only thinking of the insurance angle. Lt. Scott tells Johnny that he has questioned Carter's wife and other relatives. At his hotel, Hazel Carter is waiting for Johnny in the bar. She tells Johnny that they have a common problem. She tells Johnny that Janice's brother called her and told her that she is a suspect and she wants to get rid of the suspicion. She wants to know about how to offer a reward for information.

In Johnny's room, Hazel tells him that she is relieved that Frank had gotten the news out about their relationship. With him gone there is nothing. She loved Emil and talked to him when she heard he was leaving. She tells Johnny that Emil had enemies. She wants to offer $5,000 to Johnny to help, and he suggests that she go to the papers.

The next day the reward hits the papers and Janice calls Johnny and asks him about the reward and whether it is a trick. She tells Johnny that her brother had told her about Hazel last night. She tells Johnny that the police will have to find her, and that she will not give up, as she has to think. Lt. Scott calls Johnny and tells him that he and has a confession from Janice Lake's brother. Johnny tells Lt. Scott about meeting Janice at the beach and that the discussion with the brother was nothing. Lt. Scott tells Johnny that when Johnny mentioned the angle of a man killing Emil, Frank thought Johnny had something on him, so when the reward hit the papers, he gave up.

Johnny goes to visit Frank in his cell, and Frank tells Johnny that he never thought he would go so far as to murder Emil. Frank had been shilling for Janice for ten years. When he found out Emil was taking her out of the country, Frank went to talk to him. They argued about Janice, Carter laughed at him so he shot him. He stayed in the apartment until the crowd left and went out the back door, but Johnny finds a lot of errors in his statement. Lt. Scott comes in to tell Johnny about a shooting between two women at Hazel Carter's apartment. Johnny and Lt. Scott go to the apartment. The doctor tells them that both are still alive. Johnny talks with Janice, who tells Johnny that she hopes she killed Hazel. Johnny tells her that Frank had tried to save her so she knew that Hazel must have done it. Johnny talks to Hazel who admits killing Emil because he was going away with Janice.

Johnny was wrong from the beginning. Frank took the wrap for Janice because he thought Hazel was innocent.

NOTES:
- THIS IS A REMAKE OF "THE ALMA SCOTT MATTER" DONE BY EDMOND O'BRIEN ON 12/29/1951
- CHARLES LYONS IS THE ANNOUNCER
- MUSIC BY EDDIE DUNSTEDTER

Producer: Jaime del Valle   Writers: Gil Doud
Cast: Mary Jane Croft, Hal March, Hy Averback, Frank Nelson, Mary Lansing

◆   ❖   ◆

SHOW: THE JONATHAN BELLOWS MATTER
SHOW DATE: 6/23/1953
COMPANY: INTERCONTINENTAL INDEMNITY & BONDING CORPORATION
AGENT: ROGER STERN
EXP. ACCT: $208.60

SYNOPSIS: Roger Stern calls and tells Johnny that someone has tried to kill Jonathan Bellows. He is insured for $500,000. Go look into it; his wife Edith is expecting you.

Johnny drives to New York City and meets with Mrs. Edith Bellows. She tells Johnny that her husband was shot at in his garden. Edith tells Johnny that he is sixty-three and does not like meddlers, and the police are meddlers. Edith tells Johnny that she is mildly concerned; and Johnny tells her that the insurance company is very concerned. Johnny is told that Edith is wife number three, and that Bellows has a son, Ralph.

Edith drives Johnny to the upstate mansion in the station wagon. At the mansion, Johnny meets Ralph who tells Johnny that his father is in the library with Professor Wilt. Ralph is sure that this father will blow a fuse at Johnny's being there. Ralph tells Johnny that his father is a tough, bigoted and unreasonable man, and that he sort of likes making him blow a fuse.

Johnny meets Bellows who is playing chess with the professor. Bellows objects to the insurance company sending a meddler and tells Johnny to get out or he will have Johnny fired. Johnny gets tough and tells Bellows to sit down. Johnny reminds him that the insurance company has an interest in his life, and if there is no investigation, he will call the insurance company and tell them to cancel his policy. Johnny tells him that if he tries to get tough with Johnny again, he will turn him over his knee to give him the spankings he missed as a child. Suddenly Bellows softens and wants to talk to Johnny alone. Bellows shows Johnny a letter that threatens his life and tells him "you will pay for Ashantay." Bellows tells Johnny that he had been involved in a mining operation in Africa thirty years ago, and that his partner Frank Victor had been killed in a cave-in after an argument and that he was cleared of any guilt. Bellows has told Johnny this because he has decided to trust Johnny. Johnny asks if Frank is still alive, or is it blackmail, or a scare tactic? Bellows tells Johnny to take the station wagon back to town and stay in the Park Avenue apartment.

Johnny arrives at the apartment to a bellman that is charged with looking after Johnny's every need. Johnny calls Roger Stern and requests more information on the family, Professor Wilt and the servants. Later Johnny gets a call from Bellows, or is it Bellows? The voice tells Johnny to go to a bar and pick up a package and bring it to him. Johnny goes to the bar, picks up the package and drives it to the mansion. At the mansion, Ralph is out and Edith is leaving. Johnny goes to the library where Bellows tells Johnny that he knows nothing about a package, and then suddenly remembers that he does. As Bellows is opening the package, Johnny goes to phone a company physician when Ralph comes in. As Johnny is explaining about the package there is a massive explosion, and Bellows is killed; there was a bomb in the package.

Johnny drives back to the bar and looks for the bartender, who has gone home. The current bartender gives Johnny the address of Earl Phillips, who lives on East 157th street. Johnny goes to the apartment and gets no answer at the door. Johnny gets the landlady, "who is four years older than Grant's tomb" to open the door where Johnny finds Ernie stabbed to death. Johnny spots a trail of blood leading to a closet, and convinces the landlady to call the police. "Go down the police and call the stairs" she repeats on the way out, scared to death. Johnny opens the door and finds the man with the knife; Professor Wilt. They struggle and Professor Wilt is shot. Before he dies, Professor Wilt tells Johnny that he had once been a carnival worker and learned hypnosis. He eventually became a psychoanalyst and met Bellows through his wife. It was a good setup. When he learned of the Ashantay incident, Edith came up with the idea to get rid of him. The phone call was done under hypnosis and the opening of the package was a post-hypnotic suggestion. Wilt dies before the police arrive.

Mrs. Bellows is arrested and Johnny gives his story to the police.

NOTES:
- ROGER STERN WAS THE AGENT FOR INTERCONTINENTAL INDEMNITY & BONDING COMPANY IN THE "THE CUBAN JEWEL MATTER," BUT HE WAS KILLED IN THAT STORY. ROGER STERN ALSO APPEARS IN SEVERAL STORIES AFTER THIS ONE. SEE THE REPORTS SECTION FOR THE STORIES.
- CAST INFORMATION FROM TERRY SALOMONSON
- MUSIC BY EDDIE DUNSTEDTER
- CHARLES LYONS IS THE ANNOUNCER

Producer: Jaime del Valle   **Writers:** Les Crutchfield
Cast: Clayton Post, Virginia Gregg, Tony Barrett, Ralph Moody, Howard McNear, Martha Wentworth

◆ ❖ ◆

SHOW: THE JONES MATTER
SHOW DATE: 6/30/1953

COMPANY: CONCOURSE MUTUAL LIFE INSURANCE COMPANY
AGENT: GEORGE DEAN
EXP. ACCT: $418.40

SYNOPSIS: George Dean calls and asks Johnny how he would like to go to Vas Vegas? George tells Johnny that Lilly LaSoure has just had a $30,000 diamond necklace stolen. She still has the same two bad habits, gambling and young men.

Johnny flies to Las Vegas, Nevada, checks into the Flamingo Hotel and goes to see Lilly at her hotel. Lilly is with Eddie Lawson when he gets there. When Johnny tells Lilly why he is there, she is puzzled. Oh, the necklace! She is afraid that Johnny is going to ask all sorts of embarrassing questions. She would love to talk to Johnny, but Buck and Devastator are waiting for her. Eddie explains to Johnny that Buck is her riding instructor, and Devastator is her horse. Eddie tells Johnny that he is going to marry Lilly. Johnny is told to come to the hotel after the show; everyone involved will be there.

Johnny drives to the Lazy J Ranch and talks to Buck, who has no idea of what happened. He tells Johnny that he was there with Miss Jo, Joan Drake who had wanted to meet Lilly. Joan and Lilly had gone to change clothes and came back. Then he heard Lilly scream that her rocks were gone. That is about all. Buck has something else to tell Johnny, and he guesses that Buck is going to marry Lilly.

Johnny talks to Marshall Kimberly and gets the story of the theft. It seems that Lilly, Eddie, Joan and Buck (who is from Los Angeles, not Texas, by the way) were on the terrace when the jewels disappeared. Joan is from the east, and is a floor manager at the "Billion Dollar Club." Johnny mentions the slot machine in the Marshall's office and puts in a dollar and loses. Johnny is told that the slot machine is rigged to lose and that the proceeds go to the local orphanage.

Johnny goes to talk to Joan Drake. While Joan is playing, and losing roulette, Johnny leans that she was born to rich parents and went to a swank eastern college. Her father was involved with another woman. When everyone found out, his clients left him, his wife divorced him and he committed suicide after the other woman jilted him. Johnny asks Joan why an educated woman like her is working in Las Vegas for $50 per week, and hanging out with Lilly. Joan tells Johnny that Vegas has the glamour and glitter that she was used to.

Later that night after Lily's show everyone is there at the pool terrace. Lilly tells Johnny that she had worn the necklace for her show and, after changing clothes with Joan, she had put it in a handkerchief by her chair and it vanished. Johnny tells her that the insurance company will want more, so she tells Johnny that she had played the slot machine and won a jackpot, and that Joan was sitting there too. They were all in bathing suits, so it was hard to hide anything. Buck and Eddie walk up to Lilly and argue over who will walk Lilly to her next show.

Later that night, Joan calls and asks Johnny if the insurance company will deal for information. Johnny tells her that he must check. She also tells Johnny that her real name is Jones, and that her father was Jonathan Vanderlay Jones and that Lilly was named in his divorce as the other woman. Johnny and Joan eat dinner and Johnny wonders if Joan is out for revenge, or knows who and how the necklace was stolen. After the show, Lilly tells Johnny that she wants to drop the claim. Johnny asks Lilly who did it, or whom she thinks did it. Johnny runs through who the likely suspects are, and that he is curious now. After Lilly leaves the marshal pages Johnny, and is told that Kimberly has found Joan Drake in a parking lot, dead. Johnny goes to the scene and finds Joan, beaten in a car belonging to Buck. Her hands are rusty and greasy and the car radiator is still warm. Johnny tells Kimberly that Joan had called and wanted to deal; so maybe she did know who did it, and died trying to prove it.

Johnny goes to the pool and examines it. He wraps his room key into a handkerchief, and throws it in, and watches it float down into the drain at the deep end. Johnny goes to the pump house, shuts down the pump, and uses a brand new wrench to open the suction tank where he finds his room key and the necklace. On his way back out, the lights go out and someone pushes Johnny into the pool and swims toward him. Johnny uses the wrench to hit the swimmer. Marshall Kimberly arrives and they pull Eddie Lawson from the pool. Johnny tells Kimberly that Eddie had taken the necklace, and that Joan had found out where it was and died for her efforts.

Johnny goes to see Lilly and gives her the necklace. Johnny tells her that Joan is dead and that Eddie killed her. She tells Johnny that she really meant no harm to anyone. Lilly tells Johnny that the necklace was given to her by someone with the initials "JVJ," but they really do not mean anything to her.

Johnny notes the policy is coming up for renewal and advises against it, as Lilly is a bad risk.

NOTES:
- CAST INFORMATION FROM TERRY SALOMONSON.
- CHARLES LYONS IS THE ANNOUNCER
- MUSIC BY EDDIE DUNSTEDTER

Producer: Jaime del Valle   Writers: Les Crutchfield
Cast: Ken Christy, Mary Lansing, Victor Perrin, Hal March, Parley
           Baer, Virginia Gregg

◆ ❖ ◆

SHOW: THE BISHOP BLACKMAIL MATTER
SHOW DATE: 7/7/1953
COMPANY: NATIONAL ALL-RISK INSURANCE COMPANY
AGENT: PHILLIP SHAW
EXP. ACCT: $46.35
SYNOPSIS: Johnny is called by Phillip Shaw and told that Mrs. Bishop has been found dead. She was with Tony Grayson, a known blackmailer. It looks like Grayson killed her and then shot himself. She has a $32,000 policy with the husband as the beneficiary.

Johnny goes to New York City and talks to Mr. Bishop in his apartment, and he tells Johnny that he knew that his wife was being blackmailed. He got a phone call from a friend of Tony who told him that the blackmail would continue. Johnny is told that Mrs. Bishop was wild in her youth and that the man has some letters she wrote and he wants $100,000. Johnny also is told that Mrs. Bishop had all of the money in the family.

Johnny goes to the 5th precinct and meets Lt. Beck who tells Johnny that Bishop has been married for three years. Johnny also sees some photos of the murder scene and is told that the friend of Tony Grayson is a wino named Wilbur Truitt. Johnny calls Mr. Bishop and tells him about Truitt and then goes to the Parrot Club and finds Wilbur. For the price of a bottle, Johnny is told that Grayson has a friend named Leo Fink. Wilbur gives Johnny the address and tells him that he is the second person to ask him for that information that day. Johnny goes to Fink's address and finds Lt. Beck there. Leo Fink is dead and the room has been torn up and it looks like the killer used the fire escape. Johnny asks Lt. Beck about a glass in the pictures and is told that it had prints from Grayson's right hand. Johnny goes to see Mr. Bishop and tells him about the death of Fink, but Bishop has an alibi. Johnny goes back to talk to Lt. Beck who tells Johnny that Wilbur will not talk about who else asked him for the address. Johnny is told that the paraffin tests showed that Grayson did not fire the gun, but Mrs. Bishop did. Johnny thinks that Mrs. Bishop killed Grayson and someone she trusted took the gun and killed her.

Johnny goes back to the Parrot Club and for another bottle learns that the other man was Louis Crabb, an assassin who just walked in the door. Johnny hits Crabb with a bottle and Wilbur is shot. When Crabb wakes up he tells Johnny that he was paid by a "John Jones" to kill Fink, and will be paid tonight on the ferry, and is supposed to wear a carnation in his lapel. Johnny goes to the ferry that night with a carnation in his lapel and spots Mr. Bishop. Johnny tells him that he hired Crabb to kill Leo, and killed his wife for her money. Bishop hits Johnny and runs, but Johnny shoots him. Bishop admits to killing his wife. He found the letters and gave them to Grayson and was splitting the blackmail.

NOTES:
- THE ANNOUNCER IS CHARLES LYON
- MUSIC IS BY EDDIE DUNSTEDTER
- STORY INFORMATION OBTAINED FROM THE **KNX** COLLECTION IN THE THOUSAND OAKS LIBRARY

Producer:	Jaime del Valle	**Writers**	**Blake Edwards**
Cast:	John Stephenson, Bill Johnstone, Jack Moyles, Herb Butterfield		

❖ ❖ ❖

SHOW:	THE SHAYNE BOMBING MATTER
SHOW DATE:	7/14/1953
COMPANY:	COLUMBIA ALL RISK INSURANCE COMPANY
AGENT:	
EXP. ACCT:	$123.70

SYNOPSIS: Introduction missing.

Johnny goes to New York City to get the information on David Shayne and meets with Lt. Will Stevens, an old friend. Johnny is told that David's brother is being held, as he mailed the box and it came from California. Charles swears that he did not do it and they were very close. Johnny reminds Lt. Stevens that Cain and Abel were close also. Lt. Stevens tells Johnny that there does not seem to be a motive in the case. After his lawyer showed up, Charles hushed up and will not talk. David was a factory foreman at Bishop and Harding and was active in union affairs. Johnny talks to Charles Shayne in his cell and tells him that he is investigating his brother's death. Charles tells Johnny that he did not send in the bomb. He tells Johnny that the package came from California, where he worked in a shipyard for eight months. Johnny is told to look at the police report if he wants more answers. Johnny asks why he came back to New York, and Charley tells Johnny that he quit and came back to New York because he did not like the job.

Johnny goes to the hospital to see Mrs. Shayne. Johnny tells her that Charles is ok. She tells Johnny that she made a mistake telling the police that Charles sent the package, as he did not do it. She feels that David must have been wrong. She tells Johnny that they were in kitchen, and that the package was delivered to the factory, addressed to David. He came home and told her that the package was from Charles. Johnny then goes to see Mary Shayne, David's sister, who is also in hospital. She is sedated, but she tells Johnny that Charles did not do it, as he was helping David. She tells Johnny that Charles knows who sent the package and that David was making speeches against the Workers Protective Association and Charles was helping David in California. A man named Wagner called David all the time, and he is a lawyer. David also told someone at factory that Charles was helping him. It was Ralph Prior who he sometimes ate dinner with.

On the way out a sidewalk photographer takes Johnny's picture. Johnny takes a cab to the factory and talks to Ralph Prior. Ralph tells Johnny that Shayne was a good friend and that he had worked there for six years. He tells Johnny that he had said goodbye to David when he left work yesterday. Ralph tells Johnny that the mail comes in from mailroom and that the foreman usually sends some one from the floor to get it. Johnny goes to the mailroom and there had been a heavy package for David, and that someone picked it up. Johnny calls Lt. Stevens and tells him that David did not send the package. Lt. Stevens agrees, as the contents were high-grade dynamite. Johnny asks Lt. Stevens to pick up Ralph Prior and hold him as long a possible.

Johnny waits outside the plant until Prior is picked up. Johnny then goes to see Lt. Stevens and tells him that Charles was doing undercover work on the WPA. Lt. Stevens tells Johnny that the WPA is an extortion ring that muscles in on the local unions and forces people to pay up. The FBI has been working for over a year on busting it. Johnny is told that Prior will not talk and Johnny wants to see who bails him out. Lt. Stevens tells Johnny that John Wagner also came to see Charles. If Wagner is involved he probably threatened Charles. Johnny tells Lt. Stevens that if Charles was working with his brother, then Wagner probably threatened his family with another bomb to keep Charles quiet. So if the bomb was sent from within the factory, someone else is involved. As they are talking Lt. Stevens is told that Wagner has come in to see his client, Ralph Prior.

Johnny spots Wagner, was wearing blue suit, homburg and spats. When Wagner leaves, Johnny follows him in a cab to a waterfront dive. Johnny goes in and asks the bartender about Wagner. When Johnny asks where the back door goes, the bartender tells "Mr. Dollar" to go back there with him, as Johnny is expected. Johnny wants to make a call first but the bartender has a gun and takes Johnny back to see Wagner. Behind the backroom is an office with Mr. Wagner who tells Johnny that he is in serious trouble. Johnny is told that the photographer had taken his picture, and that they looked him up and found out who he is. Johnny is told that Al will take him out and take care of him. Johnny confirms with Wagner that Prior knew the package was coming and that they had switched the contents with the dynamite. David thought there were important papers in the package. Their people knew of the package and alerted them. A buzzer warns of trouble out front. Al shoves Johnny out the back door as Lt. Stevens comes in with Prior. Al turns to shoot Lt. Stevens, who shoots Al first. Wagner goes out the window and Johnny chases him. Johnny tackles Wagner and knocks him out. When Lt. Stevens yells at Johnny for taking a risk, Johnny tells him "You gotta be crazy to be a hero."

Wagner was head of WPA and Prior worked for him. When David told Prior of Charles' work, Prior told Wagner who had him substitute the dynamite when the papers showed up. Wagner had sprung Prior, and Lt. Stevens had followed Prior to Wagner's just in time to save Johnny.

NOTES:
- CHARLES LYONS IS THE ANNOUNCER
- MUSIC BY EDDIE DUNSTEDTER

Producer: Jaime del Valle   Writers: Blake Edwards
Cast: Junius Matthews, Frank Nelson, Clayton Post, Virginia Gregg,
            Mary Lansing, Sammie Hill, Jim Nusser

SHOW:	THE BLACK DOLL MATTER
SHOW DATE:	7/21/1953
COMPANY:	NATIONAL ALL RISK INSURANCE COMPANY
AGENT:	PHILLIP SHAW
EXP. ACCT:	$467.60

SYNOPSIS: Phillip Shaw calls Johnny about a shooting in Los Angeles. The victim was Miss Judith Thompson. Johnny is told to get the details at the office before he flies to Los Angeles.

Johnny flies to Los Angeles, California and goes to the Wentworth Hotel. Johnny meets Lt. Brickford and learns that Miss Thompson was shot once with a .38 and the police have talked to witnesses and so far there is no real reason for the killing. Johnny is told that there is a new boy friend, named William Carnes, who works for Timken Aircraft as a test pilot. Also, Miss Thompson was shot in her apartment and the boyfriend is a former military pilot. The police are sure that she went out that evening, but they do not know where. Johnny and Lt. Brickford go to talk to Bill Carnes at the Timken Aircraft plant. Johnny and Lt. Brickford meet with Mr. Timken and tell him why he is there. They are told that Bill is getting ready to take up a new airplane so Johnny and Lt. Brickford go out and watch the tests, and they are impressive. After the plane lands, they go to the office and Lt. Brickford tells Bill that Judith is dead. Bill tells Lt. Brickford that he had stayed home on the night of the killing, and then he changes his mind. He tells Johnny that he is married and separated, but he was lonesome and took Judy out that night. Bill tells Johnny that they went to the beach and played the concessions on the pier, and nothing unusual happened. Bill tells Johnny that he had split with his wife over his job. Bill really loves his wife, and does not want his name in the papers. Johnny and Lt. Brickford leave and on the way out, Bill runs after them to tell them he almost had a fight with a man running the shooting gallery on the pier. He had won a big black doll and Judy wanted it and he had to almost fight the man to get it for her. Bill tells them that Judy took the doll home, along with a lot of other trinkets. After they pull away, Lt. Brickford tells Johnny that the doll was missing when they searched the apartment, but that the trinkets were there.

Johnny and Lt. Brickford go to the apartment of the dead girl where they find the trinkets on the dresser; but there is no black doll. Johnny and Lt. Brickford go back to talk to Bill Carnes at his apartment before they head for the pier. Bill tells them that he is positive that Judy took the doll home. Bill confirms that the argument was over the doll, and that Judy took it home with her. Bill agrees to go with Johnny and Lt. Brickford to the pier to identify the man he had argued with after he is told that the doll is missing. After dinner, they all drive to the amusement pier and look for the shooting gallery. Johnny spots a black doll on the top shelf and Johnny shoots out all the targets and wins the doll. Lt. Brickford asks the man running the stand, whose name is Virgil Wellman, who was running the stand three nights ago. Lt. Brickford is told that a man named Charlie Gilbert was running the stand that night, but that he quit last night. Johnny and Lt. Brickford question Virgil and learn that he had never met Charlie until three weeks ago when he hired him, but that he had a bad temper. Lt. Brickford is sure that he has seen Virgil somewhere, and takes the doll to have it examined.

Later that night the phone rings and Lt. Brickford calls to tell Johnny that a man has been pulled from the ocean. There was no identification, but he looks like Gilbert had been described. Also, Johnny is told that Virgil Wellman, who is really Virgil Sheldon, has a narcotics record and has served five years. Johnny goes to city hall and meets Lt. Brickford and goes over the information Lt. Brickford has. Bill Carnes arrives and identifies the man who was pulled from the ocean as the man he argued with. Johnny learns that the man has been identified by his prints as Charles Sidney, alias Sidney Gilbert and Charles Gilbert, and that Gilbert was wanted by the FBI. Johnny and Lt. Brickford go back to the pier to talk to Virgil, but the gallery is closed, so they look around. Johnny tells Lt. Brickford that the doll Bill had won probably had something in it, and was supposed to be picked up by a particular party, but Carnes got there first. Johnny hears a boat pull up to the landing, and Johnny sees two men pass a crate off to two men on the landing. Johnny sees Virgil and another man bring the crate up to the pier. Lt. Brickford calls to Virgil to stop, there is shooting and Virgil is wounded and the other man is killed. Lt. Brickford opens the crate and it is full of black dolls, all stuffed with drugs.

Virgil tells Johnny about a plan to pass the dolls off to a pickup man on a certain night each week. Bill had won the doll, so Virgil had to go after it. Judith found Virgil searching her apartment, and he killed her. Virgil shot Charlie because Bill could identify him. Johnny gets to take his doll home with him. It looks awful but makes a fair ashtray.

NOTES:
- THIS IS FROM AN **AFRS** TAPE THAT CONTAINS AN ARTICLE ABOUT SIGNAL JAMMING
- THE MID-PROGRAM COMMERCIAL IS ABOUT THE PRESIDENCY OF GEORGE WASHINGTON
- CAST INFORMATION FROM TERRY SALOMONSON.
- CHARLES LYONS IS THE ANNOUNCER
- MUSIC BY EDDIE DUNSTEDTER

Producer: Jaime del Valle   **Writers:**   Blake Edwards
Cast: Dick Ryan, Bill Johnstone, Frank Nelson, Hy Averback, Bill James, Tom Hanley

❖ ❖ ❖

SHOW:	**THE JAMES FORBES MATTER**
SHOW DATE:	7/28/1953
COMPANY:	**INTERCONTINENTAL INDEMNITY & BONDING CORPORATION**
AGENT:	**ROGER STERN**
EXP. ACCT:	**$148.48**

SYNOPSIS: Roger Stern calls Johnny about James Forbes who was killed last night. It looks like and accident, but it might not be. Johnny will come to the office and get the details.

Johnny goes to New York City to meet with Roger Stern and then registers at the Madison Hotel. Johnny goes to talk with Lt. Arthur Parkhill. Johnny is told that Mr. Forbes fell over a 110-foot cliff. There is no motive but there is a wife and lots of money and $500,000 in insurance. Johnny is also told that Mr. Forbes took long walks and fell over a cliff. Financially he was doing well, and there was no suicide note.

Johnny rents a car and goes to Long Island, New York to meet Mrs. Forbes. The butler tells Johnny that she is seeing no one. Johnny tells the butler who he is, and Mrs. Forbes will see him; she forgot to tell the butler. Johnny tells her that the investigation is a routine matter. She tells Johnny that Mr. Forbes left right after dinner about 9:00 just like any other night, and the police found him. She was worried when he did not return and called William, her butler. William looked for him and then called the police, who found the body the next morning. Johnny wants to see the spot where Forbes died and William takes him there.

William tells Johnny that he has been working for the Forbes for ten years, and that theirs was a good marriage. At the shore, Johnny sees the cliff where Forbes fell. It was foggy, William tells Johnny. William tells Johnny that he is not convinced that it was an accident. This morning he felt different. He tells Johnny that Mr. Forbes knew the area, but little things have happened. Mrs. Forbes has made calls, affectionate calls, but not to Mr. Forbes. Also, whenever Mr. Forbes left on business, Mrs. Forbes went to town and returned only the day before Mr. Forbes would return. Williams tells Johnny that once the person she was in town visiting came to the house, and told Williams she had not seen Mrs. Forbes for a long time. William did not think about it at the time, but he just has to tell someone. Johnny asks William to call him if Mrs. Forbes gets anymore of the calls.

Johnny goes to his hotel and updates Lt. Parkhill. Later William calls and tells Johnny that Mrs. Forbes has received a call. She just left and was going to the city. Johnny is told that he can intercept her at the George Washington Bridge. She is driving the gray Cadillac sedan, with license plate #6A31593.

Johnny drives to the bridge and follows Mrs. Forbes south into the city. At 41st and 5th Avenue, a man gets in and for an hour she drives and talks to the passenger. At 11:30 the man gets out at 108th street and throws her a kiss. Johnny parks and follows the man to Apartment 1D where the name on the door is Roger Phillips.

Johnny calls Lt. Parkhill, who tells Johnny that he will check on the name. While Johnny is talking, a cab pulls up and Phillips gets into it. Johnny follows Phillips to the waterfront and the Blue Toad Saloon. Johnny follows Phillips into the one-room saloon and sees another man sitting with Phillips. A girl comes to Johnny's table and asks Johnny to buy her some champagne. She tells Johnny that he is too nice for this joint. She is Jane, and Johnny looks like a "Mike" to her and asks Johnny whom he is watching. She tells Johnny that the tall handsome man just passed Timmy a bundle of money. She tells Johnny that the police know Timmy, and he is a bad boy with no friends. Phillips leaves and Johnny goes to his car waits for Timmy to come out. Johnny follows Timmy to the Bayview Hotel and calls Lt. Parkhill and gives him the name. Johnny is told that Timmy Collins is an assassin and that he has an old forgery rap. Johnny is told that Phillips is a socialite playboy. Phillips comes from Cleveland, and so does Collins. Johnny is told that the police will stake out the hotel.

Next morning Lt. Parkhill tells Johnny that Phillips left Cleveland owing Collins a lot of gambling debts. Lt. Parkhill thinks that Timmy probably met Forbes and gave him a shove. Johnny suggests that Mrs. Forbes fell for Phillips and they plotted to have him killed. So Phillips made a deal with Timmy to do the job for a big payoff. Lt. Parkhill will check with the banks, and Johnny will go to see Phillips to see if he will take some bait.

Johnny goes to Phillip's apartment and tells him that he wants to talk about Mrs. Forbes, the one who picked you up last night and gave you money. Johnny tells Phillips that he is in big trouble. Johnny tells him that he knows about Cleveland and Timmy. Johnny leaves Phillips to wonder. Johnny waits for Phillips to make some calls and then calls William. He tells Johnny that Mrs. Forbes is going to meet the same man by the cliffs. Phillips took the bait.

Johnny calls Lt. Parkhill who tells Johnny that Phillips had called Collins and told him that Johnny was on to them. Johnny is told that Mrs. Forbes has withdrawn $10,000 from the bank. Lt. Parkhill picks up Johnny they drive to Long Island and go to the cliffs. Johnny spots Mrs. Forbes walking, and they stop her. Johnny and Lt. Parkhill tell her that they know all about who killed her husband and how he was killed. Johnny tells her that now they are going to kill her. Johnny and Lt. Parkhill tell Mrs. Forbes that they know all about the meeting last night, but Mrs. Forbes does not believe them. Johnny and Lt. Parkhill hide the car and let Mrs. Forbes find out for her self. Phillips and Collins arrive and try to run her down. Lt. Parkhill shoots and the car crashes. They were going to kill her. Mrs. Forbes tells Johnny everything.

NOTES:
- CHARLES LYONS IS THE ANNOUNCER
- MUSIC BY EDDIE DUNSTEDTER

Producer: Jaime del Valle   **Writers:**   Blake Edwards
Cast: Larry Thor, Jack Moyles, Mary Jane Croft, Gene Howell, Robert Griffin

◆ ❖ ◆

SHOW:	THE VOODOO MATTER
SHOW DATE:	8/4/1953
COMPANY:	INTERNATIONAL INSURANCE & BONDING COMPANY
AGENT:	NELSON PRICE
EXP. ACCT:	$461.40

SYNOPSIS: Nelson Price calls Johnny with a job in the West Indies, near St. Leger, Haiti. Claude Shelton has a big policy on his farm and is having trouble.

Johnny goes to Port au Prince, Haiti and gets a hotel room where Claude Sheldon shows up, per arrangements. Sheldon is sick and tells Johnny that there has been more trouble. He tells Johnny that he is a farmer and has been doing well until several months ago. Since then, there has been fire in the cane fields, dead cattle, and several farmers have died. Now he is sick from a voodoo curse. There is nothing wrong with him physically, and a local doctor examined him and his wife and found nothing wrong. He tells Johnny that after getting ill, Sheldon received a very low offer from a local banker acting for Arthur Cotswold, who is the richest planter in the area, and the other farmers got same offer. Sheldon collapses and Johnny takes him to the hospital where he dies. An autopsy is ordered and Johnny heads for the Sheldon's Farm in San Leger.

At the Sheldon farm there are natives and drums, and Johnny senses that something is wrong. At the door is a 7-foot, 300-pound native named Bimba. Bimba knows who Johnny is and that Sheldon is dead. Bimba tells Johnny that the drums are for Madame. She is dead and the natives are her friends. She died at the same time as her husband. Bad Voodoo, Johnny is told. Bimba tells Johnny that Cotswold is a big man, and that the drums are good voodoo for the Sheldons. Bimba takes Johnny on horseback to see the local police, Inspector George. Inspector George tells Johnny that Cotswold is very prominent, and it is better not bother him, as he has a violent temper. Inspector George hopes Johnny will not find anything wrong as he is not going to look for trouble. Inspector George tells Johnny that he is the law, but that he prefers the middle of the road.

Bimba tells Johnny that George said to forget about Cotswold, but he thinks Johnny will do what he wants, as Johnny is not afraid. As Johnny and Bimba go to see Cotswold, drums are starting again and Bimba sings something. He tells Johnny that today is papa dambala. At the Cotswold mansion Bimba tells Johnny to watch Mr. Jocelyn, as he is a bad man. At the door, Jocelyn lets Johnny in and tells him that Cotswold is expecting him. Cotswold knows why Johnny is here and tells Johnny that the farmers are suspicious and think he is responsible. He tells Johnny that he tried to help Sheldon and that he wants his land. He tells Johnny that none of his cattle are sick and that he wants the land and will do away with the sick cattle. His advice to Johnny is to go home and leave well enough alone. He is not patient man so heed his advice and do not persist. Johnny tells Cotswold that he is paid to persist.

Johnny gets an idea and sends Bimba on to the farm, as he goes back to town and talks to Inspector George who has the autopsy report. Johnny learns that Sheldon died of Brucellosis, or Bang's disease. Johnny tells inspector George that he is going to look for the cause of the infection, as only the cattle of the small farmers are infected. Johnny tells George to issue a search warrant, or he will have him held as a material witness. Johnny tells George that he has a plan. Bimba and his friends will help by setting a fire to get Cotswold out of the house. George agrees to help, reluctantly, as long as it is a harmless fire.

Johnny goes to the Sheldon farm and there is a crowd outside the house, and Johnny senses that something is wrong. Inside the house, Bimba is lying on the floor almost dead. He has been stabbed in the back. He tells Johnny that he has talked to his friends and they will help. Johnny tells Bimba that he will stay until Bimba dies. There is a voodoo burial ceremony, complete with pigeons, dead chickens, cornmeal, fire and chants. Suddenly Bimba's body sits up and then falls back.

Johnny and the Inspector go to Cotswold's and wait for the fire to start. When the house is empty, they go in to search and find nothing. In the barn Inspector George finds a hypo and a bottle that he will take to be analyzed. Cotswold appears and stops them while Jocelyn searches them. Inspector George tells Cotswold that he has a search warrant, but Cotswold tells him it is useless, and that they have made a serious mistake. Cotswold tells Johnny that the hypodermic was used to infect the cattle, but they will never tell anyone. Cotswold confirms to Johnny that Jocelyn had killed Bimba. Jocelyn walks them out towards the fields when Cotswold screams in terror from the house. In the house they find Cotswold on the floor of the study with a broken neck, and a ghostly image that looks like Bimba. Jocelyn shoots at Bimba 6 times but Bimba crushes Jocelyn. Johnny does not want to know what happened, he only wants to get back to Hartford and relax in a tub of hot mud. It looked like Bimba. Maybe it was. The natives did not find it unusual as Cotswold was a bad man, and Bimba came back to kill him. Johnny tells it just the way he saw it.

Johnny can be contacted at the Greenbriar rest home, 3rd mud pie from the left.

NOTES:

- DAMBALA (OR DAMBALLAH-WEDO) IS A SERPENT SPIRIT OF THE LOCAL REGIONS OF HAITI.
- BRUCELLOSIS OR BANG'S DISEASE, IS AN INFECTIOUS DISEASE OF FARM ANIMALS THAT IS SOMETIMES TRANSMITTED TO HUMANS. IN HUMANS THE DISEASE IS ALSO KNOWN AS UNDULANT FEVER, MEDITERRANEAN FEVER, OR MALTA FEVER. IN SUSCEPTIBLE ANIMALS, PRIMARILY CATTLE, SWINE, AND GOATS, BRUCELLOSIS CAUSES INFERTILITY AND DEATH.
- CHARLES LYONS IS THE ANNOUNCER
- MUSIC BY EDDIE DUNSTEDTER

Producer: Jaime del Valle   **Writers:** Blake Edwards

Cast: **Tudor Owen, Parley Baer, Roy Glenn, Ben Wright, Bill Conrad, Jester Hairston**

◆ ❖ ◆

SHOW: THE NANCY SHAW MATTER
SHOW DATE: 8/11/1953
COMPANY: COLUMBIA ALL RISK INSURANCE COMPANY
AGENT: PHILLIP MARTIN
EXP. ACCT: $604.65

SYNOPSIS: Phillip Martin calls Johnny with a Job. Miss Nancy Shaw the actress is insured and has just had $100,000 in jewels stolen. Johnny offers to waive his expense account just to work with Nancy Shaw—just kidding!

Johnny flies to Los Angeles, California and drives to Santa Monica to meet with Sgt. James Dodd. Sgt. Dodd tells Johnny that there have been three other robberies, all with same MO. Johnny gets a list of the stolen items and is told that Miss Shaw was robbed on the maid's night off. Johnny tells Sgt. Dodd that he will visit Miss Shaw and is told that she lives at 913 at the Artist Colony in Malibu. Sgt. Dodd will call the guard to tell him to let Johnny in. Sgt. Dodd tells Johnny that the thief probably parked on the highway and worked his way into the house.

Johnny drives to Malibu and is allowed into the colony and drives to Miss Shaw's house. Bernice the maid takes Johnny to Nancy, who is wearing a white sun suit that almost makes Johnny's hair catch on fire. Johnny has a gin and tonic with Nancy and there is small talk about Johnny and his job. Johnny goes over the list of stolen items and gets a confirmation from Nancy. Nancy suggests that they go out and sit on the beach and tells Johnny that there are plenty of trunks in the guesthouse. Nancy meets Johnny on the beach in a red bathing suit. When Nancy teases Johnny about his lack of a suntan, Johnny tells her "I'm not white, just pearl gray." They sit on the beach and there is talk of sandcastles and dreams unfulfilled. Dave Asher, Nancy's fiancé, comes to the beach and is miffed at Nancy and tells Johnny to leave, but Johnny tells him to leave. Dave tells Johnny that he has some private matters to settle, but Nancy tells Dave to leave. Dave tells Nancy that he is going to end the relationship and he leaves. Nancy tells Johnny that she should have dropped him sooner, as Dave is just a rich young man. She tells Johnny that Dave was with her on the night of the robbery. As they leave the beach Nancy asks Johnny to take her to a party that night.

At the party, Johnny and Nancy go outside to talk by the pool, and Johnny muses that being with Nancy is very nice. Nancy asks Johnny to kiss her and he does, and that was nice too. As they get ready to leave the party Dave walks up to Johnny and wants to talk to him. David tells Johnny that he does not like Johnny, or glamour-gal Nancy, so Johnny slugs Dave and he falls into the pool.

Back on the beach they talk and Johnny finally leaves at sunrise. At 4:00 PM Sgt. Dodd calls Johnny and tells him that he made the front page by putting David Asher in the pool. Sgt. Dodd tells Johnny that he has been checking on

Dave, and no one has heard of him, but he does have money. But three months ago David was broke. Johnny goes to see Nancy and Bernice tells Johnny that Nancy is not in and that she is seeing no one. Johnny notices that Bernice has been crying so Johnny runs up to Nancy's bedroom. Johnny goes in and discovers that Nancy has been beaten. Nancy tells Johnny that the doctor is on his way, but Nancy will not tell Johnny who did it. Johnny gives Nancy a sleeping pill and goes to talk to Bernice who tells Johnny that it was Dave Asher who beat her. Bernice also tells Johnny that she found a diamond on the floor after Dave left. Johnny calls Sgt. Dodd and asks if the stone is on the list. Johnny is told that there was a ring with a large diamond on the list and Johnny tells Sgt. Dodd about the beating. Bernice tells Johnny that Nancy and Dave had visited all the people who were robbed just before the robberies occurred. Johnny gets the address for Dave and arranges to meet Sgt. Dodd there.

Before Sgt. Dodd arrives, Johnny slugs his way into the apartment and breaks Dave's nose. Dave tells Johnny that he had bought the ring from some man. Johnny slugs him again and Dave admits that he was casing the houses when he went with Nancy, and that Stanley Fisher was the man who actually stole the jewelry. Dave tells Johnny that Fisher lives at the Shelton Hotel and that he has the rest of the loot. Dave tells Johnny that he beat up Nancy because he got mad at her. Sgt. Dodd comes in and tells Johnny that they know about Fisher. Sgt. Dodd takes care of Dave, and Johnny goes back to Nancy.

After things are wrapped up, Johnny visits Nancy and tells her that he will come back and visit he on his next case in California. Nancy tells Johnny that she will rob every house in California to make that happen. Nancy kisses Johnny, who asks "Are you sure my hair is not on fire?"

NOTES:
- CHARLES LYONS IS THE ANNOUNCER
- MUSIC BY EDDIE DUNSTEDTER
- A MO—MODUS OPERANDI—IS ONES METHOD OR STYLE OF OPERATION

Producer: Jaime del Valle **Writers:** Blake Edwards
Cast: Mary Jane Croft, Thelma Johnson, Peter Leeds, Vic Perrin

SHOW:	THE ISABELLE JAMES MATTER
SHOW DATE:	8/18/1953
COMPANY:	NATIONAL LIFE & CASUALTY INSURANCE COMPANY
AGENT:	DON MAYNARD
EXP. ACCT:	$335.04

SYNOPSIS: Don Maynard calls and tells Johnny that Isabelle James was murdered in Tulsa, Oklahoma. Johnny will come to the office to get the details.

Johnny goes to Tulsa, Oklahoma after getting the information on the case. At the police department Johnny meets Capt. Clifford Kissick, who would like to help Johnny, but he is stumped. Capt. Kissick tells Johnny that there have been four killings in three weeks, and Isabelle James is the latest. Johnny is told that there are no clues or witnesses, that the killing all took place in deserted areas, and that the lab thinks the killer is using a razor. Johnny is told that Dawson, Isabelle's hometown is not too far away, and Capt. Kissick tells Johnny that he had found the insurance papers. Johnny is told that her uncle, the beneficiary, is just a poor farmer who can use the money. Johnny tells Capt. Kissick that he will be there until the killer is found.

Johnny drives to the farm of Morley Parish, who is in his late fifties and suspicious of Johnny. Morley invites Johnny in when he mentions the money from the insurance. Morley opens a jug of homemade whiskey and offers it to Johnny. Johnny takes a sip and almost chokes. Morley apologizes because he did not shake the jug to make it smoother, sort of. Morley tells Johnny that he thinks the man who killed the others also killed Isabelle. She had run off to Tulsa and visited Morley occasionally. Morley tells Johnny that she never wrote, and said nothing on her last visit. Morley offers Johnny more whiskey and after a polite refusal, Morley tells Johnny that he has to finish the jug once he opens it.

Back at his hotel, Capt. Kissick calls to tell Johnny that they have a suspect. The police have a man who was following a girl. She screamed and called the police and when they got there they found that the man was carrying a straight razor. Johnny goes to see Capt. Kissick and is told that the man, Alvin Story, has said nothing. He told the police that he was just carrying the razor while he was out for a walk. Johnny and Capt. Kissick interrogate Alvin for some time and Alvin tells them he was on the way to a show downtown, but Capt. Kissick tells Alvin that he was going in the wrong direction. Capt. Kissick and Johnny have coffee and discuss Alvin. Capt. Kissick tells Johnny that it is hard to tell, as men make mistakes when they are scared. The phone rings and Capt. Kissick is told that Alvin has just confessed.

Johnny relates that Alvin looked relieved as he tells his story. He admits that killed all of the girls. He does not know why he killed them he just wanted to. He used to dream about killing women. The first one he killed on Garvey Street on the 11th. But Alvin tells Johnny and Capt. Kissick that there were only three girls not four. Alvin knows the names of the girls, and Isabelle is not one of them. He read about her in the paper but he did not do it.

The next day Johnny gets a wakeup call and is told that Morley Parish is waiting for him in the lobby. Johnny dresses goes to talk to Morley, who tells Johnny that he has come to talk about his niece. He tells Johnny that he wants the insurance money to buy some land. Johnny tells Morley that he will not get the money until he is finished with the investigation, and that the same man may not have killed Isabelle. Johnny tells Morley that the razor used on the other girls was a different razor than the one that was used on Isabelle. Johnny tells Morley that he wants him to get his money, but has to wait until the killer is caught with the same razor that killed his niece. Morley leaves and Johnny tells him he will get the money when he is convinced that the killer has changed razors.

Johnny calls Capt. Kissick, and Cliff tells him that Story killed all the girls but James. Johnny tells Capt. Kissick about the story he told to Morley, who Johnny thinks killed Isabelle for the insurance money. Johnny tells Capt. Kissick that he had not told Morley that Story had been arrested. Johnny thinks Morley will go out and try to kill some one to prove the killer has changed razors, and that he has to go to the farm to get the razor. Capt. Kissick and Johnny drive to Morley's farm and wait for him to come home for his razor. As Johnny watches from Capt. Kissick's car, Morley comes home and then leaves. Johnny stops him and Morley tells Johnny that he has business and that he is in a hurry. Johnny tells him that he will give him a ride, but Morley declines, and Johnny tells him that he is walking, but does not want a ride. Johnny asks Morley for the razor and Morley tells Johnny that that he killed Isabel. Morley tells Johnny that he sure could have used the money. He thought he had it all figured out, but you sure can't beat those scientific police methods. Morley is told that the state will take care of the farm and Morley wants Johnny to take the jug behind the stove so it will not be wasted on a stranger.

Morley gives his story to the police and confirms Johnny's suspicions.

NOTES:
- THIS IS AN **AFRS** PROGRAM, AND THE OPENING ARTICLE ABOUT THE VALUE OF THE PATENTS AND COPYRIGHTS
- THE MID-PROGRAM COMMERCIAL IS ABOUT THE PRESIDENCY OF WILLIAM HOWARD TAFT
- CHARLES LYON IS THE ANNOUNCER FOR THE OPENING OF THE PROGRAM
- MUSIC BY EDDIE DUNSTEDTER

Producer: Jaime del Valle   **Writers:** Blake Edwards
Cast: Parley Baer, Howard McNear, Joseph Du Val, Clayton Post

SHOW:	THE NELSON MATTER
SHOW DATE:	8/25/1953
COMPANY:	COLUMBIA ALL RISK INSURANCE COMPANY
AGENT:	PHILLIP MARTIN
EXP. ACCT:	$301.01

SYNOPSIS: Phillip Martin calls Johnny with a job. Carl Nelson has been shot and the beneficiary Maude Gilkerson has disappeared.

Johnny goes to New York City and goes to see Lt. Korchack who asks Johnny how much insurance "The Frog" has. Lt. Korchack explains to Johnny that Nelson got the nickname because looked like one. Lt. Korchack tells Johnny that he thinks that Carl's wife Maude knows about the killing. Johnny is told that Nelson was a hood with a record and that he had been associated with Ellis Hartje, a big gangster. Johnny tells Lt. Korchack that he has a "source" for information on how to find Maude. Johnny cabs to skid row and the Het's

Hilarity to talk to Wilbur Truit. Wilber has missed his friend "Bucko" Johnny and laments his financial downturn. He tells Johnny that he used to make fifty cents a day. Johnny asks for the location of Maude Gilkerson, and tells Wilbur that she might be worth two bottles. Johnny tells Wilbur to tell Maude that she has $10,000 coming from Carl Nelson's insurance.

Later that afternoon Wilbur calls Johnny at his hotel and tells him that Maude is not happy. She is hiding and wants to make a deal; she wants enough money to leave the country in exchange for information that is worth it. Johnny starts to go out and is met at the door by Ernie and Goon, who invite them selves in. They want to talk about why Johnny is in town. After some rough stuff, they tell Johnny to lay off the Nelson killing, or the police will investigate the Dollar killing.

Johnny goes to Maude's address and meets her. Johnny wants to know what information she has, and Maude wants all the money and tells Johnny that she must leave as soon as possible, as she does not want to die. She tells Johnny that she needs $500. Johnny gives her $200 and she tells him that Carl had been working for Hartje for a year and was worried about getting hit on the head. She tells Johnny that Carl knew a lot, and had collected enough evidence to put Hartje away, and Maude has the evidence. Johnny tells her that he will get the rest of the money in an hour and Maude gives him the key to a locker in Grand Central Station.

As Johnny walks back towards town, he sees a car following him. Johnny spots a blind beggar man and puts the key into his cup. Goon stops Johnny and puts him in the car and Ernie asks Johnny what Maude had told him. Johnny is stripped and searched and then taken to an apartment building to meet Ellis Hartje. Ellis tells Johnny that he is running things, so Johnny better cooperate. Hartje tells Johnny that he wants the information Maude has, and Johnny tells him that he only talked to her about the insurance. The phone rings and Ernie tells Hartje that Maude had given Johnny a key.

Ernie and Goon take Johnny to a warehouse in the bowery and beat him to find out where the key is. After a long beating Goon is distracted by a phone call and Johnny over powers him and then takes out Ernie. Johnny takes Ernie's gun and car and heads back to the blind beggar. Johnny gives the beggar some money to buy the key back. Johnny goes to Lt. Korchack and updates him on what has happened. Lt. Korchack arranges to have Bert and Goon picked up, and tells Johnny that Maude was pulled from the river an hour ago. Johnny and Lt. Korchack go to Grand Central Station and open the locker. Inside there is a package and Lt. Korchak is shot at. In the ensuing gunfight, Bert and Goon are killed and Lt. Korchack is wounded. Lt. Korchack goes to the Hartje penthouse with a squad of men where Hartje shoots through the door. The police go in shooting and Hartje is killed.

NOTES:
- **CAST INFORMATION FROM TERRY SALOMONSON**
- **CHARLES LYONS IS THE ANNOUNCER**

- **MUSIC BY EDDIE DUNSTEDTER**

Producer:	Jaime del Valle	Writers:	Blake Edwards
Cast:	Victor Rodman, Joseph Kearns, Herb Butterfield, Jim Nusser, James McCallion, Martha Wentworth, William Conrad		

◆ ❖ ◆

SHOW: **THE STANLEY PRICE MATTER**
SHOW DATE: **9/1/1953**
COMPANY: **WORLD INSURANCE & INDEMNITY COMPANY**
AGENT: **HANDLEY CONRAD**
EXP. ACCT: **$113.40**

SYNOPSIS: Handley Conrad calls and asks if Johnny can take a job. Handley tells Johnny that the New York police have confiscated $100,000 in jewels found in the water pipe beneath the sink of a murdered man named Wells. A client in Europe was robbed three months ago, and Handley thinks these are the same jewels, but they are not in their settings, and some have been re-cut. The police are holding Mrs. Wells who claims that the jewels are hers, but does not know how they got into the water pipes. So Johnny has to prove that he jewels are stolen.

Johnny trains to New York City and goes to see Capt. Fred Bee of the robbery detail. Fred tells Johnny of the call from Stanley Price telling them about the jewels. There was a shot and the line went dead. When they got there they found Robert Wells dead. The wife has been released due to lack of evidence. Fred tells Johnny that Wells had just returned from Europe. Stanley Price is a small time hood that has been making book lately. Mrs. Wells went back to the apartment and Fred has the apartment watched. Johnny tells Fred he has a friend who knows all about the bookmakers in the area, but Johnny will not tell Fred his name. Johnny gets a room, rents a car and drives to the Greenwich Village home of Andre Duval, an abstract painter. Johnny finally gets Andre to open the door and Johnny asks him if he knows Stanley Price. Johnny offers $25 and Andre finally remembers that Price owes him $11.80, but he still does not know where he is. Price was also in the fish business as he had brought Andre two halibut he had caught from his boat. The boat was kept at a place called Schooner Landing. Johnny drives to the waterfront and Schooner Landing where an old man tells Johnny that he knows Stan Price, but he has not seen him lately and owes him money. The man tells Johnny that Price was not a fisherman and did not know anything about running a boat even though he had a commercial fishing license. Johnny goes to the Bureau of Licenses and finds one with a picture of Price on it. Johnny then goes to see Mrs. Wells and shows her the picture of Price whom she had seen visit her husband. Johnny tells her about the call from Price and his interest in the case. Mrs. Wells is anxious to help straighten Johnny's curly hair, but Johnny opts to leave. Johnny goes to his hotel and is met by a man with a gun who wants the picture of Price.

Johnny gives the man the license and counts to twenty as he leaves, and then Johnny calls Andre and then goes to see Fred. Johnny tells Fred that it was important to the insurance company to prove the jewels were stolen in a short period of time, before they would have to turn them over to Mrs. Wells. Johnny has a hunch that it if he turns the jewels over to Mrs. Wells the case will open up very quickly. Johnny knows that only three people knew where he was staying: Mr. Conrad, Fred and Mrs. Wells. Fred is sure that Mrs. Wells told Price where Johnny was, Johnny tells him that Price has not paid Andre his $11.80, so it was not Price that held him up. Johnny tells Fred that Well's boat from Europe landed last Wednesday while Price was out fishing. When Wells arrived, Price went out fishing for two hours, came back and disappeared. Then Wells has a sink full of jewels he had dropped overboard for Price to pick up. But Johnny is not sure who killed Wells in his own apartment. The whole thing had to be planned by someone who knew when Wells would return, namely Mrs. Wells. Johnny goes to the morgue to look at Wells and Johnny tells Fred that the body is not Wells, but Stanley Price. Johnny asks Fred to let him take the jewels to Mrs. Wells, as a representative of insurance company. Johnny gets the jewels and Johnny goes to the apartment followed by two police officers. Johnny is let in and gives her the jewels, with no strings attached. Mrs. Wells is puzzled by Johnny is mixed up in this case, and he tells her that the insurance company thinks the jewels are stolen, but Mrs. Wells is not convinced. She tells Johnny it is too easy and as she tells Johnny she thinks Johnny is trying to trap her, some one knocks Johnny out. Johnny wakes up alone in the apartment and goes out to look for the police who are gone. Johnny calls Fred who tells Johnny that the police are following Mrs. Wells and Johnny tells him that she is a decoy, leading them away from Mr. Wells who left by the back door. Johnny tells Fred to meet him as Schooner's Landing. Johnny goes the landing where the old man tells Johnny that Prices' boat has been gassed up and is ready to leave. Johnny runs to the boat and jumps on to see Mr. and Mrs. Wells. Johnny is held at gunpoint as Wells takes the boats out. Mrs. Wells take the wheel and Johnny tells Mr. Wells he knows who he is. Wells tells Johnny that he killed Price because he wanted a larger cut and was calling the police. He had put the jewels in the pipe and hoped the police would not find them. A Coast Guard boat approaches and Wells tells Johnny to get on the bow. Johnny grabs a life preserver and slugs Wells with it, but not before he shoots Mrs. Wells. Johnny stops the boat for the police.

Johnny buys a good dinner for $8.75 and gets a good night's sleep.

NOTES:

- THIS IS AN **AFRS** PROGRAM THAT STARTS WITH A STORY ABOUT DO-IT-YOURSELF PROJECTS AND THE EXPERTS AT THE DEPARTMENT OF AGRICULTURE.
- CHARLES LYONS IS THE ANNOUNCER
- MUSIC BY EDDIE DUNSTEDTER
- COMMERCIAL BREAK **#2** IS ABOUT THE PRESIDENCY OF JAMES A. GARFIELD.

Producer: Jaime del Valle   **Writers:**   Blake Edwards
Cast: John Stephenson, Kenny Delmar, Jay Novello, Howard
                McNear, Mary Shipp

◆   ❖   ◆

SHOW: THE LESTER MATSON MATTER
SHOW DATE: 9/8/1953
COMPANY: COLUMBIA ALL RISK INSURANCE COMPANY
AGENT: PHILLIP JAMES
EXP. ACCT: $154.50

SYNOPSIS: Phillip James calls about an arson case. Lester Matson's plastics plant has burned and there was $700,000 in insurance. The police have found evidence of arson.

Johnny trains to New York City and rents a car. Lt. Ridgeway updates Johnny and tells him that arson definitely was involved and that a high-octane fuel in a ten-gallon can was used. Lt. Ridgeway tells Johnny that he has a lead on Lester Matson, who was at a party with his daughter that night, but he acted funny. Lt. Ridgeway has talked to Matson, but he acted scared, like he was hiding something. Johnny tells Lt. Ridgeway that the insurance coverage will not cover the actual losses in the fire.

Johnny goes to see Lester Matson in New Jersey, and Christine Matson meets Johnny in the library and Johnny tells her why he is there. She tells Johnny that she has been playing tennis, and Johnny tells her that he used to play a little, but not anymore. Mr. Matson comes in and they talk. Matson tells Johnny that the police have investigated the fire, that he was at a party with Christine and that he found out about the fire when he came home. Matson is sure that the fire was an accident but does not like the idea of a fire being started intentionally. He worries about what might have happened if it had started during the day. Johnny tells him that a pyromaniac does not target plants during the day. Matson tells Johnny that he has two more plants, so he hopes he is not an exception to the rule. Matson agrees to give Johnny as much information as he can. Johnny senses that the idea of a pyromaniac eases Matson's uneasiness as he tells Johnny what he can.

Johnny calls Lt. Ridgeway from his hotel. Johnny tells him of the firebug angle and the change in Matson's attitude. Johnny thinks that Matson may know who started the fire. Johnny tells Lt. Ridgeway that he thinks that maybe the daughter started the fire. Johnny tells Lt. Ridgeway that he has met her, and he is still smoldering. At 4:30, Johnny is in the bar "freshening up" when he is paged to the hotel phone. Christine tells Johnny that she called to talk, but she must be discrete. If certain parties saw her talking to Johnny her father's life would be in danger. Johnny agrees to meet her in a cab.

Johnny meets Christine's cab and gets in. As they drive around, she tells Johnny that her father is being blackmailed and knows who burned the plant. She tells Johnny that two men had demanded a percentage of the business and protection and they burned the plant to make their point. Her father did not tell the police because of her. The man had threatened to do something worse if he talked, and her father is afraid they meant Christine. She wants Johnny to help without making a big issue of it. She tells Johnny that her father had told her all of the details when she saw him upset. She tells Johnny that he would rather loose everything than loose her. Johnny tells her to drive to the house so he can talk to father.

At the Matson home, Christine tells her father that she has told Johnny everything, and that Johnny will not bring in the police unless necessary. Matson tells Johnny that Christine does not realize how foolish she is, and that he must think of his family, as the men will do anything. He tells Johnny that there is no alternative, and they will continue to bleed him dry and will kill Christine if he does not pay. Christine tells her father that the blackmail will kill him as it is taking his freedom and will ruin them. Johnny tells Matson that the men have effectively kidnapped his business from him, and that he has a job to do and will do it. A shot is fired through a window in the study and Matson is hit. Johnny runs outside as Christine call the doctor and hears a car starting in the front of the house. Johnny runs to the front of the house, sees the car pull away and shoots. Johnny tells a frantic Christine to stay with her father until the doctor comes. Johnny walks to the car, which is wrapped around an oak tree. Johnny sees a man halfway through the windshield man and bleeding. Another man surprises Johnny, takes his gun, and walks him up to the garage to get another car with a gun in his back. He knows Johnny is an insurance man, so Johnny will be his insurance. They walk to the garage and a car drives up. When the man turns to look, Johnny slugs him and tells the doctor to go to the house where his patient is.

Lester Matson lives, and the men were identified as Ernie Starbuck and Stan Cole. Ernie was dead in the car and Stan went to prison for life.

On the way home Johnny stops to see Christine. He agrees to have a drink with her and ends up taking the late train home.

NOTES:
- CHARLES LYON IS THE ANNOUNCER
- EDDIE DUNSTEDTER PROVIDES THE MUSIC
- THIS IS AN AFTS TAPE AND CONTAINS AN OPENING ARTICLE ABOUT THE STATE DEPARTMENT
- COMMERCIAL BREAK #2 IS ABOUT THE PRESIDENCY OF ANDREW JACKSON.

Producer: Jaime del Valle   Writers: Blake Edwards
Cast: John Larch, Hal March, Lillian Buyeff, Bill Johnstone

SHOW: THE OSCAR CLARK MATTER
SHOW DATE: 9/15/1953
COMPANY: NATIONAL LIFE & CASUALTY COMPANY
AGENT: DON MAYNARD
EXP. ACCT: $168.59

SYNOPSIS: Don Maynard calls Johnny and tells him that Oscar Clark is being held for a hit-and-run and the woman he hit was hurt. Clark has a $200,000 policy and did not know that he hit anything. Clark is also a wealthy man with influence.

Johnny goes to Miami, Florida and meets with Lt. Eddy who tells Johnny that Lucille Best is from Chicago and lives in a hotel. She has a broken leg and a back injury. She was found on the highway and requested her physician, Dr. Hawley. She told the police that she had a flat tire and a car hit her when she got out. She got the tag number and the car belongs to Oscar Clark. Clark's car has a dent and blood stains, and Clark was booked on a 318. He admitted to the police that he stopped at the Red Mill Tavern and had one drink and left at 7:20. Johnny goes to see Oscar Clark who denies everything and claims he is being framed. Johnny goes to see Dr. Hawley and he tells Johnny that Lucille is doing ok, except for the fractured leg and a back injury. He tells Johnny that Lucille came to Florida for her health and her doctor recommended him to her. He also tells Johnny that Lucille has hired a lawyer. Johnny looks at the x-rays and goes to his hotel where he is called by Lt. Eddy who tells him that the lab has made a discovery that proves Lucille is a liar. Johnny goes to see Lt. Eddy and he tells Johnny that a metal object was used to dent the fender, and that the glass from a headlight is missing. Also, the blood on the car was smeared on with a rag.

Johnny goes to see Clark and tells him of the new discoveries. Clark tells Johnny that he left his car with an attendant when he went into the tavern. When he left, his car was at the far end of the parking lot. Johnny wonders if the car could have been damaged there. Johnny goes to the Red Mill and talks to the bartender who tells Johnny that the valet is Sammie, a jockey who hurt his back in a racing accident. Johnny is told that Sammie was healed by Dr. Jones, who is no longer practicing.

Johnny leaves and waits for Sammie to leave and then follows him to a small house. Johnny goes in and talks to Sammie, who admits that Hawley thought up the idea. Hawley had fixed up Sammie's back and he dented the car to pay his bill. They picked Clark because he was rich and Hawley broke the girl's leg. Dr. Hawley walks in and shoots Sammie. He tells Johnny that he is going to have an accident. Lt. Eddy comes in and disarms Hawley. Lt. Eddy tells Johnny that they had staked out both Hawley and Sammie.

NOTES:
- THE ANNOUNCER IS CHARLES LYON

- Music is by Eddie Dunstedter
- Story information obtained from the KNX Collection in the Thousand Oaks Library

Producer: Jaime del Valle   Writers   Blake Edwards
Cast: Tom Tully, Barney Phillips, Francis X. Bushman, Parley Baer,
            Joan Miller, Sam Edwards

◆   ❖   ◆

SHOW: THE WILLIAM POST MATTER
SHOW DATE: 9/22/1953
COMPANY: COLUMBIA ALL-RISK INSURANCE COMPANY
AGENT: RAY KEMPER
EXP. ACCT: $78.05

SYNOPSIS: Ray Kemper calls and tells Johnny that Mrs. William Post has been killed. Her body was found by a detective named Sax, and her attorney George Simon. The husband is suspected of killing her.

Johnny goes to New York City and meets Lt. Roseman at the 5th precinct. Johnny is told that Teresa Post was found stabbed four times, gagged and robbed. Sax and Simon had appointments at the time, and her jewels and a cloth coat are missing. The Posts had argued and separated, and she had filed for divorce over her husband's cheating, based on evidence obtained by Sax. A mink coat was left in the closet and the husband was with Jane Hughes at the time. Johnny goes to meet Sax, who tells Johnny that it is easy to find a husband with another woman and that Post made the mistake of leaving the fur coat. Johnny goes to see George Simon who tells Johnny that he met Sax at the apartment and had been in his office all day. Johnny goes to talk to Jane Hughes, and she is a real dish! She tells Johnny that she was with Post all afternoon. Bill Post comes in and tells Johnny to leave.

Johnny goes to the apartment and meets Pete the janitor, who is singing to himself. Johnny has to pay Pete a $20 bribe to get into the apartment, where he finds nothing. On the way out Pete tells Johnny that he does not like Mrs. Post. Johnny goes to his hotel and gets a call from Lt. Roseman who tells Johnny that the cloth coat has been pawned. Johnny goes to the pawnshop and the owner tells Johnny that the man who hocked the coat was singing to himself. Johnny goes back to Pete and he denies pawning the coat. Pete is taken in and put in a lineup and is identified by the pawnshop owner. Pete tells Johnny that Mrs. Post gave him the coat. Johnny convinces Lt. Roseman to let Pete loose.

Johnny goes to see Jane again and tells her and Post that Pete killed his wife, but he needs their help to trap him. Johnny wants Jane to dress up like Mrs. Post and go to the apartment and call Pete to complain about the plumbing. Johnny and Jane go to the apartment where she buzzes Pete to fix the plumbing. Pete comes up to the apartment and tells Jane that she is dead. He killed he once and will kill her again. Johnny stops Pete and the jewels are found in a paint bucket in the basement. Pete admits that he was robbing the apartment when she came in, so he had to kill her.

NOTES:
- THE ANNOUNCER IS CHARLES LYON
- MUSIC IS BY EDDIE DUNSTEDTER
- RAY KEMPER IS ALSO THE SOUND MAN FOR THIS PROGRAM
- STORY INFORMATION OBTAINED FROM THE KNX COLLECTION IN THE THOUSAND OAKS LIBRARY

Producer: Jaime del Valle   Writers   Blake Edwards
Cast: Jack Moyles, Bill Johnstone, Benny Rubin, Charles Davis,
            Mary Jane Croft, Hy Averback, Howard McNear

◆ ❖ ◆

SHOW: THE ANITA BUDDHA MATTER
SHOW DATE: 9/29/1953
COMPANY: WORLD INSURANCE & INDEMNITY COMPANY
AGENT: HANLEY CONRAD
EXP. ACCT: $527.15

SYNOPSIS: Hanley Conrad calls and asks if Johnny is employed. Johnny is available, so Hanley tells him to go to Los Angeles, where William McEdwards was killed in a house fire

Johnny flies to Los Angeles, California, rents a car and goes to see C.H. Anderson, Chief of Police in Beverly Hills. Lt. Hankins tells Johnny that he received the call and went to the fire where he found William McEdwards, burned to death in his bedroom. The autopsy showed that McEdwards had been stabbed and beaten.

Johnny goes to Encino to talk to McEdward's wife, Pat. She tells Johnny that she had been visiting with friends in Pasadena, and left the Buddha with Charley Wilkins. Her father-in-law got the Buddha while he was in Korea and gave it to them. Her father-in-law is a production executive for a movie studio, and she knew of nothing unusual that day.

Johnny goes to his hotel and makes an appointment to see John McEdwards, William's father. When Johnny gets to the house there is a tall metal fence with four Great Danes behind it. Mr. McEdwards quiets the dogs and lets Johnny into the house. McEdwards tells Johnny that the dogs are named Samson, Delilah, Cleopatra and The Duchess. They are good dogs but very protective. Johnny is told that a friend had a man break into his house and their Great Dane caught the man and broke his neck. Johnny is told that Bill was a wonderful son and it is hard for John to deal with the loss. He tells Johnny that he had been in Korea for three months working on a movie and was digging a small dam when he found the Buddha in a box. He decided to give it to Bill and Pat when he came back. Johnny learns that Bill was pretty solid but settled down when he met Pat and had bought the insurance. The dogs start barking again and Pat comes in.

She tells Johnny and her father-in-law that Chief Anderson had called and told her that Bill had been murdered. Johnny wonders if the Buddha is involved somehow.

Johnny drives to Encino to talk to Charles Wilkins about the Buddha. After a brief history of the Buddha, Charles thinks that this is the original Anita Buddha of Contemplation, from 200 BC, and estimates that it is worth at least $150,000 and probably $500,000.

Johnny drives back to Beverly Hills to talk to Chief Anderson who tells Johnny that the Buddha is the first lead they have. Bill had no enemies, so who knew of the Buddha? Chief Anderson will check the studio and steamship and airlines, and Johnny will go back to talk to Mr. McEdwards.

Johnny drives to the McEdwards home and talks to Mr. McEdwards in the kitchen for about an hour about the case. The phone rings and Mr. McEdwards comes back looking shaken. He tells Johnny that a man on the phone said that he had Pat and that she was ok. Mr. McEdwards was told to get the Buddha and tell no one or there will be trouble. Mr. McEdwards agrees to let Johnny follow him to Charles Wilkins' home to get the Buddha. On the way back, Johnny parks out of sight and they walk into the house where Pat is waiting for them along with two men. Alan Sutker and Don Roach tell Mr. McEdwards that they are there for the Buddha. Mr. McEdwards explains that Johnny was a friend who just happened to be there when the call came. "Too bad for your friend," Sutker tells him, and then explains that he had been tracking the Buddha for a long time and had buried it after a man named Woo Sung died, under "mysterious circumstances." Sutker tells then that he had waited in Tokyo until the war was over but McEdwards got there first. Now he wants the Buddha. Mr. McEdwards wants to know which one of them killed his son, and Sutker tells him that Roach had burgled the house to get the Buddha, but Bill caught him in the act and he resisted, so he was killed. He tells Mr. McEdwards that it is of no difference that he knows this, as he will not be around to tell anyone. Sutker tells all of them to go out and get in his car. Outside Mr. McEdwards punches Roach, who hits him with his gun, driving the penned dogs crazy. Samson jumps the fence, followed by the others, who attack Roach and Sutker. After the melee, Roach is dead with a broken neck, and Sutker is crying for a doctor. Mr. McEdwards tells Johnny that the end was appropriate, as Samson was Bill's dog.

NOTES:

- THE PROGRAM I HAVE HAS A SERIOUS BLANK SPOT IN THE MIDDLE WHERE CHARLES WILKINS EXPLAINS THE HISTORY OF BUDDHA, WHICH COULD PROBABLY BE A BOOK IN ITSELF.
- CHARLES LYONS IS THE ANNOUNCER
- MUSIC BY EDDIE DUNSTEDTER

Producer: Jaime del Valle   **Writers:** Blake Edwards

Cast: James Nusser, John Stevenson, Jeanette Nolan, Sammie Hill, Herb Butterfield, Bill James, Robert Griffin, Edgar Barrier

SHOW:	**THE ALFRED CHAMBERS MATTER**
SHOW DATE:	**10/6/1953**
COMPANY:	**COLUMBIA ALL-RISK INSURANCE COMPANY**
AGENT:	**PHILLIP MARTIN**
EXP. ACCT:	**$114.05**

SYNOPSIS: Phillip Martin calls and has a job for Johnny. Phillip insures Mr. Alfred Chambers of Pittsburgh, who was shot to death yesterday, and it looks like murder. Chambers had rented a cabin on Les Chenou Island, about 30 miles south of Sault Ste. Marie, Michigan where his wife found him shot through the chest in the cabin. Johnny will leave in the morning

Johnny flies to Sault Ste. Marie, Michigan and cabs to the police department and meets Capt. George Laine. Johnny is told that Chambers had rented the Forrester cabin and spent three days alone before his wife arrived. Mr. Schoenberg took her to the island where she found her husband shot through the chest. There are no suspects and Mrs. Chambers told the police that she had separated from her husband a week before he came to the island and that Chambers had been dead for fourteen hours. Capt. Lane and Johnny travel to the island and Johnny learns that Chambers was shot outside the cabin and crawled inside, that the cabin does not have electricity, though others in the island do, and that Chambers had rented a boat to get on and off the island. Also, the coroner discovered that Chamber's shoes were still damp, and that he had been in the water with his clothes on. Capt. Lane thinks Chambers was shot while he was on the docks, fell in the water and waded to shore and was shot about five in the afternoon, four hours before darkness. Capt. Lane tells Johnny that Chambers was shot by a .22 long rifle, and that the mud on his shoes matches the mud down by the docks. Johnny and Capt Lane agree that it was probably someone on the island who shot Chambers. Johnny drives Capt Lane's car to the hotel to talk to Mrs. Chambers, who tells Johnny that this is her first visit to the island. She knew that her husband had been seeing another woman, and they had decided to separate but did not because of the publicity; her husband is in the steel business and they have two children. She had seen the girl once and tells Johnny that her name is Jane Elkins who also lives in Pittsburgh. Before this she would not have cared about the girl, but because of the children it matters. She had come to the island to talk with her husband one last time. She tells Johnny that she has thought about killing her husband, but cannot think of anyone else who would. The phone rings and Mrs. Chambers tells someone to come right up. She asks Johnny to stay as the phone call was from Jane.

Jane Elkins comes to Mrs. Chamber's room and is introduced to Johnny. She tells them that she was never in love with Mr. Chambers and had no idea he was coming here. She tells Johnny that she came up with her fiancé a week ago. Jane does not know where she was when Chambers was shot, but saw him last on Tuesday. Jane's fiancé knows about her and Chambers and did not take it too well. Jane tells Johnny that on Tuesday she went back to the house and that Charles was out on a boat. Jane tells Mrs. Chambers how sorry she is, and leaves to attend a cocktail party for her at the Weatherwaxes. Johnny gets a room and updates Capt. Laine, who will check on Jane. Johnny decides to crash the party and rents a ride on Schoenberg's boat. Johnny spots Jane and goes to talk to her. Jane threatens to have Johnny thrown out until Johnny asks her if she wants to talk to the police instead. Jane tells Johnny that Charles got back about 6:30 on the night Chambers was shot. Charles walks up and tells Johnny to leave and Johnny now knows that he is jealous and violent. Jane tells Charles that Johnny is an investigator and Johnny asks Charles where he was yesterday, and if he owns a .22 rifle. Johnny tells Charles that the bullet can be traced to the rifle it was fired from; it's called ballistics. "Isn't science wonderful?" Johnny asks and leaves. Johnny leaves but watches the Weatherwax docks. Ten minutes later Charles takes a boat to a spot 300 yards off the shore and dives into the water. Johnny rushes to the boat as Charles surfaces, pulls his gun and asks what kind of fish Charles is after. Back on the dock Johnny takes Charles to the house and asks what he was looking for. Charles tells Johnny that he did not kill Chambers but he was with him when he was killed. He had gone there to tell him to stay away from Jane and was standing on the dock when there was a shot and Chambers fell into the water. Charles thought he was dead and left in a panic. Charles remembered he had a .22 in the boat and threw it overboard. When Johnny had mentioned ballistics, Charles realized he had thrown away the one piece of evidence that would clear him so he came back to find it. Johnny tells Charles he does not believe him and Charles tackles Johnny and takes his gun and points it at Johnny's head. Johnny wrestles with him, gets the gun away from him and asks Charles why he did not fire when he had the chance. Charles tells Johnny that he is not the shooting type. Charles tells Johnny that the story he told is true, and Johnny believes him this time. Johnny is sure that if Charles did not shoot Chambers, Jane did, as she had motive, opportunity and no alibi. Charles admits that he killed Chambers and did not know that Jane had broken up with him. Chambers got nasty and Charles shot him. As they are talking a shot rings out and they run to investigate. In a small cove they find a boat and a small boy with a .22 rifle. The boy greets them and tells Charles that he lives in Fire Island and was hunting squirrels. The boy had come there on Tuesday and got two squirrels. Johnny tells him "that's not all you got."

Well that's the way things work out sometimes. You think you have a cold-blooded murder on your hands and it turns out to be young kid who shouldn't have been given a gun for his birthday. The .22 was checked by the ballistics department and proved to be the one that fired the fatal shot. At the inquest the jury returned a verdict of accidental manslaughter. However, it is doubtful that young Jimmy Bishop will ever want another gun as long as he lives.

NOTES:
- THIS PROGRAM IS VERY NOISY AND THE DETAILS WERE DIFFICULT TO HEAR IN THE MIDDLE.

- CAST CREDITS FROM THE KNX SCRIPT COLLECTION AT THE THOUSAND OAKS LIBRARY.
- CHARLES LYONS IS THE ANNOUNCER
- MUSIC BY EDDIE DUNSTEDTER

Producer: Jaime del Valle   Writers: Blake Edwards
Cast: Hal March, Marvin Miller, Jeanette Nolan, Jane Webb, Dick Beals

◆ ❖ ◆

SHOW: THE PHILIP MOREY MATTER
SHOW DATE: 10/13/1953
COMPANY: NATIONAL LIFE & CASUALTY INSURANCE COMPANY
AGENT: DON MAYNARD
EXP. ACCT: $99.38

SYNOPSIS: Don Maynard calls and asks Johnny to go to New York City, where Morley Productions is in trouble because Phil Morley has had a breakdown. Go see what you can do.

Johnny goes to New York City and meets with Milton Gradkey, the producer, who is very concerned with Phil's condition. Johnny is told that Phil is very sick, and that his doctor, Charles Ewing, told Milton that Phil had had a breakdown caused by something personal. Johnny is told that he cannot see Phil, as he is too sick, so go talk to the doctor.

Johnny goes to see Phil Morley at his apartment but is met at the door by a man who will not let him in. Phil staggers into the room, and it is clear to Johnny that Phil has had a "90 proof breakdown" and is drunk. Phil tells Johnny that he does not want insurance as he is a lousy risk, and to go away. Phil tells Johnny that he will stay drunk "until they have another blue snow."

Johnny goes to his hotel for a drink and is met in the bar by the man in the apartment, who introduces himself as Richard Long, the writer and director on the program. Richard swears to Johnny that Phil had only started drinking the night before after a call from his wife's lawyer to let him know she was divorcing him. Johnny tells Richard that he will have to report that to the Insurance Company. Johnny knows that Phil has lost other contracts for drinking and has had several wives take him to the cleaners. Richard tells Johnny that the current wife, Janet, is going to do the same as all the other wives, namely to take him for everything she can get. Johnny is told that she got what ever she asked for from Phil, just like everyone else because Phil is a nice guy who cannot say no. When the lawyer called last night Phil went for the bottle. Richard tells Johnny that Janet is a real tramp, but she played him for what he could get, and there were no witnesses.

Johnny goes to see Janet at her apartment. On the way up, Johnny meets a man rushing out of the elevator. Johnny wonders, "Now who is that man? I know him from somewhere." Janet meets Johnny at the door, and he tells her why he is there. Janet tells Johnny that that Phil has been drunk for over a month, and that she tried to help him. Besides, she tells Johnny, Phil has lots of money and he can afford a dozen more ex-wives. And as for Richard Long, he is just jealous. Janet mixes Johnny a glass of bourbon and water and they talk. When Johnny tells Janet that that he recognizes her from a picture he saw once, she shows him a photo album of her pictures, which curdles his drink, but tells Johnny that Janet is up to no good. In one of the pictures Johnny sees the man he saw leaving the building and the name comes back to him.

Johnny leaves and goes back to talk to Richard Long at this hotel. Johnny tells Richard about the man he saw, who is named Eugene Sweet. Johnny tells Richard that Sweet had been convicted of forgery in California, and Johnny had worked on the case. Johnny explains that Sweet would introduce a young woman to a rich older man, and after the wedding, Sweet would forge checks and then the girl would divorce the old man and get a nice payoff. Johnny guesses that they are probably doing the same thing to Phil. Richard tells Johnny that a man named Swift introduced Janet to Phil, but the description of Swift matches Sweet, so Johnny and Richard go back to see Janet.

When Johnny and Richard get to the apartment, they see Swift going in. While waiting for the elevator, Milton Gradkey comes down and is very upset. He tells Johnny and Richard that Phil got away from him, and that he has a gun and is probably is upstairs. When Johnny and Richard get to Janet's floor, the apartment door is open and Phil is threatening Janet and Swift. Johnny is able to talk the gun away from Phil, the police are called and Janet and Swift confess. They had fleeced Phil out of over $300,000 in forged checks and had taken advantage of his spending habits.

NOTES:

- CHARLES LYON IS THE ANNOUNCER
- MUSIC BY EDDIE DUNSTEDTER

Producer:	Jaime del Valle	**Writers:**	**Blake Edwards**
Cast:	Joe Du Val, Sidney Miller, Hy Averback, Bill Johnstone, Jeanette Nolan		

◆ ❖ ◆

SHOW:	THE ALLEN SAXTON MATTER
SHOW DATE:	10/20/1953
COMPANY:	GREAT EASTERN LIFE INSURANCE COMPANY
AGENT:	STANLEY MITCHELL
EXP. ACCT:	$119.93

SYNOPSIS: Stanley Mitchell calls and tells Johnny to go to New York and see Allen Saxton. He has recently returned from Europe with a "priceless" paining and has applied for insurance on it. Several experts claim it is a fake, and Saxon is angry because he paid $200,000 for the picture.

Johnny goes to New York City, rents a car and drives to the Saxton home in New Jersey. Saxton, who has a bad cough, tells Johnny that he had paid $200,000 for the painting in Paris, and that he was told that it was supposed to be a genuine Marchaux, and that the dealer was one of the most respected in Paris. Then a guy named Lippert tells Saxton it is a fake. As Allen takes Johnny to see the picture, Allen's daughter Barbara comes in, and starts rolling her eyes at Johnny. Johnny looks at the picture and calls it "beautiful." Allen tells Johnny that Rene Francois is in town until the painting is authenticated. Barbara wants Johnny to stay for dinner, and Allen tells Johnny to leave, as Barbara is spoiled and Allen wants to save Johnny, as he is too nice a guy. At the door Barbara throws a vase at her father and almost hits him.

Johnny goes back to his hotel to wait for the experts to analyze the paining. Johnny calls some numbers in his black book when there is a knock at the door and Barbara comes in. She apologizes for arguing with her father and tells Johnny that she is hungry and wants Johnny to take her to dinner.

After $22.78 for dinner Johnny takes Barbara home. Johnny comments that Barbara made Delilah look like a Girl Scout. After telling Barbara he will not marry her, Johnny takes her to the open front door, deposits her in the foyer and heads for the car. Barbara screams and Johnny runs in to find Allen in the library with a bloody head.

After calming Barbara, Allen tells Johnny that he had heard a noise, went down stairs and saw a man stealing the picture. The man hit him with a flashlight and cut the picture out of the frame and ran. "She didn't get you drunk and marry Barbara, did you?" asks Allen. Allen asks Johnny if he would marry Barbara for her money. Johnny answers "No, I would marry her for your money." Allen laughs and starts to worry for his picture again. The police are called and Johnny goes back to his hotel to call the Paris office of the Insurance Company and asks the manager, Howard Gilbert to check up on Rene Francois' departure from Paris, as he was not due in New York until that day. Johnny drives to the apartment of an old friend, Andre for information. Andre tells Johnny that only his landlord or a vampire would go to such extremes to be there at that hour. After slipping some money under the door, Johnny is let in and tells Andre why he is there. Johnny tells him about Saxton and the theft of the painting, and Andre denies that he would steal the picture as he could paint something better for less than $200,000. After paying a series of small bribes to cover his back rent and an overdue deli bill, Andre tells Johnny to go to the Shelton Arms Hotel and see Gasteau Chamberlay, who just arrived from Paris yesterday.

Johnny goes to his hotel and has a message from Howard Gilbert telling Johnny that Rene Francois left Paris that day and is due in New York that afternoon. Johnny drives to the Shelton Arms and knocks on the door of Chamberlay's room. Johnny invites him self in with a fake message from Francois and convinces Chamberlay to talk. After a convincing smack on the jaw, Chamberlay admits that Rene Francois had paid him $10,000 to steal the painting, which is under the pillow on the sofa. Rene Francois wanted the painting back because there was evidence that the picture was a fake and he feared for his reputation. Johnny takes

Chamberlay to the police, and Rene is picked up at the airport. Rene tells the police that he hired Chamberlay to take the painting because he had discovered that there was a possibility that the painting was a fake, and the wanted to protect his business.

Johnny goes to see Saxton, who is happy that he has his $200,000 back. Johnny tells Allen that he will have to pay the $85 Johnny paid in bribes. Barbara has a bad hangover, but is ready to go back to Hartford with Johnny. Johnny tells her no. He is an insurance man and knows a bad risk when he sees one—him.

NOTES:
- CHARLES LYON IS THE ANNOUNCER
- MUSIC BY EDDIE DUNSTEDTER

Producer: Jaime del Valle   Writers: Blake Edwards
Cast: Edgar Barrier, Hal March, Virginia Gregg, Jay Novello

SHOW: THE HOWARD ARNOLD MATTER
SHOW DATE: 10/27/1953
COMPANY: WORLD INSURANCE & INDEMNITY COMPANY
AGENT: HANLEY CONRAD
EXP. ACCT: $123.66
SYNOPSIS: Hanley Conrad calls. Howard Arnold the attorney for George Castro is insured and they do not want anything to happen to him. He called and is worried and needs protection.

Johnny goes to New York City and calls Howard Arnold. Arnold is not home, so Johnny leaves a message to call him at the Ellsworth Hotel. Johnny calls Arnold's office and he is not there either. At 7:00 PM Howard Arnold comes to Johnny's hotel room. He tells Johnny that he has not been to the office or home in several days. Howard relates to Johnny that he has had a falling out with George Castro the gangster. Howard was his attorney and he knows too much and Castro is afraid he will talk. Howard tells Johnny that their relationship has snapped and that Castro will try to liquidate him. Johnny tells Howard that he is there to stop that but George tells him that just keeping Castro's boys away is not very practical. Howard wants Johnny to keep something for him, an envelope with information about Castro. Johnny is to hold on to it for a couple hours and then will give it back to Arnold after he makes some arrangements. Johnny hides the envelope under a dresser drawer and goes out for dinner.

Johnny eats and comes back to his room to find Marty Fleet waiting for him. Marty wants the envelope but Johnny plays dumb. Marty slugs Johnny and then tears the room apart. When Johnny wakes up, the room is torn apart but the envelope is still there. Johnny calls Arnold and suggests that he take the envelope back. Arnold gives Johnny instructions to an isolated place where he is to meet

Howard to turn over the envelope. Johnny rents a car and goes to the designated spot. As Johnny gives the envelope to Howard, Marty appears and wants the envelope. Howard offers Marty $15,000 but he only wants to slug Johnny for lying. When Johnny wakes up he discovers Howard's car in a ravine burning with a man in it.

Johnny flags down a car and calls the fire department and the police. When the police arrive, Johnny gives his story to Lt. David. Johnny cannot figure out how Fleet got there so quickly as he could not have followed Arnold, and he was there when Johnny arrived. Maybe it was Howard's wife. George Castro is brought in for questioning and Mrs. Arnold identifies the body in the car based on a ring and watch. She is certain that the body is Howard's. She tells the police that Howard had not said where he was going or where he had been. You should see the people who Howard worked for. Johnny thinks that there is something odd, why Fleet only knocked Johnny out and did not kill him. George Castro is brought in and is told about Howard. "Is it such a shame," Castro tells them. Castro does not like Lt. David or Johnny and tells them that. Johnny tells Castro that Fleet killed Arnold, but Castro does not believe it. Suddenly Johnny thinks of something. Where is Fleet? Lt. David tells Castro that the politicians are not going to bail Castro out this time and Castro tells Lt. David that Fleet is in the Alton Arms Hotel. Lt. David arranges to get Fleet at the hotel, and Johnny goes to see Mrs. Arnold.

At Mrs. Arnold's home Johnny asks her about Howard and his job. She confirms to Johnny that Howard made a lot of money and that they were happy. Johnny asks her why this killing is so funny? Johnny tells her that Fleet was supposed to have killed Howard, but he did such a poor job of searching his room. Fleet met Howard and Johnny on the road but could not have followed Johnny to Howard. Someone told him where to meet us. Johnny tells her that she had told the police that she did not know me, but on the phone the first time you said you knew me. Johnny tells her that he thinks that someone hired Fleet and wanted to use him to frame Castro. Johnny tells her that the "arrangements" Howard had made were mysterious. Maybe Howard arranged to have himself killed so you and he could leave the country. "The man is the car was Fleet, wasn't it?" Johnny tells her. Howard comes into the room with a gun and tells Beth to take her car and follow him in Johnny's car. Johnny asks, and Howard tells Johnny that Fleet was in the car. They leave the house and walk to Johnny's car when a police car drives up. Howard is distracted and Johnny slugs him. Lt. David is promised an explanation in a nice loud saloon, on the expense account.

Howard and his wife are arrested and Johnny explains the whole story over drinks and dinner for Lt. David.

NOTES:
- CHARLES LYON IS THE ANNOUNCER
- MUSIC BY EDDIE DUNSTEDTER

Producer: Jaime del Valle   **Writers:**   Blake Edwards

Cast: **David Young, Jeanette Nolan, John McIntire, Hy Averback, Frank Nelson, Bill Conrad**

SHOW:	THE GINO GAMBONA MATTER
SHOW DATE:	11/3/1953
COMPANY:	INTERCONTINENTAL BONDING & INDEMNITY
AGENT:	ROGER STERN
EXP. ACCT:	$112.07

SYNOPSIS: Roger Stern calls Johnny with a job. Stern insures Barney Rico, a former gangster who has been A-Number One citizen for the past seven years. The policy was for $100,000, and Ricco was murdered yesterday. Johnny is to see Lt. Briggs at the seventh precinct for the details. Johnny will leave as soon as he can pack a bag.

Johnny trains to New York City and gets a room. Johnny arranges to meet Art Briggs over a lunch of corned beef. Lt. Briggs tells Johnny that he has no idea whom might have killed Rico, and that he used to work for the Gambona gang. Johnny tells Lt. Briggs that Rico's brother is the beneficiary. Johnny remembers that Rico was the one who testified against Gambona and had him sent back to Sicily. Gambona had also threatened to get even with Rico, who had owned a series of barbershops, and his brother Dave is scared stiff. Johnny buys lunch and goes to see Dave Rico. Dave Rico's wife tells Johnny that Dave is not home, so Johnny cabs to the main barbershop. Johnny arrives after six and knocks on the door. Johnny is about to leave when he sees a man stagger inside the shop and collapse. Johnny kicks in the door as the man collapses and Johnny hears him mumbles something. The man is Dave Rico, and he names Gambona as his killer. Johnny calls Lt. Briggs and tells him what has happened, but Art tells Johnny that Gambona is in Sicily, so maybe Dave meant the Gambona mob. Lt. Briggs will wire the authorities to make sure that Gambona is still in Sicily. Johnny goes back to the precinct and goes through the mug books to find the remaining members of Gambona's gang. One is a girl named Virginia Barrett, who sings at a club called the Pirates Den. Johnny cabs to the club on East 34th street. Johnny tells a waiter he wants to talk to Virginia, and she joins him a few minutes later. Johnny asks her if she has heard from Gino lately, and she tells Johnny that Gino is in Sicily. Johnny tells her about Dave and Barney Rico, and she is unmoved, but walks away looking worried. Johnny follows her backstage and is stopped by a large man who tells Johnny to go back outside and tries to slug him, but Johnny knocks him out. Johnny goes to the alley and sees Virginia jump into a cab. Johnny follows her in another cab to an apartment building. Johnny rings the doorbells and fakes being a flower delivery boy to get in and goes to Virginia's apartment. The man from the club runs up the stairs and stops Johnny from knocking. Johnny tells him he is on a scavenger hunt, but the man can only guarantee Johnny some broken bones. Johnny knocks and Virginia lets Johnny and Marco in. Inside the apartment Johnny finds Gino Gambona.

Gino Gambona is sitting on a chair looking at Johnny. Marco shoves Johnny into a chair and Gino asks Johnny who he is, and Johnny tells him he is an investigator for the insurance company that insured Barney Rico. Gino tells him that the company does not have to pay off on anyone, and asks how much insurance Johnny has. Gino tells Johnny that he saw him knocking on the door of the barbershop, and that he killed Dave because his name was Rico. Gino tells Johnny that Marco was one of his boys from the old days, and that he came back to the country to get something. Gino tells Johnny that as soon as the police figure out he is in the country, he will be back and no one will have seen him. Marco is told to take Johnny for a drive by the river while he and Ginny go to pick up the stuff. On the stairs a woman calls and distracts Marco, allowing Johnny to slug him. The woman was looking for someone with some flowers for her, and Johnny tells her he will personally buy her a whole acre of orchids. Johnny goes back to the apartment but Gino and Ginny are gone. Johnny calls Lt. Briggs and they take Marco to the precinct and they interrogate him, but he says nothing. Finally Marco gives in and tells Lt. Briggs that he was supposed to get ten grand for smuggling Gambona into the states, and that Gino has some money stashed somewhere. Marco tells Johnny that he was supposed to meet them at Grand Central station by the oyster bar. Johnny and Lt. Briggs rush to Grand Central and the area is staked out, but Gino and Ginny fail to show. Johnny is sure that Marco has already made arrangement to get Gambona out of the country and suspects a boat will be used. Johnny is sure that Gambona planned it to get into the country, kill the Ricos, get the money and leave as quickly as possible. Johnny and Lt. Briggs start to check all the boats that arrived within the past two days and are leaving for Italy that night. The schedules are checked and the Atlantic Star is scheduled to sail at 1:00 AM from Pier 16. Johnny and Lt. Briggs arrive at Pier 16 at 12:50 and go to see the captain on the bridge. Lt. Briggs arrests the captain and he tells Lt. Briggs that Gambona has signed on as a cook and is in the galley. Lt. Briggs and Johnny go to Stateroom D and force their way in and arrest Ginny. The boat is cleared and Johnny goes into the galley with his hand on his .38. Gino pushes the pots and pans over onto Johnny and tries to run out until Lt. Briggs shoots him.

Gino was dead. Virginia Barrett and Marco, full name Marco Dandoy got five to ten years for their parts in the crime. The Captain of the Atlantic Star got two years and Lt. Briggs got a promotion. Yours truly returned to Adelaide Jones with the flowers he had promised her, and all-in-all, everyone got just what was coming to them.

NOTES:
- THIS IS AN **AFRS** TAPE AND COMMERCIAL BREAK **#1** IS ABOUT CHILDREN'S GAMES AND THE ORIGINS OF THE TERM "G-MEN."
- COMMERCIAL BREAK **#2** IS ABOUT COINAGE AND AMERICAN ELECTIONS.
- THE ANNOUNCER IS CHARLES LYON
- MUSIC IS BY EDDIE DUNSTEDTER

Producer: Jaime del Valle   Writers: Blake Edwards
Cast: Peter Leeds, John McIntire, Virginia Gregg, Jay Novello,
            Jeanette Nolan, Clayton Post

SHOW: THE BOBBY FOSTER MATTER
SHOW DATE: 11/10/1953
COMPANY: NATIONAL MEDICAL & HOSPITALIZATION INSURANCE
AGENT: WALTER JACKSON
EXP. ACCT: $196.96

SYNOPSIS: Walter Jackson calls and asks Johnny to conduct an investigation. Walter's company writes a group health and hospitalization policy at the Riggs Bearing Company in Riggs City, Florida. They have just received a claim for the son of an employee that involved an operation by a team of neurosurgeons. Dr. Grant Howell, director of the hospital attached a report to the claim that needs investigation. Johnny is told not to spare any expense on this case. If the report is correct, there is a vicious racket spreading, a racket that victimizes children.

Johnny flies to Miami and takes a bus to Riggs City, Florida. Johnny gets a room and goes to see Dr. Howell who is expecting him. Nurse Flo Rogers tells Johnny that the doctor will give him the details. Johnny has a cigarette with Flo and she tells Johnny that the town is a little dull, and Johnny offers to fix that. Johnny sees Dr. Howell and tells him that while the claim was rather high, they are not questioning his medical ability, but are interested in the attached report. Dr. Howell tells Johnny that the report should interest the whole country, because it is about a vicious, unscrupulous racket that is a potential child killer that preys on panic and fear. Dr. Howell takes Johnny to the hospital to see Bobby Foster. In the bed is a 5-year-old boy who is in a coma, with only a fair chance of recovery if he comes out of the coma, but he will be paralyzed if he does. Dr. Howell does not know who is behind the racket, the worst one he has seen in his 40 years of being a doctor. Dr. Howell tells Johnny that there was a polio scare in town and some children came down with similar symptoms. An expert was called in, but rumors of an epidemic spread through town. The parents held a mass meeting to demand that Dr. Howell inject all the children with gamma globulin, but he refused because the treatment is hard to get unless there is a real epidemic. Dr. Howell was called to the Foster home last week, and Bobby had all the signs of cerebral embolism, an air bubble in the blood veins. Dr. Howell called in the neurosurgeons because he was not skilled enough to do the operation. The air bubble was caused by criminal negligence during a hypodermic injection. The needle marks were still on Bobby's arm, but Dr. Howell does not know who did it. He does know that other children were injected with no problems. The parents deny that the boy was treated by anyone, but they are lying. The child was sick and taken to a quack and given a shot they thought was gamma globulin. Johnny tells Dr. Howell he will go to visit the parents, but Dr. Howell tells Johnny that it will be a waste of time. They have another child, a girl, and Dr. Howell thinks that the girl has been threatened. Johnny gets a list of names from Nurse Flo, who offers to help Johnny any way she can. Johnny arranges to meet Flo for dinner at a local bar and grill, as a civic duty. Johnny cabs to the home of the Fosters, near the beach. Mrs. Foster answers the door and does not want to talk to Johnny. Johnny asks her about the injection, but she tells Johnny that Bobby did not have any shots and gets very upset. She tells Johnny that she cannot tell Johnny who gave Bobby the shot because of Margaret. Mr. Foster comes home and tells Johnny to leave. Johnny tells him he owes it to his son to talk to Johnny, but Foster knocks Johnny down.

Johnny goes to his room to shower and change clothes and then goes to the Tropics Cafe to meet Flo. Johnny tells her what happened at the Fosters and tells Flo that he is sure that the daughter's life has been threatened. Johnny tells her he will question all the parents the next day. Flo tells Johnny that she overheard the bartender tell a man where to take his child for an injection, but she could not hear where the man was told to go. Johnny tells Flo to leave and goes to the bar and drinks himself into a dark mood with double bourbons. Johnny tells Mickey the bartender that he has something that no one can help him with. The bartender thinks it is woman trouble, but Johnny tells him that the kids are sick, and that is why he is there. The bartender tells Johnny that he can get him some gamma globulin and gives Johnny an address. Johnny takes a cab to the address after getting some coffee to remove the chill from his spine. At 2 AM Johnny arrives at a deserted beach house. Johnny walks up the drive until a man calls him by name and tells him to stop. Mr. Foster grabs Johnny and searches for Johnny's gun, which he is not carrying. Foster puts Johnny into his car and drives Johnny out of town. Foster stops at a long auto trailer and Johnny is taken inside to meet Flo who tells Johnny that the bartender is her husband. Flo offers to fix a drink and asks Johnny why he was not surprised to see her. Johnny tells Flo that Foster knew Johnny's name when he went to see them, and that she and Dr. Howell were the only ones who knew he was in town. Flo tells Johnny that she is keeping Foster's child for them, and his arrival called for drastic measures. She tells Johnny that Bobby's injection was an accident, and that Mickey had given him the shot. She tells Johnny that they charge $50 for each injection of colored water. Mickey arrives and Johnny tells him that he knew they would want to talk to Johnny before he started talking to the other parents and learned their identity. Johnny tells Mickey that Flo plays a very convincing bachelor girl and talks too much. Johnny tells Mickey that Flo told him that he had killed the Foster girl. Foster rushes in very angry and slugs Mickey, allowing Johnny to take Flo's gun. Foster wants the gun to kill Mickey but Johnny tells him that Margaret is really safe, and Flo tells him the same thing.

"This case deserves publicity, Mr. Jackson. Lots of it."

NOTES:
- THIS IS AN **AFRS** TAPE AND COMMERCIAL BREAK **#1** IS FOR BENJAMIN FRANKLIN AND HIS SAYING ABOUT DEATH AND TAXES.

- BREAK #2 IS ABOUT THE STORY OF PRESIDENT BUCHANAN.
- MUSIC IS BY EDDIE DUNSTEDTER

Producer:	Jaime del Valle	Writers:	Don Sanford
Cast:	Frank Nelson, Mary Lansing, John McIntire, Jeanette Nolan, Tom Tully		

◆ ❖ ◆

SHOW:	THE NATHAN GAYLES MATTER
SHOW DATE:	11/17/1953
COMPANY:	GREAT EASTERN LIFE INSURANCE COMPANY
AGENT:	MR. BISHOP
EXP. ACCT:	$235.00

SYNOPSIS: Mr. Bishop calls and asks Johnny if he is free. Bishop tells Johnny that his company insures a New York City police officer by the name of Nathan Gayles, who was killed yesterday. Johnny remembers reading that Gayles was shot in his garage. Bishop tells Johnny to contact Gayle's partner, Sgt. Kemper of the 15th precinct.

Johnny trains to New York City and gets a room. Johnny calls Sgt. William Kemper and arranges to meet him. Sgt. Kemper tells Johnny that Gayles had been after a hood named Bancroft who had gotten tired of the chase and let the word out he was going to kill Gayles. Sgt. Kemper tells Johnny that Gayles had called in and told him he had something hot on Bancroft, and wanted Sgt. Kemper to meet him at his house. A stoolie named Virgil Cummins was supposed to give Gayles something that would fry Bancroft. Sgt. Kemper went to see Gayles and found him dead in his garage. A neighbor saw a man running away and identified him as Bancroft. But the neighbor changed his mind when Bancroft was put in a lineup; probably someone had gotten to him and changed his mind for him. The man is scared stiff for his wife and four kids. Bancroft told the police that he was with his girl friend, and the girl corroborated the story. Sgt. Kemper went looking for Cummins and found him in his room strangled with a light cord. Now there is no evidence against Bancroft. Johnny cabs to the Gayle home and talks to Evelyn Gayle, and meets her two children. She has told the children their father is away on a trip. Evelyn tells Johnny that the day Nathan was killed was their seventh anniversary and that she expected him home around six. She was at the store when Nathan got home, and she saw the police and the ambulance when she got home. She had left the kids with their grandmother as she and Nathan were going out to dinner and see a show. She knows the neighbor George Fisher and had talked to him. She told him that he should talk to the police, and that hiding a killer is no way to protect his family. Johnny tells her he will talk to Fisher and leaves. Johnny talks to Mrs. Fisher who refuses to tell Johnny where Mr. Fisher works. Johnny goes back to the hotel and calls Sgt. Kemper and has lunch. Johnny meets Sgt. Kemper in the hotel lobby and tells him that he wants to know where Mr. Fisher works. Sgt. Kemper tells

Johnny that Fisher was killed an hour ago by a hit-and-run while going to lunch with two coworkers. All three were hit, but only Fisher was killed. There was a witness who identified the car. The police found the car later, and it had been reported stolen. Bancroft was with his girl at the time and had been at his hotel all morning. The witness said there was a man driving the car, and the police are searching for prints. Sgt. Kemper also tells Johnny that they had gotten a call from a jeweler who told them that Gayles had been looking at watches, and had taken two of them home to let his wife decide which she wanted. The watches were missing when Sgt. Kemper got there, and the car glove compartment was open and empty. The watches were expensive, and an alert is out for them. Sgt. Kemper wants Johnny to try and find out if the girl, Betty Holme, has one of the watches. Sgt. Kemper tells Johnny that Betty is attractive and likes men with money. Sgt. Kemper will get Bancroft out of the way, but only for a while.

Johnny changes hotels and becomes Johnny Dollar the Texas oilman, complete with accent and boots. Johnny goes to a fur store where Betty is shopping and he pretends he is buying a fur coat for momma. Johnny wants a full-length coat and the sales lady goes to get some, allowing Betty to talk to Johnny. She offers to help Johnny with the coats and he tells her he has mink upholstery in his car, a double length Cadillac with the gold door handles. There are formal introductions and Johnny spends an hour looking at coats and orders two coats for momma. Johnny arranges for dinner and goes to his hotel to tell Sgt. Kemper what is going on. Sgt. Kemper tells Johnny that the police will keep Bancroft held as long as possible, and arranges a limo for Johnny to use. That night the limo is waiting, complete with officer Danker as a chauffeur. Johnny takes Betty to "The 21" and spends $45.95 on dinner. Johnny avoids the nightlife of the clubs by going to Betty's apartment for a glass of hot milk, on his doctor's recommendation of course. Johnny tells Betty that she is a nice girl who has everything she needs. Betty tells Johnny that she has everything but a man, and would like to get back to he farm, where she was raised. Johnny asks for the time, and Betty tells Johnny that she does not own a watch, so Johnny tells her he will buy her one, which earns him a great big kiss. Betty tells Johnny that he has a friend who has some watches he will sell wholesale, and will arrange for him to visit Johnny at his hotel. Johnny asks Betty for a favor, "could I. . .have some more milk?" Johnny meets Sgt. Kemper at his room and he arranges for Bancroft to be released. The next Morning Johnny has breakfast with Sgt. Kemper when Betty calls. She tells Johnny that the jeweler cannot come, but he gave the watches to her, and she will bring them by. Johnny is sure that Bancroft is playing it safe by not showing up. Sgt. Kemper hides when Betty arrives and shows Johnny the watches. The price for the watches is $500, and $700, wholesale. Johnny calls Sgt. Kemper in and tells him that the watches are the one Gayles had. Betty pleads innocence until Sgt. Kemper threatens Betty with jail. She tells them that Bancroft went out the servant's entrance of the hotel when he went to murder Gayles. She also tells them that she stole the car that Bancroft had used to rundown Fisher, but she had nothing to do with it. Betty is taken away and tells Johnny "Thanks, you all."

NOTES:

- DINNER IS $347.00 IN 2006 DOLLARS.
- THE WATCHES ARE PRICED TODAY AT $3700 AND $5200. PRETTY EXPENSIVE WATCHES FOR A POLICEMAN IN THE 1950'S.
- CHARLES LYON IS THE ANNOUNCER
- MUSIC IS BY EDDIE DUNSTEDTER

Producer: Jaime del Valle   Writers: Blake Edwards
Cast: Jim Nusser, Jack Moyles, Jeanette Nolan, Mary Jane Croft

◆ ❖ ◆

SHOW: THE INDEPENDENT DIAMOND TRADERS MATTER SHOW
DATE: 11/24/1953
COMPANY: ATLAS INDEMNITY INSURANCE COMPANY
AGENT: ERIC CARLSON
EXP. ACCT: $64.20

SYNOPSIS: Eric Carlson calls Johnny with a job. Atlas Indemnity insures most of the independent diamond traders. They are the small dealers on the street in New York. Two thirds have cancelled policies and gone broke. Johnny is to see E.G. Moss at the Independent Diamond Traders.

Johnny goes to New York City and phones Mr. Moss and makes an appointment. There is a light snow falling so Johnny indulges himself and walks to the office. At the Independent Diamond Traders office, a woman is talking with Mr. Moss. There is a brief argument followed by some minor passion and Mr. Moss agrees to get rid of Susan and meet the woman that night. As the woman leaves by the back entrance, Johnny is caught eavesdropping by Susan, Mr. Moss' stepdaughter. Johnny and Mr. Moss talk about the situation and Moss tends to ramble on about how two thirds of the dealers have gone out of business, some after thirty years. He has given Mr. Carlson all the details, but Johnny tells Moss that he was to fill Johnny in. Moss tells Johnny that falling prices are driving the small traders out of business. The market is rigidly controlled, but someone has flooded the market lately. Johnny tells Moss he will start asking around the other diamond houses. On the way out Johnny asks Susan to bury the hatchet. She tells Johnny that Moss is crazy over that woman and they agree to call it a draw. Johnny checks into a small hotel near the diamond district. Johnny goes to eat and comes back to his hotel where the desk clerk has a package for him. The clerk is "always on duty," but he does not know who delivered the package. In his room, Johnny opens the package to find a card from "Mona" and a pair of 10-carat diamonds. The phone rings and it is Mona. Johnny tells her that he has the package and is interested in the contents. Mona tells Johnny that she can help him, as she knows who is flooding the market. Mona wants Johnny to meet her at the Surf and Sand Club. Johnny goes to the club on Long Island to meet Mona. Johnny waits at the bar until a red headed Mona comes in. Johnny introduces himself and she takes Johnny out to her car for a drive. The car is a Mercedes Benz with a speedometer that goes up to 120 MPH, and Mona wants to try it out, until Johnny turns off the ignition. She tells Johnny that she likes to act on impulse, and that she used the diamonds to make sure Johnny would keep the blind date. Mona tells Johnny that Captain Ledru will tell him everything. Ledru did not meet Johnny, as Ledru is wanted by the police.

Mona drives to a rundown cottage where the captain is and Mona tells Ledru that Johnny was alone. Ledru tells Johnny that he is sailing tonight, and that he is the one dumping the diamonds, which he smuggles into the country. This is his last job, and Johnny is going to do one last delivery job for him. Johnny gives the diamonds back to Mona but Ledru pulls a gun. Ledru tells Johnny that the police are watching his client and Johnny must make a delivery for him. Ledru tells Johnny to get up so that he can convince Johnny, who expects a beating. They go out back to a dock where there is a cabin cruiser. Onboard Johnny and Ledru meet Mr. Moss, who tells Johnny that he is disillusioned with Mona. Ledru tells Johnny that they will kill Moss if Johnny does not do what is asked. Johnny is left alone with Moss, who tells Johnny that Mona has led him on, but he overheard a plan. Johnny thinks there is no way out and there is no way he can get past the police at the delivery point.

Ledru comes back in, but Johnny is still not sure and wants to hear more before he decides. Ledru tells Johnny that he will phone the client and tell him who Johnny is, and that Johnny is interviewing all the merchants, etc. and he wants to meet with him. The police will know Johnny is on legitimate business and will let him alone. Johnny gets an envelope and is told to bring back another one. Ledru warns Johnny that if he tries to bring back the police, Ledru will sail with Moss.

Mona drives Johnny to a gas station where Johnny calls the client and arranges the meeting. Johnny takes a cab to the client, makes the delivery, gets the money and returns to Ledru.

The boat is pulling at the ropes and is ready to go when Johnny gets back to the boat. Johnny tells Ledru that he has the money papered to his body, as the client did not want him walking around with a package. Ledru reaches to get the bow rope and Johnny pushes him into the water and gets on the boat while Mona is running helplessly on the dock. Johnny sets the wheel of the boat towards the center of the channel as Moss comes out with a gun. Moss tells Johnny that he, Ledru and Mona are all in it together, and that he did his part to get Johnny s cooperation. Everything was staged, and Susan knows nothing. Johnny takes the gun from Moss and slugs him.

Johnny calls the police from the boat and gives them a description of the Mercedes. The police catch them and they will be out of circulation for a long time

NOTES:
- CHARLES LYON IS THE ANNOUNCER
- MUSIC IS BY EDDIE DUNSTEDTER

Producer: Jaime del Valle   Writers: Dan Sanford

Cast: Howard McNear, Parley Baer, Jeanette Nolan, Virginia Gregg, Dick Ryan, John McIntire

◆ ❖ ◆

SHOW:	THE MONOPOLY MATTER
SHOW DATE:	12/1/1953
COMPANY:	CORINTHIAN ALL RISK INSURANCE COMPANY
AGENT:	MR. BRANDT
EXP. ACCT:	$62.20

SYNOPSIS: Mr. Brandt calls Johnny about a fire, but there are no details. It is the Monopoly Club in Waterbury.

Johnny rents a car and drives to Waterbury, Connecticut . The fire department is still on the site as Johnny arrives. Later, after the fire is under control, Johnny talks to the fire inspector, Captain McReedy and is told that the fire started inside; that the building is less than five years old and is licensed for public use. The alarm came in at 11:00 AM, and the owner has gone home. The firemen have found proof of arson, a Molotov cocktail.

Johnny goes to see the building owner, Gerald Hobson. He tells Johnny that he was at the site, but his nerves got the best of him so he went home. "Thank goodness for the insurance" he tells Johnny. Hobson tells Johnny that he specializes in the game Monopoly, a harmless entertainment for the factory workers. Johnny asks about gambling, but Hobson denies anything. Johnny tells him that gambling debts could cause someone to burn the building. Hobson tells Johnny that a man had come by last week and made him pay for protection. He paid the man $100 and told the police, but they found nothing.

Johnny goes to see Capt. McReedy about the possibility of extortion. Sgt. Winnick from the police arrives and Johnny talks to him about Hobson. Sgt. Winnick tells Johnny that the police had gone to see Hobson, but no one else had reported anything, so they thought a transient had taken Hobson for $100.

Johnny goes back to Hobson to tell him that he is under suspicion for setting the fire, as his story of the protection racket did not hold up. Johnny tells Hobson that he is not as cautious as the police, and tells Hobson that he has looked into his finances and Hobson gets angry. Johnny tells Hobson that he is in need of $18,000 and the insurance would help. Johnny goes back to Hartford and gets a call from Sgt. Winnick the next morning. Sgt. Winnick tells Johnny that Hobson's story is on the level, as there was another protection racket try this morning and there was a shooting at a bowling alley.

Johnny drives back to Waterbury and meets Sgt. Winnick at the bowling alley. Johnny is told that the dead man was a bystander, and that the owner, Mr. Roblinski is upset. Johnny is told that Roblinski shot the man when they told him he was a foreigner and had to pay to work in the city. Roblinski tells Johnny that Carl came in and one of the men shot Carl. Roblinski shot the other man and the shooter got away. Johnny is told that the wounded man is Paul Loaner from Chicago, and that the police are searching for the other man.

Johnny and Sgt. Winnick go to the hospital to talk to Loaner, who has little to say. Johnny tells him that he talked while he was unconscious but Loaner does not believe him, and is not going to talk. Johnny tells him that the police found a gun but Loaner tells Johnny that it is not his. To get more information, Sgt. Winnick tells Loaner that Roblinski told them Loaner was alone. Loaner tells them that he had a partner, but does not know his name. To trick Loaner, Sgt. Winnick blurts out Bert Lucas' name and Loaner is tricked into admitting Bert was his partner. Mr. Hobson comes in and Johnny apologizes for suspecting him. Hobson tells Johnny that he does not recognize Loaner. Loaner tells Johnny that he and Lucas had torched the Monopoly Club because Hobson had gone to the police. Loaner comments that they should have taken $500. On the way out, a nurse tells Johnny that she has a call for Johnny from Loaner's wife. Johnny takes the call and tells her that Paul is all right. She is just down the street and will meet Johnny downstairs so she will not have to talk to anyone. Johnny meets with the wife, and she tells Johnny that she knew something bad would happen. Johnny is told that that Bert Lucas was with Paul, and she knows where Bert is. He is at the place they burned down, and he knows he killed the man at the bowling alley.

Johnny gets Sgt. Winnick and they go to the Monopoly Club. The police go in with their Thompsons and look for Bert. They call for Lucas and are shot at, wounding an officer in the stomach. Lights are brought into the building and Lucas tries to run, but is cut down.

NOTES:
- **CHARLES LYON IS THE ANNOUNCER**
- **MUSIC IS BY EDDIE DUNSTEDTER**

Producer: Jaime del Valle   **Writers:** Gil Doud
Cast: Sammie Hill, Bill Johnstone, Stacy Harris, Parley Baer, Howard McNear, Herb Butterfield, Jeanette Nolan, Joe Du Val

SHOW: THE BARTON BAKER MATTER
SHOW DATE: 12/8/1953
COMPANY: UNIVERSAL BONDING & INDEMNITY COMPANY
AGENT: CHARLIE MAXWELL
EXP. ACCT: $604.15

SYNOPSIS: Charlie Maxwell calls and has a job for Johnny. In a rapid-fire delivery that prevents Johnny from talking, Charlie tells Johnny that he insured Mr. Frank Meadows who lives in Newport, California and that Meadows was killed last night. How long will it take for you to pack and catch a plane? Lookup Lt. Solomon of the Newport Police when you get there, Johnny. Have a good trip. "Yeah, I'll try, Mr. Maxwell" Johnny is able to get in after Charlie hangs up.

Johnny flies to Los Angeles and rents a car for the drive to Newport, California where he meets with Lt. Solomon. Johnny learns that Frank Meadows ran a charter boat business. The police got a call about shots being fired, and when they got there, Frank had been shot three times, and two bullets were missing from his gun, so he shot it out with someone. Johnny is told that the prime suspect is Frank's partner, Dave Geller, who is missing. Lt. Solomon tells Johnny that there is no reason for the killing, and that Frank and Dave got along well, so maybe it was a woman. Frank has a wife, and Dave is single and Johnny is told that Mrs. Meadows is the kind who might cause a lot of trouble under the right circumstances. Johnny goes to see Mrs. Meadows, and Johnny is inclined to agree with Lt. Solomon. She is very attractive, blond and tan, and probably in mourning, but Johnny doubts it even though the tight bathing suit was black. Johnny tells her that he was sent out to investigate the killing, and Mrs. Meadows asks how much the insurance was for. She is surprised when Johnny tells her it was $25,000, but Johnny tells her that she will not get the money until the investigation is complete and the deceased is buried. She tells Johnny that Frank was buried this morning at 8:00. Johnny asks her if she dumped him off of a surfboard and she gets indignant, but Johnny tells her he only gets like that when he sees someone so broken up. She tells Johnny that her husband is dead and nothing will bring him back. She tells Johnny that Frank and Dave did not get a long very well because they just disagreed over things. Frank had argued with Dave before their last trip, and when they came back, Lt. Solomon told her that Frank had been killed. She tells Johnny that they had gone fishing alone for yellowtail. Johnny gets a room and calls Lt. Solomon, who tells Johnny where the boats is, and that there were no tuna on the boat when it came back. Johnny has dinner and drives to the landing where the boat, the Jay Belle is tied up. Johnny goes on board and enters the cabin and is stopped by a man with a gun. Johnny is told to turn on the lights, and the man tells Johnny that Baker must have sent him, because he knows all the cops in the area. Johnny tells the man who he is and why he is there. Geller takes Johnny's ID and gun and tells Johnny he must do something about him. He tells Johnny he did not kill Frank, but will not tell him why he is hiding. There are footsteps on the dock and Dave turns out the lights. Dave tells Johnny that if something happens to him, Johnny is to go to Bernie's garage and tell Bernie that Dave sent him, and to get the tool kit. Dave goes onto the deck and there are shots. Johnny looks out of the cabin to see a tall, thin man in a white suit pointing a gun at him. The man tells Johnny that he is Barton W. Baker, and he is going to kill Johnny like he killed Dave.

Baker comes into the cabin and smiles at Johnny. Another man, Hank, asks Baker what to do with Dave, and Baker tells him to throw Dave in the water. Baker asks Johnny about the tool kit, but Johnny feigns ignorance. Hank is told to hit Johnny, which he does. Baker offers Johnny $10,000 for the toolkit. Johnny tells Baker who he is but that he cannot prove it, as his wallet is on Dave. Johnny is beaten until he faints, but Johnny does not pass on the information. Johnny wakes up on the beach looking up at the moon. Johnny gets up and sees Mrs. Meadows walking down the beach. She takes Johnny back to her house and fixes his wounds. Johnny asks her about Baker and Hank, but she does not know either of them. Johnny tells her what happened and asks her if she knows about a tool kit at Bernie's. Johnny tells her to call Lt. Solomon and borrows her car. Johnny drives to the garage and wakes up the attendant, who turns out to be Bernie. Johnny asks Bernie for the tool kit, but Bernie is hesitant to turn over the tool kit until Johnny tells him that Dave is dead, and that Lt. Solomon is on his way. Johnny tells Bernie he is an investigator and Bernie gets the box for him. Johnny opens the lock with a crowbar while a horn blows outside. Bernie goes out side, and Johnny finds nothing but new tools inside the box, all painted black except for one. Johnny scrapes some shavings off the handle and discovers the shavings are solid platinum. Bernie comes back in with Baker and Hank. Hank takes Bernie out and Baker tells Johnny that he let him live so he could lead Baker to the tools. Johnny is told that Frank was supposed to pick Baker up and land, but Frank found out about the tools. Johnny asks if Baker is an alien, and Baker confirms that he is. Baker tells Johnny that Dave and Frank had been paid to pick up Baker south of the border. Dave figured out what the tools were made of and forced him ashore and took the kit. Baker managed to phone his operatives in Los Angeles, who met the boat and killed Frank. Shots ring out and Johnny hits Baker with the wrench. Lt. Solomon comes in and Johnny tells him that he owes Mrs. Meadows an apology. Johnny gives Lt. Solomon the wrench and tells him that Baker is going to have a very expensive headache.

"On the way over to my motel, I explained the events to Solomon, who did a little mumbling and shaking himself. Then after a fresh shower and a change of clothes I went over to Mrs. Meadows and expressed my most heartfelt thanks."

Johnny spends some time in Newport and sees Mrs. Meadows a few times, but does not get much of a tan. Barton Baker comes up for trial on illegal entry, smuggling and three counts of espionage. I hope he enjoys his stay in the USA.

NOTES:
- THIS IS AN **AFRS** TAPE AND COMMERCIAL BREAK #1 IS ABOUT THE REGULATION OF TIME IN THE US.
- BREAK #2 IS ABOUT THE PRESIDENCY OF WARREN G. HARDING
- CHARLES LYON IS THE ANNOUNCER
- MUSIC IS BY EDDIE DUNSTEDTER

Producer: Jaime del Valle   **Writers:**   Blake Edwards
Cast: Frank Nelson, Jim Nusser, Mary Lansing, Clayton Post, Edgar Barrier, Junius Matthews

SHOW: THE MILK AND HONEY MATTER
SHOW DATE: 12/15/1953
COMPANY: EASTERN INDEMNITY & INSURANCE COMPANY
AGENT: MITCHELL
EXP. ACCT: $1,480.20
SYNOPSIS: Johnny is awakened by Mitchell, and asked what he knows about the

land of milk and honey. Johnny complains about being called at 4:30 am, but Mitch tells Johnny that the sun has been up for three hours in Beirut, Lebanon and is shining brightly on a happy man named Bret Cunningham on a shipwrecked yacht. Cunningham is happy to the tune of $90,000. Johnny does not blame him and starts to go back to sleep. Mitch tells Johnny that the yacht went down in clear weather and a calm sea. "Well I've always wondered what milk and honey taste like," replied Johnny.

Johnny flies to Beirut, Lebanon and gets a room at the Saint George Hotel and finds Bret Cunningham thirty-five minutes later in the EsSuido, a swank casino. Chips and a brunette named Najia surround Cunningham at the roulette table. Johnny introduces himself and tells Cunningham that he wants to talk about the shipwreck. Cunningham asks for the insurance check but Johnny only has questions. Cunningham tells Johnny that the boat hit a derelict and sank in less than three minutes. Johnny questions the story, but Cunningham tells Johnny that he will be in the casino when Johnny is ready to pay off. Johnny goes to the harbor and talks to Commissioner Floreaux who tells Johnny about the wreck of the "Happy Times." The story was confirmed in writing by one of the eight-man crew who survived the sinking. A gunboat went to the scene the next day, found the derelict and destroyed it and the yacht was detected in 70 fathoms of water. Johnny learns that Cunningham was in route from Istanbul to Beirut and that he spends a lot of time here gambling, with a different girl on every trip. Johnny wonders why there were only two survivors out of a crew of eight. Johnny gets the name of the survivor, Casimir Andesku, and finds him on a narrow twisting street named El Akbad. Johnny knocks and the door is opened and Johnny is told that it is feeding time for his birds, so Casimir cannot talk. Johnny tells Casimir who he is and Johnny is invited in. While he feeds the birds, Casimir tells Johnny that he takes one of his favorites with him on all his voyages. He tells Johnny the same story that Floreaux had told Johnny, but Johnny tells Casimir that wants the real one. Casimir tells Johnny how poor he is, and that he only wants 10% of the claim. Johnny offers $500, but Casimir will tell him nothing. Johnny leaves and sends a radiogram to the intelligence division of the police in Istanbul and goes back to the hotel. Cunningham calls Johnny and offers to sign a quitclaim for the wreck, so Johnny heads for the casino to meet with him.

Johnny is stopped by a police officer at the casino, and Johnny sees remains of an automobile accident. Johnny spots Floreaux and is told that Cunningham's car was just blown up by a bomb. Johnny tells Floreaux about the offer of the release, which only confuses the situation. After a quick investigation by Floreaux, Johnny is driven back to his hotel where Najia is waiting for him in the lobby. She does not wince when Johnny tells her that Cunningham is dead. She tells Johnny that she like something better than Cunningham or Johnny, money, $90,000 to be exact. Johnny tells her that the money will go to the estate and Najia tells Johnny that she is Mrs. Bret Cunningham. Johnny calls Floreaux, who calls the casino manager who confirms the marriage. Johnny calls Istanbul and speaks with Chief Inspector Devriki. He tells Johnny that they know that

Cunningham's boat sailed on the 24th of November, but their problem is with the motor schooner the El Hussein, that was being towed by Cunningham's boat. They have no record of the owner, one Casimir Andesku. Johnny goes back to see Andesku, but he has disappeared, complete with his birds. Johnny rents a motor launch, complete with skipper, winch and 100 fathoms of steel chain and grappling hooks. Four hours later they arrive at the site of the wreck and start fishing. Two hours before sundown they hook something and are shot at from the shore as they try to pull it up. Back in port, Johnny shows Commissioner Floreaux their catch. It is the transom of a lifeboat with the name "El Hussein" on it. A sunburned Johnny goes to see Najia and she asks for the insurance check. Johnny asks about Casimir and is told that he is a nothing. Johnny accuses her of fraud and murder and tells her that someone sank the El Hussein and then put in a claim for the yacht. Najia is ready to seduce Johnny, but Johnny tells her she cannot spend the money in prison. Najia tells Johnny that Bret had lost $10,000 to Casimir in Istanbul, and could not pay. Casimir did not like that, because he is a big time gambler and businessman. It was Casimir who suggested sinking the El Hussein and splitting the money 50-50. However Bret won a lot of money and wanted to pay off Casimir and keep the insurance money. The call to Johnny was to try and get a better deal from Casimir, but Casimir killed Cunningham. Casimir has taken the yacht to a small place called Kibati. Johnny and Floreaux drive to Kibati and find the yacht in a small inlet, where it had been hastily disguised. Johnny finds Casimir on the boat with his birds, which Casimir tells Johnny need their sleep and object to the sound of guns. Casimir tells Johnny that Cunningham's fate was most just. Johnny tells him about being shot at, and Casimir tells him that refraction had ruined his aim. Floreaux tells Casimir that he has enough to arrest him and tells Casimir to leave with him. Casimir starts to plead for his birds and shoots at Johnny and Floreaux. Casimir is killed and Johnny tells Floreaux that Casimir was right about one thing. The birds did object to the noise.

Incidental Remarks: I still would like to know what milk and honey taste like."

NOTES:

- THIS IS AN **AFRS** TAPE AND COMMERCIAL BREAK **#1** IS ABOUT HOUSEKEEPING IN THE GOVERNMENT.
- BREAK **#2** IS ABOUT THE PRESIDENCY OF CHESTER **A.** ARTHUR
- THE SCRIPT SPELLS LILLIAN BUYEFF'S NAME "BYEFF"
- CHARLES LYON IS THE ANNOUNCER
- MUSIC IS BY EDDIE DUNSTEDTER

Producer: **Jaime del Valle**   **Writers:**   **Sidney Marshall**
Cast: **Don Diamond, Ramsey Hill, Hal March, Lillian Buyeff, Ben Wright, Jay Novello**

❖

SHOW:	THE RUDY VALENTINE MATTER
SHOW DATE:	12/22/1953
COMPANY:	COUNTY COURT, KINGS COUNTY
AGENT:	
EXP. ACCT:	$10.85

SYNOPSIS: This is the same story as the previous program from 12/30/1950, but with different cast members. The story takes place in New York City

NOTES:
* THE ANNOUNCER IS CHARLES LYON
* MUSIC IS BY EDDIE DUNSTEDTER
* STORY INFORMATION OBTAINED FROM THE KNX COLLECTION IN THE THOUSAND OAKS LIBRARY

Producer: Jaime del Valle   Writers   Gil Doud
Cast: Sidney Miller, Bill Johnstone, Jack Moyles, Jeanette Nolan, Joseph Kearns, Clayton Post, Tom Hanley, Bill James

❖

SHOW:	THE BEN BRYSON MATTER
SHOW DATE:	12/29/1953
COMPANY:	KEYSTONE MUTUAL ASSURANCE COMPANY
AGENT:	ED MURPHY
EXP. ACCT:	$823.82

SYNOPSIS: Ed Murphy calls and he wants Johnny to come to his office. It is about Ben Bryson. Johnny tells Ed that it was too bad Ben died that way. Ed tells Johnny that Ed should have died a year ago.

Johnny cabs to Ed's office where he tells Ed how close he was to Ben and it was too bad that he missed the curve and crashed into the Pacific where the body was never found. Ed tells Johnny that the company had started getting complaints about unpaid claims they had settled previously. The company looked into the matter and discovered that Ben had embezzled $80,000 from his accounts. Ed gives Johnny a ticket for San Francisco, California, but Johnny wants to pass on this case. Ed tells Johnny he can't, as too many questions need to be answered. Johnny agrees to do it because Ben was his friend. Johnny flies to San Francisco and gets a room at the Fairmont Hotel. Johnny cabs to Ben's apartment in the Franciscan Arms, a luxury building with a manager named Maurice, who has a real gardenia in his lapel. The manager, for $20, tells Johnny that Ben had been living there for six months and was a free spender. Mrs. Kearns was a friend of Ben's and they were inseparable. Johnny wants to talk to her, but he is told that she is away. Maurice tells Johnny that it is a tragic coincidence that

Mrs. Kearns' husband also died in a tragic accident. Johnny visits the bar and the bartender remembers Ben, who spent a lot of time there with Alvie Kearns. He had been there the night he died, with Alvie. Johnny realizes that he needs to talk to Alvie, as so far he has nothing to go on. Maurice calls Johnny two days later and for $20, he tells Johnny that Mrs. Kearns has written to have her mail forwarded to Panama City. Johnny flies to Panama City, Panama and is met by Captain Devano of the police. He tells Johnny that he received his radiogram and tells Johnny that Mrs. Kearns is registered in a small hotel near the waterfront. Johnny goes to the small hotel and speaks to Mrs. Kearns, who only wants to forget about Ben after the horrible accident. She tells Johnny that they were going to get married and that she came to Panama to get away from the memories. Johnny mentions Ben's wealth and she is surprised, as she thought that Ben worked for an insurance company, and besides, her husband left her a lot of money. She was only married for ten months. Johnny offers her a cigarette, but she does not smoke. Johnny walks through the apartment and asks her where the smoke came from that he smelled when he got there. Johnny starts to open a closet when Mrs. Kearns turns out the lights and Johnny is hit on the head. Johnny wakes up to find Alvie staring at him. She tells Johnny that she hit him, but Johnny tells her that he knows what is happening as only Ben Bryson shreds his cigarette butts like the ones in the ash tray. Johnny tells her that Ben Bryson hit him.

Johnny buys some aspirin, gives Ben's description to Capt. Devano and goes to bed. The next morning Johnny is met at breakfast by Mrs. Kearns. She tells Johnny that Ben did not hit him; it was a friend of hers. She tells Johnny that Ben is dead, and she is the one who tore up the cigarette papers. Johnny is sure that Ben is still alive and it hurts hard to learn that he has been stealing. Now he is alive, and Johnny has to catch him and take him back. Capt. Devano comes to see Johnny and tells him that they have found Ben. Johnny and Capt. Devano drive to the harbor where they are told that Ben is living on a boat there. Johnny goes onto the boat and Ben tells him to come on in and asks why it had to be him. Ben tells Johnny that Alvie was not supposed to come for six months. Ben tells Johnny that he stole the money for Alvie so that he could live her life style, and that they were going to go to South America to start again. Johnny asks Ben why she still has her apartment, but Ben tells Johnny that she has moved out. Ben pulls a gun and tells Johnny that he is going to go on, and will kill Johnny if he needs to. Ben locks Johnny in the boat and drives away. Capt. Devano finds Johnny and tells him that Ben was able to take the car because he was not paying attention. The police are alerted and after two hours Capt. Devano is called and told that Ben and Alvie have been found. They were driving on a mountain road, missed a curve and the car crashed into the ocean. Johnny rents a boat and diver and goes to the site of the accident. The diver goes down and reports that Alvie is dead, but Ben is not in the car. The same pattern; a crash and a missing body. Johnny climbs up the rocks and finds Ben in a crevasse, broken and dying. Ben tells Johnny that it was just like they did in San Francisco, only real this time. Johnny tells Ben that Alvie is dead and Ben tells Johnny that he made her come with him. She told him that she did not love him and was only after his money. Ben tells Johnny that he would do the same thing again if he could. The money is in his coat and he tells Johnny to give it to Ed and dies.

Johnny encloses a cashiers check for the $72,652 recovered from Ben Bryson, embezzler.

NOTES:
- THIS PROGRAM WAS REDONE WITH BOB BAILEY AS "THE CONFIDENTIAL MATTER"
- CHARLES LYON IS THE ANNOUNCER
- MUSIC IS BY EDDIE DUNSTEDTER

Producer: Jaime del Valle   Writers: Les Crutchfield
Cast: Bill Johnstone, Jack Edwards, Joe Du Val, Lillian Buyeff,
            Jeanette Nolan, Tom Tully

◆   ❖   ◆

SHOW: THE FAIRWAY MATTER
SHOW DATE: 1/5/1954
COMPANY: COLUMBIA ALL RISK INSURANCE COMPANY
AGENT: SAM HARRIS
EXP. ACCT: $25.95

SYNOPSIS: Sam Harris calls to alert Johnny of a Fairway Airlines plane crash in Hartford, Connecticut. Sam is sure that a bomb caused the accident, and thirteen people were killed. The company wants to place responsibility and do what ever it can. Contact the airline representative Mr. Reed.

Johnny goes to the scene of the crash. The plane had been airborne less than a minute when it exploded and destroyed two houses on the ground killing at least 6 people. Johnny meets a hysterical Carl Reed of the airline who is talking to an equally hysterical Mrs. Goodhugh about a daughter she fears was on the plane. The daughter was on the plane, but she has not been told yet. Carl tells Johnny that the explosion was in the tail of the plane; that the CAB is on the way; and that the State Police are in charge of the investigation.

Johnny goes to find Captain Jim Lenhart of the State Police in the hangar where the bodies are being collected. They wonder if the crash was murder with a motive, suicide or just a maniac.

The next day Johnny learns that nitroglycerine was the explosive. A tip to the police brings in Wilbur Wheeler, a maintenance worker for the airlines for questioning. Wilber is very nervous and asks what the police have on him. He admits that he had been in love with Shirley Goodhugh, a stewardess, and had fought with a copilot when Wilbur learned that Shirley was going to marry him instead. Wilbur had threatened the copilot and his plane, and knew that made him a suspect. He had heard of the crash on the radio and came back to work to help out. After questioning he is released and a police tail is placed on him.

Johnny relates that on the list of dead passengers, one man named Rupert Stone could not be located because of bogus information. Johnny and Capt. Lenhart go to visit a Mrs. Graham who is distraught over the loss of her husband. She tells Johnny and Capt. Lenhart that her husband had gone to Boston to visit his brother's grave, as he was a religious man. On the way out Jim calls the case a rotten mess and admits that he could not ask Mrs. Graham if her husband's cancer could had caused him to commit suicide. They leave to go have a drink, but are interrupted with the news that the explosive was found to have been in a first aid box in the rear of the airplane.

Wilber Wheeler is brought in for more questioning. After a very nervous interview Wilber tells Capt. Lenhart that he has worked for the airlines for a year and a half, yet does not know about the first aid kit carried on by Miss Goodhugh. Wilbur denied knowing anything about the nitroglycerine. Wilbur is held for a lie detector test and an interview with the police psychologist. Johnny and Jim search Wilbur's room and find no radio, which Wilbur said he had listened to, and no newspapers are found.

On the next day the lie detector test proves negative and the psychologist says that Wilbur has a severe guilt complex. Carl Reed calls to report that another stewardess named Alice Turner is missing and a search of her apartment uncovered her shot dead. Johnny and Capt. Lenhart go to the apartment and Carl tells them that she was originally scheduled to fly on the plane that crashed but had switched at the last minute with Shirley Goodhugh. Johnny is told that the stewardesses often switched flights among themselves. It seems now that the case against Wilbur is not very sound. Johnny and Capt. Lenhart go to visit Mrs. Goodhugh and learn nothing new other than Shirley was called shortly before the flight and that one of the girls was sick. They are told that there were six girls in Hartford who swapped flights if one was sick. Johnny and Capt. Lenhart talk to the other girls and learn nothing.

On the way home, a man named Moran meets Johnny in the hallway of his apartment, and Moran wants to talk. Moran tells Johnny that he knew Alice and that he was to blame for the accident. Moran tells Johnny that a man named Arthur Church was using Alice as a courier for drugs, which were carried in the first aid kit. She wanted out and Moran was hiding her. Alice had arranged a meeting with the Feds and Church had found out and killed her. Moran warned her to stay hidden and she had gotten Shirley to take her flight. Moran also tells Johnny that Church had hidden the explosives on the plane in Alice's kit, which was kept at the airport and picked up by Shirley.

Johnny and the Capt. Lenhart go to Church's apartment with Moran. Moran goes in and calls for Church, but he opens fire and kills Moran, and Capt. Lenhart kills Church.

NOTES:

- THIS **AFRS** PROGRAM STARTS WITH A STORY ABOUT THE POST OFFICE AND RURAL ROUTES.
- COMMERCIAL BREAK #2 IS ABOUT THE PRESIDENCY OF JOHN TYLER.

- THIS IS A REMAKE OF THE FAIRWAY MATTER OF 7/11/1951
- MUSIC IS BY EDDIE DUNSTEDTER
- CHARLES LYON IS THE ANNOUNCER

Producer: Jaime del Valle   Writers: Gil Doud
Cast: Wally Maher, Howard McNear, Unknown

SHOW: THE CELIA WOODSTOCK MATTER
SHOW DATE: 1/12/1954
COMPANY: WASHINGTONIAN LIFE INSURANCE COMPANY
AGENT: MR. MILLER
EXP. ACCT: $73.60

SYNOPSIS: Captain Lyle Woodstock returns Johnny's call. Woodstock tells Johnny that there is no trouble with his wife's disappearance. At least not yet. Johnny rents a car and drives to Bridgeport, Connecticut to meet with Captain Lyle Woodstock—captain only because he owns a 64-foot schooner. Lyle says that he has discharged the servants and had lied to Mr. Miller about fearing for his wife's life. He had wasted money on a detective, David Slater, to follow his wife and asked the insurance company for help. Woodstock gives Johnny a folder about his wife, who is 27. He met her in Mexico and married her. They both like adventure. Woodstock is suspicious as Celia has been seeing too much of Dr. Masterson in town. She sees him three times a week but she seems very healthy. Now she had disappeared. Johnny goes to see Slater, who tells Johnny of the doctor visits and of losing her on a train to New York City after taking $2000 from the bank. Slater had overheard a phone conversation with a man named Sprague. Johnny decides to tell Woodstock he is dropping the case as he gave up chasing wives a long time ago. At the Woodstock house, a nervous man with a gun meets Johnny at the door. Johnny is locked in a closet and the man leaves. Johnny breaks out of the closet and finds Celia Woodstock on the floor shot. Johnny tries to call the police but the phone is dead, so he calls the police from a neighbor's phone. The police arrive and take Celia to the hospital. Johnny tells his story to Lt. Al Jester. Johnny remembers the man carrying a cheap nickel-plated .32. The police find another body upstairs and Johnny goes up with Lt. Jester.

In a bedroom they find Capt. Woodstock with a .38 beside him. He has been shot in the back. Johnny gets a room and the next day he talks to Dr. Masterson's former nurse, Janet Squire. Janet tells Johnny that she did not know of any romantic involvement between Dr. Masterson and Celia Woodstock, nor does she know a man named Sprague. Johnny checks in with Jester and learns nothing. Johnny goes to see Dr. Masterson who wants his name kept out of the papers. He tells Johnny that that Celia came to him for a sinus condition. She seemed satisfied with her husband and looked forward to a trip to South America. He tells Johnny that during one visit Mrs. Woodstock became hysterical when the receptionist mentioned a call for "Mrs. Emil Sprague." Johnny reports in to Lt. Jester and learns that Celia was shot with a .38, Lyle by a .32; and there is no sign of Sprague. Around midnight Celia recovers consciousness and at 3 AM talks to Johnny and Jester. She tells them that she was in the house when Emil killed Woodstock and that she is really Mrs. Sprague. She married Lyle in Mexico and Emil found out and wanted money. She met him in New York and gave him the $2000. Then he followed her to Bridgeport and forced her to take him to see Lyle. Lyle shot her and Sprague shot Lyle. Emil has an apartment on Commerce Street.

Johnny and Jester go to the apartment around 3:30 AM and surround it. Johnny sees Sprague watching them from the window as they go in. Johnny calls on a pay phone and urges Sprague to surrender. He tells Johnny that he shot Woodstock because he though Celia was dead. Sprague runs from the apartment shooting and is killed.

I understand that the lawyers are now working to kick the bigamist wife out of the estate.

NOTES:
- THIS PROGRAM HAS AN **AFRS** ARTICLE ABOUT THE ATTORNEY GENERAL.
- COMMERCIAL BREAK **#2** IS ABOUT THE PRESIDENCY OF JAMES MADISON.
- THIS PROGRAM IS A REPEAT OF THE SAME STORY DONE BY EDMOND O'BRIEN IN MARCH, 1951
- MUSIC IS BY EDDIE DUNSTEDTER
- CHARLES LYON IS THE ANNOUNCER

Producer:	Jaime del Valle	**Writers:**	Gil Doud
Cast:	Howard McNear, Victor Rodman, Ken Christy, Virginia Gregg, Bill Conrad, Edgar Barrier, Jim Nusser		

SHOW:	THE BEAUREGARD MATTER
SHOW DATE:	1/26/1954
COMPANY:	PLYMOUTH MUTUAL INSURANCE COMPANY
AGENT:	DAVE BRACE
EXP. ACCT:	$203.40

SYNOPSIS: Dave Brace calls and tells Johnny that sapphires are bad luck. Johnny tells Dave that black cats are bad luck too, but Dave tells Johnny that cats do not get stolen. Dave tells Johnny that the stones are worth $30,000 and mentions Benny Stark. Johnny remembers him as a jewel thief, and Dave tells Johnny that Benny called from Rockport, Illinois and wants to make a deal. The client is Ellen Beauregard, a big wheel in Rockport society. Dave has already made reservations and told Benny that Johnny is coming.

Johnny flies to Rockport, Illinois, gets a room at the Bleeker Hotel and waits for Benny Stark to call. Johnny is visited in his room by Jarad Beauregard, the uncle of Ellen Beauregard. Jarad tells Johnny that Ellen does not use the best judgment and Johnny tells Jarad that thinks he will be able to recover the necklace. Jarad tells Johnny that the necklace was an engagement present from Phil Avery, her fiancé. Johnny gets a call from Benny, and he tells Johnny to go to the Pink Pigeon at 9:00. Benny tells Johnny that he has been double-crossed had has some information for him. Jarad tells Johnny that Ellen is impulsive and leaves. Johnny rents a car and calls on Ellen Beauregard. As Johnny walks to the house Johnny sees a man and the maid "engaged" in the sunroom. The maid answers the door, and she knows who Johnny is and goes to get Ellen. The man from the sunroom, who is Phil Avery, comes out and tells Johnny that he hopes that Johnny can recover the necklace, as the insurance will not cover the sentimental value. Ellen meets Johnny and she tells him that Phil is impulsive, but does not mean any harm. She shows Johnny the safe where the necklace was kept, and tells Johnny that the house was empty when it was stolen. She warns Johnny that Uncle Jarad means well, but is a little vague. As Johnny leaves he sees someone at the coach house. Johnny goes there to meet Lois the maid and takes some papers from her meant for the incinerator. A nervous Lois is called to the house and in the papers Johnny finds a .32 revolver with one chamber fired. Ellen finds Johnny and tells him not to believe Lois, as she as caught her in all sorts of lies. Ellen has been planning to let her go, but Uncle Jarad raised objections. Johnny goes back to his hotel room and finds a man there who asks Johnny if he knows Benny Stark. The man is chief of police Cotton, and he tells Johnny that he found Johnny's name where Benny had written it down. Johnny tells Chief Cotton why he is there and about the appointment later that night with Benny. Chief Cotton tells Johnny that Stark was killed a few hours ago by a .32. Johnny gives him the gun he took from Lois and tells Chief Cotton where he got it. Chief Cotton recognizes the gun as belonging to Jarad Beauregard. Chief Cotton tells Johnny that the family is not as wealthy as it used to be, but Jarad seems to have a lot of money lately. Phil has been in Rockport for a couple years and is a civic leader. There is a knock at the door and Chief Cotton goes to the bathroom to listen as Lois comes in. She tells Johnny that she found the gun under her mattress and wants it back. Johnny tells her it is not that simple and calls Chief Cotton into the room.

Johnny buys lunch for the president of the Central City Bank and learns that the Beauregards are aristocratic socially, but they are broke and mortgaged to the hilt. Jarad seems to have a lot of money lately, probably borrowed from Phil Avery, a go-getter who has been elected to the bank's board of directors. He has several jobs and has had to postpone the wedding. Lois is a pretty little girl and what Johnny has heard is probably gossip. Johnny goes to see Chief Cotton, who is talking to Phil Avery, who tells Johnny that Lois is not involved with the theft or the murder. Chief Cotton is going to search the house and Phil goes to see Lois. Johnny shows Chief Cotton a photo of the necklace and asks if anyone in town could make a duplicate of it. Johnny is told that someone would have to go to Chicago for that. Chief Cotton arranges for a local jeweler to give the Chicago police the technical information on the necklace. Back in his room, Ellen calls Johnny and asks him to come to dinner. Johnny rents a car and drives to Ellen's. Johnny is about to play billiards with Phil when Chief Cotton calls. He tells

Johnny that the jeweler who made the copy has been located and that the client was a girl who fits the description of Ellen Beauregard. Johnny tells him that he has found the necklace and Chief Cotton is on his way. Uncle Jarad tells Johnny that he has discovered the family secret and Johnny asks him to get Ellen and bring her to the billiards room. In the billiards room Johnny breaks the balls on the billiards table and tells Phil that Lois is only an innocent bystander, even though he found the necklace hidden in her room. Johnny tells Phil that the family is broke and looked at Phil as a way to get money, but Phil was playing the same game. Johnny tells him that Ellen was the key to open any door in town and that he used his last money to buy the necklace. Then he saw the Beauregard's accounts at the bank and discovered they were even broker than he was, so he brought Benny Stark in. But Benny told Phil that the necklace was a fake and Phil thought Benny was trying to double cross him and killed him. Phil is told that Ellen sold the necklace a week after he gave it to her and had an imitation made, and Phil had taken the imitation necklace to Lois' room to frame her. Phil pulls a gun on Johnny and when Ellen opens the door and distracts him, Johnny hits him with his pool cue. Johnny tells Ellen that Phil had had the safe broken into and then killed his partner. Johnny tells Ellen that she has committed fraud by submitting a claim on a necklace that she had already sold. Johnny is sure that the insurance company will prosecute, and that Chief Cotton is on his way.

NOTES:
- THIS **AFRS** PROGRAM STARTS WITH A STORY ABOUT THE IMPROVEMENTS IN COMMUNICATION AND CHANGES IN THE CABINET.
- COMMERCIAL BREAK **#2** IS ABOUT THE PRESIDENCY OF TEDDY ROOSEVELT.
- THIS PROGRAM WAS REMADE WITH BOB BAILEY IN AUGUST OF **1953** AS "THE KRANESBURG MATTER"
- CHARLES LYON IS THE ANNOUNCER
- MUSIC IS BY EDDIE DUNSTEDTER

Producer: Jaime del Valle   **Writers:** Les Crutchfield
Cast: Howard McNear, Unknown

◆ ❖ ◆

SHOW: THE PAUL GORRELL MATTER
SHOW DATE: 2/2/1954
COMPANY: PLYMOUTH INSURANCE COMPANY
AGENT: GEORGE POST
EXP. ACCT: $369.80

SYNOPSIS: George Post calls and asks about Johnny's trip to Arizona. Johnny tells George he was told to come out in a hurry and only knows that $100,000 was stolen and two guards were killed. George tells Johnny that if he is willing to take a chance, they might be able to crack the case.

Johnny flies to Phoenix, Arizona and notes that the newspapers were reporting the death of an unidentified man who would later be part of Johnny's investigation. George has the newspaper on his desk and tells Johnny that the two guards were disarmed and killed to prevent identification of the robbers. The man in the paper, Palovic, was the only other witness, and that Palovic was the other robber, but the newspapers and police do not know that. Palovic had called George to tell that he had split up with his partner, Paul Gorrell, as there was not supposed to be any shooting during the robbery, but Gorrell shot the guards in cold blood. Palovic told George he was on parole and would go back to jail for 20 years if he told the police. He wanted the insurance company to stop Gorrell from enjoying the blood money and told George where Gorrell was and what his plans were. Gorrell is still in Phoenix, and Johnny thinks the case should be turned over to the police. George tells Johnny that Gorrell has mailed the money to someplace in or near Los Angeles. George tells Johnny that Gorrell has arranged to share a ride to Los Angeles, and Johnny figures he will be the third man in the car. Johnny is leery but accepts the case. Johnny realizes that if the insurance company involved the police, they would spend all their time pursuing Gorrell and not the money. Johnny also realizes he is working behind the law's back, which he does not like. Johnny does not like the getaway method because Gorrell would be in charge, and Johnny could not risk taking a gun. Johnny phones the driver, a Mr. Bovey, and he tells Johnny that he already has two men and a woman, and another passenger would be too many. Johnny arranges to come to his house, and if there is room, he will go. The next morning Johnny goes to Bovey's house and Gorrell arrives and tells Bovey his partner will not be coming. Johnny is introduced and tells Gorrell he is from Connecticut. Johnny describes Gorrell as one who would be able to blend in anywhere. The woman, Miss Shelton, arrives and the car is loaded. Gorrell asks to drive and Johnny sits in the back with Shelton. Bovey gets nervous when Gorrell drives in the wrong direction, and Johnny wonders if he was trying to avoid roadblocks. Johnny notices a green coupe following them as they pull out and Gorrell notices him looking around. Later that evening, in Blithe, California, the car overheats and Bovey looks for a mechanic who tells Bovey that the water pump is bad and that he cannot get one until morning. All of them start to walk to a motor court when the green coupe drives up beside them and Gorrell tries to get away from it. The car drives on, and Gorrell tells them he though it was somebody he did not want to talk to, but Johnny noticed him mechanically reach for his automatic. Johnny is sure he is back to being an uncontrollable killer.

Johnny wants to call the police, but he does not. They get rooms and Gorrell comes to see Johnny and tells that he had gotten into trouble in Phoenix and wants Johnny to tell the others why he acted like he did. Gorrell tells Johnny that he only has six dollars, and had lost his money in a poker game and had run out on the men in the game. Gorrell asks Johnny to help him straighten things out when he gets to Los Angeles. In Los Angeles, Johnny goes with Gorrell to the Prince Hotel on Spring Street to pick up personal things he had shipped out before the trip. Gorrell tells Johnny that when he gets the suitcase he can pay off the guys following him. Gorrell offers Johnny $25 to pick up the suitcase for him. Johnny and Gorrell get rooms at the hotel and Johnny gets the receipt for the suitcase. Johnny calls the police, tells them his story, and arranges to meet a plain-clothes office near the express office. Johnny meets Sgt. Mason, shows his ID, and tells why he is playing the case like he is. Johnny gets the suitcase and Sgt. Mason follows Johnny into the hotel. Johnny knocks at the door but Gorrell does not answer. Johnny goes in, but Gorrell is gone. Johnny asks Sgt. Mason to go with him to his room and open the suitcase, but Mason tells him he has no right to open someone's personal property and leaves. Johnny checks the suitcase at a bus station and goes back to wait. Miss Shelton visits Johnny and tells him to pack up and get out of town because he is involved with some bad people as Gorrell is using him. She also tells Johnny that some men had come for Gorrell, the same ones in the green car. There is a knock at the door and Gorrell tells Johnny to let him in. Gorrell is shot and staggers into the room. Shelton tries to leave but Johnny wants answers. She tells Johnny that two men in Phoenix roped her into it, and paid her $200 to go with Gorrell and follow him. She heard them talking about a robbery and killing and caught on to what was happening. They were the ones who pulled the robbery in Phoenix. There were four men who planned it, but Gorrell tried to take the money for himself. They also mentioned a phone call from a punk named Palovic. The men were trying to find out where the money was, and she figured that Johnny was the man who Gorrell told them had the suitcase. Johnny calls Sgt. Mason and the hospital. Fifteen minutes later Johnny opens the door to find two men with guns. Johnny tells them that Gorrell talked to him before he passed out. Johnny tells the man to look in the dresser for a claim check and the man gets it, but it does not have a name on it. There is another knock and Sgt. Mason is at the door. Gorrell starts to mumble and Johnny slugs the man and lets Sgt. Mason into the room. Johnny is told that Gorrell will probably not live to enjoy his money, and not to play lone wolf on any more cases, but to level with the police.

NOTES:
- THIS **AFRS** PROGRAM STARTS WITH A STORY ABOUT THE PATENT AND COPYRIGHTS PROCESSED BY THE DEPARTMENT OF COMMERCE.
- COMMERCIAL BREAK **#2** IS ABOUT THE PRESIDENCY OF ZACHARY TAYLOR.
- CHARLES LYON IS THE ANNOUNCER
- MUSIC IS BY EDDIE DUNSTEDTER

Producer: Jaime del Valle **Writers:** Gil Doud
Cast: James McCallion, Parley Baer, Jack Edwards, Jane Webb, Jack Moyles, Tom Tully

◆ ❖ ◆

SHOW: THE HARPOONED ANGLER MATTER
SHOW DATE: 2/9/1954

COMPANY:	**WASHINGTONIAN LIFE INSURANCE COMPANY**
AGENT:	**PHILLIP MARTIN**
EXP. ACCT:	**$1,043.90**

SYNOPSIS: Phillip Martin calls and asks Johnny if he has his passport ready. Johnny asks "Where to now?" and Phil tells Johnny that he is going to a small town on the French Riviera called Cassis. Phil has a death claim on a policy for Arnold Bernier. The policy is for $75,000 and written thirty-three years ago. Johnny asks if Phil never expects his clients to die, and Phil tells Johnny that Arnold died with a fishing spear through his back. Johnny will be ready in an hour.

Johnny flies to Cassis, France and rents a 1937 Maybach Victoria and breaks down twice. Johnny gets to the office of Count Lazlo Zandescu, who asks for the check and tells "my darling Mr. Dollar" that he is like a charge 'd affaires for the bereaved. He tells Johnny that Bernier was involved in the latest and most ungentlemanly sport of skin diving. He had been down for an hour when someone went down and brought him up. Zandescu considers the case closed and wants the check. When Johnny mentions that the widow might have killed Arnold, Zandescu tells Johnny that she could never do such a thing. Johnny goes to the Bernier villa to meet the widow Magda Bernier, who tells Johnny that Arnold was a wonderful provider, but her husband's death is of no importance to her and to get all of his future information from the local police. Johnny meets Insp. Laniel, who tells Johnny that skin-diving was a fatalistic past time of Bernier, whose body was discovered by David North, an American scientist. North was returning to the surface and found Bernier's body inside a grotto with a spear through it. Laniel has no personal suspects and tells Johnny that Magda has no financial motivation, as Bernier was an immensely wealthy man. Bernier was retired and his attorney says his affairs are in perfect order and there were no personal enemies. Johnny gets a call from David North, who wants to talk about the murder of Arnold Bernier. North tells Johnny to meet him in a café, and that he was told that Johnny was there by Magda, his future wife.

Johnny waits for an hour when Zandescu shows up and asks Johnny about the check. The murder is of no consequence now to Zandescu, as he knows who killed Bernier. It has to be David North, because he has provided the proof by his suicide. "Oh, did I forget to tell you? They are taking his body from the bottom of the gulf even now." Johnny rushes to the beach were a boat is bringing the body to shore. Insp. Laniel orders North taken to a doctor and tells Johnny that North apparently went diving rather than keeping his appointment. He had been down for fifty minutes when the crew became concerned and found North in the same grotto where Bernier was found. North's aqualung was working, he had a scalp wound on his head and a fishing spear was found near him. Insp. Laniel tells Johnny that he has just found evidence that North killed Bernier, so a suicide would have closed the case.

Johnny goes to Insp. Laniel's office to wait for North to wake up. Insp. Laniel tells Johnny that North had run out of funds and Zandescu saw an opportunity to make a commission and persuaded Bernier to loan North $2,000. Insp. Laniel thinks that North's getting friendly with Magda provided a reason to kill Bernier, save his ship, and get the girl. North will tell them if they are right when he wakes up. Johnny goes to see Magda and she tells him that David worships her and would do anything for her, even murder. She tells Johnny that the talk of marriage was nothing and that she had been in the house all morning and seldom swims. Johnny goes to check up on North but Insp. Laniel tells Johnny that North just died. Johnny drives to Marseilles and is passed by a big limousine with Magda Bernier in it. Johnny drives to the home of Armond Gottier and is told to call his office. When Johnny tells him that Magda is the number one suspect in Bernier's killing, he lets Johnny in. Gottier tells Johnny that Bernier had given Magda her own fortune, one she could not spend in a lifetime and the balance goes to charitable institutions. Johnny brings up North's youth, but Gottier tells Johnny that Magda would not give up her life style for a temporary amusement. Johnny tells Gottier that there is another man in her life, and that Gottier should have gotten rid of Magda's perfume before he let Johnny in. Johnny goes back to Insp. Laniel and asks him to send a diver to the grotto, and he will have an answer to the murder. Insp. Laniel acts as diver and goes down to the grotto. Forty-five minutes later Insp. Laniel surfaces and gives Johnny a small wooden box marked "Marine Specimens." As Johnny looks at the contents of brown looking weeds, Zandescu points a spear gun at Johnny's back. He tells Johnny that Insp. Laniel is at the entry of the grotto and will soon drown. Zandescu tells Johnny that he figured out his drug smuggling plan too quickly. He tells Johnny that he buys the hashish in the Red Sea area for practically nothing with Bernier's money and transports it with North's ship and hides it in the grotto to sell when the time is right. Bernier found the warehouse so he had to kill him. North was going to get a box to show Johnny when he was killed. Johnny suddenly throws the box at Zandescu.

"Things happened pretty fast just about then. The box hit Zandescu in the chest, the spear missed me by slightly less than a hair, my fist hit Zandescu's jaw, and he hit the water. Oh, a jolly good time was had by all, including Insp. Laniel. I managed to raise some help from the shore and get a diver down to him before his oxygen ran out. Zandescu wound up in the local jail where charges are being preferred against him now: two counts of homicide, two of attempted homicide and a slight case of drug smuggling. I did not see Magda Bernier again. I didn't think I could take any more of that. When you honor the death claim, send the check care of Armond Gottier, Marseilles."

NOTES:
- THIS **AFRS** PROGRAM STARTS WITH A STORY ABOUT THE WEATHERMEN IN THE DEPARTMENT OF COMMERCE.
- COMMERCIAL BREAK **#2** IS ABOUT THE PRESIDENCY OF JOHN ADAMS.
- THE MAYBACH WAS A HIGH-END AUTOMOBILE MADE IN GERMANY FROM 1921 UNTIL 1940
- CHARLES LYON IS THE ANNOUNCER
- MUSIC IS BY EDDIE DUNSTEDTER

Producer: Jaime del Valle   Writers: Sidney Marshall
Cast: Howard Culver, Larry Dobkin, Virginia Gregg, Lou Krugman

SHOW: THE UNCUT CANARY MATTER
SHOW DATE: 2/16/1954
COMPANY: EASTERN INDEMNITY & INSURANCE COMPANY
AGENT: MR. HARRISON
EXP. ACCT: $373.25

SYNOPSIS: Mr. Harrison calls and wants Johnny to go to Beverly Hills to find an uncut canary, an uncut orange-yellow 89-carat diamond insured for $125,000 that has disappeared. Johnny tells Harrison that he'll see what he can do.

Johnny goes to Los Angeles, California and to the Johanna Jewelry store, the last resting place of the diamond. Johnny asks for Johanna and the manager tells Johnny that Madam Johanna is very tired. Johnny tells the manager, Mr. Carter, that if Johanna wants to file a claim, it will be on his time, not hers. Johanna comes from her office and Johnny is shown to her office. She tells Johnny that she purchased the diamond in Rio over a year ago. She is taking her time planning the cutting of the diamond as one wrong move will shatter the stone and make it worthless. Her father learned that the hard way 25 years ago with a stone similar to the canary. She tells Johnny that it was gone last night when she and Carter came to watch the stone being cut. She has two excellent cutters: Adolph Spiers and Hans Plessman, and they have been with her for over 30 years. All of them have the combination, but none of her employees would have stolen it. As she is talking, Adolph calls and tells her to send the police to his house and he will give them the uncut canary.

Johnny calls Chief Anderson of the Beverly Hills police, and Lt. Hankins comes to pick up Johnny. Johnny is told that the robbery chief is ill, so Lt. Hankins is on the case for the Chief. Lt. Hankins tells Johnny that Johanna is always looking for a way to make a buck and that the canary supposedly can not be cut; she bought it under the market price and has held it for over a year. There is also a rumor that Johanna also needs money. At Adolph's house no one answers the door so Johnny and Lt. Hankins go out back and hear a car running in the closed garage. In the garage they find Adolph Spiers dead. While the police do their work, Johnny calls Johanna at her home and office, and them calls Mr. Carter, but no one is home at either number.

Johnny cabs to the apartment of Hans Plessman, the other diamond cutter. At the door Plessman wants the lenses he ordered from Albert. Johnny tells him who he is and wants to talk about the stone. When Plessman asks why Johnny did not question Adolph, Johnny tells him that Adolph is dead, and probably murdered. "Nonsense!" he tells Johnny. "He did not steal the stone, I did!" Plessman then clams up and will say nothing, even to the police. At police headquarters, Lt. Hankins tells Johnny that they have little to hold Plessman on. The coroner calls and tells them that Adolph probably did not die of carbon monoxide poisoning.

Johnny cabs to Charles Carter's apartment where Carter is doing a head stand in his shorts. Carter tells Johnny that it is good for the internal organs. Johnny wants to know where he was this evening, and Carter tells Johnny that he was at the beach exercising. Carter is not surprised that Adolph is dead, as he was in lousy shape. Johnny tells Carter that shape had nothing to do with it. Carter tells Johnny that Johanna was not with him, and that she is a gentle soul and the epitome of womanhood, and not one to be maligned. Carter also tells Johnny that he does the headstand twice a day for 30 minutes.

Johnny calls Lt. Hankins and is told that Plessman still refuses to talk. Over a cup of coffee, Johnny remembers the comment Plessman had made at his door, and Johnny checks the yellow pages, and calls the optician Albert Schoenbeck at home. Schoenbeck tells Johnny that he had made lenses for Johanna and her father, and that he had made lenses for a refractometer for Plessman. Schoenbeck explains to Johnny that a refractometer is used to measure the bending of light through a stone, which tells what type of stone is. He confirms Johnny's thoughts that it could also be used to spot imperfections in a stone.

Johnny cabs to Johanna's house and asks her about the rumors of financial problems. If they were true, Johnny tells her, the insurance on an uncut or un-cuttable diamond would help. She calls it nonsense and tells Johnny that he had better leave, as he has gone too far. Johnny mentions Adolph's murder and she tells Johnny that does not know about it. Johnny tells her that some one took the stone from him, or killed him to stop him from talking about who did. She calls that unbelievable, but Johnny tells her that it is not as unbelievable as the conversation she had with him after he had died. She tells Johnny that she knows about Hans and that her lawyer is arranging bail. She is not going to change her story of the phone call either.

Because it is too late to get a cab, Johnny walks back to town and thinks about the problem. It takes about an hour to get to a phone to call Lt. Hankins who tells Johnny that Plessman has been sprung and went home. Johnny goes to Plessman' home and asks him if he has cut the stone yet. Plessman tells Johnny that he was just getting ready to and Johnny asks to watch with Johanna, who is also there. Plessman tells Johnny that Adolph would have smashed the stone, just as he did for Johanna's father 25 years ago, but that the refractometer will make the difference. Plessman tells Johnny that he could not let Adolph do that to his Johanna, as he was going to give it to Johanna as a gift and had to stop him. Plessman takes the stone and instructs Johanna on how to cut the stone, and she splits it perfectly. Plessman tells Johnny that Adolph would have ground it to bits, and that he has saved her business. Plessman starts to tell Johnny that once it is cut and polished, but he starts getting weak and lies down. Johanna tells Johnny that Plessman had called her to tell her that he had hidden the stone in her house and that he had killed Adolph. The stone will accomplish everything he wanted, but she would have rather smashed it than to have Plessman do what he did.

NOTES:

- CHIEF ANDERSON AND LT. HANKINS WERE ALSO CHARACTERS IN "THE ANITA BUDDHA MATTER"
- CHARLES LYON IS THE ANNOUNCER
- MUSIC IS BY EDDIE DUNSTEDTER

Producer: Jaime del Valle   Writers: Sidney Marshall
Cast: William Johnstone, John Stevenson, Hal March, Virginia
           Gregg, Fritz Feld

◆   ❖   ◆

SHOW: THE CLASSIFIED KILLER MATTER
SHOW DATE: 2/23/1954
COMPANY: EASTERN INDEMNITY & INSURANCE COMPANY
AGENT: TED ALBRIGHT
EXP. ACCT: $191.15

SYNOPSIS: Ted Albright calls Johnny at 4:00AM. Frank Harvey has been murdered. Johnny will grab the first plane out.

Johnny goes to Chicago, Illinois and is met by Ted Albright and a winter blizzard. Ted tells Johnny that Frank was at the office until 6:45 and that a truck driver found his body out on Mannheim Road and that he had been shot three times. Ted is really on edge as he tells Johnny that he had to drive back from Milwaukee with his wife and has had no sleep.

Johnny goes to see Lt. Franchetti who tells him that the bad weather will hold down crime, except for the rise in deaths from yacky-dak—antifreeze that the bums drain from car radiators and drink. It is really deadly. Johnny is told that Harvey was killed trying to sell his car, a 1953 Cadillac convertible, and that he had been running an ad in the papers. A garage mechanic had seen Harvey talking to a customer who drove off with him around 6:55. The truck driver found Harvey at 8:37 in a snow bank. Lt. Franchetti is sure that they should be able to identify the gun, and that an APB is out for the car, which is still missing. A call comes in and Johnny goes with Lt. Franchetti to Mannheim Road where Harvey's car has been found. The owner of a beer and hamburger joint found the car in the parking lot and called the police. There are bloodstains all over the seat and a woman's compact on the floor.

Johnny goes back to the insurance office to talk to Ted Albright. Johnny asks him, since he was Frank's boss, did he have any girlfriends. Ted tells Johnny that he did not know of any, and that there were no recent claims either. Ted tells Johnny that Frank only had a $10,000 policy, with his mother as the beneficiary. A man calls and wants to bargain for information on the killing. "You gotta make a living you know, what with the high cost of living." Johnny agrees to meet Mr. Taggert at the Biloxi Hotel at Wells and Grand. Johnny cabs to the hotel and meets Mr. Taggert with $20 to help combat the high cost of living, which must have included garlic and bourbon. Taggert shows Johnny the register where a woman named Alma Carter had checked in, scared and frightened, and she had stains on her coat. She was listening to the news broadcasts all night and had asked Taggert to buy her a paper. The compact in the news suggested to Taggert that he better call the insurance company. Johnny knocks on the door of room 14 and talks to Alma Carter. She asks Johnny why an insurance man would want to talk to a stranger in her room. Johnny tells her that they are not strangers, as he saw her picture on Ted Albright's desk, Mrs. Albright.

Mrs. Albright tells Johnny that she was with Frank Harvey last night. Frank was going to talk to a prospect and had asked her to come along, and that Ted thought she was in Milwaukee. Frank introduced the man, but she did not hear the name. The man asked Frank to drive out Mannheim Road to his house where the man asked him to stop, and then just shot Frank. She jumped out of the car ran and fainted by a shack. She got a lift to town and got a room at the hotel. She did not call the police because she was out with a man who was not her husband and involved in a murder. She just wanted to avoid scandal.

Johnny takes Mrs. Albright to Lt. Franchetti where she makes a statement and is held as a material witness and a pickup is ordered for Ted Albright. Johnny is told that the mechanic, Will Zeigler has looked at the mug books, but has not found any one. Johnny goes to his hotel room and is called by Ted Albright. Ted is in the lobby and he wants to talk. Ted comes to Johnny's room and asks Johnny if he knows about his wife Alma. He tells Johnny that he had suspected she was seeing Frank, and that he went to Milwaukee to check on her story. Johnny tells Ted to turn himself in to the police, which Ted agrees to do.

Johnny goes to the garage to talk to Will Zeigler. Johnny tells him who he is and that he wants to ask questions. He tells Johnny that it was rough; he was standing right there when the man picked up Harvey. He tells Johnny that he had never seen the man before, and that he had never seen Ted Albright either. Zeigler tells Johnny that there was nothing strange about the man, so he must be a psycho. He sees the ad, figures he will take the man out in country and kill him and steal the car. Zeigler tells Johnny that a car thief will take the car when no one is around, but this guy puts himself here where Zeigler can see him and does not back out when Harvey picks up the girl at the insurance building. Zeigler tells Johnny to tell Lt. Franchetti that one of those guys I picked out is a psycho.

Johnny goes back to talk to Alma and asks her what kind of work the man they picked do? She tells Johnny that all they talked about was cars, and that there was a sweet odor, like nail polish remover about him. Johnny cabs back to the garage and Zeigler is gone, so Johnny goes to his rooming house where Zeigler is getting clothes to take to the cleaners. Johnny wants to talk about the psycho theory, as Zeigler might be right. Johnny tells Zeigler that he has another angle; the man may have had plans for the girl too. Zeigler shows Johnny a fancy $100 jacket, and tells Johnny that there is nothing like nice clothes and a fancy car, and Harvey's car was a dreamboat! With a car like that and clothes like these he could really get the girls. Johnny notes that there are a lot of clothes going to the cleaners, and asks Zeigler if it is hard to get the acetone out of your clothes? "Yeah, that stuff really clings" he tells Johnny. "That is what Mrs. Albright said,"

Johnny tells him. Zeigler tells Johnny that she a classy dame. Johnny tells Zeigler that he knew he was the killer because of the remark about picking up the girt at the insurance company. Zeigler tries to pull a gun and Johnny shoots at him. Zeigler says he always gets excited at the wrong time, like with the car. He ruined the upholstery and had to ditch the car.

NOTES:
- CAST INFORMATION FROM TERRY SALMONSON
- CHARLES LYON IS THE ANNOUNCER
- MUSIC IS BY EDDIE DUNSTEDTER

Producer: Jaime del Valle   Writers: Sidney Marshall
Cast: Bob Bailey, Bill Conrad, Junius Matthews, Virginia Gregg,
           Sidney Miller, Fred MacKaye

◆ ❖ ◆

SHOW: THE ROAD-TEST MATTER
SHOW DATE: 3/2/1954
COMPANY: CONSOLIDATED INDEMNITY COMPANY
AGENT: MR. KING
EXP. ACCT: $217.40

SYNOPSIS: Mr. King calls from Consolidated Indemnity and tells Johnny that he has to do this job for him. Allied Motors has a new car that is crashing. Go out and find out what is happening.

Johnny flies to Detroit, Michigan and goes the Allied Motors test track. Johnny has to talk his way through security, and looks for Mr. McGregor. Johnny explains to McGregor why he is there and McGregor tells Johnny that he is testing the model three years out. He has been there for 25 years and this model makes a lot of changes. There have been three other crashes, but they have the best engineers working on the cars. Johnny is taken to see the car and is told that they look sharp, but have all fallen apart. The drivers have been told to give the car everything, but they are afraid. Johnny suspects a grudge, but is told that there is no sign of sabotage. McGregor tells Johnny that the drivers are experienced but that the designers are new and that McGregor will leave the motives to Johnny.

Johnny gets the address of the last man who was killed and visits Mrs. Grace Johnson, who has a "for sale" sign on the front yard. She tells Johnny that she is moving, as there is no reason to stay. Johnny asks her if anyone would have wanted her husband out of the way, and she tells Johnny that they had not been getting along, so she turned to a friend and started thinking about getting Steve out of the way. She tells Johnny that the man has not been to see her since. The man is Joe Simmons—a former test driver.

Johnny confirms that Simmons had quit after Steve Johnson was killed, and that he had moved out of his rooming house. Johnny finds Simmons at a local bar and talks to him. Johnny asks Simmons for help and tells him about Mrs. Johnson. Simmons tells Johnny that Steve was his friend and that Steve knew about his being with the wife. Simmons tells Johnny that he quit driving, as the car is not right. It handles like a dream, and then just goes apart. Johnny asks about bugs put in the cars or if a driver was in the way. Simmons tells Johnny that his hunch is bad as he cannot get to the cars because of security, and he would have to want to do it. Joe gets up to leave and Johnny tells him not to leave town.

Johnny goes to the hotel and calls McGregor who is not in. Lt. Farish meets Johnny in the hotel lobby and tells Johnny that he wants to talk to Johnny about the case. Johnny tells of the possible involvement of Joe Simmons and Grace Johnson. Lt. Farish tells Johnny that there is a problem with his theory; Simmons no longer works at the plant and there has been another crackup. Lt. Farish tells Johnny that the police cannot get involved, so it is his baby. The police want Johnny to go to work driving the cars; it is that important. "Oh, the things I get involved in!" laments Johnny.

At the track McGregor is working on a wrecked car when Johnny asks about why the car went to pieces. Johnny asks to be put into a car. Johnny and McGregor go to his office and talk over a drink of Scotch. Johnny is told that he will not be needed. McGregor lets Johnny listen to a memo telling the Allied executives that the design should be dropped in the interests of safety, and that they should return to the traditional means of designing cars. He tells Johnny that he will get the driving job if they do not accept the recommendation.

Johnny convinces the head office to continue the tests for one week, and goes to see the head designer, Ted Brand. They talk over something to drink, coffee. Ted is only 22 or 23 but is the chief designer. Ted tells Johnny that the car is perfect on paper and should handle like a dream. He also tells Johnny that the old guys just hate progress.

Johnny cabs to see McGregor after dinner. His wife answers the door and tells Johnny that he is not home and will probably stay the night at the plant because they are working him so hard. She would love to talk to Johnny and tells him that Ken loves his job and has turned down a pension. He works hard, but has so much on his mind and wants to make one more showing before he quits. Johnny asks her not to tell McGregor that he was there. She tells Johnny that Ken had given a lifetime of loyalty, but is now outdated, so how would Johnny feel?

Lt. Farish calls Johnny and tells him that McGregor has been killed at the plant. Johnny goes to the plant and meets Lt. Farish who tells Johnny that there were signs of a struggle and Johnny tells him that McGregor had stayed the night. Lt. Farish tells Johnny that McGregor had left at midnight for an hour and that Simmons had left much earlier. Johnny goes to Kirby's Bar, but Simmons is not there.

Back at his hotel, a man who wants to talk about the car meets Johnny. He tells Johnny that he might be a stoolie, but he had nothing to do with the killing of McGregor. He tells Johnny that McGregor had picked up Simmons and brought him back to the plant and that Simmons and McGregor were in it together. They were worried about Johnny driving and Simmons had to talk McGregor into fixing the car so Johnny would get the business. Simmons was working for a stockholder who was kicked out of management when he was found to have been involved in the rackets. The man wanted to hurt the company and had the means to do it. McGregor was sore at being eased out and Simmons knew it and got the old man to go in deeper. Simmons killed him when he would not go further. The man tells Johnny that Simmons is expecting him at the Kearns Hotel and Johnny calls Lt. Farish.

Johnny meets Lt. Farish at the hotel and the man tells Lt. Farish that Simmons has a gun. The man goes into the room and Johnny and Lt. Farish follow him in. There are shots and Simmons is killed.

The name of the stockholder has been submitted and the police are holding him. Johnny believes that he should be able to repay the claims paid by the company, from jail.

NOTES:
- CHARLES LYON IS THE ANNOUNCER
- MUSIC IS BY EDDIE DUNSTEDTER

Producer:	Jaime del Valle	Writers:	David Chandler
Cast:	Fred MacKaye, Bill Johnstone, Virginia Gregg, Ted Bliss, Clayton Post, Hy Averback, Eleanor Audley, Joseph Kearns		

◆ ❖ ◆

SHOW:	THE TERRIFIED TUAN MATTER
SHOW DATE:	3/9/1954
COMPANY:	WASHINGTONIAN LIFE INSURANCE COMPANY
AGENT:	TOM BENSON
EXP. ACCT:	$2,296.45

SYNOPSIS: Tom Benson calls and tells Johnny that a man and his wife, Harrison and Mada Langley, have two policies with double indemnity for $125,000 each. The underwriter has written to say that someone is trying to kill them. They live in Kuala Lumpur.

Johnny goes to Kuala Lumpur, Federated States of Malaya, gets a room at the Coliseum Hotel, and goes to see George Allister, the local rubber and tea broker. After Allister's complaining about the climate, Johnny mentions the murder claim from Langley. Johnny is told that the whole thing is rubbish from a diseased mind, and that the jungle and terrorists have gotten to him. Johnny is told that the plantation is in territory held by the terrorists. Johnny is also told that no one in his or her right mind would live there, and that an investigation is a waste of time. Johnny asks Allister why he stays if the hates the country so much and Allister tells Johnny that he is making too much money to leave.

Johnny rents a 1949 armor-plated Ford and drives to the Sundown Rubber Plantation. The guard at the plantation tells Johnny to talk to Tuan Crawford because Tuan Langley is sick because his wife has disappeared. Johnny goes to Langely's house and walks in. Langley meets Johnny with a gun and accuses him of killing his wife and trying to kill him. Johnny shows Langley his ID and takes the .38 Webley from him, firing a shot in the process. As Johnny fixes a drink, Langley reads the identification papers and finally believes that Johnny is there to help. Langley tells Johnny that he has been threatened by terrorists and has been helpless to stop it. Langley tells Johnny that Mada has disappeared and that is why he is upset. Crawford comes in to investigate the shots and accuses Johnny of being a vulture gathering for the feast. Crawford tells Johnny that he will take Johnny on a tour of the plantation. Langley tells Johnny that Crawford has been carrying on with his wife, and that he has a motive to kill him.

Johnny talks to Crawford about the situation and he tells Johnny that Langley gets threatening notes and phone calls, but no one ever sees them. Crawford tells Johnny that Langley had been carrying a gun everywhere and spying on Mrs. Langley and him, but there was nothing. Crawford shows Johnny some cut wire and cut trees and a bloody sleeve. Crawford thinks Langley faked the whole thing to get the insurance money on his wife as there is a $50,000 note coming due soon, and Langley needs the money.

Back at the house the servant Bandar tells Johnny that Langley has left for Kuala Lumpur after he received a telephone call. He left taking a .45 automatic with him and said something about giving Dollar something to investigate. Johnny calls Allister who confirms that he had called Langley about some rubber shipments. Allister tells Johnny that he had mentioned Langley's wife casually and Allister tells Johnny that he just finished having a drink with her at the Coliseum Hotel bar.

Johnny rushes back to town and goes to see Allister, who tells Johnny that he has not seen Langley. Allister tells Johnny that Mada claims that she was on a shopping trip. Johnny tells Allister to call the police and asks him if he knows who holds the note on Langley's plantation. Allister tells Johnny that he holds the note. Johnny goes to Mrs. Langley's room and she tells Johnny that she thinks Harry is just in a lather over the plantation and all the work. She tells Johnny that she was there during the raid and was packing for her trip. Johnny tells her that Crawford and Langley say she disappeared. But she tells Johnny that Bandar and Harry knew she was coming to the hotel, and that Harry is going to meet her here. She tells Johnny that she was a former chorus cutie when she met Harry, and she is going to ask him to take her to Singapore. Shots ring out and they fall to the floor. The shots came from another hotel room across the street, and Johnny rushes to the other hotel where the clerk says a man named Harrison Langley rented the room. Johnny goes back to Mada's room to discover that she is gone. Johnny contacts the police, who eventually decide to pick up Langley.

At the hotel bar Johnny sees Langley and goes to talk to him. Langley admits that he came there to kill her as they walk to a small garden where they talk. Langley tells Johnny that his wife no longer loves him, and that she and Crawford love each other and only want his money. They want Langley declared mentally incompetent to get the money. The threats and terrorist activity were a front, so he came here to kill her, as there is no other answer. He tells Johnny that he has walked the streets all afternoon thinking about the situation and that he should have gone and killed her. Johnny takes his .45 and determines that it has not been fired. Johnny tells Langley to wait and makes three calls. Johnny learns that the bullets from Mada's room were from a .38; that Bandar admitted that Mada had told him to say that she had disappeared; that Crawford is in Kuala Lumpur and will return by midnight. Also Johnny learns that Crawford took his gun and Langley's .38 Webley; and that the clerk at the hotel identified the man who checked in as Crawford. Johnny drives back to the plantation with Langley and along the way he hears an explosion on the road. They come upon an armored car and find Crawford and Mada in the car. Crawford has the .38 and Johnny thinks that he was the target. Langley is bitter because Mada only wanted money but she schemed and connived to get it all, but she did not succeed. She was a tramp. Langley breaks down at last and cries for his wife.

Johnny could not prevent the loss of Mada Langley, but everyone seems to have lost something.

NOTES:
- According to an Indonesian associate, the local word for "sir" or "mister" is tuan, not taun as it is listed in some catalogs.
- Charles Lyon is the announcer
- Music is by Eddie Dunstedter

Producer:	Jaime del Valle	**Writers:**	**Sidney Marshall**
Cast:	Howard McNear, Ben Wright, Jack Edwards, Bill Johnstone, Jack Moyles, Virginia Gregg		

◆ ❖ ◆

SHOW:	**THE BERLIN MATTER**
SHOW DATE:	3/16/1954
COMPANY:	**CAMDEN LIFE & FIDELITY COMPANY, LTD.**
AGENT:	**DAVE HOPKINS**
EXP. ACCT:	**$693.03**

SYNOPSIS: Dave Hopkins calls and asks if Johnny has a German visa, and Johnny tells him he sleeps with it under his pillow. Sam Harvey is a consulting engineer who has just upped his insurance to $50,000 and changed beneficiaries to a new wife. Now he is dead.

Johnny flies to Berlin, West Germany and checks in at the Waldenstern Hotel. Johnny then cabs to the police to meet with Lt. Wilhelm Meissner, who updates Johnny on the case. Johnny is told that Sam Harvey was found in the harbor and was identified by papers on his body. Johnny reviews the report and notes that his body was found in Spandau, in the British Zone, but Johnny thought he worked in the American Zone. Lt. Meissner shows Johnny the map of Berlin, with Spandau in the British Zone, just above the French Zone. Lt. Meissner thinks that Harvey probably died in the French Zone and the river currents took him to Spandau. The area of the French Zone is rough, and Harvey is not the first person to be dumped in the river there. A friend of Harvey, Paul Turner, made a positive identification, informed his wife in Vienna, and buried the body. Johnny buys Willie a beer and then goes to see Paul Turner.

Paul tells Johnny that he does not know who killed Sam, and that he probably went to the beer festival in the area, got drunk and fell into the river. Paul tells Johnny that he never mentioned insurance, but his wife is worth every penny of the insurance. She is in Vienna and will be here soon. Paul tells Johnny that there have been a lot of tears over Sam, so try to be gentle and polite. Paul is a German interpreter for the Army, a really nice job. Paul has wire that says Elsa is over her illness, and will be there at 18:00 tonight. Paul and Johnny go to pick up Sam's wife at Templehof Airport. Paul tells Johnny that he will know her when he sees her, as they had palled around before Sam married her. They meet Elsa, who is confused about who Paul is. It has been a long time she tells Johnny. Johnny tells Elsa why he is there. She tells Johnny that she was in Vienna when Sam died, and that she has to live there because of the refugee problems. Johnny goes to his hotel and has knockwurst and sauerkraut with black beer for dinner and 10 hours of sleep with no dreams.

The next morning Lt. Meissner calls and Johnny is told that there is a barge in the British Zone; "I vill send zee car, you vill get dressed and meet zee car and and you vill come!" Johnny meets Lt. Meissner on the barge and Lt. Meissner's attitude goes from "Johnny" to "Herr Dollar." On the barge is a dead man, Curt Hausman, captain pilot of the barge. Under his arm is a letter he had started to write. Lt. Meissner translates the letter that says, "If you wish of Sam Harvey to know, come you to the barge." The letter is addressed to Johnny Dollar.

Lt. Meissner wants to know what Johnny said to Turner and Harvey's wife that caused the murder of the boat captain. Johnny is told that that Hausman was a thief and a black-marketeer and a smuggler. He was also an eel, very slippery with no evidence to convict him when caught. Johnny notes that Hausman was found near the same area where Sam Harvey was found, so he must have known something and someone killed him. Captain Hausman has a friend named Mary Fuller, an American entertainer, who came to entertain the American troops and decided to stay. She works at a carnival at Zielendorf.

Johnny and Lt. Meissner go to see Mary Fuller. Lt. Meissner tells Mary that Curt is dead and she starts to cry. Mary does not know why he would be writing a letter to Johnny. She does not know who killed Curt but she knows that Sam owned the barge with Curt and was a thief with him. Sam worked as an engineer when the barge business was slow. Mary tells them that she knew his wife and was her shopper. Sam would give her money and she would buy goods in the French and British zones and send them to her. She shows Johnny a pair of pierced earrings. Sam had liked them and she bought some for his wife and then had her ears pierced. She also tells them that she does not know Paul Turner.

Johnny goes to Paul Turner and gets the address for Elsa. Johnny goes to apologize to her and to give her the papers for the insurance money. She tells Johnny that she will send them to Johnny by messenger. Johnny tells her that she is a very beautiful woman and asks her to put her hair up for him to see how she would look. Johnny tells her that she is beautiful with her hair that way. Johnny cabs back to Mary and asks for the wife's address in Vienna.

Johnny takes a plane to Vienna. A woman at the address Johnny got from Mary tells Johnny that Mrs. Harvey is dead; she died yesterday. She received a wire last week and it was given to the woman who took care of her, and that the woman arranged for the funeral when she died. Johnny guesses that this other woman moved out after she died. Yes, she did the woman tells him

Back in Berlin, Johnny goes back to see Elsa and Paul is there. Elsa has the papers and gives them to Johnny who tears them up and asks for her real name. Johnny tells Paul that he knows everything. Sam's wife was ill and Elsa had taken care of her. The tip-off was the pierced ears. Sam's real wife had them and Elsa did not. Johnny figures that Paul was in on Sam's murder to get in on the smuggling business. Paul tells him that Curt did not want Paul in on the deal and so Paul killed him. Paul pulls a gun but Johnny beats it away from him. Elsa tells Johnny that she has nothing, and even paid for the funeral, so she deserves something, as Vienna is not so nice. Johnny says she will have to talk to a nice guy name Willie.

NOTES:
- THERE IS A VERY PROPER GERMAN CLICKING OF HEELS EVERY TIME WILHELM MAKES A POINT.
- JOHN LUND TWICE MAKES A SLIP AND ASKS WHY "PAUL'S" WIFE HAS NOT SHOWN UP INSTEAD OF "SAM'S" WIFE.
- CHARLES LYON IS THE ANNOUNCER
- MUSIC IS BY EDDIE DUNSTEDTER

Producer: Jaime del Valle   Writers: Morton Fine,
                                                 David Friedkin
Cast: Benny Rubin, Edgar Barrier, Gerry Gaylor, Hal March,
            Virginia Gregg

◆   ❖   ◆

SHOW: THE PINEY CORNERS MATTER
SHOW DATE: 3/23/1954
COMPANY: TRI-STATE ASSURANCE COMPANY, LTD
AGENT: BOB CRALE
EXP. ACCT: $120.70

SYNOPSIS: Bob Crale from Tri-State tells Johnny that he has a letter about the killing of Martha Williams. "Look close to home," it says. The letter is from anonymous in Piney Corners Pennsylvania. Bob tells Johnny that Martha died a month ago and the company is ready to pay off the $10,000 policy.

Johnny goes to Piney Corners, Pennsylvania and meets Jake Finley, the constable. Jake tells Johnny that he has no real facts and that it could have been hunters. But she was shot with a squirrel rifle, notes Johnny. The police in Philadelphia could not identify the bullet and everyone here has one of those rifles Jake tells Johnny. Jake agrees to take Johnny out to see Ben Williams, but Johnny will have to pay for the gas, as the town does not have much money.

Johnny and Jake drive to the farm and stop to talk to the Keelers, the neighbors. Mrs. Keeler knows that Johnny is with Tri-State. She tells Johnny that the Williams are good neighbors and that Martha had been an invalid after an operation last year. Mrs. Keeler tells Johnny that Ben has been hanging around a girl, a real flibbertigibbet. The girl is Flora Lane who works at the Inn. Johnny tells Mrs. Keeler that the company appreciated her letter and she asks Johnny how he knew it was she. Johnny tells her that he had guessed she had sent the letter.

Johnny and Jake examine the most likely place for the shot, right next to a survey marker for a highway that would have made the land worth something. Jake explains how Martha was sitting by the window and someone shot her and got away. Johnny asks if the girl in town is pretty and if Ben was seeing her beforehand. Jake tells Johnny that Ben eats most of his evening meals there. Martha would be an invalid as long as she lived, but Jake relates that Ben is not the type. Jake tells Johnny that Mrs. Keeler liked Martha but never really liked Ben, so don't pay too much attention to her.

Johnny and Jake walk down to the farmhouse and Tom Smith, the hired man, meets them at the door and tells them that Ben is not there. Johnny asks Tom where he was when Martha was killed and Tom gets real excited and tells Johnny that he was nowhere near the place when Mrs. Williams was shot and leaves. Jake tells Johnny that Tom tends to get excited and is not too long on brains. He is also a dead shot and never misses.

Jake and Johnny go back to town when Ben does not show up. Johnny goes to the Piney Inn for dinner and meets the waitress, Flora Lane. Flora recommends the pot roast and Johnny asks to talk to her. She is surprised that Johnny found her so fast; she thought they would have a chance, as Ben would never have given her a minute while his wife was alive. "Doesn't being acquitted mean anything," she asks. She thought that Johnny knew that four years ago she was a housekeeper in Chicago where the wife died. The police said that she wanted to marry the husband and tried her for murder, but she was acquitted. Johnny finishes dinner and goes to see Jake and tells him that Flora had told Johnny the whole story. Johnny tells Jake that he thinks he could make a case against Ben. Jake tells Johnny that the farm is mortgaged to the hilt, and that Ira Keeler has a $7,500 note on the farm for a loan he had made to Ben to pay for the operation. However, the farm is only worth $4,500. Johnny asks if Ben has a squirrel rifle, but Jake says he only has a shotgun. Johnny tells Jake that he had noticed that the hooks on the mantle were made for a longer rifle and Jake remembers seeing one there, a long time ago. Johnny and Jake go back out to see Ben, who is home. They go back to the kitchen, where the fire is warming the house and talk. They tell Ben that they want to talk about who killed Martha. Johnny tells Ben that he has an idea, but it is only an idea. Johnny tells Ben that it looks like he killed Martha, and Flora could be the reason. Johnny notes that Mrs. Keeler thinks Ben killed Martha, and what about your squirrel rifle? Ben tells Johnny that the squirrel rifle was stolen the week before Martha was killed. Martha knew who took it and had asked Ben not to report it. Only Mrs. Keeler and Tom were in the house that week, and Tom is crazy about guns.

Jake and Johnny go to the shack Tom uses and Tom stops them with a gun. Johnny asks to look at his gun and finds that it is a .22. Johnny asks Tom what he did with Ben William's rifle, and Tom tells Johnny that Ira Keeler gave him $3 for it three weeks ago, a week after Martha was shot. Tom tells Johnny that he would never hurt Mrs. Williams. Besides the gun has never been used as it has rust in the barrel. Johnny takes Jake's car back to see Ira Keeler, and Mrs. Keeler meets Johnny at the door. She tells Johnny that the letter was a terrible thing to do, and that she does not hate Ben. She notes that a woman on a farm wants more than hard work, and Ben would not pay attention to her. Johnny goes in to find Ira Keeler working on his books. Johnny asks Ira about Ben's squirrel gun and Ira replies that Tom probably stole it. Johnny tells him that it was stolen from Ben. Johnny looks at the rifle over the fireplace, and there is rust all over the breech and sees that the hooks on the mantle have been there for years. Johnny tells Ira that he knows who killed Martha. Johnny relates that most people kill for hate or gain, and this one was done for gain. Johnny asks who benefits, Ben did at first, but someone would benefit more, someone who made a $7,500 loan out of kindness, something that was not in Ira's nature. Ira tells Johnny that it was not kindness; it was good business at the time. If the road had gone though the farm would have been worth twice that amount. Johnny tells Ira that the hooks do not fit the rifle that is on it. Ira finishes the books and tells Johnny that farming involves risks and often mistakes. He knew he made a mistake as soon as he pulled the trigger and takes Johnny out to behind the barn where the rifle is buried.

NOTES:

- CREDITS FROM TERRY SALOMONSON'S LOG BOOK.
- CHARLES LYON IS THE ANNOUNCER
- MUSIC IS BY EDDIE DUNSTEDTER
- THIS PROGRAM WAS DONE BY BOB BAILEY AS "THE SHADY LANE MATTER"

Producer: Jaime del Valle   **Writers:** Les Crutchfield
Cast: Jess Kirkpatrick, Parley Baer, Ralph Moody, Mary Lansing, Sam Edwards, Virginia Gregg

◆ ❖ ◆

SHOW: THE UNDRIED FIDDLE BACK MATTER
SHOW DATE: 3/30/1954

COMPANY: EASTERN INDEMNITY INSURANCE COMPANY
AGENT: TOM HARRISON
EXP. ACCT: **$480.30**

SYNOPSIS: Johnny is called by Tom Harrison and told about Edwin Colton, a lumber baron in Portland. There has been a $10,000 payroll robbery committed by his son, and he wants the money back in 48 hours.

Johnny flies to Portland, Oregon, and goes to the Colton Building where Mr. Colton wants action. Johnny is told that his son went to the bank to pick up the payroll money and just disappeared, he is sure of it. Colton only wants the money back. Johnny goes to see the police and Det. Podlas tells Johnny that Colton got the money from the bank, got into a cab and disappeared. The payroll money was in $20's, $10's, and $5's and Colton had a black satchel that was chained to his waist. Det Podlas gets a phone call and Colton's body has been found.

Johnny goes to a lumber mill on the Willamette River where he meets Cam Rogers who tells Johnny that he was checking on the crossfire and fiddleback, which is a grain pattern used by violin makers. There were three logs in the kiln that the old man was going to use for a desk for his son. When he checked inside he found the body with the empty moneybag. Cam is upset that the bloodstains have ruined the wood just like the son was ruined.

Johnny goes to visit the widow, and she knows that her husband is dead. She is sure that Eddie did not steal the money. Johnny calls Det. Podlas and is told that the cause of death was a concussion while erect, and that the cab company has been called. Johnny cabs to the cab company and finds the driver who took Colton to his home in the 900 block of Chestnut where Colton met his blonde wife. Johnny goes to the address on Chestnut and Francine Martin is not at home. Johnny rents a car and goes to see Mr. Colton who tells Johnny that he knows about Francine, and calls her a hustler who used to be a clerk, but was fired 10 days ago. Johnny gets her personnel records and learns that she made a play for all the men in the office. Johnny also learns that her brother is Max Wilkowski, who is a cabby. Johnny goes to the cab company and Max tells Johnny that Francine wanted the best out of life and was leaving for Mexico on payday. Johnny follows Max home where Francine meets him. Johnny goes in and meets Francine who tells Johnny that Eddie was going to get a divorce, and that they were going to live in Mexico. She tells Johnny that Eddie took the money to the mill while she packed, and that she used to date Cam Rogers who was sure he would get her.

Johnny leaves to go to the police but finds Cam Rogers in the back seat. Cam tells Johnny to drive to the mill and tells him that Eddie was supposed to end up in the river but the plant was busy, so he hid him in the kiln. Johnny causes the car to skid and Cam is thrown across the front seat. Later Johnny finds the money in the trunk of Cam's car.

NOTES:
- THE ANNOUNCER IS CHARLES LYON
- MUSIC IS BY EDDIE DUNSTEDTER

- STORY INFORMATION OBTAINED FROM THE **KNX** COLLECTION IN THE THOUSAND OAKS LIBRARY

Producer:	Jaime del Valle	Writers	Sidney Marshall
Cast:	Clayton Post, Ralph Moody, Jack Moyles, Bill Conrad, Virginia Gregg, Mary Jane Croft, Bill James		

◆ ❖ ◆

SHOW:	THE SULPHUR AND BRIMSTONE MATTER
SHOW DATE:	4/6/1954
COMPANY:	EASTERN INDEMNITY INSURANCE COMPANY
AGENT:	PHILIP MARTIN
EXP. ACCT:	$585.60

SYNOPSIS: Phillip Martin calls and asks what Johnny knows of hydroelectric dams. There is a completion clause on a project in Venezuela, and the project is in trouble. Asa Travers had wired about problems and was killed. "I wonder if coffee is any cheaper in Venezuela?" Johnny muses.

Johnny goes to Caracas, Venezuela and meets Sr. Metarzza, Asa Travers' partner. They fly to the dam site in a Cessna piloted by Metarzza and Metarzza tells Johnny that he knows of no reason why Travers was killed and that the federal police are on the case. The government is financing the dam and it is interested in the dam's completion. Metarzza admits that there have been problems with equipment and lost or stolen material, but he thinks that there are some dishonest men involved and maybe someone is trying to slow things down to get the project to run over the scheduled date.

At the work site Johnny goes to the construction office and runs into a young lady. Inside Johnny asks for Capt. Borros, and the straw boss, Bill Anthony gives Johnny a hard time. Bill does not need anyone poking around slowing things down. He tells Johnny that Capt. Borros has gone to Travers' house, about 10 miles from here. Get a company jeep and driver; it will get you out of here. Johnny asks about the girl and Bill tells him that she was Filomena Travers, Asa Travers' widow. Johnny tells Bill that their business must have been real important as neither one had wiped the lipstick from their chins!

Johnny goes to the motor pool and gets Pedro to take him to Travers' home. Pedro knows why Johnny is there and he knows that when evil men bring evil things it will bring evil. He tells Johnny that the dam is evil; and that it is not right to change the course of a river. Sr. Travers was destroyed by his evil. At Travers' house Johnny hears shots coming from a barn. In the barn is Filomena using her shooting gallery, and she is quite proficient. She tells Johnny that she is using a .38 on a .45 frame, but it is not the same gun that killed Asa. She tells Johnny that Capt. Borros has gone, but she knows why Johnny is there. She is not grief stricken either, as she always looks forward, not to the past. Sr. Metarzza arrives and tells Johnny that they must return to the dam as Capt. Borros has halted all work on the dam.

At the work site the equipment is idle and Capt. Borros is talking to Bill Anthony. Capt. Borros tells Johnny that he halted work to stop irreparable damage to the site. Anthony was going to blast a passage way to the river and was using too much dynamite, and it would have caused a massive landslide. Capt. Borros has discovered that more than twice as much dynamite than is required has been used. Johnny and Capt. Borros start to go and check on the charges, but someone has set them off.

The investigation showed that the proper amount of dynamite had been taken from the storehouse, that 25 cases was the proper amount, and that the charges were set off by a crude firing device found in the woods over the site. The damage is not as great as was thought, and can be bypassed. Sr. Metarzza tells Johnny that he is going to Caracas to talk to people who can countermand Capt. Borros' orders. Capt. Borros tells Johnny that he knows that there are always men who can be bought. There have been 8 men killed by accidents so far, and he stopped construction to save lives.

As Johnny prepares to eat at the mess hall that night, Mrs. Travers calls him. She is going to Caracas and wants Johnny to visit her there. She remembers that Asa had told her that the works of the devil always carry the odor of sulfur and brimstone and that there is an old sulfur mine close to the location of the blast. Johnny asks Pedro about the mine and he knows that it is there but has not been worked for many years. Pedro takes Johnny to the mine, and Pedro tells Johnny that there is evil in the mine. In the mine Johnny finds dynamite cases, some empty, some full. That explains where the extra dynamite came from. Behind the cases Johnny finds the body of Bill Anthony, and a gun with the initials "GM" on the butt. Johnny realizes that Gertulio Metarzza is the owner of the construction company. Johnny tells Capt. Borros what he has uncovered, and they both leave for Caracas.

Johnny checks into the Grand Palacio Hotel and notices that the sulfur dust from the mine had turned the silver coins in his pocket almost black. Johnny goes to the Hippodromo Nacional to see Filomena Travers, and she is surprised to see him there. Johnny notes the lack of grief in her voice and tells her about the sulfur mine, and that Capt. Borros is going to pick up Sr. Metarzza right now. Filomena pays for her drink with a coin that is almost black. She tells Johnny that the coin had been given to her so that she could burn a candle for her husband and that Pedro de la Questa had given it to her. Johnny finds Capt. Borros and they both go back to the construction site to see Pedro. When they arrive at the dam site, they see Pedro with a box of dynamite. Capt. Borros prepares to fire but Johnny asks to try to talk to Pedro, but Pedro warns Johnny off. Pedro tells Johnny that the blast will prevent the evil, it will not stop the dam but it will be a sign from heaven. Pedro tells Johnny that the dam will drown his wife, who is buried in the valley where the dam would cover it. They wish to drown her grave to make filthy money, so how could he allow it. Pedro tells Johnny that he killed Travers because he would not listen, and that Anthony had followed him to the mine. Capt. Borros fires at Pedro to scare him and Johnny tackles Pedro. Capt. Borros tells Johnny that he did not hit Pedro, as he did not want to risk hitting the dynamite. Johnny muses that the dynamite could have gone off when he dropped the crate!

NOTES:
- CHARLES LYON IS THE ANNOUNCER
- MUSIC IS BY EDDIE DUNSTEDTER

Producer: Jaime del Valle **Writers:** Sidney Marshall
Cast: Howard Culver, Don Diamond, Lillian Buyeff, Jay Novello, Donald Lawton

◆ ❖ ◆

SHOW: THE MAGNOLIA AND HONEYSUCKLE MATTER
SHOW DATE: 4/13/1954
COMPANY: EASTERN FIRE & CASUALTY COMPANY
AGENT: GIL RANDALL
EXP. ACCT: $176.45

SYNOPSIS: Gil Randall calls Johnny and boy you are in luck to get away from all this rain and cold, basking in the magnolias and honeysuckle. You are going to Charleston, South Carolina. The Ambrose Cooper Paper Company caught fire and burned last night and it was the second fire in two years. It killed a secretary and cost us $100,000, unless you can prove it was arson. "Maybe the mint juleps are in bloom there too" muses Johnny.

Johnny goes to Charleston, South Carolina and rents a car to drive to the paper company and meets with Lt. Hervey. Johnny is told that there is no question of arson, as the fire burned real fast up front. Lt. Hervey tells Johnny that Robert and Norman Cooper run the company for their mother, Alice. The floor in Norman's office shows signs of deep scorching, signs of an amateur. The night watchman found the fire and turned in the alarm at 4:17. He was burned trying to pull Felicia Farrell, Norman's secretary, out of the building. It does not make much sense, why was the girl there at 4 in the morning. Norman took her out last night but now has disappeared.

Johnny goes to visit Alice Cooper at her mansion, and Robert, her brother-in-law is there too. Robert thinks Johnny should be looking in the criminal part of Charleston and not here. Alice tells Johnny that Norman is away on a hunting trip, and that he left at midnight. Robert blurts out that Norman had nothing to do with the fire and Alice tells Johnny that he leaves at midnight to get to the hunting camp at dawn. Norman had taken Felicia to a company dance that night and had taken her home by eleven. She was an attractive girl, but not the type for Norman.

Johnny goes to the plant, but Lt. Hervey had gone. Johnny eats at a restaurant near the paper plant and the waiter tells Johnny that it was real pretty. He saw it last night because the night man was sick and he had to work for him. There was no one around except Horace Singleton the night watchman. He came into the restaurant and had been nipping and wanted some company. Horace was talking about how happy he would be when he retired. He always seemed to spend his money on booze. That was just before the fire started. The waiter tells Johnny that he never thought to tell that to the police.

Johnny gives the information to Lt. Hervey, and they drive to Horace's shack, which is on fire. They break in and find Horace's body with an empty bottle in his hand. At least he answered one question; he did not start the last fire as no liquor smells like gasoline. Back at Lt. Hervey's office, they figure that the arsons are being used to cover up another crime. The coroner's report says that Felicia's lungs were not burned or seared, so she was asphyxiated before the fire started. Lt. Hervey gets a call that Norman Cooper has been picked up for speeding, and Felicia's hand bag and a couple of gasoline cans were in the trunk of his car.

Norman is brought in and is not upset. He tells Johnny and Lt. Hervey that he heard the news on the radio and sped back to town. He tells them that he had brought Felicia home around 11:45 and went home. She must have forgotten her purse in car. He tells Johnny that he always carries gas in his car, in case he runs out on the road. Last night was the only time he had taken Felicia out as his regular date, Maryanne James, had stood him up. He tells Johnny that Felicia's regular boy friend is Robert Cooper, the man his mother is going to marry.

Johnny goes to talk to Maryanne, but she is not home, and a neighbor tells Johnny that she works at a botanical garden in the area. Johnny drives to the garden and gets on her guide boat to talk to her. Johnny tells her that he wants to cut the botanical talk. Johnny tells her who he is and wants to talk about Felicia Farrell. Maryanne tells Johnny that the only thing she knows about Felicia is what she read in the paper. Johnny tells her that Norman said she knows about Felicia, but she tells Johnny that Norman is a darlin' thing, but gets the craziest ideas. She tells Johnny that she does not make enough money to buy the clothes necessary to see people like him. Johnny suddenly "finds" some money in the boat and gives it to her and she suddenly becomes more talkative. Of course, she knows Felicia, how silly to say she didn't. She was going to go to the dance with Norman but got a headache and asked Felicia to go for her. She had never gone with Norman before, and she never went out with Robert. One of them is lying, and it is not Maryanne.

Johnny goes back to the hotel and calls Lt. Hervey, who has been checking the financial records. Lt. Hervey tells Johnny that Felicia had been making regular deposits for the past two years and there was a corresponding withdrawal in Robert's account. Also, Felicia has a safety deposit box, and Johnny joins Lt. Hervey to open it. At the bank, Johnny learns that the box is owned jointly by Felicia and Maryanne James, who had both been in earlier that day. In the box is a marriage license issued the year before to Robert and Felicia. So Felicia must have been blackmailing Robert who was planning to marry Mrs. Cooper. And, Robert probably killed the watchman when he caught him killing Felicia. Johnny thinks that Maryanne was in today to get the marriage certificate to blackmail Robert with, and Robert may try to get her too. Johnny drives to Maryanne's place where Norman is waiting for Maryanne to come home. Norman tells Johnny that she was going to meet someone at the garden after work, some sort of business arrangement. Johnny and Lt. Hervey rush to the garden and find Robert's car in the parking lot with Maryanne's. Johnny and Lt. Hervey search the grounds and hear screams and then shots. Johnny shoots at and hits Robert and he throws his gun down. Robert tells Johnny that she should not have tried to blackmail me. There is nothing worse than blackmail. Johnny says Felicia could think of something worse!

NOTES:
- **CREDITS FROM TERRY SALOMONSON**
- **CHARLES LYON IS THE ANNOUNCER**
- **MUSIC IS BY EDDIE DUNSTEDTER**

Producer: Jaime del Valle   **Writers:** Sidney Marshall
Cast: Hal March, Herb Butterfield, Lee Patrick, Bill Johnstone, Howard McNear, Virginia Gregg

SHOW: THE NATHAN SWING MATTER
SHOW DATE: 4/20/1954
COMPANY: GREAT EASTERN LIFE INSURANCE COMPANY
AGENT: MR. MITCHELL
EXP. ACCT: $176.45

SYNOPSIS: Mr. Mitchell calls and Johnny tells him that he is completely available. Mitchell tells Johnny that Nathan Swing is insured, but his body was found in the Los Angels harbor. Contact Sgt. Matthews.

Johnny goes to Los Angeles, California and meets Lt. Matthews. Johnny is told that Nathan Swing had a police record, and had been shot once in the chest and once in the shoulder. A stoolie has told the police that some of Dorando's boys had met with Swing, but Swing was a small time crook. After the killing, the special investigator Dan Fletcher, who is after Dorando on vice matters, suddenly calls off the investigation. Dorando was supposed to appear tomorrow, but now "there is not enough evidence." Lt. Matthews tells Johnny that Fletcher is thought to be an honest man.

Johnny goes to meet with Daniel Fletcher, but he is not in the office that day. A call to Lt. Matthews gets Johnny Fletcher's home address. Johnny goes to the house, which is in a very nice area and the butler opens the door. Johnny introduces himself to Fletcher and tells him that he is there to talk about the murder of Nathan Swing. Johnny thought that Fletcher might know something about Swing. Fletcher tells Johnny to call him tomorrow, but Johnny tells him that he will see what Jimmy Dorando has to say, and Fletcher gets anxious. Fletcher tells Johnny that he knows about people who beat around the bush and throw their weight around. Fletcher threatens Johnny that he will have his job, but Johnny tells him that he will stay on the case until his insurance company says to stop.

Fletcher's daughter Mary comes in and he tells her to go back to bed, she should not be up. She asks if it is about Jimmy and she starts crying and Fletcher tells Johnny to leave.

Johnny goes to his hotel and calls Lt. Matthews. Johnny asks for the address for Jimmy Dorando. Lt. Matthews tells Johnny that it will be better to go to his café later tonight, when some undercover officers can be there to watch out for Johnny. Johnny goes to the café and asks for Dorando. Johnny gets a scotch and water and when a muscleman named Tony approaches Johnny to ask why he wants to see Dorando. Johnny tells him it is about Nathan Swing and Johnny is taken to see Jimmy Dorado in his office. "What are you investigating?" asks Jimmy. Johnny tells him about the Swing murder and Jimmy tells Johnny that he does not know anything about Swing. Also, he does not like Johnny, so don't bother me any more. Johnny goes out of the office and starts to leave when he sees Mary Fletcher go back to Dorando's office. Johnny waits outside until she leaves. She drives west and Johnny follows her to a deserted pier. She is trying to jump when Johnny pulls her back and takes her crying to her car to talk. Johnny tells her who he is and she tells him that he should have let her jump, as she does not want to talk about anything. She tells Johnny she only saw Nathan Swing once, the night she killed him.

Mary stops crying and admits to Johnny that she killed Swing, even though it will ruin her father. She had been seeing Jimmy for a long time and her father found out when Jimmy told him. Jimmy told him that Mary had killed Swing, and to call off the investigation because Jimmy has the gun that Mary used. Swing had come in to talk to Jimmy about some sort of bet. There was an argument and Swing pulled a gun. Jimmy took it away and Swing went after Jimmy with a poker. She picked up the gun and shot Swing. Johnny tells her that now that Dorando is in a better position now because he has the gun. Johnny tells her that he will try to get the gun away from Dorando. She can lie long enough for your father to prosecute him, and then you can talk to the police.

Johnny drives back to Dorando's café and tries to think of some way to get the gun. Johnny remembers an alley behind the café and a window in Jimmy's office. Johnny walks back to the window and hears Dorando and Tony talking until the window is shut. Johnny sees Jimmy take the gun from a safe, put it in a box and give it to Tony. Johnny follows Tony to Union Station where he is about to put the box in a public locker. Johnny tries to get the gun and Tony runs down the platform shooting. Tony runs into a tunnel and Johnny hits him. Johnny gets the gun and calls Lt. Matthews. Johnny gets Dorando's address in Beverly Hills and tells Lt. Matthews to meet him there. Johnny drives to Dorando's house and climbs the fence into the yard and tries the to open the French doors to the study when the lights go out. Dorando is there when Johnny wakes up and Johnny wants to know who hit him. Dorando tells Johnny that he is trespassing and that he could kill him. Dorando tells Johnny that he had found the box, but the gun is missing and Dorando figures that Johnny was the one that killed Tony. Johnny tries to fool Dorando and stall for time until the police get there. Dorando starts to shoot Johnny when Mary comes out with the gun. Dorando and Mary fire at the same time and Mary is hit. Mary tells Johnny that she is sorry she hit him. She had looked for him at the café and then came here. She got the gun and dies before telling Johnny any more.

Dorando is dead and Fletcher will not have to prosecute him.

NOTES:
- CREDITS FROM TERRY SALOMONSON
- CHARLES LYON IS THE ANNOUNCER
- MUSIC IS BY EDDIE DUNSTEDTER

Producer:	Jaime del Valle	Writers:	Blake Edwards
Cast:	Clayton Post, Tim Graham, Dick Ryan, William Johnstone, Virginia Gregg, Jay Novello, David Young		

◆　❖　◆

SHOW:	THE FRUSTRATED PHOENIX MATTER
SHOW DATE:	4/27/1954
COMPANY:	WASHINGTONIAN LIFE INSURANCE COMPANY
AGENT:	MR. BRADLEY
EXP. ACCT:	$153.50

SYNOPSIS: Mr. Bradley calls and asks if Johnny has read any good books lately, specifically books by Martin Vaneberg? Martin has not written anything for twenty years, but wanted to change the beneficiary of his $25,000 policy. The police are looking for his wife after Martin was killed.

Johnny goes to Chicago, Illinois, gets a room at the Sherman House and cabs to the offices of the newspaper to brush up on recent history on Vaneberg. The editor suggests Johnny talk to Richard Hanley, a critic and confidant of Vaneberg for 20 years. Vaneberg's wife would be a better source, as Hanley was her first husband. Johnny cabs to Hanley's apartment and Hanley offers to tell Johnny either about the man or the writer. Hanley tells Johnny that Vaneberg was a genius as a writer in the thirties, but he followed that with twenty years of desolate life. Hanley had tried to get Vaneberg to write again for many years, but the vows were many and the accomplishments few. Hanley also tells Johnny that he had not planned to give Vaneberg his wife and Hanley has not seen either of them in five weeks. Johnny is told that Vaneberg had nothing, and there was no reason for anyone to kill him.

Johnny goes to see Lt. Worshak who tells Johnny that Vaneberg was shot in his apartment around 11 PM with a .25 Beretta. Nobody heard the shots; nobody saw anyone go in our out. Dalton Towler found the body at 3 AM this morning. Towler was working on some earth shattering poems and wanted to show them to Vaneberg. The police found a portable typewriter in the apartment but no manuscript.

Johnny visits Dalton Towler in Newberry Park, talking to a pair of uninterested squirrels. Johnny introduces himself and wants to talk about Vaneberg. Towler tells Johnny that Vaneberg is the final degradation of genius. Towler tells Johnny that Martin Vaneberg is not dead, as a soul such as his will rise from his ashes and write again like the Phoenix. Johnny asks who would want to kill Vaneberg; and the answer is any of the hack writers of the world. Towler tells Johnny that the wife, Elaine, was a dedicated servant to Vaneberg, and that Towler had never considered the insurance as a motive. Towler tells Johnny that Elaine was typing a manuscript at Martin Hanley's apartment.

Johnny goes back to Hanley's apartment to ask about what Towler had told him. Hanley tells Johnny that he did not mention the manuscript because his attorney was out of town and he wanted to consult with him first. Hanley expects her tonight at eight and Johnny tells Hanley that he and Lt. Worshak will be there also. Hanley tells Johnny that Elaine had left at midnight; an hour after Martin was killed. Johnny cabs to see Lt. Worshak and finds him running out into a car. Johnny is told that a woman has taken an overdose and is in the hospital with a signed Vaneberg book, and the police had found a .25 Beretta under her pillow.

At the hospital an intern tells Johnny and Lt. Worshak that the patient is 30, Caucasian, complains of an overdose, has normal vital signs, and her stomach has been pumped. Johnny notes that the signs do not point to an overdose and the intern agrees. In the room the woman is pleading for Martin Vaneberg to forgive her, as she did not mean to do it. She does not care who Johnny and Lt. Worshak are. Martin was her only true love and she worshiped him. Lt. Worshak recognizes her as Dolly Darling, a stripper. Even so, she tells them that she loved Martin; and that they were secret lovers. Lt. Worshak mentions the laws against suicide and filing a false crime report and suddenly her agent Sammie Farwell is a rat, as it was his idea. He told her it would be a great gimmick and now she is going to get nothing out of it. Lt. Worshak tells her that she probably will get 30-90 days, depending on the judge.

Lt. Worshak confirms that the stunt had nothing to do with Vaneberg's murder. Johnny checks out most of Vaneberg's former haunts and ends up at Towler's apartment. Johnny asks Towler about the poems he rushed to Vaneberg. He tells Johnny that they were just drivel and that he had destroyed them. Johnny asks if he had destroyed Vaneberg's manuscript as well, but Towler tells Johnny that he had not found a manuscript. Towler tells Johnny that Vaneberg was writing under contract to someone. Towler had seen it and it was filth. He would have destroyed it but it was gone. When Elaine found out what he was doing she left him. When Johnny mentions the police looking for the manuscript, Towler tells Johnny that if the material came out it would be worse than murder. Johnny calls Lt. Worshak and learns that Elaine has been found, in the river. She has been shot as well and Hanley is in the hospital with a breakdown. Johnny's job is done but he is curious about the gun and the manuscript. If someone knew enough to use a Beretta in Dolly's stunt, before the police knew what kind of gun it was, maybe there is a motive there. Johnny and Lt. Worshak go to visit Sammie Farwell to see if they can find that motive. In the hallway they hear shots and go in to find Towler in the office burning the manuscript, and Farwell dead in the other room with a Beretta on the desk. Towler tells Johnny that he knew there had been a serious disagreement between Vaneberg and Farwell over Farwell's attention to Elaine. Farwell ended up shooting Vaneberg and then Elaine. Towler did not go to the police because he was only interested in the manuscript. Towler was tipped to the identity of the killer by a friend after Johnny's visit. He came up and demanded the manuscript from Farwell and they fought over the gun. All in all, things have turned out quite well in Towler's opinion.

NOTES:

- THIS IS AN **AFRS** TAPE, AND THE FIRST COMMERCIAL BREAK IS ABOUT THE AGRICULTURE DEPARTMENT
- THE MID-PROGRAM COMMERCIAL BREAK IS ABOUT THE PRESIDENCY OF BENJAMIN HARRISON
- CREDITS FROM TERRY SALOMONSON
- CHARLES LYON IS THE ANNOUNCER
- MUSIC IS BY EDDIE DUNSTEDTER

Producer: Jaime del Valle   Writers: Sidney Marshall
Cast: Dan O'Herlihy, Ken Christy, Junius Matthews, William
            Conrad, Virginia Gregg

SHOW: THE DAN FRANK MATTER
SHOW DATE: 5/4/1954
COMPANY: COMMONWEALTH MUTUAL ASSURANCE COMPANY
AGENT: JIM BATES
EXP. ACCT: $194.90

SYNOPSIS: Jim Bates calls Johnny and asks "if a chief of police got killed, what would be the most likely reason for it?" Jim has a hunch on this one, because the chief is middle aged, shot with his own gun in his own house. The beneficiary is a twenty seven year old wife of eight months, the $50,000 policy is seven months old, and the wife filed a claim within 24 hours of his death. Johnny thinks he had better look into it.

Johnny goes to the great lakes town Middleboro and the home of Dan Frank. Johnny meets Pete Parker, a reporter for the local paper and a little drunk. Pete had just asked the wife about insurance; Dan had some and Laura will probably get it. Pete tells Johnny to watch himself as the town looks sleepy, but it is wide open with rackets and everything. The Chief gets $6,000, but look at his house and his wife. . .very expensive. Dan was involved all right.

Mrs. Frank meets Johnny and is surprised to learn that they are paying so promptly, but gets angry when she learns Johnny is an investigator. She knows they are trying to get out of paying the policy. Laura shows Johnny where Dan fell and tells Johnny that there was a noise and Dan went down to investigate and was shot with his own gun. She tells Johnny that Dan had enemies because of his job. Johnny tells her that 24 hours is too quick to file a claim and Laura tells Johnny to talk to Max Beely.

Johnny meets Max Beely, who tells Johnny that he can prove that she did not kill Dan; he was there. He and Dan were going fishing, so he spent the night at the house. He heard someone in the hall and went out when Laura turned on the lights, and the shots rang out. Laura was standing next to her room when Dan was shot. Max makes a good alibi, as he is the city attorney. Max tells Johnny that that Laura has a cash register inside of her and Dan found out too late. "So that is why he needed to get involved in the rackets?" asks Johnny. Max is caught off guard and agrees. The city commissioner, Mr. Corbit, comes in and tells Johnny that Eddie Sales killed Dan because Dan had sent Sales to jail and Sales swore he would get even, and that Sales was paroled last week. Find Sales and you will find the key to the killing and the rackets Johnny is told.

Outside Laura honks her car horn at Johnny, who confirms that Max gave her an alibi. She tells Johnny that she is ready to be friendly and cooperative. A car speeds by and shots are fired and Laura asks why someone would shoot at Johnny, but he thinks the shots were for Laura.

Johnny finds Pete in a bar and asks for more information about Laura. Pete tells Johnny that Laura is a four-star tramp, a former dancer and the former girlfriend of Eddie Sales. Pete tells Johnny that he is in love with Laura and that she was his girl before Eddie Sales. Pete notes that the gun was found beside Dan; and everyone assumed he was shot with it, but it took the police two days to find out Dan had been shot with his own gun. Pete gets a call from the office and learns there is a fire at Laura Frank's place and they cannot get inside.

At the scene of the fire Johnny and Pete can only watch as the house is destroyed. Laura is in a car with Max Beely and she is sure that someone is after her. She tells Johnny that she had taken a nap and woke up with the house in flames. Max notes that the house is insured as well; and Pete tells her that now all her assets are in cash. Johnny thinks it may be Eddie's work. There are shots and they see a man staggering out of the basement of the house—it is a badly burned Eddie Sales.

At the hospital, the doctor says the odds are against Eddie. Johnny cannot figure the shots, they came before he got out of the house. The phone rings and Laura needs to talk to Johnny at the lunchroom across the street. Johnny tells Pete to stay there and goes to meet Laura, who asks Johnny if he thinks she is attractive. She asks Johnny to turn in his report so she can get the money. Johnny wants to know why she heard the noise, and why she sent Dan downstairs and why she turned on the lights making him a perfect target. Johnny is going to wait to see what Eddie says, and if he says nothing, she is in the clear. Laura offers Johnny $10,000 to file a positive report. Pete comes into the lunchroom and tells Johnny that a fireman told him that the cellar door was padlocked from the outside, and that Eddie fired the shots to open the door. So maybe Eddie was supposed to die in the fire, right Laura? Pete asks Johnny what he wanted to see him about and Johnny tells Pete that he did not call him and they rush back to the hospital room. Johnny realizes that Laura called him to get him out of the room. Inside, Johnny sees Beely coming out of the elevator because the commissioner called him. They go back to the room to find no policeman at the door and commissioner Corbit holding a pillow over Eddie Sale's face. Max is sure now that Corbit was in charge of the rackets, and Corbit pulls a gun. When Johnny asks Corbit why he had Dan killed, Max tells Johnny that he and Dan were going fishing so that Dan could spill the beans about the rackets and Laura found out and tipped off Corbit. Eddie hid out in Laura's house and she locked him in. Corbit heads for a window and falls out. Laura comes in and tells Johnny that now there are no witnesses. Johnny tells her that her insurance claim really is a confession. The claim says that they found Dan frank shot with his own gun, but the police did not find that out for two days. So how did you know, Mrs. Frank?

NOTES:
- THIS IS AN **AFRS** PROGRAM THAT HAS A STORY ABOUT THE SEAL OF THE US AND THE SWIMMING VARIETY.
- THE MID-PROGRAM COMMERCIAL IS ABOUT THE PRESIDENCY OF JOHN QUINCY ADAMS
- CAST CREDITS FROM TERRY SALOMONSON
- CHARLES LYON IS THE ANNOUNCER
- MUSIC IS BY EDDIE DUNSTEDTER
- THIS PROGRAM WAS DONE BY BOB BAILEY AS "THE OPEN TOWN MATTER"

Producer: Jaime del Valle   **Writers:** Les Crutchfield
Cast: Jim Nusser, Peter Leeds, Virginia Gregg, Joseph Kearns, Frank Nelson, Joe Du Val

◆ ❖ ◆

SHOW: THE AROMATIC CICATRIX MATTER
SHOW DATE: 5/11/1954
COMPANY: EASTERN MARITIME & INSURANCE COMPANY
AGENT: JAMES HARRINGTON
EXP. ACCT: $196.10

SYNOPSIS: Johnny is called by James Harrington and told that the cabin cruiser of Thomas Bellamy exploded and he was killed, and there was a $10,000 policy. James notes that this is the second husband lost in boating accident in three years.

Johnny goes to the British Colony of Bermuda and gets a room at the Bermudian Hotel. Johnny goes to the office of Harrington, but it is closed so Johnny goes to see Inspector Brice who tells Johnny that the explosion killed Bellamy and almost destroyed the boat, which was at the dock in St. George's harbor. Johnny goes to the Bellamy residence where a young lady on a motorbike greets him. Betty Bellamy introduces herself and tells Johnny that "old poopsie" Harrington told her that he was coming. She tells Johnny that Thomas Bellamy was her stepfather, and that her father was killed the same way. She tells Johnny that Thomas was murdered but not by his wife, and Betty suspects poopsie.

Johnny goes to the Bellamy perfume factory and meets Michael Forrest who tells Johnny that he heard Thomas and Harrington arguing about some trust agreements. Michael tells Johnny that Mrs. Bellamy and Mr. Harrington are in the lab. While they are talking there is an explosion and Harrington staggers out, and Johnny goes in to get Mrs. Bellamy. Harrington tells Johnny that Mrs. Bellamy had just lit a cigarette, but there was nothing in the lab that was flammable. Johnny goes to the boat and meets Michael who tells Johnny that there was ether and benzene in the lab that Harrington had suggested as a new way to process the perfume. Johnny goes to the police who tell Johnny that Mrs. Bellamy is ready to confess. Johnny goes to the hospital, but the doctors will not let him in. Johnny meets Dr. Randall who tells Johnny about a cicatrix, which is an internal scar. Insp. Brice arrives and tells Johnny about a confession by Betty, and that the estate of £5000 would go to Betty. Johnny goes to see Betty who tells Johnny that she wants to apologize to poopsie because her mother has just died, and Betty tells Johnny that she hated her mother. Johnny goes back to see Dr. Randall who tells Johnny that the cicatrix was a mental scar on Betty caused by the death of her father, and had caused her to go to a sanatorium. Johnny goes to Harrington's office and he tells Johnny that he had suggested the solvents, but there was no record of purchases. Harrington tells Johnny that he remembers the smell of ethyl oxide, which was not the same as medical ether, and that he had joked that Dr. Randall should be there. Johnny goes to a chemist shop and gets the evidence he needs; Miss Betty Bellamy was the purchaser. Johnny calls Insp. Brice and learns that Betty is missing. Johnny eats dinner and finds Betty on the hotel terrace. Betty tells Johnny that she has found love, and that Mike had suggested coming to the hotel. Insp. Brice arrives and tells Johnny that he will get Michael while Johnny occupies Betty until the doctor arrives.

NOTES:
- THE ANNOUNCER IS CHARLES LYON
- MUSIC IS BY EDDIE DUNSTEDTER
- STORY INFORMATION OBTAINED FROM THE KNX COLLECTION IN THE THOUSAND OAKS LIBRARY

Producer: Jaime del Valle   **Writers**   **Sidney Marshall**
Cast: Ben Wright, Tudor Owen, Virginia Gregg, Hal March, Eric Snowden

◆   ❖   ◆

SHOW: THE BILKED BARONESS MATTER
SHOW DATE: 5/18/1954
COMPANY: EASTERN INDEMNITY & INSURANCE COMPANY

AGENT: **BEN TURNER**

EXP. ACCT: **$50.45**

SYNOPSIS: Ben Turner calls and asks Johnny how he likes hobnobbing around nobility. Johnny is going to meet Olga Zharvas who had $100,000 in furs and jewelry stolen from her penthouse last night. A former photographer husband just filed for bankruptcy and she has been seen with him lately.

Johnny drives to New York City and the penthouse of the baroness. Inside she tells Johnny that the maid is off and she is on the way out to a cocktail party. She has told the police everything and tells Johnny to see them. She relents and tells Johnny that she noticed the items missing at about 3:00 when she got home. She had some friends over, they went to a show and then to dinner and Thomas Bentley, her former husband brought her home. Now she really must go as good friends are irreplaceable, but the jewels are insured.

Johnny talks to the staff of the hotel and only learns that Olga's place is a gathering place for every screwball in New York. Johnny goes to see Lt. Lewisson, who tells Johnny that it probably was an inside job. The only way in was with a key and whoever did it knew exactly where to go. Also, Olga gives out keys like trinkets, so it could have been anyone. Lt. Lewisson agrees with Johnny that no one could have gotten out with the furs without being seen. The doorman says that one of her friends, Vasily Udescu stayed behind and that he has a record for running a confidence game and shoplifting furs. Lt. Lewisson thinks that the case might be closed when they pick Vasily up. Johnny thinks that is not the case; as he has not had an easy case in three years and doubts Lt. Lewisson has had one either.

Johnny goes to the studio of Thomas Bentley, where a photo shoot is underway. During a quick break Johnny introduces himself and is told to come back some other time. Johnny thinks that it is funny how he is in full operation when he is supposed to be broke. Bentley tells Johnny that there is no tie-in between the robbery and him. Olga always moves upwards and never would get involved in fraud to help out a former husband. He tells Johnny that he went to see her because he wanted a $20,000 loan from Olga, but she would not give it to him so the creditors are letting him run the shop until he gets the money to pay his bills. A muscleman actor wants to talk about using a loincloth to show off his body. "The body of Hercules and the brain of a second-class ape" notes Bentley. Thomas asks if Johnny could offer a reward for the return of the goods, just out of curiosity. Johnny calls Lt. Lewisson and learns that Udescu has been picked up with some the jewels in his apartment.

At Lewisson's office Udescu is complaining about being treated like a common criminal and will sue them for every penny. Lt. Lewisson shows him some jewels that are covered by the policy. Udescu tells them that he was at the party last night and did not go out because he had seen the play and did not want to be bored and he knows nothing about the jewels. Johnny now has some of the jewels but still needs to find $87,000. Johnny goes to the Plaza Hotel, and Tom Bentley calls tells Johnny that he knows where the loot is. Johnny calls Lt. Lewisson and goes to meet Bentley at his studio, but Lt. Lewisson is there already. Lt. Lewisson tells Johnny that Tom Bentley is in the back of the studio dead, shot by the .357 magnum rifle lying next to him on the floor. Johnny goes back to the office with Lt. Lewisson and meets Olga and the model he had seen earlier at Bentley's studio, Herta Werner. Olga is ready to sign a complaint when Herta reminds her of the secret cabinet in the den where she had placed the jewels during a taffy pull. She had forgotten about them and had included them in the list of items stolen. Poor, dear Vasily. Olga signs a statement about the jewels and leaves with Herta. Lt. Lewisson calls down stairs and there is nothing new on the killing: no prints and no witnesses.

Johnny cabs to the apartment of Herta Werner, who is expecting him. Johnny reminds her how she had batted her eyes at him at police headquarters and asks her how much she wants to give him information and she wants $1,000, which will require a lot of information. The apartment is covered with pictures of Harley Townsend, the model Johnny had seen at the studio complaining about the loincloth. Harley is Herta's soon to be ex-husband. Herta tells Johnny that Harley has a key to Olga's apartment. He was at the party and left at 12:30 and came back at 1:30 with Tom Bentley. Bentley had called today at 7:00 and Harley blew up. He said he would not settle for $10,000 when he could get $50,000. Harley told Bentley he had better wait for him and get over there, and he took some cartridges with him. She does not know where Harley is, either. Johnny cabs back to Lt. Lewisson and tells him of the conversation. Lt. Lewisson thinks that Bentley and Harley worked the job together; Bentley wants $20,000 to turn the stuff back in and Harley objects and kills him. Now they need to find Harley. Johnny thinks that maybe someone posing as a service man could have gotten upstairs, but the street was torn up for repairs, preventing a pickup and would not be fixed until today. Johnny and Lt. Lewisson go to the building and check with the superintendent who tells them that the street is fixed and the service people are coming in regular now. There is a new laundry man there now. Maybe he will take something out as he probably is in the laundry room now. Johnny and Lt. Lewisson go to the laundry room and find Harley pushing a laundry cart out. Lt. Lewisson calls out for Harley to stop but Harley pulls a gun and fires. Harley is shot and killed and in the laundry cart are the furs and jewels. They were kept in a storage room over night. Johnny notes that they need to go to the shooting range more often, as one of the coats has a hole in the sleeve.

NOTES:
- CREDITS FROM TERRY SALOMONSON
- CHARLES LYON IS THE ANNOUNCER
- MUSIC IS BY EDDIE DUNSTEDTER

Producer: Jaime del Valle   **Writers:** Sidney Marshall
Cast: Hal March, Mary Lansing, Parley Baer, Bill Johnstone, Peter Leeds, Jay Novello, Virginia Gregg, Joe Du Val

❖ ❖ ❖

SHOW:	THE PUNCTILIOUS FIREBUG MATTER
SHOW DATE:	5/25/1954
COMPANY:	EASTERN INDEMNITY & FIRE COMPANY
AGENT:	JEFF CONNORS
EXP. ACCT:	$309.25

SYNOPSIS: Jeff Connors calls and asks Johnny to come to Dallas. There is a firebug on the loose and there have been four fires in four weeks. One every Tuesday night.

Johnny goes to Dallas, Texas and meets with Jeff Connors who outlines the fires so far, with claims of $95,000. The fire starts every Tuesday at 11:00PM. Lt. Len Borchart says that the bug may be in the insurance office, but there is no reason to suspect anyone. Jeff is sure he will lose his job if the fires do not stop. Lt. Borchart calls and there has been another fire in an apartment building. Jeff realizes that the policy was just written that week.

Johnny and Jeff go to the site and meet Lt. Borchart. There is not much to do until the building cools down in the morning. Johnny is told that a man in the building reported the fire, but he was trapped in the building and does not know his wife and kids died in the building. By 1:00 AM the only witness has died on the way to the hospital. Lt. Borchart tells Johnny that he will find evidence of a candle fuse when they search the ashes. Lt. Borchart suspects someone in the office and mentions that Jeff's personal problems are not keeping him from working. His wife has been sick and he recently lost a child in a house fire.

Johnny goes to the office and finds a woman there. She is Sally Martin, Jeff's secretary. She tells Johnny that she came by to get some paperwork ready for Jeff after a date. The papers are for the building that just burned. Sally suggests to Johnny that Jeff answer any more questions. Sally's date, Bill Trendler comes in and Sally relates the details of their date, but Bill seems to know nothing about it.

Later after a short nap Johnny has breakfast and meets with Lt. Borchart, who tells Johnny that there was a 1953 Ford involved in a hit and run in the area of the fire last night; and it was registered to Jeff Connors. The report detailed how Connor's car was at the scene around 9:00 PM. Johnny tells Lt. Borchart that Jeff was driving a Plymouth Coupe when he picked him up at the airport. Lt. Borchart tells Johnny that the police have issued an APB for Connors. Johnny takes a cab to the Connors home. The wife tells Johnny that Jeff went to have his car fixed. Johnny tells her that he came to see her. She tells Johnny how Jeff fell apart when they lost their son. He bottled up his emotions and would not talk about it. He has been depressed since the recent fires and she suggested moving or sports. Jeff has been out on Tuesdays lately.

Johnny checks out the other fire locations and finds nothing. Johnny calls Lt. Borchart and learns that Sally and Bill's story checks out. Bill Trendler used to work for Jeff, but quit to open a bowling alley. Johnny goes to the bowling alley and talks to Bill about the fires. In his office, Johnny asks Bill about working for Jeff. Bill tells Johnny that he was just not a good insurance agent. He relates that Jeff came here occasionally, and he last saw him four weeks ago with Sally. Johnny is suspicious about Bill's story. Johnny calls Sally from the hotel but she is not in. Lt. Borchart calls and tells Johnny that they have found Jeff's car, in 12 feet of water. Johnny goes to the location and when the car is lifted from the river, there is no one in it. Lt. Borchart drops Johnny off at the hotel and then Johnny goes to talk to the elevator man in Jeff's office. Johnny learns that Sally Martin had been there, and someone was waiting for her in a car. Johnny cabs to Sally's apartment and pounds on the door. Sally lets Johnny in and Johnny asks her where Jeff is and Sally says she does not know where Jeff is. She tells Johnny that Mrs. Connors called last night. She usually calls on Tuesday's to get information on new policies, but had called today and got the address for a new apartment policy. Johnny rushes to the apartment building and meets Lt. Borchart. Sally's car is in the alley as they move in. Johnny and Lt. Borchart find Jeff in the car. He tells them that wanted to handle this him self. He tells Johnny that he ditched the car to cover up the problem. Jeff tells Johnny that his wife is in the building, setting the fuse and Lt. Borchart goes in to get her. Jeff tells Johnny that Sally is not involved. It does not make much sense that his wife is a firebug. She was such a lovely girl.

Johnny has seen fires burn everything, but this is the first time he has ever seen a fire burn the heart out of a man. He does not want to ever see that again.

NOTES:
- CHARLES LYON IS THE ANNOUNCER
- MUSIC IS BY EDDIE DUNSTEDTER

Producer: Jaime del Valle   **Writers:**   Sidney Marshall
Cast: Hal March, Barney Phillips, Jeanne Bates, Sam Edwards, Virginia Gregg, Jim Nusser

SHOW:	THE TEMPERAMENTAL TOTE BOARD MATTER
SHOW DATE:	6/1/1954
COMPANY:	WASHINGTONIAN LIFE INSURANCE COMPANY
AGENT:	BEN GORDON
EXP. ACCT:	$354.95

SYNOPSIS: Ben Gordon calls Johnny with a strange case. Luis Alvarado owns a racetrack in Puerto Rico. He was found with a winning ticket on a long shot in his hand.

Johnny goes to San Juan, Puerto Rico, checks in at the Carib Hilton and meets Captain Cardinas. Capt. Cardinas tells Johnny that the insurance has nothing to do with his murder as Tony Randolph, the gambler, has been trying to buy the racetrack, but Luis threw him out. Luis was last seen at 6:00 PM and he was killed with a .38 at about 4:00 AM this morning. Tony has an alibi—he was asleep. The winning ticket was $72.00 to win, but it has no bearing on the murder. Capt. Cardinas tells Johnny that Luis and his brother Jose were very close. But so were Cain and Abel notes Johnny.

Johnny goes to the racetrack offices where he meets Maria Roldan, Jose's secretary. She was expecting Johnny and tells him that she has to work but also acts as hostess to special guests. She tells Johnny that she can meet him at 8:00 that night. Johnny cabs to Tony Randolph's hotel and meets him. Tony admits to Johnny that he wanted to buy the racetrack, but the boys are playing hard to get. As for the fight with Luis, well they were just clowning around. Tony does not know who killed Luis; he was a nice guy. Tony tells Johnny that he will use his connections to look into the murder for Johnny.

Johnny goes back to the track to meet with Jose but Capt. Cardinas is there and tells Johnny that Jose has been shot at his home. Johnny and Capt. Cardinas go to Jose's home and meet his son, Tomas. In the living room is a dead man with a .38 near his hand. He is Julio Mendoza, a former employee. Tomas tells Johnny that he heard angry voices and then heard his father cry out. Tomas brought his .45 Colt automatic to the room and Julio shot at him, so he shot Julio. Tomas tells Johnny that his father is unconscious and has a bad heart. Johnny is told that Julio ran a pari-mutuel machine at the track and was fired by Luis for cheating. Johnny speculates that the pari-mutuel ticket under Julio's arm has something to do with it. The ticket was on the same horse as the ticket that was in Luis' hand.

Johnny goes to his hotel and eats. Capt. Cardinas calls and tells him that Julio's gun is the same one that killed Luis, so case closed. Later Tony Randolph calls Johnny to tell him that Mendoza is the wrong cookie. Some one has figured out how to beat the races. Go ask Jose Alvarado about it.

Johnny cabs to Maria's address and meets her in her swank apartment. She is dressed and ready to go. But Johnny wants to ask some questions about the pari-mutuel machines first. Maria tells Johnny that the pari-mutuel machine records each ticket and it places the total bets on the tote board. The system is automatic and foolproof. The pari-mutuel system only pays out as much money as is bet, but $21,000 was bet on the fourth race and $26,000 has been paid out, all on $10 winning tickets. Maria tells Johnny that she saw the bookkeeper's totals last night after the track closed. Luis and Jose usually were the only ones to see the figures but she saw them because she stayed late. She tells Johnny that Tomas is in charge of the guards and security, and that Julio Mendoza ran a $10 machine.

Johnny cabs to Capt. Cardinas' office, but he is unimpressed with the information because the machine cannot be fixed and each ticket has a unique number punched on it. Johnny borrows a car and goes to talk to Tony Randolph again. Johnny wants to know whom Tony is gunning for to get Johnny off the hook. Johnny wants some professional advice: what if someone figures out how to beat the system and Luis found out and some one killed him. Tony tells Johnny that in order to beat the system you could print your tickets. You could use the recorded numbers to print your own tickets with the tote board off. Johnny goes back to Capt. Cardinas with his theory. Johnny learns that the head bookkeeper left after the seventh race for a personal matter and has been killed in an auto accident. Capt. Cardinas gets a phone call and learns that the gun found by Julio was registered to Jose Alvarado. Johnny calls Maria and asks to see her.

Capt. Cardinas and Johnny go to the racetrack and the watchman tells them that no one is there. They spot a light in the ticket office and Johnny figures that some one is running the machines by hand. The person in the office hears them and calls out. Capt. Cardinas yells "police" and there are shots. Tomas Alvarado is wounded and does not want to die at the track. Tomas confesses to the murder of Julio and Luis, but recants after he learns he will live. Capt. Cardinas tells Johnny that he will take care of the unfinished business while Johnny goes to see Maria.

Johnny goes to see Maria to take care of his unfinished business. Johnny tells her of the events of the night and she tells Johnny that Tomas would have had everything if he had waited. Johnny tells her that there was probably some woman working with him. "What did you do with the tickets?" Johnny asks her, "sell them to a fence?" Johnny tells her that she tipped her hand when she told Johnny that she had seen the bookkeeper's report, but she did not know that he had left early. Johnny drops her at the police station.

Jose was still too ill for visitors and Johnny did not get to see him. How can you give $50,000 in one hand and take away a son with the other?

NOTES:
- CAST FROM RADIOGOLDINDEX
- WRITER FROM TERRY SALMONSON
- CHARLES LYON IS THE ANNOUNCER
- MUSIC IS BY EDDIE DUNSTEDTER

Producer: Jaime del Valle   Writers: Sidney Marshall
Cast: Hal March, Edgar Barrier, Don Diamond, Lillian Buyeff, Ted de Corsia

◆   ❖   ◆

SHOW: THE SARAH DEARING MATTER
SHOW DATE: 6/8/1954
COMPANY: FEDERAL LIFE INSURANCE COMPANY
AGENT: ED GROSS
EXP. ACCT: $372.25

SYNOPSIS: Ed Gross calls and wants Johnny to investigate the death of Sarah Dearing, the silent movie actress who retired in the twenties and supposedly died in a fire. There is a rumor that she did not die from the fire, and her estate is the beneficiary of her policy.

Johnny flies to the Inglewood International Airport and drives to Palma,

California. Johnny visits the Palma News and asks for the editor and runs into trouble, he is expecting a man and meets a woman, Maggie Lacey; and no, she does not need any printing supplies. Johnny tells her that he wants some information on the article about Sarah Dearing's death and he tells her who he is and why he is looking into the death. Maggie tells Johnny that the coroner says she was burned to death, but Maggie found a medicine bottle in the ruins and the contents were for a very powerful medicine. She thinks that the two men who visited her caused the fire. She tells Johnny that there are two men who visit her every year on her birthday, and Maggie took their picture last year. They left on the 6:20 bus and the fire started at 8:00. Maggie tells Johnny that Sarah was a recluse and died broke. There was just enough money to pay Hilda Brower, the maid.

Johnny visits Dan Cox, the sheriff, and Dan tells Johnny that the reports are unfounded. As for the drugs, they could have been purchased anywhere, and the two men are old friends who come every year, and no, I will not give you their names. Dan tells Johnny that Sarah did not commit suicide and preferred solitude. As for her health, she was always was in frail health. Also, the coroner felt that an autopsy was not needed, and Dan is also the coroner.

Johnny visits Hilda Brower, the maid, who is very upset. She tells Johnny that she had been to the movies and there was a fire when she came back. She tried to rescue Sarah but could not. She knows nothing of the two men and cannot say any more, so go away. Dan Cox drives up and tells Johnny to leave them in peace and do not trespass on the property again. On the way out, Johnny notices that there are four photographs of the same man on a table.

Back at the newspaper office, Johnny asks Maggie for the picture of the two men, and one of the men is the man in the photos in Sarah's house. Johnny borrows the photo, and heads for the Hollywood Library. Johnny spends four hours looking through the standard casting directories and finds his man in the 1928 edition. His name was Neville Thomas and his agent was Matty Freeman. Johnny phones the artist's guild and discovers that Matty now runs a restaurant. Johnny visits the restaurant and is met by Matty Freeman. Johnny shows Matty the photo and tells him that he has a witness to his being in Palma. He tells Johnny that he was in the business when Sarah was acting. Johnny tells Matty that he has an opportunity to clear his name of suspicion, but Matty tells him that Sarah died in a fire. Johnny wants to know where Neville is, but Matty does not know where he is. When Johnny mentions getting police assistance, Matty tells him that Neville is in his office.

In the office Neville tells Johnny that Sarah was a vixen and a temperamental woman. Neville last saw her when they made their final picture, but Johnny tells him he was there on the day she died. Neville admits he did visit occasionally; that Sarah was in love with him but he only pitied her. He had read that she died in a fire, but Neville can prove he was in Matty's apartment at the time. Johnny realizes that their alibis are well rehearsed and on the way out he sees Dan Cox talking to Matty. Johnny gets a room in a hotel, takes a shower and takes a sleeping pill. Later the phone rings and Maggie is calling. She has to see Johnny right away. She is in Hollywood and will meet Johnny in the lobby in five minutes.

When Maggie gets there Johnny is still half-asleep from the pill. Maggie has done some research on Sarah Dearing and shows Johnny a picture of the people who will be receiving her estate: Hilda, Matty, Neville and Dan. Johnny sends a wire and goes back to bed. Ed Gross calls Johnny about the wire and wants to know what is up. Ed tells Johnny that he has received a letter from the estate; and Dan Cox mailed it. Johnny drives back to Palma and goes to see Hilda and finds out his is expected, as Dan Cox is there. Dan tells Johnny that Hilda is ill and cannot be disturbed. Johnny reads the picture caption and Dan tells him that Johnny probably thinks that the four of them killed Sarah for the estate. Dan tells Johnny that Sarah was not murdered. She was dead when the fire started. Hilda came home, found the open bottle of sedatives and thought that Sarah had committed suicide, so to protect her reputation she set the fire to destroy the evidence. Johnny is ready to report death by suicide, but Dan tells Johnny that there is more. After Matty and Neville had visited, Sarah had another visitor, who is down the hall. Johnny is introduced to Dr. James Harding, and he tells Johnny that he has broken up his first vacation in years. Dr. Harding tells Johnny that he was an old friend of Sarah's and her doctor. He had stopped by on his way to the desert, and Sarah was very ill and was dying and was in a great deal of pain. So he administered the sedatives to ease her pain, and she died peacefully. Dr. Harding then went to Dan's office and left a death certificate on Dan's desk and left. Hilda returned and found the sedatives, and the rest you know. Dan reported that Sarah died in the fire so that he would not have to charge a dear old friend for arson. Hilda did set the fire, but do you think she committed a crime? Johnny says no, and leaves.

NOTES:
- THIS IS AN **AFRS** PROGRAM THAT STARTS WITH A STORY ABOUT THE PRESIDENCY OF JAMES MONROE
- THE MID-PROGRAM IS ABOUT THE STATE DEPARTMENT
- CAST INFORMATION FROM TERRY SALOMONSON
- CHARLES LYON IS THE ANNOUNCER
- MUSIC IS BY EDDIE DUNSTEDTER

Producer: Jaime del Valle   **Writers:** Don Sanford
Cast: Joe Du Val, Lillian Buyeff, Tom Tully, Jeanette Nolan, Don Diamond, Bill Johnstone, Jack Edwards

SHOW:	THE PATTERSON TRANSPORT MATTER	
SHOW DATE:	6/15/1954	
COMPANY:	EASTERN INDEMNITY & INSURANCE COMPANY	
AGENT:	TOM BENSON	
EXP. ACCT:	$184.45	

SYNOPSIS: Tom Benson wants Johnny to go to Kansas City as fast as possible;

maybe he can stop a homicide. The Patterson Transportation Company has had a series of six robberies and beatings. The last driver is in the hospital.

Johnny flies to Kansas City, Missouri and is met by Walt Hendricks, VP of the Patterson Transport Company who outlines the events so far. Walt explains that the man will buy something C.O.D. and have it delivered to a vacant house and then beats the driver. The police have been riding with the drivers, but the last man got beaten in his own garage after coming home from a movie with his wife. Johnny gets a room and a Patterson car for his use. Johnny talks to Lt. Herman about the robberies and learns that each one has either been at the farthest point in the route or the last stop on the route, like the robber is familiar with the routine of the drivers. He has gotten more violent with each robbery, and Lt. Herman thinks he must be a psycho. The description of the man notes a limp in the left leg. A look at the map shows that the robberies seem to form a rough circle. They know Milton Speers is next and are watching him. Lt Herman hopes the man will try when the police are on a truck. A report comes in about a Patterson truck involved in an accident where the driver killed. The truck was in for repairs and was being test-driven by Milton Speers.

Johnny and Lt. Herman drive to the scene and learn that the truck suddenly veered into a parked car. The driver did not die from the impact, so maybe he had a heart attack. Johnny wonders why the truck was being test driven on a residential street, and why it was going fast enough to cause skid marks before it crashed, and why it was Milton Speers. Mrs. Robertson, a local woman, is upset and wants to talk to Lt. Herman. She tells him that the citizens need to be protected, as they cannot even park their cars on the street without drunk drivers hitting them. She tells Lt. Herman that she was in her apartment playing wist when the accident happened. The driver had to be drunk, because she saw one man walk away from the crash and go off limping down the street.

Johnny gets the driver's statements for all of the accidents and the driver who was beaten last night dies. Johnny meets Walt Hendricks, who tells Johnny that Milt had a perfect record. Johnny tells Walt that, according to the police, Speers was the next driver to be hit. Walt tells Johnny that Speer's truck broke down and he went out alone to test the truck. Counting Speers, every driver has been hit. Johnny gives 8-5 the robber will try something.

Johnny goes back to Lt. Herman's office and learns that Speers died from a .25 bullet in the brain. Lt. Herman gets a phone call from Mrs. Robertson who has just seen the man in the truck outside her apartment.

Johnny and Lt. Herman go and talk to Mrs. Robertson, who tells them that the same man she saw this morning was looking at her car. She is positive about the man because he was limping and wearing a gray suit and went into the bar at the corner. In the bar, Johnny spots the man and they search him. The man is Gerald Wesley, and he tells Lt. Herman that he just got into town and was looking at the car out of curiosity. Lt. Herman takes Wesley down to the office and Wesley has nothing to say. He knows nothing about the robberies but had read about them in the papers and has just come from Folsum Prison in California. Lt. Herman wires Folsum and they verify that Wesley had been paroled the day before. Mrs. Robertson looks at a line-up and makes a perfect identification, of Sgt. Grayson.

Johnny goes back to the garage where Walt is looking for drivers. Johnny tells him that the man is familiar with the routine, so maybe money is the frosting and he has a grudge. Walt tells Johnny that the company has a good labor record, and he even called Mrs. Thompson his former secretary. She used to work for the company and was involved in a car accident and was crippled. She talked to her husband who knew about the company through her, but they could think of nothing. Mr. Thompson thought he knew the pattern and had warned Milt to be careful. Johnny goes to the hotel and calls Tom Benson to have him look through the records on the Thompson accident. In forty-five minutes Tom calls back and tells Johnny that the Thompsons had been at a party at the company and Mr. Thompson had had too much to drink. On the way out he drove into the wrong lane, and a delivery truck hit him. The driver was killed and Mrs. Thompson suffered two broken vertebrae. Mrs. Thompson gets a lifetime income of $100 a month and the husband just got out of the hospital. Johnny visits the Thompsons and is met by a practical nurse and then talks to Mrs. Thompson. Mrs. Thompson is very appreciative but still would like to be able to be up and about. Her husband Charlie just left, and he feels terrible about the drivers and has been so worried. He has wanted to ride along with the drivers and protect them. He has felt so protective ever since the accident. He is wonderfully forgiving. He told her that the robber would go from one driver to another. He is determined that nothing will happen. He is going to protect Mr. Hendricks. Johnny calls the police and then calls Walt Hendricks but gets a busy signal. Johnny drives to the garage, but Walt is not in the office. Johnny goes to the garage and calls for Mr. Thompson only to be answered by shots which Johnny returns. Walt comes out of an office and they find Charlie Thompson dead. Johnny tells Walt that someone had to stop him.

Ballistics verified that Thompson's gun had killed Speers. Johnny talks to Mrs. Thompson, who somehow believes that her husband died a hero while capturing the bandit single-handed.

NOTES:
- THIS IS AN **AFRS** PROGRAM THAT STARTS WITH A STORY ABOUT THE PRESIDENCY OF GROVER CLEVELAND
- THE MID-PROGRAM IS ABOUT THE VALUE OF THE WORLD SECURITY
- CAST INFORMATION FROM TERRY SALOMONSON
- CHARLES LYON IS THE ANNOUNCER
- MUSIC IS BY EDDIE DUNSTEDTER

Producer:	Jaime del Valle	**Writers:** Sidney Marshall
Cast:	Clayton Post, Hal March, Ed Begley, Hy Averback, Jim Nusser, Lee Patrick, Virginia Gregg	

SHOW: THE ARTHUR BOLDRICK MATTER
SHOW DATE: 6/22/1954
COMPANY: CORINTHIAN ALL RISK INSURANCE COMPANY
AGENT:
EXP. ACCT: $77.30
SYNOPSIS: This is the same program as the previous story aired on 6/16/1951, but with a different cast and crew. The story takes place in Hartford, Connecticut.

NOTES:
* THE ANNOUNCER IS CHARLIE LYON
* MUSIC IS BY EDDIE DUNSTEDTER
* STORY INFORMATION OBTAINED FROM THE KNX COLLECTION IN THE THOUSAND OAKS LIBRARY

Producer: Jaime del Valle   Writers   Gil Doud
Cast: Lou Krugman, Parley Baer, Jeanette Nolan, Tom Tully, Frank
           Nelson, Mary Lansing, Virginia Gregg, Charles Calvert

SHOW: THE WOODWARD MANILA MATTER
SHOW DATE: 6/29/1954
COMPANY: COLUMBIA ALL RISK INSURANCE COMPANY
AGENT: RALPH WEADON
EXP. ACCT: $2,611.80
SYNOPSIS: Ralph Weadon calls to tells Johnny that the burglary take is about $55,000 and that an American clerk named Blake has disappeared. Johnny will be staying at the Hotel Tondo, and Ralph will contact him if he gets additional information.

Johnny flies to Manila, Philippines to investigate a burglary and is met by Floyd McDonald and Irving Morgan of the Woodward Hardware Company who take him directly to the office. McDonald tells Johnny that he had discovered the loss on Monday morning when he found the safe open. McDonald tells Johnny that the U. S. headquarters required them to keep the money on hand for monthly shipments home. The managers disagree over the clerk, Dan Blake. McDonald trusts Dan, and Morgan feels he is guilty as he had access to the office. Blake has been missing four days with no sign, but it is easy to drop out of site in the area.

In his room, Johnny orders gimlets and waits for his luggage as he watches the harbor area. Johnny then goes to the police and talks to Sgt. Malvar who is not looking for Dan Blake. He has captured the thief, a local man named Miguel who is a professional thief. Miguel cannot tell the police where he was that night, and was caught robbing another store last night, but he does not have money. Johnny talks to Miguel who tells Johnny that he does not work and has two daughters who work in prison. He has no money, and if he did then why steal 5 pesos? Sgt. Malvar tells Johnny that the daughters are out of prison and stay away because Miguel steals their money. Johnny thinks it is easier for Sgt. Malvar to grill Miguel than look for the real thief.

Johnny goes to the Woodward office and meets Charlotte Page, the niece of owner. She shows Johnny the office layout. Johnny tells her that it looks bad for Dan, but she cannot believe he did it. She tells Johnny that she saw him occasionally and knows of no problems. Johnny is shown the office safe under the rug in the office. Charlotte tells Johnny that everyone trusted Dan, but he did not know the combination. Johnny gets Dan's address and goes to Dan's room. Johnny finds a good biography of Dan Blake from the things in his room, and learns that he was in the Merchant Marine had had traveled in the Philippines. Johnny goes to the police and tells Sgt. Malvar of Dan's travels in the islands. Sgt. Malvar tells Johnny that Dan has been found in a dugout and taken aboard a ship. He had been shot many times and is dead, but the money has not been found yet.

Sgt. Malvar tells Johnny that the man was Dan Blake because he had told the ship captain his name before he died. Johnny calls McDonald to come and look at the body. McDonald and Johnny go to look at the body and confirm it is Dan. Johnny tells McDonald that Dan was found in a dugout in Tayabas Bay. He had been shot in the back four times when Captain Covar, the captain of an inter-island schooner found him. He was alive for a while but no money was found. McDonald takes Johnny to the docks where they rent a boat to find Captain Covar. They locate the "Sea Nymph," which is a wreck, and go aboard and talk to Captain Covar. He tells Johnny that Sgt. Malvar says Covar has the money and that he better give it to him. Johnny tells Covar that there is over $75,000 missing from the robbery. Covar tells Johnny that he found the man in a dugout, a Morro craft, and there was no money in it. He lived 15-20 minutes and said little. Covar gets angry when Johnny questions him and tells Johnny that the police are getting papers to search the boat. Covar tells Johnny that plenty could have happened on the way to Tayabas Bay, as the Huks would do anything for money. Johnny leaves the boat and is not sure of Covar, as he may be lying. Later, Johnny sees Sgt. Malvar's report and also learns that McDonald is deeply in debt. Johnny does not think it wise to question McDonald, so he goes to see Morgan, who tells Johnny that McDonald told him that the money is gone for good. Johnny tells him that the Huks can be a handy people to have around. Johnny asks how well he knows of McDonald's personal life, and Morgan tells Johnny they are friends and that he sees McDonald socially. Johnny asks Morgan if McDonald owes him money too, as McDonald owes a lot of money to a lot of people. Johnny asks if McDonald could have stolen the money and Morgan is sure that he is not the kind of man to do such a thing. Morgan tells Johnny that McDonald usually has dinner at the Merchants Club and Johnny leaves to question McDonald at home. Morgan wants to stay away from this thing.

At McDonald's home Johnny sees Capt. Covar running out of the front door. "Forget you saw me," he says as he runs. Johnny tries to stop him but he gets away. Johnny goes to the house and meets Charlotte. She tells Johnny that Covar had been there with her and that he hit her and demanded the money, so she gave it to him. She had the money and was holding it for Dan, who kept calling her name while he died. She tells Johnny that they wanted to get away to have a life of their own. Johnny calls Sgt. Malvar and meets him at the harbor police and they go out after Covar. Sgt. Malvar tells Johnny that the police doctor says Dan was choked to death by Covar to learn about the money. Johnny and Sgt. Malvar find Covar after 30 minutes and the police open up with machine gun. Covar fires back and hits a searchlight. Covar's crew turns on him and he shoots them. The police machine gun cuts him down.

NOTES:

- SEE THE ORIGINAL PROGRAM OF **11/25/1950** FOR COMMENTS ON THE LOCAL NATIVES
- THIS IS AN **AFRS** PROGRAM THAT BEGINS WITH AN ARTICLE ABOUT THE WEATHER DEPARTMENT
- THE MID-PROGRAM BREAK IS ABOUT THE PRESIDENCY OF THEODORE ROOSEVELT
- THE ANNOUNCER IS CHARLES LYON
- MUSIC IS BY EDDIE DUNSTEDTER.
- CAST INFORMATION FROM TERRY SALOMONSON

Producer:	Jaime del Valle Writers: Gil Doud
Cast:	Ed Begley, Lillian Buyeff, Jay Novello, Berry Kroeger, Joe Kearns, Don Diamond

◆ ❖ ◆

SHOW:	THE JAN BREUGEL MATTER
SHOW DATE:	7/6/1954
COMPANY:	EASTERN INDEMNITY & INSURANCE COMPANY
AGENT:	TOM LESLIE
EXP. ACCT:	$135.85

SYNOPSIS: Tom Leslie is sending Johnny a check for $25,000 to buy a picture in Detroit. It is called "The River" and was pained by Jan Breugel. It was stolen eleven years ago. Johnny does not like paying for stolen property, but the company does not want to take a $125,000 loss. Johnny will do it but he won't like it.

Johnny flies to Detroit, Michigan and cabs from the Statler Hotel to the Masterson Gallery. A nervous man named Merwin Hacker, the general factotum, meets Johnny. Hacker takes Johnny to Masterson's office where he is expected. Masterson thinks that being a go between is novel. He tells Johnny that a man came in and wanted a painting appraised, and it was the Breugel. Masterson tried to detain him but he left. Yesterday he called back to offer Masterson a commission to get the insurance company here today at four o'clock. It is 2:30 now, so you have time to figure out how to capture the man. Johnny tells Masterson that the statute of limitations has run out, and there is nothing he can do to the man. But it is worth it to get a masterpiece back into the world.

Johnny cabs to the police and meets Lt. Griswald who gets the case file for the original robbery, but the file has nothing to say. Lt. Griswald thinks that Selena Jeffers, the daughter of the owner, was involved. She was 18 at he time and had fallen in love with the painting, but he could not prove it. Johnny does not want to make the deal but will have to.

Johnny goes back to the gallery and the phone rings at 4:00. Johnny is told to go to 2135 N. DeVersey and have the cash with him. Johnny tells the man that he is going to bring an expert and the man says to bring anyone Johnny wants. Johnny goes to the Jeffers estate and talks to Selena. Johnny asks if she wants to buy the picture, but she has no interest. Johnny asks her to go along to identify the picture, and to help identify the man if possible. She agrees to go with him.

The next day Johnny cashes the check and goes to the apartment. The name on the door was Eddie Travers. Johnny has the money and wants to see the painting. Selena is positive that the painting is real, so Johnny gives the money to Eddie, who starts to count it while Selena leaves. Eddie cannot figure the insurance companies, why should they care? Johnny takes the painting to Masterson and then goes to his hotel.

Johnny goes to the airport to leave and is stopped by Merwin Hacker. Johnny tells Hacker that he took the painting to the gallery and Hacker tells Johnny that he thinks the painting is a forgery. Hacker drives Johnny back to the gallery and shows Johnny the painting. Hacker tells Johnny that he was preparing the painting for storage and was nervous and his hand slipped. He shows Johnny a paint chip. Under the paint chip there is a different type of paint underneath. Johnny asks about the experts on art forgery and Hacker refers him to Steven Durwood. Johnny calls Lt. Griswald and he orders a pick up on Eddie Travers. Steven Durwood looks at the picture and tells Johnny to come back in an hour. Johnny goes to see Selena and tells her of the forgery. She offers Johnny a drink and she tells him more is involved. The painting was her childhood image of perfection, but there is no proof that the picture is the same. If it was the one that was stolen, she will pay the $125,000 to the insurance company. Back at Durwood's studio, he is at a loss. The painting is a genuine 17th century painting in appearance, but the flecks of paint on the flowers are strange, as only on the flowers is there moderm paint. Steven tells Johnny that some forgers use an electric oven to age a painting and maybe the forger slipped up and left a clip on that comer. Lt. Griswald calls and they have Eddie Travers. Johnny cabs to police headquarters and Eddie has little to say. Johnny tells him that he could be held for fraud and bunco for selling a fake painting; and that is worth 10 to 20 years. "Yeah, the job seemed too easy" Eddie tells them. He tells Johnny that the man who hired him is Merwin Hacker. Johnny calls the gallery and Hacker has gone for the day. Johnny and Lt. Griswald go to the Hacker's house, which is a farm. In the barn is a workshop for making forgeries. In the back they find Hacker dead. Johnny takes the painting to the gallery and gives it to Masterson, who tells Johnny that Hacker had been there for 15 years. Johnny tells Masterson that Hacker had been forging paintings, but not passing them, he is the one who did that. Johnny tells Masterson that Hacker disclosed the forgery because he found out you were shortchanging him. Masterson admits that he stole the painting from Selena Jeffers because it was the first one they had made and the paint had started to chip. Too bad your detective work is for nothing because of the statute of limitations Masterson tells Johnny. Johnny tells him that Hacker is dead and there is no limitation on murder. A paraffin test shows Masterson had fired a gun and Travers identifies him as Merwin Hacker.

NOTES:
- THIS IS AN **AFRS** PROGRAM THAT BEGINS WITH AN ARTICLE ABOUT TIME AND THE DEPARTMENT OF COMMERCE
- THE MID-PROGRAM BREAK IS ABOUT THE PRESIDENCY OF FRANKLIN PIERCE
- MUSIC IS BY EDDIE DUNSTEDTER
- CHARLES LYON IS THE ANNOUNCER

Producer: Jaime del Valle   Writers: Sidney Marshall
Cast: Parley Baer, Howard McNear, William Johnstone, Jack
           Moyles, Hal March, Virginia Gregg

◆　❖　◆

SHOW: THE CARBONIFEROUS DOLOMITE MATTER
SHOW DATE: 7/13/1954
COMPANY: EASTERN INDEMNITY & INSURANCE COMPANY
AGENT: BILL WESLEY
EXP. ACCT: $2,074.05

SYNOPSIS: Bill Wesley calls and asks Johnny what he knows about oil wells, and Johnny tells him that he would not mind owning one. Bill has a policy on the Van Oosterhaut Oil Company equipment, and they have lost $60,000 in equipment and Pieter Oosterhaut wants an investigator.

Johnny flies to the Van Oosterhaut Oil Company in Madan, Sumatra and meets with Pieter Van Oosterhaut who tells Johnny that he is a gambler and that he needs Johnny to keep the game honest. He tells Johnny that a landslide has destroyed his rigging equipment and that the explosion was set. Other things have happened as well and there is no doubt that sabotage is involved. The local authorities sent a man to investigate, but he is against Pieter too. Pieter wants Johnny to stay for three weeks until his drilling permit expires.

Johnny gets a room and calls the government offices and then goes for dinner. A lovely young woman helps him with the menu. Her name is Fredrika Reynolds, Pieter's daughter. She wants Johnny to convince Pieter to accept the insurance money, because her husband is an oilman and he says there is no oil there. She tells Johnny that there are always accidents; maybe these were due to old equipment. Johnny tells her that Pieter has a stronger case. She tells Johnny that a man's life is worth more than $60,000, that her father has a weak heart, and Johnny could lose his life too. Johnny has Sambal Goreng for dinner.

Johnny goes to bed early but Inspector Pajak calls on Johnny and asks for his gun. The magazine is full and the gun is clean. Insp. Pajak tells Johnny that he had gone to Pieter's office and had called his office. "What caliber killed Pieter" Johnny asks. "It was a .38, but how did you know?" asks Insp. Pajak. "Intuition" Johnny tells him. Johnny and Insp. Pajak go to the oil shack and Pieter's body is there. Johnny learns that Fredrika had told the inspector that Johnny was the last to see Pieter. Insp. Pajak asks if there is anything different in the office, and Johnny only notes some metal canisters. Insp. Pajak tells Johnny that they came in after Johnny left. They are well borings and indicate that the well is dry. Insp. Pajak tells Johnny that Fredrika is distraught from the news of her father, and is going to leave Madan. Johnny tells Insp. Pajak he will stay to find out why Pieter was murdered.

Johnny gets a call from Don Reynolds, who wants to see Johnny. Don knows who shot Van Oosterhaut. Reynolds comes in seven minutes later and tells Johnny that he does not want the inspector involved. Johnny is told that Sunga Tabaran is a wildcatter, and Pieter had tangled with him over some oil leases. Pieter won and Sunga said he would get even. He came back about the time of the sabotage and Sunga was Insp. Pajak's expert. They had a fight the other day, and Sunga is in Madan now.

Johnny goes to see Sunga Tabaran in a small bungalow. Johnny introduces himself and wants to talk, but Sunga tells Johnny it is too early. Johnny tells him that murder is not particular about the hours it keeps. Johnny notes that it is dawn yet he is dressed and asks about the argument with Van Oosterhaut. Sunga tells Johnny that he is looking around and trying to judge him, but he will disappoint Johnny. On the way out, Johnny says to extend his condolences to Fredrika; her purse is on the table. Johnny leaves and wonders why is Fredrika there? Johnny takes a rickshaw to Pieter's office and then to the hotel. Inspector Pajak meets Johnny in the lobby and warns him not to interfere in internal affairs.

Johnny goes to the shop of Herr DeGroot and shows him part of an oil sample. DeGroot knows that they are from Van Oosterhaut's well because they are specimens of carboniferous dolomite, which is a great signifier of oil 100-500 feet below the service. Don Reynolds has been bringing them in regularly, so why did he not tell Pieter? Johnny calls Reynolds and Sunga, but they are both out. Johnny calls the airport and the controller tells him that both Reynolds and Sunga have left for the oil fields and that Reynolds came in twice last night.

Johnny goes to Insp. Pajak and tells him that the evidence adds up to murder. Reynolds knew that Pieter would hit oil so he tried to stall Pieter until the permit would run out and then drill him self. Pieter must have found out and Reynolds killed him. Fredrika went with Sunga to the oil field to confirm her suspicions and Reynolds followed them.

Johnny and Insp. Pajak rent a plane and go to the drilling area, and there is no one around when they arrive. Johnny spots Reynolds with a nitroglycerine tube in his hand and realizes that he is going to shoot the well. He tells Johnny that he is going to try to blast through some rock. Johnny tells Reynolds to drop the nitro or he will shoot. Reynolds runs to the well and Johnny shoots the nitro tube in Reynolds hand, causing it to explode and kill Reynolds. Insp. Pajak is ready to arrest Johnny until he sees Fredrika and Sunga tied up in the tool shed and realizes that Reynolds was going to kill them.

The trip home did not seem half as long as the walk to the tool shed to see it Sunga and Fredrika were alive. They were.

NOTES:
- THIS IS AN **AFRS** PROGRAM THAT BEGINS WITH A STORY ABOUT HOUSE KEEPING WITHIN THE GOVERNMENT
- THE MID-PROGRAM BREAK IS ABOUT TAXES
- CAST FROM JERRY SALOMONSON.
- MUSIC IS BY EDDIE DUNSTEDTER
- CHARLES LYON IS THE ANNOUNCER
- JOHNNY IS CARRYING AN AUTOMATIC.

Producer: Jaime del Valle   Writers: Sidney Marshall
Cast: Hal March, Edgar Barrier, Virginia Gregg, Jay Novello, Hy Averback, Marvin Miller

◆   ❖   ◆

SHOW: THE JEANNE MAXWELL MATTER
SHOW DATE: 7/20/1954
COMPANY: CORINTHIAN LIFE INSURANCE COMPANY
AGENT: MR. SEMPLIN
EXP. ACCT: $265.85

SYNOPSIS: Johnny calls Mr. Semplin in Boston and gets the name of the police contact for the Jean Maxwell case. Johnny asks Semplin if the case is murder or suicide.

Johnny rents a car and drives to the Boston, Massachusetts police headquarters. Johnny tells Lt. DeRosa that the insurance company is nervous about a possible suicide case and that the girl's mother is the beneficiary and is an invalid. Lt. DeRosa tells Johnny that the mother has taken up with old boy friend. Lt. DeRosa tells Johnny that the girl was found in shallow water near a bridge and that it did not look like suicide. The bridge was too low, and a suicide never does it without taking off coat and shoes, and her purse was missing. She was 21 years old and very pretty. The Inquest will be in two days. Johnny wants to dig up his own background information.

Johnny goes to the site where the body was found, and placement of body indicates she going towards Boston, not away. Johnny goes to Jeanne's apartment and talks to Mary O'Neal, Jeanne's roommate. Mary tells Johnny that it is a great shock and that she never thought Jeanne would do this. She expected trouble as Jeanne lived too fast after her mother went into the hospital, as there were too many men. One is Harold Correy, who is a truck driver for Seaboard Trucking Company. Jeanne saw other men when he was gone. Johnny wants to look at her things and he goes through a locked dresser that contains nothing but clothes, perfume and jewelry, and a gold house key with a heart shaped head. Johnny keeps the key, as he wants to find out who made it.

Johnny calls Seaboard Trucking Company and is told that Correy is out of town and due back at 3 A.M. Johnny calls Jeanne's employer and goes to see Mr. Hollis at home where Johnny also meets Mrs. Hollis. Johnny tells Mr. and Mrs. Hollis that he suspects murder, as Jeanne did not do any of the things suicides normally do. Mr. Hollis tells Johnny that he knew nothing of Jeanne's private life, as he had no right to know, but he knew of the invalid mother. Johnny thinks there was only one man with enough money to buy expensive things. Hollis tells Johnny that he will get the names of Jeanne's co-workers if Johnny will call in the morning.

Johnny goes to see Correy at 10:30 and he tells Correy that it looks like murder. Correy tells Johnny that she would never kill herself. He last saw her Tuesday and left Wednesday morning on a run and Johnny tells Correy that he could have done it before he left. Correy tells Johnny that he wanted to marry Jeanne and throws Johnny out.

Johnny calls Lt. DeRosa, who tells Johnny the cause of death is suicide. The autopsy says she died of carbon monoxide poisoning. She killed herself and someone probably moved body to avoid embarrassment.

Johnny goes to see Lt. DeRosa and to see the autopsy report which points to car exhaust but also shows severe concussion. Johnny is still convinced that Jeanne was killed. Johnny shows Lt. DeRosa the key and asks if he can find where it was made and Lt. DeRosa tells Johnny he will do what he can.

Johnny goes to see Paul Anderson, the boy friend of the mother. Paul tells Johnny that the mother was 17 when Jeanne was born. He met Jeanne first and realized she was a cheap opportunist. He did what he could for the mother and did not send her to a home to get her out of the way. Paul does not know anything about the gold the key and tells Johnny that he knew very little about Jeanne.

Johnny goes to Mary's apartment and she cannot remember anything additional. She tells Johnny that Jeanne had never mentioned Paul Anderson to her, and that she never knew how Jeanne was able to put her mother in a nursing home. Johnny talks to six of Jeanne's co-workers and finds nothing. The police find a goldsmith who made key. Johnny talks to him. The Jeweler remembers that a councilman's wife came in the same day. The gold key was made for a man named Carter. It was made for a cottage on the bay. Johnny tells Lt. DeRosa about cottage but Lt. DeRosa cannot assign men to search cabins in the area, as it is county responsibility. Johnny searches real estate offices and on the 3rd day hits pay dirt. An agent remembers renting a cottage to J.E. Carter and the rent has been paid by cashier's check since May. They go to cottage where Johnny looks through the cottage. On the way out, Johnny locks the door with the gold key.

Johnny goes to Mr. Hollis and tells him he thought he would get away with it. Johnny tells Hollis that he rented cottage and bought the key and killed Jeanne. Hollis admitted he was infatuated with Jeanne and wanted to break it off. Jeanne left and committed suicide in the car. Johnny tells Hollis it was not suicide and Hollis agrees to go to the police. Mrs. Hollis comes in and tells Johnny that she had lost her husband and had found out about them. She went out and waited and caught them and killed the girl and carried her to the car.

Remarks: "I don't know what sticklers the Massachusetts courts of law are, but Jeanne Maxwell was not killed by the wronged wife. She was unconscious but alive when Hollis put her into the car trunk. She died there by carbon monoxide."

NOTES:

- THIS PROGRAM IS AN **AFRS** PROGRAM WITH AN ARTICLE ON THE PRESIDENCY OF JAMES MONROE
- THE MID-PROGRAM BREAK IS ABOUT THE FUNCTIONS OF THE VARIOUS DEPARTMENTS OF THE GOVERNMENT.
- THIS IS A REPEAT OF THE PROGRAM OF **3/6/1953**, BUT WITH MINOR MODIFICATIONS AND A DIFFERENT CAST.
- THE ANNOUNCER IS CHARLES LYON
- MUSIC IS BY EDDIE DUNSTEDTER

Producer:	Jaime del Valle Writers: Gil Doud
Cast:	Parley Baer, Howard McNear, Virginia Gregg, Hal March, William Johnstone, Jack Moyles

◆ ❖ ◆

SHOW:	THE RADIOACTIVE GOLD MATTER
SHOW DATE:	7/27/1954
COMPANY:	CORINTHIAN INSURANCE COMPANY
AGENT:	ED TRASK
EXP. ACCT:	$165.45

SYNOPSIS: Ed Trask calls and wants Johnny to go to the Washington Research Hospital in South Bend. There has been a robbery and $150 worth of gold isotope has been stolen.

Johnny goes to South Bend, Indiana and cabs to the hospital where Dr. Reed McKinlock is in charge. Johnny is told that the missing gold is a lethal weapon as it is highly radioactive and is used in treating tumors. It is stored in glass vials in lead boxes in a safe. There were only four ounces, and other materials in the vault were worth much more. The gold had been used the day before and was found missing this morning and the box had been left behind. Nurse Doris Florea tells Johnny that it was her fault. She checks the vault and locks it, at least she thinks it she locked it. The vault was open this morning, so she forgot to lock it.

Johnny goes to police headquarters and sees Lt. Aridos, where the police are trying to close the details. There have been no leads from the staff and the news media have been notified. Johnny gets a list of the hospital staff and heads back to the hospital. Lt. Aridos stops Johnny and tells him that they have a lead, and they head to a pawnshop owner who thinks he has the gold. The man, Mr. Parker is glad to see the police. He knows it is the right stuff as a man came in with three ounces of gold leaf he said he got it from his office windows. The gold is in the back office and Parker will not get near "that atomic bomb stuff." Parker tells Johnny that the man brought it to the shop in an envelope. While Lt. Aridos gets a lead box, Johnny gets the address of the seller. Parker tells Johnny that he would go to the hospital to get checked, but a man must make a buck. Johnny and Lt. Aridos head to the hospital to see Dr. McKinlock, who is working with Steve Wrojak, who has a suspected malignancy, when they get there. Dr. McKinlock gets a Geiger counter and the gold is not radioactive.

Johnny gets a hotel room and is called in the middle of the night. Dr. McKinlock wants him to come in to the hospital. Doris Florea is hysterical and thinks she is dying from radiation poisoning. Johnny arrives at the hospital and Dr. McKinlock tells Johnny how she came in and was crying, so the night doctor called him in. She has some radioactive exposure, but it is too early to tell. They go in and ask her what she is guilty of and she tells Johnny that she is careless and incompetent and that she exposed herself to the radioactivity night after night. She tells them that she has been shortcutting the safety procedures, but she did not take the gold. She is only guilty of leaving the gold in the treatment room where anyone could take it.

Johnny tells Lt. Aridos the good news and Johnny is told that every crank in town is calling the police. Johnny goes to the hospital and continues the questioning. Dr. McKinlock comes in and tells Johnny about finding radioactivity in the hallway. They follow the signals from the Geiger counter and find a rubbish cart in a closet. Johnny calls Lt. Aridos with a name of orderlies and other staff who are brought to the hospital for testing, but none of the staff show any signs of contamination.

Johnny goes to the hotel and Lt. Aridos calls and wants to pick him up. An eight-year-old boy was found playing with a bottle from the hospital with traces of gold in it. At the hospital, the boy's mother, Mrs. Thatcher, tells Johnny that Bobby was playing in the back yard. She had gone out to get him, saw the bottle and brought him into the hospital. Bobby told her that he found the bottle in the next-door neighbor's yard. Mr. and Mrs. Wrojak the neighbors are having a 50th anniversary party tonight. A check of the hospital records show that Mr. Wrojak was there on the day of the theft. Johnny and Lt. Aridos go to visit Wrojak, who tells them that it is too bad that they find out tonight, on their anniversary. They go to the workshop to talk. Mr. Wrojak knows that they are after the gold. He has it in the workshop and tells Johnny that he had used the rubbish cart to get it out of the building. Mr. Wrojak took it to make a ring for he and his wife

Anna. After fifty years she deserves something nice for her golden anniversary. Mr. Wrojak knows it was wrong, but he did what he had to do to make a gift for Anna. Mr. Wrojak does not read in English so he does not know about the news, but he will pay back the hospital.

NOTES:
- ACCORDING TO TERRY SALMONSON, THE ORIGINAL TITLE WAS "THE GOLDEN RING MATTER"
- CAST INFORMATION FROM TERRY SALMONSON.
- CHARLES LYON IS THE ANNOUNCER
- MUSIC IS BY EDDIE DUNSTEDTER

Producer: Jaime del Valle   Writers: Sidney Marshall
Cast: Lou Merrill, Joseph Kearns, Jeanne Bates, Hy Averback, Howard McNear, Mary Jane Croft

◆ ❖ ◆

SHOW: THE HAMPTON LINE MATTER
SHOW DATE: 8/3/1954
COMPANY: WORLDWIDE MARITIME & INSURANCE COMPANY
AGENT: JACK LORING
EXP. ACCT: $158.55

SYNOPSIS: Jack Loring calls about an easy job. All Johnny has to do is to fly to Sault Ste. Marie, sit back and look important and watch the Coast Guard do all the work. Jack tells Johnny that a man named Carl Richards set off a bomb on the ore boat Hampton Queen and the damage is about $160,000. Johnny is needed as a formality.

Johnny flies to Sault Ste. Marie, Michigan and meets Coast Guard Commander Winter. Johnny tells Cmdr. Winter that he understands Carl Richards is the main suspect. Johnny is told that Richards operates a supply boat and had called on the Hampton Queen yesterday at 13:00. Richards came up the Jacobs ladder himself, went below and then left. The explosion happened later and an engine room hand saw Richards in the room where the explosion took place. When the supply boat landed, Richards was not there. Elsa Richards, the daughter, does not know what happened to her father and has dared to Coast Guard to charge her. Cmdr. Winters wonders what the motive was, as Richards has an excellent reputation.

Johnny goes to the Richards supply boat and Miss Elsa Richards stops him. She tells Johnny that she has nothing to say to him because he is not interested in the truth. Johnny notes the odd cargo and asks Elsa about the blasting powder.

Johnny goes to the Shoreview Hotel and finds Capt. Torgeson, who does not know where Richards is. Capt. Torgeson knows that Richards is not responsible for the blast, because he has known him for 25 years. Nor does he know why Richards went below decks. Johnny is told that the blast went off in an empty storage locker, but if they wanted to do some real damage the engines were near by. Capt. Torgeson tells Johnny that Richards has never said a bad word or cheated anyone, so Johnny asks why Richards disappeared.

Back at the Coast Guard a report comes in from the station in Three Harbors. A man tried to sneak aboard a Hampton Lines boat there and was shot. The man was Carl Richards. Johnny and Cmdr. Winter pick up Elsa and they fly to Three Harbors. Johnny, Elsa and Cmdr. Winter meet the man who shot Richards, and Elsa goes in alone to be with her father. Bill Fraser tells Johnny that he was standing the night watch and saw the dinghy under the stern. He haled it and got shot at, so he shot back and got a lucky shot. Fraser tells Johnny that the dinghy was carrying blasting powder. Fraser tells Johnny that Three Harbors is the closest port to Canada, so maybe Richards was going there. Cmdr. Winter gets a call and another Hampton boat has had an explosion.

Johnny and Cmdr. Winter go to Parisian Island, and go aboard the James K. where the skipper, Capt. Hartzel, shows them the damage that looks just like what was done on the Hampton Queen. The blast looks like it came from inside the central pipe in the ceiling.

In the morning Johnny calls Cmdr. Winter and learns that the Richards inquest is finished, the verdict was justifiable homicide, and the funeral is this afternoon. Johnny requests an autopsy and then Johnny searches the supply boat and finds nothing. Johnny gets a call from Jack Loring who learns that another boat is damaged. Loring tells Johnny that he has had all the boats tied up for the time being. Johnny tells him to cancel the order for 24 hours. Johnny calls the hospital and there is no report on the autopsy. At the dry dock Johnny sees Captain Hartzel who tells Johnny that he has not seen Richards for three weeks. Johnny asks Hartzel for a crew list and gets a list from the Hampton Queen and takes the information he was looking for to Cmdr. Winter. On each list, there is a substitute sailor for Bill Fraser. Johnny calls Three Harbors and learns that Richard died from drowning, not from gunshots. Also, Fraser has shipped off on another boat and Elsa is on the supply boat heading out. Johnny and Cmdr. Winter take a plane out to intercept them. Johnny tells Cmdr Winter that he had a hunch and the booby traps tipped him off. If Fraser were bringing in contraband the booby traps would be perfect to cover up anything that was discovered. And they only needed one in-bound trip to get the goods. Richards probably was covering for his daughter by destroying the evidence and they killed him. Nice people! Johnny and Cmdr. Winter board the Agnes Hampton to look for Fraser. Near the engine room Fraser tells to them to go above decks. He laughs and tells them he will sink the ship, as he has a real charge this time. Fraser taunts Johnny to take him. Fraser tells Johnny that he has a bangalor torpedo and can set it off from anywhere on the boat. Johnny tries to get close enough to jump him while Cmdr. Winters stalls for time by telling Fraser that Elsa is going to Canada without him. Johnny is able to jump Fraser and knock him unconscious. Johnny tells Cmdr. Winter that Fraser had gotten to the pipe before Johnny hit him, but the bomb was a dud. Elsa Richards had run out on Fraser and was picked up by the Canadian authorities.

NOTES:

- THIS IS AN **AFRS** PROGRAM THAT BEGINS WITH A STORY ABOUT THE COLLECTION OF TAXES.
- THE FINAL BREAK IS ABOUT THE PRESIDENCY OF ABRAHAM LINCOLN
- THE BANGALORE TORPEDO WAS USED AS A MEANS OF EXPLODING BOOBY TRAPS AND BARRICADES LEFT OVER FROM THE BOER AND RUSSO-JAPANESE WARS.
- THE CAST CREDITS ARE GIVEN AS: JIM NUSSER IS JACK LORING, HY AVERBACK IS COMMANDER WINTERS, LEE PATRICK IS ELSA RICHARDS, ED BEGLEY IS CAPT. TORGESON, CLAYTON POST IS CAPT. HARTZEL, HAL MARCH IS BILL FRASER
- CHARLES LYON IS THE ANNOUNCER
- MUSIC IS BY EDDIE DUNSTEDTER
- THIS IS THE LAST AVAILABLE PROGRAM WITH JOHN LUND

Producer:	Jaime del Valle	Writers:	Sidney Marshall
Cast:	Jim Nusser, Hy Averback, Lee Patrick, Ed Begley, Clayton Post, Hal March		

◆ ❖ ◆

SHOW:	THE SARAH MARTIN MATTER
SHOW DATE:	8/10/1954
COMPANY:	WASHINGTONIAN LIFE INSURANCE COMPANY
AGENT:	ED REYNOLDS
EXP. ACCT:	$318.05

SYNOPSIS: Ed Reynolds calls Johnny and asks him to go to Milwaukee and check out Joe Martin. His business has gone to pot, there are shortages in his accounts, and he has separated from his wife who Joe had said was trying to kill him.

Johnny flies to Milwaukee, Wisconsin and is paged at the airport. Johnny answers the page and is met by police Lt. Hanks who tells Johnny that Joe Martin is dead. Johnny goes to Joe's home at Whitefish Bay and learns that Joe was killed the previous night by two shots from a .32. His stepdaughter Hazel Martin had discovered Joe less than an hour ago. Hazel tells Johnny that she did not live at the house, and that her mother killed Joe. Hazel tells Johnny that she came to the area to visit a client and decided to stop by and visit her dad, who she had last seen two months ago. Hazel tells Johnny that Joe had made her the beneficiary of the $65,000 policy, and claims that her mother tried to kill Joe after they separated by starting a fire at his house.

Johnny goes to the Schroeder Hotel and is called by Mrs. Sarah Martin who tells Johnny that she has some information. Johnny goes to the Juneau Hotel to meet Mrs. Martin and is told that she had called the office and was told about Joe, and that Johnny was investigating. Sarah tells Johnny that they had been estranged for a year, and that she had made enemies of all their friends. Sarah tells Johnny that she was at Lake Geneva and had been at a movie when Joe was killed, and has proof. Sarah tells Johnny that she has a Smith and Wesson .32, so Johnny takes her to the police.

At the police department, Johnny meets a Mr. Everett Norvell who tells Johnny that he killed Joe Martin. Everett tells Johnny that he was an insurance salesman and that Joe owed him money. They had fought and Everett stabbed Joe. Everett wants to talk to the reporters and get photographed, but Johnny calls him a "Confessin' Sam." Johnny goes to Joe's office and hires a CPA to go over the books. Johnny also talks to the secretary, Esther Buchwald. Esther tells Johnny that Joe was a fool to get involved with those two harpies, and that he had no enemies. Lt. Hanks calls Johnny, and he tells Johnny that there has been a gas heater explosion at the cabin in Lake Geneva. Johnny goes to the cabin where a .32 was found in the rubbish. The gun is the murder weapon, and was registered to Joe.

Johnny goes back to the office and the CPA has found a $20,000 shortage in the books. Joe has lunch with Hazel, and tells her about the gun. Hazel tells Johnny that Joe had not used the gun in three years, and had given it to the boyfriend of his secretary, Everett Norvell. Johnny goes to the office and talks to Esther who tells Johnny that Everett had juggled the books, and that Joe had found out. Esther tells Johnny that she is an old maid and Everett was the only man who paid any attention to her. Johnny calls the police and Everett is arrested.

NOTES:
- THE ANNOUNCER IS CHARLES LYON
- MUSIC IS BY EDDIE DUNSTEDTER
- STORY INFORMATION OBTAINED FROM THE KNX COLLECTION IN THE THOUSAND OAKS LIBRARY

Producer: Jaime del Valle   **Writers**   Sidney Marshall
Cast: Jay Novello, John McIntire, Howard McNear, Virginia Gregg, Mary Jane Croft, Jeane Cagney, Lou Merrill

SHOW: THE HAMILTON PAYROLL MATTER
SHOW DATE: 9/5/1954
COMPANY: CORINTHIAN INSURANCE COMPANY
AGENT: BILL FEDDERSON
EXP. ACCT: $417.65

SYNOPSIS: Bill Fedderson calls Johnny and asks if he remembers the Hamilton Payroll Robbery two and a half years ago. The robbers wore Halloween masks and got away with $85,000. Bill tells Johnny that the money has turned up in Tijuana. See Captain Reyes for details.

Johnny goes to Tijuana, Mexico, gets a room at the Reforma Hotel and goes to see Capt. Reyes who tells Johnny that three bills have been traced to the area, all 20's. Señora Rosa Fuentes runs a quinta and made the deposit, which was made from the rental money. Currently there are five Americans staying there. The guests include a Miss Jamison from Kansas City, Mr. Haines and his wife from Los Angeles, and Mr. Burke and Mr. Behrens from New York.

Johnny goes to the quinta acting as a tourist and meets the Haines, who tell Johnny that they are on their honeymoon. Johnny meets Burke, who Johnny recognizes as a New York numbers racket member named Callenti. Burke tells Johnny that he is on vacation, and invites Johnny to go to the jai alai games with him. Johnny gets a room and meets Dorothy Jamison who knows that Johnny is an insurance investigator, because Burke told her. Johnny goes to update Capt. Reyes and learns that Behrens has been found shot to death by a .38. Johnny is told that Behrens was a Patterson New York police officer. Capt. Reyes gets a call and learns that another $20 has surfaced at the jai alai fronton, and it was passed by Mrs. Haines. Johnny goes to the fronton and talks to the cashier, Louis Campos who tells Johnny that he works at a bank, and knows how to spot wanted currency. Johnny watches a match and Burke comes in and Johnny tells him about the robbery. Burke bets Johnny $20 that a certain player will win the match, and Johnny wins the bet. Burke pays Johnny with a $20 and the bill is clean. Johnny updates Capt. Reyes and learns that the Haines are clean.

Johnny goes to the quinta and searches the rooms and finds nothing. Johnny has a drink with Dorothy who tells Johnny that Mr. Haines is interested in why Johnny is there. Capt. Reyes arrives and tells Johnny that Mr. Haines has been killed. He was found near where Behrens was found, and was shot six times. His wife was found nearby and taken to the hospital. Johnny goes to the hospital and Mrs. Haines tells Johnny that she and her husband were robbed and everything they had was taken except her rings. She admits that she only had two bills left, and her husband had told her that he might go to prison because she took the money from his wallet to play at the fronton. She also tells Johnny that the man who robbed them bragged about killing Behrens. Johnny finds a receipt for a package at the post office and finds a package with the rest of the money.

NOTES:
- THE ANNOUNCER IS CHARLES LYON
- MUSIC IS BY EDDIE DUNSTEDTER
- STORY INFORMATION OBTAINED FROM THE KNX COLLECTION IN THE THOUSAND OAKS LIBRARY

Producer: Jaime del Valle   Writers   Sidney Marshall
Cast: Lou Krugman, Don Diamond, Virginia Gregg, Jim Backus,
          Hans Conried, Mary Jane Croft

SHOW: THE GREAT BANNOCK RACE MATTER
SHOW DATE: 9/12/1954
COMPANY: SEABOARD MUTUAL LIFE INSURANCE COMPANY

Agent: **Bill Blake**
Exp. Acct: **$1,207.90**

Synopsis: Bill Blake calls ask Johnny if he wants to go to Scotland. The village of Roxburgh has a race called the Bannock Race. Miss Elsie McLeod won this year and then died. She ate the bannock she had made and died of poison. Bill wants Johnny to find out if she was married.

Johnny flies to Roxburgh, Scotland and goes to meet inspector Michaels of Scotland Yard who tells Johnny that there was no record of Miss McLeod ever being married. She was born in the village, became an actress and came back to run a curio shop. Insp. Michaels tells Johnny that the bannocks have to do with the Battle of Culloden where Prince Charlie was defeated. The bannock is an oatcake and every year the village holds a race to see who can make theirs the quickest. This year Elsie won and ate her bannock and died after the Earl of Roxstane handed the bannock to her. Elsie has a cousin who is her next of kin, and he is running the shop now.

Johnny goes to visit the Earl of Roxstane who calls the thought of marriage nonsense. While talking the Earl's fiancée Alice Merrick comes in and tells Johnny that at their engagement party, Elsie said in an odd manner that she would have to present her husband. Johnny goes to the shop and meets Alfred, who tells Johnny that he saw the race and tells Johnny that there were stoves at one end of the town, and Roxstane was at the other. The contestants made their batter at home. Johnny inspects the living room, and Alfred is nervous, so Johnny calls for Insp. Michaels. The inspector arrives and he and Johnny remove a number of bank passbooks from different banks in different cities. Insp. Michaels suspects that they were from blackmail. Johnny is told that Lord Roxstane is really Henry Claridge, and that his title is inherited.

Johnny flies to the town of Frontignan in the south of France and spots Miss Merrick there. Johnny goes to see Pierre le Blanc, a collector of theater programs where Johnny finds a program from 1940 for the play "Gay Lady Gay" where Elsie had a role. Johnny goes to a local photographer and meets Miss Merrick again. Johnny tells her that he has proof that Elsie had married Henry in 1940. Alice tells Johnny that Henry feared Elsie.

Johnny goes back to Roxstane and he tries to bribe Johnny, and tells him that he and Elsie were only married for two days and never saw her again until he got the title. He tells Johnny that Elsie tried to blackmail him, but he did not kill her. Johnny goes to see Alfred and tells him that he will not inherit Elsie's money. Johnny goes to see Insp. Michaels and they go see the Earl and Alice and tell them that he cannot give the insurance money because Roxstane is a suspect. While they are talking shots are heard and the bullets come through he curtains. The police arrest Alfred and Johnny tells him that he killed Elsie. He tells Alfred that he made two batches of bannocks and the inspector can prove it by the crumbs in his pockets.

Notes:
- **The announcer is Charlie Lyon**

- MUSIC IS BY EDDIE DUNSTEDTER
- STORY INFORMATION OBTAINED FROM THE KNX COLLECTION IN THE THOUSAND OAKS LIBRARY

Producer:	Jaime del Valle	**Writers**	**Gibson Scott Fox**
Cast:	Howard McNear, John McIntire, Lou Merrill, Virginia Gregg, Alex Harford, Jay Novello		

◆　❖　◆

SHOW:	THE UPJOHN MATTER
SHOW DATE:	9/19/1954
COMPANY:	CONTINENTAL FIRE & CASUALTY COMPANY
AGENT:	MATT BRANDON
EXP. ACCT:	$293.65

SYNOPSIS: Matt Brandon calls Johnny from St. Louis and is in court with the Upjohn Printing Company case. Johnny is told that Tierney was in the building on the night of the fire and there has been a lot of expert testimony by the attorney Eggleston. Johnny will come out to testify.

Johnny flies to St. Louis, Missouri and goes to the courtroom. Johnny is called to testify and tells the court that he has been an investigator for seven years, had spent four years in the Army Air Corps, and was a member of the New York Police Department. Johnny also has a number of letters of reliability from the insurance companies he has represented. Johnny testifies that he was called in to investigate a fire at the Upjohn Printing Company and found evidence of celluloid and paraffin wicks. Johnny states that Pat Tierney improvised the method and that he had ink from the plant on his clothes. The case is closed and goes to the jury.

Johnny goes to talk to Tierney and gives him the option of talking to him, or hoping on the jury. Johnny really wants Upjohn, who paid Tierney to set the fire. Johnny wants Tierney to will tell the court he was hired. Tierney refuses to cooperate with Johnny.

The jury comes back and Tierney is found guilty. On the way out, Tierney calls to Johnny that he wants to talk. Johnny talks to Tierney in his cell and he tells Johnny that he was paid $2,500 by Upjohn, and that he contacted Upjohn through a friend. Tierney changes his story to Johnny several times, and Johnny reminds him that his sanity has been proven. Tierney finally admits that he met Upjohn in a bar a month before the fire. He knew that Upjohn was in financial trouble and got $3,500, which he has hidden in a can in a vacant lot. Johnny goes to the police and Upjohn is arrested.

NOTES:
- THE ANNOUNCER IS CHARLIE LYON
- MUSIC IS BY EDDIE DUNSTEDTER
- THIS STORY WAS INCORPORATED INTO "THE BENNET MATTER"

- STORY INFORMATION OBTAINED FROM THE **KNX** COLLECTION IN THE THOUSAND OAKS LIBRARY

Producer:	Jaime del Valle	Writers	E. Jack Neuman
Cast:	Joe Du Val, Joe Kearns, John McIntire, Jay Novello, Bob Sweeney		

Index

VOLUME ONE: PAGES 1–414

VOLUME TWO: PAGES 415–995

VOLUME THREE: PAGES 996–1203

B

BACKGROUND

C

CASE LOCATIONS

CAST MEMBERS

CATALOGED STORIES

H

HOME ADDRESS

HOTELS USED

M

MARITAL STATUS

MUSIC SUPERVISION

P

PHONE NUMBER

POISONS USED

R

RECURRING CHARACTERS